FOUNDATIONS OF MARKETING

JOHN FAHY AND DAVID JOBBER

SIXTH EDITION

FOUNDATIONS OF MARKETING

JOHN FAHY AND DAVID JOBBER

Mc
Graw
Hill

SIXTH EDITION

Foundations of Marketing, Sixth Edition
John Fahy and David Jobber
ISBN-13 9781526847348
ISBN-10 1526847345

Published by McGraw-Hill Education
338 Euston Road
London
NW1 3BH
Telephone: +44 (0) 20 3429 3400
Website: www.mheducation.co.uk

British Library Cataloguing in Publication Data
A catalogue record for this book is available from the British Library

Library of Congress Cataloguing in Publication Data
The Library of Congress data for this book has been applied for from the Library of Congress

Portfolio Manager: Rosie Churchill
Content Product Manager: Ali Davis
Marketing Manager: Katarzyna Rutkowska

Text design by Kamae Design
Cover design by Adam Renvoize
Printed by Bell & Bain Ltd, Glasgow

ISBN-13 9781526847348
ISBN-10 1526847345
eISBN-13 9781526847355

Dedication

To my Mum, Martha
Who has seen many changes in her time

John Fahy

About the Authors

John Fahy is Professor of Marketing at the University of Limerick in Ireland and Adjunct Professor of Marketing at the University of Adelaide, Australia. He has a distinguished track record of teaching and research in the fields of marketing and business strategy. In particular, he is known for his work in the area of marketing resources and capabilities, and how these factors impact on organizational performance. He is a founder member of the MC21 group, which has conducted research on marketing resources and performance across 15 countries. An eclectic thinker, his work draws on insights from marketing strategy, behavioural economics, evolutionary psychology and neuroscience. Other current research interests include customer value, evolutionary perspectives on marketing, and strategic leadership. He is the author of dozens of refereed journal articles on marketing and strategy, which have been published in leading titles, including the *Journal of Marketing, Journal of International Business Studies, Journal of Business Research, Journal of Marketing Management, European Journal of Marketing, International Business Review* and the *Sloan Management Review*. His *Journal of Marketing* paper on sustainable competitive advantage has been cited more than 1,800 times. He is also the winner of several major international research awards such as the AMA Services Marketing Paper of the Year Award and the Chartered Institute of Marketing Best Paper Award at the Academy of Marketing Annual Conference.

Professor Fahy is also a renowned teacher, with a particular expertise in working with MBA and executive groups, and was awarded the prestigious Shannon Consortium Regional Teaching Excellence Award in 2012. His skills have been in demand around the world – he has worked with students in Australia, Japan, Hungary, Ireland, New Zealand, Russia, Singapore, the UK and the USA. The focus of his executive work is on bridging the gap between academic insight and the commercial realities facing organizations. He has been extensively involved in both open and custom programmes in Ireland and abroad with companies such as Abbvie, Alexion, Analog Devices, Fexco, Glanbia, Pfizer, Promet and Syngenta. He is the author of several award-winning business case studies and has also been involved in the development of new pedagogical materials such as a series of business videos where he interviews some leading marketing managers about recent strategic initiatives in their organizations. Further details can be found at www.johnfahy.net.

Professor Fahy currently holds the Chair in Marketing at the University of Limerick. Prior to this he worked at Trinity College, Dublin, and he holds a master's degree from Texas A&M University and a Doctorate from Trinity College. Outside of work his passions include family, music, sport, food and travel.

David Jobber is an internationally recognized marketing academic. He is Professor of Marketing at the University of Bradford School of Management. He holds an honours degree in Economics from the University of Manchester, a master's degree from the University of Warwick and a doctorate from the University of Bradford.

Before joining the faculty at the Bradford Management Centre, David worked for the TI Group in marketing and sales, and was Senior Lecturer in Marketing at the University of Huddersfield. He has wide experience of teaching core marketing courses at undergraduate, postgraduate and post-experience levels. His specialisms are industrial marketing, sales management and marketing research. He has a proven, ratings-based record of teaching achievements at all levels. His competence in teaching is reflected in visiting appointments at the universities of Aston, Lancaster, Loughborough and Warwick in the UK, and the University of Wellington, New Zealand. He has taught marketing to executives of such international companies as BP, Croda International, Allied Domecq, the BBC, Bass, Royal & Sun Alliance, Rolls-Royce and Rio Tinto.

Supporting his teaching is a record of achievement in academic research. David has more than 150 publications in the marketing area in such journals as the *International Journal of Research in Marketing, MIS Quarterly, Strategic Management Journal, Journal of International Business Studies, Journal of Management, Journal of Business Research, Journal of Product Innovation Management* and the *Journal of Personal Selling and Sales Management*. David has served on the editorial boards of the *International Journal of Research in Marketing, Journal of Personal Selling and Sales Management, European Journal of Marketing* and the *Journal of Marketing Management*. He has acted as special adviser to the Research Assessment Exercise panel that rates research output from business and management schools throughout the UK. In 2008, he received the Academy of Marketing's Life Achievement award for distinguished and extraordinary services to marketing.

Brief Table of Contents

Part 1: The Market-Led Organization 1

Part 2: Creating Customer Value 163

Part 3: Delivering and Managing Customer Value 251

Detailed Table of Contents

Case list

Vignette list

Critical Marketing Perspective

Preface to the Sixth Edition

In the relatively short period between each new edition of *Foundations of Marketing*, it is remarkable how much the field changes. New concepts emerge, older ideas evolve, new innovative practices enter the arena, and the fortunes of leading businesses throughout the world rise and fall. What is also evident is how much the pace of change is accelerating. Facebook's mantra for its developers – 'move fast and break things' – seems to have been adopted as the business philosophy of many technology companies. What it means is that the innovation may not be perfect but speed is everything. Another phrase to come into the lexicon is that we are living in a VUCA world – that is, one that is volatile, uncertain, complex and ambiguous. When we look at the current fusion of technologies, including artificial intelligence, robotics, nanotechnology, the Internet of Things and autonomous vehicles, to name just a few, characteristics such as complex and ambiguous certainly seem appropriate. And, to further illustrate the pace of change, it has been estimated that 90 percent of the world's data has been generated in the past two years! That alone is a mind-boggling statistic.

What all of this means is that the world of marketing is changing and looks as though it will continue to change at an ever accelerating pace. This presents a challenge for researchers, educators and students to try to frame and understand these developments. Of course many of the core fundamentals have an enduring quality. Great marketing is still about building value propositions and marketing programmes based on deep customer insights. But the processes and technologies underpinning how this is done continue to evolve. There seems to be little doubt that marketing, with its far-reaching societal implications, will remain a fascinating arena for research, study and work.

The sixth edition

Before you dive in to the detail of the chapters, below is an overview of some of the main features of this sixth edition.

Digital marketing

It is probably fair to say that, for many, digital marketing was a topic that was not well understood and probably taken to mean something to do with the likes of search engine optimization or advertising on Facebook. So while earlier it may have played a role as something of an exotic visitor, digital marketing is now living up to its name in that no area of marketing has been untouched by digital. And that is how this book deals with the subject matter. Issues relating to digital are discussed throughout the text, wherever it is appropriate. For example, web analytics, Big Data and social listening are transforming the world of market research so these are discussed in Chapter 4, where we examine marketing research and customer insights. Digital technology is enhancing the ability of companies to engage in personalized marketing, essentially segments of one, so we discuss this topic in Chapter 5's review of segmentation, targeting and positioning. Social influencers are having a profound impact on the buying decision process, so we discuss this in the consumer behaviour chapter (Chapter 3), and so on. That said, we have allocated a separate chapter in this edition to online marketing communications (Chapter 11), to reflect the importance of the research and innovations taking place in that space. The year 2017 was a red letter one, in that it represented the first time that digital advertising spend globally exceeded that of television. This new chapter provides an overview of the essential digital communications tools available to the marketer.

Critical marketing perspectives

While the world economy hurtles along, there have been many academics and commentators whose research provides pertinent pause for thought. A number of books in the area of political economy either question the merits of capitalism or are predicting its demise in the very near future. The consequences of the capitalist project are everywhere to be seen, from pollution-induced climate change to the depletion of the Earth's resources to the ever widening gap between the rich and poor to the human suffering caused by global migration. Throughout the world, the practice of marketing is inextricably linked with the well-being of society.

Therefore, it cannot be viewed in an ideologically neutral way. This book invites the reader to critically reflect on the principles and practice of marketing throughout. In particular, it includes 12 Critical Marketing Perspective vignettes that outline contentious aspects of marketing and invite the reader to evaluate arguments from both sides of the debate, along with a guide to further reading on the subject matter.

From marketing to strategy

The central defining issue in marketing is the creation, delivery and communication of customer value. The book opens with a focus on value, which provides an architecture as it expands to explore the relevant dimensions of the topic. Nevertheless, more than ever, marketing activities need to be planned carefully as well as inform the organization's strategic vision. A chapter on planning and strategy has been restored as the concluding topic in this book, to tie these themes together.

New concepts and developments

The pace of change in the field, discussed earlier, has meant that there is a rich variety of new themes and developments included in each chapter of this edition. These include, to name but a few: the move to omni-channel marketing, where organizations try to systematically manage the increasing number of touchpoints they have with their customers; personalized pricing, whereby online prices vary from customer to customer; data mining and the legislation governing the management of customer data; how the purchase of online advertising has become increasingly automated; and the changing nature and shape of the customer journey.

Learning about marketing

Marketing is an interesting and exciting subject that is at the core of our lives both as consumers and as employees or managers in organizations. Therefore the focus of this book has always been on blending conceptual insights with the contemporary world of marketing practice. As such it retains the popular features of previous editions and adds several new ones.

Insights from the world of practice feature in myriad ways. Each chapter begins with a Marketing Spotlight focusing on the marketing activities and challenges facing some well-known global enterprises, which sets the scene for the content that follows. In addition, there are more than 40 new Marketing in Action vignettes throughout the book that focus on the activities of a variety of organizations, large and small, public and private. Roughly one-third of these organizations are based in the UK/Ireland, one-third in Europe and one-third are from around the world, giving a wide geographic breadth. Each of these inserts contains discussion questions designed to improve critical thinking and learning. In addition, 12 new end-of-chapter cases with a similarly wide geographic spread are included to provide more detailed problems for analysis and discussion.

Although the text is foundational, it also provides students with an introduction to many of the concepts in the marketing literature. Included, among other topics, are consumer culture theory, semiotics, multisensory marketing, experiential marketing, search engine optimization, ambient marketing, value co-creation and marketing metrics. These concepts are presented in an accessible way, to enable students to learn both the classic and contemporary elements of effective marketing.

Acknowledgements

Our thanks go to the following reviewers for their comments at various stages in the text's development:

Nathalie Dens, University of Antwerp

Caitlin Ferreira, University of Cape Town

Jonathan Ivy, Lancaster University

Zhongqi Jin, Middlesex University

Mandy Jones, Cape Peninsula University of Technology

Abraham Joseph, Coventy University, London Campus

James Lappeman, University of Cape Town

Anna-Carin Nordvall, Umea University

Michael Redwood, University of Bath

Vicky Roberts, Staffordshire University

Andrea Rumler, Berlin School of Economics and Law

Anita Wade, Dublin City University

Sara Leroi-Werelds, Hasselt University

We would also like to thank the following contributors for the material which they have provided for this textbook and its accompanying online resources:

Glyn Atwal, Burgundy School of Business

David Brown, Northumbria University

Irena Descubes, ESC Rennes School of Business

Geraldine Lavin, National University of Ireland Maynooth

Valerie McGrath, Institute of Technology Tralee

Tom McNamara, ESC Rennes School of Business

Christina O'Connor, National University of Ireland Maynooth

Marie O'Dwyer, Waterford Institute of Technology

Mariusz Soltanifar, University of Groningen and Hanze University of Applied Sciences

Vicky Roberts, Staffordshire University

Authors' acknowledgements

We would particularly like to thank Dr Christina O'Connor, Dr Marie O'Dwyer and Mariusz Soltanifar (PhD Candidate) for their insightful contributions to this edition of the book. We would also like to thank our colleagues, case contributors and the reviewers who have offered advice and helped develop this text. We are indebted again to our editors Rosie Churchill and Matthew Simmons for their invaluable support and assistance, and extend our gratitude to Alice Aldous, Alison Davis, Ben King and Lynn Brown.

Every effort has been made to trace and acknowledge ownership of copyright and to clear permission for material reproduced in this book. The publishers will be pleased to make suitable arrangements to clear permission with any copyright holders whom it has not been possible to contact.

Picture acknowledgements

The authors and publishers would like to extend thanks to the following for the reproduction of images, advertising and logos:

Exhibits

1.1: Gritsana P / Shutterstock; 1.2: gresei / Shutterstock; 1.3: The Photo Works / Alamy Stock Photo; 1.4: Daniel Krason / Shutterstock; 1.5: Reproduced with permission from Toms Group A / S, Robert Boisen / Like Minded; 1.6: Grzegorz Czapski / Shutterstock; 1.7: Reproduced with permission from Health Service Executive, Ireland; 1.8: LunaseeStudios / Shutterstock; 2.1: SB_photos / Shutterstock; 2.2: Denis Belitsky / Shutterstock; 2.3: Heineken UK®; 2.4: noomcpk / Shutterstock; 2.5: amer ghazzal / Alamy Stock Photo; 2.6: Reproduced with permission from Amnesty International and Walkter Werbeagentur AG; 2.7: Reproduced with permission from The Surfrider Foundation, surfrider.org; 2.8: LunaseeStudios; 2.9: jackie ellis / Alamy Stock Photo; 2.10: Reproduced with permission of madebywave. Images show Kalahari Beach Bag, madebywave collection and madebywave founder Victoria Bakir visiting her team of craftsmen in Indonesia; 2.11: Sorbis / Shutterstock; 3.1: Home Bird / Alamy Stock Photo; 3.2: Sergey Ryzhov / Shutterstock; 3.3: char abumansoor / Alamy Stock Photo; 3.4: Goran Jakus / Shutterstock; 3.5: Reproduced with permission from Porsche Cars Great Britain; 3.6: Peter Horree / Alamy Stock Photo; 3.8: Instagram / iamgalla; 4.1: Reproduced with permission from Spotify; 4.2: © Jeffrey Blackler / Alamy; 4.5: Adam Hester / Blend Images; 4.6: Tooykrub / Shutterstock; 5.1: tomas devera photo / Shutterstock; 5.2: jeremy sutton-hibbert / Alamy Stock Photo; 5.3: reproduced with permission from Cuddledry®. Image credit: Charlie Goggs; 5.4: charnsitr / Shutterstock; 5.5 alekso94 / Shutterstock; 5.6: monticello / Shuttestock; 5.7: david a eastley / Alamy Stock Photo; 6.1: 2p2play / Shutterstock; 6.2: Bborriss.67 / Shutterstock; 6.3: reproduced with permission from Continental Tyres; 6.4: D. Callcut / Alamy Stock Photo; 6.5: Innocenti / Image Source; 7.1 Copyright AIG Japan Holdings; 7.2 Alistair Laming / Alamy Stock Photo; 7.3: Dmitry Birin / Shutterstock; 7.4: Natee Meepian / Shutterstock; 7.5: chrisdorney / Shuttestock; Exhibit 7.6: reproduced with permission from NHSBT / www.blood.co.uk; Exhibit 7.7: Reproduced with the kind permission of Brass Agency. Artist: Alex Lucas, Photographer: Ed Waring; 7.8: Djohan Shahrin / Shutterstock; 7.9: Reproduced with permission from Kolle Rebbe; 8.1: Reproduced with permission from camelcamelcamel; 8.2: charnsitr / Shutterstock; 8.3: Timothy A. Clary / Getty; 8.4: Reproduced with permission from Transavia; 8.5: DMstudio House / Shutterstock; 8.6: Bloomberg / Getty images; 8.7: volkerpreusser / Alamy Stock Photo; 8.8: Reproduced with permission from P&O Cruises; 8.9: ROPI / Alamy Stock Photo; 9.1: Reproduced with permission from PRS research; 9.2: Bjoern Wylezich / Shutterstock; 9.3: Rob Wilson / Shutterstock; 9.4: James W Copeland / Shutterstock; 9.5: jax10289 / Shutterstock; 9.6: Thinglass / Shutterstock; 9.7: Martin Good / Shutterstock; 10.1: Reproduced with permission from Aston Martin; 10.2: Dimitrios Kambouris / Getty; 10.3: Dominique Berbain / Gamma Rapho / Getty images; 10.4: Miquel Benitez / Getty Images Entertainment; 10.5: Mark Collinson / Alamy Stock Photo; 10.6: Kristoffer Tripplaar / Alamy Stock Photo; 11.1: Pieter Beens / Shutterstock; 11.2: Featureflash Photo Agency / Shutterstock; 11.3: pio3 / Shutterstock; 11.6: Nielsen Norman Group 2006; 11.7: Photo provided courtesy of Booking.com; 11.8: AugustSnow / Alamy Stock Photo; 11.9: Jan Kruger / Stringer / Getty; 11.10: © Google; 11.12: Reproduced with permission from Edgewell; 11.13: ksokolowska / Shutterstock; 11.14: Reproduced with permission from MailChimp; 12.1: Denys Prykhodov / Shutterstock; 12.2: JPstock / Shutterstock; 12.3: roger parkes / Alamy Stock Photo; 12.4: chrisdorney / Shutterstock; 12.5: Sheila Fitzgerald / Shutterstock; 12.6: Reproduced with permission from Qualcomm; 12.7: Josephnator / Shutterstock; 12.8: Jonathan Weiss / Shutterstock; 12.9: Sasa Wick / Shutterstock

Part opening images

1: Alastair Wallace/Shutterstock; 2: stokkete © 123RF.com; 3: Shutterstock/William Potter.

Chapter opening images

1: A.Ricardo/Shutterstock; 2: Rich Carey/Shutterstock; 3: True Images/Alamy Stock Photo; 4: Scharfsinn/Shutterstock; 5: Chris Willson/Alamy Stock Photo; 6: Vytautas Kielaitis/Shutterstock; 7: Zapp2Photo/Shutterstock; 8: Panint Jhonlerkieat/Shutterstock; 9: ChameleonsEye/Shutterstock; 10: natthi phaocharoen/Shutterstock; 11: IgorGolovniov/ Shutterstock; 12: Evan el-Amin/Shutterstock.

Case images

1: pingdao/Shutterstock; 2: Christian Bertrand/Shutterstock; 3: TarikVision/Shutterstock; 4: Gavyn Pedley and Aisling Mooney; 5: DenisMArt/Shutterstock; 6: Action Plus Sports Images/Alamy Stock Photo; 7: Chrispictures/Shutterstock; 8: Helen89/Shutterstock; 9: Casimiro PT/Shutterstock; 10: vengerof/Shutterstock; 11: Willy Barton/Shutterstock; 12: Russell Hart/Alamy Stock Photo

Guided Tour

Chapter Outline and Learning Outcomes

The topics covered and a set of outcomes are included at the start of each chapter, summarizing what to expect from each chapter.

MARKETING SPOTLIGHT

Beyonce: super brand and innovative marketer

Beyonce Knowles-Carter is someone who needs no introduction. Half of a powerhouse couple, along with her husband Jay Z, her net worth is estimated at US$350 million and together they are music's first billion-dollar couple. Born in Houston, Texas, she became famous as part of all-girl R&B group Destiny's Child, before leaving to forge her own solo career in 2002. Since then she has gone from strength to strength. Aside from hugely successful records and Grammy awards, there are movie appearances, clothes lines, perfume deals, and partnerships with leading brands such as Pepsi, McDonald's and Apple. Beyonce is more than just a musician and business mogul, she is also a very savvy marketer in an industry characterized by rapid technological and consumer changes.

A case in point was the launch of her self-titled, fifth studio album, released in December 2013, which was innovative in both its content and distribution. The record, which had been a year and a half in the making, was shrouded in secrecy. When all of the 14 songs were recorded, 17 music videos were created, which added an extra layer of difficulty to keeping the project secret. However, this would also set it apart from competing records in that a 'visual' album was a relatively new concept. But it was her launch of the new record that really caught the attention. Normally new albums are launched with the initial release of a single followed by an intensive round of television inter-

Marketing Spotlight

A lively vignette begins each chapter to introduce the main topic and show how marketing works in real life.

Marketing in Action

In each chapter you'll find these fun, informative examples of marketing in action, which show how the issues covered in the chapter affect real-life companies and products. Each Marketing in Action vignette has a Critical Thinking box to provoke discussion and encourage critical reflection on that topic.

Marketing in Action 1.1
Hyundai: recreating Shackleton's epic journey

Critical Thinking: Below is a review of Hyundai's 2017 advertising campaign for its Santa Fe brand. Read it and look at the videos of the making of the advert online. Assess how effective it is in its use of emotion. How relevant is emotion to the selling of a car, for example?

Put yourself in the shoes of a consumer goods marketer. Your product is a shampoo or a TV or a bank. Can you think of something that you can say about your product that will both distinguish it from your competitors but, more importantly, that will get the attention of and engage potential customers. And remember, these customers not only have lots of other things competing for their time and attention, but they are constantly exposed to marketing messages, most of which they ignore. It is no wonder, then, that companies will go to extraordinary lengths to try to create content that will cut through this saturated marketplace and communicate messages to a potential

Critical Marketing Perspective 1.1
Marketing: good or evil?

It is possible to look at marketing from different standpoints. A positive view ing provides significant benefits to society. For example, the innovative ef provide us, as consumers, with a world of choice and diversity. A search o to find information on anything that we want; with an Apple app on their i longer need a stethoscope to examine patients, and websites like Amazon an shop from the comfort of our desks. The innovations of tomorrow will bring ing products, services and solutions. Second, as the practice of marketing ticular needs are increasingly being met. If we eat only gluten-free products, have a passion for Japanese origami, there are organizations that will fulfil the collect more information about their customers, they will tailor solutions to requirements. Finally, the competition between firms continually forces the services and products, and deliver extra value to customers. For example, low

Critical Marketing Perspective

Critical Marketing Perspective boxes are located throughout the book, designed to highlight ethical issues, and provoke discussion and critical reflection.

Exhibit 1.1 Coca-Cola Life failed to meet the needs of its target market segment and was withdrawn after less than three years.

Table 1.2 Marketing planning activities

Main activities in the marketing planning process	Relevant chapters
Business mission and strategy	Chapter 12
Environmental and customer analysis	Chapters 2 to 4
Marketing objectives	Chapter 12
Marketing strategy	Chapter 5
Marketing actions	Chapters 6 to 11
Evaluation of performance	Chapter 12

e achievement of corporate goals through meeting and For example, Netflix has added to its successful movie how content. In addition, all of its content is available vourite movies and shows while on the move – a sig-

analyses and choices, which are detailed in Table 1.2. The ges will be developed in greater detail at certain times will examine marketing planning in greater detail in ith an assessment of the situation that the organization

Exhibits, figures and tables

We've included a hand-selected array of contemporary adverts and images to show marketing in action. Key concepts and models are illustrated using figures, tables and charts.

End-of-chapter case studies

Every chapter has its own case study, directly relating to the issues discussed and designed to bring the theories to life. See page xx for a full list of companies and issues covered. Questions are included for class work, assignments and revision, and to promote critical reflection.

Case **1**
GoPro: riding the waves of a changing market

Introduction

Twelve thousand feet above Navarre Beach, Florida, Patrick Remington hangs from the landing skids of a small helicopter with his two, equally brazen, friends. Equipped with a pair of black flip-flops, cargo shorts, a parachute and a visorless helmet with a mounted GoPro HERO3 action camera, he prepares for flight with animated yells, echoed by his dangling partners. On the count of three, the trio release their grip, the

high-definition video into a captivating four-minute clip, ready for sharing on YouTube.

Who is GoPro? A company overview

Entrepreneur and adrenaline-junkie Nicholas Woodman founded California-based action camera and accessories manufacturer GoPro after struggling to capture immersive footage of his Australian surfing vacation.

Summary

This chapter has examined the key activities of market segmentation, market targeting and positioning. The following issues were addressed.

1. The process of market segmentation: not all consumers in the market have the same needs and we can serve them better by segmenting the market into groups with homogeneous needs.

2. A variety of bases are available for segmenting both consumer and industrial markets, and often a combination of bases is used to effectively segment markets. In consumer markets, behavioural variables such as benefits sought and purchase behaviour are particularly powerful bases for segmentation. Choice criteria are a key factor in segmenting organizational markets.

3. The five criteria for successful segmentation: effective, measurable, accessible, actionable and profitable.

4. The four generic target marketing strategies: undifferentiated marketing, differentiated marketing, focused marketing and customized marketing. Differentiated and focused marketing have their unique strengths and weaknesses, while customized marketing continues to grow in popularity.

5. The definition of personalization and the growing role of the personalization strategy for changing consumer demographics.

6. What is meant by the concept of positioning, why it is important, and the need for clarity, consistency, credibility and competitiveness in a positioning statement. Consumers buy benefits, not products or services, and positioning is the key to conveying these benefits.

7. The concept of repositioning and the four repositioning strategies: image repositioning, product repositioning, intangible repositioning and tangible repositioning. Repositioning is challenging and should be undertaken with great care.

Study questions

1. Discuss the advantages and related challenges of segmenting the market.
2. You have been asked by a client company to segment the confectionery market. Use at least three different bases for segmentation and describe the segments that emerge.
3. Many consumer goods companies have recently been experimenting with the possibilities of a customized target marketing strategy. What are the advantages and limitations of such a strategy?
4. Research has emerged that views the targeting of particular segments as overdone. Discuss the merits and weaknesses of the mass marketing approach of appealing to as large a slice of the market as possible.
5. A friend of yours wants to launch a new breakfast cereal on the market but is unsure how to position

End-of-chapter material

The Chapter Summary reinforces the main topics, to make sure you have acquired a solid understanding. Study questions allow you to apply your understanding and think critically about the topics. Suggested reading and References direct you towards the best sources for further research.

Tour our video and digital resources

In addition to the great study tools available for student and lecturers through Connect™ there is a host of support resources available to you via our website:

Ad Insight

Throughout the book you will find QR codes that link to carefully selected TV advertising campaigns via company YouTube videos. To access the videos, download a QR code reader app to your smartphone and scan the codes with your camera.

Marketing Showcase

We are excited to offer an exclusive set of new video cases to lecturers adopting this text. Each video illustrates a number of core marketing concepts linked to the book, to help students to see how marketing works in the real world. This fantastic video resource will add real value to lectures, providing attention-grabbing content that helps students to make the connection between theory and practice.

What do the videos cover?

The videos offer students insights into how different organizations have successfully harnessed the elements of the marketing mix, including discussions about new product development, pricing, promotion, packaging, market research, relationship and digital marketing. The videos feature interviews with business leaders and marketing professionals, researched and conducted by Professor John Fahy, to ensure seamless integration with the content of the new edition of this text.

How can I use them?

To ensure maximum flexibility for teaching purposes, the videos have been edited to focus on key topics so that short extracts can easily be integrated into a lecture presentation or delivered in a tutorial setting to spark class discussion. To ensure painless preparation for teaching, each video is accompanied by PowerPoint slides, teaching notes and discussion questions.

Some highlights of the video package include:

- an interview with **Paddy Power**, communications director of the eponymous bookmaker, who reveals the story behind its ground-breaking and often controversial marketing campaigns
- a first-hand account of how a young student entrepreneur set up the thriving **SuperJam** brand, taking his homemade preserves from the kitchen table to the supermarket
- the marketing director of **Burnt Sugar**, luxury toffee confectioner, explaining how his company has used innovative online forums, events and other customer feedback to develop and promote its products.

How do I get the videos?

The full suite of videos is available exclusively to lecturers adopting this textbook. For ultimate flexibility, they are available to lecturers through Connect.

If you are interested in this resource, please contact your McGraw-Hill representative or visit **www.mheducation.co.uk**

MARKETING

McGraw-Hill Connect Marketing is a learning and teaching environment that improves student performance and outcomes while promoting engagement and comprehension of content.

You can utilize publisher-provided materials, or add your own content to design a complete course to help your students achieve higher outcomes.

PROVEN EFFECTIVE

INSTRUCTORS

With McGraw-Hill Connect Plus Marketing, instructors get:

- simple **assignment management**, allowing you to spend more time teaching

- **auto-graded** assignments, quizzes and tests

- **detailed visual reporting**, where students and section results can be viewed and analysed

- sophisticated **online testing** capability

- a **filtering and reporting** function that allows you to easily assign and report on materials that are correlated to learning outcomes, topics, level of difficulty, and more; reports can be accessed for individual students or the whole class, as well as offering the ability to drill into individual assignments, questions or categories

- **instructor materials** to help supplement your course.

Get Connected. Get Results.

STUDENTS

With McGraw-Hill Connect Marketing, students get:

Assigned content

- Easy **online access** to homework, tests and quizzes.

- **Immediate feedback** and 24-hour tech support.

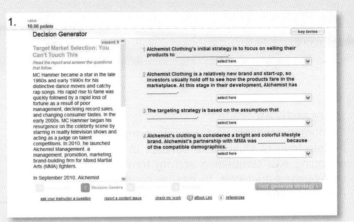

With McGraw-Hill SmartBook, students can:

- Take control of your own learning with a personalized and adaptive reading experience.

- Understand what you know and don't know; SmartBook takes you through the stages of reading and practice, prompting you to recharge your knowledge throughout the course for maximum retention.

- Achieve the most efficient and productive study time by adapting to what you do and don't know.

- Hone in on concepts you are most likely to forget, to ensure knowledge of key concepts is learnt and retained.

ACCESS OPTIONS

|MARKETING

Is an online assignment and assessment solution that offers a number of powerful tools and features that make managing assignments easier, so faculty can spend more time teaching. With Connect Marketing, students can engage with their coursework anytime and anywhere, making the learning process more accessible and efficient.

Interactives

Encourage students to formulate a marketing strategy or illustrate a concept in an engaging and stimulating activity format with step-by-step guidance, to ensure conceptual understanding is tested and applied.

Videos

Promote engagement and student understanding, offering content in a fresh format and reinforcing key concepts. Videos feature interviews from business leaders and marketing professionals, allowing students to learn from real-world strategies and campaigns.

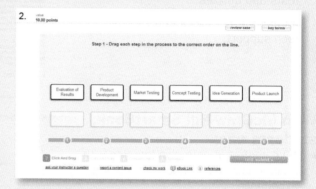

Cases

Allow the student to learn how to analyse cases and check they have understood what they have read, while learning from market-leading brand names.

Multiple-Choice Questions

Check students' knowledge and conceptual understanding. Quick to answer and give students immediate feedback.

Pre-built assignments

Assign all of the autogradable end-of-chapter material as a ready-made assignment with the simple click of a button.

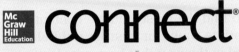

Fueled by LearnSmart—the most widely used and intelligent adaptive learning resource—SmartBook is the first and only adaptive reading experience available today. Distinguishing what a student knows from what they don't, and honing in on concepts they are most likely to forget, SmartBook personalizes content for each student in a continuously adapting reading experience. Valuable reports provide instructors insight as to how students are progressing through textbook content, and are useful for shaping in-class time or assessment.

LearnSmart™

LearnSmart is the most widely used and intelligent adaptive learning resource that is proven to strengthen memory recall, improve course retention and boost grades. Distinguishing what students know from what they don't, and homing in on concepts they are most likely to forget, LearnSmart continuously adapts to each student's needs by building an individual learning path so students study smarter and retain more knowledge. Real-time reports provide valuable insight to instructors, so precious class time can be spent on higher-level concepts and discussion.

Let us help make our content your solution

At McGraw-Hill Education our aim is to help lecturers to find the most suitable content for their needs delivered to their students in the most appropriate way. Our **custom publishing solutions** offer the ideal combination of content delivered in the way that best suits lecturer and students.

Our custom publishing programme offers lecturers the opportunity to select just the chapters or sections of material they wish to deliver to their students from a database called CREATE™ at

http://create.mheducation.com/uk/

CREATE™ contains more than two million pages of content from:
- textbooks
- professional books
- case books – Harvard Articles, Insead, Ivey, Darden, Thunderbird and BusinessWeek
- Taking Sides – debate materials.

Across the following imprints:
- McGraw-Hill Education
- Open University Press
- Harvard Business Publishing
- US and European material.

There is also the option to include additional material authored by lecturers in the custom product – this does not necessarily have to be in English.

We will take care of everything from start to finish in the process of developing and delivering a custom product to ensure that lecturers and students receive exactly the material needed in the most suitable way.

With a Custom Publishing Solution, students enjoy the best selection of material deemed to be the most suitable for learning everything they need for their courses – something of real value to support their learning. Teachers are able to use exactly the material they want, in the way they want, to support their teaching on the course.

Please contact **your local McGraw-Hill representative** with any questions or alternatively contact Marc Wright e: marc.wright@mheducation.com.

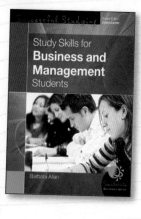

Part 1

The Market-Led Organization

Chapter 1

The Nature of Marketing

Chapter outline

What is marketing?

The development of marketing

The scope of marketing

Marketing and business performance

Planning marketing activity

Learning outcomes

By the end of this chapter you will:

1 Understand what marketing is

2 Understand the nature of customer value

3 Describe how marketing thought has developed over the years

4 Explain the scope of marketing

5 Analyse the impact of marketing activity on organizational performance

6 Critique the role of marketing in society

Beyonce: super brand and innovative marketer

Beyonce Knowles-Carter is someone who needs no introduction. Half of a powerhouse couple, along with her husband Jay Z, her net worth is estimated at US$350 million and together they are music's first billion-dollar couple. Born in Houston, Texas, she became famous as part of all-girl R&B group Destiny's Child, before leaving to forge her own solo career in 2002. Since then she has gone from strength to strength. Aside from hugely successful records and Grammy awards, there are movie appearances, clothes lines, perfume deals, and partnerships with leading brands such as Pepsi, McDonald's and Apple. Beyonce is more than just a musician and business mogul, she is also a very savvy marketer in an industry characterized by rapid technological and consumer changes.

A case in point was the launch of her self-titled, fifth studio album, released in December 2013, which was innovative in both its content and distribution. The record, which had been a year and a half in the making, was shrouded in secrecy. When all of the 14 songs were recorded, 17 music videos were created, which added an extra layer of difficulty to keeping the project secret. However, this would also set it apart from competing records in that a 'visual' album was a relatively new concept. But it was her launch of the new record that really caught the attention. Normally new albums are launched with the initial release of a single followed by an intensive round of television inter-views and performances. Beyonce took a completely different approach. The night before the album was released, she posted a short 15-second clip on Instagram with the message 'Surprise'. The album was available only on iTunes with, again, the reason being that Apple was viewed as the best company to help keep the launch a secret. In addition, fans could only buy the album as a whole and not the singles separately as normal. A media frenzy ensued. Facebook mentions saw a 1,300 per cent spike, she had more than 1.2 million mentions on Twitter, and Google searches of the phrase 'Beyonce's new album' reached 70 million-plus, with the result that revenues on the first weekend of release alone reached almost US$10 million.

Why did Beyonce take such a radical and risky approach to the launch of her fifth album? Two elements of contemporary marketing – surprise and scarcity – help to explain its success. In the media-saturated world that we live in, getting attention for products and services has never been more difficult. Beyonce's surprise move created an immediate buzz that garnered attention for the album. Paradoxically, making a product scarce helps to foster demand for it, a technique that has been used in the past by companies like Apple and Zara. Limiting its release to iTunes created an element of scarcity and exploited the modern social phenomenon of FOMO (fear of missing out) in a way that drove instant purchases.

When it came to the 2016 launch of her next album, *Lemonade*, Beyonce added some new twists to these techniques. Coinciding with her performance at the Super Bowl halftime show in February of that year, she released a single, 'Formation', without any warning on her YouTube or Tidal (the streaming service founded by Jay Z) accounts. In an unusual move, the song was not listed on YouTube so it was not possible to just search 'Beyonce Formation'. Instead fans had to visit her website in order to find the link to the video, driving traffic to her site, which also features a merchandise store and links to purchase music. Two months later, she formed a clothing col-laboration with British high-street brand Topshop, launching her Ivy Park 'athleisure' clothing brand. Queues formed at Topshop stores around the world and the launch crashed the company's website. Fresh from all this publicity, the album was released in April immediately following a HBO special of the same name and again without any warning. Once again the internet went wild, leading 24 April to become known as Lemonade Day. A week later her world tour began. *Lemonade* became the highest-grossing album of 2016, with 2.5 million physical and digital units sold, while her world tour grossed more than US$256 million.

(continued)

As we can see, Beyonce is far more than just a singer – she is a well-crafted and very well-marketed brand. She appeals to her target market of 18–35-year-old females by portraying herself as a strong, independent woman. In her songs, she is not afraid to tackle difficult social issues such as gender, female empowerment and race inequality in her native USA. She has multiple income streams from record and concert ticket sales, merchandise, her clothing, vegan and perfume lines, as well as her acting roles, brand endorsements and appearance fees. And she is clearly not afraid to use innovative and risky marketing tactics to communicate with and engage her ever growing fan base.[1]

The activities of companies both reflect and shape the world in which we live. For example, some have argued that the invention of the motor car has defined the way we live today because it allowed personal mobility on a scale that had never been seen before. It contributed to the growth of city suburbs, to increased recreation and to an upsurge in consumer credit. It gave us shopping malls, theme parks, motels, a fast-food industry and a generation of road movies. In a similar vein today, the development of the smartphone created a new form of mobility on a scale never seen before. Users have instant access to any information they might require, and everything from news to event bookings to shopping to entertainment can be had at the touch of a few buttons. With this has also come a variety of new phenomena such as smartphone addiction, technostress and data mining.

Therefore, the world of business is an exciting one, where there are new successes and failures every day. The newspaper industry was once all powerful and the main means by which consumers learned about what was happening in the world. It continued to thrive with the arrival of radio and television, and complemented these media. But the internet has changed the way that news is both captured and communicated, with the result that many newspapers are either struggling or failing. Not too long ago, Sony dominated the gaming business with its PlayStation consoles and exciting range of games. While trying to strengthen the functionality of its PlayStation 3, it wasn't alive to the threat posed by the Nintendo Wii, whose ease of use, lower price points and broader appeal enabled it to capture a leading share in the market. And now both organizations must respond to an increasing customer preference for online play in virtual worlds.

At the heart of all of this change is marketing. Companies succeed and fail for many reasons, but very often marketing is central to the outcome. The reason for this is that the focus of marketing is on customers and their changing needs. If you don't have customers, you don't have a business. Successful companies are those that succeed not only in getting customers but also in keeping them through being constantly aware of their changing needs. The goal of marketing is long-term customer satisfaction, not short-term deception or gimmicks. This theme is reinforced by the writings of top management consultant Peter Drucker, who stated:[2]

> *Because the purpose of business is to create and keep customers, it has only two central functions – marketing and innovation. The basic function of marketing is to attract and retain customers at a profit.*

What does this statement tell us? First, it places marketing in a central role for business success since it is concerned with the creation and retention of customers. The failure of many products, particularly those in sectors like information technology, is often attributed to a lack of attention to customer needs. For example, Microsoft developed a new version of its Windows operating system, Windows 8, in order to appeal to a growing segment of consumers using hand-held tablet devices rather than traditional personal computers. However, its launch was generally considered a failure as poor design and usability issues meant a low level of uptake of the system by existing Microsoft users, while it also failed in its important task of kick-starting sales of Microsoft's own tablet devices. Similarly, in 2014, Coca-Cola launched its new sub-brand, Coca-Cola Life, to appeal to 35–55-year-old consumers looking for a lower-calorie drink than regular Coke but also with natural sweetness rather than the artificial flavours added to its diet drinks. However, within three years the product was axed as it became clear that it was neither healthy enough nor natural enough to appeal to the target market (see Exhibit 1.1).[3] Second, it is a reality of commercial life that it is much more expensive to attract new customers than to retain existing ones. Indeed, the costs of attracting new customers have been found to be up to six times higher than the costs of retaining existing ones.[4] Consequently, market-orientated companies recognize the importance of building relationships with customers by providing satisfaction, and attracting new customers by creating added value. Grönroos stressed the importance of relationship building in his definition of marketing, in which he describes the objective of marketing as to establish, develop and commercialize long-term customer relationships so that the objectives of the parties involved are met.[5] Third, since most markets are characterized by strong competition, the statement also suggests the need to monitor and understand competitors, since it is to rivals that customers will turn if their needs are not being met. The rest of this chapter will examine some of these ideas in more detail.

Exhibit 1.1 Coca-Cola Life failed to meet the needs of its target market segment and was withdrawn after less than three years.

What is marketing?

The modern **marketing concept** can be expressed as 'the achievement of corporate goals through meeting and exceeding customer needs better than the competition'. For example, Netflix has added to its successful movie rental and streaming services by providing original TV show content. In addition, all of its content is available on mobile devices, allowing customers to watch their favourite movies and shows while on the move – a significant advantage over cable operators. Three conditions must be met before the marketing concept can be applied. First, company activities should be focused on providing **customer satisfaction** rather than, for example, simply producing products (see Exhibit 1.2). This is not always as easy as it may first appear. Organizations almost by definition are inward-looking, with a focus on their people, their operations and their products. Research has demonstrated the disconnect that often exists between managerial perceptions of levels and drivers of customer satisfaction and those of their customers. One study found that managers systematically overestimate the levels of customer satisfaction, attitudinal loyalty and perceived value. Second, managers tend to underestimate the importance of customer perceptions of quality in driving their satisfaction, and of satisfaction in driving loyalty and complaint behaviour.[6]

The customer may often appear to be at some remove from the organization and, when their needs are changing rapidly, companies can lose touch with them. For example, until recently, Finland's Nokia was the world's dominant mobile-phone manufacturer by some distance. However, its failure to recognize the shift in consumer tastes towards more technologically advanced smartphones meant that its sales collapsed and it was rapidly overtaken by Apple and Samsung. Its Mobile Devices and Services division was subsequently sold off to Microsoft in 2013.

Second, the achievement of customer satisfaction relies on integrated effort. The responsibility for the implementation of the concept lies not just within the marketing department but should run right through production, finance, research and development, engineering and other departments. The fact that marketing is the responsibility of everyone in the

Exhibit 1.2 The Duracell brand owned by P&G has built a strong reputation in the marketplace as a longer-lasting battery.

Duracell Ad Insight: Brand advertising focuses on key benefits such as battery life.

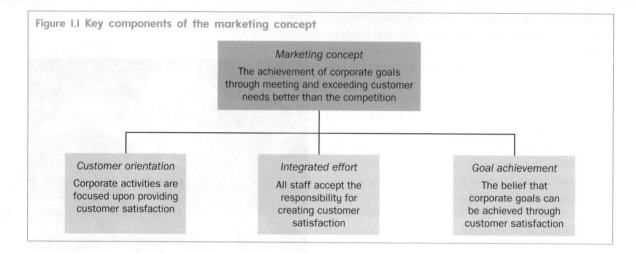

Figure I.I Key components of the marketing concept

Marketing concept
The achievement of corporate goals through meeting and exceeding customer needs better than the competition

Customer orientation
Corporate activities are focused upon providing customer satisfaction

Integrated effort
All staff accept the responsibility for creating customer satisfaction

Goal achievement
The belief that corporate goals can be achieved through customer satisfaction

organization provides significant challenges for the management of companies. Finally, for integrated effort to come about, management must believe that corporate goals can be achieved through satisfied customers (see Figure 1.1). Some companies are quicker and better at recognizing the importance of the marketing concept than others. For example, Nike was a late entrant into the running shoe business dominated by brands such as Reebok and Puma, but it has established itself as the world's leading sportswear company, through the delivery of powerful brand values (see Exhibit 1.3).

In summary, companies can be viewed as being either inward looking or outward looking. In the former, the focus is on making things or providing services but with significant attention being paid to the efficiency with which internal operations and processes are conducted. Companies that build strategy from the outside in start with the customer and work backwards from an understanding of what customers truly value. The difference in emphasis is subtle but very important. By maintaining an outside-in focus, companies can understand what customers value and how to consistently innovate new sources of value that keep bringing them back.[7] Doing so efficiently ensures that value is created and delivered at a profit to the company – the ultimate goal of marketing.

Exhibit I.3 Nike's 'Risk Everything' campaign for the 2014 FIFA World Cup focused on familiar Nike themes of what winners must do to succeed.

The nature of customer value

One of the most important tasks in marketing is to create and communicate value to customers, to drive their satisfaction, loyalty and profitability.[8] Generally speaking, customer value is framed as a dual exchange concept. First, in order to be successful, firms have to create perceived value for customers. But customers too return value to firms, both directly through purchases and indirectly through referrals, word-of-mouth promotion and even suggestions for product and service modifications. Above and beyond these ideas of value as exchange, the concept can also be considered at a social level, in terms of benefit from both the individual's and society's point of view – a fundamental theme that is explored throughout this book. And, at a third level, value can also be considered in a semiotic sense, where cultural meanings are mediated through consumption, and constantly reconstructed among multiple actors.[9] This is the fundamental premise of Consumer Culture Theory (CCT), which is explored in greater detail in Chapter 3.

If delivering **customer value** is the key to building a successful business, how can a firm know if it is creating such value? This has proved to be a troublesome problem for many companies. For example, some firms add new features to products and hope that this will attract customers. Others engage in new marketing activities such as advertising campaigns, Facebook competitions or the creation of retail experiences. And still others may seek to exploit consumer preferences for economy by offering products or services at lower prices. But the key question is: do consumers see any of these changes as being beneficial to them and worth any of the costs that they may have to incur in order to obtain these benefits? Consequently, customer value is often expressed in terms of the definition below and it is important to note that it is customers and not organizations that define what represents value:

Exhibit 1.4 This campaign by accommodation website Airbnb conveys the unique benefits it offers to its customers.

$$\text{customer value} = \text{perceived benefits} - \text{perceived sacrifice}$$

Perceived benefits can be derived from the product (for example, the hotel room and restaurant), the associated service (for example, how responsive the hotel is to the specific needs of customers) and the image of the company (for example, is the image of the company/product favourable?). Conveying benefits is a critical marketing task and is central to positioning and branding, as we shall see in Chapters 5 and 6 (see Exhibit 1.4).

Perceived sacrifice is the total cost associated with buying the product. This consists not just of monetary costs, but also the time and energy involved in the purchase. For example, with hotels, good location can reduce the time and energy required to find a suitable place to stay. But marketers need to be aware of another critical sacrifice in some buying situations: the potential psychological cost of not making the right decision. Uncertainty means that people perceive risk when purchasing. Therefore, hotels like the Marriott or restaurants like McDonald's aim for consistency so that customers can be confident of what they will receive when they visit these service providers.

A further key to marketing success is to ensure that the value offered exceeds that of competitors. Consumers decide on purchases on the basis of judgements about the value offered by different suppliers. Once a product has been purchased, customer satisfaction depends on its perceived performance compared with the buyer's expectations and will be achieved if these expectations are met or exceeded. Expectations are formed through pre-buying experiences, discussions with other people, and suppliers' marketing activities. Companies need to avoid the mistake of setting customer expectations too high through exaggerated promotional claims, since this can lead to dissatisfaction if performance falls short of expectations.

In the current competitive climate, it is usually not enough simply to match performance and expectations. Expectations need to be exceeded for commercial success so that customers are delighted

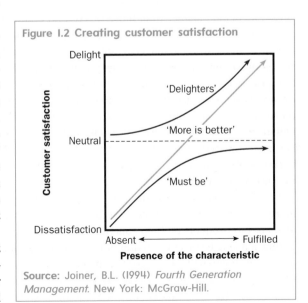

Figure 1.2 Creating customer satisfaction

Source: Joiner, B.L. (1994) *Fourth Generation Management.* New York: McGraw-Hill.

with the outcome. In order to understand the concept of customer satisfaction, the Kano model (see Figure 1.2) helps to separate characteristics that cause dissatisfaction, satisfaction and delight. Three characteristics underlie the model: 'must be', 'more is better' and 'delighters'.

Those characteristics recognized as 'must bes' are expected and thus taken for granted. For example, commuters expect planes or trains to depart on time and for schedules to be maintained. Lack of these characteristics causes annoyance but their presence only brings dissatisfaction up to a neutral level. 'More is better' characteristics can take satisfaction past neutral and into the

Exhibit I.5 As part of its 'Generosity Campaign', the Danish chocolate maker Anthon Berg developed the 'Generous Upgrader' at Copenhagen Airport, where passengers could scan their tickets and if they had a poor seat – for example, at the back of the plane – they would get a complimentary box of chocolates and Anthon Berg flying merchandise.

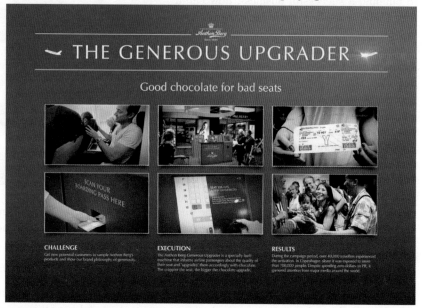

positive satisfaction range. For example, no response to a telephone call can cause dissatisfaction, but a fast response may cause positive satisfaction. The usability of search results is an example of 'more is better' and has become a key differentiating factor in the search engine industry, which has allowed Google to become the dominant player. 'Delighters' are the unexpected characteristics that surprise the customer (see Exhibit 1.5). Their absence does not cause dissatisfaction, but their presence delights the customer. For example, tourists who have found that a holiday destination has exceeded their expectations through the quality of customer service that they have received will often be delighted and are likely to recommend the destination to friends and colleagues. Although modern organizations offer an innumerable variety of products and services, the following four core forms of customer value have been identified.[10]

Price value: one of the most powerful customer motivations to purchase is because a product is perceived as being cheaper than those offered by competitors. This has been exploited in many industries, such as air travel (Ryanair), food retailing (Aldi), car rental (easyCar), and so on. These types of organization recognize that, in their markets, some consumers will forgo extra product features in order to avail themselves of low prices (see market segmentation in Chapter 5). They respond by providing basic products at low prices. For example, low-fares airlines have stripped away many of the features that used to characterize air travel, such as in-flight meals, airport check-ins and no baggage restrictions. Consumers who want these features are now charged extra for them and the profitability of low-price companies is further enhanced by the high degree of attention they pay to the efficiency of their operations. Food retailer Aldi has an estimated annual turnover of €40 billion and is one of Germany's most successful companies. Its business proposition is to offer customers a limited range of own-label products at permanently low prices in a no-frills environment.

Performance value: in the same way that some customers have a preference for low price, others are more concerned about product performance. What they are looking for is the latest features, and they are attracted to products by their functionality and perceived quality levels. The priority for companies operating in this space is to be consistently innovative, exploiting changes and discontinuities in technology in order to deliver products with attractive features and functionality. For example, the UK electronic products manufacturer, Dyson, has a team of 420 engineers and scientists working on product ideas and the firm has been responsible for innovations like the cyclonic vacuum cleaner, the Airblade electric hand dryer and the

Contrarotator, which was the world's first washing machine with two counter-rotating drums for a better clean. Firms like Dyson aim to provide value to customers based on the functionality and performance features of their products and services.

Emotional value: one of the big challenges facing the modern firm is to find effective ways to differentiate products based on performance elements. If one looks at the car industry, for example, the technical differences between cars in particular categories such as economy cars and family saloons are marginal. Most have very similar designs, functionality and features, and different manufacturers frequently share time on the same production lines. Similarly, for a whole array of consumer products such as basic electrical appliances, the brands of competing firms are regularly manufactured by a small number of companies and technical differences between them are minimal. Consequently, the only real difference that exists between these brands is in the mind of the consumer and this is what is known as emotional value (see Marketing in Action 1.1). Some consumers may prefer Volvo cars because they believe them to be safer than competing brands (technically this is not the case) and as a result remain loyal Volvo buyers. This kind of emotional value is created through marketing activity, as we shall discuss throughout this text. It also helps to explain why some consumers will pay huge premiums for luxury brands (e.g. Chanel, Hermès) and why others will queue for hours to be the first among their peers to own certain products (e.g. iPad, Kate Moss clothing).

Marketing in Action 1.1
Hyundai: recreating Shackleton's epic journey

> **Critical Thinking:** Below is a review of Hyundai's 2017 advertising campaign for its Santa Fe brand. Read it and look at the videos of the making of the advert online. Assess how effective it is in its use of emotion. How relevant is emotion to the selling of a car, for example?

Put yourself in the shoes of a consumer goods marketer. Your product is a shampoo or a TV or a bank. Can you think of something that you can say about your product that will both distinguish it from your competitors but, more importantly, that will get the attention of and engage potential customers. And remember, these customers not only have lots of other things competing for their time and attention, but they are constantly exposed to marketing messages, most of which they ignore. It is no wonder, then, that companies will go to extraordinary lengths to try to create content that will cut through this saturated marketplace and communicate messages to a potential audience.

A recent example is Hyundai's campaign for its Santa Fe car brand in 2017. In it, it chose to focus on the 100th anniversary of an epic expedition by the explorer Sir Ernst Shackleton to cross Antartica. In 1917, Shackleton took a team of 27 men with him, with the aim of becoming the first man to cross the continent. However, his ship became trapped in pack ice and he had to give up on his dream in order to save his men. The Hyundai campaign was fronted by Patrick Bergel, Shackleton's great grandson, who undertook the gruelling journey across the coldest and driest continent on the Earth by car. To build an emotional connection with the original expedition, the names of original crew members and their descendants were engraved on the car. Despite temperatures of minus 30 degrees Celsius and frequent snow storms, the team drove 15–20 hours/day for 30 days to complete the crossing, making the Santa Fe the first passenger car brand to have made this journey. Content surrounding the event was posted on YouTube, Facebook and Instagram in 42 of Hyundai's markets. Unsurprisingly, the campaign was hugely successful, with more than 100 million YouTube views, the highest ever for a car brand. The limited 'Endurance edition' of the Santa Fe brand in the UK showed a year-on-year sales increase of more than 100 per cent (see Exhibit 1.6).

(continued)

Some aspects of this campaign are particularly noteworthy. First, there is the powerful use of emotion. Several of the descendants of those who took part in the original expedition feature in the video, reconnecting to the spirit and bravery of Shackleton and his men. Hyundai was able to embrace that fundamental together-ness in its philosophy of 'Together for a better future'. Second, the campaign empha-sizes the importance of great storytelling. From the time that we are children we are

Exhibit 1.6 The Hyundai Santa Fe.

listening to and sharing stories, so storytelling is a fundamental aspect of being human. Brands both tell their own stories or connect with other stories, such as in this case. In the same way, the Sainsbury's Christmas 2014 ad connected to the centenary of another historic event – the playing of a football game during the First World War between the two warring sides, on Christmas Day 1914. As products and services become increasingly hard to distinguish at a technical level, it is no surprise that brands look to deeper levels of meaning to both engage audiences and, of course, drive sales.

Based on: Anonymous, 2018[11]

Relational value: another important motive to purchase is the quality of service received by the customer. This presents a particular opportunity in the case of service businesses (see Chapter 7), such as a restaurant meal, or business taxation services, which are not easy to evaluate in advance of purchase. When the customer finds a good-quality service provider, they may be willing to stay with this provider and, as the relationship builds, a high level of trust becomes established between the parties. Central to this is the notion of the **lifetime value of a customer**, which is recognition by the company of the potential sales, profits and endorsements that come from a repeat customer who stays with the company for several years. But relational value is not restricted just to service businesses. All kinds of organizations are now becoming proficient users of **customer relationship management** (CRM) systems to get to know their customers better and to interact with them on a regular basis (see Chapter 7). Even fast-moving consumer goods brands such as innocent and Walkers have sought to build stronger relationships with core customers through running events that customers can enjoy (innocent village fetes, Walkers 'Do Us a Flavour'), while in turn the company benefits not only from customer loyalty but also the creation of new product ideas that come from the marketplace. In other words, value is increasingly being seen as not something that is created by organizations for customers but rather something that is co-created between organizations and customers.[12]

The challenge for organizations, then, is to try to become a value leader on one of these four dimensions. Those that do achieve these leadership positions, such as Ryanair (price value leader in aviation) or Louis Vuitton (emotional value leader in luxury fashion goods), tend to be significantly more successful than their peers. This is because they have a clearly defined **customer value proposition** or unique selling point (USP), which is a reason why customers return to them again and again. It is not normally possible for companies to compete on more than one dimension as to do so would mean presenting a confusing message in the mar-ketplace. However, the proposition may evolve over time. For example, innocent drinks initially captured a share of the market through the quality of its smoothies (performance value) but this was quickly supplanted by the personality of the brand – its humorous, quirky approach to business and its cause-related activity (emotional value).

The key role of customer value enables us to offer the following definition of **marketing**:

Marketing is the delivery of value to customers at a profit.

Therefore we see that the two core elements of marketing are value and profit. Organizations must create and deliver some form of value for some customer group. But they also must be able to do this in a manner that enables them to generate a profit, otherwise their business will be unsustainable. For example, Norwegian Air is a budget airlines that has expanded into providing low fares on long-haul flights such as across the Atlantic. However it recorded significant losses in 2017 and many commentators have questioned the viability of its strategy.[13] Being consistently able to provide value and generate profit is a characteristic of the most successful companies, such as Apple and Samsung.

The development of marketing

The origins of modern marketing can be traced to the Industrial Revolutions that took place in Britain around 1750, and in the USA and Germany around 1830.[14] Advances in production and distribution, and the migration of rural masses to urban areas, created the potential for large-scale markets. As business people sought to exploit these markets, the institutions of marketing, such as advertising media and distribution channels, began to grow and develop. Marketing as a field of study began in the early part of the twentieth century, growing out of courses that examined issues relating to distribution.[15] The focus of marketing courses in the 1950s and 1960s was on 'how to do it', with an emphasis on the techniques of marketing.[16] This was followed by a focus on the philosophy of marketing as a way of doing business and on the nature and impact of marketing on stakeholders and society in general. More recently, the impact of technology on both consumers and marketing has been the predominant focus of both academic research and the general business press.

Despite this long tradition, there is no guarantee that all companies will adopt a **marketing orientation**. Many firms today are characterized by an inward-looking stance, where their focus is on existing products or the internal operations of the company, that can be traced all the way back to the emergence of mass production in the USA in the 1920s and 1930s. Figure 1.3 (a) illustrates **production orientation** in its crudest form. The focus is on current production capabilities. The purpose of the organization is to develop products or services, and it is the quality and innovativeness of these offerings that are considered to be the key to success. For example, a report on the funds management industry in the UK found that, in general, the sector was characterized by a lack of customer focus and a lack of effective market segmentation, with the result that many products being offered were unsuitable and potential sales were being lost.[17]

Many other organizations are characterized by what can be described as an excessive sales focus. They may possess good products and services but believe that the focus of marketing should be on ensuring that

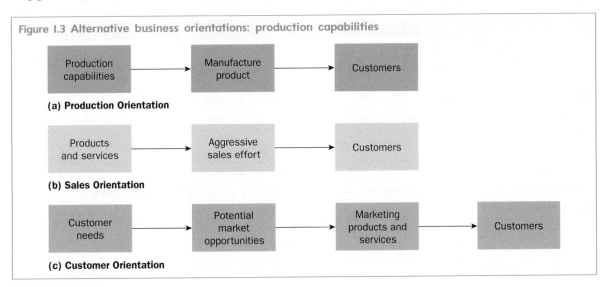

Figure 1.3 **Alternative business orientations: production capabilities**

(a) Production Orientation
Production capabilities → Manufacture product → Customers

(b) Sales Orientation
Products and services → Aggressive sales effort → Customers

(c) Customer Orientation
Customer needs → Potential market opportunities → Marketing products and services → Customers

customers buy these offerings (see Figure 1.3 (b). This is an approach that is often traced back to the post-Second World War period in the United States, when the engines of mass production generated a surplus of products in the market and aggressive sales efforts were required in order to persuade customers to buy. Many industries, such as pharmaceuticals, rely heavily on sales forces to push products in the marketplace.

The failure of many businesses that were excessively product or sales focused then led to increasing attention to the needs of customers. This orientation is shown in Figure 1.3 (c). Because customer-orientated companies get close to their customers, they understand their needs and problems. Market research is a critically important activity that will be discussed in more detail in Chapter 4. Customer needs and preferences change rapidly, and close contact with them is necessary to understand these changes. Throughout the book we will describe examples of organizations that have changed their marketing strategies in response to customer changes.

Sometimes these three orientations are presented as being chronological, with the production orientation (c.1930s), followed by the **sales orientation** (c.1950s), and then the customer orientation emerging in the 1960s and 1970s. But it is quite clear that, in the world of practice, all three orientations are still commonplace. Significant attention has also been paid to newer business orientations that have been emerging in recent years, particularly the **societal marketing concept**, which is frequently referred to as sustainable marketing. One of the major concerns for both business and society is that the resources of the planet are finite and business activity places significant demands on these limited resources. The societal marketing concept holds that marketing strategy should deliver value to customers in a way that maintains or improves both the consumer's and society's well-being. This means that, as well as meeting customer needs, businesses should also engage in activities such as reducing pollution, as well as developing corporate social responsibility programmes. The societal marketing concept will be dealt with in greater detail in Chapter 2.

Finally, there is also an increasing recognition that a focus on customer needs does not always deliver the kinds of insights that businesses expect. Consumers may not always be able to articulate their needs and wants, and it is also up to organizations to lead markets from time to time. These **market-driven or outside-in firms** seek to anticipate as well as identify consumer needs and build the resource profiles necessary to meet current and anticipated future demand. For example, it is generally considered that Apple has become one of the world's most successful and profitable companies not by responding to customer needs but by actually leading them, through the creation of products like the iPhone. In the same vein, Vargo and Lusch have called for a move away from the economic model of marketing based on notions of manufactured goods and transactional exchanges to one that is based more clearly on relational exchanges between entities where value is co-created rather than determined by one entity and exchanged with another.[18] Recent developments, such as the rapid growth of social media, further illustrate the important role of the customer in co-creating value.

In short, the differences between market-orientated businesses and internally orientated businesses are summarized in Table 1.1. These can be considered to be two ends of a spectrum. Market-driven businesses

Table 1.1 Market-orientated businesses versus internally orientated businesses

Market-orientated businesses	Internally orientated businesses
Customer concern throughout business	Convenience comes first
Know customer choice criteria and match with marketing mix	Assume price and product performance key to most sales
Segment by customer differences	Segment by product
Invest in market research (MR) and track market changes	Rely on anecdotes and received wisdom
Welcome change	Cherish status quo
Try to understand competition	Ignore competition
Marketing spend regarded as an investment	Marketing spend regarded as a luxury
Innovation rewarded	Innovation punished
Search for latent markets	Stick with the same
Be fast	Why rush?
Strive for competitive advantage	Happy to be me-too

display customer concern throughout the business; they understand the criteria customers use to choose between competing suppliers; they invest in market research and track market changes; they regard marketing spend as an investment, and are fast and flexible in terms of their pursuit of new opportunities.

The scope of marketing

So far in this chapter our focus has been on the application of marketing in commercial contexts – that is, its use by companies with products or services to sell. But it is clear from simple observation that the marketing concept, and marketing tools and techniques, is in evidence in many other contexts too. For example, political parties are often criticized for their overuse of marketing. They are heavy users of marketing research to find out what the views of the voting public are; the candidates they put forward for election are often carefully selected and 'packaged' to appeal to voters. They are also extensive users of advertising and public relations to get their message across. In fact, the success of both Barack Obama and Donald Trump in the US Presidential elections has been variously attributed to the marketing activities that supported their campaigns (see Marketing Spotlight 12.1). This is because value exchange is a key element of marketing, as we have seen. Organizations create some form of value and exchange it for something that they need. In the case of politics, it is the creation of policy platforms in exchange for votes in an election.

Evidence of the application of marketing can be found in many other contexts (see Marketing in Action 1.2). Educational institutions have become more market-led as demographic changes have given rise to greater competition for students, whose choices are increasingly being influenced by the publication of performance-based league tables. Universities are responding by developing new logos and rebranding themselves, conducting promotional campaigns, and targeting new markets such as mature students and those from other countries around the world. They are also using the kinds of segmentation techniques employed by companies to identify potential 'customers', as well as customer service training to convert enquiries into 'sales'.[19] The use of marketing takes many forms in the arts and media. It has been argued that many media vehicles, such as newspapers and television channels, are being 'dumbed down' in order to appeal to certain market segments and to maximize revenues, in the same way that many artistic organizations would be criticized for putting revenues ahead of quality and originality by producing art that appeals to a mass audience.

Marketing in Action 1.2
Metro Trains: Dumb Ways to Die

Critical Thinking: Below is a review of Metro Trains' highly successful 'Dumb Ways to Die' campaign. Read it and consider the reasons for its success. What other social marketing campaigns have you been impressed by?

Communicating to young people regarding risks to their health is particularly challenging as marketers always run the risk of adding yet another item to a list of 'don'ts', such as 'don't smoke', 'don't do drugs', etc. This is precisely the challenge that Metro Trains Melbourne faced when developing a campaign to try to reduce the number of unnecessary deaths happening on its network, particularly at stations and level crossings. Added to that, the company had a modest budget of AU$300,000 to spend, meaning that it had to be very innovative in order to get its message across.

The creative strategy that it adopted was a clever one. Rather than coming across as authoritarian or 'parental' and giving the audience yet another message that it didn't want to hear, the company decided to create content that its younger audience would want to seek out and share. But how could it make rail safety engaging? The key insight underlying the campaign was that most rail accidents were avoidable and usually caused by people doing things like running on tracks or driving around barriers because they couldn't be bothered to wait – in other words, dumb behaviour.

(continued)

This insight became the theme for a catchy three-minute music video that showed cartoon characters dying in really dumb ways. The last three characters all died in rail accidents leading to the core message that, of all the dumb ways to die, getting hit by a train is the dumbest. The video was posted on YouTube and could be downloaded free of charge from iTunes. Traditional media, like radio, cinema and station posters, were combined with social channels such as Soundcloud and Instagram to drive traffic to the video on YouTube. The novel campaign received extensive coverage in the Australian media and more than 200 cover versions and parodies of the song were recorded, amplifying the campaign.

The campaign was highly successful. The YouTube video received more than 44 million views in its first five months and its enduring popularity is reflected by the fact that it had had more than 170 million views by September 2018. The video was also one of the most shared of all time, while the song itself was so popular that it entered the singles charts in 28 countries. The extensive global coverage the campaign received was estimated to be worth in the region of AU$60 million, a far cry from its initial budget. And, most important of all, near misses and accidents around trains fell by more than a third following the campaign. Metro Trains followed up this success by releasing *Dumb Ways to Die – The Games*, a free smartphone gaming app. In it, players travel by train across a new world filled with new characters and try to keep them alive as they compete in 28 of the dumbest sports ever invented. In-game purchases and in-game advertising helped to make this stage of the campaign self-financing. Again this innovative approach has been highly successful and the game has been downloaded more than 108 million times and played over 5.88 billion times globally. Its self-funding nature means that Metro Trains now has the resources to continue to communicate its messages around rail safety.

Based on: Anonymous, 2014;[20] Anonymous, 2017;[21] Bronswell, 2013[22]

RNLI (Royal National Lifeboat Institution) Ad Insight: Advertising can be used to present powerful social messages.

Social marketing refers to the use of marketing techniques in order to change or maintain people's behaviour for the benefit of the individual or society as a whole (see Exhibit 1.7). Familiar social campaigns include, for example, anti-smoking, drink aware, sun safety, water safety, sexual health and exercise. It is sometimes seen as restricted to a client base of not-for-profit organizations, health services groups and government agencies. However, as organizations increasingly recognize their societal responsibilities, many are getting involved in social programmes. In addition, the scope of social marketing has

Exhibit 1.7 Ireland's Health Service Executive smoking cessation campaign was led by Gerry Collins and his family. Gerry, who was a lung cancer patient, died in 2014.

grown significantly over the years to embrace cultural theory, critical perspectives and systems-level theory, giving rise to a greater emphasis on the notion of social good.[23]

The range of potential applications for marketing has given rise to much debate among marketing scholars regarding the scope of marketing.[24] In particular, the challenge has been to find a core concept that effectively integrates both business and non-business, or social, marketing. For example, initially the idea of a transaction was put forward, but not all marketing requires a transaction or sale. Kotler then put forward the notion of exchange, implying that any exchange between two parties can be considered marketing.[25] However, this is also clearly problematic as many exchanges, such as favours given by family members, are not marketing activities. Throughout this book, we place customers at the core of marketing and detail the processes through which organizations understand and respond to their ever changing needs and wants.

Marketing and business performance

Does marketing work? Surprisingly, this is a controversial question, with many people arguing that, yes, of course it does, while others are less sure. The difficulty surrounds both the definition and the intangibility of marketing. Many organizations think they are engaging in marketing but may simply be conducting selling or promotional campaigns and, if these activities do not achieve their intended objectives, they may feel that their marketing efforts have been ineffective. But what we will learn throughout this book is that selling or promotion is only part of the marketing process. It can also be difficult to predict in advance whether a marketing or promotional campaign is going to work. Sometimes campaigns can be very successful (see Marketing in Action 1.3). New campaigns can drive the sales of stagnant brands, as happened in the case of Magnum ice cream, which had been suffering flat sales throughout Europe. Aimed at women and using a combination of television advertising, outdoor advertising and internet advertising, the Magnum 7 Deadly Sins campaign lifted sales of the brand by 20 per cent in one year.[26]

Marketing in Action 1.3
Bolia.com: furniture as fashion

Critical Thinking: Below is a review of a successful turnaround by the Scandinavian furniture brand Bolia. Read it and consider the reasons why its change of marketing approach was successful. Can you think of any other examples of successful marketing campaigns?

Bolia.com is an example of a brand which shows that an understanding of customer value combined with innovative communications can assist any company faced with significant marketing challenges. The Danish furniture retailer was founded in 2000 and quickly built a reputation in the market for selling cool Scandinavian designs, both online and in physical stores, to customers in Denmark, Sweden and Norway. However, the global financial crisis of 2008 posed significant challenges for the young company. One-third of all furniture purchases are related to consumers moving house and the collapse of the property market had a huge impact on a premium brand like Bolia. Competitors slashed their prices, causing Bolia's revenues to slump and turning profits to losses in both 2008 and 2009. The company's products were not the problem but the economic crash had made consumers very cautious and reluctant to part with their cash. It could choose to cut its prices like everyone else but such a move is frequently a race to the bottom. Bolia needed to create a desire to buy furniture beyond the occasion of moving house.

Bolia's customers are typically under 45 years of age, with the majority being in their thirties. The company's qualitative research on this age group showed that many didn't see moving home as a functional activity but rather as a more emotional milestone signifying progress in their lives. From this research Bolia gleaned the idea of treating furniture more in terms of what is says about its owner, in same way as clothing or perfume might. In other words, furniture can be a vehicle for expressing personal identity and not just something associated with house moves (see the discussion

(continued)

earlier in this chapter on the idea of meaning as customer value). One of Bolia's new taglines was 'the spaces we create are who we are'. With marketing budgets limited due to declining sales, some innovative thinking was required in order to communicate this new positioning. So instead of creating lots of imagery of lovely-looking tables, chairs and sofas like most other furniture brands, Bolia included cutting-edge fashion models and fashion imagery that would not look out of place for a perfume brand. It was woven through all shopper contact points, not just in advertising but also in physical stores, its website, social media and its product catalogue.

Thinking like a fashion brand also led to new media choices and product decisions. The proportion of spend going to TV and digital has grown, while investments in more traditional media like newspapers and magazines have been phased out. Its product range was organized into a portfolio of seasons, enabling the company to launch six to eight 'collections' per year. The change of strategy has been highly successful. The numbers visiting the company's online and physical stores have been rising year on year since 2010. While rivals were cutting prices after the recession, Bolia's marketing approach strengthened its quality perception, allowing it to actually steadily increase prices. By 2016, it was estimated that the campaign had generated incremental revenues of €182 million and profits of €12 million despite the difficult market circumstances that it had faced. Adopting a market-led approach rather than merely reacting to the challenges it faced helped turn the company's fortunes around.

Based on: Anonymous, 2017;[27] Gladstone, Samuelsen and Winther-Puopinel, 2016[28]

In many companies, marketing is seen as the central engine of business growth. For example, Nestlé is a huge global company, with 8,000 products (a figure that grows to 20,000 when local variations are included) and an annual marketing budget of €18 billion. Reckitt Benckiser, the world's largest manufacturer of household cleaning products, spends an average of 12 per cent of sales on marketing and is a market leader in its business. These kinds of firms see marketing expenditure as an investment, not a cost, and continue to spend money on marketing even during recessions when sales and demand drop (see Exhibit 1.8). A case in point is the Berocca vitamin tablet brand, owned by the German corporation, Bayer. It was launched on the Irish market in 2001 but thanks mainly to an investment level of 25 per cent of turnover on marketing, it saw sales rise from an initial level of just €500,000 to over €4 million by 2010. This gave it a 40 per cent share of the Irish market, making it one of the best markets in the world for Berocca on a per capita basis.[29] For some, though, the issue is not whether marketing works but rather that it works too well. Marketing has been the subject of a great deal of criticism.[30] It has been equated with trickery and deception, and with persuading people (often those on low incomes) to buy products they do not really need. Some of the main controversies surrounding marketing are summarized in Critical Marketing Perspective 1.1.

In short, marketing works. Succeeding in making it work in any particular situation is the challenge. In this regard some issues relating to the nature and impact of marketing need to be borne in mind.

Exhibit 1.8 With its Coors Lite brand struggling in the UK market, Molson Coors spent £20 million on a marketing campaign fronted by Jean Claude van Damme that transformed its fortunes.

Critical Marketing Perspective 1.1
Marketing: good or evil?

It is possible to look at marketing from different standpoints. A positive view holds that marketing provides significant benefits to society. For example, the innovative efforts of companies provide us, as consumers, with a world of choice and diversity. A search on Google allows us to find information on anything that we want; with an Apple app on their iPhones, doctors no longer need a stethoscope to examine patients, and websites like Amazon and eBay allow us to shop from the comfort of our desks. The innovations of tomorrow will bring us new and appealing products, services and solutions. Second, as the practice of marketing improves, our particular needs are increasingly being met. If we eat only gluten-free products, love skydiving and have a passion for Japanese origami, there are organizations that will fulfil these needs. As firms collect more information about their customers, they will tailor solutions to meet specific user requirements. Finally, the competition between firms continually forces them to improve their services and products, and deliver extra value to customers. For example, low-fares airlines have revolutionized air travel and enabled people who traditionally flew infrequently to travel to new destinations much more often.

At the same time, marketing is also the subject of some trenchant criticism. For example, it is seen as not only fulfilling needs but also creating unnecessary wants. Critics argue that companies use sophisticated marketing techniques to create aspirations and to get consumers to buy products they don't really need, with the result that many consumers find themselves building up significant debts. Consumer credit levels are at an all-time high in many developed countries. Related to this is the rise of materialism in society. Proponents of this view suggest that the modern consumer has become obsessed with consumption – as illustrated, for example, by the growth in Sunday shopping. Psychologists argue that this rise in consumption has done little to make people feel happier and better about themselves. At the same time as materialism is rising, there are growing concerns that the world's resources are being rapidly depleted and that current levels of consumption are not sustainable into the future. Third, there are concerns with the way in which marketers target vulnerable groups like children, where the skills of child psychologists are used to find more and novel ways to instil brand preferences in the very young. Finally, there are concerns with the ways in which marketing activity appears to have invaded all aspects of society. Public leisure events such as sports, shows and concerts now usually have a corporate partner, with the result that events aimed at teenagers may be sponsored by an alcoholic drinks organization, for example. Pressures on the public funding of schools, hospitals, and so on, also create opportunities for corporations to tie in with these entities, which is often ethically questionable.

Resolving such a debate is very difficult, but the core of the issue lies in the key components of the definition of marketing – namely, value and profit. When organizations provide genuine value to customers, marketing is doing what it should, and both firms and society benefit. When firms create an illusion of value or seek to exploit customers for profit, then consumers and society do not benefit. Like all professions, marketing has its unscrupulous practitioners, and there will always be individuals and organizations who will seek to exploit vulnerable customers. But, in an information-rich world, such practitioners can and should be named and shamed.

Suggested reading: James, 2007;[31] Klein, 2000;[32] Linn, 2004[33]

Reflection: Critically evaluate the arguments above and develop your own opinion on whether marketing is good or evil.

Marketing and performance

The adoption of the marketing concept will improve business performance – that is the basic premise. Marketing is not an abstract concept; its acid test is the effect that its use has on key corporate indices such as profitability and market share. Extensive research has been conducted that has sought to examine the relationship between marketing and performance. The results suggest that the relationship is positive.

Narver and Slater, for instance, looked closely at the relationship between marketing orientation and business performance.[34] They collected data from 113 **strategic business units (SBUs)** of a major US corporation. In the main, their study found that the relationship between market orientation and profitability was strongly linear, with the businesses displaying the highest level of market orientation achieving the highest levels of profitability, and those with the lowest scores on market orientation having the lowest profitability figures. As the authors state: 'The findings give marketing scholars and practitioners a basis beyond mere intuition for recommending the superiority of a market orientation.' Another study examining firm performance over a nine-year period provided further support for the adoption of a market orientation, which was seen to have a positive effect in both the short and long term. Sustained advantages were achieved by firms that had adopted a market orientation earlier than competitors and it had a more pronounced effect on profits than on sales because of the focus on customer retention rather than merely acquisition.[35]

It is surprising, then, that marketing has not had the influence in corporate boardrooms that its importance would seem to justify. A study in the UK found that only 21 per cent of chief executive officers (CEOs) in FTSE 100 companies had worked in marketing before going into general management, and only five of the FTSE 100 companies had dedicated marketing directors on their boards.[36] A study of German firms found that the influence of the marketing department on key decision areas such as strategy, new product development and pricing has been in decline, and that it is ceding its influence to the sales department.[37] Doyle argues that the reason for marketing's relatively low status is that the links between marketing investments and the long-term profitability of the organization have not been made clear.[38] Too often, marketers justify their investments in terms of increasing customer awareness, sales volume or market share. Doyle proposes the concept of **value-based marketing**, where the objective of marketing is seen as contributing to the maximization of **shareholder value**, which has become the overarching goal of chief executives in more and more companies. This approach helps to clarify the importance of investment in marketing assets such as brands and marketing knowledge, and helps to dissuade management from making arbitrary cuts in marketing expenditure, such as advertising, in times of economic difficulty.

To further explore the link between marketing activities and firm performance, Rust et al. have identified a **chain of marketing productivity**, which demonstrates how marketing investments eventually are reflected in firm outcomes. The chain begins with a firm's strategy, such as its product strategy or promotion strategy, which is then translated into specific tactics such as an advertising campaign or a loyalty programme, for example. These campaigns have an impact on customers (attitudes or satisfaction), which in turn feeds through to market impacts (e.g. market share) and financial impacts (e.g. profitability), and ultimately to the value of the firm. In other words, a variety of factors influenced by marketing activity such as marketing capabilities, marketing assets and marketing actions can impact upon firm value.[39,40] Further research has found that, where this marketing activity is measured, significant performance benefits accrue and a market orientation combined with systems for measuring marketing performance have been found to further enhance financial performance.[41,42] As a result, the title chief marketing officer (CMO) has emerged to reflect the importance of marketing to the overall performance of the organization. Chief marketing officers usually have a seat in the corporate boardroom.

Planning marketing activity

Finally, in some organizations, marketing can be a haphazard activity done in response to particular opportunities or in times of difficulty or crisis. However, attention to marketing must be consistent as markets change and nothing lasts for ever. For example, the past decade has seen a dramatic growth in the use of digital marketing techniques. Marketers have very quickly had to develop an understanding of a range of new fields, such as search engine optimization, search advertising, social media and programmatic advertising (see Chapter 11). But, rather than rushing in and following these new trends, as many marketers have, a more carefully planned approach is preferable. Marketers certainly needed to consider the opportunities provided by these new methods, but they also needed to focus on their overall goals and objectives, and then evaluate the potential roles (if any) that digital tools might play in their efforts.

Therefore, for marketing efforts to be effective, it is essential that a planned approach is taken. The process by which businesses analyse the environment and their capabilities, decide upon courses of marketing action and implement those decisions is called **marketing planning**. The following key questions need to be asked when thinking about marketing planning decisions:

Table 1.2 Marketing planning activities

Main activities in the marketing planning process	Relevant chapters
Business mission and strategy	Chapter 12
Environmental and customer analysis	Chapters 2 to 4
Marketing objectives	Chapter 12
Marketing strategy	Chapter 5
Marketing actions	Chapters 6 to 11
Evaluation of performance	Chapter 12

- Where are we now?
- Where would we like to be?
- How do we get there?

The process of answering these questions involves some analyses and choices, which are detailed in Table 1.2. The themes and issues emerging during each of these stages will be developed in greater detail at certain times throughout specific chapters of this book and we will examine marketing planning in greater detail in Chapter 12. The marketing planning process begins with an assessment of the situation that the organization currently finds itself in. This requires conducting both an external analysis of the industry and the environment that it is operating in, and an internal analysis or audit of its activities. When this information has been collected and considered, the organization can then begin to shape its strategy by considering which parts of the market to focus on and deciding on the objectives it seeks to achieve in the given planning period.

Once decisions have been made about where the organization wants to go, the next steps involve deciding on how to get there. At a strategic level, the fundamental decisions revolve around **market segmentation**, **market targeting** and **positioning**, and these issues will be examined in detail in Chapter 5. Executing these strategic choices involves a series of action items that have traditionally been labelled the **marketing mix**, comprising the 4Ps of product, price, place and promotion. **Product** decisions refer to the choices that are made regarding products/services combinations that an organization might choose to offer, and may encompass decisions surrounding branding, customer relationships and customer loyalty, for example. We shall explore these questions in more detail in Chapters 6 and 7. **Price** refers to all the decisions that are made regarding the different price points that are used for products in the company's range, as well as decisions regarding the raising or lowering of prices in response to competitor activity and customer demand. Pricing is examined in detail in Chapter 8. **Place** is a term that is used to describe where customers can buy a product or service, and deals with the distribution of goods from companies to customers. This is an aspect of marketing that is changing rapidly as more consumers opt for making purchases online, and place is discussed in detail in Chapter 9. Finally, **promotion** describes the ways in which organizations communicate with customers both to create awareness of their offerings and to try to engage with and persuade consumers to purchase. A wide variety of promotional options are open to organizations, ranging from television advertising to Google Adwords to ambient campaigns. Promotional decisions are discussed in detail in Chapters 10 and 11.

In addition, several other 'Ps' have been identified that can be considered part of the marketing mix. In the case of services businesses, for example, three additional variables – namely, people, process and physical evidence – have been proposed (see Chapter 7). A total of 12 variables were initially identified by Borden, which demonstrates the breadth of activities that need to be considered when putting marketing programmes into action.[43]

The final elements of the marketing planning process involve organizing the people and structures to implement the chosen programme, and carrying out all the necessary actions. Then, once the plan has been implemented, all that remains is the very important issue of assessing whether or not it has been effective in achieving its goals. One of the criticisms that has traditionally been levelled at marketing is that it is weak on measurement and it is not always possible to gauge whether marketing programmes have had the desired effects. However, there is now a very useful suite of metrics that are available to marketers and these are discussed in Chapter 12.

Summary

This chapter has introduced the concept of marketing, and discussed how and why organizations become market oriented. In particular, the following issues were addressed.

1. What is meant by the marketing concept? The key idea here is that it is a business philosophy that puts the customer at the centre of things. Implementing the marketing concept requires a focus on customer satisfaction, an integrated effort throughout the company and a belief that corporate goals can be achieved through customer satisfaction.

2. The idea of customer value, which is the difference between the perceived benefits from consuming a product or service and the perceived sacrifice involved in doing so. Customers are faced with a wide variety of choices in most instances, therefore companies need to clearly spell out what value they are offering and this forms their customer value proposition.

3. That marketing as both a field of study and a field of practice is constantly evolving. The way that we think about marketing has moved from an internal focus on production and sales towards a more outward-looking focus on customers and markets. These market-driven organizations are better placed to succeed in rapidly changing competitive environments.

4. That marketing planning is an important activity to ensure marketing effectiveness. There are a number of critical steps in the marketing planning process, namely, the business mission and strategy, the marketing audit, marketing objectives, marketing strategy, marketing actions and evaluation of performance.

5. That marketing works and there is a strong relationship between a marketing philosophy and business performance. Academic research in the field of market orientation and ample evidence from practice attest to the power of marketing in assisting organizations to achieve their goals.

6. That the scope of marketing is broad, involving non-business as well as business contexts. Political parties, educational institutions, sporting organizations, religious organizations and others are regular users of marketing.

7. That marketing is also controversial and that it has many negative connotations relating to the creation of unnecessary desires among consumers, that it exploits vulnerable groups and that it results in depletion of the world's resources. An informed perspective on both the merits and risks associated with marketing and commerce generally is important.

Study questions

1. Discuss the development of marketing. What are the critical ways in which marketing has changed over the years?

2. Identify two examples of organizations that you consider provide customer value, and describe how they do it.

3. Marketing is sometimes considered to be an expensive luxury. Respond to this claim by demonstrating how a marketing orientation can have a positive impact on business performance.

4. Marketing is central to how we live our lives. Discuss.

5. Rather than assisting in the creation of value, marketing is responsible for many of society's ills. Discuss.

6. Visit www.marketingpower.com and www.exchange.cim.co.uk. Select any story currently featuring that interests you and summarize the three key learning points from the article.

Suggested reading

Dawar, N. (2013) When marketing is strategy, *Harvard Business Review*, 91(12), 100–8.

Homberg, C., Vomberg, A., Enke, M. and **Grimm, P.** (2015) The loss of the marketing department's influence: is it really happening? And why worry? *Journal of the Academy of Marketing Science*, 43, 1–13.

Hult, G., Morgeson, F., Morgan, N. and **Mithas, S.** (2017) Do managers know what their customers think and why? *Journal of the Academy of Marketing Science*, 45, 37–54.

Karababa, E. and **Kjellgaard, D.** (2014) Value in marketing: toward socio-cultural perspectives, *Marketing Theory*, 14(1), 119–27.

Kumar, V. (2015) Marketing as a discipline: what has happened and what to look out for, *Journal of Marketing*, 79, 1–9.

Kumar, V., Keller, K. and **Lemon, K.** (2016) Mapping the boundaries of marketing: what needs to be known (Introduction to Special Issue), *Journal of Marketing*, 80, 1–5.

Vargo, S. and **Lusch, R.** (2004) Evolving to a new dominant logic for marketing, *Journal of Marketing*, 86(1), 1–17.

Verhof, P. and **Lemon, K.** (2013) Successful customer value management: key lessons and emerging trends, *European Management Journal*, 31, 1–15.

References

1. **Barry, A.** (2016) Why Beyonce is a business genius, *TheJournal.ie*. Available at www.thejournal.ie/beyonce-business-money-2740599-Apr2016/ (accessed 18 June 2018); **Jacobs, E.** (2014) How to market brand Beyonce, *Ft.com*. Available at www.ft.com/content/9ebce5a6-43d0-11e4-8abd-00144feabdc0 (accessed 18 June 2018); **Philp, D.** (2014) Get classy: comparing the massive marketing of *Anchorman 2* to the non-marketing of Beyonce's *Beyonce* album, *Journal of the Music & Entertainment Industry Educator's Association*, 14, 219–48.

2. **Drucker, P.F.** (1999) *The Practice of Management*. London: Heinemann.

3. **Roderick, L.** (2017) 'Coca-Cola Life's' demise always felt inevitable, *MarketingWeek.co.uk*. Available at www.marketingweek.com/2017/04/06/coke-lifes-demise/ (accessed 3 August 2018).

4. **Rosenberg, L.J.** and **Czepeil, J.A.** (1983) A marketing approach to customer retention, *Journal of Consumer Marketing*, 2, 45–51.

5. **Grönroos, C.** (1989) Defining marketing: a market-oriented approach, *European Journal of Marketing*, 23(1), 52–60.

6. **Hult, G., Morgeson, F., Morgan, N.** and **Mithas, S.** (2017) Do managers know what their customers think and why? *Journal of the Academy of Marketing Science*, 45, 37–54.

7. **Day, G.S.** and **Moorman, C.** (2010) *Strategy From the Outside-in: Profiting From Customer Value*. New York: McGraw-Hill.

8. **Kumar, V.** and **Reinartz, W.** (2106) Creating enduring customer value, *Journal of Marketing*, 80, 36–68.

9. **Karababa, E.** and **Kjellgaard, D.** (2014) Value in marketing: toward socio-cultural perspectives, *Marketing Theory*, 14, 119–27.

10. **Fahy, J.** (2012) Creating a winning customer value proposition, in S. Harwood (ed.) *Best Practices in Successful Businesses: A Collection of Tutorials*. USA: Walker Publications, 78–87.

11. **Anonymous** (2018) Hyundai Motor Company: Shackleton's return, *Warc.com*. Available at www.warc.com/content/article/cannes/hyundai_motor_company_shackletons_return/122319 (accessed 23 May 2018).

12. **Vargo, S.** and **Lusch, R.** (2004) Evolving to a new dominant logic for marketing, *Journal of Marketing*, 86(1), 1–17.

13. **Anonymous** (2018) Norwegian Air makes bigger than expected net loss, *FT.com*. Available at www.ft.com/content/c2e417b0-1249-11e8-8cb6-b9ccc4c4dbbb (accessed 3 August 2018).

14. **Fullerton, R.** (1988) How modern is modern marketing? Marketing's evolution and the myth of the 'production era', *Journal of Marketing*, 52, 108–25.

15. **Jones, D.** and **Monieson, D.** (1990) Early development of the philosophy of marketing thought, *Journal of Marketing*, 54, 102–13.

16. **Benton, R.** (1987) The practical domain of marketing, *American Journal of Economics and Sociology*, 46(4), 415–30.

17. **Davis, P.** (2005) Attack on 'outdated' marketing, *Financial Times*, Fund Management Supplement, 30 May, 1.

18. **Vargo, S.** and **Lusch, R.** (2004) Evolving to a new dominant logic for marketing, *Journal of Marketing*, 86(1), 1–17.

19. **Boone, J.** (2007) Private school's marketing pays off, *Financial Times*, 4 May, 3.

20. **Anonymous** (2014) Metro Trains: Dumb Ways to Die, *Warc.com*. Available at www.warc.com/content/article/cannes/metro_trains_dumb_ways_to_die/ (accessed 31 July 2018).

21. **Anonymous** (2017) Metro Trains Melbourne: Dumb Ways to Die – The Games, *Warc.com*. Available at www.warc.com/content/article/cannes/metro_trains_melbourne_dumb_ways_to_die_the_games/111498 (accessed 31 July 2018).

22. **Brownsell, A.** (2013) 'Dumb Ways to Die': the story behind a marketing phenomenon, *Campaignlive. co.uk*. Available at www.campaignlive.co.uk/article/dumb-ways-die-story-behind-global-marketing-phenomenon/1187124 (accessed 31 July 2014).

23. **Gordon, R., Russell-Bennett, R.** and **Lefebvre, R.** (2016) Social marketing: the state of play and brokering the way forward, *Journal of Marketing Management*, 32, 1059–82.

24. See, for example, **Foxall, G.** (1984) Marketing's domain, *European Journal of Marketing*, 18(1), 25–40; **Kotler, P.** and **Levy, S.** (1969) Broadening the concept of marketing, *Journal of Marketing*, 33, 10–15.

25. **Kotler, P.** (1972) A generic concept of marketing, *Journal of Marketing*, 36, 46–54.

26. **Coulter, D.** (2004) Magnum 7 Sins: driving women to sin across Europe, *Warc.com*. Available at https://www.warc.com/content/article/A79862_Magnum_Magnum_7_Sins/79862 (accessed 26 October 2018).

27. **Anonymous** (2017) Bolia.com: building a big brand, with a small budget, *Warc.com*. Available at www.warc.com/content/article/euro-effies/boliacom_building_a_big_brand_with_a_small_budget/112886 (accessed 23 March 2018).

28. **Gladstone, M., Samuelsen, L.** and **Winther-Poupinel, J.** (2016) Bolia.com: selling sofas in a financial meltdown, *Warc.com*. Available at www.warc.com/content/article/ipa/boliacom_selling_sofas_in_a_financial_meltdown/108055 (accessed 23 March 2018).

29. **O'Connell, S.** (2009) Vitamin ad provides flat market with some fizz, *Irish Times*, 15 October, 22.

30. **Klein, N.** (2000) *No Logo*. London: HarperCollins.

31. **James, O.** (2007) *Affluenza*. London: Vermilion.

32. **Klein, N.** (2000) *No Logo*. London: HarperCollins.

33. **Linn, S.** (2004) *Consuming Kids: The Hostile Takeover of Childhood*. New York: The New Press.

34. **Narver, J.C.** and **Slater, S.F.** (1990) The effect of a market orientation on business profitability, *Journal of Marketing*, 54(October), 20–35.

35. **Kumar, V., Jones, E., Venkatesan, R.** and **Leone, R.** (2011) Is market orientation a source of sustainable competitive advantage or simply the cost of competing? *Journal of Marketing*, 75, 16–30.

36. **Terazono, E.** (2003) Always on the outside looking in, *Financial Times*, Creative Business, 5 August, 4–5.

37. **Homberg, C., Vomberg, A., Enke, M.** and **Grimm, P.** (2015) The loss of the marketing department's influence: is it really happening? And why worry? *Journal of the Academy of Marketing Science*, 43, 1–13.

38. **Doyle, P.** (2000) *Value-based Marketing*. Chichester: John Wiley & Sons.

39. **Rust, R., Ambler, T., Carpenter, G., Kumar, V.** and **Srivastava, R.** (2004) Measuring marketing productivity: current knowledge and future directions, *Journal of Marketing*, 68(4), 76–89.

40. **Hanssens, D., Rust, R.** and **Srivastava, R.** (2009) Marketing strategy and Wall Street: nailing down marketing's impact, *Journal of Marketing*, 73(6), 115–18.

41. **O'Sullivan, D.** and **Abela, A.** (2007) Marketing performance measurement ability and firm performance, *Journal of Marketing*, 71(2), 79–93.

42. **Frosen, J., Luoma, J., Jaakkola, M., Tikkanen, H.** and **Aspara, J.** (2016) What counts versus what can be counted: the complex interplay of market orientation and market performance measurement, *Journal of Marketing*, 80, 60–78.

43. **Borden, N.** (1964) The concept of the marketing mix, *Journal of Advertising Research*, June, 2–7.

Appendix I.I Careers in marketing

Choosing a career in marketing can offer a wide range of opportunities. Table A1.1 outlines some of the potential positions available in marketing.

Table AI.I Careers in marketing

Marketing positions	
Marketing executive/co-ordinator	Management of all marketing-related activities for an organization.
Brand/product manager	A product manager is responsible for the management of a single product or a family of products. In this capacity, he or she may participate in product design and development according to the results of research into the evolving needs of their customer base. In addition, marketing managers develop business plans and marketing strategies for their product line, manage product distribution, disseminate information about the product, and co-ordinate customer service and sales.
Brand/marketing assistant	At the entry level of brand assistant, responsibilities consist of market analysis, competitive tracking, sales and market share analysis, monitoring of promotion programmes, etc.
Marketing researcher/analyst	Market researchers collect and analyse information to assist in marketing, and determine whether a demand exists for a particular product or service. Some of the tasks involved include designing questionnaires, collecting all available and pertinent information, arranging and analysing collected information, presenting research results to clients, making recommendations.
Marketing communications manager	Manages the marketing communications activity of an organization, such as advertising, public relations, sponsorships and direct marketing.
Customer service manager/executive	Manages the service delivery and any interactions a customer may have with an organization. Role can be quite varied, depending on industry.
Sales positions	
Sales executive/business development	Aims to develop successful business relationships with existing and potential customers. Manages the company's sales prospects.
Sales manager	Plans and co-ordinates the activities of a sales team, controls product distribution, monitors budget achievement, trains and motivates personnel, prepares forecasts.
Key account executive	Manages the selling and marketing function to key customers (accounts). Conducts negotiations on products, quantities, prices, promotions, special offers etc. Networks with other key account personnel influential in the buying decision process. Liaises internally with all departments and colleagues in supplying and servicing the key account. Monitors performance of the key account.

(continued)

Sales support manager	Provides sales support by fielding enquiries, taking orders and providing phone advice to customers. Also assists with exhibitions, prepares documentation for brochures and sales kits, and commissions market research suppliers for primary data.
Merchandiser	Aims to maximize the display of a company's point-of-sale displays, and ensures that they are stocked and maintained correctly.
Sales promotion executive	Aims to communicate product features and benefits directly to customers at customer locations through sampling, demonstrations and the management of any sales promotion activities.
Telesales representative	Takes in-bound or makes out-bound calls, which are sales related.
Advertising sales executive	Sells a media organization's airplay, television spot or space to companies for the purpose of advertising.
Retailing positions	
Retail management	Plans and co-ordinates the operations of retail outlets. Supervises the recruitment, training, conduct and work of staff. Maintains high levels of customer service. Manages stock levels.
Retail buyer	Purchases goods to be sold in retail stores. Manages and analyses stock levels. Obtains information about the range of products available. Manages vendor relations.
Advertising positions	
Account executive	Helps devise and co-ordinate advertising campaigns. Liaises with clients, obtaining relevant information from them such as product and company details, budget and marketing goals, and marketing research information. Briefs other specialists in the agency (such as creative team, media planners and researchers) on client requirements, to develop the details of a campaign. May present draft campaign suggestions to clients, along with a summary of the expenditure involved, and negotiate and arrange for modifications if required. May supervise and co-ordinate the work of the relevant production departments so that the campaign is developed as planned to meet deadlines and budget requirements.
Media planner/buyer	Organizes and purchases advertising space on television, radio, in magazines, newspapers or on outdoor advertising. Liaises between clients and sellers of advertising space to ensure that the advertising campaign reaches the target market.
Public relations positions	
Public relations executive	Helps to develop and maintain a hospitable, friendly public environment for the organization. This involves liaising with clients, co-ordination of special events, lobbying, crisis management, media relations, writing and editing of printed material.
Press relations/corporate affairs	Develops and maintains a good working relationship with the media. Creates press releases or responds to media queries.

(continued)

Digital marketing positions	
Digital marketing executive	Oversees all aspects of digital campaigns. Planning, organizing, executing and evaluating campaigns. Liaises with and manages specialist third-party providers.
SEO/PPC executive	SEO (search engine optimization) managers are responsible for activities designed to ensure the highest positions on organic search rankings and web traffic. PPC (pay per click) managers are responsible for all advertising campaigns on search engines such as Google and Bing.
Social media marketing executive	Oversees all the organization's social media marketing activities both paid for (such as Facebook advertising) and organic, such as content strategies on Snapchat, Instagram, etc.
Content marketing executive	Plans, organizes and executes all content campaigns. Responsible for content creation for different channels, such as websites, social media platforms and digital advertising. May liaise and interact with specialist content agencies and/or manage a team of content writers/editors.
Email manager	Responsible for designing, developing, executing and evaluating email campaigns.
Analytics manager	Responsible for managing the various analytics platforms in the organization, such as website and social analytics. Generates insights from analytics and assesses the effectiveness of campaigns. Responsible for a wide variety of metrics, such as bounce rates, retention rates, etc.
User experience (UX) manager	Responsible for monitoring and managing the user experience such as, for example, why do users abandon certain webpages, or why do they not complete purchases. Responsible for development and design changes to the website and social channels.

1

GoPro: riding the waves of a changing market

Introduction

Twelve thousand feet above Navarre Beach, Florida, Patrick Remington hangs from the landing skids of a small helicopter with his two, equally brazen, friends. Equipped with a pair of black flip-flops, cargo shorts, a parachute and a visorless helmet with a mounted GoPro HERO3 action camera, he prepares for flight with animated yells, echoed by his dangling partners. On the count of three, the trio release their grip, the pulsating beat of Rich Aucoin's 'Yelling in Sleep' drops and we share in the heart-wrenching moment of free flight from the adrenaline-fuelled skydiver's remarkable point of view. Having demonstrated his aviating prowess, Patrick treats the roused viewer to a cool and casual landing on the white sands of Navarre, as puzzled beachgoers acknowledge his startling arrival. In close pursuit is one of his jumping partners, also sporting a mounted GoPro action camera, who adds a sand-displacing tumble and cry of muffled profanities to the manoeuvre. Eager to show the world his adventurous spirit and daring day out, Patrick compiles the footage from his jump (and that of his friend, for comic effect), and slickly edits the high-definition video into a captivating four-minute clip, ready for sharing on YouTube.

Who is GoPro? A company overview

Entrepreneur and adrenaline-junkie Nicholas Woodman founded California-based action camera and accessories manufacturer GoPro after struggling to capture immersive footage of his Australian surfing vacation. In 2002, surfing videography was limited to the third-person perspective, captured from the shore or by a friend in the water sacrificing their own leisure to film. Dissatisfied, Woodman tinkered in vain with a disposable Kodak camera and broken surf leash turned wrist strap, in pursuit of immersive point-of-view (POV) footage from within the barrel of the waves. On his return to California, an impassioned Woodman travelled the North American coast in his 1974 Volkswagen bus selling Indonesian bead-and-shell belts to fuel a vision that, just a decade later, on its initial public offering, would be valued at US$3 billion.

Through creativity and perseverance, Woodman successfully engineered a functional wrist strap. ▶

However the inability of existing imaging devices to withstand the unforgiving bombardment of Californian waves quickly became overt. Unperturbed, he liaised with Chinese camera manufacturer Hotax to augment the young company's fledgling offerings with modified 35-millimetre devices. In September 2004, at a trade show in San Diego, the first HERO action camera and wrist strap combination was sold, inaugurating Woodman's commitment to delivering 'the world's most versatile camera'. While promotional efforts were limited to energetic trade show appearances, incessant surf shop cold calling and QVC demonstrations, GoPro generated US$350,000 in its first full year of trading.

In 2006, GoPro transitioned from film to digital technology, coinciding with the acquisition of blossoming video-streaming website YouTube by technology conglomerate Google, which initiated the self-documentation revolution. Revenues exceeded US$8 million in the following year, with the organization invigorated by the rapidly materializing demand for superior video-recording capabilities, endowed by increasingly robust hardware and stimulated by Woodman's racing-car-induced epiphany that GoPro's appeal could extend far beyond its surfing origins. Riding the momentum of growing performance, GoPro endeavoured to expand its niche distribution strategy, with a partnership with American outdoor recreation store REI initiating a torrent of global agreements that placed GoPro products in more than 40,000 stores, ranging from specialist sports and consumer electronics retailers to supermarkets, across 100 countries. GoPro technology continued to develop, with the company's first high-definition device introduced in 2009, superseded by periodic hardware updates and complementary mounts and accessories designed to enable unique perspectives. Exploration of the virtual reality, drone and broadcasting industries offered further opportunities for expansion.

GoPro's target market

GoPro was founded by an action-sport enthusiast for fellow adrenaline junkies, with affinities ranging from BASE jumping to surfing. Bound by adventure sports' physically demanding nature, the core target market was primarily populated by digital natives, 55 per cent of whom are inclined to engage in self-documentation on social media. In homage to the company's extreme origins, the brand name GoPro and omnipresent slogan 'be a HERO' resonate with the typical aspirations of the youthful and daring action sport enthusiast target market. GoPro's corporate culture emulated this audacious segment, transcending the charismatic CEO referred to as the 'Mad Billionaire', to include many of the organi-

Exhibit Cl.I GoPro founder and CEO Nicholas Woodman.

zation's workforce. Woodman astutely leveraged his active team to generate immersive content, encouraging San Diego-based employees to spend every Thursday afternoon pursuing their passions while equipped with HERO devices as part of the 'live it, eat it, love it' initiative. The result of this initiative, combined with a customer base with an affinity for death-defying stunts, according to head of global business development and content acquisitions at GoPro, Adam Dornbusch, is that 'they [users] were doing things with cameras better than anything we could script'.

As footage featuring astounding human feats circulated on social media, the burgeoning brand inevitably garnered attention from outside the action-sport niche. By developing a device that produced seamless footage across a plethora of strenuous environments, GoPro was inadvertently bestowed with a product that appealed to the technology- and mobility-hungry masses. When GoPro outsold Sony at Best Buy in December 2010, it was evident that the HERO had penetrated the mainstream imaging device market, with its target market evolving to include both millennials and Generation Xers who wanted a durable, affordable and high-quality action camera, be it for everyday use or for more adventurous applications.

User-generated content (UGC)

The most satisfying thing for me about GoPro is when I go on Facebook, on GoPro's page, and see how many people around the world are so stoked on GoPro and their HERO camera, and more than that, they're stoked to share the photos and videos that they're capturing with each other online, and share it with us. So if you go to GoPro's Facebook page, it's sort of like the world brought to you by you.

Nicholas Woodman (GoPro, 2011)

To 'inspire the masses to get their camera, go out and create content', GoPro curated a roster of approximately 140 social influencers. While athletes remain paramount, musicians, fashion designers and television personalities, among others, increasingly affiliated with the brand. With existing influencers boasting an accumulative social following of more than 80 million, GoPro's preference for those with an affinity for social media is overt. Furthermore, the roster radiated charisma, replete with extrovert and personable characters such as MotoGP superstar Valentino Rossi, skateboarding prodigy Ryan Sheckler, surfer-turned-model Alana Blanchard and television personality Alton Brown. In collaboration with GoPro Productions, influencers produced scripted content including themed mini-series and 'Creative Tips' instructional videos, in addition to exercising their creative agency to showcase their own lifestyles.

GoPro engaged influencers in a manner that transcended typical sponsorship activity, developing initiatives that encouraged camaraderie, competition and passion among what GoPro executives affectionately call the 'GoPro Family', exemplified by the 2014 'Share the Stoke' campaign. One month before the launch of the HERO4, influencers received an exclusive package complete with HERO4, accessories and a booklet showcasing prizes ranging from a day with Woodman to a dedicated GoPro billboard, which were available to the influencers that generated the most social media engagement with content captured on their new HERO. Two weeks into the campaign, an additional element was revealed, as consumers were enticed to interact with influencers' content for the chance to win prizes that included a 'one of everything we make' package and a seven-day resort getaway. Stimulating the engrossment was a live leader board, accessible online to both consumers and influencers, tracking interactions and ranking influencers accordingly. Influencer enthusiasm was palpable, with 3,193 pieces of content produced under the auspices of the campaign, while 8.3 million consumer interactions far surpassed the target of 3 million.

Joining social influencers at the 'top of the food chain' that GoPro leverages to entice content creation are the events and brands with which it partners. Adventure sports events initially claimed precedence, with big-ticket events such as the Nike Skateboarding Street League, the World Surf League and the ESPN X Games brandishing GoPro affiliation, in addition to smaller events such as the Grom Games and the GoPro Open Shortboard Competition. This was followed by associations with the PGA golf tour, the National Hockey League and the Tour de France professional cycling race, where producers set out to capture 'life inside the tour'. Participants' GoPro-related knowledge and skills were also expanded through initiatives designed to encourage brand engagement, exemplified at the Grom Games where contestants in the underage surf competition earned additional points through immersive content creation. Events were also leveraged as rich sources of content, with GoPro's title event at the 2016 ESPN X Games – the GoPro Ski Big Air Competition – starring in the competition's inaugural POV livestream broadcast on Twitter's Periscope and Instagram alongside spectator-submitted content.

Software enhancements, such as the development of the GoPro app in 2012, assisted in the production of suitable content. Remodelled as GoPro Capture, a mobile application, compatible with iOS, Android and Apple Watches, it was capable of controlling HERO devices, highlighting key moments in real time, capturing high-resolution still images from live footage, while facilitating sharing on the GoPro Channel and social media. By the end of 2015, Capture had accrued 24 million downloads. Content was shared on GoPro's Facebook, Twitter, Instagram and Pinterest channels. Not surprisingly, engagement levels with GoPro's event-oriented content were higher than those of competitors and even social influencers. For example, in 2015, nine of the top ten most liked Instagram posts featured UGC, while a festive campaign highlighting the year's best user and athlete-generated content garnered 20 million engagements. The brand was also able to effectively exploit technology developments by the social media companies, such as Twitter hashtags (#GoProChat) and live streaming. Of course, the video content community, YouTube, proved to be a veritable hotbed of UGC activity, with Woodman accrediting the site with the surge in demand for video devices that stimulated GoPro's early growth. In 2009, coinciding with the company's social network debut, the GoPro Channel was established on YouTube (and on GoPro.com), through which user-generated and professional content was broadcast and amplified. As the GoPro Channel's audience grew, so too did HERO sales, while a 71 per cent increase in content broadcast via the Channel in 2014 earned the company top spot on YouTube's brand channel leader board. This momentum persisted through 2015, as broadcast content rose 175 per cent to reach 2,092 unique items, generating 1.01 million daily organic views and enabling GoPro to become one of just four brands to surpass one billion views.

Finally, of its many collaborations it is its partnership with Red Bull that has been one of the most

▶ significant in helping to grow the brand. Following the success of the famous 2012 Stratos Jump, the partners entered into an official multi-year agreement in 2016, with GoPro ceding equity in return for the title of official POV camera supplier to the entirety of Red Bull's 1,800 events across 100 countries, in addition to shared licensing agreements and the assurance of prominence on Red Bull's enviable social media empire and distribution network, consisting of Red Bull.com, Red Bull TV and the Red Bull Content Pool.

Challenges on the horizon

Over the last decade, jeopardized by the proliferation of increasingly sophisticated smartphones, the global imaging device (cameras and camcorders) market within which GoPro operates has experienced dramatic decline. In the once-lucrative North American market, the number of imaging device units sold in 2016 totalled just 15 million compared with 69 million in 2010, while 2016 alone saw digital camera sales fall by 16 per cent in the United Kingdom and 15 per cent in China. Despite this dramatic market contraction, the action camera sector, pioneered by GoPro, saw consistent year-on-year growth from 2004. The sector is forecast to reach a value of US$3.4 billion by 2021, with annual volume sales expected to rise from 7.4 million units to 24 million. Consumer trends fuelling this growth include millennials' desire to lead an active lifestyle while simultaneously sharing their exploits on social media, in addition to the booming adventure tourism industry.

Rampant sector growth has attracted competition from established camera manufacturers including Sony, Kodak, Polaroid and Panasonic, in addition to ambitious action camera start-ups such as Contour, Ion and Chinese challenger brand Xiao whose offering 'is almost exactly a GoPro' at half the price. GPS specialist Garmin has also audaciously entered the market, promoting its 'feature-rich, easy-to-use' VIRB action camera with a laudable team of athletes, including X-Games snowboarding gold medallists Mark McMorris and Silje Norendal, through conspicuous event sponsorships that include the Red Bull Air Race World Championship, and with a digital library of thrilling POV videos that emulate those attributed to GoPro.

GoPro's revenues peaked at US$1.6 billion in 2015. Since then the company has struggled, with sales falling back to just over US$1 billion in 2017 and it posted its first significant loss of over US$400 million in 2016. Its share price has had a similarly turbulent ride. In its initial public offering (IPO) in 2014, the shares were priced at US$24 and quickly surged to a high of US$93 before falling all the way back to just over US$8 by end of 2017. Various reasons have been put forward for the company's troubles. Despite having the strongest brand reputation in the sector, new rivals have eaten into its revenues and profitability by offering products of similar quality at more competitive prices, forcing it to discount some of its marque brands such as HERO5 and HERO6. It has also been criticized for its lack of innovation, for failing to match the speed with which innovative features and benefits are offered by smartphone manufacturers, for example. A further reason for the fall in its share price specifically has been investor concerns that the company is limited to just one product category, namely, the action camera. It tried to respond to this problem with the development of its KARMA drone, priced at US$1,000. However, the product was beset with problems, with videos of it crashing popping up frequently on YouTube. The innovation turned out to be an expensive failure, which was abandoned by the company in 2016. The brand built on action and adventure might just be facing its biggest challenges ever.

Questions

1. How did the development of GoPro meet the changing needs of consumers in the marketplace?
2. Evaluate the forms of customer value provided by GoPro.
3. Evaluate the promotional techniques used by the company to build its brand.
4. What new market challenges face the brand and how should it respond?

This case was prepared by Adam Reynolds, Dr Conor Carroll and Professor John Fahy, University of Limerick, from various published sources as a basis for class discussion rather than to show effective or ineffective management.

Chapter 2

The Global Marketing Environment

Chapter outline

The macroenvironment

Economic forces

Social forces

Political and legal forces

Ecological forces

Technological forces

The microenvironment

Environmental scanning

Learning outcomes

By the end of this chapter you will:

1 Understand what is meant by the term 'marketing environment'

2 Explain the distinction between the macro- and microenvironment

3 Analyse the impact of economic, social, political and legal, physical and technological forces on marketing decisions

4 Critique the nature of corporate social responsibility and ethical marketing practices

5 Analyse the impact of customers, distributors, suppliers and competitors on marketing decisions

6 Explain how companies respond to environmental change

Adidas: selling shoes made of ocean plastic

In 1949, Adi Dassler registered 'Adi Dassler Adidas Sportschuhfabrik', known as Adidas today, and set to work with 47 employees in the small German town of Herzogenaurach. After 70 years of operations, in 2017, Adidas was in the top 100 of Interbrand's 'Best Global Brands 2017' list, ranked number 55, with a brand value of US$7.9 billion.[1] Employing 56,888 people from more than 100 countries, Adidas produces more than 900 million product units every year and generates sales of US$25.739 billion (all figures relate to 2017).[2]

The power of sports to positively impact individuals, groups and societies is more important today than ever before. The current influx of people seeking asylum in Germany to escape political persecution, war and terror makes this a challenging time for the country. However, this is also a time that holds many opportunities if people, politicians and companies join forces in a positive shared vision. Enter 'We Together' (*Wir Zusammen*), a business-driven integration initiative driving long-term projects to integrate refugees into the business community, and German society more broadly. A broad collaborative platform, We Together is the result of proactive measures taken by Adidas and 36 other German companies aligned under the shared mission of creating an inclusive, diverse and flourishing society. On a global level, Adidas has been working with the non-governmental organization Luftfahrt ohne Grenzen (Wings of Help) since 2012 to provide and donate products to refugee camps in Syria and Turkey on a regular basis. It also provides support to refugee camps and programmes in Greece, Italy, Turkey, Iraq, and along the Balkan route.

Sustainability is a big part of Adidas's business strategy and, in 2016, the company launched its Sustainability Strategy. Deeply rooted in the company's core belief that sport has the power to change lives, the Strategy translates the Group's sustainable efforts into tangible goals and mea-surable objectives until 2020. In 2016, Adidas eliminated plastic bags in its 2,900 retail stores around the world, saving 70 million plastic shopping bags by switching to paper. James Carnes, Adidas vice president of global brand strategy, told *Fortune*: 'Plastic bags are always a problem because they aren't a renewable resource. They are trash', 'Good plastics have the potential to be reused but plastic bags are bad plastics.'[3]

According to CEO, Kasper Rorsted, Adidas sold a million pairs of shoes made from ocean plastic in 2017.[4] What contributed to this number is a close collaboration with Parley for the Oceans, which is an environmental initiative addressing major threats to the world's oceans, the most impor-tant ecosystem of the planet, to develop products made from recycled marine plastic. The latest study pub-lished by Scientific Reports in March 2018[5] revealed that the area known as the Great Pacific Garbage Patch is about 1.6 million square kilometres in size – up to 16 times bigger than pre-viously estimated. Instead of remaining waste, Adidas has found a smart way to use recycling to its (and the planet's) benefit. It introduced three versions of the UltraBoost shoe in 2017. On average, each pair reuses

Exhibit 2.1 The UltraBoost Adidas shoe

(continued)

11 plastic bottles and incorporates recycled plastic into the laces, heel webbing, heel lining and sock liner covers.

This move towards sustainability proposed by Adidas is a small change in the way products are manufactured and recycled, but on a global scale can have a huge impact. 'Take, for instance, the fact that Americans alone use an average of 500 million plastic straws every day,[6] which inspired the Be Straw Free campaign by the National Parks Service.' This habit has huge consequences: that plastic waste winds up in our oceans, polluting the water and killing animals, only to eventually make its way back to us through the food we eat (and the micro plastics in it). High-performance shoes made from marine plastic are part of a larger sustainability push by the company. In 2017, Adidas unveiled the company's first performance products – soccer jerseys and running shoes – that were mass produced with plastic found in the oceans. These lines were a limited release, but they resonated with shoppers.

Beyond the use of recycled plastics, shoe makers generally have become more innovative and experimental in how they manufacture, source materials and use technology to make sneakers. A shortlist of new initiatives includes Adidas's 3D-printed shoes, Reebok's use of futuristic liquid material and 3D drawing, Nike's personalized marathon running shoes for elite athletes, and Under Armour's connected footwear with built-in sensors. Growing use of new technologies and awareness of environmental impact are two of the hallmarks of this industry sector.

 Video: UltraBoost X – Greater Every Run

A market-orientated firm needs to look outwards to the environment in which it operates, adapting to take advantage of emerging opportunities and to minimize potential threats. In this chapter we will examine the **marketing environment**, and how to monitor and adapt to it accordingly. In particular, we will look at some of the major forces that impact upon organizations, such as economic, social, legal, physical and technological issues. Firms need to monitor the rapid changes taking place in these forces in order to be prepared to compete in an increasingly interdependent global economic environment.

The marketing environment is composed of the forces and actors that affect a company's ability to operate effectively in providing products and services to its customers. Distinctions have been drawn between the **macroenvironment** and the **microenvironment** (see Figure 2.1). The macroenvironment consists of a number of broader forces that affect not only the company, but also the other actors in the environment. These can be grouped into economic, social, political/legal, physical and technological forces. These shape the character of the opportunities and threats facing a company, and yet are largely uncontrollable. The microenvironment consists of the actors in the firm's immediate environment or business system that affect its capabilities to operate effectively in its chosen markets. The key actors are suppliers, distributors, customers and competitors.

Figure 2.1 The marketing environment

The macroenvironment

This chapter will focus on the major macroenvironmental forces that affect marketing decisions. Typically there are six forces that need to be examined – namely, economic, social, political, legal, ecological and technological. Together these forces can be grouped using the acronym PESTEL, which is often used to describe macroenvironmental analysis. Later in the chapter we will introduce the four dimensions of the microenvironment, some of which will then be dealt with in greater detail throughout the book. The changing nature of the supply chain and customer behaviour will be dealt with in detail in Chapter 3, while the issue of distributors and the impact of digitalization on distribution channels is explored in depth in Chapter 9.

Economic forces

Through its effect on supply and demand, the economic environment can have a crucial influence on the success of companies and their **sustainable competitive advantage**. It is important to identify those economic influences that are relevant and to monitor them. We shall now examine three major economic influences on the marketing environment of companies: economic growth and unemployment; interest rates and exchange rates; and taxation and inflation.

Economic growth and unemployment

The general state of both national and international economies can have a profound effect on an individual company's prosperity. Economies tend to fluctuate according to the 'business cycle'. Most of the world's economies went through a period of significant growth from the early to mid-2000s, driven mainly by rising demand in developing economies like China and the availability of cheap credit in the developed markets of the West. The fortunes of many sectors, such as retailing, services, consumer durables and commodities, closely mirror this economic pattern. For example, the rising demand for oil meant a rapid growth in wealth for oil-rich states like the United Arab Emirates (UAE), resulting in a retail, hotel and property boom in states such as Dubai or Abu Dhabi. The global financial crisis (GFC) of 2008, followed by a sudden scarcity of credit, gave rise to a significant downturn in the economies of Europe in particular. Several countries, such as Greece, Ireland, Italy, Portugal and Spain, suffered severe financial crises caused by excess levels of personal, corporate and sovereign debt built up during the boom years. Greece's economy collapsed, with growth levels at zero and unemployment doubling since 2011 to almost one-third of the population (see Table 2.1). Youth unemployment (those younger than 25 years) is a particular problem in some countries, with levels as high as 43.7 per cent and 34 per cent in Greece and Spain respectively,[7] all of which has a very negative effect on levels of consumer demand for products and services. A major marketing problem is predicting the next boom or slump that will influence the **purchasing power** of customers. Germany, which for years lagged behind average growth in Europe, has become the quickest country to recover from the GFC, with many of its major firms reporting record profits. Investments made during periods of low growth can yield rich returns when economies recover and boost customer spending.

Low growth rates and high unemployment levels have a direct impact on the way consumers behave. Because they feel less well off, they are likely to purchase less, buy smaller quantities and/or switch to cheaper alternatives such as discount or retailer brands. But opportunities can also arise. Because consumers pay fewer visits to beauty salons and spas, for example, manufacturers may sell more beauty products to be applied at home. This is also the time when companies tend to cut back on advertising budgets, which has particular implications for marketing. For instance, lack of confidence caused by Brexit means that many marketers are cutting back or moving budgets to cost-efficient digital channels. According to the Bellwether Report – a trusted quarterly poll of senior marketers from some of the UK's biggest spenders on media – 80 per cent of companies froze or reduced budgets (69 and 11 per cent, respectively).[8] The variation in unemployment levels and associated growth rates in some of the world's economies is illustrated in Table 2.1.

A key challenge for marketers will be to anticipate the implications of the changing patterns of global economic growth. While growth in the traditional powerhouses of the world economy, such as Europe, remains slow (see Table 2.1), other economies are racing ahead. China has grown so rapidly in the past decade that it is now the world's second-largest economy. The remaining BRIC nations (Brazil, Russia and India, as

Table 2.1 Growth rates and unemployment rates (percentage) in selected countries, 2018

Country	Growth rate[9]	Unemployment rate[10]
Czech Republic	3.5	2.4
Japan	1.2	2.7
Iceland	3.2	2.8
Mexico	2.3	3.4
Germany	2.5	3.6
Turkey	4.4	10.1
Italy	1.5	10.8
Spain	2.8	16.6
Greece	2.0	20.9
South Africa	1.5	27.6

Source: International Monetary Fund and Statista.

well as China) have also experienced strong growth, while the term CIVETS (Colombia, Indonesia, Vietnam, Egypt, Turkey, as well as South Africa) has been used to describe the newest group of countries likely to grow rapidly. As these countries build factories, roads and shopping centres, they need resources such as oil, copper, coal, and so on, and the continent of Africa – traditionally the world's poorest region – is rich in these resources, with the result that huge levels of Chinese investment have poured into Africa.

In specific industries, new opportunities are emerging all the time. For example, Nokia has been very successful in its efforts to gain a large share of the Indian market through its provision of low-cost telecommunications products, while H&M has located much of its production in countries like Cambodia and Myanmar (see Marketing in Action 2.1). Similarly, China with its rapid economic growth and increased urbanization has growing problems with pollution leading to respiratory issues and death. One Canadian company, Vitality, which is based in Edmonton, Alberta, collects air from the Canadian Rockies and compresses it into containers for sale in heavily polluted cities. A single eight-litre bottle of compressed Canadian air – which comes with a specially designed spray cap and mask – holds around 160 breaths and costs C\$32 (US\$24) per bottle. Global environmental trends need to be monitored for the emergence of new opportunities and threats.

Interest rates and exchange rates

One of the levers that the government uses to manage the economy is interest rates; the interest rate is the rate at which money is borrowed by businesses and individuals. Throughout the world, interest rates are at historically low levels. One of the results of this has been a boom in consumer borrowing for capital investments such as housing. This has meant significant sales and profit rises for construction companies and global furniture retailers like IKEA. While taking on debt to buy homes and cars has traditionally been considered acceptable, what is worrying policy-makers is the high levels of consumer debt arising particularly from the overuse of credit cards. Total household borrowing as a percentage of gross domestic product (GDP) has risen considerably over the past two decades, but the rate of growth has been variable. Denmark had the highest level of consumer debt in Europe in 2015 at almost 300 per cent of net disposable income, followed by the Netherlands, Norway and Switzerland.[11] Overall, changes in interest rates are usually followed quickly by changes in consumer behaviour.

Exchange rates are the rates at which one currency buys another. With the formation of the European Union (EU), exchange rates between most European countries are now fixed. However, the rates at which major currencies like the US dollar, the euro, sterling and the yen are traded are still variable. These floating rates can have a significant impact on the profitability of a company's international operations. For example, in 2015, the Chinese Government devalued its currency, the yuan, against the US dollar. Because the value of the yuan has loosely tracked the dollar, it was being dragged higher as the US dollar rose in anticipation of rising US interest rates. This had the impact of making Chinese goods exported to the US relatively more expensive than those coming from rival countries such as Japan and South Korea.[12] Devaluing the currency makes Chinese exports such as consumer electronics and machinery relatively cheaper but makes travel abroad by Chinese citizens relatively more expensive.

Taxation and inflation

There are two types of personal taxes: direct and indirect. Direct taxes are taxes on income and wealth, such as income tax, capital gains tax, inheritance tax, and so on. Income tax is important for marketers because it determines the levels of disposable income that consumers have. When taxes fall, consumers keep a greater portion of their earnings and have more money to spend. It also increases the levels of discretionary income

Marketing in Action 2.1
H&M: offering fashion and quality at the best price

Critical Thinking: Below is a review of some of the controversy surrounding clothing manufacturers like H&M, who outsource manufacturing to developing economies. Read it and critically reflect on this popular trend.

The H&M group is a global fashion and design company with more than 4,700 stores in 69 markets as well as a strong digital presence. The company was founded by Erling Pedersson, who opened his first fashion retail store, Hennes (which is the Swedish word for 'hers'), in 1947. After acquiring the hunting apparel and equipment retailer, Mauritz Wildforss, the company name was changed to Hennes & Mauritz, and men's fashion was included in the product range. Since then H&M has played a significant role in democratizing fashion and bringing trends once reserved for the upper classes to the masses. Today, The H&M group is one of the leading fashion companies worldwide, with the brands H&M and H&M Home, COS, Other Stories, Monki, Weekday, Cheap Monday and ARKET, and headquarters located in Stockholm, Sweden. H&M employs 171,000 people and generated sales including VAT of SEK232 billion in 2017 (equal to US$26 billion). H&M brands are united by a passion for fashion, design and quality, and the drive to dress customers in a sustainable way.

The clothing industry is currently characterized by a fast-fashion model, which puts an emphasis on the speed with which new designs and styles are brought to market, quick turnover of products, and a focus on low-cost production and low prices. These features present a challenge for businesses that wish to operate in a sustainable manner. Even though H&M is a member of the Fair Labour Association, which aims to improve working conditions in factories, the company has been hit with a slew of bad press after a series of mass fainting incidents at partner factories in Cambodia. Further revelations included H&M's links with clothing factories in Myanmar, where children as young as 14 toiled for more than 12 hours a day. Myanmar, formerly known as Burma, has become a popular manufacturing destination for many retailers, including Marks & Spencer, Tesco, Primark, C&A, Aldi and Gap.

Overall, H&M has had both positive and negative press coverage on its sustainability initiatives, as detailed below.

The positive

- H&M surpassed Walmart as the world's largest buyer of organic cotton, consuming more than 15,000 tonnes in 2010, an increase of 77 per cent on the previous year.
- It is a founding member of the Better Cotton Initiative, which introduces more sustainable practices at every step of the cotton production supply chain.
- It has experimented with other eco-fibres, including recycled polyester, recycled polyamide, recycled plastic, organic linen, recycled cotton, recycled wool, Tencel® and organic hemp.

(continued)

The negative

■ Reports from Human Rights Watch detailed the criminally abusive conditions in Cambodia's garment factories, displaying the impoverished conditions under which many of the young female workers live.

■ A Greenpeace report alleged that H&M-affiliated factories are discharging hazardous chemicals into rivers in China or Indonesia.

■ Workers demanding better conditions and benefits destroying the production line of a Chinese-owned factory in Myanmar in one of the most violent labour disputes in the country in years.

Based on: Chapman, 2018;[13] Eriksen, 2017;[14] Farmbrough, 2018;[15] Jensen, 2017[16]

Video: H&M orders on hold in Myanmar after factory riot

that they have – that is, the amount of money available after essentials, such as food and rent, have been paid for. At this point consumers move from needs to wants, and a great deal of marketing activity is aimed at trying to convince us where we should spend our discretionary income.

Indirect taxes include value added tax (VAT), excise duties and tariffs, and are taxes that are included in the prices of goods and services that we buy. They have major implications for marketing mix variables such as price. Changes in VAT rates need to be passed on to customers and this can cause problems for firms trying to compete on the basis of low price. Differences in indirect tax levels across national boundaries give rise to the problem of *parallel importing*, whereby goods are bought in a low-cost country for importation back into a high-cost country. This presents a challenge for distributors in the high-cost country, who are not permitted to get access to this source of supply. Variations in tax levels impact on consumer demand. For example, in 2016, the World Health Organization (WHO) recommended the imposition of a 20 per cent tax on sugary drinks, suggesting that such a move would result in 'proportional reductions in consumption', something that was deemed desirable in the light of the global obesity epidemic particularly among children. The tax has been introduced in several countries, including the UK and Ireland, despite strong opposition from drinks manufacturers. Norway has gone even further, with the government imposing an 83 per cent tax on sugar-containing ready-to-eat products and 42 per cent on drinks.

Finally, inflation is a measure of the cost of living in an economy. The inflation rate is calculated by monitoring price changes on a basket of products such as rent/mortgage repayments, oil, clothing, food items and consumer durables. The rising price of commodities like oil and wheat feeds through to consumers in the form of higher fuel bills and higher bread and pasta prices. Rapid rises in inflation also reduce the future value of savings, investments and pensions. Governments are acutely sensitive to inflation figures and increase interest rates to keep inflation under control.

Overall economic movements feed through to marketing in the form of influencing demand for products and services, and the level of profitability that accrues to the firm from the sales of goods.

Social forces

When considering the social environment, two major aspects need to be examined, namely demographic changes and the cultural differences that exist within and between nations. Further aspects of the social environment will be explored in the next chapter when we examine consumer behaviour in greater detail.

Demographic forces

The term demographics refers to changes in population. The most significant factor from society's point of view is the dramatic growth in the world's population in the past 200 years (see Figure 2.2). On the one hand, this presents opportunities for marketers in the form of growing markets, but on the other hand it raises questions about the sustainability of this global growth. The planet's resources are finite, meaning that pressure is increasing on the limited supplies of water, food and fuel. For example, the fishing industry supports 520 million people, or 8 per cent of the global population, but if current overfishing levels continue, commercial fishing will collapse before 2050. Some species, such as tuna, marlin and swordfish, have fallen in numbers by as much as 90 per cent since the 1950s. Innovative solutions to this challenge are likely to generate significant returns for organizations. Variations in population growth are also important. Although China dropped its one-child policy in 2015, growth is slowing in the developed world and most increases are forecast in Africa, Asia and Latin America. In response, Unilever is trying to sell more soap to rural customers in African countries, which improves hygiene and cuts down on diseases. Worldwide, there are 3.4 billion rural consumers, and about 3 billion of them live in developing countries in Asia and Africa. They are not all poor; in many countries, a rural middle class is emerging or expanding. Technology is making it easier to connect with rural consumers in so-called media dark areas. For instance,

Figure 2.2 The dramatic growth in global population presents a major challenge to us all

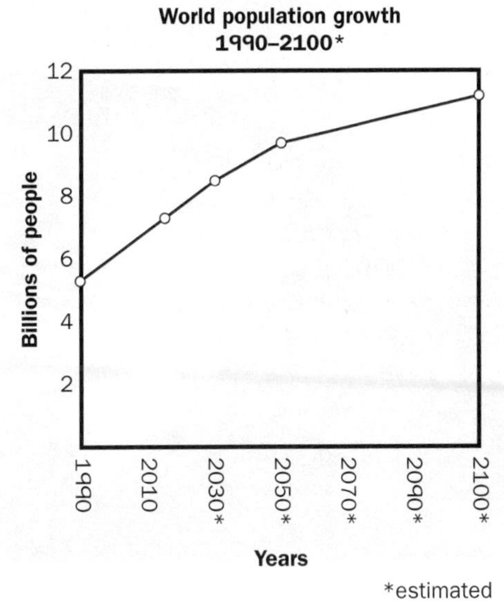

World population growth 1990–2100*

Billions of people (y-axis: 2, 4, 6, 8, 10, 12)

Years (x-axis: 1990, 2010, 2030*, 2050*, 2070*, 2090*, 2100*)

*estimated

Source: Data from United Nations Department for Economics and Social Affairs, Population Division, *World Population Prospects: The 2015 Revision.*

mobile phone companies like Vodafone in Africa and Digicell in the Caribbean have generated significant profits from providing telephony in these regions.

Globalization has given rise to two other interesting demographic effects, namely population migration between countries and the rise of middle and wealthy classes in countries with a low average GDP per capita. The continued integration of Europe has resulted in significant movements of labour from the poorer areas of Central and Eastern Europe to the wealthier Western European countries. These patterns are being played out around the world, and the number of international migrants – persons living in a country other than where they were born – has continued to grow rapidly in recent years, reaching 258 million in 2017, of which 106 million were born in Asia.[17] The United Nations estimates that the number of migrants could reach 405 million by 2050. Changes in immigration controls, such as the number of student visas issued, impact upon the level of demand for university places. Global economic prosperity has also given rise to significant segments of

wealthy consumers in countries with low average wages, such as Russia and Indonesia. For example, the fastest-growing markets for advertising expenditure are in Latin America and Asia Pacific as these economies grow.

A major demographic change that will continue to affect demand for products and services is the rising proportion of people over the age of 60 and the decline in the younger age group. Figure 2.3 shows projections for the growth of this segment up to 2050. The rise in the over-55-year-old group creates substantial marketing opportunities because of the high level of per

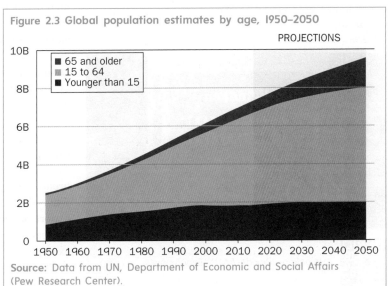

Figure 2.3 Global population estimates by age, 1950–2050

PROJECTIONS

- ■ 65 and older
- ■ 15 to 64
- ■ Younger than 15

(y-axis: 0, 2B, 4B, 6B, 8B, 10B)

(x-axis: 1950, 1960, 1970, 1980, 1990, 2000, 2010, 2020, 2030, 2040, 2050)

Source: Data from UN, Department of Economic and Social Affairs (Pew Research Center).

Exhibit 2.2 Cruise holidays are particularly popular with the 'grey' consumer

capita income enjoyed by this group in developed countries. They have much lower commitments in terms of mortgage repayments than younger people, tend to benefit from inheritance wealth and are healthier than ever before. Pharmaceuticals, health and beauty, technology, travel, financial services, luxury cars, lavish food and entertainment are key growth sectors for this market segment (see Exhibit 2.2). The overall implication of these trends is that many consumer companies may need to reposition their product and service offerings to take account of the rise in so-called 'grey' purchasing power. For example, almost one-fifth of skiers at US resorts are aged over 55 and have been dubbed locally as the 'greys on trays'!

Finally, one of the emerging demographic trends is the growth in the number of household units and falling household sizes. People are choosing to get married later or stay single, divorce rates are rising and family sizes are smaller than they traditionally have been. Combined with high incomes and busy lives, these trends have led to a boom in connoisseur convenience foods and convenience shopping. Companies like Northern Foods and Marks & Spencer, in particular, have catered for this market very successfully. Demand for childcare and homecare facilities has also risen.

Cultural forces

Culture is the combination of values, beliefs and attitudes that is possessed by a national group or subgroup. Cultural differences have implications for the way in which business is conducted. For example, because of the growth of markets like China, India and Singapore, more and more westerners are doing business in these countries and are finding significant differences in the way things are done. Westerners tend to view contracts as set in stone, while those from the East take a more flexible view. In the East, a penchant for harmony means that decision-making tends primarily to be a rubber-stamping of a consensus already hammered out by senior management. The Western obsession with using logic to unravel complex situations is likely to be viewed as naive by those in the East. These kinds of differences are deeply culturally bound in the complex social networks of the East versus the greater levels of independence experienced by those living in the West.[18]

Exhibit 2.3 The hugely popular Heineken 'Worlds Apart' campaign of 2017 aimed to show how conversation can bridge the divide between people from different subcultures.

Heineken: 'Worlds Apart' Experiment.

International marketers need to pay particular attention to the possible impact of culture. For example, MTV – which was the traditional, all-American music channel – developed 141 channels broadcasting in 32 languages to 160 countries. While these could be viewed as vehicles for the export of American culture to new countries, the company is careful to reflect local cultures; for example, 45 per cent of what is shown on MTV Arabia in the Middle East is locally produced and the remainder is translated.[19]

Even within particular countries, however, it is important to bear in mind that many subcultures also exist. The rapid movement of global populations, described above, has meant that ethnically based subcultures have sprung up in most developed countries, creating potentially lucrative niche markets for products and services. For example, there are an estimated 3.5 million people of Turkish origin living in Germany, more than 5.5 million Moroccans living in Spain, and 800,000-plus people living in Italy are of Albanian origin. In addition, social trends and fashions give rise to their own particular subcultures, whose members dress and behave in certain ways. Culture is a central factor when developing marketing communications and is frequently a focus of advertising messages such as in the Guinness *Sapeurs* campaign or the Heineken *Worlds Apart* campaign (Exhibit 2.3).

Political and legal forces

Marketing decisions can be also influenced by political and legal forces, which determine the rules in which businesses operate. Political forces describe the close connections that politicians and senior business people often have, sometimes referred to as crony capitalism. These relationships are often cultivated by organizations, both to monitor the political mood and also to influence it. Companies sometimes make sizeable contributions to the funds of political parties in an attempt to maintain favourable relationships. The types of sectors where crony capitalism is most pervasive include resources, defence, ports and airports, real estate, and utilities and telecoms, while the problem is greatest in countries like Hong Kong, Russia, Malaysia, Ukraine and Singapore.[20] The importance of political connections has been demonstrated by a study which showed that 'politically connected firms' are three times more likely to be bailed out during a financial crisis than those that are not.[21] During the global financial crisis in 2008, Lehman Brothers was allowed to fail but Goldman Sachs was rescued, leading it to earn the nickname 'Government Sachs'. The extent to which businesses try to influence the political process is illustrated by the level of lobbying that takes place. Earlier in this chapter, we saw how world fishing stocks are being depleted yet successful lobbying by national fishing groups has given the industry globally an estimated US$35 billion a year in cheap fuel, insurance, and so on.[22] It is estimated that there are more than 30,000 lobbyists in Brussels trying to influence EU policy-making, which almost matches the 31,000 staff employed by the European Commission.[23] Some of the proposals that businesses have lobbied against include restrictions on online and mobile phone advertising to reduce spam, tougher packaging rules to reduce waste, and stricter testing and labelling for chemicals. As an example of how unbalanced lobbying can be, it is estimated that the big tobacco companies spent more than €3 million trying to weaken proposed anti-smoking legislation in 2014, while one of the smallest lobbying groups in Brussels is the consumer protection lobby.[24]

Political decisions can have major consequences for businesses (see Exhibit 2.4). For example, they can lead to the creation or removal of industries and businesses. Producing and selling marijuana is illegal in most countries but, in 2014, Colorado became the first state in the USA to allow the legal sale of the substance, creating a new industry, with producers, distributors and customers, as well as a new source of tax revenue for the state. In 2016, the Venezuelan government was ordered to pay the Canadian mining firm, Rusoro Mining, for expropriating its investment in the country. Decisions can severely impact existing business, such as the US decision to invade Iraq, which resulted in some leading American companies becoming the targets for attack and some American products being boycotted. German businesses lobbied against proposed sanctions for Russia following its intervention in Ukraine in 2014 as it is Germany's 11th biggest export market, worth an estimated €36 billion and supporting 300,000 jobs. Political turmoil in the region had a huge impact on Turkey's very important tourism industry, which saw visitor numbers plummet by almost 12 million between 2014 and 2016. Usually, political forces have a more gradual and subtle effect, as illustrated by European politicians' pursuit of a common European Union.

Exhibit 2.4 The granting of drilling and mining rights are important political decisions and a frequent source of controversy

The European Union

In the past, the basic economic unit has been the country, which was largely autonomous with regard to the decisions it made about its economy and levels of supply and demand. But, for the past three decades, all this has been changing rapidly, driven mainly by the globalization of business. The world's largest companies, like Amazon, Apple, Google, Samsung, Facebook, AT&T, Microsoft, Verizon, Walmart, ICBC and others, are now larger than most countries in economic terms. At the same time, countries have been merging together into economic areas to more effectively manage their affairs. Most European countries are now part of the European Union (EU), the North American countries have grouped together into an economic area known as NAFTA (the North American Free Trade Agreement), the Pacific Rim countries are part of a group known as the ASEAN (Association of South East Asian Nations), and there's also the African Union (AU).

The advent in 1986 of the Single European Act was the launch pad for an internal market in the EU. The intention was to create a massive deregulated market of 320 million consumers by abolishing barriers to the free flow of products, services, capital and people among the then 12 member states. The current EU members are Austria, Belgium, Bulgaria, Croatia, Cyprus, Czech Republic, Denmark, Estonia, Finland, France, Germany, Greece, Hungary, Ireland, Italy, Latvia, Lithuania, Luxembourg, Malta, Netherlands, Poland, Portugal, Romania, Slovakia, Slovenia, Spain, Sweden and the UK, notwithstanding the potential exit of the latter (see Marketing in Action 2.2). The euro is the most tangible proof of European integration – the common currency in 19 out of 28 EU countries and used by some 338.6 million people every day. The benefits of the common currency are immediately obvious to anyone travelling abroad or shopping online on websites based in another EU country, making travel, price comparisons and cross-border trade easier.

One of the main outcomes of economic union is that the prospects for adopting what is known as a pan-European or standardized strategy across Europe are improved. Standardization appears to depend on product type. In the case of many industrial goods, consumer durables (such as cameras, toasters, watches, radios) and clothing (Gucci shoes, Benetton sweaters, Levi's jeans) standardization is well advanced. However, for many fast-moving consumer goods (fmcg), standardization of products is more difficult to achieve because of differences in local tastes. Nevertheless, it is an approach that is increasingly being adopted by companies. For example, Lastminute.com, which is aiming to position itself as a leisure, entertainment and travel retailer, has created a Europe-wide promotional campaign based on the idea of customers telling unforgettable stories, under the tagline 'Stories start here …'.

Marketing in Action 2.2
Brexit: The future of 'Brand Britain'

Critical Thinking: Below is an overview of Brexit consequences for marketers. Read it and consider other examples of how Great Britain leaving the EU influences marketing decisions. What would you advise companies operating and planning to establish their presence in Great Britain to do?

By deciding to leave the European Union, Great Britain, the world's fifth largest economy, has become a major source of uncertainty, not only in Europe but in America and the world as well. Brexit has caused multiple consequences for marketing activities. It is clear that the rise of nationalism will result in more protected markets and more localized marketing. Localization will transform how we think about and manage global brands, and marketing in general. Companies will have to go through a cultural transformation as they shift from globalization to localization. First, local brand relevance demands local market creativity and local authenticity. And, second, sharing information and learning within the enterprise is the new essential. Marketing budgets are likely to be scrutinized and frozen, even curtailed, and investment in innovation might be pared down as companies retrench. For example,

(continued)

80 per cent of senior marketers polled in a Bellwether study in 2017 reported that they had frozen or reduced marketing budgets.

Furthermore, Great Britain, as no longer part of the EU single market, loses its influence in top markets, as trading outside of the EU bloc, it will be faced with higher tariffs and trade costs, and new barriers to doing business and marketing products. Beyond the export question, there are various thorny regulatory issues for marketers to pick through. Britain has its own independent regulatory body in the Advertising Standards Authority, so Brexit would not alter the ethical standards that British marketers and brands already adhere to. However, in areas such as consumer protection, product law and copyright, Brexit could potentially create a two-tier system because Britain would no longer be bound by rules governing the rest of the EU.

Britain's marketing, technology and creative industries are highly diverse and multinational, so curbs on EU immigration would affect many businesses' recruitment practices. Figures from data intelligence company DueDil show that more than a fifth of British start-ups are led by foreign entrepreneurs, while the number of tech directors in Britain from EU countries has grown by 176 per cent since 2010. Further development will be hindered by making it more difficult for talent from the continent to live and work in Britain.

Brexit may also redefine what it means to be British. It may be seen as a withdrawal from the global stage and a rejection of modernity, detracting from one of the key marketing advantages for British brands abroad. Countless brands trade on their British heritage, so any change in perception of the country could have implications for their positioning overseas.

Based on: Bacon, 2016;[25] Parsons, 2017[26]

Video: UK ad industry urges clarity on Brexit immigration strategy | Marketing Media Money

Pro-competitive legislation

Political action may also translate directly into legislation and less formal directives, which can have a profound influence on business conduct. One of the key areas in which regulators act is ensuring that competition is fair and legal and operates in such a way that consumers and society benefit. Formerly, the control of monopolies in Europe was enacted via Article 86 of the Treaty of Rome, which aimed to prevent the 'abuse' of a dominant market position. However, control was increased in 1990 when the EU introduced its first direct mechanism for dealing with mergers and takeovers: the Merger Regulation. This gave the Competition Directorate of the European Commission jurisdiction over 'concentrations with a European dimension'. Over the years, the Commission has challenged the activities of major global companies, most notably Google. An example is the unexpectedly large fine the European Commission slapped on Google – €2.4 billion (US$2.7 billion) – as a result of a case that began in 2010 when the UK shopping comparison engine Foundem complained to the Commission that Google was promoting its own rival service, then called Google Product Search and later renamed Google Shopping, to the detriment of competitors. The case grew as other European and US companies jumped on the bandwagon that didn't want to buy ads that Google promised to place at the top of the search results page, insisting instead that Google display 'organic' results. This was followed by a further record fine of €4.3 billion in 2018 for abuse of the market position held by its dominant Android operating system.[27] 'Google announced that it 'respectfully disagrees' with the Commission's decision and intends to appeal it. That's a difficult path to take – just ask Microsoft, which fought the Commission with all it could and lost all of its appeals in eight years of litigation. In fact, the Commission has a strong record in abuse of monopoly position cases. From 2000 to 2011, the EU's General Court did not fully annul a single one of the 14 Commission decisions that were appealed to it, though it cancelled parts of four decisions. Competition bodies also operate at a national level, such as the Office of Fair Trading in the UK and the Competition Authority in Ireland, where they monitor local-level competition issues.

Consumer legislation

Regulators also enact legislation designed to protect consumers. Many countries throughout Europe have some form of Consumer Protection Act that regulates how businesses interact with consumers and how they advertise their products. These acts typically outlaw practices that are deemed to be unfair, misleading or aggressive. For example, promotions and product information must be clear and claims – such as that a product is friendly to the environment – must be backed up with evidence. This legislation is then enforced through a body such as the National Consumer Agency in Ireland. For example, because of a global obesity epidemic, restaurants around the world are being required to state the number of calories in everything on their menus. The need for this kind of consumer protection is illustrated by the marketing of products like breakfast cereals and soft drinks, which frequently portrays these products as being much healthier than they actually are. Consumers are also protected when shopping online in the EU, where regulations allow a 14-day 'cooling off' period for consumers, with some exceptions, the right to clear information about the seller, delivery company and additional taxes and charges, the right to a refund for delay or non-delivery and the right to return faulty goods.

In short, political and legal decisions can change the rules of the business game very quickly. For example, in 2018, EU General Data Protection Regulation (GDPR) came into effect. Described as the most ground-breaking piece of EU legislation in the digital era, the GDPR is designed to harmonize data privacy laws across Europe, to protect and empower all EU citizens' data privacy and to reshape the way organizations across the region approach data privacy. Data breaches and the misuse of consumer data by corporations has become a major concern for legislators. Some of the features of the legislation include very clear consent required before data can be held, the right of the individual to be delisted and have their history cleared, and mandatory reporting of data security breaches. Fines for breaches of the legislation are up to €20 million, or 4 per cent of worldwide annual turnover (whichever is greater) (see Critical Marketing Perspective 10.1).

In many instances, firms and industries create voluntary codes of practice in order to stave off possible political and legal action.

Codes of practice

On top of the various laws that are in place, certain industries have drawn up codes of practice – sometimes as a result of political pressure – to protect consumer interests. The UK advertising industry, for example, has drawn up a self-regulatory Code of Advertising Standards and Practice designed to keep advertising 'legal, decent, honest and truthful' and, in 2010, this code was extended to cover Facebook pages, Twitter feeds and online banner advertising. However, these codes are frequently violated as advertisers push the boundaries of what is socially acceptable in order to increase the level of likes, shares and comments on social media (see Exhibit 2.5).

Similarly, the marketing research industry has drawn up a code of practice to protect people from unethical activities such as using marketing research as a pretext for selling. However, many commentators are critical of the potential effectiveness of voluntary codes of conduct in industries like oil exploration and clothing manufacture.[28] Firms like Coca-Cola and PepsiCo in the USA have begun to restrict sales of soft drinks in schools, in an effort to appease critics and stave off regulation such as that imposed in France, which banned school-based vending machines.

Marketing management must be aware of the constraints on its

Exhibit 2.5 This Protein World 'Are You Beach Body Ready' campaign was banned in the UK over body confidence and health concerns.

activities brought about by the political and legal environment. It must assess the extent to which there is a need to influence political decisions that may affect operations, and the degree to which industry practice needs to be self-regulated in order to maintain high standards of customer satisfaction and service.

Ecological forces

The explosion in the world's population and the resulting economic growth has brought the issue of environmental sustainability to centre-stage. Everything that we need for our survival and well-being depends directly or indirectly on the natural environment. Some of the key sustainability challenges that have emerged in recent decades are outlined below.

Climate change

Climate change has been one of the most hotly debated topics in recent years. Most commentators argue that human activity is hastening the depletion of the ozone layer, resulting in a gradual rise in world temperatures, which is melting the polar ice caps and causing more unpredictable weather extremes like droughts, floods and hurricanes. Contrarian views suggest that global warming is largely the result of a natural cycle and find supporting evidence in the fact that global temperatures grew at a far slower rate between 1998 and 2013 than they had in the 1990s. In effect, for businesses, this means seeking ways to reduce CO_2 emissions and a ban on the use of chlorofluorocarbons (CFCs). Such initiatives will be necessary as higher taxes on SUVs have caused their sales levels in Western Europe to fall quickly. However, the response of some companies has left a lot to be desired, as shown in Marketing in Action 2.3. Opportunities are also being created by the use of route-planning software for transport companies to reduce emissions, and internet matching systems to fill empty vehicles.

Marketing in Action 2.3
The Volkswagen emissions scandal

Critical Thinking: Below is a review of Volkswagen, which was caught attempting to cheat engine emissions tests. Read it and think of examples of other businesses that have behaved in an unethical manner.

German car companies have built a global reputation for the quality and performance levels of their many brands. However, this reputation was significantly damaged in 2015 when it emerged that the country's largest car maker, Volkwagen (VW), had been involved in an elaborate attempt to beat the emissions tests that monitor the levels of nitrogen oxide emitted by vehicles contributing to air pollution, smog and even death. The problem surfaced when the Environmental Protection Agency (EPA) in the USA found that cars being sold there had a defeat device (or software) in diesel engines that detected when the car was being tested and changed its performance results accordingly. Under test conditions, the cars met emissions standards but, in real driving conditions, the cars' emissions were up to 40 times the permitted levels. VW had been engaged in a major marketing push for its diesel vehicles in the USA, ironically putting a focus on the cars' low emissions, under the label 'Clean Diesel'.

At first the company insisted that the scandal was a fraud pulled off by some rogue engineers. Eventually, the attempted cover-up was exposed and VW's chief executive, Martin Winterkorn, was forced to step down. Initially, the problem appeared to be related only to US diesels, but the company subsequently admitted that some 11 million cars, including 8 million in Europe, were fitted with the defeat device. To add to the problems, internal VW investigations also uncovered 'irregularities' in CO_2 emissions and fuel consumption figures. The impact for Volkswagen has been huge. The company announced plans in 2015 to refit the affected vehicles across its VW, Audi and Skoda

(continued)

ranges, and set aside US$7 billion to cover the cost of rectifying the problem. In the USA, more than US$25 billion has already been paid to the authorities in fines, penalties and restitution for the more than half a million vehicles sold there. Fines for the much larger number of vehicles sold in Europe (8 million) have yet to be paid. Total compensation costs ranging from the loss of resale value of the cars to pollution liabilities could cost the company anything up to US$100 billion. And the bad news for VW appears to just keep on coming. In 2018, the company came under fire again when it emerged that it has been conducting experiments in which monkeys and humans were required to breathe car fumes for hours at a time.

Based on: Connolly, 2018;[29] Hotten, 2015;[30] Parloff, 2018[31]

Exhibit 2.6 Droughts and famines brought on by climate change have been the focus of attention of numerous non-governmental organizations (NGOs) such as Amnesty International.

Climate change has the potential to have a major impact on business and society (see Exhibit 2.6). For example, air travel is very much taken for granted, and has boomed in recent years due to economic prosperity and the marketing activities of low-cost airlines. But airplanes are significant users of limited fossil fuels like oil, and CO_2 emissions from international aviation have doubled since 1990. Ultimately, this may mean consumers choosing to fly less or even being encouraged to fly less, which will have significant implications for the aviation industry. These kinds of changes have already happened in the business of patio heaters, which grew in popularity due to smoking bans and a preference by consumers for eating and drinking outdoors. But the gas-powered heaters can emit as much CO_2 per year as one and a half cars, and companies like DIY chain B&Q have stopped selling them.

Pollution

The quality of the physical environment can be harmed by the manufacture, use and disposal of products. The production of chemicals that pollute the atmosphere, the use of nitrates in fertilizer that pollutes rivers, and the disposal of by-products into the sea have caused considerable public concern. Rapidly growing economies like China and India have particular problems in this regard, with China having overtaken the USA as the world's biggest emitter of CO_2. Coal provides 80 per cent of China's energy and it is anticipated that it will continue to do so for the next half-century. Factory and car emissions have meant that air pollution has become a major problem in Beijing. Water pollution has also reached serious levels, with an estimated 90 per cent of the water running through cities being polluted.[32]

Pressure from regulators and consumer groups helps to reduce pollution (see Exhibit 2.7). Denmark has introduced a series of anti-pollution measures, including a charge on pesticides and a CFC tax. In the Netherlands, higher taxes on pesticides, fertilizers and carbon monoxide emissions are proposed. Cities around the world are banning cars. Copenhagen prioritizes bicycles over cars and is aiming to be carbon neutral by 2025, while Helsinki is aiming to build a public transport system that is so good no one will want a car by 2050.[33] Not all of the activity is simply cost raising, however. In Germany, one of the marketing benefits of its involvement in green technology has been a thriving export business in pollution-control equipment.

Animal testing of new products

To reduce the risk of them being harmful to humans, potential new products such as shampoos and cosmetics are tested on animals before launch. This has aroused much opposition. One of the major concepts key to the initial success of UK retailer the Body Shop was that its products were not subject to animal testing. This is an example of the Body Shop's ethical approach to business, which also extends to its suppliers. Other larger stores, responding to Body Shop's success, have introduced their own range of animal-friendly products. Many other companies follow the overall practices in order to avoid any form of **animal cruelty**. Companies are coming to realize that treating animals humanely and concern over their welfare is good business.

Use of environmentally friendly ingredients

The use of biodegradable and natural ingredients when practicable is favoured by environmentalists. The toy industry is one that has come in for criticism for its extensive use of plastics and other environmentally unfriendly products. Consequently, start-up companies like Green Toys and Anamalz have used a different approach. The for-

Exhibit 2.7 This advert from the Surfrider Foundation (surfrider.org) powerfully illustrates the problem of excessive pollution of our oceans and waterways.

WHAT GOES IN THE OCEAN GOES IN YOU.

A RECENT STUDY FOUND THAT 35% OF FISH SAMPLED OFF THE WEST COAST HAD INGESTED PLASTIC. FIND OUT HOW YOU CAN HELP. VISIT WWW.SURFRIDER.ORG MAKE THE PLEDGE. BAN THE BAG.

SURFRIDER FOUNDATION

mer makes toys from recycled plastic milk containers, which are sold in recycled cardboard, while Anamalz uses wood instead of plastic. The humble light bulb is a classic example of a product made from environmentally unfriendly ingredients. It wastes huge amounts of electricity, radiating 95 per cent of the energy it consumes as heat rather than light, and its life span is relatively short. This is because existing light bulbs use electrodes to connect with the power supply and also include dangerous materials like mercury. Researchers at a company called Ceravision in the UK have developed an alternative that does not require electrodes or mercury, uses very little energy and should never need changing. These types of innovation illustrate the business opportunities that are created through the monitoring of the marketing environment.

Recyclable and non-wasteful packaging

The past 20 years or so have seen significant growth in recycling throughout Europe. Cutting out waste in packaging is not only environmentally friendly but also makes commercial sense. Thus companies have introduced concentrated detergents and refill packs, and removed the cardboard packaging around some brands of toothpaste, for example. The savings can be substantial: in Germany, Lever GmbH saved 30 per cent by introducing concentrated detergents, 20 per cent by using lightweight plastic bottles, and the introduction of refills for concentrated liquids reduced the weight of packaging materials by a half. Many governments have introduced bans on the ubiquitous plastic bags available at supermarkets and convenience stores as they give rise to pollution and are slow to biodegrade, which has major implications for packaging manufacturers.

The growth in the use of the personal computer has raised major recycling issues as PCs contain many harmful substances and pollutants. EU legislation is forcing manufacturers to face up to the issue of how these products are recycled, with some of the costs being absorbed by the companies and the rest by the consumer. Hewlett-Packard set up a team to re-examine how PCs are made and to design them with their disposal in mind. The team conducted projects such as using corn starch instead of plastic in its printers, redesigning packaging and cutting down on emissions from factories.[34] The Waste Electrical and Electronic

Equipment (WEEE) Directive became European law in 2003 and imposed the responsibility for the disposal of electrical products on manufacturers. Consumers are entitled to return old electrical goods to sellers, which are charged with recycling them, though the cost of this activity has largely been passed on to consumers through an additional recycling levy. One of the consequences of the Directive has been an increased focus by manufacturers on the ease of recycling of their products.

Conservation of scarce resources

Recognition of the finite nature of the world's resources has stimulated a drive towards conservation. This is reflected in the demand for energy-efficient housing and fuel-efficient motor cars, for example. In Europe, Sweden has taken the lead in developing an energy policy based on domestic and renewable resources. The tax system penalizes the use of polluting energy sources like coal and oil, while less polluting and domestic sources such as peat and wood chip receive favourable tax treatment. The UK is experiencing a boom in the installation of solar panels in response to the creation of incentives for households that generate surplus electricity that is exported back into the grid.[35] Companies manufacturing solar panels and related products stand to benefit from this trend. Toyota's development of its Prius model – a hybrid petrol-electric car – has been an unprecedented success; so much so, that the company has struggled to meet demand for it.

There is increasing recognition that water may become the next scarce resource that needs to be conserved as it is estimated that only 1 per cent of the world's water is fit for human consumption. This has major implications for the lucrative global bottled water industry. The industry has been growing globally at a rate of 10 per cent per year and is estimated to reach a value in the region of US$350 billion by 2021.[36] The lifestyle brand, Fiji water, is sourced in Fiji but travels 10,000 miles to Europe and beyond, while one in three Fijians does not have access to safe drinking water. Furthermore, millions of barrels of crude oil are used in the making of 300 billion plastic bottles per year, 90 per cent of which are disposed of after one use and take 1,000 years to biodegrade. Water scarcity also has implications for soft drinks manufacturers like PepsiCo and Coca-Cola, which are accused of causing water shortages near production plants in developing countries.

Organizational responses to the issue of scarce resources can have interesting effects. For example, European law commits countries to generating 30 per cent of their electricity from renewable sources by 2020. This has given rise to a rapidly growing wind turbine industry, which has had two consequences. First, wind turbines are very unpopular with local residents due to their size and impact on the skyline. As a result, many wind farms have been moved offshore but the cost of producing electricity this way is estimated to be three times the current wholesale price.[37]

In summary, the demands that global economic growth are placing on the natural environment are very significant. Consequently, attention is now being given to the extent to which businesses behave responsibly and ethically.

Corporate social responsibility

Corporate social responsibility (CSR) is a widely used term that describes a form of self-regulation by businesses based on the ethical principle that a person or an organization should be accountable for how its actions might affect the physical environment and the general public. Concerns about the environment, business and public welfare are represented by pressure groups such as Greenpeace, Corporate Watch and Oxfam. The term **green marketing** is used to describe marketing efforts to produce, promote and reclaim environmentally sensitive products.[38]

Marketing managers need to be aware that organizations are part of a larger society and are accountable to that society for their actions. Such concerns led Toyota to recall about 645,000 vehicles worldwide to fix an electrical problem that could stop air bags from inflating in a crash. The recall covered certain Toyota Prius and Lexus RX and NX SUVs. Also covered were some Toyota Alphard, Vellfire, Sienta, Noah, Voxy, Esquire, Probox, Succeed, Corolla, Highlander, Levin and Hilux models. All were produced from May 2015 to March 2016. The automaker said an open electrical circuit could occur over time that would set off an air bag warning light and could stop the side and front air bags from deploying. Through its dealer network the company offered to inspect serial numbers on sensors and replace them if necessary at no cost to owners.[39] Similarly, Honda recalled nearly 1.2 million Accord vehicles produced between 2013 and 2016, after receiving multiple reports of the cars' battery sensors causing fires in the engine. The Japanese firm admitted that the sensors, which notify drivers when there is a problem with the battery, may not be 'sufficiently sealed' against moisture. As a result, substances like road salt can enter the sensor and cause it to short, potentially leading to fires.[40]

The societal marketing concept is a label often used to describe how the activities of companies should not only consider the needs of customers but also society at large. For example, like many global banks, the Brazilian bank Itau has been encouraging customers to move away from paper bank statements. However, this campaign had a particular resonance in Brazil where the excessive use of paper is strongly associated with deforestation. The company decided to communicate its message in a 'paperless' fashion with a primary focus on TV and cinema advertising that featured a baby

Exhibit 2.8 Budweiser's 2017 Super Bowl advert addressed the topical and controversial issue of immigration. Watch it at https://www.youtube.com/watch?v=FIgIFRtWJYs.

laughing hysterically as some paper was torn. 'Baby Paperless' was a huge success, becoming the most viewed online ad in Brazil, as well as driving Itau to become the number-one bank in terms of brand recall in the country. Similarly, advertising such as Budweiser's 2017 Super Bowl ad may address social issues. The 60-second spot showcases the story of the brand's immigrant founder, Adolphus Busch. Titled 'Born the Hard Way', it dramatizes Busch's travel from Germany to the United States (see Exhibit 2.8). Upon arrival, he is shoved by an American man and told: 'You're not wanted here. Go back home.' The ad addresses a significant problem of refugees and puts the heated issue in front of millions of Americans by paying tribute to immigrants who overcame hardships to succeed. It was released just days after President Donald Trump signed an executive order limiting travel into the United States for citizens of seven countries in the Middle East and Africa.[41]

Corporate social responsibility is no longer an optional extra but a key part of business strategy that comes under close scrutiny from pressure groups, private shareholders and institutional investors, some of whom manage ethical investment funds. Businesses are increasingly expected to adapt to climate change, biodiversity, social equity and human rights in a world characterized by greater transparency and more explicit values.[42] Two outcomes of these developments have been the growth in social reporting and cause-related marketing.

Social reporting is where firms conduct independent audits of their social performance and report the results. The practice is a form of self-regulation and some firms, like Baxter International, Inc. and Shell, have been producing such reports since the mid-1990s. Currently, most of the world's largest companies produce sustainability reports.

Cause-related marketing is a commercial activity by which businesses and charities or causes form a partnership with one another in order to market an image, product or service for mutual benefit (see Exhibit 2.9). Cause-related marketing works well when the business and charity have a similar target audience.

Exhibit 2.9 As part of its 'One for One' campaign, the Canadian shoe company TOMs partners with over 100 NGOs in 60 countries distributing a free pair of shoes for every pair purchased from the company.

Exhibit 2.10 The beach and travel accessories brand MadeByWave works with a small community of suppliers in Indonesia sustaining their traditions and craftsmanship

For example, in 2010 the Indian telecommunications company Aircel partnered with the World Wide Fund for Nature-India (WWF-India) to launch a 'Save the Tigers' initiative, in response to the dwindling number of tigers, India's national animal. The centrepiece of the campaign was a powerful television advertising campaign, featuring Stripey, eagerly waiting for its mother to return while gunshots interrupt the scene. Similarly, companies like TOMS footwear are an example of businesses that have social causes at the heart of everything they do. The Canadian company was set up in 2006 by Blake Mycoskie after he had travelled through Argentina and witnessed the hardships faced by children growing up without shoes. He pioneered the idea of 'one for one' whereby, for every pair of shoes bought, a pair was donated to a child in need.[43]

Ethics are the moral principles and values that govern the actions and decisions of an individual or group.[44] They involve values about right and wrong conduct. There can be a distinction between the legality and ethicality of marketing decisions. Ethics concern personal moral principles and values, while laws reflect society's principles, and standards that are enforceable in the courts. Many businesses look to position themselves as ethical brands, as shown in Exhibit 2.10.

Not all unethical practices are illegal. For example, it is not illegal to include genetically modified (GM) ingredients in products sold in supermarkets; however, some organizations (such as Greenpeace) believe it is unethical to sell GM products when their effect on health has not been scientifically proven. However, regulators so far appear to favour the stance taken by businesses. For example in 2013, the Obama administration in the USA signed legislation protecting biotech companies from litigation in regard to the making, selling and distribution of genetically modified seeds and plants despite environmental concerns. Similarly, mobile phone manufacturers are ensuring that handsets conform to international guidelines on the specific absorption rate of radiation emissions and the industry has contributed millions of dollars to research on the issue.[45]

Many ethical dilemmas derive from a conflict between profits and business actions. For example, by using child labour, the cost of producing items is kept low and profit margins are raised. In 2006, secret footage aired on a news bulletin on the UK's Channel 4 showed clearly underage workers making Tesco own-label clothing in a factory in Bangladesh. Tesco, it emerged, was unaware that the factory produced clothes for it – it is a member of the Ethical Trading Initiative, which is a UK-based group that requires independent monitoring of the global supply chain. In 2013, an eight-storey building housing another clothing firm in Dhaka, Bangladesh, collapsed, resulting in more than 1,000 deaths. Significant concerns were raised about the safety and working conditions in these factories, which produce cheap products for sale by firms such as Walmart, Benetton and JC Penney. Because of the importance of marketing ethics, each of the chapters in this book includes a key ethical debate discussing the positions taken by supporters and critics of marketing on a variety of core themes. The debate on corporate social responsibility (CSR) is summarized in Critical Marketing Perspective 2.1.

The consumer movement

The 'consumer movement' is the name given to the set of individuals, groups and organizations whose aim is to safeguard consumer rights. For example, various consumers' associations in Europe campaign on behalf of consumers and provide information about products, often on a comparative basis, allowing consumers to make more informed choices between products and services.

Critical Marketing Perspective 2.1
CSR or PR?

For many years now, debate has raged regarding how socially responsible companies should be. Businesses do not operate in isolation, but are intrinsically linked to the economic, social, physical and political environments in which they operate. To many, their record in being sensitive to the needs of these environments is not one to be proud of. The abuse of human resources in the form of poorly paid workers, working in dangerous conditions, and child labour has been highlighted. Environmental damage through pollution, deforestation and the illegal dumping of waste has rightly been criticized. There is also the exploitation of consumers through the maintenance of artificially high prices and the corruption of the political process throughout the world. The list goes on. Riots between protesters and police at major government and economic conferences highlight the extent of the divide between business and some sections of society.

As a result of societal pressure for change, corporate social responsibility (CSR) has become part of the language of the corporate boardroom. All major corporations have CSR initiatives and many publicize these in their annual reports and/or social reports. As far back as 1953, Shell Oil Company set up the Shell Oil Foundation, which, since its formation, has contributed in the region of $500 million to the development of the communities where Shell employees live and work. In 2014, the food giant Kellogg's caved in to public pressure and announced that it would only buy palm oil from suppliers who can prove that they actively protect rainforests and peat lands, and respect human rights. Some 30,000 square miles of rainforest has been destroyed in the past 20 years to supply the global food industry with a cheap source of palm oil to make packaged foods, ice cream and snacks, endangering indigenous peoples and local habitats. Triple bottom-line accounting has grown, whereby firms demonstrate not only their economic performance but also their social and environmental performance.

At the same time, however, there are commentators who trenchantly argue that these kinds of investments are completely wrong. This stance has been most famously taken by the US economist Milton Friedman. In his view, the mission of a business is to maximize the return to its owners and shareholders; he advocated that anything that detracts from that mission should be avoided, and that society's concerns are the responsibility of government. Similarly, Robert Reich, who served as US Labor Secretary under Bill Clinton, has argued that companies cannot be socially responsible and that activists are neglecting the important task of getting governments to solve problems. Added to this is the growing line of research which shows that CSR does not work – in other words, that CSR has a negative effect on corporate performance.

So it remains very much a matter of debate as to whether the current trend in CSR activity reflects a greater concern from businesses about their impact on the environment or whether this is simply a rather large public relations exercise. Many critics would suggest the latter as companies respond to increasing scrutiny from non-governmental organizations and the public at large. The term 'greenwashing' has been coined to describe organizations that have an environmental programme while at the same time their core business is inherently polluting or unsustainable. A CSR initiative may create a feel-good factor within a business and may satisfy commentators and shareholders, but the ultimate test is whether businesses will consistently put principle before profit. This dilemma has been illustrated by the trials of brands like The Body Shop, Ben & Jerry's and innocent Ltd that have faced the challenge of staying true to their ethical values as they have grown in scale. Enlightened long-term self-interest would appear to be the best approach for corporations to take.

Suggested reading: Bakan (2004)[46]; James (2007)[47]; Sekerta and Stimel (2011)[48]

Reflection: Is it appropriate that a business should put society's interests ahead of its own?

As well as offering details of unbiased product testing and campaigning against unfair business practices, consumer movements have been active in areas such as product quality and safety, and information accuracy. Notable successes have been improvements in car safety, the stipulation that advertisements for credit facilities must display the true interest charges (annual percentage rates), and the inclusion of health warnings on cigarette packets and advertisements.

Such consumer organizations can have a significant influence on marketing practices. For example, the Belgian consumer group Test-Achats brought a case to the European Court of Justice on the equal treatment of males and females in the provision of goods and services. The court ruled in its favour, meaning that insurance companies who had traditionally offered cheaper car insurance to female drivers would no longer be able to do so from December 2012. However, the industry has been slow to implement these changes with price differences between the genders continuing to persist in some markets.[49] In the UK, the Office of Fair Trading is seeking to enable consumers to more easily take legal action against companies that have harmed them through anti-competitive practices.

The consumer movement should not be considered a threat to business, but marketers should view its concerns as offering an opportunity to create new products and services to satisfy the needs of these emerging market segments. For example, growing concern over rising obesity levels in the developed world has led McDonald's to make significant changes to its menu items and marketing approach. It introduced a number of healthy options to its menus, including salads and fruit bags, which helped the company to return to profitability after some years of poor performance. Its *Global Best of Green* social report highlights advances made in energy efficiency, sustainable packaging and recycling of uniforms that it hopes will boost its image. European firms that have made it to the list of the world's most ethical companies are included in Table 2.2.

Table 2.2 The world's most ethical companies, 2017[50]

Name	Business	Country
Accenture	Business services	Ireland
Capgemini	Consulting services	France
DCC	Conglomerate	Ireland
Delphi Automotive plc	Automotive	UK
EDP Energias de Portugal SA	Energy & utilities	Portugal
H&M	Apparel	Sweden
IBERDROLA	Energy & utilities	Spain
illycafè	Food, beverage & agriculture	Italy
L'Oréal	Heath & beauty	France
Marks & Spencer	Retail	UK
Microsoft	Technology	UK
National Grid	Energy & utilities	UK
Northumbrian Water Group	Energy & utilities	UK
PepsiCo	Food, beverage & agriculture	USA
PKN ORLEN S.A.	Oil & gas, renewables	Poland
Schneider Electric	Diversified machinery	France
TE Connectivity	Electronics & semiconductors	Switzerland
The Rezidor Hotel Group	Lodging & hospitality	Belgium
Volvo Car Group	Automotive	Sweden

Source: Data from Kauflin, J. (2017) The world's most ethical companies 2017, *Forbes*, 14 March.

Technological forces

People's lives and companies' fortunes can both be affected significantly by technology. Technological advances have given us body scanners, robotics, camcorders, computers and many other products that have contributed to our quality of life. Many technological breakthroughs have changed the rules of the competitive game.

For example, the launch of the computer has decimated the market for typewriters and has made calculators virtually obsolete. Companies, like Skype, that have pioneered telephone calls over the internet have revolutionized the telecoms business and reduced revenues for international calling to virtually zero. Mobile phone services are being used by pharmaceutical companies to tackle the damaging trade in counterfeit drugs in developing countries like Ghana and Nigeria. Consumers in these countries that buy medicines, scratch off a panel on the packaging that reveals a code. They text this code to a computer system that comes back with a message that the drug is genuine and safe.[51] Monitoring the technological environment may result in the identification of opportunities and major investments in new technological areas. For example, the US company Tesla is recognized as one of the most innovative businesses in the world. Founded in 2003, the company has focused on sectors in emerging technology like electric cars, lithium ion batteries, and solar panels and roof tiles. However, the challenges involved in pursuing such new opportunities are illustrated by its results to date. For example, in 2017, the company posted revenues of almost US$12 billion but accumulated losses for the same period of US$1.6 billion.

New potential applications for technology are emerging all the time. For example, money – which has been the foundation for the market economy for generations – is becoming increasingly redundant. In Japan there has been a huge growth in the use of e-cash facilities where consumers buy smart cards that are topped up on a monthly basis and can be used for everything from transport systems to shops and cafés. The growth in cashless transactions has continued to accelerate with the emergence of mobile payment and digital wallet services provided by the likes of Apple Pay and Google Pay. And new currencies such as crypto-currency Bitcoin offer yet another alternative to cash. Based on new technologies like blockchain and distributed ledgers, crypto-currencies can exist without reliance on existing central banking systems. Although still emerging, crypto-currencies are already in use in some Nordic countries, like Denmark, Sweden and Finland, where they can be used to purchase everything from tattoos to hotel stays.

The speed with which technology can become part of our lives is illustrated by the rapid penetration of application software, or apps. An app is a computer program that allows a user to perform a single task or several related tasks (see Table 2.3). The frustrating task of finding a cab has been revolutionized by the Uber app. The application allows users to hail and pay for the cab using an app. Drivers accept the journey on their phones and passengers can see the driver's name and photo so they know who to accept. The key to successful technological investment is, however, market potential, not technological sophistication for its own sake (see Exhibit 2.11 and Marketing in Action 2.4). The classic example of a high-technology initiative driven by technologists rather than pulled by the market is Concorde. Although technologically sophisticated, management knew before its launch that it never had any chance of being commercially viable. Large numbers of Internet businesses have failed for the same reason.

Table 2.3 Software applications and their uses

Context	Applications
Travel	Airbnb (accommodation), Google Maps (maps), Google Flights (flights), Skyscanner (flights)
Social media	Facebook (social networks), Instagram (picture posting), Snapchat (picture messaging), Pinterest (photographs), Tumblr (blogging)
Games	Candy Crush Saga, Google Play Games, GameSpot, Words with Friends, Pokémon Go, Rave
Communication	WhatsApp (messaging), Skype (video calls), Viber/Telegram (calls and messages)
Entertainment	Netflix (TV/movies), YouTube (live streaming), TED (talks, speeches)
Sport	BetFair (betting), LiveScore (scores), Sky Sports (information, video)
Music	Spotify (music streaming), Shazam (finding music), Soundcloud (store recordings), Ticketmaster (buying tickets)
Holidays	DuoLingo (langauges), Google Translate (translation), Trivago (price comparison), TripAdvisor (reviews), XE Currency (currency exchange rates)
Education	Coursera (digital lecturers), iTunes U (university courses), Khan Academy (maths and science), My Class Schedule (timetabling)
Work	DropBox (file exchange), Evernote (note taking), Slack (project planning)

Exhibit 2.11 Brands like Samsonite show that even the lowly suitcase can be enhanced through the application of technology.

Technological change impacts on the practice of marketing all the time. For example, in 2013, Tesco installed high-tech screens in its petrol stations that scanned customers' faces as they waited at checkouts, to determine their age and sex. This information is then used to tailor the types of adverts that are broadcast while customers are in the store.[52] One of the biggest shifts to take place in marketing in the past decade has been the reallocation of marketing budgets away from traditional media like television and newspapers to advertising on websites and social media. The growth in areas like search engine marketing and programmatic ad buying is examined in more detail in Chapter 11.

In summary, a wide variety of forces in the macoenvironment impact upon business. Their common characteristics are that they are outside the control of the organization and can represent either an opportunity or a threat to its future. Analysing all of these potential variables, and being able to anticipate the kind of impact that they can have, is a particularly demanding task, which we shall examine in more detail in the section on environmental scanning.

Marketing in Action 2.4
Netflix: Watch anywhere. Cancel at any time.

> **Critical Thinking:** Below is a review of how Netflix targets its programming to different audiences in the USA. Read it and reflect on the markets that some of your favourite programmes are aimed at.

Netflix is a streaming media provider based in the United States. Founded in California in 1997, the company started as a small DVD-by-mail service in the USA and specialized in streaming media and video on demand over the years. The number of Netflix streaming subscribers has been constantly increasing, surpassing the 100 million mark in the second quarter of 2017. Although more than half of Netflix's streaming subscribers are located in the United States, the company's presence is growing worldwide. Some of the most important markets for Netflix include Mexico, Brazil and Argentina. Netflix's penetration in these markets stood as high as 72 per cent in the second quarter of 2017. Netflix's global expansion has a direct impact on its earnings, as the company's annual revenue increased more than tenfold between 2005 and 2016.

Netflix's main competitors in the subscription video on demand (SVoD) service market in the USA are Amazon Prime and Hulu Plus. However, while Netflix maintains in the region of 52 million streaming subscribers there, about 37 per cent stated that they streamed content on a weekly basis in 2016. In line with the growth in number of users, this high level of usage of the medium and the associated rise in 'binge watching', where viewers watch entire shows in one sitting, have helped to drive the company's revenues. Original programming has been central to this growth in heavy usage of the medium. Netflix made a move into the distribution of original TV series in 2013, with the political drama *House of Cards*, starring Kevin Spacey and Robin Wright. The series, watched by 4.9 million viewers aged 18 to 49 within the first 35 days of its Netflix premiere date,

(continued)

is one of Netflix's biggest successes in original programming. The female-prison based drama *Orange is the New Black*, the documentary *Making a Murderer* and the series *Fuller House* are some examples of well-received original programmes distributed by Netflix.

Although the United States is still the most important regional market for Netflix, multicultural consumers are a large and growing segment of the US market and are transforming the American mainstream. More than 50 per cent of millennials are multicultural and 21 of the top 25 metro areas have more multicultural residents than non. There's no question that many leading brands are tailoring products and services to this important demographic. Especially for millennials, these brands want to engender loyalty early on while a group is establishing and growing its buying power. These brands, including Netflix, use social media to interact with customers.

Netflix is an example of a brand that tries to tailor its offerings to unique audiences and its demographics, particularly among an ever-growing multicultural audience in the USA. As such it offers programming such as *Luke Cage* (one of Marvel's first African American superheroes) and *Narcos* (based on the Medellin drug cartel leader Pablo Escobar, appealing to a Hispanic as well as mainstream audience), and stars such as Aziz Ansari (young, affluent and often Asian, interested in politics). The company monitors demographic trends and changes in consumer behaviour to challenge even the most established content publishers and producers.

Based on: Wilhelm-Volpi, 2017[53]

 Video: Inside Netflix's plan to get the entire world watching

The microenvironment

In addition to the broad macroeconomic forces discussed above, a number of microeconomic variables also impact on the opportunities and threats facing the organization. While these are also generally outside the control of the organization, managerial decisions and activities can exert some influence on them. We shall introduce each of these in turn, and deal with them in greater detail throughout the book.

Customers

As we saw in Chapter 1, customers are at the centre of the marketing effort and we shall examine customer behaviour in great detail in Chapter 3. Ultimately customers determine the success or failure of the business. The challenge for the company is to identify unserved market needs and to get and retain a customer base. This requires sensitivity to changing needs in the marketplace and also having the adaptability to take advantage of the opportunities that present themselves.

Distributors

Some companies, such as mail-order houses, online businesses and service providers, distribute directly to their customers. Most others use the services of independent wholesalers and retailers. As we shall see in Chapter 9, these middlemen provide many valuable services, such as making products available to customers where and when they want them, breaking bulk and providing specialist services such as merchandising and installation. Developments in distribution can have a significant impact on the performance of manufacturers. For example, the growing power of online retailers such as Amazon and Apple has affected the sales and profitability of both manufacturers and offline retailers.

Suppliers

Not only are the fortunes of companies influenced by their distributors, they can also be influenced by their suppliers. Supply chains can be very simple or very complex. For example, the average car contains about

15,000 components. As a result, the car industry is served by three tiers of suppliers. Tier-one companies make complete systems, such as electrical systems or braking systems. They are served by tier-two suppliers, which might produce cables, for example, and are in turn supplied by tier-three suppliers which produce basic commodities such as plastic shields or metals. Just like distributors, powerful suppliers can extract profitability from an industry by restricting the supply of essential components and forcing the price up.

Competitors

Levels of competition vary from industry to industry. In some instances, there may be just one or two major players, as is often the case in formerly state-run industries like energy or telecommunications. In others, where entry is easy or high profit potential exists, competition can be intense. For example, when messaging apps were developed to replace traditional SMS messaging, a wide range of brands quickly entered the space and tried to achieve market dominance, including WhatsApp, GroupMe, Line, WeChat, MessageMe, Kik, Tango and many others. To be successful in the marketplace, companies must not only be able to meet customer needs but must also be able to gain a differential advantage over competitors. As we saw in the previous chapter, this can be done by gaining a leadership position in the delivery of some form of customer value.

A very popular tool for analysing the microenvironment is Porter's 'five forces' model. Porter was interested in why some industries appeared to be inherently more profitable than others, and concluded that industry attractiveness was a function of five forces: the threat of entry of new competitors; the threat of substitutes; the bargaining power of suppliers; the bargaining power of buyers; and the rivalry between existing competitors. Each of these five forces, in turn, comprises a number of elements that combine to determine the strength of each force, as shown in Figure 2.4. So, for example, industries that have high barriers to entry but relatively low levels of buyer/supplier power, low threat of substitutes and relatively benign competition will be more attractive than industries with the opposite set of forces. For example, high barriers to entry and high levels of competitive rivalry between major players such as Amazon, Sony and Apple may already have made the e-reader business unattractive for some potential entrants. We shall now look briefly at each of the forces in turn.

The threat of new entrants

Because new entrants can raise the level of competition in an industry, they have the potential to reduce its attractiveness. The threat of new entrants depends on the barriers to entry. High entry barriers exist in some industries (e.g. pharmaceuticals), whereas other industries are much easier to enter (e.g. restaurants).

Key entry barriers include:

- Economies of scale
- Capital requirements
- Switching costs
- Access to distribution
- Expected retaliation.

The bargaining power of suppliers

The cost of raw materials and components can have a major bearing on a firm's profitability. The higher the bargaining power of suppliers, the higher these costs. The bargaining power of suppliers will be high when:

- There are many buyers and few dominant suppliers
- They offer differentiated, highly valued products
- Suppliers threaten to integrate forward into the industry
- Buyers do not threaten to integrate backwards into supply
- The industry is not a key customer group to the suppliers.

A firm can reduce the bargaining power of suppliers by seeking new sources of supply, threatening to integrate backwards into supply and designing standardized components so that many suppliers are able to produce them.

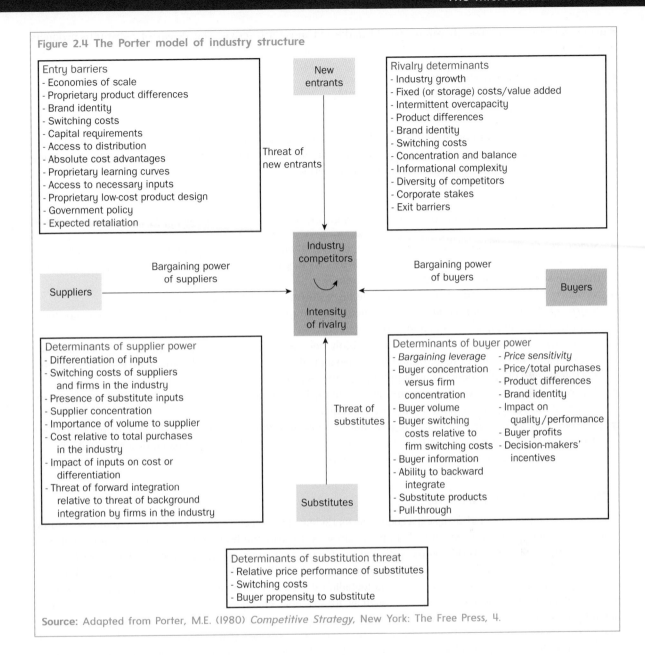

Figure 2.4 The Porter model of industry structure

Entry barriers
- Economies of scale
- Proprietary product differences
- Brand identity
- Switching costs
- Capital requirements
- Access to distribution
- Absolute cost advantages
- Proprietary learning curves
- Access to necessary inputs
- Proprietary low-cost product design
- Government policy
- Expected retaliation

New entrants

Threat of new entrants

Rivalry determinants
- Industry growth
- Fixed (or storage) costs/value added
- Intermittent overcapacity
- Product differences
- Brand identity
- Switching costs
- Concentration and balance
- Informational complexity
- Diversity of competitors
- Corporate stakes
- Exit barriers

Industry competitors

Intensity of rivalry

Suppliers

Bargaining power of suppliers

Bargaining power of buyers

Buyers

Determinants of supplier power
- Differentiation of inputs
- Switching costs of suppliers and firms in the industry
- Presence of substitute inputs
- Supplier concentration
- Importance of volume to supplier
- Cost relative to total purchases in the industry
- Impact of inputs on cost or differentiation
- Threat of forward integration relative to threat of background integration by firms in the industry

Threat of substitutes

Determinants of buyer power
- *Bargaining leverage*   - *Price sensitivity*
- Buyer concentration   - Price/total purchases
  versus firm   - Product differences
  concentration   - Brand identity
- Buyer volume   - Impact on
- Buyer switching   quality/performance
  costs relative to   - Buyer profits
  firm switching costs   - Decision-makers'
- Buyer information   incentives
- Ability to backward
  integrate
- Substitute products
- Pull-through

Substitutes

Determinants of substitution threat
- Relative price performance of substitutes
- Switching costs
- Buyer propensity to substitute

Source: Adapted from Porter, M.E. (1980) *Competitive Strategy*, New York: The Free Press, 4.

The bargaining power of buyers

As we shall see in Chapter 9, the concentration of European retailing has raised buyers' bargaining power relative to that of manufacturers. The bargaining power of buyers is greater when:

- There are few dominant buyers and many sellers
- Products are standardized
- Buyers threaten to integrate backwards into the industry
- Suppliers do not threaten to integrate forwards into the buyer's industry
- The industry is not a key supplying group for buyers.

The threat of substitutes

The presence of substitute products can lower industry attractiveness and profitability because they put a constraint on price levels. For example, tea and coffee are fairly close substitutes in most European countries.

Raising the price of coffee, therefore, would make tea more attractive. The threat of substitute products depends on:

- Buyers' willingness to substitute
- The relative price and performance of substitutes
- The costs of switching to substitutes.

The threat of substitute products can be lowered by building up switching costs, which may be psychological – for example, by creating strong distinctive brand personalities and maintaining a price differential commensurate with perceived customer values.

Industry competitors

The intensity of rivalry between competitors in an industry depends on the following factors.

- *Structure of competition*: there is more intense rivalry when there are a large number of small competitors or a few equally balanced competitors; there is less rivalry when a clear leader (at least 50 per cent larger than the second) exists with a large cost advantage.
- *Structure of costs*: high fixed costs encourage price cutting to fill capacity.
- *Degree of differentiation*: commodity products encourage rivalry, while highly differentiated products that are hard to copy are associated with less intense rivalry.
- *Switching costs*: when switching costs are high because a product is specialized, the customer has invested a lot of resources in learning how to use a product or has made tailor-made investments that are worthless with other products and suppliers, rivalry is reduced.
- *Strategic objectives*: when competitors are pursuing build strategies, competition is likely to be more intense than when playing hold or harvest strategies.
- *Exit barriers*: when barriers to leaving an industry are high due to such factors as lack of opportunities elsewhere, high vertical integration, emotional barriers or the high cost of closing down a plant, rivalry will be more intense than when exit barriers are low.

Environmental scanning

The practice of monitoring and analysing a company's marketing environment is known as **environmental scanning**. Two key decisions that management need to make are what to scan and how to organize the activity. Clearly, in theory, every event in the world has the potential to affect a company's operations, but a scanning system that could cover every conceivable force would be unmanageable. The first task, then, is to define a feasible range of forces that require monitoring. These are the 'potentially relevant environmental forces' that have the most likelihood of affecting future business prospects – such as, for example, changes in the value of the yen for companies doing business in Japan. One popular technique for managing this complex task is the development of scenarios – that is, the creation of fictitious future situations that combine a number of possible variables. The advantage of scenario planning is that it enables managers to consider and discuss how they would handle likely future changes in the business environment.[54] The second prerequisite for an effective scanning system is to design a system that provides a fast response to events that are only partially predictable, emerge as surprises and grow very rapidly. This has become essential due to the increasing turbulence of the marketing environment.

In general, environmental scanning is conducted by members of the senior management team, though some large corporations will have a separate unit dedicated to the task. The most appropriate organizational arrangement for scanning will depend on the unique circumstances facing a firm. Environmental scanning provides the essential informational input to create a strategic fit between strategy, organization and the environment (see Figure 2.5). Marketing strategy should reflect the environment even if this requires a fundamental reorganization of operations (see Chapter 12).

Companies respond in various ways to environmental change (see Figure 2.6).

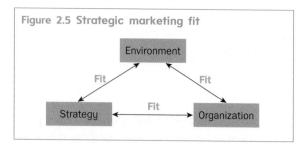

Figure 2.5 Strategic marketing fit

Ignorance

If environmental scanning is poor, companies may not realize that salient forces are affecting their future prospects. They therefore continue as normal, ignorant of the environmental issues that are threatening their existence, or the opportunities that could be seized. No change is made.

Delay

The next response, once the force is understood, is to delay action. This can be the result of bureaucratic decision processes that stifle swift action. The slow response by Kodak to the threat posed by the popularity of digital cameras and smartphones, for example, was thought, in part, to be caused by the bureaucratic nature of its decision-making. 'Marketing myopia' can slow response through management being product focused rather than customer focused. A third source of delay is 'techno-

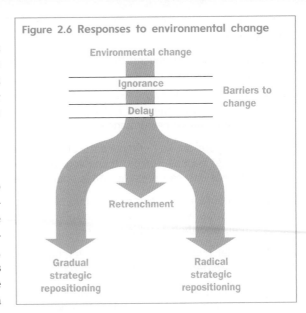

Figure 2.6 Responses to environmental change

logical myopia'; this occurs where a company fails to respond to technological change. The fourth reason for delay is 'psychological recoil' by managers who see change as a threat and thus defend the status quo. These are four powerful contributors to inertia.

Retrenchment

This sort of response deals with efficiency problems but disregards effectiveness issues. As sales and profits decline, the management cuts costs; this leads to a period of higher profits but does nothing to stem declining sales. Costs (and capacity) are reduced once more, but the fundamental strategic problems remain. Retrenchment policies only delay the inevitable.

Gradual strategic repositioning

This approach involves a gradual, planned and continuous adaptation to the changing marketing environment. Faced with a customer base that was increasingly critical of its poor customer service, resulting in falling profits, the low-cost airline Ryanair hired a chief marketing officer (CMO), redesigned its website to make it more user-friendly and introduced a host of other changes to try to improve its reputation in the marketplace.

Radical strategic repositioning

If its procrastination results in a crisis, a company could have to consider a radical shift in its strategic positioning – the direction of the entire business is fundamentally changed. For example, Dell Computer Corporation, a former leader in personal computer manufacturing, had suffered several years of decline as customers switched to the attractive products offered by rivals like Apple and Samsung. In 2013, it was taken private by a consortium of investors as part of a strategy to try to rebuild the business by moving away from PC manufacturing and focusing instead on the provision of business services to the corporate sector. Radical strategic repositioning is much riskier than gradual repositioning because, if unsuccessful, the company is likely to fold.

In summary, perhaps the single biggest challenge faced by organizations is anticipating and responding to change. The pace of change in the environment is being accelerated particularly by developments in technology but also by sometimes more subtle economic and social changes. The PESTEL framework helps managers to think about these challenges. Consulting organizations and future think-tanks also provide insights to help business leaders anticipate the changes coming down the line.

Summary

This chapter has introduced the concept of the marketing environment. In particular, the following issues were addressed.

1. That the marketing environment comprises a micro- and macroeinvironement. What happens in these environments is largely uncontrollable by firms but can have a significant impact on organizational performance.

2. There are six key components of the macroenvironment: economic forces, social forces, legal forces, political forces, technological forces and ecological forces. Changes on each of these dimensions can present either opportunities or threats to the firm.

3. Economic forces comprise economic growth and unemployment, interest rates and exchange rates, as well as taxation and inflation. They largely impact upon how well off consumers feel, and their resulting propensity to buy goods and services.

4. Social forces are made up of demographic changes and cultural differences. Sensitivity to cultural differences between countries is a particularly crucial issue in international marketing.

5. 'Political and legal forces' describes the regulatory environment in which organizations operate. Regulation may be enacted at a national or European level, and is mainly designed to protect the interests of consumers and to ensure a fair competitive playing field for organizations.

6. Changes in the ecological environment have been the focus of a great deal of attention in recent years. This encompasses concerns regarding climate change, pollution, scarce resource conservation, recycling and non-wasteful packaging, environmentally friendly ingredients and animal testing. Sustainability is a central challenge facing businesses, and the relationship between marketing and society is a central theme of this book.

7. The term technology is used widely to describe information technology but also developments in nanotechnology, artificial intelligence, and so on. Technology is the engine as well as one of the outputs of modern business, and needs to be carefully monitored as changes in this area can make businesses obsolete very quickly.

8. There are four key components of the microenvironment: suppliers, distributors, customers and competitors. They combine and interact to influence both the profitability of industries and the performance of individual organizations.

9. Environmental scanning is the process of examining the company's marketing environment. Firms exhibit a number of different responses to environmental change, including no change through ignorance, delay and retrenchment, through to gradual or radical repositioning.

Study questions

1. Visit www.trendwatching.com. Read its latest trend briefing and consider the impact of this trend for a brand of your choice.
2. Corporate social responsibility (CSR) activities are largely an exercise in public relations by major corporations. Discuss.
3. Discuss the alternative ways in which companies might respond to changes in the macroenvironment.
4. In 2013, Shell's scenario planning department presented two visions of the future labelled 'mountains' and 'oceans'. See http://www.shell.com/global/future-energy/scenarios/new-lens-scenarios.html. Select one scenario and outline its implications for energy companies.
5. Visit www.business-ethics.com/. Select any two of its 'popular stories' and discuss their implications for both business and society.
6. Discuss any three technologies and consider their impact on marketing.

Suggested reading

Bloomberg, J. (2018) Digitization, digitalization, and digital transformation: confuse them At Your Peril, *Forbes*, 29 April.

Jackson, R.W. and Wood, C.M. (2014) The marketing environment: a new paradigm, *Academy of Marketing Studies Journal*, 17(1): 35–50.

Jha, S., Parulkar, I., Krishnan, R. and Dhanaraj, C. (2016) Developing new products in emerging markets, *MIT Sloan Management Review*, 57(3): 55–62.

Roxburgh, C. (2009) The use and abuse of scenarios, *McKinsey Quarterly*, November, 1–10.

Royte, E. (2008) *Bottlemania: How Water Went on Sale and Why We Buy It*. London: Bloomsbury Publishing Inc.

Sekerta, L. and Stimel, D. (2011) How durable is sustainable enterprise? Ecological sustainability meets the reality of tough economic Times, *Business Horizons*, 54: 115–24.

Webster, F.E. and Lusch, R.F. (2012) Elevating marketing. Marketing is dead! Long live marketing!, *Journal of the Academy of Marketing Science*, 41: 389–99.

References

1. **Interbrand** (2017) Best global brands. Available at http://interbrand.com/best-brands/best-global-brands/2017/ranking/adidas/ (accessed 16 May 2018).

2. **Adidas profile** (2018) Adidas at a glance. Available at https://www.adidas-group.com/en/group/profile/ (accessed 16 May 2018).

3. **Kell, J.** (2016) Here's how Adidas plans to drastically cut down on waste, *Fortune*, 14 April. Available at http://fortune.com/2016/04/14/adidas-cuts-water-waste-usage/ (accessed 16 May 2018).

4. **Kharpal, A.** (2018) Adidas sold 1 million shoes made out of ocean plastic in 2017, CNBC, 14 March.

5. **Lebreton, L. et al.** (2018) Evidence that the Great Pacific Garbage Patch is rapidly accumulating plastic, *Scientific Reports*, 22 March.

6. **Prisco, J.** (2018) The last straw: is time up for this plastic relic? CNN, 15 January.

7. **Statistica.com** (2018) Youth unemployment rate in EU member states as of May 2018. Available at www.statista.com/statistics/266228/youth-unemployment-rate-in-eu-countries/ (accessed 16 August 2018).

8. **Parsons, R.** (2017) Marketing budgets take a hit as Brexit uncertainty bites, *Marketing Week*, 18 October. Available at https://www.marketingweek.com/2017/10/18/marketing-budgets-take-a-hit-as-brexit-uncertainty-bites/ (accessed 28 May 2018).

9. **World Economic Outlook** (2018) International Monetary Fund. Available at http://www.imf.org/external/datamapper/NGDP_RPCH@WEO/OEMDC/ADVEC/WEOWORLD (accessed 28 May 2018).

10. **Statistica.com** (2018) Youth unemployment rate in EU member states as of May 2018. Available at www.statista.com/statistics/266228/youth-unemployment-rate-in-eu-countries/ (accessed 16 August 2018).

11. **OECD** (2017) Household debt. Available at www.data.oecd.org/hha/household-debt.htm (accessed 5 June 2018).

12. **Inman, P.** (2015) Why has China devalued its currency and what impact will it have? *TheGuardian.com*. Available at www.theguardian.com/business/2015/aug/11/china-devalues-yuan-against-us-dollar-explainer (accessed 5 June 2016).

13. **Chapman, B.** (2018), H&M, Asda and Next supplier polluted river with chemicals linked to cancer and death, investigation finds, *Independent.co.uk*. Available at www.independent.co.uk/news/business/news/hm-asda-next-supplier-leaks-cancer-causing-chemicals-factories-aditya-birla-india-a8232231.html (accessed 16 August 2018).

14. **Eriksen, E.** (2017) Mass fainting in H&M factory in Cambodia, *ScandAsia.com*. Available at www.scandasia.com/mass-fainting-in-hm-factory-in-cambodia/ (accessed 16 August 2016).

15. **Farmbrough, H.** (2018) H&M is pushing sustainability hard, but not everyone is convinced, *Forbes.com*. Available at www.forbes.com/sites/heatherfarmbrough/2018/04/14/hm-is-pushing-sustainability-hard-but-not-everyone-is-convinced/#7942b3d97ebd (accessed 16 August 2018).

16. **Jensen, N.** (2017) Angry workers damage H&M factory in Mynamar, *Scandasia.com*. Available at www.scandasia.com/angry-workers-damage-hm-factory-in-myanmar/ (accessed 16 August 2018).

17. **United Nations** (2017) *International Migration Report 2017 Highlights*, 21 May.

18. **Matthews, R.** (2005) US grapples with 'language of love', *Financial Times*, 13 January, 9.

19. **Edgecliffe-Johnson, A.** (2007) MTV tunes in to a local audience, *Financial Times*, 16 October, 16.

20. **Anonymous** (2014) Planet plutocrat, *The Economist*, 15 March, 53–4.

21. **Faccio, M., Masulis, R. and McConnell, J.** (2006) Political connections and corporate bailouts, *Journal of Finance*, 61(6).

22. **Anonymous** (2014) In deep water, *The Economist*, 22 February, 47–9.

23. **Traynor, I.** (2014) 30,000 lobbyists and counting: is Brussels under corporate sway? *TheGuardian.com*. Available at www.theguardian.com/world/2014/may/08/lobbyists-european-parliament-brussels-corporate (accessed 5 June 2018).

24. **Traynor, I.** (2014) 30,000 lobbyists and counting: is Brussels under corporate sway? *TheGuardian.com*. Available at www.theguardian.com/world/2014/may/

08/lobbyists-european-parliament-brussels-corporate (accessed 5 June 2018).

25. **Bacon, J.** (2016) What would Brexit mean for marketers? *Marketingweek.com*. Available at www.marketingweek.com/2016/05/05/what-would-brexit-mean-for-marketers/ (accessed 16 August 2018).

26. **Parsons, R.** (2017) Marketing budgets take a hit as Brexit uncertainty bites, *Marketing Week*, 18 October. Available at https://www.marketingweek.com/2017/10/18/marketing-budgets-take-a-hit-as-brexit-uncertainty-bites/ (accessed 28 May 2018).

27. **Smyth, P.** (2018) Google fined €4.3bn by EU over Android software market abuse, *IrishTimes.com*. Available at www.irishtimes.com/business/technology/google-fined-4-3bn-by-eu-over-android-software-market-abuse-1.3568786 (accessed 16 August 2018).

28. **Klein, N.** (2000) *No Logo*. London: HarperCollins.

29. **Connolly, K.** (2018) VW condemned for testing diesel fumes on humans and monkeys, *The Guardian.com*. Available at www.theguardian.com/business/2018/jan/29/vw-condemned-for-testing-diesel-fumes-on-humans-and-monkeys (accessed 17 April 2018).

30. **Hotten, R.** (2015) Volkswagen: the scandal explained, *BBC.com*. Available at www.bbc.com/news/business-34324772 (accessed 17 April 2018).

31. **Parloff, R.** (2018) How VW paid $25 billion for 'Dieselgate' – and got off easy, *Fortune.com*. Available at http://fortune.com/2018/02/06/volkswagen-vw-emissions-scandal-penalties/ (accessed 17 April 2018).

32. **Coonan, C.** (2008) Great pall of China, *Innovation*, January, 36–7.

33. **Vidal, J.** (2016) How are cities around the world tackling air pollution? *TheGuardian.com*. Available at www.theguardian.com/environment/2016/may/17/how-are-cities-around-the-world-tackling-air-pollution (accessed 7 June 2018).

34. **Harvey, F.** (2004) PC makers set to face costs of recycling, *Financial Times*, 4 February, 13.

35. **Harvey, F.** and **Simpson, L.** (2010) Outlook sunny for solar panels as homeowners go green, *Financial Times*, 25 August, 8.

36. **Anonymous** (2018) The global bottled water market: expert insights and statistics, *Blog.MarketResearch.com*. Available at blog.marketresearch.com/the-global-bottled-water-market-expert-insights-statistics (accessed 7 June 2018).

37. **Anonymous** (2014) Rueing the waves, *The Economist*, 4 January, 23–4.

38. For a discussion of some green marketing issues, see **Pujari, D.** and **Wright, G.** (1999) Integrating environmental issues into product development: understanding the dimensions of perceived driving forces and stakeholders, *Journal of Euromarketing*, 7(4): 43–63; **Peattie, K.** and **Ringter, A.** (1994) Management and the environment in the UK and Germany: a comparison, *European Management Journal*, 12(2): 216–25.

39. **Anonymous** (2018) Toyota recalls 645,000 vehicles; air bags may not inflate, *USA Today*, 31 January.

40. **Iyengar, R.** (2017) Honda recalls more than a million cars over battery fires, *CNN Money*, 14 July.

41. **O'Reilly, L.** (2017) Budweiser's Super Bowl ad will tell the story of its immigrant cofounder's journey to the US – but the brand says it's not making a political statement, *Business Insider*, 30 January.

42. **Elkington, J.** (2001) *The Chrysalis Economy*. Oxford: Capstone.

43. **Townsend, J.C.** (2014) A better way to 'buy one, give one', *Forbes.com*. Available at www.forbes.com/sites/ashoka/2014/10/08/a-better-way-to-buy-one-give-one/#7eed9a86485e (accessed 7 June 2018).

44. **Berkowitz, E.N., Kerin, R.A., Hartley, S.W.** and **Rudelius, W.** (2000) *Marketing*, Boston, MA: McGraw-Hill.

45. **Jack, A.** (2008) An unusual model for good causes, *Financial Times*, 5 June, 16.

46. **Bakan, J.** (2004) *The Corporation*. London: Constable.

47. **James, O.** (2007) *Affluenza*, London: Vermilion.

48. **Sekerta, L.** and **Stimel, D.** (2011) How durable is sustainable enterprise? Ecological sustainability meets the reality of tough economic times, *Business Horizons*, 54, 115–24.

49. **Meadows, S.** (2017) Men still paying more than women for car insurance five years after EU ruling, *Telegraph.co.uk*. Available at www.telegraph.co.uk/insurance/car/men-still-paying-women-car-insurance-five-years-eu-ruling/ (accessed 16 August 2018).

50. **Kauflin, J.** (2017) The world's most ethical companies 2017, *Forbes*, 14 March.

51. **Anonymous** (2011) Not just talk, *The Economist*, 29 January, 61–2.

52. **Hawkes, S.** (2013) Shoppers' faces to be scanned in advertising push at Tesco petrol stations across the UK, *Telegraph.co.uk*, 3 November.

53. **Wilhelm-Volpi, L.** (2017) Netflix a great example of multicultural marketing, *Spotright.com*. Available at www.http://spotright.com/2017/02/27/netflix-a-great-example-of-multicultural-marketing/ (accessed 7 June 2018).

54. **Roxburgh, C.** (2009) The use and abuse of scenarios, *McKinsey Quarterly*, November, 1–10.

Fjällräven and the global marketing environment

Introducing Fjällräven

Fjällräven (Swedish for 'Arctic Fox') is a prestigious outdoor clothing and equipment manufacturer, founded by Åke Nordin in Örnsköldsvik, northern Sweden, in 1960. A decade previously, as a teenage outdoor enthusiast, he had noticed the limitations of available backpacks, so constructed a robust cotton rucksack with wooden external frame and leather straps. Using this technical knowledge to sell expedition equipment to the military, he expanded to sell durable, classically styled and functional outdoor equipment to a broader market.

Fjällräven's most famous products are its Greenland coat and its Kånken backpack. The Kånken backpack, at around £85, is relatively expensive, but hard-wearing, timeless and extremely practical. As most Swedish schoolchildren carry a Kånken backpack, Swedes consider Fjällräven part of the national heritage. At around £400, the Greenland coat is also expensive but extremely durable and waterproof, favoured by Arctic explorers and serious mountaineers.

Fjällräven has eight different outdoor clothing product ranges, although some of the differences between them are relatively nuanced, which allow it to target customer categories that are slightly distinct from one another and provide products that closely address different customers' needs and usage occasions. Fjällräven is also very popular in other Scandinavian countries, and increasingly in Germany, which now accounts for its greatest number of sales at almost 50 per cent (Fenix Outdoor Annual Report, 2017). Elsewhere the brand is less well known, although there is a current push to establish Fjällräven in the USA and Canada.

Fjällräven belongs to the Fenix Outdoor Group, a profitable organization that also owns other outdoor brands such as Primus (manufacturer of camping stoves), Brunton (specializing in solar-powered electrical equipment for expeditioners), Swedish outdoor clothing specialist Tierra, and boot manufacturer Hanwag. Fenix entered North America recently, with Fjällräven its only brand there. It has opened

Fjällräven-only shops in major urban centres of the USA and Canada, which are near prime trekking country, whereas elsewhere Fjällräven shares shelf space with competitors, even when sold through the dominant Finnish outdoor clothing retailer Partioaitta, which is part of the Fenix group. Many of Fenix's warehousing and marketing functions are in the Netherlands and Colorado, USA, but Fjällräven retains its distinctive Swedish identity and culture – not least because foreign consumers associate its country of origin with an outdoor tradition and high product quality. It opened a flagship store in Oslo, Norway, in 2015 and targets annual double-digit growth in profit before tax. Its major challenges include raising brand awareness within its less developed markets, attracting customers from different cultures who will nonetheless embrace its distinctively Scandinavian ethos and identity, and defending against powerful competitors such as The North Face and Patagonia. Fenix Outdoor Group's sales recently surged to €500 million per year (Fenix Outdoor Annual Report, 2017).

Mission, values and ethos

Fjällräven is environmentally conscious. Its founder's love of the great outdoors is shared by its employees and customers, infiltrating the company ethos. In addition to its focus on functional, timeless and durable outdoor equipment, the brand seeks to act responsibly towards people, animals and nature. It sponsors a professorship to protect the endangered Arctic fox, and champions conservation initiatives. Fjällräven owns a flock of geese to ensure that down for its jackets is sourced humanely. It also promotes healthy outdoor lifestyles. For example, it organizes the annual Fjällräven Classic multi-day walking events in four countries, in which thousands of participants embark on self-guided trekking tours in stunning locations. The brand has a strong online presence, and engages its audiences through various corporate social responsibility initiatives and careful customer relationship management. Indeed, the Fjällräven Classic multi-day trekking events in Sweden, the USA, Hong Kong and Denmark are intended to combine these two areas by bringing together customers and encouraging peer-to-peer relationships and brand affinity in a spirit of customer co-creation, but also by creating an event that is sustainable, environmentally sound and encourages a broad range of stakeholders to behave ethically towards the countryside.

Fjällräven's product ranges and market territories

As Fjällräven has become more well known internationally, it has attracted many customers who may be considered its focal audience – outdoor enthusiasts who require durable, timeless and highly functional clothing that is specially designed for their specific needs, and is priced accordingly. However, it has also attracted many customers who are less motivated by exploring and adventures, and more so by fashion statements. Although this incremental interest and revenue stream is not problematic in itself, it is important for the brand not to become too dependent on a customer segment that is likely to be fickle. Likewise, if the brand becomes too closely tied to servicing the needs of urban fashionistas, they would be likely over time to demand stylistic and functional product features that could make those products unacceptable to the core audience. Moreover, by becoming increasingly associated with these new 'brand fans', Fjällräven risks inadvertently changing the positive brand associations held by its traditional customers, losing credibility and alienating its core audience. Entering new markets allows Fjällräven to acquire new customers who are outdoor enthusiasts, rather than running out of such customers in its home market and needing to amend its brand proposition for a more mainstream audience.

By having eight well-established product lines, Fjällräven has effectively created sub-brands with which its more loyal customers are familiar. For example, its Keb range comprises technical trekking equipment, which would attract customers who undertake multi-day expeditions, whereas its Kiruna range would appeal to more casual users who might wear the clothes on day trips or even every day. Fjällräven's iconic Kånken backpack is similarly split into variants entitled Original, Mini, Laptop 13, Laptop 17, Big and Maxi, thereby suiting different usages and customer groups while leveraging on the significant brand recognition and equity enjoyed by Kånken in Sweden.

In the second decade of the twenty-first century, Fjällräven's global sales have increased by between 10 and 20 per cent year on year, and net profits began to grow rapidly (by 20 per cent and more) during the middle years of that decade. While sales in Sweden are strong, they are relatively static due to saturation. The brand enjoys similarly high and steady sales within other Nordic countries (Norway, Finland, Denmark and Iceland), which share many cultural values and topographical characteristics with Sweden and, in some cases, have linguistic similarities. However, Sweden and these territories have a combined population of only around 27 million. Sales within Benelux (Belgium, the Netherlands and Luxembourg) have risen healthily in recent years, and account for around 50 per cent higher volumes than Sweden. However, these countries are only marginally more populous (with 29 million people) than the Nordic countries and, due to being low lying, have none of the wilderness areas closely associated with the brand's usage. Sales in Germany have increased rapidly, and total sales in that territory are now greater than in the rest of non-Scandinavian Europe. Sales in non-Nordic Europe outside Germany, and in North America, have grown strongly in recent years and each accounts for nearly three times as many sales as the home market of Sweden.

Fjällräven's core customers and their other brands

Fjällräven's products reflect the activities that are most popular among its core customers – hiking and mountaineering, cycling (trail and road), skiing (downhill and cross-country), and running. Fans of these activities often undertake related hobbies such as camping, orienteering, rock climbing and kayaking, which presents potential opportunities for selling associated products to loyal brand fans. In many countries, people who undertake these activities are more likely to lead 'middle class' lifestyles and enjoy relative job security and higher wages. People are often motivated to engage in these activities to escape from the everyday pressures of their careers and urban existences, for health benefits, to meet like-minded people and to enjoy the great outdoors. It is commonplace for customers to have several different usage occasions. For example, a consumer might run locally twice a week, undertake a 10-mile walk each weekend within an hour's drive of home, and complete a full-week expedition in more distant and challenging mountains once a year. Such a consumer might demand different products for each type of usage, needing them to match the terrain, weather and physicality of the exercise. Fjällräven products may be considered relatively expensive, 'high end', durable and prestigious. It is not unusual for outdoor enthusiasts to wear certain outdoor brands in everyday situations, to identify themselves to like-minded people, or express their identity and sense of adventure. Some of the main competing brands are as follows:

- The North Face – US manufacturer of mountaineering and expedition clothing such as down jackets, with a heavy presence in North America and Europe

- Patagonia – US manufacturer of technical outdoor clothing, such as waterproof outer jackets; the organization has a clearly stated ethical stance; its founder, Yvon Chouinard, gives his staff leave to pursue outdoor activities, and a recent advertising campaign urged customers not to buy any clothing on that day, to ease the pressure on recycling

- Arcteryx, Mammut, Haglofs and Black Diamond – other manufacturers of high-end technical outdoor equipment and expedition gear.

Consumers of outdoor clothing are motivated to adopt a brand if it offers highly functional or comfortable products that are more durable or manufactured to a higher standard, that are attractive or more environmentally friendly, or that have been recommended by peers (through word of mouth and e-word of mouth). They may also wish to adopt brands that offer superior technical support and customer advice, better retail premises, closer customer relationship management and social media presence and, depending on the market segment, differentiated pricing points. Although Fjällräven is less well known outside northern Europe than most of its North American competitors, it is well regarded by those familiar with it, and it benefits from country-of-origin effect insofar as Sweden is associated with quality brands, strong build quality, an ethical and inclusive culture and, perhaps most importantly, a tradition and heritage of outdoor adventure.

Questions

1. What opportunities are presented to Fjällräven by entering new markets?
2. What macroenvironmental and microenvironmental factors should Fjällräven consider when expanding?
3. What are the major threats facing Fjällräven as it enters new markets, and how may it mitigate the risks from these?
4. What might be considered the internal strengths and weaknesses of the Fjällräven brand?

This case was prepared by David Brown, Northumbria University, UK from various published sources as a basis for class discussion rather than to show effective or ineffective management.

Source

Key source: Fenix Outdoor Group Annual Report 2017, available at http://www.fenixoutdoor.se/wp-content/uploads/2018/03/Annualreport_2017.pdf, accessed 21 May 2018.

Chapter 3

Understanding Customer Behaviour

Chapter outline

The dimensions of customer behaviour

Who buys?

How they buy

What are the choice criteria?

Influences on consumer behaviour

Influencer marketing

Influences on organizational buying behaviour

Learning outcomes

By the end of this chapter you will:

1 Understand the key dimensions of customer behaviour

2 Explain the different roles played in a buying decision

3 Compare and contrast different theories of the buying decision process

4 Understand the differences between consumer and organizational buyer behaviour

5 Analyse the main influences on consumer behaviour – personal and social

6 Understand how influencer marketing is used by marketers, and appreciate its uses and limitations

7 Analyse the main influences on organizational buying behaviour – the buy class, product type and purchase importance

8 Critique the role of marketing activities in consumption decisions

9 Develop a better understanding of one's own consumption choices

Fortnite

Every so often a game comes along that conquers the hearts, minds and thumbs of gamers everywhere. Fortnite is the latest in this category and has leapt to great popularity with its Battle Royale mode. Fortnite is a video game, which its maker, Epic Games, is calling the biggest in the world, with 3.4 million reported users as of February 2018. The game combines Minecraft resource collecting and building with team-based survival shooting games. Fortnite parachutes 100 players out of a plane onto an island and requires them to scavenge for weapons and other resources, build defensive structures and vanquish opponents in a quest to become the last player standing. The game pits the 100 players against one another while a mysterious cloud steadily reduces the size of the war zone, creating knife-edge and climatic gun fights. It is free to play and is playable on game systems, computers and mobile phones alike, but players pay for accessories and costumes for their characters. While Fortnite can be played solo, users often team up with a friend or group of friends. Playing Fortnite is often a social experience as friends can team up in pairs or fours. If they're not together physically, they communicate – over FaceTime, a headset linked to a game system, or the like – to co-ordinate strategy, alert teammates to threats, root for one another and trade banter. Although it is just a shooting game, players will develop strategic thinking, forward planning and creative approaches to combat. It teaches a deep amount of collaboration in working together and saving teammates.

Since its release in September 2017, the game has been downloaded to personal computers and video game consoles more than 40 million times. With so many children devoting hours to Fortnite many parents are concerned about the harmful effects that the long playing durations and violent content are having on their children, and there are fears it could cross the divide between hobby and obsession. 'Many studies have shown that playing violent video games is associated with real-life aggressive behaviour and less pro-social behaviour,' says Catherine Hallissey, a child and educational psychologist based in Ireland. 'In addition, there is the potential of any highly interesting and rewarding activity, such as video gaming, becoming addictive, leading to family conflict.' Fortnite isn't the first mass online shooter to develop a fanatical following. However, what sets it apart is its child-friendly gloss. Battles typically last around 20 minutes, meaning a game can easily be squeezed in before homework but also giving it a one-last-go quality. It is this aspect of Fortnite – its powerful addictive tendencies – that has prompted alarm, with one mother going on ITV's *This Morning* show to explain how Fortnite had negatively impacted on her son's behaviour.

However, not all agree that Fortnite can have a negative impact on player behaviour. For example, Andrew Reid, who is a doctoral researcher of serious games at Glasgow Caledonian University, has stated that 'mother worrying' mega-hit Fortnite is not addictive, it's just that people can't stop playing it, which is something completely different. He further states, 'We must be careful when using this term. Addiction is a psychological disorder that pertains to habitual and excessive activity. Video-game addiction has suggestively been defined as the excessive consumption of games that conflict with everyday living.' Studies suggest that gaming disorder affects only a small proportion of people who engage in digital- or video-gaming activities, according to the World Health Organization. However, it believes that people who partake in gaming should be alert to the amount of time they spend on gaming activities, particularly when it is to the exclusion of other daily activities, as well as to any changes in their physical or psychological health and social functioning that could be attributed to their pattern of gaming behaviour.

There is also a concern that Fortnite's violence, however slapstick, may have an unhealthy impact on behaviour. Fortnite involves firearms and is recommended for ages 12 and up. However, its graphics are free of blood and gore. Although adults may worry that shooting games cultivate

(continued)

aggression, C. Shawn Green, an Associate Professor of Psychology at the University of Wisconsin-Madison who researches video games, notes that, 'there's really no evidence that playing a violent video game would take someone who has absolutely no violent tendencies and suddenly make them violent'. However, Catherine Hallissey adds: 'A 2012 study used brain scans to show that playing violent video games has the potential to desensitize gamers to real-life violence and suffering. When that is combined with the still-developing frontal lobe of adolescents, the negative potential is increased. The US Army uses these types of games to recruit soldiers [and] to train them.' The electronic games market, people's desires to play and pay for online games, and the conflicting views on their impact on player behaviour raise some interesting questions about consumer behaviour, which is the focus of this chapter.[1]

Our lives are full of choices. We choose which universities we would like to attend, what courses we would like to study, what careers we would like to pursue. On a daily basis we make choices about the food we eat, the clothes we buy, the music we listen to, and so on. The processes by which we make all these choices and how they are influenced are of great interest to marketers as well as to consumer researchers. Companies with products or services to sell want to know us, what we like and dislike, and how we go about making these consumption decisions. As we saw in Chapter 1, this kind of in-depth knowledge of customers is a prerequisite of successful marketing; indeed, understanding customers is the cornerstone upon which the marketing concept is built. How customers behave can never be taken for granted and new trends emerge all the time, such as the current popularity of social networking or the increase in digital consumption, which will be explored later in this chapter. There are a variety of influences on the purchasing habits of customers and our understanding of these influences is constantly improving. Successful marketing requires a great sensitivity to these subtle drivers of behaviour and an ability to anticipate how they influence demand.

In this chapter we will explore the nature of customer behaviour; we will examine the frameworks and concepts used to understand customers; and we will review the dimensions we need to consider in order to grasp the nuances of customer behaviour and the influences upon it.

The dimensions of customer behaviour

At the outset, a distinction needs to be drawn between the purchases of private consumers and those of organizations. Most consumer purchasing is individual, such as the decision to purchase a chocolate bar on seeing an array of confectionery at a newsagent's counter, though it may also be by a group such as a household. In contrast, in organizational or business-to-business (B2B) purchasing there are three major types of buyer. First, the industrial market concerns those companies that buy products and services to help them produce other goods and services, such as the purchase of memory chips for mobile telephones. These industrial goods can range from raw materials to components to capital goods such as machinery. Second, the reseller market comprises organizations that buy products and services to resell. Online retailers and supermarkets are examples of resellers and we will look at these in some detail in Chapter 9. Third, the government market consists of government agencies that buy products and services to help them carry out their activities. Purchases for local authorities and defence are examples of this.

Understanding the behaviour of this array of customers requires answers to the following core questions (see Figure 3.1).

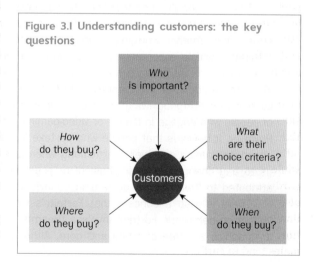

Figure 3.1 Understanding customers: the key questions

Who is important?

What are their choice criteria?

How do they buy?

Customers

Where do they buy?

When do they buy?

- *Who* is important in the buying decision?
- *How* do they buy?
- *What* are their choice criteria?
- *Where* do they buy?
- *When* do they buy?

The answers to these questions can be derived from personal contact with customers and, increasingly, by employing marketing research, which we will examine in Chapter 4. In this chapter we examine consumer and organizational buyer behaviour. The structure of this analysis will be based on the first three questions: who, how and what. These are often the most intractable aspects of customer behaviour; it is usually much more straightforward to answer the last two questions, about where and when customers buy.

Who buys?

Blackwell, Miniard and Engel[2] describe five roles in the buying decision-making process.

1 *Initiator*: the person who begins the process of considering a purchase. Information may be gathered by this person to help the decision.
2 *Influencer*: the person who attempts to persuade others in the group concerning the outcome of the decision. Influencers typically gather information and attempt to impose their choice criteria on the decision.
3 *Decider*: the individual with the power and/or financial authority to make the ultimate choice regarding which product to buy.
4 *Buyer*: the person who conducts the transaction. The buyer calls the supplier, visits the store, makes the payment and effects delivery.
5 *User*: the actual consumer/user of the product.

Multiple roles in the buying group may, however, be assumed by one person. In a toy purchase, for example, a girl may be the initiator and attempt to influence her parents, who are the deciders. The girl may be influenced by her sister to buy a different brand. The buyer may be one of the parents, who visits the store to purchase the toy and brings it back to the home. Finally, both children may be users of the toy. Although the purchase was for one person, in this example marketers have four opportunities – two children and two parents – to affect the outcome of the purchase decision. For example, since 2015, Microsoft has been European partner with the CoderDojo Foundation and Movement. CoderDojo and Microsoft are working together to encourage more young people to give coding a try. In 2017, Microsoft announced that it would extend this partnership further by sponsoring the CoderDojo Coolest Projects Showcase, an event celebrating standout projects in 'dojos' – free coding clubs for young people. Microsoft's association with CoderDojo helps to market its brand to a youth market by creating brand awareness, building its brand image and building positive attitudes towards Microsoft among a younger audience.[3]

The roles played by the different household members vary with the type of product under consideration and the stage of the buying process (see Exhibit 3.1). For example, men now do a very significant portion of household grocery shopping, while women are increasingly visitors to DIY and hardware shops. Other interesting differences have also been observed. Women, who tend to take their time and browse in a retail environment, are more time conscious and goal directed online, while males tend to surf and browse many websites when

Exhibit 3.1 'Flash' all-purpose cleaners' 2018 TV advert challenges traditional household roles. It features a man using the household cleaning product rather than a woman, which has normally been the case in the past.

shopping on the internet. Also, the respective roles may change as the purchasing process progresses. In general, one or other partner will tend to dominate the early stages, then joint decision-making tends to occur as the process moves towards final purchase. Joint decision-making is more common when the household consists of two income earners.

Most organizational buying tends to involve more than one individual and is often in the hands of a decision-making unit (DMU), or **buying centre**, as it is sometimes called. This is not necessarily a fixed entity and may change as the **decision-making process** continues. Thus a managing director may be involved in the decision that new equipment should be purchased, but not in the decision as to which manufacturer to buy it from. The marketing task is to identify and reach the key members in order to convince them of the product's worth. But this is a difficult task as the size of the decision-making groups in organizations is on the increase. It can also be difficult as the 'gatekeeper' is an additional role in organizational buying. Gatekeepers are people like secretaries, who may allow or prevent access to a key DMU member. The salesperson's task is to identify a person from within the decision-making unit who is a positive advocate and champion of the supplier's product. This person (or 'coach') should be given all the information needed to win the arguments that may take place within the DMU.

Exhibit 3.2 Advertising by shower manufacturers such as Mira has enabled them to build a high level of consumer recognition, and hence reduce the influence of 'deciders' making choices in-store.

The marketing implications of understanding who buys lie within the areas of marketing communications and segmentation. An identification of the roles played within the buying centre is a prerequisite for targeting persuasive communications. As we saw earlier, the person who actually uses or consumes the product may not be the most influential member of the buying centre, nor the decision-maker. Even when they do play the predominant role, communication to other members of the buying centre can make sense when their knowledge and opinions act as persuasive forces during the decision-making process. For example, recommendations from plumbers influence the majority of shower purchase decisions by consumers planning to install or replace shower units in their homes. Therefore, brands like Mira (see Exhibit 3.2) have sought to build awareness in the consumer market to reduce the influence of these 'deciders' in the purchasing decision.

How they buy

Attempting to understand how consumers buy and what influences their buying decisions have been the core questions examined in the field of consumer behaviour. It is a rich arena of study, drawing on perspectives from disciplines as wide ranging as economics, psychology, sociology, cultural anthropology and others. The dominant paradigm in consumer behaviour is known as the **information processing approach** and has its roots in cognitive psychology. It sees consumption as largely a rational process – the outcome of a consumer recognizing a need and then engaging in a series of activities to attempt to fulfil that need. But an alternative paradigm, known as **consumer culture theory (CCT)**,[4] views consumption as a much less rational or conscious activity (see **Critical Marketing Perspective 3.1**). In it, consumption is seen as a more socio-cultural or experiential activity that is laden with emotion, and helps to explain, for example, why consumers derive pleasure from shopping or search for certain meanings in the brands they choose (see Exhibit 3.3).

CCT theorists focus on understanding the interrelationships between various material, economic, symbolic, institutional and social relationships and their effects on consumers, the marketplace, other institutions and society. Researchers typically draw from and build on theories rooted in sociology, anthropology, media studies and communications, history, literary criticism and semiotics, gender theory and cultural studies, to

Critical Marketing Perspective 3.1
Neuromarketing: friend or foe?

Understanding consumers' decision-making process is one of the important goals of marketing. However, traditional tools used in marketing research, such as surveys, interviews and observation, are often inadequate to analyse and study consumer behaviour. These traditional methods fail to take into account that, often, people's decisions are influenced by several unconscious mental processes. This may mean that a consumer may be unwilling or unable to explain their behaviour or the choices they make. This is where neuromarketing can provide valuable information. Neuromarketing is an emerging field in which academic and industry research scientists employ neuroscience techniques to study marketing practices and consumer behaviour. The emergence of neuromarketing has significantly advanced conventional marketing research, illuminating how unconscious responses and emotions impact consumers' perception and decision-making processes.

Researchers use medical technologies such as functional magnetic resonance imaging (fMRI), eye tracking, behavioural experiments, sensor-based methods, body signal measures (biometrics), electromyography (EMG), brain signal measures (neurometrics) and electrical activity/ electroencephalography (EEG), to analyse changes in activities in various parts of the brain, the decisions being made by consumers and also what part of the brain is telling them to do that.[5]

However, there are certain ethical concerns associated with neuro-marketing. Most ethical objections to neuromarketing refer to risks of harm and violation of rights. Critics argue that, by scanning consumers' brains and possibly discovering a 'super-effective' communications technique, corporations will be able to 'push the buy button' in a consumer's brain, thereby being able to manipulate consumers' behaviour. Therefore, the main concerns are that neuromarketing may cause harm through its immediate effects on individual consumers and long-term effects on society as a whole.

Suggested reading: Alviro et al., 2018;[6] Flores et al., 2014;[7] Miletti et al., 2016;[8] Stanton et al., 2017[9]

Reflection: Consider the arguments for and against the use of neuromarketing. Put forward your own point of view on this matter.

---

develop a better understanding of consumers. CCT research has tended to address four key theoretical domains and their various points of intersection:

1. Consumer identity projects
2. Marketplace cultures
3. The socio-historic patterning of consumption
4. Mass mediated marketplace ideologies and consumer interpretative strategies.[10]

The CCT approach places consumers in a wider context than the information processing approach. It has led to increased use of forms of consumer research such as introspection, narrative analysis/ inquiry and ethnography. Introspection is a form of structured self-reflection that can be used to examine a range of consumption practices and provide a more in-depth understanding of consumers' behaviour, e.g. consumers' music consumption, film consumption or choice of holiday destination. Narrative analysis/inquiry attempts to better understand

Exhibit 3.3 In the competitive world of cosmetics, brand consumption is heavily influenced by perceptions of self identity.

the relationship between the experiences of the consumer and brands, companies, advertisements and interpersonal exchanges through the consumer's narrative account. It can be used to better understand details of how purchase decisions are made and what influences the choices made. In the digital world, online blogs and diaries can provide valuable introspective and narrative analysis insights that can aid marketers in their decision-making.[11] Ethnography has also become popular due to greater acceptance of the CCT approach. It is a qualitative research method that seeks to understand environmental, social, cultural and psychological influences on consumers. It involves observing people and their actions rather than asking them to self-report what they do (see Chapter 4). For example, German household goods manufacturer Miele used ethnography to learn about its consumers' behaviour. It observed constant cleaning in homes where some family members were suffering from allergies. As a result, it designed a vacuum cleaner with a traffic-light indicator that shows when a surface is dust free.[12] In recent years, there has been increased use of digital ethnographic research. For example, marketers can now observe consumers' online behaviour through the use of social media analytics and can observe consumers' responses to marketing stimuli through the use of eye-tracking research.[13]

The main differences between the two modes of thinking about consumer behaviour (the information processing approach and consumer culture theory) are summarized in Table 3.1. While this chapter is largely structured around the information processing approach, the broader perspectives brought by consumer culture theory are incorporated into the discussion.

Table 3.I **The information processing approach vs. consumer culture theory**

Attribute	Information processing approach	Consumer culture theory
Level of analysis	Individual	Society
Focus	Cognitive processes	Context of consumption
Purpose of consumption	Utilitarian	Experiential
Process of consumption	Logical	Random
Key consumption influence	Rationality	Social

Figure 3.2 **Types of consumer decision**

Extended problem solving	Habitual problem solving
Limited problem solving	Variety-seeking behaviour

Both traditions enrich our understanding of why consumers behave as they do and we also need to take account of the different kinds of decisions that consumers engage in (see Figure 3.2). *Extended problem solving* occurs when consumers are highly involved in a purchase, perceive significant differences between brands and there is an adequate time available for deliberation.[14] It involves a high degree of information search, as well as close examination of the alternative solutions using many choice criteria.[15] It is commonly seen in the purchase of cars, consumer electronics, houses and holidays, where it is important to make the right choice. Information search and evaluation may focus not only on which brand/model to buy, but also on where to make the purchase. The potential for post-purchase dissatisfaction or **cognitive dissonance** is greatest in this buying situation.

A great deal of consumer purchases come under the mantle of *limited problem solving*. The consumer has some experience with the product in question so that information search may be mainly internal through memory. However, a certain amount of external search and evaluation may take place (e.g. checking prices) before the purchase is made. This situation provides marketers with some opportunity to affect the purchase by stimulating the need to conduct a search (e.g. advertising) and reducing the risk of brand switching (e.g. warranties).

Habitual problem solving occurs in situations of low consumer involvement and a perception of limited differences between brands. It will take place, for example, when a consumer repeat-buys a product while carrying out little or no evaluation of the alternatives, such as groceries purchased on a weekly shopping trip. He or she may recall the satisfaction gained by purchasing a brand, and automatically buy it again. Advertising may be effective in keeping the brand name in the consumer's mind and reinforcing already favourable attitudes towards it.

Finally, consumers also engage in *variety-seeking behaviour* in situations characterized by low product involvement but where there are significant perceived differences between brands. For example, consumers may switch from one brand of biscuit to another, simply to try something new. The use of sales promotions by firms, such as extra free products and product sampling, are designed to encourage variety-seeking behaviour.

From the perspective of the information processing approach, the typical decision-making process for consumers and organizations is shown in Figure 3.3. This diagram shows that buyers typically move through a series of stages, from recognition that a problem exists to an examination of potential alternatives to a purchase and the subsequent evaluation of the purchase. Organizational buying is typically more complex and may involve more stages. However, as we saw above, the exact nature of the process will depend on the type of decision being made. In certain situations some stages will be omitted; for example, in a routine re-buy situation such as reordering photocopying paper, the purchasing officer is unlikely to pass through the third, fourth and fifth stages of organizational decision-making (search for suppliers and analysis, and evaluation of their proposals). These stages will be bypassed as the buyer, recognizing a need, routinely reorders from an existing supplier. In general, the more complex the decision and the more expensive the item, the more likely it is that each stage will be passed through and that the process will take more time.

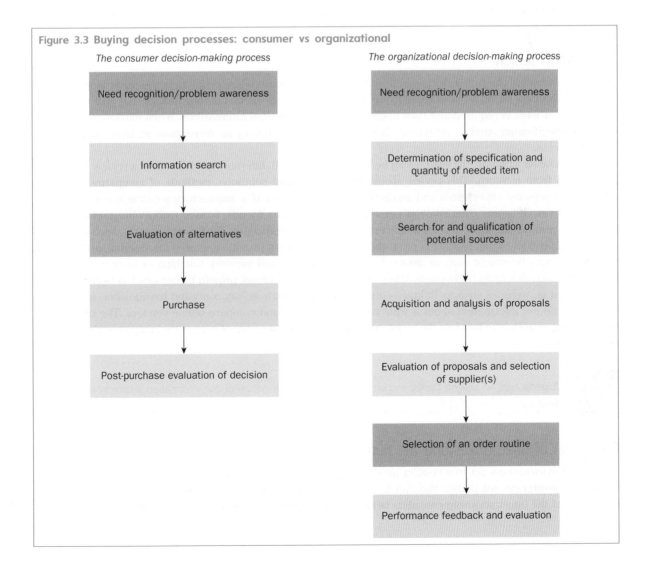

Figure 3.3 Buying decision processes: consumer vs organizational

The consumer decision-making process

- Need recognition/problem awareness
- Information search
- Evaluation of alternatives
- Purchase
- Post-purchase evaluation of decision

The organizational decision-making process

- Need recognition/problem awareness
- Determination of specification and quantity of needed item
- Search for and qualification of potential sources
- Acquisition and analysis of proposals
- Evaluation of proposals and selection of supplier(s)
- Selection of an order routine
- Performance feedback and evaluation

Need recognition/problem awareness

Need recognition may be functional and occur as a result of routine depletion (e.g. petrol, food) or unpredictable (e.g. the breakdown of a car or washing machine). In other situations, consumer purchasing may be initiated by more emotional needs or by simply imagining or daydreaming about what an experience may be like. Marketing campaigns frequently try to tap directly into emotional needs as a way of initiating consumption and driving brand preference.

The need recognition stage has a number of implications for marketing. First, marketing managers must be aware of the needs of consumers and the problems they face. Sometimes this awareness may be due to the intuition of the marketer who, for example, spots a new trend (such as the early marketing pioneers who spotted the trend towards fast food, which has underpinned the global success of companies like McDonald's and KFC). Dove is another brand that spotted a new trend and took note of the positive body movement. It has worked hard to connect its brand image to social ideals and, thanks to a decade of 'Real Beauty' campaigns, the personal care products company has successfully associated itself with the goal of positive body image. Alternatively, marketing research could be used to assess customer problems or needs (see Chapter 4). Second, marketers should be aware of need inhibitors – that is, those factors that prevent consumers from moving from need recognition to the next stage of the buying decision process. For example, ASOS recognized that overcoming the need inhibitor – delivery costs – is important. To overcome this inhibitor, it was one of the first online retailers to introduce free standard delivery for customers spending more than €25. Third, marketing managers should be aware that needs may arise because of stimulation. Their activities, such as developing advertising campaigns and training salespeople to sell product benefits, may act as cues to need arousal.

Information search

The second stage in the buyer decision-making process will begin when problem recognition is sufficiently strong. In the case of an organizational buying decision, the decision-making unit (DMU) will draw up a description of what is required and then begin a search for potential alternatives. When marketers can influence the specification that is drawn up, it may give their company an advantage at later stages in the buying process.

In a consumer situation, the search may be internal or external. Internal search involves a review of relevant information from memory. This review would include potential solutions, methods of comparing solutions, reference to personal experiences and marketing communications. If a satisfactory solution is not found then an external search begins. This involves personal sources such as friends, family, work colleagues and neighbours, and commercial sources such as advertisements and salespeople. Third-party reports, such as *Which?* reports and product testing reports in print and online media, may provide unbiased information, and personal experiences may be sought such as asking for demonstrations, and viewing, touching or tasting the product. Information search largely takes place online and one of the significant growth businesses has been intelligent agents – that is, websites such as Rakuten.com (previously known as buy.com) and trivago.com, which allow buyers to find out information about a wide range of products and compare online vendors. The objective of **information search** is to build up the **awareness set** – that is, the array of brands that may provide a solution to the problem.

Expedia.com Ad Insight: Digital marketing has changed the nature of our information search when booking holidays.

Evaluation of alternatives and the purchase

Reducing the awareness set to a smaller group of options for serious consideration is the first step in evaluation. The awareness set passes through a screening filter to produce an **evoked set**: those products or services that the buyer seriously considers before making a purchase. In a sense, the evoked set is a shortlist of options for careful evaluation. The screening process may use different choice criteria from those used when making the final choice, and the number of choice criteria used is often fewer.[16] In an organizational buying situation, each DMU member may use different choice criteria. One choice criterion used for screening may be price. For example, transportation companies whose services are below a certain price level may form the evoked set. Final choice may then depend on criteria such as reliability, reputation and flexibility. The range of choice criteria used by customers will be examined in more detail later.

Consumers' level of involvement is a key determinant of the extent to which they evaluate a brand. Involvement is the degree of perceived relevance and personal importance accompanying the brand choice.[17] When engaging in extended problem solving, the consumer is more likely to carry out extensive evaluation. High-involvement purchases are likely to include those incurring high expenditure or personal risk, such as car or home buying. In contrast, low-involvement situations are characterized by simple evaluations about purchases. Consumers use simple choice tactics to reduce time and effort rather than maximize the consequences of the purchase.[18] For example, when purchasing baked beans or breakfast cereals, consumers are likely to make quick choices rather than agonize over the decision. Research by Laurent and Kapferer has identified four factors that affect involvement:[19]

1 *Self-image*: involvement is likely to be high when the decision potentially affects one's self-image. Thus purchase of jewellery, clothing and cosmetic surgery invokes more involvement than choosing a brand of soap or margarine.
2 *Perceived risk*: involvement is likely to be high when the perceived risk of making a mistake is high. The risk of buying the wrong house is much higher than that of buying the wrong chewing gum, because the potential negative consequences of the wrong decision are higher. Risk usually increases with the price of the purchase.
3 *Social factors*: when social acceptance is dependent upon making a correct choice, involvement is likely to be high. Executives may be concerned about how their choice of car affects their standing among their peers in the same way that peer pressure is a significant influence on the clothing and music tastes of teenagers.
4 *Hedonistic influences*: when the purchase is capable of providing a high degree of pleasure, involvement is usually high. The choice of restaurant when on holiday can be highly involving since the difference between making the right or wrong choice can severely affect the amount of pleasure associated with the experience.

The distinction between high-involvement and low-involvement situations is important because the variations in how consumers evaluate products and brands lead to contrasting marketing implications. The complex evaluation in the high-involvement situation suggests that marketing managers need to provide a good deal of information to assist the purchase decision, such as through employing a well-trained, well-informed sales force. In low-involvement situations, providing positive reinforcement through advertising as well as seeking to gain trial (e.g. through sales promotion) is more important than providing detailed information. The increased use of price comparison websites has further assisted the evaluation of alternatives, as outlined in Marketing in Action 3.1.

Post-purchase evaluation of the decision

The creation of customer satisfaction is the real art of effective marketing. Marketing managers want to create positive experiences from the purchase of their products or services. Nevertheless, it is common for customers to experience some post-purchase concerns; this is known as cognitive dissonance. Such concerns arise because of an uncertainty surrounding the making of the right decision. This is because the choice of one product often means the rejection of the attractive features of the alternatives.

There are four ways in which dissonance is likely to be increased: owing to the expense of the purchase; when the decision is difficult (e.g. there are many alternatives, many choice criteria, and each alternative offers benefits not available with the others); when the decision is irrevocable; and when the purchaser is inclined to experience anxiety.[20] Thus it is often associated with high-involvement purchases. Shortly after

Marketing in Action 3.1
Price comparison websites

Critical Thinking: Below is a review of the role of price comparison websites in the evaluation of alternatives phase of the buying decision process. Read it and critically evaluate the pros and cons of using these sources of information.

Online shoppers are a frugal bunch. Customers want items quickly, and from the cheapest reliable seller. Price comparison engines or comparison shopping engines group products together based on price, shipping rates and seller ratings so consumers can compare products easily in one place. Consumers are increasingly relying on such price comparison sites to gain knowledge about the market. Shoppers are increasingly going online to price comparison sites and using the information gathered there to help them make offline, in-store purchases, or 'web-to-store' shopping. The detailed information presented in price comparison site search results (e.g. retailer ratings, frequency of retailers offering the product at the same price, retailer price level) may influence subsequent price evaluations. Online shoppers are generally not going direct to an online retailer's website any more. Instead, consumers are accessing products online through search engines and price comparison engines such as Google Shopping, Amazon Product Ads and Pricegrabber. For example, in the insurance industry, while comparison sites are best known for motor and home insurance, there are now many other types of cover that can be searched for, including pet, travel and small business insurance. In recent years, more and more niches have been added to suit a variety of needs, including telematics (also known as black box insurance) for young drivers, specialist policies for tenants and holiday home owners, along with a host of other financial services, utilities and broadband products.

It is estimated that more than 11 million people use price comparison sites and it's clear why they appeal. First, they can reduce consumers' search cost by bringing different providers onto the same platform. As such, consumers no longer need to go to each individual provider's website to extract information. Second, by grouping different product/service features, they assist consumers in navigating through the complicated product/service options and help to simplify their decision-making process. Third, the value-added functions allow consumers to select the best deal available on that price comparison website according to their chosen criteria. As the name suggests, price is what most of these sites provide their rankings on. Nevertheless, some price comparison websites have been innovative in how they provide the price rankings. For instance, Skyscanner provides the option of allowing the consumer to choose the date of travel and rank potential travel destinations by price. Such value added services add another layer of convenience to consumers.

However, the use of price comparison websites is not without its problems. Research by the Competition and Markets Authority (CMA) found that consumers did not typically think price comparison websites were pushing any particular supplier or product, and often described them as 'unbiased' or 'there to help consumers'. Not every insurer and every insurance product will be on a particular site – this is why the CMA recommended that consumers should use several sites to ensure they are covering all the bases. Consumers are not generally aware of the business models driving these commercial organizations. They provide their services to consumers free of charge because they make money by charging a commission to suppliers – be they energy companies, insurers or lenders – when we switch or sign up via their platform. Therefore, while price comparison sites have certainly increased competition and aid consumers in evaluating alternatives, it should always be remembered that, despite the customer benefits offered, the business model is one that is based on making a profit through commission on sales.

Based on: MacArthur, 2015;[21] Arora, 2016;[22] Anonymous, 2018;[23] Europe Economics, 2017;[24] Barrett, 2018[25]

purchase, car buyers may attempt to reduce dissonance by looking at advertisements and brochures for their model, and seeking reassurance from owners of the same model. Some car dealers, such as Toyota, seek to reduce this 'buyer remorse' by contacting recent purchasers by letter to reinforce the wisdom of their decision and to confirm the quality of their after-sales service. Organizations frequently solicit customer reviews of products and services, which are made available online and provide future customers with a better idea of what to expect. Managing expectations is a key part of reducing dissonance.

The consumer decision journey

Perspectives on how consumers move through the buying decision process have changed through taking account of the easy access to information and media-rich environments in which we now live. The concept of the **consumer decision journey** has been advanced to describe how consumption decisions are made today.[26] Among the significant trends that have been observed is that the number of alternatives considered may actually grow rather than reduce during the decision-making process. This is due to the ease of access to information about alternatives available both offline and online. A second major feature is the more active post-purchase experience, where the unwrapping and unboxing of purchases may be filmed and shared, along with a significant growth in the use of social media and online reviews to post positive and negative commentary on goods and services. Some aspects that appear to improve the customer journey experience include a fully digitized journey, high levels of customer convenience and customization of the journey.[27]

What are the choice criteria?

The various attributes (and benefits) a customer uses when evaluating products and services are known as **choice criteria**. They provide the grounds for deciding to purchase one brand or another. Different members of the buying centre may use different choice criteria. For example, purchasing managers who are judged by the extent to which they reduce purchase expenditure are likely to be more cost conscious than production engineers who are evaluated in terms of the technical efficiency of the production process they design. Four types of choice criteria are listed in Table 3.2, which also gives examples of each.

Technical criteria are related to the performance of the product or service, and include reliability, durability, comfort and convenience. Many consumers justify purchase decisions in rational technical terms but, as we shall see, the true motives for purchasing are often much more emotional. Some technical criteria, such as reliability, are particularly important in industrial purchasing. Many buying organizations are unwilling to trade quality for price. A 2018 *Harvard Business Review* study showed that although price is an important consideration in industrial buying, a full range of rational and emotional factors can influence business purchases.[28] Infosys, the Indian business consulting and information technology services firm, is a good example of how a B2B seller can benefit from focusing on quality rather than low price. Core to the company's brand strategy was quality and value over price, and this has meant that Infosys has walked away from lucrative deals below a certain price point that might compromise its reputation for quality. This quality guarantee has allowed Infosys to charge a premium for its service, leading to higher margins and securing long-term revenue through retained customers.[29]

Table 3.2 Choice criteria used when evaluating alternatives

Type of criteria	Examples
Technical	Reliability Durability Performance Style/looks Comfort Delivery Convenience Taste
Economic	Price Value for money Running costs Residual value Life cycle costs
Social	Status Social belonging Convention Fashion
Personal	Self-image Risk reduction Morals Emotions

Economic criteria concern the cost aspects of purchase, and include price, running costs and residual values (e.g. the trade-in value of a car). However, it should not be forgotten that price is only one component of cost for many buying organizations. Increasingly, buyers take into account life-cycle costs – which may include productivity savings, maintenance costs and residual values as well as initial purchase price – when evaluating products. Marketers can use life-cycle cost analysis to break into an account. By calculating life-cycle costs with a buyer, new perceptions of value may be achieved.

Social and personal criteria are particularly influential in consumer purchasing decisions. Social criteria concern the impact that the purchase makes on the person's perceived relationships with other people, and the influence of social norms on the person. For example, in the early days the manufacturers of personal computers and mobile phones, such as Apple, IBM and Motorola, sought to sell them on the basis of their technical and economic criteria. But as the technology underpinning these products becomes similar for all vendors, new forms of differentiation, such as colour, shape, appearance and emotional attributes, all became important. Recent research has demonstrated the powerful social effects of consumption. Simply wearing clothes sporting well-known labels such as Lacoste and Tommy Hilfiger has been shown to generate perceptions of higher status, increase participation in shopping mall surveys and improve the wearer's job prospects and ability to solicit funds for a charity.[30]

Exhibit 3.4 Drinks brands like Corona Extra are heavy users of emotional advertising.

Personal criteria concern how the product or service relates to the individual psychologically. Emotions are an important element of customer decision-making (see Exhibit 3.4).

Personal criteria are also important in organizational purchasing. Risk reduction can affect choice decisions since some people are risk averse and prefer to choose 'safe' brands. The classic IBM advertising campaign that used the slogan 'No one ever got fired for buying IBM' reflected its importance. Suppliers may be favoured on the basis that certain salespeople are liked or disliked, or due to office politics where certain factions within the company favour one supplier over another.

Marketing managers need to understand the choice criteria being used by customers to evaluate their products and services. Such knowledge has implications for priorities in product design, and the appeals to use in advertising and personal selling.

Western Sydney University Ad Insight: An emotional appeal is used to illustrate the power of education.

Influences on consumer behaviour

The main influences on consumer behaviour are summarized in Figure 3.4. Personal influences describe those drivers that relate to the individual, while social influences take account of the drivers that arise from the contexts in which we live.

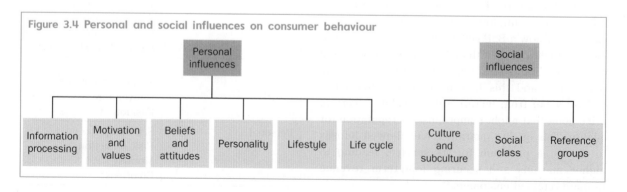

Figure 3.4 Personal and social influences on consumer behaviour

Personal influences

The six personal influences on consumer behaviour are: information processing, motivation, **beliefs** and **attitudes**, personality, lifestyle, and life cycle.

Information processing

The term **information processing** refers to the process by which a stimulus is received, interpreted, stored in memory and later retrieved.[31] It is therefore the link between external influences including marketing activities and the consumer's decision-making process. Two key aspects of information processing are perception and learning.

   Perception is the complicated means by which we select, organize and interpret sensory stimulation into a meaningful picture of the world.[32] We receive these external stimuli through our different senses, such as hearing a familiar jingle, seeing a YouTube video or encountering the familiar smell of a favourite coffee shop. The sensation of touch has been important in the success of Apple's products. Companies now place a significant emphasis on trying to present a multi-sensory experience for their customers as a way of attracting our attention (often subconsciously) and of differentiating their offerings from competitors. For example, Toyota produced a pop-up ad of a Toyota Camry's dashboard. Once the viewer placed their thumbs on the sensor tabs in the advert, the sensors activated a heart rate monitor that registered the user's pulse, the monitor on the advertisement lit up to show the user's heart rate and it emitted a leather new-car smell. Other car brands have also developed innovative ways of creating a multi-sensory experience (see Exhibit 3.5).

Exhibit 3.5 The Porsche Sound Lab was a pop-up store in the form of a modern music store to give customers the virtual experience of driving the car.

   Three processes may be used to sort, into a manageable amount, the masses of stimuli that could be perceived. These are **selective attention**, **selective distortion** and **selective retention**. Selective attention is the process by which we screen out those stimuli that are neither meaningful to us nor consistent with our experiences and beliefs. In our information-rich world, selective attention represents a major challenge for marketers. Various studies have shown that consumers are exposed to a huge volume of marketing messages but attend to a very small percentage of them. For example, one study has found that consumers could recall only an average of 2.21 advertisements that they had ever seen.[33] Creative approaches such as humour, shock, sex and mystery are used by advertisers to try to capture consumer attention. Position is also critical; objects placed near the centre of the visual range are more likely to be noticed than those on the periphery. This is why there is intense competition to obtain eye-level positions on supermarket shelves. We are also more likely to notice those messages that relate to our needs (benefits sought)[34] and those that provide surprises (e.g. substantial price reductions).

   When consumers distort the information they receive according to their existing beliefs and attitudes this is known as selective distortion. We may distort information that is not in accord with our existing views. Methods of doing this include thinking that we misheard the message and discounting the message source. Consequently, it is very important to present messages clearly without the possibility of ambiguity and to use a highly credible source. **Information framing** or priming can affect interpretation. 'Framing' refers to ways in which information is presented to people. Levin and Gaeth[35] asked people to taste minced beef after telling half the sample that it was 70 per cent lean and the other half that it was 30 per cent fat. Despite the fact that the

Exhibit 3.6 Luxury brands like Calvin Klein are frequent users of black and white imagery to convey elegance and luxury.

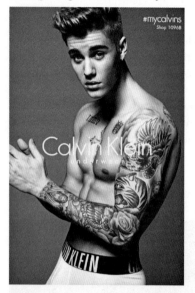

two statements are equivalent, the sample that had the information framed positively (70 per cent lean) recorded higher levels of taste satisfaction.

Priming involves using stimuli to encourage people to behave in certain ways. For example, when consumers arrive at a supermarket it takes a while for the mind to get into shopping mode. Therefore retailers term the area just inside the entrance as the decompression zone – where people are encouraged to slow down and look at special offers – which is then followed by the chill zone containing books, magazines and DVDs.[36] Colour is another important influence on interpretation (see Exhibit 3.6). Blue and green are viewed as cool, and evoke feelings of security. Red and yellow are regarded as warm and cheerful, but have also been found to have an aphrodisiac effect on men without an awareness on their part that this is the case.[37] By using the appropriate colour in pack design it is possible to affect the consumer's feelings about a product. However, it is important to remember that colour is also subject to different interpretations across different cultures.

Selective retention refers to the fact that only a selection of messages may be retained in memory. We tend to remember messages that are in line with existing beliefs and attitudes. Marketers are also interested in how we make sense of marketing stimuli such as the processes by which a leading sportsperson can cause us to select particular brands.

Learning takes place in a number of different ways. These include conditioning and cognitive learning. **Classical conditioning** is the process of using an established relationship between a stimulus and a response to cause the learning. Thus, advertising of soft drinks will typically show groups of people having fun and, when this type of advertising is constantly repeated, a certain level of conditioning takes place, creating an association between drinks consumption and happiness. This helps to explain why big, well-known brands advertise repeatedly. For example, the energy drink Red Bull repeatedly uses quirky, humorous advertising to appeal to its target market of young adults.

Operant conditioning differs from classical conditioning in terms of the role and timing of the reinforcement. In this case, reinforcement results from rewards: the more rewarding the response, the stronger the likelihood of the purchase being repeated. Operant conditioning occurs as a result of product trial. The use of free samples is based on the principles of operant conditioning. For example, free samples of a new shampoo are distributed to a large number of households. Because the use of the shampoo is costless it is used (desired response), and because it has desirable properties it is liked (reinforcement) and the likelihood of its being bought is increased. Thus the sequence of events is different for classical and operant conditioning. In the former, by association, liking precedes trial; in the latter, trial precedes liking. A series of rewards (reinforcements) may be used over time to encourage the repeat buying of the product.

The learning of knowledge, and the development of beliefs and attitudes without direct reinforcement is referred to as **cognitive learning**, which stresses the importance of internal mental processes. The learning of two or more concepts without conditioning is known as **rote learning**. Having seen the headline 'Lemsip is for flu attacks', the consumer may remember that Lemsip is a remedy for flu attacks without the kinds of conditioning and reinforcement previously discussed. **Vicarious learning** involves learning from others without direct experience or reward. It is the promise of the reward that motivates. Thus we may learn the type of clothes that attract potential admirers by observing other people. In advertising, the 'admiring glance' can be used to signal approval of the type of clothing being worn or the alcoholic beverage being consumed. We imagine that the same may happen to us if we dress in a similar manner or drink a similar drink.

Reasoning is a more complex form of cognitive learning and is usually associated with high-involvement situations. For example, a detailed online product review or a sales presentation enables consumers to draw their own conclusions through reasoning, having been presented with some facts or assertions. Whatever form of learning is used, marketers are particularly interested in both the recognition and recall of messages, as we shall see in Chapter 10.

Our understanding of how people perceive stimuli and learn is improving all the time. **Semiotics** is the study of the correspondence between signs and symbols, and their roles in how we assign meanings. Symbols in logo design and advertising are given meanings by the consumers that interpret them as such. For example, the striding man on a bottle of Johnnie Walker whisky symbolizes the journey we take through life and this journey was the centrepiece of the Johnnie Walker 'Keep Walking' campaign. In psychology and brain research, significant attention is being devoted to trying to understand the subconscious as it would appear that much of our decision-making is done there without us realizing it (as we saw in Critical Marketing Perspective 3.1). For example, it has been argued that we often make snap judgements that are superior to those that we think a great deal about.[38]

Motivation

Given the endless array of choices that are available to us, what are the motives that cause us to select one experience over another or choose to spend our time or money in certain ways? A key part of this issue (and of the debates about marketing generally) is the distinction between needs and wants. Critics of marketing argue that it creates excessive wants and desires among consumers, leading to all types of maladaptive behaviours such as addictive consumption, compulsive shopping disorder (CSD), consumer debt and the waste of the planet's scarce resources.

One of the best-known theories of motivation is Maslow's Hierarchy of Needs. The psychologist Abraham Maslow sought to explain how people grow and develop, and proposed that we move through a hierarchy of motives. First we must satisfy our basic *physiological needs* for food, clothing and shelter, then we move to *safety needs* such as protection from danger and accidents, then to the need for *belongingness* such as love and family relationships, then to the needs for *esteem and status*, and then to the final, highest level of need, namely *self-actualization*, which is essentially our understanding of whatever the meaning of life is for us. From a marketing point of view, different products can be seen as fulfilling different needs, such as security systems for safety, club memberships for status, and travel and education for self-actualization. However, consumers do not progress rigidly up the hierarchy but may place emphasis on different levels at different times, and the same product may satisfy different needs for different people.

Consequently, new explanations of fundamental human needs are becoming more popular. For example, evolutionary psychologists argue that we have four basic human needs that have derived from our evolution as a species and can be observed in different cultures during different time periods. These are the need to survive, to reproduce, to select kin and to reciprocate. These fundamental motives can be observed in the consumption of everything from cookery books (survival) to cosmetic surgery (reproduction) to Christmas gift giving (reciprocation).[39]

Beliefs and attitudes

A thought that a person holds about something is known as a 'belief'. Beliefs about oneself, known as the **self-concept**, are very important because this drives a signification element of consumption. For example, the viral video from Dove called 'Evolution', which was part of the Real Beauty campaign, was a significant hit because it shows how perceptions of beauty are distorted in the media.

Consumers increasingly use brands to convey their identity by wearing branded clothes or even having brands tattooed on their bodies. Marketing people are also very interested in consumer beliefs because these are related to attitudes. In particular, misconceptions about products can be harmful to brand sales. Duracell batteries were believed by consumers to last three times as long as Ever Ready batteries, but in continuous use they lasted more than six times as long. This prompted Duracell to launch an advertising campaign to correct this misconception.

An 'attitude' is an overall favourable or unfavourable evaluation of a product or service. The consequence of a set of beliefs may be a positive or negative attitude towards the product or service. Changing attitudes is an important step in convincing consumers to try a brand. For example, prior to 2010, Old Spice was seen as a brand for older generations, and the younger market had a negative attitude towards it and saw it as a stagnant and uninteresting brand. The introduction of its humorous 'The Man Your Man Could Smell Like' advertisements helped change attitudes towards the brand and make it more appealing to a new younger demographic.[40] By changing the brand name and packaging of its value range to M Savers, the UK supermarket chain Morrisons was successful in changing attitudes and growing sales of this sub-brand.

Understanding beliefs and attitudes is an important task for marketers. For example, the attitudes of the 'grey market' (those over the age of 50 years) are not well understood. Some companies, such as Gap, have explicitly targeted this segment, but Gap was forced to close its Forth & Towne outlets after heavy losses. Brands like Amazon's Kindle and Apple's iPhone and iPad have proved to be particularly popular with the grey market because they are larger than other portable devices and are very easy to use. Some firms are trying to understand older people better. Kimberley-Clark, a maker of consumer products, has built a mock-up of what a senior-friendly shop might look like in the future. Ford has also created a 'third-age suit' for car designers to wear to help them understand the needs of older people: the suit thickens the waist, stiffens the joints and makes movement more cumbersome.[41] This large and relatively well-off 'grey market' is likely to be the subject of significant marketing effort in the years to come.

Personality

Just from our everyday dealings with people we can tell that they differ enormously in their personalities. **Personality** is the sum of the inner psychological characteristics of individuals, which lead to consistent responses to their environment.[42] There are several theories of personality but the most accepted today is the big five, and the extent to which one varies on these dimensions ranges from high to low.[43] The big five are:

1   Openness to new experience, novelty seeking, etc.
2   Conscientiousness, which is self-control, reliability, etc.
3   Agreeableness, which is warmth, friendliness, etc.
4   Stability, such as emotional stability
5   Extraversion – that is, the extent to which people are outgoing and talkative or not.

The extent to which we possess each of these traits will be reflected in our behaviour and in our consumption choices. For example, conscientiousness is generally low in juveniles and increases with age. The consumption of high-maintenance products, pets, personal grooming and home fitness equipment is an indicator of high conscientiousness.

G-Shock Ad Insight: This Casio G-Shock advertisement promotes the brand's tough and durable characteristics.

This concept – personality – is also relevant to brands (see Marketing in Action 3.2). 'Brand personality' is the characterization of brands as perceived by consumers. Brands may be characterized as 'for adventure seekers' (Red Bull), 'for winners' (Nike) or 'self-important' (L'Oréal). This is a dimension over and above the physical (e.g. colour) or functional (e.g. taste) attributes of a brand. By creating a brand personality, a marketer may generate appeal to people who value that characterization. For example, one of the longest-running fictional brands is James Bond; a variety of car makers and technology companies have attempted to bring his cool, suave and sexy personality into their brands by placing them in Bond movies.

Marketing in Action 3.2
Virgin brand personality

Critical Thinking: Below is a review of the importance of brand personality and an overview of how Virgin's brand personality has helped to distinguish it from competitors and build a loyal customer base.

A brand personality is something to which a consumer can relate. It helps define the character of a brand and facilitates the emotional connection between a brand and its target audience. Brand personality is simply the way a brand presents itself to the world. It includes how a brand looks, sounds, feels and behaves, and it is the most immediate way for customer to understand 'who' the brand is and be attracted to find out more. When all competitors in a particular industry do, more or less, the same thing, it becomes increasingly difficult to differentiate on brand positioning alone. Corporate

(continued)

culture as experienced by the unique personality of a brand can often set companies in these indus-tries apart. Brand personality is a critical part of developing a well-rounded brand strategy. A consis-tent brand personality gives a consumer a seamless experience and a consistent message about what a brand stands for. When executed strategically, brand personality empowers a brand to create strong, invaluable brand equities and loyal customers. In essence, it's less about *what* these compa-nies do to provide value to customers and more about *how* they provide that value.

Virgin is a brand that has a very distinct brand personality that helps it to stand out from the competition. Virgin is often described as maverick, rebellious and even a bit edgy – but that is combined with a sense of fun and appreciation of pleasure. It's that combination of personality traits that has enabled Virgin to challenge and shake up many industries while keeping a strong emotional appeal to customers. Virgin's clear, recognizable, attractive and distinctive personality ensures it stands out. The Virgin brand identity is highly consistent across industries, countries and over time: the red colour, the upbeat tone of voice and the 'naughty' behaviour are all part of cre-ating success for the maverick Virgin and the maverick Richard Branson.

One of its core values is to disrupt industries while providing heartfelt service – all the while having fun. Whether it is selling holidays or mobile phone contracts, it always makes sure fun shines through in its products and services, by placing it at the heart of its marketing. For example, when it launched Virgin Atlantic, it didn't have the budget to take on British Airways' marketing campaigns. Instead, Richard Branson put himself front and centre of the brand – giving Virgin a personality that British Airways didn't have. Ever since then, it has been thinking up fun ways to stand out from the crowd and draw the media's attention to the company. It's done everything from breaking world records to teasing competitors, and taking part in outlandish adventures that have got it noticed. Virgin also maximizes social media to enhance customer loyalty through events, promotions and sales; it opens lines of communication to generate buzz from satisfied customers and quickly addresses the concerns of disgruntled ones. Virgin continues to consistently make headlines by letting its brand personality shine through everything it does and by having fun.

Based on: Million, 2018;[44] Anonymous, 2018;[45] Branson, 2016;[46] Anonymous, 2015[47]

Lifestyle

Lifestyle patterns have been the subject of much interest as far as marketing research practitioners are con-cerned. The term 'lifestyle' refers to the pattern of living as expressed in a person's activities, interests and opinions (the AIO dimensions). Lifestyle analysis (psychographics) groups consumers according to their beliefs, activities, values and demographic characteristics (such as education and income). For example, the advertising agency Young & Rubicam identified seven major lifestyle groups that can be found throughout Europe and the USA:

1   *The mainstreamers*: the largest group. Attitudes include conventional, trusting, cautious and family centred. Leisure activities include spectator sports and gardening; purchase behaviour is habitual, brand loyal and in approved stores.
2   *The aspirers*: members of this group are unhappy, suspicious and ambitious. Leisure activities include trendy sports and fashion magazines; they buy fads, are impulse shoppers and engage in conspicuous consumption.
3   *The succeeders*: those that belong to this group are happy, confident, industrious and leaders. Leisure activ-ities include travel, sports, sailing and dining out. Purchase decisions are based on criteria like quality, status and luxury.
4   *The transitionals*: members of this group are liberal, rebellious, self-expressive and intuitive. They have unconventional tastes in music, travel and movies; and enjoy cooking and arts and crafts. Shopping behav-iour tends to be impulsive and to involve unique products.
5   *The reformers*: those that belong to this group are self-confident and involved, have broad interests and are issues orientated. They like reading, cultural events, intelligent games and educational television. They have eclectic tastes, enjoy natural foods, and are concerned about authenticity and ecology.

6   *The struggling poor*: members of this group are unhappy, suspicious and feel left out. Their interests are in sports, music and television; their purchase behaviour tends to be price based, but they are also looking for instant gratification.

7   *The resigned poor*: those in this group are unhappy, isolated and insecure. Television is their main leisure activity and shopping behaviour is price based, although they also look for the reassurance of branded goods.

Lifestyle analysis has implications for marketing since lifestyles have been found to correlate with purchasing behaviour.[48] A company may choose to target a particular lifestyle group (e.g. the mainstreamers) with a product offering, and use advertising that is in line with the values and beliefs of this group (see Exhibit 3.7). For example, Benecol's range of cholesterol-lowering foods is marketed at consumers who seek to have a healthy lifestyle. As information on the readership/viewership habits of lifestyle groups becomes more widely known so media selection may be influenced by lifestyle research.

Exhibit 3.7 The increased popularity of the 'outdoor' lifestyle has enabled brands like Regatta to grow across Britain and Ireland.

A typical example of a popular lifestyle that has grown significantly in recent years is surfing. Originating in the South Pacific, surfing was formerly popular in just some select areas, such as Hawaii, California and Australia. In the past decade, its popularity has soared and participation rates around the world have grown dramatically. It is characterized by its own surf culture, such as dressing in boardshorts or driving 'woodies' – station wagons used to carry boards. Many brands have capitalized on this opportunity, most notably the Australian clothing brand Billabong and the US brand Hollister, and marketers aiming to target surfers can do so through particular magazines, events, television programmes and social networks.

Life cycle

In addition to the factors we have already examined, consumer behaviour may depend on the 'life stage' people have reached. A person's life-cycle stage is of particular relevance since disposable income and purchase requirements may vary according to life-cycle stage. For example, young couples with no children may have high disposable income if both work, and may be heavy purchasers of home furnishings and appliances since they may be setting up home. When they have children, their disposable income may fall, particularly if they become a single-income family and the purchase of baby and child-related products increases. At the empty-nester stage, disposable income may rise due to the absence of dependent children, low mortgage repayments and high personal income. Research has shown that, when children leave a home, a mother is likely to change 80 per cent of the branded goods she buys regularly and that they are more likely than any other group to decide which brands they want to buy once in a store than beforehand.[49] Both these issues have important marketing implications.

Social influences

The three social influences on consumer behaviour are: culture, social class and reference groups.

Culture

As we noted in Chapter 2, **culture** refers to the traditions, taboos, values and basic attitudes of the whole society within which an individual lives. It provides the framework within which individuals and their lifestyles develop, and consequently affects consumption. For example, in Japan it is generally women that control the family finances and make all the major household spending decisions. As a result, many financial services firms are developing investment products targeted specifically at Japanese women. Within cultures there are also a variety of subcultures that influence consumer behaviour and marketing, as we saw in Chapter 2.

The most notable trend in the past three decades has been the increased internationalization of cultures. Products and services that previously may have been available only in certain countries are now commonplace. For example, speciality cuisines like Japanese sushi, Korean barbecue and Cajun food can now be found in major cities throughout the world. Allied to this, though, is the growing domination of some cultures. For example, the success of American fast-food chains and social media companies represents a major challenge to smaller, local enterprises in many parts of the world.

Social class

Long regarded as an important determinant of consumer behaviour, the idea of social class is based largely on occupation (often that of the chief income earner). This is one way in which respondents in marketing research surveys are categorized, and it is usual for advertising media (e.g. newspapers) to give readership figures broken down by social class groupings. Some countries are significantly more class conscious than others, such as the UK and India, and movement between the classes is difficult. In others, such as Brazil and China, rising incomes are creating large new middle- and upper-class segments, which is significantly driving demand for international and luxury brands respectively. For example, such is the demand for golf courses in China that many are being built without planning permission and others are not being called golf courses to get around planning legislation.

However, the use of traditional social class frameworks to explain differences in consumer behaviour has been criticized because certain social class categories may not relate to differences in disposable income (e.g. many self-employed manual workers can have very high incomes). The National Statistics Socioeconomic Classification system (NSSEC) in the UK aims to take account of this situation by identifying eight categories of occupation, as shown in Table 3.3. Consumption patterns are likely to vary significantly across these categories. For example, research on the social class of British grocery shoppers has found that the highest proportion of AB (managerial/professional) shoppers frequent Sainsbury's; Asda attracts a significantly higher share of people in lower supervisory and technical occupations; while Tesco's profile mirrors that of society in general.[50] An interesting trend in the growing middle-class segment is that consumers are becoming more cost-conscious and this has contributed to the growth of the discounters. Lidl has now overtaken Waitrose to become Britain's seventh largest supermarket by share of the groceries market. Furthermore, its rival Aldi has cemented its spot in fifth position ahead of Co-op. Britain's big four grocers (Tesco, Sainsbury's, Asda and Morrisons) are losing market share to the discounters.[51]

Table 3.3 Social class categories

Analytic class	Operational categories	Occupations
1	Higher managerial and professional occupations	Employers in large organizations; higher managerial and professional
2	Lower managerial and professional occupations	Lower managerial occupations; higher technical and supervisory occupations
3	Intermediate occupations	Intermediate clerical/administrative, sales/service, technical/auxiliary and engineering occupations
4	Small employers and own-account workers	Employers in small, non-professional and agricultural organizations, and own-account workers
5	Lower supervisory and technical occupations	Lower supervisory and lower technical craft and process operative occupations
6	Semi-routine occupations	Semi-routine sales, service, technical, operative, agricultural, clerical and childcare occupations
7	Routine occupations	Routine sales/service, production, technical, operative and agricultural occupations
8	Never worked and long-term unemployed	Never worked, long-term unemployed and students

Reference groups

A group of people that influences an individual's attitude or behaviour is called a **reference group**. Where a product is conspicuous (for example, clothing or cars) the brand or model chosen may have been strongly influenced by what buyers perceive as acceptable to their reference group; this may consist of the family, a group of friends or work colleagues. Some reference groups may be formal (e.g. members of a club or society), while others may be informal (friends with similar interests). Reference groups influence their members in a number of ways, such as providing peers with information about products, by influencing peers to buy products and by individual members choosing certain products because they feel that this will enhance their image within the group. The role of reference groups is now more important than ever given that certain groups choose to live a very 'public' life through social networks. Different types of reference groups exist. *Membership* groups are those to which a person already belongs, and can be with friends, club members or classmates. An interesting marketing development has been the growth of brand communities, which are social relationships based around interest in a product (see Chapter 6). *Aspirational* groups are those that a person would like to belong to – for example, people often aspire to the lifestyle of sports stars or celebrities. Finally, *avoidance* groups are those that people choose to distance themselves from because they do not share the values of such a group.

A key role in all reference groups is played by the opinion leader. Opinion leaders are typically socially active and highly interconnected within their groups. They also have access to product information, and influence the behaviour and purchase choices of group members. Given advances in social networking technology, their influence can be highly significant. Therefore, they are the focus of attention from marketers, who aim to identify them and to encourage them to influence their peers through buzz marketing techniques. They are also critical to the adoption of new products, as demonstrated in Figure 3.5.

A related issue is the 'herd mentality' of consumption behaviour. People are social animals and tend to follow the crowd, therefore companies are looking at ways of exploiting this to increase sales. For example, researchers in the USA created an artificial music market in which people downloaded previously unknown songs. What they found was that when consumers could see how many times the tracks had been downloaded, they tended to select the most popular tracks. As a result, many websites now include features like 'other customers have bought' tabs. Similarly, 'smart cart' technology is being pioneered in supermarkets to exploit this herd instinct. Each cart has a scanner that reads products that have been chosen and relays the information to a central computer. When a shopper walks past a shelf of goods, a screen on the shelf can tell her/him how many people in the shop have already selected that particular product. Studies have shown that, if the number is high, he or she is more likely to choose it, so this method can be used to increase sales without offering discounts, for example. In summary, the behaviour of consumers is affected by a variety of factors. There is a range of personal influences and some social influences that all combine to make up the

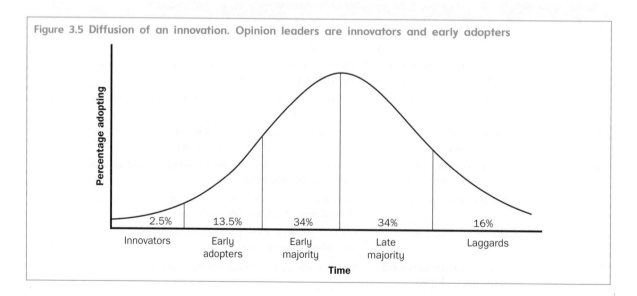

Figure 3.5 Diffusion of an innovation. Opinion leaders are innovators and early adopters

nature of the relationships that individuals have with products and services. More recently, influencer marketing has become an important factor affecting consumers' purchasing intentions. This is the focus of the following section.

Influencer marketing

Influencer marketing involves using individuals that have social media influence to reach consumers. It harnesses the growing impact of digital technologies to influence consumers' brand awareness, attitudes and purchase intentions.

The impact of digital technologies

The internet has become a major transformational force in consumers' lives. With 55 per cent internet penetration worldwide in 2018 and a whopping 4.021 billion internet users and 3.196 billion active social media users across the world, it has become indispensable to consumers in the context of their everyday lives.[52] Digital technology has allowed for greater customization of products, services and promotional messages. It has enabled marketers to adapt elements of their marketing mix to consumers' needs more quickly and efficiently, and has allowed marketers to build and maintain relationships with consumers on a much larger scale. It has also allowed for the collection and analysis of increasingly complex data about consumers, their buying patterns and personal characteristics, which can then be used to target smaller and increasingly more focused groups of consumers (see Chapter 4). Finally, digital technologies have enabled consumers to engage in increasing amounts of consumption online, e.g. browsing, shopping, reading and writing online reviews, searching for information, evaluating alternatives and consuming media.

The digital consumer

As digital consumers we use social media to connect with others, to consume content others have created (e.g. music, videos, games, reviews), to create our own content (e.g. posting updates, pictures, videos, reviews) and to control the information and image we project to others (see Figure 3.6).[53] Therefore digital technologies, and social media in particular, have revolutionized consumer behaviour and have led to the emergence of a new type of consumer, the digital consumer, who actively likes to 'search, surf and share' online.

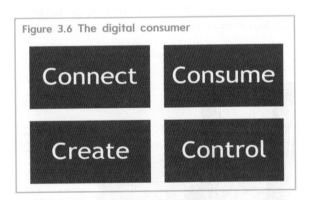

Figure 3.6 The digital consumer

Connect   Consume

Create   Control

The growth of social media influencers

As TV viewership continues to decline and traditional channels like TV and display ads are becoming increasingly less effective, brands have had to alter their approach to marketing and leverage the power of social media. One way in which they can achieve this is through the use of influencer marketing.[54]

Influencer marketing involves the use of social media influencers to drive a brand's message to reach target segments. A social influencer is simply a person who can influence other people. In the beginning, many influencers were celebrities; however, nowadays influencers can be ordinary people who may be admired by others or viewed as trendsetters, and who have the potential to influence their family, friends and followers. Companies invite and pay these influencers, who have thousands or even millions of followers, to act as brand ambassadors and help spread conversations about their brand online. These influencers can be fitness gurus, gaming addicts, beauty bloggers, fashionistas, social media stars or others. They typically use a variety of social media platforms, such as Facebook, Twitter, Instagram and YouTube to publicize product information and the latest promotions to their online followers. Collectively, these social media influencers are referred to as social media stars, brand influencers and digital influencers, and terms like YouTubers, Instagrammers, Viners, Snapchatters, vloggers and bloggers are used to describe platform-specific users.[55]

Impact

A strength of influencer marketing is that it allows brands to partner with creators that develop content perceived to be authentic and relatable to their audience. Usually, their audience has come to know them over a period of time, and has seen their reviews of a range of different products and services. When an influencer voices their opinion and integrates a brand into their feed, it connects with their audience in a much more powerful way than simply getting a video view or an ad impression.[56] Through marketing and advertising with top social media influencers, the relationships and relevancy these influencers have with their followers ensures that audiences will not only see the brand an influencer is promoting, but will also be more likely to act, prompted by the influencer's recommendation and endorsement.[57]

Influencers are often perceived by consumers to be more credible, trustworthy and knowledgeable compared to celebrity endorsers, due to their amicability and their ability to build a rapport with consumers. They have become a particularly important information source for businesses targeting a young demographic.[58] According to a recent Nielsen report, influencer marketing yields returns on investment (ROI) 11 times higher than digital marketing. The report highlights that, although celebrity endorsement is instrumental in raising brand awareness among consumers, social media influencers play a highly significant role in driving product engagement and brand loyalty as they are more capable of communicating to a niche segment.[59]

Research from *Forbes* magazine further supports the positive impact of influencers, stating that 92 per cent of consumers trust influencers more than an advertisement or traditional celebrity endorsement.[60] In addition, recent research has found that social media influencers have even greater impact on consumer brand awareness and purchase considerations than was thought, as 21 per cent of consumers across the USA and Europe said they had purchased a product or service based on a social influencer post. This research also showed that images and video content are the most preferred types of influencer content, with Facebook, Instagram and YouTube the most favoured platforms for following influencers.[61] In order to assess the effectiveness of influencer marketing, reach, impressions, click-through rates, engagement and ROI metrics of the influencer can be tracked. In addition, marketers can also use influencer marketing to better understand consumer needs and priorities.[62]

Exhibit 3.8 Nespresso used influencer marketing to connect with millennials.

There have been numerous examples of brands that have successfully used influencer marketing to connect with consumers. For example, in 2016, Nespresso launched an Instagram influencer campaign to make the product known to a younger generation of coffee drinkers. Nespresso chose top influencers Adam Gallagher, who is admired for his classic and effortless style, and Aimee Song, a top fashion blogger, to post about the brand on Instagram. Both influencers reached different audiences, but their personas, centred on elegance and good taste, were an excellent fit for Nespresso and allowed the brand to access a previously untapped market: millennials (see Exhibit 3.8).[63]

Challenges

As more and more companies and brands harness the power of influencer marketing, questions about its effectiveness arise. One concern is the cost associated with its use. Influencer marketing can be expensive as companies pay influencers to promote their brand on social media. The cost of using influencer marketing varies from influencer to influencer and may be affected by the social media platforms used, the influencer's following, the level of engagement required, the product in question, the extent of the campaign and whether the influencer is being engaged with directly or through a talent agency.[64]

Recent research by Emarketer has found that companies are paying the most for celebrity influencer posts, especially on certain social media platforms. It found that, on average, posts by celebrities with at least 1 million followers cost nearly £65,000 each, with Facebook posts demanding a leading rate of approximately £75,000. In certain industries, the costs were even higher, with some premium fashion brands, for example, paying celebrity influencers more than £160,000 per post. When it came to so-called micro-influencers (those with 10,000 or fewer followers), prices averaged at close to £1,350 per post, with YouTube and Facebook commanding the highest prices.[65]

Another challenge is that many influencers are becoming commercial and money-driven, and this may mean that they may be less committed to some of the brands they recommend, focusing more on the money to be made. Influencers are also competing to work with brands, and this increased competition between influencers may diminish their connection with their audience. An additional problem is that some brands overuse social media influencers by choosing many influencers for a campaign, some of whom may be irrelevant for the brand and the target audience.[66] When choosing an influencer, a brand must ensure that they are aligned with the brand's overall content strategy and brand image. The influencer should be connecting with a relevant audience and should be a good fit to the brand.[67]

One of the biggest challenges facing the future of influencer marketing is the lack of regulation around its use. In some countries, there is no consumer protection legislation governing the advertising sector and no specific reference to blogging or social media influencers in general consumer law.[68] In those countries where consumer protection legislation is in place to regulate influencer marketing, there is an onus on influencers to state if they are being paid to promote a brand. These influencers must clearly use tags like #ad on paid-for posts to show that paid-for product promotion is involved. Action can be taken against those influencers who fail to do so. For example, the Advertising Standards Authority (ASA) in the UK has upheld a number of complaints against brands that have failed to provide sufficient clarity in publicising their commercial relationships with bloggers, vloggers and other social media influencers.[69] Consumers have also become increasingly sceptical of some influencers as awareness increases of the heavily curated, edited and photoshopped images some of them post. This scepticism was further exacerbated when two Instagram accounts called @Bullshitcallerouter and @Bloggersunveiled debuted in early 2018, exposing the use of photoshopping and cosmetic enhancements by some Irish influencers.

Despite these challenges, the future of influencer marketing looks bright. Companies are now recognizing that influencers are masters at **e-WOM** (electronic word-of-mouth). They can take on the role of forming consumers' opinions on products and services, and the e-WOM produced by these influencers can be substantial. By building influencer marketing and e-WOM into their marketing strategies, it can give companies an opportunity for open dialogue and information flow. Influencer budgets continue to rise, creators are learning more about how to integrate brands in a more sophisticated and authentic way, and the industry as a whole is attempting to adopt best practices to drive even more value for everybody involved.[70] We will now turn to the factors that influence the buying behaviour of organizations.

Influences on organizational buying behaviour

Organizational buying is characterized by a number of unique features. Typically, the number of customers is small and order sizes large. For example, in Australia just two companies, Coles and Woolworths, account for more than 70 per cent of all products sold in supermarkets, so getting or losing an account with these resellers can be crucial. Organizational purchases are often complex and risky, with several parties having input into the purchasing decision, as would be the case with a major information technology (IT) investment. The demand for many organizational goods is derived from the demand for consumer goods, which means that small changes in consumer demand can have an important impact on the demand for industrial goods. For example, the decline in the sale of DVDs has had a knock-on effect on the demand for DVD component parts. When large organizational customers struggle, this impacts on their suppliers. Most major car manufacturers, such as Ford, General Motors, Daimler Chrysler and Volkswagen, have demanded significant price cuts from their suppliers in recent years. However, at the same time suppliers have faced rising steel and raw material costs, which has affected profitability and forced some out of business.[71] On the other hand, some suppliers, like Intel, have done an exceptional job of building their brands and creating an awareness of the presence of their products in the offerings of other companies. Organizational buying is also characterized by the prevalence of negotiations between buyers and sellers; and in some cases reciprocal buying may take place where, for example, in negotiating to buy computers a company like Volvo might persuade a supplier to buy a fleet of company cars.

Figure 3.7 shows the three factors that influence organizational buying behaviour and the choice criteria that are used: the buy class, the product type and the importance of purchase.[72]

The buy class

Organizational purchases may be distinguished as either a **new task**, a **straight re-buy** or a **modified re-buy**.[73] A new task occurs when the need for the product has not arisen previously so that there is little or no relevant experience in the company, and a great deal of information is required. A straight re-buy occurs where an organization buys previously purchased items from suppliers already judged acceptable. Routine purchasing procedures are set up to facilitate straight re-buys. The modified re-buy lies between the two extremes. A regular requirement for the type of product exists, and the buying alternatives are known, but sufficient change (e.g. a delivery problem) has occurred to require some alteration to the normal supply procedure.

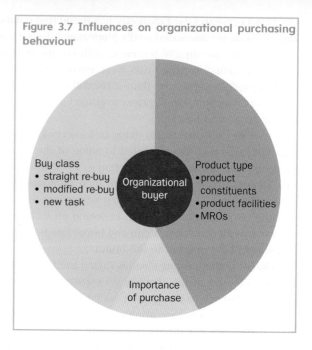

Figure 3.7 Influences on organizational purchasing behaviour

The buy classes affect organizational buying in the following ways. First, the membership of the DMU changes. For a straight re-buy possibly only the purchasing officer is involved, whereas for a new buy senior management, engineers, production managers and purchasing officers may be involved. Modified re-buys often involve engineers, production managers and purchasing officers, but not senior management, except when the purchase is critical to the company. Second, the decision-making process may be much longer as the buy class changes from a straight re-buy to a modified re-buy and to a new task. Third, in terms of influencing DMU members, they are likely to be much more receptive to new task and modified re-buy situations than straight re-buys. In the latter case, the purchasing manager has already solved the purchasing problem and has other problems to deal with.

The first implication of this buy class analysis is that there are big gains to be made if a company can enter the new task at the start of the decision-making process. By providing information and helping with any technical problems that can arise, the company may be able to create goodwill and 'creeping commitment', which secures the order when the final decision is made. The second implication is that, since the decision process is likely to be long and many people are involved in the new task, supplier companies need to invest heavily in sales personnel for a considerable period of time. Some firms employ 'missionary' sales teams, comprising their best salespeople, to help secure big new-task orders.

The product type

Products can be classified according to four types: materials, components, plant and equipment, and maintenance, repair and operation (MRO):

1 materials – to be used in the production process, e.g. aluminium
2 components – to be incorporated in the finished product, e.g. headlights
3 plant and equipment – for example, earth-moving equipment
4 products and services for MRO – for example, spanners, welding equipment and lubricants.

This classification is based on a customer perspective – how the product is used – and may be employed to identify differences in organizational buyer behaviour. First, the people who take part in the decision-making process tend to change according to product type. For example, senior management tend to get involved in the purchase of plant and equipment or, occasionally, when new materials are purchased if the change is of fundamental importance to company operations, e.g. if a move from aluminium to plastic is being considered. Rarely do they involve themselves in component or MRO supply. Similarly, design engineers tend to be involved in buying components and materials, but not normally MRO and plant equipment. Second, the decision-making process tends to be slower and more complex as product type moves along the following continuum:

$$MRO \rightarrow components \rightarrow materials \rightarrow plant\ and\ equipment$$

The importance of purchase

A purchase is likely to be perceived as being important to the buying organization when it involves large sums of money, when the cost of making the wrong decision – for example, in terms of production downtime – is high and when there is considerable uncertainty about the outcome of alternative offerings. In such situations, many people at different organizational levels are likely to be involved in the decision and the process will be long, with extensive search for and analysis of information. Thus extensive marketing effort is likely to be required, but great opportunities present themselves to sales teams who work with buying organizations to convince them that their offering has the best pay-off; this may involve acceptance trials (e.g. private diesel manufacturers supply railway companies with prototypes for testing), engineering support and testimonials from other users. Additionally, guarantees of delivery dates and after-sales service may be necessary when buyer uncertainty regarding these factors is pronounced.

Features of organizational purchasing practice

Within the purchasing function, a number of trends have occurred that have marketing implications for supplier firms. The relentless drive for efficiency by businesses has been one of the key factors behind the growth of just-in-time purchasing, online purchasing and centralized purchasing. At the same time, these developments have often strengthened relationships between buyers and their suppliers, and we have seen a significant growth in relationship marketing and reverse marketing.

The **just-in-time (JIT)** concept aims to minimize stocks by organizing a supply system that provides materials and components as they are required. The total effects of JIT can be enormous. Purchasing inventory and inspection costs can be reduced, product design can be improved, delivery streamlined, production downtime reduced and the quality of the finished item enhanced. Very close co-operation is required between a manufacturer and its suppliers. An example of a company that employs a JIT system is the Nissan car assembly plant in Sunderland in the UK. Nissan adopts what it terms 'synchronous supply': parts are delivered only minutes before they are needed. For example, carpets are delivered by Sommer Allibert, a French supplier, from its facility close to the Nissan assembly line in sequence for fitting to the correct model. Only 42 minutes elapse between the carpet being ordered and its being fitted to the car. This system also carries risks, however: the 2011 earthquake in Japan caused delays to the introduction of two new Toyota Prius models, and impacted on production in other global companies such as Caterpillar and General Motors.

The growth in the use of the internet has given rise to the development of online purchasing. Two main categories of marketplaces, or exchanges, have been created: **vertical electronic marketplaces** are industry specific, such as sites for the automotive and healthcare industries (e.g. www.covisint.com); **horizontal electronic marketplaces** cross industry boundaries and cater for supplies such as MROs (e.g. www.dgmarket.com) and services (www.upwork.com). Companies seeking supplies post their offers on these websites. Potential vendors then bid for the contracts electronically. Some companies report significant improvements in efficiency from managing their purchasing this way, through reducing the number of procurement staff involved in processing orders and increasing the potential global spread of vendors. This heightened competition presents challenges for suppliers. Social media platforms such as Facebook and LinkedIn have become a popular mechanism for firms to source employees and suppliers.

Where several operating units within a company have common requirements, and where there is an opportunity to strengthen a negotiating position by bulk buying, centralized purchasing is an attractive option. Centralization encourages purchasing specialists to concentrate their energies on a small group of products, thus enabling them to develop an extensive knowledge of cost factors and the operation of suppliers.[74]

For example, increasing concerns over the costs of healthcare have meant that many hospitals have centralized purchasing in procurement departments rather than devolving the activity to doctors and nurses as had been the case in the past. As a result, many contracts are put out to tender, often on a pan-European basis, with vendors selected on the basis of quality, cost and ability to deliver over a number of years. The net effect of this is that orders are much more difficult to secure but, once secured, are likely to be more long lasting. At the same time, organizational buying has become increasingly characterized by very close relationships between buyers and sellers. **Relationship marketing** is the process of creating, developing and enhancing relationships with customers and other stakeholders (see Marketing in Action 3.3). For example, Marks & Spencer has trading relationships with suppliers that stretch back almost a century. Such long-term relationships can have significant advantages for both buyer and seller. Risk is reduced for buyers as they get to know people in the supplier organization and know who to contact when problems arise. Communication is thus improved, and joint problem solving and design management can take place, with suppliers becoming, in effect, strategic

Marketing in Action 3.3
General Electric

> **Critical Thinking:** Below is a review of some of the innovative marketing conducted by General Electric (GE), which is a leader in social media. Read it and consider how social media marketing could be used by other business-to-business firms.

Social media marketing might initially appear to be the sole preserve of the business-to-consumer (B2C) marketer. However, according to a 2018 research study into B2B social media marketing by Omobono, not only can business-to-business (B2B) marketers benefit from social media, but it could be their most effective marketing channel of all. General Electric (GE) is one of the most exciting B2B companies and was an early mover on social media. GE are not necessarily going for direct sales via social media as their sales efforts take place elsewhere. Social media is used by the company to remain top of mind and to dust off this company founded back in the nineteenth century.

GE has been using Instagram to highlight its most important technological advancements, and in 2016, with the help of BBDO New York, the company created buzz by creating Invention Donkey, a character that 'hijacked' GE's Twitter account for the day, providing custom video tweets to those with questions about GE's latest technology. Previously, GE has used Instagram to give enthusiasts a behind-the-scenes look at what is happening at the company, even giving top Instagram influencers – the best way to get bonus marketing and PR – as well as a handful of super fans a chance to tour a GE aviation facility in Ohio, where the most advanced jet engines in the world are tested. Both influencers and fans shared their experiences via the widespread platform Instagram offered, while GE took a social media time travel throughout the company's 120-year history, posting a range of material, from archive photos from the 1939 World's Fair to today's awe-inspiring technological advances. GE gained more than 3,000 new followers thanks to more than 200,000 social media interactions and 3.5 million views.

GE has been nominated for, and has won, numerous awards, such as Best Brand on Vine, Best Fortune 500 Brand on Social Media, Twitter and Instagram categories. GE's much lauded approach was to humanize its brand, educate its followers and of course post stunning visuals of its technology in action. According to Linda Boff, GE chief marketing officer, 'Social started because we wanted to be having conversations with people: consumers, employees, investors, and anybody else that shares our passions. We try hard to focus on where we have the greatest opportunity to tell our story in a rich, accessible way.'

Based on: Chaffey, 2018;[75] Shahari, 2017;[76] Anonymous, 2018;[77] Meistrell, 2016[78]

partners. Sellers gain through closer knowledge of buyer requirements, and many companies have reorganized their sales forces to reflect the importance of managing customer relationships effectively – a process known as key account management. New product development can benefit from such close relationships. The development of machine-washable lamb's wool fabrics and easy-to-iron cotton shirts came about because of Marks & Spencer's close relationship with UK manufacturers.[79] The issue of relationship marketing will be dealt with in more detail in Chapter 7.

The traditional view of marketing is that supplier firms will actively seek out the requirements of customers and attempt to meet those needs better than the competition. However, purchasing is now taking on a more proactive, aggressive stance in acquiring the products and services needed to compete. This process, whereby the buyer attempts to persuade the supplier to provide exactly what the organization wants, is called **reverse marketing**.[80] Syngenta, an international supplier of chemicals, uses reverse marketing very effectively to target suppliers with a customized list of requirements concerning delivery times, delivery success rates and how often sales visits should occur. The growth of reverse marketing presents two key benefits to suppliers who are willing to listen to the buyer's proposition and carefully consider its merits: first, it provides the opportunity to develop a stronger and longer-lasting relationship with the customer; second, it could be a source of new product opportunities that may be developed to a broader customer base later on.

Finally in B2B contexts, a firm may not actually make a purchase but rather it simply leases a product. A lease is a contract by which the owner of an asset (e.g. a car) grants the right to use the asset for a period of time to another party in exchange for the payment of rent.[81] The benefits to the customer are that a leasing arrangement avoids the need to pay the cash purchase price of the product or service, is a hedge against fast product obsolescence, may have tax advantages, avoids the problem of equipment disposal and, with certain types of leasing contract, avoids some maintenance costs. These benefits need to be weighed against the costs of leasing, which may be higher than outright buying.

Summary

This chapter has examined the nature of customer behaviour and the key influences on customer behaviour. The following key issues were addressed.

1. The differences between consumer and organizational buying behaviour. In the latter, the buying decision process involves more stages, the input of more parties and greater levels of negotiation. Technical and economic choice criteria tend to play a greater role in organizational buying.

2. Who buys – the five roles in the buying decision-making process: initiator, influencer, decider, buyer and user. Different people may play different roles, particularly in a family purchase and, for marketers, identifying the decider is critical.

3. There are two main theories of consumer behaviour: the information processing approach, which sees consumption as a rational, utilitarian process, and consumer culture theory, which sees consumption as a social activity rooted in contexts.

4. The buying decision process, involving the stages of need recognition, search for alternatives, evaluation of alternatives, purchase and post-purchase evaluation. In the case of high-involvement purchases, consumers will typically go through all these stages, whereas in a low-involvement situation, they may move directly from need recognition to purchase.

5. The main choice criteria used in making purchase decisions – namely, technical, economic, social and personal criteria. In consumer buyer behaviour, social and personal criteria are very important as consumers build their identities through product and service selection.

6. The main influences on consumer buying behaviour: personal influences and social influences. At any given time, there are myriad factors that may influence a consumer's purchase decision. Deeply embedded emotional elements such as conditioning, learning, attitudes and personality are key drivers of consumption decisions.

(continued)

7. The impact of influencers on consumer purchase decisions. Influencer marketing involves using individuals that have social media influence to reach consumers. It harnesses the growing impact of digital technologies to influence consumers' brand awareness, attitudes and purchase intentions.

8. The main influences on organizational buying behaviour: the buy class, the product type and the importance of purchase. For example, a major investment in plant and equipment that is critical to the organization and is a new task purchase will necessitate the involvement of many parties in the organization and will take time before a decision is made.

9. The key features of organizational purchasing practice: just-in-time purchasing, online purchasing, centralized purchasing, relationship marketing, reverse marketing and leasing. Organizational purchasing at one level presents opportunities for reverse marketing and relationship building with suppliers, but at a different level is driven by efficiency concerns that are managed through centralized and online purchasing.

Study questions

1. What are the differences between organizational buying behaviour and consumer buying behaviour?

2. Choose a recent purchase that included not only yourself but also other people in making the decision. What role(s) did you play in the buying centre? What roles did these other people play and how did they influence your choice?

3. Compare and contrast the information processing approach and the consumer culture approach to our understanding of how consumers behave in the ways that they do.

4. Review the choice criteria influencing some recent purchases, such as a hairstyle, a meal, etc.

5. Describe the recent trends in just-in-time purchasing, online purchasing and centralized purchasing. Discuss the implications of these trends for marketers in vendor firms.

6. Outline the benefits and challenges associated with using influencer marketing. Highlight some of the main social media influencers relevant to your market, age group and interests. Assess the extent to which these influencers have affected your awareness of brands, attitudes towards brands and your purchase intentions.

Suggested reading

Almquist, E., Cleghorn, J. and **Sherer, L.** (2018) The B2B elements of value, *Harvard Business Review*, 96(2), 72–81.

Anderson, J.C., Narus, J.A. and **van Rossum, W.** (2006) Customer value propositions in business markets, *Harvard Business Review*, 84(3), 90–9.

Arnould, E. and **Thompson, C.** (2005) Consumer culture theory (CCT): twenty years of research, *Journal of Consumer Research*, 31(4), 868–82.

Gladwell, M. (2005) *Blink: The Power of Thinking Without Thinking.* London: Allen Lane.

Lim, X.J., Radzol, A., Cheah, J. and **Wong, M.W.** (2017) The impact of social media influencers on purchase intention and the mediation effects of consumer attitude, *Asian Journal of Business Research*, 7(2), 19–36.

Miller, G. (2009) *Spent: Sex, Evolution and the Secrets of Consumerism.* London: William Heinemann.

Spenner, P. and **Freeman, K.** (2012) To keep your customers, keep it simple, *Harvard Business Review*, 90(5), 108–14.

Stanton, S., Sinnott-Armstrong, W. and **Huettel, S.** (2017) Neuromarketing: ethical implications of its use and potential misuse, *Journal of Business Ethics*, 144(4), 799–811.

Wisenblit, J., Priluck, R. and **Pirog, S.** (2013) The influence of parental styles on children's consumption, *Journal of Consumer Marketing*, 30(4), 320–7.

References

1. **Sheppard, C.** (2018) What's Fortnite's age rating certificate, how many children play the video game and what did the NCA say about child grooming? *Sun*, 12 April; **Robertson, A.** (2018) Fortnite: what is the 'addictive' viral game and why are parents so worried? *Daily Record*, 12 March; **Damour, L.** (2018) Parenting the Fortnite addict, *New York Times*, 30 April; **Anonymous** (2018) Should parents worry that their kids are playing Fortnite: Battle Royale? *Irish Independent*, 15 March; **Stewart, C.** (2018) Fortnite gamers not addicted claims expert, *Scottish Herald*, 29 March.

2. **Blackwell, R.D., Miniard, P.W.** and **Engel, J.F.** (2000) *Consumer Behaviour*. Orlando, FL: Dryden, 174.

3. **Anonymous** (2017) Microsoft to sponsor CoderDojo Coolest Projects Showcase 2017, *Irish Tech News*, 13 June.

4. **Arnould, E.** and **Thompson, C.** (2005) Consumer culture theory (CCT): twenty years of research, *Journal of Consumer Research*, 31(4), 868–82.

5. **Nyoni, T.** and **Wellington Garikai, B.** (2017) Neuromarketing methodologies: more brain scans or brain scams? *Journal of Economics and Finance*, 21(3), 30–8.

6. **Alviro, L., Constantinides, E.** and **Franco, M.** (2018) Consumer behaviour: marginal utility as a parameter in neuromarketing research, *International Journal of Marketing Studies*, 10(1), 90–106.

7. **Flores, J., Baruca, A.** and **Saldivar, R.** (2014) Is neuromarketing ethical? Consumers say yes. Consumers say no, *Journal of Legal, Ethical and Regulatory Issues*, 17(2), 77–91.

8. **Mileti, A., Guido, G.** and **Prete, I.** (2016) Nanomarketing: a new frontier for neuromarketing, *Psychology and Marketing*, 33(8), 664–74.

9. **Stanton, S., Sinnott-Armstrong, W.** and **Huettel, S.** (2017) Neuromarketing: ethical implications of its use and potential misuse, *Journal of Business Ethics*, 144(4), 799–811.

10. **Anonymous** (2018) About CCT. Available at http://cctweb.org/about (accessed 7 June 2018).

11. **Szmigin, I.** and **Piacentini, M.** (2015) *Consumer Behaviour*. London: Oxford University Press.

12. **Burrows, D.** (2014) How to use ethnography for in-depth consumer insight. Available at https://www.marketingweek.com/2014/05/09/how-to-use-ethnography-for-in-depth-consumer-insight/ (accessed 7 June 2018).

13. **Rewinska, D.** (2017) 6 creative examples of ethnographic research in action. Available at https://www.flexmr.net/blog/qualitative-research/2017/1/creative-examples-of-ethnographic-research.aspx (accessed 7 June 2018).

14. **Engel, J.F., Blackwell, R.D.** and **Miniard, P.W.** (1990) *Consumer Behavior*. Orlando FL: Dryden, 29.

15. **Hawkins, D.I., Best, R.J.** and **Coney, K.A.** (1989) *Consumer Behavior: Implications for Marketing Strategy*. Boston, MA: Irwin, 30.

16. **Kuusela, H., Spence, M.T.** and **Kanto, A.J.** (1998) Expertise effects on prechoice decision processes and final outcomes: a protocol analysis, *European Journal of Marketing*, 32(5/6), 559–76.

17. **Blackwell, R.D., Miniard, P.W.** and **Engel, J.F.** (2000) *Consumer Behavior*. Orlando, FL: Dryden, 34.

18. **Elliot, R.** and **Hamilton, E.** (1991) Consumer choice tactics and leisure activities, *International Journal of Advertising*, 10, 325–32.

19. **Laurent, G.** and **Kapferer, J.N.** (1985) Measuring consumer involvement profiles, *Journal of Marketing Research*, 12(February), 41–53.

20. **Hawkins, D.I., Best, R.J.** and **Coney, K.A.** (1989) *Consumer Behavior: Implications for Marketing Strategy*. Boston, MA: Irwin.

21. **MacArthur, B.** (2015) The top 3 comparison shopping engines for online merchants, *YOTTAA*, 14 December.

22. **Arora, N.** (2016) Is that a good price? How online research affects in-person purchases, *Wisconsin School of Business*, 21 January.

23. **Anonymous** (2018) Everything you need to know about price comparison sites, *Telegraph*, 1 February.

24. **Europe Economics** (2017) Price comparison websites: consumer saviour or cause for concern? *Europe Economics*, 12 April.

25. **Barrett, C.** (2018) Price comparison websites are far from epic, *Financial Times*, 29 September.

26. **Court, D., Elzinga, D., Mulder, S.** and **Jorgen Vetvik, O.** (2009) The consumer decision journey, *McKinsey Quarterly*, 3, 1–11.

27. **Dias, J., Ionitiu, O., Lhuer, X.** and **van Ouwerkerk, J.** (2016) The four pillars of distinctive customer journeys, *McKinsey Quarterly*, August, 1–5.

28. **Almquist, E., Cleghorn, J.** and **Sherer, L.** (2018) The B2B elements of value, *Harvard Business Review*, 96(2), 72–81.

29. **Abraham, M.** (2015) Unlocking the influence of brand in the B2B space, *Brand Cap*, June.

30. **Anonymous** (2011) I've got you labelled, *The Economist*, 2 April, 74.

31. **Engel, J.F., Blackwell, R.D.** and **Miniard, P.W.** (1990) *Consumer Behavior*. Orlando, FL: Dryden, 363.

32. **Williams, K.C.** (1981) *Behavioural Aspects of Marketing*. London: Heinemann.

33. **Lindstrom, M.** (2009) *Buyology: How Everything We Believe About Why We Buy is Wrong*. London: Random House Books, 38.

34. **Ratneshwar, S., Warlop, L., Mick, D.G.** and **Seegar, G.** (1997) Benefit salience and consumers' selective attention to product features, *International Journal of Research in Marketing*, 14, 245–9.

35. **Levin, L.P.** and **Gaeth, G.J.** (1988) Framing of attribute information before and after consuming the product, *Journal of Consumer Research*, 15(December), 374–8.

36. **Anonymous** (2008) The way the brain buys, *The Economist*, 20 December, 99–101.

37. **O'Morain, P.** (2008) The fascinating facts about ladies in red, *Irish Times HealthPlus*, 11 November, 14.

38. **Gladwell, M.** (2005) *Blink: The Power of Thinking Without Thinking.* London: Allen Lane.

39. **Saad, G.** (2007) *The Evolutionary Bases of Consumption.* Hillsdale, NJ: Lawrence Erlbaum.

40. **De Mers, Y. (2016)** Five examples of rebranding done right, *Forbes*, 7 July.

41. **Anonymous** (2016) The grey market: older consumers will reshape the business landscape, *The Economist*, 7 April.

42. **Kassarjan, H.H.** (1971) Personality and consumer behavior: a review, *Journal of Marketing Research*, November, 409–18.

43. **Miller, G.** (2009) *Spent: Sex, Evolution and the Secrets of Consumerism.* London: William Heinemann.

44. **Million, M.** (2018) Virgin America: a lesson in brand personality. Available at https://www.fullsurge.com/blog/virgin-america-lesson-brand-personality (accessed 14 May 2018).

45. **Anonymous** (2018) What is brand personality? Available at http://www.opento.com/blog/brand_personality (accessed 14 May 2018).

46. **Branson, R.** (2016) The golden rule of marketing. Available at https://www.virgin.com/richard-branson/golden-rule-marketing (accessed 14 May 2018).

47. **Anonymous** (2015) Four branding ideas you can learn from Virgin Airline. Available at http://www.activecamps.com/lets-talk-camp/2015/10/4-branding-ideas-you-can-learn-from-virgin-airline (accessed 14 May 2018).

48. **O'Brien, S.** and **Ford, R.** (1988) Can we at last say goodbye to social class? *Journal of the Market Research Society*, 30(3), 289–332.

49. **Carter, M.** (2005) A brand new opportunity in the empty nest, *Financial Times*, 5 December, 14.

50. **Anonymous** (2005) This sceptred aisle, *The Economist*, 6 August, 29.

51. **Anonymous** (2017) Lidl tops Waitrose to become UK's seventh biggest grocer, *BBC*, 22 August.

52. **Hootsuite** (2018) Global Digital Report 2018, *Hootsuite: We Are Social.*

53. **Hoffman, D., Novak, T.** and **Stein, R.** (2013) The digital consumer, in R. Belk and R. Llamas (eds) *The Routledge Companion to Digital Consumption.* Oxon: Routledge.

54. **Anonymous** (2016) What is influencer marketing? *Mediakix*, 1 February.

55. **Lim, X.J., Radzol, A., Cheah, J.-H.** and **Wong, M.W.** (2017) The impact of social media influencers on purchase intention and the mediation effects of consumer attitude, *Asian Journal of Business Research*, 7(2), 19–36.

56. **Wong, R.** (2018) TV may affect the brain, but influencer marketing affects the heart, *Adweek*, 26 January.

57. **Anonymous** (2016) What is influencer marketing? *Mediakix*, 1 February.

58. **Sassine, R.** (2017) What is the impact of social media influencers? *Digitalmeup*, 6 April.

59. **Tapinfluence** (2017) What is influencer marketing? Available at https://www.tapinfluence.com/blog-what-is-influencer-marketing/ (accessed 14 May 2018).

60. **Sassine, R.** (2017) What is the impact of social media influencers? *Digitalmeup*, 6 April.

61. **Anonymous** (2018) The psychology of following: how social influencers impact purchasing behaviour, *Agility PR Solutions*, 3 January.

62. **Anonymous** (2016) What is influencer marketing? *Mediakix*, 1 February.

63. **Anonymous** (2016) Nespresso's Instagram influencer marketing campaign, *Mediakix*, 8 January.

64. **Lua, A.** (2018) How much does social media influencer marketing cost? *Buffer*, 4 April.

65. **Annicelli, C.** (2017) Influencer marketing prices rising in the UK, *Emarketer*, 3 August.

66. **Sassine, R.** (2017) What is the impact of social media influencers? *Digitalmeup*, 6 April.

67. **Wong, R.** (2018) TV may affect the brain, but influencer marketing affects the heart, *Adweek*, 26 January.

68. **Fox, J.** (2018) Commission to review role of social media influencers, *RTE*, 19 January.

69. **Anonymous** (2018) UK public wants rules on social influencers tightened up, *Promo Marketing*, 15 February.

70. **Wong, R.** (2018) TV may affect the brain, but influencer marketing affects the heart, *Adweek*, 26 January.

71. **Simon, B.** (2005) Car parts groups face a depressed future, *Financial Times*, 18 May, 31.

72. **Cardozo, R.N.** (1980) Situational segmentation of industrial markets, *European Journal of Marketing*, 14(5/6), 264–76.

73. **Robinson, P.J., Faris, C.W.** and **Wind, Y.** (1967) *Industrial Buying and Creative Marketing.* Boston, MA: Allyn & Bacon.

74. **Briefly, E.G., Eccles, R.W.** and **Reeder, R.R.** (1998) *Business Marketing.* Englewood Cliffs, NJ: Prentice-Hall, 105.

75. **Chaffey, D.** (2018) Using social media marketing in B2B markets, *Smart Insights*, 6 April.

76. **Shahari, F.** (2017) B2B social media case study: General Electric. Available at https://cloudrock.asia/blog/b2b-social-media-case-study-general-electric (accessed 14 May 2018).

77. **Anonymous** (2018) The 8 best B2B social media success stories the world has ever seen. Available at http://cultbizztech.com/the-8-best-b2b-social-media-success-stories-the-world-has-ever-seen (accessed 14 May 2018).

78. **Meistrell, M.** (2016) Top B2B social media case studies for 2016. Available at https://trueinfluence.com/b2b-social-media-case-studies-for-2016 (accessed 14 May 2018).

79. **Thornhill, J.** and **Rawsthorn, A.** (1992) Why sparks are flying, *Financial Times*, 8 January, 12.

80. **Blenkhorn, D.L.** and **Banting, P.M.** (1991) How reverse marketing changes buyer–seller roles, *Industrial Marketing Management*, 20, 185–91.

81. **Anderson, F.** and **Lazer, W.** (1978) Industrial lease marketing, *Journal of Marketing*, 42(January), 71–9.

'*D*oes our brand suck?' This is not a question that is often raised in marketing or board meetings. However, a quick search on Google may reveal what some consumers *really* think and feel about the company's brand. Customers who have been waiting to talk to a call centre operator, only to be shifted to another operator or a computerized robotic-voice menu system are left annoyed and frustrated. Potential customers who have been given the cold shoulder in a high-end boutique experience feelings of anger and contempt. These dissatisfied consumers frequently harbour strong feelings and thoughts about revenge, and – depending on the severity of the 'offence' – some even go as far as to act on them.

Call out culture

The empowered consumer is not afraid to call brands to account. Euromonitor International identified *call out culture* in its Top 10 Global Consumer Trends for 2018. Consumers are increasingly taking a stand, and negative opinions and experiences are likely to be shared, facilitated by near instantaneous online communication and the widespread use of social media. It has never been easier for consumers to take on global brands, with potentially damaging consequences for brand image and the bottom line. In a US survey, nearly half of people have used social media to complain about a business. And this matters. Who hasn't read an online review when buying a book, consumer electronics contraption, or before booking a hotel or restaurant?

TripAdvisor is the world's largest travel site, which allows users to upload hotel and restaurant reviews. Although some hospitality brands, such as Four Seasons Hotel London at Park Lane, enjoy a maximum five-star rating, it is apparent that many other luxury hotels do not always meet the expectations of the discerning traveller. Another review site is Trustpilot, which gives customers an amplified voice to provide feedback on their online experience. For example, Ryanair.com has a Trust Score of 1.5/5 based on 2,525 reviews. Reviews of headlines posted, such as 'Rip off', 'Worst budget airline',

'Never again this **** company' and 'Worst company in the world', certainly do not paint an ideal picture of the low-cost airline. It is the collective experiences – positive and negative – of other genuine consumers that provide the consumer with information that enables them to decide whether to select one brand over another.

Brand hate

Consumers are often left emotionally outraged, fuming or angry by company failures, and they want their feelings to be known by as many people as possible. They want to hurt the organization guilty of ruining their experience. These extremely disgruntled customers, who want to let off steam, make their suffering public, harm the brand reputation and thus get revenge, can also turn to brand-specific websites such as ihateryanair.co.uk to share their grievances. In acute cases, this can result in consumers' attitudes being permanently changed to an enduring hatred of the brand, and some of these individuals become – and remain – vocal about it. Former customers who have felt extreme negative emotions about a company's brand might therefore develop a strong and persistent negative attitude about the company and its brands in general. This attitude risks contagion to other potential consumers via ferocious negative feedback online and offline.

Belief-driven buyers

This is, however, just the tip of the iceberg. Brand scandals increasingly seem to be an omnipresent phenomenon as the string of high-profile corporate scandals continues to dominate the media space.

The arrest of two African-American men in a Philadelphia Starbucks in April 2018 had put the coffee chain on the defensive. Although Starbucks' CEO had apologized following accusations of racial profiling by the company, the company was not let off the hook. #DeleteStarbucks continue to trend on social media and the brand saw a 21-point decrease in its 'Buzz score', a reputational tracker.

In addition, consumers are more willing than ever to 'punish' companies. A 2017 Edelman Earned Brand survey of 14,000 people in 14 countries found that 57 per cent of consumers will buy or boycott a brand solely because of its position on a social or political issue. These so-called *belief-driven buyers* were dominant among the millennial generational segment, and most active in developing countries such as China and India.

#Activism

'Hashtag activism' is a clear illustration of consumers using social media such as Twitter not only to raise awareness of underlying issues but to exert pressure on corporations to change business practices. These are not so-called 'extremists', but regular consumers. In other words, anti-brand sentiment is no longer an exception, but has evolved into mainstream experience. For example, #BoycottUnited was rapidly adopted when a United Airlines passenger was filmed by another passenger being brusquely and forcibly removed from an overbooked aircraft.

Conversations about United Airlines quickly dominated social media and #BoycottUnited, #BoycottUnitedAirlines and #NeverAgainFlyUnited were just some of the many hashtags that came to characterize the desire of many customers to punish the brand. The majority of these people were not directly involved in the service failure. It ignited a media firestorm, which continued in the public domain via popular network US talkshow hosts, who were quick to cruelly mock the airline. Additionally, nearly US$1 billion was temporarily wiped off the company's market value. The incident had even attracted the attention of US policy-makers and the company's chief executive officer, Oscar Munoz, was convoked to, and harshly scolded at, a four-hour congressional hearing.

The hashtag #DeleteFacebook is another manifest example of consumers attacking a company in the light of allegations that the personal data of about 50 million Facebook users, including CEO Mark Zuckerberg's own personal data, had been harvested and shared with third parties, which included Donald Trump's presidential campaign managers. A total of 177,000 people have already signed a Change.org petition asking Facebook to provide drastically better protection of their data. Facebook is a case where its CEO is a well-known personality who has already attracted extreme negative attitudes (e.g. #Zucked, #Zucked Over) towards himself and his corporate creation. Once again, US Congress convoked a CEO for a gruelling examination of corporate ethical, and potentially legal, failures. The Facebook privacy crisis just might have long-lasting repercussions for the company, as well as the entire Big Data sector across the world.

Message amplification

Negative publicity can certainly spread like wildfire: 24/7 news cycles, combined with social media offer a lightning-fast media outlet leviathan. Moreover, the

▶ intervention of key opinion influencers can vastly amplify the anti-brand message. For example, WhatsApp co-founder Brian Acton, and Elon Musk, CEO of Tesla and Space X, endorsed the #DeleteFacebook campaign. Celebrities such as Cher and Will Ferrell have decided to avoid the brand by boycott, and have closed their accounts. Indeed, the use of celebrities to promote numerous boycott campaigns has a long history. For example, former *Baywatch* actress and model, Pamela Anderson, has been an ambassador for animal rights group PETA for more than 20 years and has campaigned against a series of companies, including KFC and SeaWorld.

Moral agenda

Consumers may boycott a brand because of its perceived disrespect for human rights, the natural environment or involvement in unethical business practices. However, it seems that consumers are becoming more concerned beyond the traditional realms of corporate social responsibility. For example, the #GrabYourWallet campaign encourages consumers to boycott brands associated with presidential politics: the Trump family itself.

The politicization of many issues has indeed forced companies to take a political position. In a US survey, two-thirds of consumers say it is important for brands to take public stands on social and political issues. Kellogg's, BMW, Visa and Lufthansa are among a number of companies that took the decision to withdraw advertising from the news and opinion website Breitbart.com, which is widely perceived to be an outlet for the alt-right political movement. In a similar vein, brands such as United Airlines, Delta Air Lines and Hertz terminated ties with the National Rifle Association (NRA) following the Florida shooting incident in February 2018. Consumers are ready and willing to punish companies for perceived moral shortcomings.

Reputational crisis

Brands have never been under such intense scrutiny. The implications of this evolution may have a major impact on the bottom line. The reputational crisis that engulfed Facebook (#DeleteFacebook) resulted into a loss of nearly US$50 billion in market value in two days following revelations of data breach allegations. It is likely that Facebook will be able to ride out the storm, but consumers are less willing to forgive companies that fall short, and governments are becoming less likely to ignore big business's perceived ethical failures.

Loss of trust and a damaged reputation after the perceived brand failure of many high-profile brands might be felt for many years. The long-established US bank Wells Fargo created as many as 2 million fake bank and credit card accounts between 2011 and 2015. A subsequent survey of bank customers found that negative perceptions of Wells Fargo had increased from 15 per cent to 52 per cent, while 30 per cent of Wells Fargo customers surveyed claim they are actively exploring leaving the bank and 14 per cent say they have already decided to switch banks. More than half of non-Wells Fargo customers say they are not likely to join the bank. This is without doubt a shot across the bow for all companies steering into dangerous ethical waters.

Brand redemption

No company or organization is immune from consumers taking direct action as a result of reputational loss. A recent example is the NGO Oxfam, which lost 7,000 regular donors after it was revealed that the aid agency's staff had sexually exploited victims of the Haiti earthquake in 2010.

Organizations such as Oxfam, Facebook, Starbucks, United Airlines and Wells Fargo obviously need to restore their reputations if they are to win back the trust and loyalty of consumers – past, present and future. However, this is no straightforward task. As with companies accused of 'greenwashing', consumers can easily detect a 'public relations redemption' campaign that simulates the impression of a company's efforts at brand image salvation.

Although many brands may polarize, it doesn't mean that they have to 'suck'. Brand managers need to be aware of what can be done to avoid or dissipate #BrandHate.

Questions

1. Conduct a search on the internet, including anti-brand sites, in order to identify the potential causes and consequences of brand hate.
2. Using the consumer decision-making process, discuss how and why consumers reject brands.
3. What advice would you give to brand managers whose brands have become victims of brand hate?

This case was prepared by Glyn Atwal, Burgundy School of Business, and Douglas Bryson, Rennes School of Business, from various published sources as a basis for class discussion rather than to show effective or ineffective management.

Chapter 4

Marketing Research and Customer Insights

Chapter outline

The role of customer insights

Marketing information systems

Market intelligence

Approaches to conducting marketing research

Stages in the marketing research process

Learning outcomes

By the end of this chapter you will:

1   Understand the importance of marketing information and customer insights

2   Explain what is meant by a marketing information system

3   Analyse the main types of internal market information

4   Explain what is meant by market intelligence

5   Understand the opportunities and challenges presented by Big Data

6   Understand the different dimensions of marketing research

7   Explain the main stages in the marketing research process

8   Describe the differences between qualitative and quantitative research

The future looks bright for electric vehicles

The possibility of owning an electric car is looking more likely as research within the automobile industry states that, by 2025, one in every six new cars will be electric, with Europe having the highest electric vehicle penetration, followed by China.[1] By 2024, it is anticipated that the cost of electric car ownership (buying and fuelling) in countries such as Germany will be the same as a conventional petrol or diesel model. To add to this, motorists will not have to fret about the range offer as, by the 2020s, the distance between charges will go to 400 miles and above, from 100–150 miles today. Various car companies are leading the way, such as the Swedish firm Volvo, which has announced that, from 2019, it will launch only hybrid, plug-in hybrid or 100 per cent electric cars.[2]

This is an exciting time in the automobile industry, with BMW, Ford, GM, Honda, Hyundai, Nissan, Tesla Motors, Toyota, Volkswagen, Volvo and many more racing to compete in this market, with sparking new and innovative product designs. Despite this race, the electric vehicle market is still very niche;[3] how much do these companies understand about what all customers need and want in a new electric vehicle?

In a response to this gap in market knowledge, General Electric (GE) carried out a survey that looked at the needs of drivers when considering purchasing an electric vehicle. The survey of 1,000 car owners in 2017, with 50 per cent driving gas-powered and 50 per cent currently driving a hybrid or electric vehicle identified the following three needs.

1 The Green Team, known as **'Environmentally Conscious'** – who view EVs as 'symbolizing their commitment to the planet, sustainability and fossil fuel independence'.
2 The Wow Factor, known as **'Technology and Car Driven'** – who view 'technology as cool – representing the cutting-edge innovation that puts them ahead of the pack'. This group typically reflects early adopters.
3 The Wallet Matters, known as **'Frugal Drivers'** – who view EVs as a way of 'permanently reducing their travel costs – with the added benefit of being environmentally friendly'.

Ultimately, IPOS research suggests that automakers can confidently target millennials, who have an early adoption attitude and broad tech knowledge. However, automakers will also need to note that traditional features such as safety and design cannot be overlooked and that consumer needs are understood.[4] This research serves to support existing theory on consumer EV adoption. Significant advancements are being made in the consideration of consumer adoption of EVs, which are deemed a more disruptive innovation in transportation technology and ultimately pose a different behavioural demand on the consumer.[5] Interestingly from this research, consumers' perception of EVs as the cars of the future is hindering adoption as they are not yet perceived to be the cars of the present (not needed as yet). However, this therefore challenges EV manufacturers to continuously re-innovate EVs in order to enhance consumers' perception of them as an innovation over time.

The challenge for the automobile makers is to ensure the balance of thorough customer insight and research in conjunction with their desire to be the most innovative electric vehicle manufacturer in the world. The future of EVs is now here.

The role of customer insights

Customer insights play a significant role in decision-making[6] and it is clear that more or better research was required with the spectacular failures of the likes of New Coke, WAP technology and Google Wave. We will never know the level of insight that was or was not gleaned, but what is certain is that truly market-led companies recognize that they need to always be in touch with what is happening in the marketplace.

Customer needs are continually changing, often in ways that are very subtle. To innovate new forms of value for customers, accurate and timely customer insights are very important. The term **customer insight** can be defined as 'knowledge about the customer' that is valuable for a firm and that is distinct from customer information. It is important for firms to understand that 'information requires transformation to generate insight'.[7] These insights can inform everything from product innovation to product design and features, advertising campaign themes and so on (see Exhibit 4.1). For example, streaming giant Spotify cleverly used its own customer insight in its end-of-year campaigns, with advertisements that tuned in to people's listening choices from 2017 and translated them into 2018 'goals'. These hilarious advertisements were based on what its customer base (audience) might do in 2018 based on the events, cultural and political, of 2017.[8]

Exhibit 4.1 Spotify's use of data-driven customer insight from 2017 presented humorous outdoor global advertisements in 2018.

 Spotify Ad Insight: This outdoor global series of advertisements utilized customer data from 2017 to gain insight for design of 2018's 'goals' campaign.

For some companies, no major strategic decisions are made without first researching the market. But this activity goes far beyond commercial organizations. For example, political parties and record companies are heavy users of marketing research and often stand accused of over-dependence on it to shape everything from manifestos to new albums. Therefore organizations have a huge appetite for information to help them make the correct decisions. This information can play a key role in a whole variety of choices, including whether there is a market for a new product, what our current customers think of our service levels, how our brands are performing in the market, how effective our latest promotional campaign has been, and so on.

This chapter will examine the types of information that are available and how they can be used to assist better decision-making. Given the information age that we live in, this is a crucial activity, as organizations frequently suffer more from a surplus rather than a deficit of information.

It is clear that an increasing range of information sources available through a mass of media channels, together with more effective data capture methods, are creating new challenges for generating customer insight from this information, and managing its dissemination and use.[9] Being able to intelligently sort through all the information that is potentially available and convert it into usable customer insights is an important marketing task.

As a result, the marketing research industry is a huge one, estimated to be worth more than US$44.5 billion globally in 2016 and growing at a rate of 3.7 per cent annually, with an additional US$23.7 billion additional revenue generated from players for whom this is not a primary activity.[10] Table 4.1 provides details of levels of marketing research expenditure throughout the world. Market research also tends to follow market development. For example, some of the highest growth rates for market research have been in Africa, which achieved the position of fastest-growing region at 22.7 per cent. This growth is attributed to countries like Nigeria and Kenya, which have widened their measure of the research markets. Understandably these growing economies have attracted the interest of marketers.[11] The highest expenditure per capita is to be found in Europe. Defining the boundaries of marketing research is not easy. Casual discussions with customers at exhibitions or monitoring online forums can provide valuable informal information about their requirements, competitor activities and future happenings in the industry. More formal approaches include the conducting of marketing research studies or the development of marketing information systems. This chapter focuses on these formal methods of information provision.

Marketing information systems

Given the wide variety of information sources that an organization can potentially access, decisions about which types of information to gather are crucial. In the main, these are driven by what questions need to be answered. For example, if a company wants to examine whether there have been any changes in attitude towards its brand following on from recent marketing activities, it may informally monitor conversations that are happening online or more formally carry out periodic market research using customer panels that track changes in how the brand is perceived. For every research question, there is always a menu of answers and the main categories of information available are shown in Figure 4.1, which outlines the components of a **marketing information system**.

A marketing information system is defined as:[12]

a system in which marketing information is formally gathered, stored, analysed and distributed to managers in accord with their informational needs on a regular planned basis.

The system is built on an understanding of the information needs of marketing management, and supplies that information when, where and in the form that the manager requires it. Marketing information system (MkIS) design is important since the quality of a marketing information system has been shown to influence the effectiveness of decision-making.[13] The MkIS comprises four elements: internal market information, market intelligence, marketing research and environmental scanning (see Figure 4.1). The last element – environmental scanning – is discussed in Chapter 2 and each of the other elements will be examined in detail in this chapter. The volume of market information and insight that is to be managed clearly shows how important it is to effectively design and use a MkIS.

Marketing information systems should be designed to provide information and insights on a selective basis where it is useful in assisting decisions. Senior management should conspicuously support use of the system.[14] These recommendations are in line with Ackoff's view[15] that a prime task of an information system is to eliminate irrelevant information by tailoring what is provided to the individual manager's needs. It is also consistent with Kohli and Jaworski's view that a market orientation is essentially the organization-wide generation and dissemination of, and responsiveness to, market intelligence.[16]

Marketing research is more likely to be used if researchers appreciate not only the technical aspects of research, but also the need for clarity in report presentation and the political dimension of information provision. It is unlikely that marketing research reports will be used in decision-making if the results threaten the status quo or are likely to have adverse political repercussions. Therefore, perfectly valid and useful information may sometimes be ignored in decision-making for reasons other than difficulties with the way the research was conducted. However, accurate and timely customer insights are crucial to an organization becoming a truly market-led enterprise.

Table 4.1 Global marketing research expenditure 2016 (selected countries)

Country	Turnover in US$ million	Spend per capita in US$
UK	6,642	101.29
France	2,334	36.13
Sweden	357	35.75
Germany	3,321	33.34
Norway	107	20.37
Denmark	121	21.21
USA	19,487	60.28
Switzerland	205	24.61
Australia	791	32.56
Finland	91	16.51
Netherlands	460	27.03
Ireland	80	17.11
Belgium	143	12.64
Canada	345	9.52
New Zealand	86	18.21
Japan	1,891	14.90
Italy	614	10.13
Singapore	173	30.87
China	1,884	1.36

Source: Esomar (2017) *Global Market Research 2017: An Esomar Industry Report.*

Figure 4.1 The marketing information system (MkIS)

Internal market information — Environmental scanning — The marketing information system (MkIS) — Market intelligence — Marketing research

Internal market information

A very good place for an organization to begin answering a research problem is by looking at what information it currently already has available to it. This can take many forms. For example, it could include the review of the organization's website to collect detailed information about browsing and buying, as well as about the personnel working in the organization, such as salespeople or customer service people, who may have useful information regarding what is happening in the market.

Fashion retailer Zara encourages staff to have casual chats with consumers. This prized information shared by consumers about quality and new trends that they would like to see on the racks is recorded.[17] What also is essential is that employees are motivated to share this information and that systems are put in place to record, store and make available these customer insights. Advances in information technology (IT) mean that the retention of this type of information has improved dramatically. It can also help firms find and open new markets, deliver improved services to customers and streamline internal marketing processes.[18] Internal market information is particularly useful when companies want to get to know their current customers better. To do this the following techniques are used.

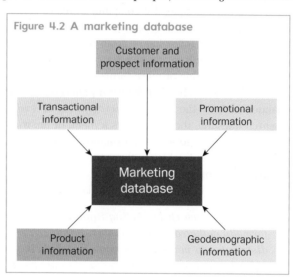

Figure 4.2 A marketing database

Marketing databases

Companies collect data on customers on an ongoing basis. Figure 4.2 shows the sort of information that is recorded and stored on a database. This will typically include each customer's key details such as their name, address and telephone number, along with transactional data such as type and frequency of purchase and purchase value. Transactional data may be sufficiently detailed to allow frequency, recency and amount of category (FARC) information to be extracted for each customer. Frequency refers to how often the customer buys. Recency measures when the customer last bought; if customers are waiting longer before they re-buy

Exhibit 4.2 Loyalty card schemes are used extensively by organizations to build up databases of customers.

(i.e. recency is decreasing) the reasons for this (e.g. less attractive offers or service problems) need to be explored. Amount measures the amount a customer has bought, usually in value terms, and category defines the type of product bought. Promotional information records responsiveness to promotional campaigns, while product information will include which products have been promoted, who responded, when and where. Finally, geodemographic information (which will be explored in more detail in Chapter 5) includes details of the location where customers live, and their social and lifestyle activities.

For example, retailers collect these data through loyalty card schemes, which are popular with supermarkets, department stores and so on (see Exhibit 4.2). Customers collect points that can be redeemed for cash or gifts, while at the same time the retailer collects valuable information about the customer each time the card is used (see Marketing in Action 4.1).

Banks have become heavy users of this type of information as they seek to manage more carefully consumers that have taken on debts such as mortgages and credit cards. Banks get information from a number of sources, including their own records, their links to other payment organizations, such as Visa and MasterCard, and specialist credit-checking agencies. Through the examination of this information, they can develop relatively accurate predictions of which customers are likely to default on a loan, or they can intervene earlier before debts become significant. Over the past five years, how people shop has changed, particularly with the growth of online retailers, with online sales of non-food items soaring from 11.6 per cent in 2012 to 24.1 per cent in 2017.[19] Companies like Amazon have grown rapidly, largely due to the management of consumer purchase information, which provides very detailed insights into consumers, and the types and number of products purchased. This can be seen through Amazon's very smart integrated recommendations system, which is neatly incorporated into every part of the purchasing system, or its use of database information to create emailed recommendations to account holders. The actual buying information of others has allowed for the accurate prediction of recommendations for other consumers when browsing the same or similar products.

Marketing in Action 4.1
Costa Coffee Club

Critical Thinking: Below is a review of a campaign conducted by Costa Coffee targeted at its Club members. Read it and critically evaluate why the promotion was so successful and the ways in which firms can use existing customer information better.

Almost all service organizations, such as hairdressers, coffee shops, DIY retailers and supermarkets, offer customers the opportunity to participate in a loyalty scheme or club. Some businesses use these simply as a way of rewarding regular visitors with discounts in an attempt to retain these customers. So, for example, a coffee shop may have a scheme whereby every 10th coffee is free or, alternatively, you collect points that can be redeemed against future purchases. Increasingly even coffee shops are using sophisticated data mining to glean as much information as possible about customers in order to maximize revenues and profits. Costa Coffee used a strategy of personalized communications with its members in order to increase sales. The company has a wide variety of touchpoints with its customers, including in-store purchases, Facebook contact, SMS messaging and email contact. These were aggregated to develop a more accurate profile of customers, ranging from heavy, loyal users to those who were lapsing or had lapsed. Communications were tailored specifically to each of these different customer groups. For example, if heavy users visited seven times per month, double points could be offered for an eighth visit. Email was the primary means chosen as it allowed for a volume of messages at low cost and the opportunity for interaction, as well as the facility to accurately measure response. Facebook was used in a similar way, allowing response via SMS, Facebook or email.

The results of the campaign were significant. In-store visits increased by 47 per cent and average spend per customer rose by 50 per cent. Points redemption rates increased by 84 per cent – nine times the target set – and the campaign as a whole generated £21 million in additional revenues for Costa.

Based on: Arnett (2013);[20] Direct Marketing Association (2012)[21]

Website analysis

For today's companies, website analysis forms a critical source of information for the marketing database. Measurements of the areas of the site most frequently visited, which products are purchased and the payment method used can be made. Indeed, one of the challenges of website analysis is coping with the vast volumes of data that can be produced. Whatever the challenges of measuring the size of the audience from an advertising point of view, there are several aspects to how consumers behave while visiting a website that owners should record and monitor. First, where did they come from – for example, did they come via a search engine or from a link on another site? In this case the use of keywords, branded and not branded, and phrases are important to identify that the right prospects. Second, where do they go once they are on the site? What options are selected, what visuals are viewed, and so on. How long did they spend on the website and what proportion of visitors

Exhibit 4.3 Consumer behaviour on websites can be analysed using Google Analytics.

'bounced' away from the site within a few seconds? This analysis may observe the top page entries as well as the top viewed pages. Did they respond to particular offers, promotions or site design changes? Most websites use Google Analytics or Bing Analytics to monitor these patterns and results are available on a daily or weekly basis (see Exhibit 4.3). And, if the company is an online retailer, what percentage of consumers proceeded to the checkout and, for those that didn't, at what stage in the buying process did they drop out? This web traffic data may also include performance data from campaigns or events. For example, PopUpRaces.ie is a professional race timing and event management business that operates online only. Each week they will contact their members with updates of upcoming race events. In this case, web analytics can be gathered on the number of click-throughs from a weblink inserted in a PopUpRace.ie email, as well as general activity on the member's viewing time and number of events attended.

Some of the key metrics for website analysis include the number of unique visitors, and information on these visitors and their levels of engagement with the site. Measurement of these variables is improving all the time, although some are still open to manipulation. *Unique users* (when a person visits a website) is a popular metric for measuring the number of visitors to a site. But it is problematic because 2 million unique users could mean anything from 2 million people visiting the site once, to one person visiting it 2 million times. It is impossible to know for sure. Information about website visitors is best captured by having them register to use the site, where they provide details of who they are and what they are interested in. *Page views* has been a popular way of measuring website engagement but many modern websites use a technology that allows pages to update parts of themselves, such as a share-price ticker, without having to reload and redraw the rest of the page. Therefore a user spending the entire day on Yahoo! Finance, for example, counts as only one page view. Thus more emphasis is now being put on website *interactivity*. 'Bounce rate', 'visit duration' and 'engagement time' suggest how long one or more people are interacting with a page, which in turn gives an indication of how 'engaged' they are, as does counting the number and types of comments left by visitors.

Market intelligence

Internal market information is very useful for developing deep insights about current customers, but is less useful for learning about potential new customers and competitor activity. For answers to these questions, the organization needs to begin looking outwards to what is happening in the marketplace. **Market intelligence** is something of a catch-all term to describe the systematic collection of data on what is happening in a market, including gathering information on customers, competitors and market developments. Increasingly, the term 'Big Data' is used to describe the wide range of external sources of information that can be used to aid marketing decision-making.[22] Everything that a modern customer does, such as websites searched, social media activity, telephone use, loyalty card use, purchases made, and so on, leaves a trail. The collection, aggregation and analysis of all of this information is becoming increasingly sophisticated, supported by vast data storage capabilities, faster software and people equipped with the necessary analytical skills.

Big Data characteristics

A number of key characteristics, known as the 4 Vs, have been identified and expanded upon to demonstrate how Big Data differs from other forms of data analysis that have existed up to now. The first is *Volume*. It is estimated that Walmart collects more than 2.5 million petabytes of data every hour from its customers' transactions. A petabyte is the equivalent of about 20 million filing cabinets' worth of text. The second is *Velocity*.

Data provided by mobile phones, credit card transactions and consumers checking in on social media sites are now real time or almost real time. The third is *Variety*.[23] However, the American multinational technology company, IBM, cites a fourth V in the form of *Veracity* (see Exhibit 4.4). This characteristic identifies the uncertain and imprecise nature of the data and is considered just as significant as the original 3 Vs.

Much debate exists in terms of the number of characteristics, and some scholars have suggested at least 7 Vs with the additional 3 Vs identified as *Variability, Visualization and Value*.[24] Data visualization refers to the techniques use in the encoding of information as a visual object. This ultimately serves to communicate information clearly and efficiently to the data user.

Exhibit 4.4 The four Vs of Big Data

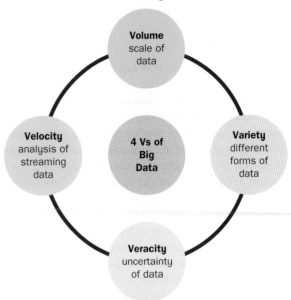

Big Data analysis

Big Data analysis enables marketers to answer all sorts of questions about customers. Do they buy products from competitors? What other categories of products and services are they interested in? What are their hobbies and interests? For example, supermarkets might provide the credit and debit card data of their customers to an analytics firm, which can then look for information that it already has on those card numbers from other companies to begin to build a profile of where customers are spending their money.[25] This can then be used to create offers designed to encourage consumers to spend more or to switch from competitors. Life insurance companies have begun to aggregate data about individuals from records like drug purchases, magazine subscriptions, credit card spending and social media activity like Facebook profiles, to determine whether they have sedentary, active or risk-taking lifestyles, all of which helps to determine their risk profile. Business-to-business firms use Big Data to find optimal price points for the thousands of product variants that many of them offer. As we have seen, data are increasingly being aggregated from a wide variety of sources. However to date, Big Data analysis is not for everyone. For smaller organizations or those without the resources to devote to Big Data initiatives, another source of market intelligence is secondary research.

The challenges with Big Data

As much as Big Data presents significant opportunities for businesses to understand the needs and wants of their customers, it is important to be aware of the challenges it presents. The first is the same as with all other data: is it reliable and valid? Second, Big Data is susceptible to robustness issues and spurious results if not analysed in a systematic way. This can also lead to the manipulation of the data (e.g. shaping the data to support a predetermined product or campaign idea). Third is the issue of ethics. An OECD (2016) report[26] identified the forms of Big Data most commonly used for social research as administrative data, records of commercial transactions, social media and other internet data, geospatial data and image data. These data differ from traditional research data (e.g. surveys) in that they have not been generated specifically by researchers for research purposes. As a result, the usual ethical protections that are applied at several points in the research data life cycle have not taken place[27] (see Figure 4.3). Finally the issue of privacy in relation to Big Data has come to the fore, with the emergence

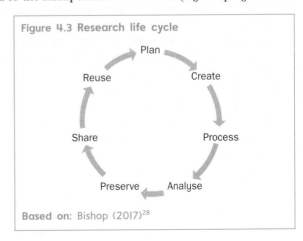

Figure 4.3 Research life cycle

Based on: Bishop (2017)[28]

of the European Union's General Data Protection Regulation (GDPR), enacted on 25 May 2018 to address this growing area of data availability (see Critical Marketing Perspective 4.1 and 10.1).

Social listening

As social media platforms have grown, so too has our ability to engage, participate and to contribute to online conversations through tweeting, liking a page, providing a review, suggesting solutions on a discussion forum, providing information on a message board, and so on. As a result of this interactivity, an increasing number of companies, governments and even political campaigns have started listening in on social media to gauge sentiments and public opinion. Even as far back as 2003, Oreo was monitoring public sentiment expressed about trans fats in its cookies. As a result, Oreo cut trans fats from its snack products. However, the question of measurement in relation to the comments posted online is significant in order to ensure accuracy. Therefore many marketers are likely to employ listening platforms that collect comments across different social media venues such as Twitter and Facebook as an aggregate or present them as venue-specific metrics. There are shortcomings if social media metrics do not account for differences across platforms.[29] Overall, this listening process challenges the methodology of the traditional asking process. For example, in the asking process, the researchers work rigorously on creating focused questionnaires and discussion guides to gather responses from consumers, as we shall see in the section on questionnaire design later in this chapter. Researchers using social media have access to the responses, opinions and thoughts of consumers on various brands regardless of whether they have even requested this opinion. This is important because it marks a significant change in the role of consumers. Social media platforms provide a voice for consumers, where they initiate changes they want, and potentially products or services to be developed or enhanced.[30]

Webscraping

As a result of the volumes and intensity at which data are being generated, larger companies have moved from the traditional manual copy-and-paste technique in favour of using a webscraping software program that is used to extract unstructured content from websites and convert the data into useful information. Webscraping, commonly known as web data extraction or web harvesting, is very much the first stage of the data-mining process, which will lead to analysis. Webscraping can be utilized in multiple ways to help business development, as described below.

1 **Price competitiveness and price comparison:** retailers such as Amazon will use webscraping not only to monitor their competitors' prices, such as those of Walmart, but to also improve their product attributes. In terms of price comparison, companies such as Booking.com will focus on site-specific webcrawling or price comparison website crawls to extract prices and product descriptions for analysis and comparison.

2 **To gather public opinion and to provide better-targeted ads to customers:** this is the scraping of data on what people are saying about certain companies and their products. This scraping will also assist in enabling ads to be better targeted to customers, with scraping largely based on number of customers to the page as well as extracting their behaviour and sentiment.

3 **Search engine results for SEO tracking:** this is the scraping of organic search results in order to find out what particular search terms are being used to reach the business and its competitors (see Chapter 11).

4 **Online reputation and the detection of fraudulent reviews:** the reputation of an organization is extremely important, and therefore it is necessary to scrape reviews of opinion leaders, trending topics, sentiment and demographic information to enable management of reputation. Through the detection of illegal writing of fake reviews, scraping detects which reviews to block, streamline or verify.

5 **The tracking of online presence and custom analytics:** in order to keep an eye on competitors, webscraping can extract details on business profiles and competitor reviews. In addition to this, for new websites or channels, custom analytics and duration information is extracted to get to know viewer behaviour.[31]

Ultimately, webscraping is an efficient tool that can make data gathering fast and scheduled. Traditionally, businesses have always listened out and sought information on their customers and competitors, but now they can monitor the movements of these groups automatically through webscraping technology.

Critical Marketing Perspective 4.1
Illegal harvesting of data on social media platforms: the Facebook–Cambridge Analytica data scandal

Big Data has been described as 'new oil'[32] due to the value that can be extracted from it. This was the case for Cambridge Analytica when it harvested data from an estimated 87 million Facebook users based on their profiles, to assist with insight for two of the most significant events within US and EU history: Donald Trump's election to the US Presidency and the UK 'Brexiting' the European Union. Facebook CEO Mark Zuckerberg has apologized repeatedly for the breach of data, which has wiped US$60 billion from Facebook's value[33] and concerned 2.2 billion monthly active users. But how did this happen?

It has emerged that Cambridge Analytica (CA), a data analytics company that worked with Donald Trump's election team and the winning Brexit campaign, obtained user data through a Facebook-linked app named 'thisisyourdigitallife'. Through the app, CA member Aleksandr Kogan paid Facebook users in exchange for a detailed personality test, supposedly for academic research purposes. Users consented and signed up, but controversary surrounds the ability of the app to pull personal data from the user's Facebook-linked friends' profiles without their consent, to build a system that could profile individual US voters in order to predict voting patterns, target them with personalized political advertisements and, ultimately, influence their voting decisions.[34] CA transformed the data into a political messaging weapon. This marketing activity included hyper targeting of voters during the presidential campaign to convince them to support Trump in the 2016 presidential election. For example, one highly personalized messaging advert contained a picture of a dictionary with the caption, 'Look up marriage and get back to me.' This was a compelling message for the conscientious who yearned for a source of order and structure in society. Another example was of a campaign advert containing a picture of a smiling male (father) and young female (daughter) at a shooting range, with the caption 'Not just our right. Our responsibility. Defend the Second Amendment.' Again this emotive topic appealed to the basic human rights of voters.[35]

This breach by CA went against Facebook's 'platform policy', which allowed collection of friends' data only to improve user experience on the app, and barred it being sold on or used for advertising, which CA had done.[36] Employer Christopher Wylie of CA stated, 'We exploited Facebook to harvest millions of people's profiles. And built models to exploit what we knew about them and target their inner demons. That was the basis the entire company was built on.'[37]

In 2016, Facebook had found out that information had been harvested on an unprecedented scale and approached CA to delete this data. But this never happened. At the time Facebook failed to alert users and took only limited steps to recover and secure the private information of more than 50 million individuals. However, Facebook has taken steps to create a tool that will tell users whether they were one of the 87 million users affected by this breach.[38] One of the largest data breaches in history caused CA to cease operations due to the loss of confidence of customers and suppliers. But will this put a stop to any further breaches or will it be the start of many more to emerge?

Reflection: How should Facebook seek to rebuild the trust of its users in general and do you think the value of the insight from the Facebook users' profiles is significant enough to really influence or persuade the ultimate voting decision of US voters in the presidential election?

Marketing research

If organizations cannot find the answers they are looking for through either existing internal information or market intelligence, then there is always the option of a marketing research study. **Marketing research** is defined as the systematic design, collection, analysis and reporting of data relevant to a specific marketing situation. Marketing research describes a broad range of potential activities, many of which are quite different from one another and therefore it can be classified in a number of different ways. For example, distinctions have been drawn between ad hoc and continuous research, custom and syndicated research, and also between exploratory, descriptive and casual research.

Ad hoc and continuous research

Ad hoc research focuses on a specific marketing problem and involves the collection of data at one point in time from one sample of respondents, such as a customer satisfaction study or an attitude survey. **Continuous research** involves conducting the same research on the same sample repeatedly to monitor the changes that are taking place over time. This form of research plays a key role in assessing trends in the market and one of the most popular forms of continuous research is the consumer panel.

When large numbers of consumers are recruited to provide information on their purchases over time, together they make up a **consumer panel**. For example, a grocery panel would record the brands, pack sizes, prices and stores used for a wide range of supermarket brands. By using the same consumers over a period of time, measures of brand loyalty and switching can be achieved, together with a demographic profile of the type of person who buys particular brands. Tesco has created a Shopper Thoughts panel comprising 60,000 households, some of which are not regular Tesco customers. Part of the research process is a facility called Net Chats, which is available in real time to Tesco management. Questions are posed to panel members in the morning, with responses from members received by the end of the day. This complements the behavioural data available through the Tesco loyalty card programme, to give the company a very complete view of the grocery shopper.

As this example shows, recent years have seen a significant growth in the use of technology in consumer panel research, with studies being conducted online or over the telephone, as well as face to face. Once participants are familiar with the researchers and have indicated a willingness to participate, then these more remote research approaches can work very effectively. For example, Metro Ireland, which markets a free newspaper to Dublin commuters, set up an online panel of 2,000 18- to 44-year-old urban dwellers, to which it sent six waves of questions and a series of mini-polls over 18 months. The insights derived from the panel informed Metro's decisions regarding everything from its editorial content to its marketing strategies to attract advertising.

The rapid growth of online blogs and discussion forums has given rise to a variant on the traditional customer panel. These types of discussion boards are everywhere on the internet, discussing anything from the best types of cosmetics, latest food and gym trends to the merits of new electronic gadgets. In most instances, they have not been formally created by corporations but the frank nature of the debate that often takes place on them makes them appealing to managers (see Marketing in Action 4.2). Some companies track these discussion groups to see what is being said about their brands and what trends are emerging. It is also a very cost-effective form of research as much of the monitoring can be done electronically. However, because this monitoring is generally covert, it may be disturbing for participants to learn that what they have to say is being studied by companies.

Marketing in Action 4.2
Open and closed online research communities

Critical Thinking: Below is a review of a discussion on the ideal participants in online research communities. Read it and reflect on the advantages and disadvantages for companies like easyJet and United Biscuits in engaging with participants in traditional consumer panels versus online research communities.

The market research environment appears to be changing, with a decline in response rates to surveys both online and offline, towards more engaged online consumers increasingly completing online reviews of products, services and companies. This shift may also be as a result of the potential savings resulting from self-documentation and analysis, estimated to be approximately 40 per cent when compared to that of traditional research.

The 'My Starbucks Idea' community exemplifies the increasing role that consumers play in research, posing their own questions and agenda setting for innovation. This is an example of an open community where anyone can join by simply creating an account and starting to participate.

(continued)

However, there are also closed communities, such as easyJet plc online research community (ORC) and United Biscuits ORC, through which membership is approved and by invitation only to specific individuals. easyJet ORC was established in 2008 and consists of approximately 1,800 members (600 female, 1,200 male). This type of research community employs voting polls, discussion forums, virtual focus groups, blog environments and functionality to allow community members to upload personal details, photos and videos. Each community has a dedicated moderator who posts email requests to members to contribute to the ORC on a specific topic of interest to the members on approximately a twice-weekly basis. Participants are not paid, but in the case of the easyJet ORC they are placed in a weekly free flights prize draw or similar incentives.

What is interesting about some of these closed communities is the method by which they select members – the 'ideal participants'. Some communities have a registration questionnaire, which determines the appropriateness of that individual within the community. But what makes a participant ideal? Research suggests that an ideal participant is one who possesses some form of social capital. This depends on the following two variables: (1) the trustworthiness of the social environment (that the participant trusts the market researchers to reciprocate in the future – e.g. sharing a summary of market research with the community – then the participant is more likely to take an active part in the community); (2) the extent of obligations to be met.

Despite the shift towards a more instant and consumer direct research community, it is clear, just as in traditional research, that trust is as important as the market research process itself for sharing ideas and passing on information.

Based on: Heinze, Ferneley and Child (2013)[39]

Custom and syndicated research

Custom research is research that is conducted for a single organization to provide specific answers to the questions that it has. But because companies have such an appetite for market information, an industry has grown up in the provision of **syndicated or omnibus research**. This is research that is collected by firms on a regular basis and then sold to other firms. Among the most popular types of syndicated research are retail audits and television viewership panels.

Major research firms, like the Nielsen Company, conduct **retail audits**. By gaining the co-operation of retail outlets (e.g. supermarkets), sales of brands can be measured by means of laser scans of barcodes on packaging, which are read at the checkout. Although brand loyalty and switching cannot be measured, retail audits can provide an accurate assessment of sales achieved by store. For example, Nielsen's BookScan service provides weekly sales data on more than 300,000 titles, collected from point-of-sale information from a variety of retailers.

A television viewership panel measures audience size on a minute-by-minute basis. Commercial breaks can be allocated ratings points (the proportion of the target audience watching) – the currency by which television advertising is bought and judged. In the UK, the system is controlled by the Broadcasters' Audience Research Board (BARB) and run by AGB and RSMB. AGB handles the measurement process and uses 'people meters' to record whether a set is on or off, which channel is being watched and, by means of a hand console, who is watching. Because of concerns about the extent to which viewers actually watch advertising, audience measurement companies are now providing measures of the viewership of advertising breaks as well as programmes. Technological developments continue to revolutionize television audience measurement. Personal video recorders (PVRs) build up a profile of viewers' likes and dislikes, and record their favourite programmes automatically, but the box also relays every button press on its remote control back to the manufacturer, providing exact details of what programmes people watch on which channels. A further challenge is presented by the growth in TV viewing on personal devices such as tablets and smartphones. Software has been developed that monitors the programming delivered from TV services like BBC iPlayer to an IP (internet protocol) address. It shows what programming is being viewed but not who is viewing it.[40]

Exploratory, descriptive and causal research

Finally, distinctions can also be drawn between exploratory, descriptive and causal research. **Exploratory research** is employed to carry out a preliminary exploration of a research area to gain some initial insights or to form some research hypotheses. It can be conducted in a variety of ways, such as examining secondary data that are available, conducting a focus group interview with some key customers or depth interviews with industry experts. To develop stronger conclusions about a research problem, **descriptive research** needs to be conducted. This may involve a survey of a large sample of customers that is representative of a population as a whole and allows the researchers to be confident that their views accurately represent those of the market. Finally, **causal research** seeks to establish cause-and-effect relationships. The most popular form of causal research is experimentation, where different variables are manipulated such as packaging design or advertising theme, and the effects of these changes on consumers are monitored. The processes through which these different forms of research are conducted are examined next.

Primary and secondary research

Because the data come to the researcher 'second-hand' (i.e. other people have compiled them), it is known as **secondary research**. (When the researcher actively collects new data – for example, by interviewing respondents – this is called primary research.) Secondary research should be carried out before primary research. Without the former, an expensive primary research survey might be commissioned to provide information that is already available from secondary sources. Increasingly, a significant amount of market information is available for purchase through companies like Mintel, Euromonitor and others.

There is a very wide variety of secondary sources of data available. These include government and European Commission statistics, publishers of reports and directories on markets, countries and industries, trade associations, banks, newspapers, magazines and journals. The range of sources of information available to researchers in the European Union is included in Appendix 4.1, which lists some of the major sources classified by research question.

Given the amount of potential sources of information that are available globally, for many the first port of call is an internet search engine, which can support the collection of both primary and secondary data. The amount of data stored on servers and that is uploaded online daily is a great source of information about the market and consumers (see Tables 4.2 and 4.3).

Table 4.2 Examples of secondary data sources online

Data about companies and organizations	Data about consumers
■ Directories ■ Companies' webpages (including social media) ■ Market research companies and databases ■ Government reports ■ Research results ■ Official statistics ■ Website and service analytics	■ Blogs ■ Social media pages ■ Databases ■ Browser data (site activity) ■ Search history ■ Purchase history

Table 4.3 Examples of primary data sources online

Qualitative	Quantitative	Mixed method
■ Video clips ■ Activity-capturing software ■ Users, experience recording ■ Netnography – online observations	■ Online surveys (e.g. Survey Monkey, Qualtrics) ■ Log files ■ Database records	■ Skype, Google Hangout, Whatsapp, QQ, Snapchat – variety of communicators ■ Chats, discussion forums, group discussion tools ■ Email conversations ■ Mystery shoppers

Approaches to conducting marketing research

There are two main ways for a company to carry out marketing research, depending on the situation facing it. It might either carry out the work itself or employ the services of a market research agency. Where the study is small in scale, such as gathering information from libraries or interviewing a select number of industrial customers, companies may choose to conduct the work themselves. This is particularly feasible if a company has a marketing department and/or a marketing research executive on its staff. Other companies prefer to design the research themselves and then employ the services of a fieldwork agency to collect the data. Alternatively, where resources permit and the scale of the study is larger, companies may employ the services of a market research agency to conduct the research. The company will brief the agency about its market research requirements and the agency will do the rest. The typical stages involved in completing a market research study are described next; full-service agencies generally conduct all the activities described below.

The leading marketing research firms in the world are shown in Table 4.4.

Table 4.4 World's leading marketing research firms, 2016

Name	Country	Employees	Revenue (US$ million)
Nielsen Holdings NV	USA	43,000	6,309
The Kanter Group	UK	30,000	3,847
QuintilesIMS	USA	50,000	3,301
Gartner. Inc	USA	15,000	2,445
Ipsos	France	16,600	1,962
GfK	Germany	13,069	1,677
Information Resources, Inc.	USA	4,700	1,026
Westat, Inc.	USA	1,900	512
INTAGE, Inc	Japan	2,431	440
dunnhumby Ltd	UK	2,071	429

Source: Esomar (2017) Global Market Research 2017: An Esomar Industry Report.

Stages in the marketing research process

Figure 4.4 provides a description of a typical marketing research process. Each of the stages illustrated will now be discussed.

Initial contact

The process usually starts with the realization that a marketing problem requires information to aid its solution. Marketing management may contact internal marketing research staff or an outside agency. Where an outside agency is being used a meeting will be arranged to discuss the nature of the problem and the client's research needs. If the client and its markets are new to the agency, some exploratory research (e.g. a quick online search for information about the client and its markets) may be conducted prior to the meeting.

Research brief

At a meeting to decide what form the research will need to take, the client explains the marketing problem and outlines the company's research objectives. The information that should be provided for the research agency includes the following.[41]

- *Background information*: the product's history and the competitive situation.
- *Sources of information*: the client may have a list of industries that might be potential users of the product. This helps the researchers to define the scope of the research.

- *The scale of the project*: is the client looking for a 'cheap and cheerful' job or a major study? This has implications for the research design and survey costs.
- *The timetable*: when is the information required?

The client should produce a specific written **research brief**. This may be given to the research agency prior to the meeting and perhaps modified as a result of it but, without fail, should be in the hands of the agency before it produces its **research proposal**. The research brief should state the client's requirements and should be in written form so that misunderstandings are minimized.

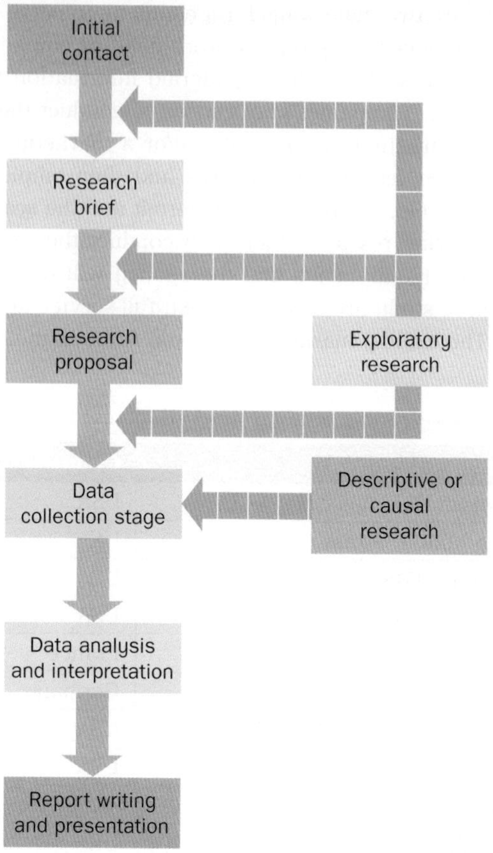

Research proposal

A research proposal lays out what a marketing research agency promises to do for its client and how much this will cost. Like the research brief, the proposal should be written in a way that avoids misunderstandings. A client should expect the following to be included.

- *A statement of objectives*: to demonstrate an understanding of the client's marketing and research problems.
- *What will be done*: an unambiguous description of the research design – including the research method, the type of sample, the sample size (if applicable) and how the fieldwork will be controlled.
- *Timetable*: if and when a report will be produced.
- *Costs*: how much the research will cost and what, specifically, is/is not included in these costs.

Figure 4.4 The marketing research process

Data collection

During the main data collection phase of the study, a variety of techniques can be employed to deal with the questions under consideration. Researchers usually draw a distinction between qualitative and quantitative research. **Qualitative research** involves a semi-structured, in-depth study of small samples in order to gain deep customer insights. Some of the key qualitative techniques include focus-group interviews, depth interviews, observation studies and ethnographic research. **Quantitative research** is a structured study of small or large samples using a predetermined list of questions or criteria and the statistical analysis of findings. Typical quantitative techniques include surveys and experiments. Traditionally, qualitative research was seen as being useful during exploratory research but then needed to be supplemented by quantitative research if a descriptive study was necessary. However, this is no longer the case. The findings of many quantitative studies have proven to be erroneous, while improvements in qualitative research techniques mean that they may yield more useful insights (see Table 4.5 for a breakdown of research expenditure patterns). We will now examine some of the major data collection techniques in more detail.

Table 4.5 Market research expenditure by type (%),* 2017

Method	France	Germany	Italy	Japan	Finland	Sweden	UK
Focus group	5	5	4	7	4	3	3
Depth interview	2	2	2	10	1	2	2
Online qualitative	2	2	2	1	2	2	1
Other qualitative	1	0	1	3	1	0	1
Total qualitative	**10**	**10**	**8**	**21**	**8**	**7**	**8**
Telephone survey	10	26	9	1	25	24	5
Postal survey	1	2	1	7	10	13	2
Face-to-face	11	17	11	7	13	6	6
Online survey	29	34	12	50	30	31	30
Automated digital/electronic	22	3	0	0	5	7	0
Other quantitative	2	4	1	0	0	2	10
Total quantitative	**75**	**88**	**85**	**79**	**92**	**89**	**54**

Source: Esomar, Global Market Research, 2017.

*Figures may not add up to 100 due to rounding.

Focus group discussions

Focus groups involve unstructured or semi-structured discussions between a moderator or group leader, who is often a psychologist, and a group of consumers (see Exhibit 4.5). The moderator has a list of areas to cover within the topic, but allows the group considerable freedom to discuss the issues that are important to them. By arranging groups of 6–12 people to discuss their attitudes and behaviour, a good deal of knowledge may be gained about the consumer. This can be helpful when constructing questionnaires, which can be designed to focus on what is important to the respondent (as opposed to the researcher) and worded in language the respondent uses and understands. Sometimes focus groups are used to try to generate new product ideas, through the careful selection of participants who have a flair for innovation or a liking for all things new.

Exhibit 4.5 Focus group interviews such as this one are a very popular form of market research.

Focus groups take place face to face, but the rise of the internet has led to the creation of online focus groups. The internet offers 'communities of interests', which can take the form of chat rooms or websites dedicated to specific interests or issues (see Marketing in Action 4.2). These are useful forums for conducting focus groups or at least for identifying suitable participants. Questions can be posed to participants who are not under time pressure to respond. This can lead to richer insights since respondents can think deeply about the questions put to them online. Another advantage is that they can comprise people located all over the world at minimal cost. Furthermore, technological developments mean it is possible for clients to communicate secretly online with the moderator while the focus group is in session. The client can ask the moderator certain questions as a result of hearing earlier responses. Clearly, a disadvantage of online focus groups compared with the traditional form is that the body language and interaction between focus group members is missing.[42]

Depth interviews

Depth interviews involve the interviewing of individual consumers about a single topic for perhaps one or two hours. The aims are broadly similar to those of the group discussion, but depth interviews are used when the presence of other people could inhibit the expression of honest answers and viewpoints, when the topic requires individual treatment (as when discussing an individual's decision-making process) and where the individual is an expert on a particular topic. For example, depth interviews have been used to conduct research on wealthy Americans to try to understand their attitudes and opinions on money and how they spend it. This was deemed to be a method that was superior to focus groups or surveys, where it was felt that respondents would be reluctant to talk about these issues. A technique called 'snowballing' was also used, where interviewees would recommend others that they thought would be willing to participate in the research.[43]

Care has to be taken when interpreting the results of these kinds of qualitative research because the findings are usually based on small sample sizes, and the more interesting or surprising viewpoints may be disproportionately reported.

Observation

Observation research involves gathering primary data by observing people and their actions. These types of studies can be conducted in real situations such as traffic counts on public streets or in contrived situations such as hall tests where research subjects are presented with a mock shopping aisle and their behaviour is monitored. Observation studies can have a number of advantages. First, they do not rely on the respondent's willingness to provide information; second, the potential for the interviewer to bias the study is reduced; and, third, some types of information can be collected only by observation (for example, a traffic count). Observation studies are particularly popular in the retail trade where a great deal can be learned by simply watching the behaviour of shoppers in a supermarket or clothing shop. Many retail innovations, including store layout and the positioning of products, have arisen as a result of observation studies of consumer behaviour.

Observation studies can be conducted by either human or, increasingly, mechanical means, such as video recording, and may be conducted with or without the customer's knowledge. Camera phones are the latest technology to be used for observation studies, with problems arising when they are used covertly. Samsung, the world's leading manufacturer of camera phones, has even banned their use in its factories, fearing industrial espionage.[44] Some technologies allow researchers to bypass what consumers say and observe instead what they do. For example, by using eye-tracking technology researchers observe which parts of an advertisement are viewed first by a subject and the design of print advertisements is greatly influenced by this kind of research. Advertisers are also extensive users of online eye tracking to monitor website behaviour and the attention paid to online display ads. Facial imaging software enables the reaction of the viewer to the advert to be measured as it can pick up smiles, frowns and so on with the result that the effectiveness of online adverts can be measured more accurately.[45] **Neuromarketing** research, which involves observing brain responses to marketing stimuli, promises to provide an even deeper understanding of why consumers behave in the ways that they do, as we saw in Critical Marketing Perspective 3.1).

Ethnographic research

One of the criticisms of research techniques like focus-group interviews is that they are somewhat contrived. Groups of people, who may or may not know one another, are brought together in boardroom-type settings and expected to provide insights into their thoughts, feelings and opinions. In such settings consumers may find it difficult or be unwilling to fully engage. As a result, many research companies are borrowing from the kinds of techniques that are employed by anthropologists and biologists, which place an emphasis on the observation of species in their natural settings. This type of research is known as **ethnographic research** and it may involve a combination of both observation and in-depth or focus-group interviewing.

In ethnographic studies, researchers decide what human behaviours they want to observe. They then go out into the field and record what consumers do, how they live their lives, how they shop, and so on (see Exhibit 4.6). For example, IKEA makes it its business to understand, learn and adapt to the changing cultures that exist today. The company frequently does home visits and – in a practice that blends research with reality TV – will even send an anthropologist to live in a volunteer's home. In one study, IKEA put up cameras in people's homes in Stockholm, Milan, New York and Shenzhen, China, to better understand how people use their sofas. They learned a lot from this study, particularly that people do all kinds of things except sitting and watching TV! The IKEA study found that, in Shenzhen, most of the subjects sat on the floor using the sofas as a backrest. This insight was fascinating considering that IKEA sofas had not been designed to accommodate people sitting on the floor and using a sofa like a prop. But now maybe they will![46]

One of the key advantages of the ethnographic approach is that researchers often find things they didn't even realize they should have been looking for. Having recorded these activities, consumers are interviewed to

Exhibit 4.6 The home furnishings company, IKEA, is a frequent user of ethnographic research around the world.

try to gain insights into the motivations and attitudes that underpin their actions. When all these data have been collected, they are analysed using qualitative software packages that search for common patterns of behaviour and generate clusters of consumers. Ethnographic findings are often reported using visual as well as written means. This provides a mechanism for senior executives to get close to consumer groups they may never come into contact with in their own daily lives because of physical distance and/or social class disparities. An increasingly popular form of ethnography is online ethnographic studies, better known as netnography (see Marketing in Action 4.3).

Ikea Ad Insight: The new IKEA TV spot for the Belgian market shows a couple of older figure skaters once again enjoying 'skating' and reliving their passion in their transformed living room. IKEA's mission is to get Belgians to fully enjoy their homes, their times and their lives based on insight gleaned through ethnographic studies.

Marketing in Action 4.3
Using netnography to understand the wine tourism experience

Critical Thinking: Below is a review of some of the netnographic research conducted in the wine tourism industry. Read it and reflect on the advantages and disadvantages of netnography as a research tool across other industries.

Wine tourism is a form of special interest tourism that is seen as a complementary vector of the wine industry with the tourism industry. France is a perfect example of this, as its wine regions are regarded as major tourist destinations. In 2016, 10 million wine tourists visited these

(continued)

destinations, representing €5.2 billion in terms of expenditure. From 2009 to 2016, the average growth rate of wine tourists visiting French wine destinations was 33 per cent. The wine tourism experience comprises visits to vineyards, wineries, wine festivals and wine shows, or staying overnight at vineyards.

Research was undertaken in the French Cognac Delimited Region, a region well known for its long wine history and for its international brand, to understand the wine tourism experience. A netnography study was the chosen technique in comparison to other qualitative research techniques due to its distinctive value in telling a story, understanding complex social phenomena, as well as assisting the researcher in developing themes from the consumer's point of view. The researchers identified the largest travel-related website, TripAdvisor, as an online community most relevant to study the wine tourist experience, focusing on online reviews posted relating to the Cognac area. By August 2016, there were 5,552 reviews on the TripAdvisor page for Cognac. Further refinement of the review page, with careful selection of postings linked to visits to vineyards, wineries, wine festivals, and/or experiencing the attributes of a grape wine region as the primary motivating factors for visitors, resulted in 825 original reviews forming the final data.

After rigorous coding, results emerged identifying that education and entertainment are viewed as integral to the wine tourism experience, from 90 per cent of the reviews analysed. However, references relating to the aesthetic dimension (appreciation of the 'winescape') were limited to 10 per cent of reviews, and only six of the 825 reviews related to the escapist dimension in the consumers' evaluations. This general observation illustrates that the existing tourism offers in the Cognac area focus mainly on the absorption side of the experience, either passive or active, and thus neglect the immersion aspect.

As a result of the insight gathered through the netnographic approach, the researchers recommended that Cognac tourist professionals could support their offer's competitive differentiation with a larger variety of visiting packages, including activities such as concerts, grape harvesting time, exhibitions, festivals, cooking workshops and craft seminars based on Cognac-style accommodation, and so on. In particular, it would be essential to diversify offers related to the escapist dimension with activities such as hiking or cycling in vineyards, ballooning over vineyards, horseback riding and carriage tours in vineyards.

Based on: Thanh and Kirova, 2018[47]

Surveys

Surveys remain the major market research technique (see Table 4.5) and typically involve the following key decisions:

- Who and how many people to interview: the sampling process.
- How to interview them: the survey method.
- What questions to ask: questionnaire design.

Sampling process   Figure 4.5 offers an outline of the **sampling process**. This starts with the definition of the population – that is, the group that forms the subject of study in a particular survey. The survey objective will be to provide results that are

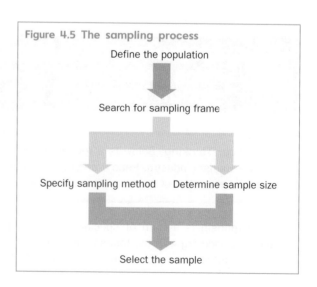

Figure 4.5 The sampling process

Define the population

Search for sampling frame

Specify sampling method   Determine sample size

Select the sample

representative of this group. Sampling planners, for example, must ask questions like 'Do we interview purchasing managers in all software development firms or only those that employ more than 50 people?'

Once the population has been defined, the next step is to search for a sampling frame – that is, a list or other record of the chosen population from which a sample can be selected. Examples include the electoral register and the *Kompass* business directory of companies. Researchers then choose between three major sampling methods: simple random sampling (where the sample is drawn at random and each individual has a known and equal chance of being selected); stratified random sampling (where the population is broken into groups and a random sample is drawn from each group); and quota sampling (where interviewers are instructed to ensure that the sample comprises a required number of individuals meeting pre-set conditions, such as a set percentage of small, medium-sized and large companies).

Finally, the researcher must select an appropriate sample size. The larger the sample size the more likely it is that the sample will represent the population. Statistical theory allows the calculation of sampling error (i.e. the error caused by not interviewing everyone in the population) for various sample sizes. In practice, the number of people interviewed is based on a balance between sampling error and cost considerations. Fortunately, sample sizes of around 1,000 (or fewer) can provide measurements that have tolerable error levels when representing populations counted in their millions.

Survey method Four options are available to those choosing a survey method: face-to-face interviews, telephone interviews, mail surveys or online surveys. Each method has its own strengths and limitations. Table 4.6 gives an overview of these.

Table 4.6 A comparison of survey methods

	Face to face	Telephone	Mail	Online
Questionnaire				
Use of open-ended questions	High	Medium	Low	Low
Ability to probe	High	Medium	Low	Low
Use of visual aids	High	Poor	High	High
Sensitive questions	Medium	Low	High	Low
Resources				
Cost	High	Medium	Low	Low
Sampling				
Widely dispersed populations	Low	Medium	High	High
Response rates	High	Medium	Low	Low
Experimental control	High	Medium	Low	Low
Interviewing				
Control of who completes questionnaire	High	High	Low	Low/high
Interviewer bias	Possible	Possible	Low	Low

A major advantage of face-to-face interviews is that response rates are generally higher than for telephone interviews or mail surveys.[48] It seems that the personal element in the contact makes refusal less likely. Face-to-face interviews are more versatile than telephone and mail surveys. The use of many open-ended questions on a mail survey would lower response rates[49] and time restrictions for telephone interviews would limit their use. Probing for more detail is easier with face-to-face interviews. A certain degree of probing can be achieved with a telephone interview, but time pressure and the less personalized situation will inevitably limit its use.

Face-to-face interviews do, however, have their drawbacks. They are more expensive than telephone, mail and internet surveys. The presence of an interviewer can cause bias (e.g. socially desirable answers) and lead to the misreporting of sensitive information. There is also the challenge for researchers in the recruitment and interviewing process not to disclose their bias or views, as a means to avoid alienation of the participants. However, in particularly emotionally sensitive cases, interviewers may face disclosure. For example, Goodrum and Keys[50] research centred on participants who had abortions. The interviewer in this case was intent not to reveal her pro-choice ideology, but in one interview setting she felt compelled to reveal her position in order to help calm the participant.

In some ways, telephone interviews are a halfway house between face-to-face and mail surveys. They generally have a higher response rate than mail questionnaires but a lower rate than face-to-face interviews; their cost is usually three-quarters of that for face-to-face but higher than for mail surveys; and they allow a degree of flexibility when interviewing. However, the use of visual aids is not possible and there are limits to the number of questions that can be asked before respondents either terminate the interview or give quick (invalid) answers in order to speed up the process. The use of computer-aided telephone interviewing (CATI) is growing. Centrally located interviewers read questions from a computer monitor and input answers immediately.

Given a reasonable response rate, mail survey research is normally a very economical method of conducting research. However, the major problem is the potential for low response rates and the accompanying danger of an unrepresentative sample. Nevertheless, using a systematic approach to the design of a mail survey, such as the total design method (TDM),[51] has been found to have a very positive effect on response rates. The TDM recommends, as ways of improving response rates, both the careful design of questionnaires to make them easy to complete, as well as accompanying them with a personalized covering letter emphasizing the importance of the research. Studies using the TDM on commercial populations have generated high response rates.[52]

Online research is now the most popular method of conducting research, accounting for 27 per cent of all expenditure globally. The countries with the highest spend on online research as a percentage of total spend include Japan (50 per cent), New Zealand (44 per cent), Australia (44 per cent each) and Canada (39 per cent).[53] The internet questionnaire is usually administered by email, or signals its presence on a website by registering key words or using banner advertising on search engines to drive people to the questionnaire. The major advantage of the internet as a marketing research vehicle is its low cost, since printing and postal costs are eliminated, making it even cheaper than mail surveys. In other ways, its characteristics are similar to mail surveys: the use of open-ended questions is limited; control over who completes the questionnaire is low; interviewer bias is low; and response rates are likely to be lower than for face-to-face and telephone interviews.

When response is by email, the identity of the respondent will automatically be sent to the survey company. This lack of anonymity may restrict the respondent's willingness to answer sensitive questions honestly. A strength of the internet survey is its ability to cover global populations at low cost, although sampling problems can arise because of the skewed nature of internet users. These tend to be from the younger and more affluent groups in society. For surveys requiring a cross-sectional sample this can be restricting.

Questionnaire design To obtain a true response to a question, three conditions are necessary. First, respondents must understand the question; second, they must be able to provide the information; and, third, they must be willing to provide it. Figure 4.6 shows the three stages in the development of the questionnaire: planning, design and pilot.

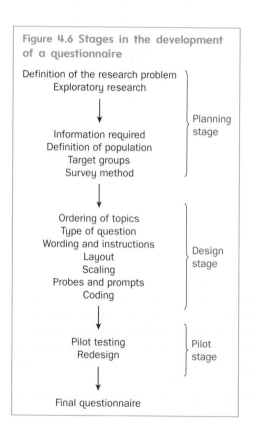

Figure 4.6 Stages in the development of a questionnaire

Definition of the research problem
Exploratory research

↓

Information required
Definition of population
Target groups
Survey method

} Planning stage

↓

Ordering of topics
Type of question
Wording and instructions
Layout
Scaling
Probes and prompts
Coding

} Design stage

↓

Pilot testing
Redesign

} Pilot stage

↓

Final questionnaire

Table 4.7 Poorly worded questions

Question	Problem and solution
What type of wine do you prefer?	'Type' is ambiguous: respondents could say 'French', 'red' or 'claret', say, depending on their interpretation. Showing the respondent a list and asking 'from this list . . .' would avoid the problem.
Do you think that prices are cheaper at Tesco than at Aldi?	Leading question favouring Tesco; a better question would be 'Do you think that prices at Tesco are higher, lower or about the same as at Aldi?' Names should be reversed for half the sample.
Which is more powerful and kind to your hands: Ariel or Bold?	Two questions in one: Ariel may be more powerful but Bold may be kinder to the hands. Ask the two questions separately.
Do you find it paradoxical that X lasts longer and yet is cheaper than Y?	Unfamiliar word: a study has shown that less than a quarter of the population understand such words as paradoxical, chronological or facility. Test understanding before use.

The planning stage involves the types of decision discussed so far in this chapter. It provides a firm foundation for designing a questionnaire, which provides relevant information for the marketing problem that is being addressed.

The design stage deals with the actual construction of the survey instrument and involves a number of important decisions. The first relates to the ordering of topics. It is sensible to start with easy-to-answer questions, in order to relax the respondent, and leave sensitive questions until last. Effective questionnaires are well structured and have a logical flow. Second, the type of question needs to be decided. Generally, three types are used: dichotomous questions (allow two possible answers, such as 'Yes'/'No'), multiple-choice questions, which allow more than two answers, and open questions, where the respondents answer by expressing their opinions.

Great care needs to be taken with both the wording and instructions used in the questionnaire and its layout. Questionnaire designers need to guard against asking ambiguous or leading questions, and using unfamiliar words (see Table 4.7). In terms of layout, the questionnaire should not appear cluttered and, where possible, answers and codes should each form a column so that they are easy to identify.

The use of 'scales' is very common in questionnaire design. For example, respondents are given lists of statements (e.g. 'My company's marketing information system allows me to make better decisions') followed by a choice of five positions on a scale ranging from 'strongly agree' to 'strongly disagree'. 'Probes' are used to explore or clarify what a respondent has said. Following a question about awareness of brand names, the exploratory probe 'Any others?' would seek to identify further names. Sometimes respondents use vague words or phrases like 'I like going on holiday because it is nice.' A clarifying probe such as 'In what way is it nice?' would seek a more meaningful response. 'Prompts', on the other hand, aid responses to a question. For example, in an aided recall question, a list of brand names would be provided for the respondent. Coding involves the assignment of numbers to specific responses in order to facilitate analysis of the questionnaire later on.

Once the preliminary questionnaire has been designed it should be piloted with a representative subsample, to test for faults. Piloting tests the questionnaire design and helps to estimate costs. Face-to-face piloting, where respondents are asked to answer questions and comment on any problems concerning a questionnaire read out by an interviewer, is preferable to impersonal piloting where the questionnaire is given to respondents for self-completion and they are asked to write down any problems found.[54] Once the pilot work proves satisfactory, the final questionnaire can be administered to the chosen sample.

Data analysis and interpretation   Basic analysis of questionnaire data may be at the descriptive level (e.g. means, frequency tables and standard deviations) or on a comparative basis (e.g. t-tests and cross-tabulations). More sophisticated analysis may search for relationships (e.g. regression analysis), group respondents (e.g. cluster analysis), or establish cause and effect (e.g. analysis of variance techniques used on experimental data).

When interpreting marketing research results, great care must be taken. One common failing is to infer cause and effect when only association has been established. For example, establishing a relationship that sales rise when advertising levels increase does not necessarily mean that raising advertising expenditure will lead to an increase in sales. Other marketing variables (e.g. sales force effect) may have increased at the same time as the increase in advertising. A second cautionary note concerns the interpretation of means and percentages. Given that a sample has been taken, any mean or percentage is an estimate subject to 'sampling error' – that is, an error in an estimate due to taking a sample rather than interviewing the entire population. A market research survey which estimates that 30 per cent of males but only 25 per cent of females smoke, does not necessarily suggest that smoking is more prevalent among males. Given the sampling error associated with each estimate, the true conclusion might be that there is no difference between males and females.

Report writing and presentation   Crouch suggests that the key elements in a research report are as follows:[55]

1   Title page
2   List of contents
3   Preface – outline of agreed brief, statement of objectives, scope and methods of research
4   Summary of conclusions and recommendations
5   Previous related research – how previous research has had a bearing on this research
6   Research method
7   Research findings
8   Conclusions
9   Appendices.

Sections 1–4 provide a concise description of the nature and outcomes of the research for busy managers. Sections 5–9 provide the level of detail necessary if any particular issue (e.g. the basis of a finding or the analytical technique used) needs checking. The report should be written in language the reader will understand; jargon should be avoided.

Good decision-making is at the heart of effective marketing. The ability to understand customer needs, to design products and services to meet those needs and to develop appropriate ways of communicating with customers all require timely and accurate market information. But marketing research is also not without its societal problems and some of these issues are raised in Critical Marketing Perspective 4.2.

Critical Marketing Perspective 4.2
Market research – fact or fiction?

Market research is one of the most visible faces of marketing. At some stage or other, nearly everyone participates in a survey, whether it is in a retail environment, a university or at home via telephone, post or, increasingly, by pressing the red button on their television remote controls. Consumers are also invited to participate in focus groups, depth interviews and ethnographic research. While all this research provides answers, it also seems to be raising some very fundamental questions.

The first concerns the widespread usage to which research is being put. It is virtually impossible now to pick up a newspaper or watch the television without seeing the results of some survey or other being presented. It may be about the most mundane of matters, such as how much time is

(continued)

spent cleaning the kitchen floor or who people think is the most eligible film star. The more outrageous the survey or its findings, the more likely it is to be picked up by news bulletins or discussed on radio talk shows. In other words, surveys have become the news and for 24-hour news channels they represent a relatively cheap and useful time filler. For example, many people missed the irony of Sky News charging viewers to vote by text on whether they thought they were paying too much for their mobile phone bills.

The sheer prevalence of surveys and their findings raises two other fundamental questions: who sponsored the study and how was it conducted? The former is crucial because it demonstrates that many of the surveys in the media are, in truth, public relations pieces being put out by particular companies or brands. For example, our floor cleaning survey is likely to have originated from a cleaning products company; that the majority of workers favour emailing colleagues over face-to-face meetings is likely to come from a business communications company, and so on. Sometimes, this can be relatively harmless fun but in other instances it can be very serious if the subject matter relates to food, family health and the like. The surfeit of visual, audio and print media means that there is always an outlet for these kinds of PR exercises. The consumer should take care to know who sponsored any study that receives media coverage.

After reading this chapter, you should also be critical of how studies are being conducted. What were the sampling frame and the sample size? Are the findings valid (the research measured what it intended to measure), reliable (similar findings would be found if the study were repeated) and representative (the study accurately represents the larger population)? For all the survey findings that are presented regularly, this type of detail rarely is. In its absence, it is impossible to conclude that the research was conducted scientifically. Unfortunately, time-pressed consumers rarely seek out this information and tend to take survey results at face value.

Market research suffers from other problems, too. In some instances it is used to gather competitor intelligence. Questionable practices include using student projects to gather information without the student revealing the identity of the sponsor of the research, pretending to be a potential supplier who is conducting a telephone survey to understand the market, posing as a potential customer at an exhibition, bribing a competitor's employee to pass on proprietary information, and covert surveillance such as through the use of hidden cameras. The practice of selling in the guise of marketing research, commonly known as 'sugging', also occurs from time to time. Despite the fact that it is not usually practised by bona fide marketing research agencies but, rather, unscrupulous selling companies who use marketing research as a means of gaining compliance to their requests, it is the marketing research industry that suffers from its aftermath.

Market research is an important vehicle by which organizations can learn more about their customers, and develop products and services that meet their needs. Properly conducted, it can yield invaluable insights, and can be the difference between success and failure in business. But its reputation is being sullied by the prevalence of 'bogus' surveys and other questionable practices. This raises the issue of whether research deals with the facts or is an exercise in fiction.

Reflection: Select any three studies that you have heard or seen being publicized in the media. Investigate them and, using the criteria discussed above, evaluate the quality of the research that has been undertaken.

Summary

This chapter has examined the nature and role of marketing information and customer insights. The following key issues were addressed.

1. The importance of marketing research and customer insights: customer insights are key if an organization is to be truly market led. They can provide answers to all sorts of marketing questions that the organization may face.

2. The nature of marketing information systems: these are systems in which marketing information is formally gathered, stored and distributed on a regular, planned basis.

3. The three main types of market information: internal market information involves the collection and examination of data available internally to the organization; market intelligence involves the gathering of information on what is happening in the marketplace generally; while marketing research is conducted to examine specific research questions that the firm has.

4. The term 'Big Data' refers to the collection, aggregation and analysis of data from multiple sources in order to aid marketing decision-making. The availability and suitability of new technologies has given rise to an increased use of this type of information. The continual development of Big Data illustrates the growth in this area and the associated challenges, alongside the emergence of the GDPR, software programs, and platforms such as webscraping and social listening.

5. The approaches to conducting research: marketing research can be conducted either by the organization itself or by employing the services of a professional marketing research firm. Large-scale, complex research work is best conducted by a professional firm.

6. The stages in the market research process: these include initial contact, the research brief, the research proposal, exploratory research, the main data collection phase, data analysis and report writing/presentation.

7. Qualitative research techniques: a range of semi-structured research techniques including focus groups, depth interviews, observation studies, ethnographic research, and so on.

8. The four main survey methods: namely face-to-face, telephone, mail and internet. Each has its unique advantages and disadvantages, and the decision as to which to use should be guided by the nature of the study, the respondents and the cost.

Study questions

1. What are the differences between qualitative and quantitative research? Explain the roles played by each.
2. Outline the main stages in the marketing research process, identifying particularly the kinds of difficulties that might be faced at each stage.
3. Market research is being trivialized by the number of surveys that are being reported in the media. Discuss.
4. Many firms are now investing heavily in analysing their own customers through CRM and website analysis. What are the advantages and disadvantages of this trend for both firms and consumers?
5. Discuss and debate the definition of the 7 Vs of Big Data. Are there any Vs missing, in your opinion?
6. What are the opportunities and challenges for companies using social media listening?
7. Discuss the recent rise of ethnography and netnography as methods to study consumer behaviour. What are the ethical implications of these approaches?
8. Visit www.surveymonkey.com and learn about how to create and administer a survey.

Suggested reading

Carson, D., Gilmore, A. and **Gronhaug, K.** (2001) *Qualitative Marketing Research*. London: Sage Publications.

Graves, P. (2010) *Consumerology*. London: Nicholas Brealey.

McAfee, A. and **Brynjolfsson, E.** (2012) Big Data: the management revolution, *Harvard Business Review*, 90(10): 60–8.

McKenna, B., Myers, M.D. and **Newman, M.** (2017) Social media in qualitative research: challenges and recommendations, *Information and Organisation*, 27: 87–99.

Poynter, R. (2010) *The Handbook of Online and Social Media Research: Tools and Techniques for Market Researchers*. London: John Wiley & Sons.

Said, E., McDonald, E., Wilson, H. and **Marcos, J.** (2015) How organisations generate and use customer insight, *Journal of Marketing Management*, 31(9/10): 1158–79.

Verhof, P., Kooge, E. and **Walk, N.** (2016) *Creating Value with Big Data Analytics: Making Smarter Marketing Decisions*. London: Routledge.

References

1. **USB** (2017) Global Auto Survey.
2. **Vaughan, A.** (2017) Electric cars to account for all new vehicle sales in Europe by 2015, *Theguardian.com*, 13 July.
3. **Research and Markets** (2017) Global electric vehicle market research report insights, opportunity analysis and market shares and forecast 2017–2023.
4. **Kiser, J.** and **Essery, M.** (2017) An IPOS point of view: is there a target market for electric vehicles? *Ipsos.com*, April.
5. **Rezvani, Z., Jansson, J.** and **Bodin, J.** (2017) Advances in consumer electric vehicle adoption research: a review and research agenda. *Transportation Research* Part D, 34: 122–36.
6. **Said, E., McDonald, E., Wilson, H.** and **Marcos, J.** (2015) How organisations generate and use customer insight, *Journal of Marketing Management*, 31(9/10): 1158–79.
7. **Said, E., McDonald, E., Wilson, H.** and **Marcos, J.** (2015) How organisations generate and use customer insight, *Journal of Marketing Management*, 31(9/10): 1158–79.
8. **Jardin, A.** (2017) Spotify sets out your 2018 'goals' in this year's data-driven holiday campaign, A*dage.com*, 28 November.
9. **Said, E., McDonald, E., Wilson, H.** and **Marcos, J.** (2015) How organisations generate and use customer insight, *Journal of Marketing Management*, 31(9/10): 1158–79.
10. **Esomar** (2017) Global Market Research 2017: An Esomar Industry Report.
11. **Esomar** (2017) Global Market Research 2017: An Esomar Industry Report, 14.
12. **Jobber, D.** and **Rainbow, C.** (1977) A study of the development and implementation of marketing information systems in British industry, *Journal of the Marketing Research Society*, 19(3): 104–11.
13. **Van Bruggen, A., Smidts, A.** and **Wierenga, B.** (1996) The impact of the quality of a marketing decision support system: an experimental study, *International Journal of Research in Marketing*, 13: 331–43.
14. **Piercy, N.** and **Evans, M.** (1983) *Managing Marketing Information*. Beckenham: Croom Helm.
15. **Ackoff, R.L.** (1967) Management misinformation systems, *Management Science*, 14(4): 147–56.
16. **Kohli, A.** and **Jaworski, B.** (1990) Market orientation: the construct, research propositions and marketing implications, *Journal of Marketing*, 54: 1–18.
17. **Varma, A.** (2017) Zara's secret to success lies in Big Data and an agile supply chain, https://www.Straitstimes.com/lifestyle/fashion/zaras-secret-to-success-lies-in-big-data-and-an-agile-supply-chain (accessed 25 May 2017).
18. **Nakata, C., Zhu, Z.** and **Izberk-Bilgin, E.** (2011) Integrating marketing and information services functions: a complementarity and competence perspective, *Journal of the Academy of Marketing Science*, 39, 700–16.
19. **Bowsher, E.** (2018) Online retail sales continue to soar, *Financial Times*, 11 January. Available at https://www.Ft.com/content/a8f5c780-f46d-11e7-a4c9-bbdefa4f210 (accessed 15 May 2018).
20. **Arnett, G.** (2013) Are loyalty cards really worth it? *Guardian.co.uk*, 31 October.
21. **Direct Marketing Association** (2012) Costa Coffee Club loyalty programme, *Warc.com*.
22. **Davenport, T.** (2006) Competing on analytics, *Harvard Business Review*, 84(1): 98–107.
23. **McAfee, A.** and **Brynjolfsson, E.** (2012) Big Data: the management revolution, *Harvard Business Review*, 90(10): 60–8.
24. **IBM** (2018) Big Data & Analytics Hub, http://www.Ibmbigdatahub.com/infographic/four-vs-big-data (accessed 22 May 2018).
25. **Chartier, T.** (2016) Vertigo over the seven Vs of Big Data. *Journal of Corporate Accounting*, 27(5): 81–2.
26. **OECD** (2016) Research ethics and new forms of data for social and economic research, *OECD Science, Technology and Industry Policy Papers*, 34. Paris: OECD Publishing, http://dx.doi.org/10.1787/5jln7vnpxs32-en.
27. **Ferguson, D.** (2013) How supermarkets get your data – and what they do with it, *Guardian.co.uk*, 8 June.

28. **Bishop, L.** (2017) Big Data and data sharing: ethical issues. UK Data Service, UK Data Archive.

29. **Schweidel, D.** and **Moe, W.** (2016) Listening in on social media: a joint model of sentiment and venue format choice, *Journal of Marketing Research*, 51(4): 387–402.

30. **Pettit, A.** (2011) The promises and pitfalls of SMR: prevailing discussions and the naked truth, *Marketing Research*, Fall: 15–21.

31. **Anonymous** (2018) Webscraping: top 15 ways to use it for business, *www.Agenty.com*, May.

32. **Buckingham, D.** (2011) Why we believe that data is the new oil, *www.Marketingweek.com*, 12 July.

33. **Kanter, J.** (2018) 2nd Cambridge Analytica whistle blower says app and quizzes like 'Sex Compass' gathered data from way more than 87 million Facebook users, *http://uk.Businessinsider.com*, 17 April.

34. **Hicks, M.** and **Ellis, C.** (2018) The Cambridge Analytica and Facebook data scandal: how to tell if your data was shared, *www.Techradar.com*, 10 April.

35. **Hern, A.** (2018) Cambridge Analytica: how did it turn clicks into votes? *Theguardian.com*, 6 May.

36. **Cadwalladr, C.** and **Graham-Harrison, E.** (2018) Revealed: 50 million Facebook profiles harvested for Cambridge Analytica in major data breach, *www.TheGuardian.com*, 18 March.

37. **Cadwalladr, C.** and **Graham-Harrison, E.** (2018) Revealed: 50 million Facebook profiles harvested for Cambridge Analytica in major data breach, *www.Theguardian.com*, 18 March.

38. **Hicks, M.** and **Ellis, C.** (2018) The Cambridge Analytica and Facebook data scandal: how to tell if your data was shared, *www.techradar.com*, 10 April.

39. **Heinze, A.**, **Ferneley, E.** and **Child, P.** (2013) Ideal participants in online market research, *International Journal of Market Research*, 55(6): 769–89.

40. **Asquith, R.** (2014) Why multi-screen television moves the audience measurement goalposts, *Guardian.co.uk*, 15 May.

41. **Crouch, S.** and **Housden, M.** (1999) *Marketing Research for Managers*. Oxford: Butterworth Heinemann, 253.

42. **Gray, R.** (1999) Tracking the online audience, *Marketing*, 18 February, 41–3.

43. **Birchall, J.** (2005) Rich, but not fortune's fools, *Financial Times*, 13 December, 13.

44. **Harper, J.** (2003) Camera phones cross moral, legal lines, *Washington Times*, Business, 15 July, 6.

45. **Anonymous** (2011) The all-telling eye, *The Economist*, 22 October, 90–1.

46. **Kowitt, B.** (2015) How IKEA took over the World, *Fortune.com*. Available at www.http://fortune.com/ikea-world-domination/ (accessed 1 June 2018).

47. **Thanh, T.V.** and **Kirova, V.** (2018) Wine tourism experience: a netnography study, *Journal of Business Research*, 83: 30–7.

48. **Yu, J.** and **Cooper, H.** (1983) A quantitative review of research design effects on response rates to questionnaires, *Journal of Marketing Research*, 20 February, 156–64.

49. **Falthzik, A.** and **Carroll, S.** (1971) Rate of return for close v open-ended questions in a mail survey of industrial organisations, *Psychological Reports*, 29: 1121–2.

50. **Goodrum, S.** and **Keys, J.** (2007) Reflections on two studies of emotionally sensitive topics: bereavement from murder or abortion, *International Journal of Social Research Method*, 10(4): 249–58.

51. **Dillman, D.** (1978) *Mail and Telephone Surveys: The Total Design Method*. New York: John Wiley & Sons.

52. **Fahy, J.** (1998) Improving response rates in cross-cultural mail surveys, *Industrial Marketing Management*, 27, November, 459–67; **Walker, B.**, **Kirchmann, W.** and **Conant, J.** (1987) A Method to improve response rates in industrial mail surveys, *Industrial Marketing Management*, 16, November, 305–14.

53. **Esomar** (2017) Global Market Research 2017: An Esomar Industry Report.

54. **Reynolds, N.** and **Diamantopoulos, A.** (1998) The effect of pretest method on error detection rates: experimental evidence, *European Journal of Marketing*, 32(5/6): 480–98.

55. **Crouch, S.** (1992) *Marketing Research for Managers*. Oxford: Butterworth Heinemann, 253.

Appendix 4.I: Sources of European marketing information

Is there a survey of the industry?

Datamonitor provides global market research on the industry profile of countries.

Euromonitor GMID Database has in-depth analysis and current market information in the key areas of country data, consumer lifestyles, market sizes, forecasts, brand and country information, business information sources and marketing profiles.

Reuters Business Insight Reports are full-text reports available online in the sectors of healthcare, financial services, consumer goods, energy, e-commerce and technology.

Key Note Reports cover size of market, economic trends, prospects and company performance.

Mintel Premier Reports cover market trends, prospects and company performance.

Esomar is a global insights community that provides opinion, social research and data analytics in an annual Global Market Esomar Industry Report.

Snapshots on CD-Rom The 'Snapshots' CD series is a complete library of market research reports, providing coverage of consumer, business-to-business and industrial markets. Containing 2,000 market research reports, this series provides incisive data and analysis on more than 8,000 market segments for the UK, Europe and the USA.

British Library Market Research is a guide to British Library Holdings. It lists titles of reports arranged by industry. Some items are available on inter-library loan; others may be seen at the British Library in London.

International Directory of Published Market Research, published by Marketsearch.

How large is the market?

European Marketing Data and Statistics Now available on the Euromonitor GMID database.

International Marketing Data and Statistics Now available on the Euromonitor GMID database.

CEO Bulletin

A–Z of UK Marketing Data

European Marketing Pocket Book

The Asia Pacific Marketing Pocket Book

The Americas Marketing Pocket Book

Where is the market?

Regional Marketing Pocket Book

Regional Trends gives the main economic and social statistics for UK regions.

Geodemographic Pocket Book

Who are the competitors?

British companies can be identified using any of the following:

Kompass (most European countries have their own edition)

Key British Enterprises

Quarterly Review – KPMG

Sell's Products and Services Directory (Gen Ref E 380.02542 SEL)

For more detailed company information consult the following:

Companies Annual Report Collection Carol: company annual reports online at www.carol.co.uk

Fame DVD (CD-Rom service)

Business Ratio Reports

Retail Rankings

Overseas companies sources include:

Asia's 7,500 Largest Companies

D&B Europa

Dun's Asia Pacific Key Business Enterprises

Europe's 15,000 Largest Companies

Major Companies of the Arab World

Million Dollar Directory (US)

Principal International Businesses

What are the trends?

Possible sources to consider include the following:

The Book of European Forecasts Now available on the Euromonitor GMID database

Marketing in Europe

European Trends

Consumer Europe Now available on the Euromonitor GMID database

Consumer Goods Europe

Family Expenditure Survey

Social Trends

Lifestyle Pocket Book

Drink Trends

Media Pocket Book

Retail Business

Mintel Market Intelligence

OECD (Organisation for Economic Co-operation and Development)

EU statistical and information sources

'Eurostat' is a series of publications that provide a detailed picture of the EU; they can be obtained by visiting European Documentation Centres (often in university libraries) in all EU countries; themes include general statistics, economy and finance, and population/social conditions.

Eurostat Yearbook

European Access is a bulletin on issues, policies, activities and events concerning EU member states.

Marketing and Research Today is a journal that examines social, political, economic and business issues relating to Western, Central and Eastern Europe.

European Report is a twice-weekly news publication from Brussels on industrial, economic and political issues.

European Survey Research Association provides co-ordination in the field of survey research in Europe and fosters a link between European survey researchers. Responsible for publishing the journal *Survey Research Methods*.

Abstracts and indexes

Business Periodicals Index

ANBAR Marketing and Distribution Abstracts

ABI Inform

Research Index

Times Index

Elsevier Science Direct

Emerald

Wiley Interscience and Boldideas

Guides to sources

A great variety of published information sources exists; the following source guides may help you in your search:

Marketing Information

Guide to European Marketing Information

Compendium of Marketing Information Sources

Croner's A–Z of Business Information Sources

McCarthy Cards: a card service on which are reproduced extracts from the press covering companies and industries; it also produces a useful guide to its sources: *UK and Europe Market Information: Basic Sources*

Statistics

Guide to Official Statistics

Sources of the Unofficial UK Statistics

Sources: the authors thank the University of Bradford School of Management Library for help in compiling this list.

Listening to the vegan consumer: the case of Moodley Manor

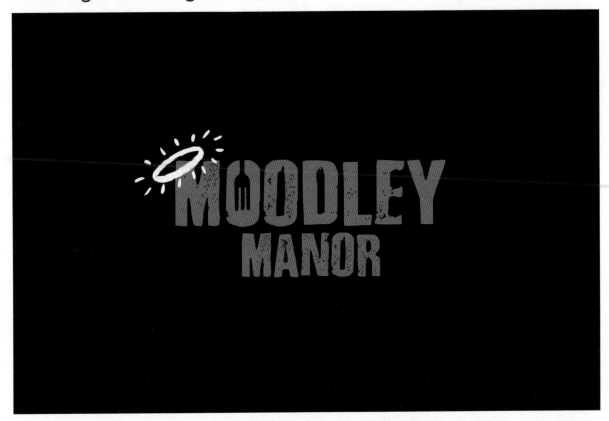

Introduction

Moodley Manor was established by two passionate foodies who realized a need among the vegan community for fresh, exciting and utterly delicious meat-free options. Armed with its motto, 'All Taste . . . No Sacrifice', this business has been changing the way vegans eat since 2014.

For as long as he can remember, co-founder Gavyn Pedley has always been interested in the provenance of food, but meeting his now wife and business partner Aisling brought his desire for good food to the fore. It was the beginning of something great and something more radical as Gavyn decided to adopt a vegan diet himself. After many meals together, Aisling and Gavyn realized that, as vegans, it was virtually impossible to eat out in restaurants, with many of their dates ending up with them sharing a plate of chips. This marked the beginning of a taste-driven food business for vegans.

Understanding the market

Despite the data-filled world we live in, statistics on vegetarianism and veganism in Ireland are very limited and difficult to retrieve. In launching the business, Moodley Manor read market reports to gain customer insights. However, as there was very little published information available on the market for vegan products in Ireland, the founders needed to do primary research themselves. As a start-up business in 2013, they encountered the challenge faced by the majority of start-up businesses – they had no budget to use the services of a market research agency. As a result, Moodley Manor had to think of innovative ways to do market research.

The first critical decision it needed to make was to agree on what food products would sell. While the co-founders knew how they shopped for vegan products, they needed to find out how other people searched for and bought these products. Aisling set about actively engaging with consumers to understand more about their needs and habits. Her first interaction with the vegan market was through an online survey aimed at capturing their purchasing habits: what they bought, why they bought and where they shopped. As a result of this initial contact and insightful feedback, Aisling set about building the home website and ultimately a 'community' of vegan followers under the Moodley Manor brand, linking into Facebook, Twitter and Instagram networks to build advocates for the brand.

During this early stage of development, and to help understand buyer behaviour in this niche market, the co-founders sourced a range of food and non-food vegan products and sold them online. Their online store stocked third-party products based on a range of luxury offerings, from chocolates and sauces to body washes and shampoos, which they also sold as luxury gift boxes. The store provided Moodley Manor with its first sales and allowed it to get to know its consumers – and ultimately to put a 'face' to its potential consumers. This helped to develop the company's understanding of the vegan consumer as it could analyze the website data to see what search terms brought people to the website, what captured their attention while on the website, what products they purchased and how they paid for the products. After observing consumer behaviour and seeing that there was a gap for vegan products in Ireland, Gavyn and Aisling were more determined than ever to sell products for this growing and what they considered an unserved market.

Through continual online promotion directed at early adopters and online influencers across various groups such as 'I'm a Little Vegan', the Vegetarian Society of Ireland, vegan events in Ireland as well as regional vegan groups, the Moodley Manor brand gained momentum in the first year and, more importantly, the business developed its reputation as a valued and trusted name among the vegan communities both in Ireland and the UK. Rather than base its research solely on its own interactions with current and potential consumers, the company began to engage more frequently in an ongoing process of social listening. This involved using social media research that listens to consumers who are participating in discussion forums, Facebook pages, Twitter conversations, voluntarily and eagerly pushing spontaneous responses outwards among their peer groups, listeners as well as brands. As a result of this social listening process, the business was in an informed position to create and develop a product range to satisfy the frustrated vegan.

Developing the product range

In 2014, the first product idea was that of a non-dairy cheese offering. During this testing and development phase, Moodley Manor continued to engage in ongoing market scanning to identify new trends and to track the activities of competitors. Frustratingly, during the test phase, the non-dairy cheese market opened up with two bigger competitors emerging with new cheese products. As these products were already gaining a foothold in the marketplace, Gavyn and Aisling felt that it wasn't in the interests of their fledgling business to tackle the two competitors head on, so it was back to the drawing board.

Rather than focus on a single product, they reviewed their research and, based on their social listening, they realized that the business needed an offering to satisfy a range of needs among vegan consumers. This also made strong business sense as they would develop the business based on a product range as opposed to a single product. Taking this on board, the business identified a significant gap in the market for something that had great taste with a texture to match – a product that vegans could get their teeth into, just as meat eaters do! As a result, the founders decided to create plant-based 'meat' alternative products. These products had to satisfy the need for comfort for meal occasions from a 'weekend fry-up' to a sandwich, something that had the texture and 'bite' of classic meats but with better health benefits. In 2015, after spending significant time understanding the needs of the community, Moodley Manor became one of the first producers of 100 per cent plant-based meat in Ireland, with the launch of Moodley Meats Badass Bacon and Boss Burgers (see Exhibits C4.1 and C4.2).

The product launch began with a phased teaser release to see if people were interested. If potential consumers were interested in the product, they were required to sign up online and pay for the product in

Exhibit C4.1 Moodley Manor Badass Bacon launched in April 2015 as a bacon-style meat alternative, designed to be used in the same way as traditional meat bacon. The slices of bacon are thick cut (3 mm), flavoured with hickory smoke and glazed with maple syrup.

Exhibit C4.2 Moodley Manor Boss Burgers, launched in April 2015, are large and much like beef, and marketed as the only real substitute for beef burgers while also being healthier than real meat burgers.

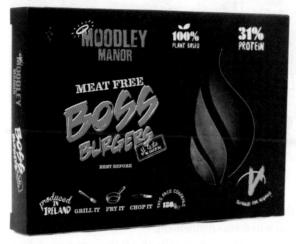

advance. The pre-sales model worked effectively from inception, with consumers ordering online before the launch and, within four months, demand was so large that it aided entry to retail customers. This buy-in by consumers provided a cost-effective way of validating the market for the company's products and also brought its products to the attention of retailers.

For this business, market research was a continuous listening process as it constantly scanned the market for new trends and developments within its field of food. To ensure a growing consumer base, each product bought in the early stages of the business was personally delivered by the co-founders as it provided a good opportunity for them to engage directly with consumers to get feedback and to help foster brand loyalty.

During the launch phase of the first two vegan meat products, Moodley Manor actively continued to capture the reactions of its consumers. One successful way it did this was through the 'You decide what's next poll' on it website. This poll provided a list of product ideas and its online community helped guide the decision of what product would be launched next. As a result, in August 2015, 'Savage Sausages' were launched online and into a national retailer. It emerged that, between May and December 2015, the business had made and delivered more than 25,000 vegan meals.

The feedback from consumers didn't stop there – the online vegan community was seeking an offering for the Christmas season. The business launched a family-size roast leading up to Christmas 2015, due to growing demand for a family-satisfying centrepiece for a festive meal. Following the incredible reception, including many endorsements by prominent figures in the food industry, Moodley continued to release it in two sizes for online purchase, with in-store purchase from February 2016 onwards.

Expanding the business

Given the success of asking consumers what they wanted, the business continues to use the customer poll approach to decide on which products to launch. It has now set up a survey using an online survey tool and rolls it out via its Facebook page and through trusted partners. These polls are used in conjunction with internal business development and have resulted in Moodley Manor adding to its range with vegan mince, garlic mayonnaise, salami slices and chicken.

The development of its vegan chicken came from a different route than usual for Moodley Manor and opened up a new line of business for it. In 2016, it was approached by Token, an event space containing a bar, a retro arcade, a pinball parlour and a restaurant selling high-end fast food. It wanted the founders to develop a vegan chicken product for its menu. As a result, Moodley Manor made three different versions, which were tested by the restaurant staff and, with a few tweaks, Chick-Hun was born. The company now provides its products as ingredients to a number of food outlets, such as restaurants and takeaways, and these businesses account for up to 40 per cent of revenues.

In 2017, the business wanted to look at ways to reduce its dependence on its biggest client, a large food retailer. In tandem with this, the need for more presence offline was highlighted online by consumers who wanted to know how to get their hands on the range of delicious food products. As a result, Moodley Manor brought the 'Eat My Veg Food Truck' on the road (see Exhibit C4.3). As well as providing another revenue stream for the business, the co-founders and their team use the food truck as a live testing environment for new products. Now, along with online feedback through Facebook, Twitter and Instagram, the company has direct access to its customers and their reaction to its products. The team found it interesting to see its community of customers grow and to watch their interactions in the queue for food. Gavyn observed that, through going to the food truck, consumers were in effect stepping into the business and saying something publicly about their love of vegan food. The food truck has been to trade shows, festivals and business parks, but the team has found that it is public parks with well-publicized events that produce the best sales and customer interactions. Festivals in particular might seem like a good place for a vegan food offering. However, while multi-day festivals were good to attend as this gave people the opportunity to get to know the brand over the duration of the event, it was hard to generate enough revenue to cover the high cost of having the food truck on-site.

Given the size of the UK market, it made sense for the team to look at expanding there. In 2016, Moodley Manor started with online sales in the UK to test the market through organic growth. When its customer base grew and was more established, it partnered with its first UK distributor. This process continued, with the business carefully selecting new distribution partners that it felt understood its product range. One of its most successful partnerships is with TheVeganKind, a distributor, online vegan supermarket and vegan subscription box provider based in Glasgow. Given the nature of their business, this was a perfect match for the co-founders and a significant percentage of UK sales are through this distributor.

Using the research to understand the customer

Moodley Manor's research helped it to get to grips with its market, starting with gaining a clear understanding of its consumer. The initial image of the vegan was explored with the aid of a section on the original webpage, 'Tell your vegan story', as well as through continuous discussions with vegan communities online. Based on these shared stories and the research collected through the online vegan community, the company soon realized that the consumer for vegan products was a much more complex character. It identified three categories of consumer, from the ethically motivated vegan to the health-motivated vegan and finally to the meat reducers/avoiders. These profiles tended to cross a broad age range, from mid- to late teens right up to 40 year olds and older. Despite the profiles of the health-motivated vegans and meat reducers/avoiders sounding similar, Moodley Manor soon recognized that they were distinctly different in

Exhibit C4.3 Moodley Manor's Eat my Veg Food Truck in action.

their needs, and also presented challenges in terms of ways to form engagement.

In order to engage with all three types of consumer, Aisling and Gavyn returned continuously to their online community for inspiration and discussion in understanding what consumers actually want in their food. It emerged that the preconceived image of the 'virtuous vegan' was just one perspective and that there was an emergence of the vegan addicted to fast food. This was also in addition to 'non-vegetarian' consumers who seek healthiness, attractiveness and convenience. The Moodley Manor consumer was identified as having three core values in terms of taste, value and freshness (see Figure C4.1). In this insight, Gavyn and Aisling realized that their consumer is one who yearns for 'All Taste . . . No Sacrifice', and desires good-tasting fast food while remaining true to the virtues of being a vegan.

Conclusion

The Moodley Manor business is a small but powerful vegan business, which has utilized a listening process, whether through traditional face-to-face interactions, polling or through social media research, to extract key consumer insights to develop its product – and its big vegan personality. The business brand was designed to be an expression of the business partners' personalities as well as being relatable to the community of vegans throughout Ireland and beyond. The rock'n'roll, delicious but indulgent personality of the brand has supported the inroads that the business has made socially on radically reimagining the vegan.

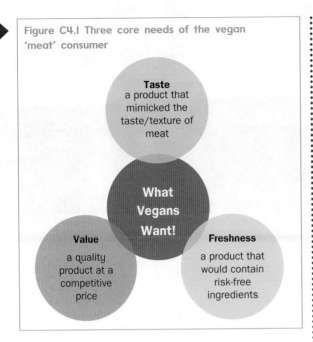

Figure C4.1 Three core needs of the vegan 'meat' consumer

Taste
a product that mimicked the taste/texture of meat

What Vegans Want!

Value
a quality product at a competitive price

Freshness
a product that would contain risk-free ingredients

Today, Gavyn and Aisling have become advocates for the same networks that they use for business support, as well as utilizing Facebook, Twitter and Instagram to engage in conversations with large groups and influencers in the vegan space. However, it is the contact with individual consumers in person – through doorstep delivery, its Eat My Veg Food Truck and its online presence – that has ensured the business has remained approachable and friendly, while driving innovation and satisfying the needs of vegan customers. Using their online social community, these co-founders are seeking to further expand in the UK market and beyond. This drive has been accompanied by new research insight that has identified a trend towards UK adults adopting vegan buying behaviours, and Britain being perceived as more vegan friendly than ever before.

The question emerges, will Moodley Manor be able to continue to grow and develop its unique offering while ensuring that it is continuously listening and asking questions of its growing consumer base?

Questions

1. Discuss the ways in which Moodley Manor engages in market research. Is each of the methods sustainable as the business grows?
2. What are the limitations regarding Moodley Manor's approach to market research?
3. Discuss Moodley Manor's approach to the use of social media listening?
4. Discuss three additional approaches you would suggest Moodley Manor should use. Justify your suggestion in each case.
5. How has the research enabled Moodley Manor to be more consumer oriented in its approach, and do you think this has led to the discovery of different segments of consumers?

This case was prepared by Christina O'Connor and Geraldine Lavin, Maynooth University, Ireland from various published sources as a basis for class discussion rather than to show effective or ineffective management. Their thanks go to Gavyn and Aisling, the co-founders of Moodley Manor, who have been giving of their time from 2015 to 2018 through a series of interviews.

Sources

Cleary, C. (2017) The rise of veganism: we are what we eat, *Irish Times Online*. Available at https://www.irishtimes.com/life-and-style/food-and-drink/the-rise-of-veganism-we-are-what-we-don-t-eat-1.3287187, accessed 5 April 2018.

Moodley Manor website (n.d.) **https://www. moodleymanor.com**.

Mooney, A. and **Pedley, G.** (2015) Moodley Manor Business Plan.

Pettit, A. (2011) The promises and pitfalls of SMR: prevailing discussions and the naked truth, *Marketing Research*, Fall: 15–21.

Reed, Z., McIlveen, H. and **Strugnell, C.** (2000) The retailing environment in Ireland and its effect on the chilled ready meal market, *Journal of Consumer Studies & Home Economics*, 24(4): 234.

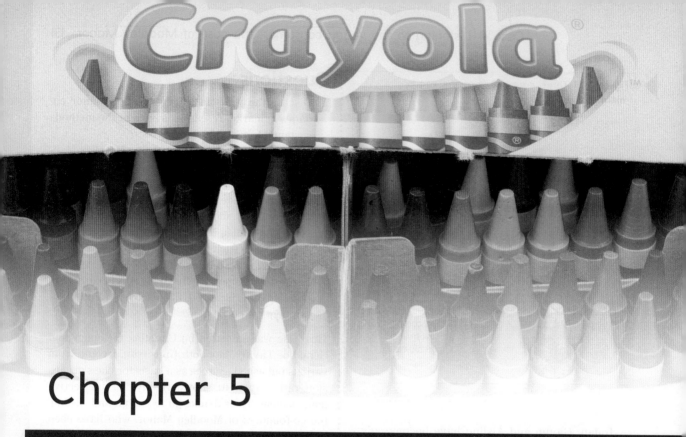

Chapter 5

Market Segmentation, Targeting and Positioning

Chapter outline

Segmenting consumer markets

Consumer segmentation criteria

Segmenting organizational markets

Criteria for successful segmentation

Target marketing

Positioning

Repositioning

Learning outcomes

By the end of this chapter you will:

1 Understand what is meant by market segmentation

2 Explain the methods used to segment both consumer and organizational markets

3 Explain the criteria for effective segmentation

4 Compare and contrast the four market targeting strategies – undifferentiated, differentiated, focused and customized marketing

5 Explain the concept of positioning and the keys to successful positioning

6 Analyse the concept of repositioning and the repositioning options available to the firm

7 Critique the role of market segmentation and targeting in society

Making Crayola the champion of creativity for tech-savvy kids

One of the most notable features of developing consumer markets is the emergence of new technologies for younger and younger consumers. Understanding and developing products and services for this quickly changing generation presents challenges and opportunities for marketers. This challenge has been particularly vivid for the wax-stick producer Crayola, with the traditional business rooted so far from the information age.

Formed in 1885, Crayola has produced art products for home and school use, and it has watched the change in 'play' over the generations, particularly in recent years as children have become more digitally savvy, and interactive toys like tablets and Hatchimals have become the preferred form of play. In response Crayola has been working to maintain its relevance with consumers (particularly teens) as a champion of creativity, remaining engaged with consumers on what they say, how they say it and where they say it! Crayola has invested significant revenue, with US$11.5 million spent on advertising in the USA in 2016 to help reinvigorate the brand for today's tech-savvy kids and to bring adults back to their childhood, playing on the emotional trigger of nostalgia and childhood memories.

Some of Crayola's efforts include fun collaborations with nail colours with Sally Hansen, and a lip colour collection with Clinique, which have been designed to attract the female market – teenagers, and adults along with their kids. Many art-focused offerings, like the Color Alive franchise, include a digital component that lets artists bring their drawings to life through an app. This has certainly reached the main target segment, the tech-savvy kid who wants to 'play' digitally. The brand is also expanding its Crayola Experience retail stores, which promote activities alongside products. The brand recognizes the importance of selling experiences to mall-weary shoppers and typically is located within a mall to attract families and young children to experience Crayola first-hand.

However, it was the simple removal of an old crayon – the Dandelion colour – and its replacement that caused the sensational revival of the tech-savvy consumer's interest. Crayola intended to announce Dandelion's demise in a much-promoted Times Square event on 31 March, National Crayon Day, in 2017. But a Target store shopper noticed the missing yellow and tweeted a picture, along with the message 'Bye-bye Dandelion. I never thought you were a weed. Hasn't @Target ever heard of a #SpoilerAlert!!!' Crayola responded, immediately serving up a social media missive about Dandelion's wanderlust and desire to start his retirement tour of schools and landmarks early. Rather than stealing Crayola's thunder, the tweet brought the campaign into the mainstream, with major news outlets covering the story.

The first week of the Dandelion announcement generated almost 5 billion impressions across Crayola's social media platforms. Consumers were voting among five possible names, such as Bluetiful and Dreams Come Blue, whittled down from 300,000 consumer suggestions. The campaign also paved the way for more spin-off social media feeds, which largely attracted adults and teenagers to follow and comment. Crayola also has sought to personalize its crayons, as a way of bringing them to life, with characters that are visible and fun for the younger segment of its market. This is merely the start, but the question remains whether Crayola can creatively reach and connect with the tech-savvy kid living within a tech-obsessed pop culture. Although kids are the main target audience, attracting adults and bringing them back to their childhood has been deemed a valuable target, as Crayola recognizes the role of the adult in purchasing and encouraging creative play through traditional analogue products such as Crayola.[1]

In our review of customer behaviour in Chapter 3, we saw that there are a variety of influences on the purchase decisions of customers. Their needs and wants vary and, no matter how good a company's product or service is, not all customers will want it or will be willing to pay the same price for it. For example, some consumers may feel that saving their money in order to be able to travel to New Zealand to do a bungee jump is a good idea, while others might rather spend their money now on the latest fashions in order to look good. While both these groups of consumers may have some similarities in their preferences, they also have some key differences. Therefore, to implement the marketing concept and satisfy customer needs successfully, different product and service offerings must be made to the diverse customer groups that typically comprise a market.

Exhibit 5.1 The Audi Q5 through its React 2018 campaign, focuses on its intuitive technology, like adaptive cruise control and self-learning personal route functions. It is as if the new Audi Q5 has a brain.

The technique used by marketers to get to grips with the diverse nature of markets is called **market segmentation**. Market segmentation is defined as 'the identification of individuals or organizations with similar characteristics that have significant implications for the determination of marketing strategy'.

Thus, market segmentation involves the division of a diverse market into a number of smaller submarkets that have common features. The objective is to identify groups of customers with similar requirements so that they can be served effectively, while being of a sufficient size for the product or service to be supplied efficiently (see Exhibit 5.1). Market segmentation, by grouping together customers with similar needs, provides a commercially viable method of serving these customers. It is therefore at the heart of strategic marketing, since it forms the basis by which marketers understand their markets and develop strategies for serving their chosen customers better than the competition. For example, a study of UK mobile phone consumers examined their attitudes to three dimensions of the purchase, namely consumer innovativeness, the need for emotion and prestige price sensitivity. From these variables four distinct clusters or segments emerged – cognitive adopters, prestige-seeking emotional innovators, emotional adopters and prestige-seeking cognitive innovators – with implications for positioning and the use of rational or emotional appeals in marketing communications.[2]

There are a number of reasons why it is sensible for companies to segment their markets (see Figure 5.1). Most notably, it allows companies the opportunity to enhance their profits. Many customers are willing to pay a premium for products or services that match their needs. For example, first-class air travellers regularly pay thousands of euros for long-haul flights, though the additional costs of catering for these customers is only marginally higher than that of catering for economy-class customers. In product categories like 'all-in-one' PCs, where all the key internal computer parts such as processors and graphic cards are encased with the monitor, consumers have the option of paying more than €1,200 for a top-of-the-range Apple iMac or approximately half that amount for models on offer from companies like Lenovo and Hewlett-Packard. Both of these price points and product offerings will appeal to different segments of the market.

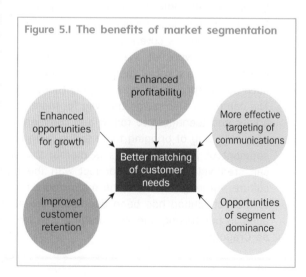

Figure 5.1 The benefits of market segmentation

Enhanced profitability

Enhanced opportunities for growth

More effective targeting of communications

Better matching of customer needs

Improved customer retention

Opportunities of segment dominance

Second, through segmenting markets, companies can examine growth opportunities and expand their product lines. For example, in marketing its over-the-counter cough medicines, the Pfizer corporation offers different products for different types of cough under the Benylin brand. In its children's medicines range, it offers separate products for chesty coughs, dry coughs and night coughs, while there are five different cough brands in its adult range. Finally, in many competitive markets, companies are not able to compete across all segments effectively; by segmenting markets, companies can identify which segments they might most effectively compete in and develop strategies suited to those segments. For example, in the audio equipment business, one of the leading brands is Bose, which has built a global reputation as a manufacturer of high-quality sound systems that are available only through select stores and at premium prices. By pursuing this strategy, Bose has successfully differentiated itself from competitors like Sony, Samsung and Pioneer, and, despite its premium prices, still has sales revenues of almost US$4 billion per annum.

Segmenting consumer markets

Consumer segmentation criteria may be divided into three main groups: behavioural, psychographic and profile variables. Since the purpose of segmentation is to identify differences in behaviour that have implications for marketing decisions, behavioural variables, such as benefits sought from the product and buying patterns, may be considered the ultimate basis for segmentation. **Psychographic segmentation** is used when researchers believe that purchasing behaviour is correlated with the personality or lifestyle of consumers. Having found these differences, the marketer needs to describe the people who exhibit them, and this is where **profile segmentation** such as socio-economic group or geographic location is valuable.[3] For example, a marketer may see whether there are groups of people who value low calories in soft drinks and then attempt to profile them in terms of their age, socio-economic groupings, etc. Figure 5.2 shows the major segmentation variables used in consumer markets and Table 5.1 describes each of these variables in greater detail.

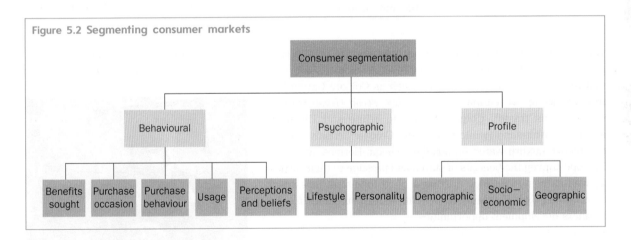

Figure 5.2 Segmenting consumer markets

Consumer segmentation criteria

Table 5.1 shows the variety of criteria that might be considered when segmenting a consumer market. In practice there is no prescribed way of segmenting a market, and different criteria and combinations of criteria may be used. In the following paragraphs we will examine some of the more popular bases for segmentation. It is also critical for marketers to remember that consumer psychographics and behaviour patterns change over time, so that consumers do not necessarily remain in the same segments but may move between them. It is important therefore that segmentation analyses are done with the most up-to-date information.

Benefits sought

Benefit segmentation provides an understanding of why people buy in a market, and can aid the identification of opportunities. It is a fundamental method of segmentation because the objective of marketing is to provide customers with benefits that they value. For example, a basic product like toothpaste can confer a

Table 5.1 Consumer segmentation methods

Variable	Examples
Behavioural	
Benefits sought	Convenience, status, performance
Purchase occasion	Self-buy, gift, special occasions
Purchase behaviour	Brand loyal, brand switching, innovators
Usage	Heavy, light
Media behaviour	Snapchat, Instagram, Netflix, radio
Psychographic	
Lifestyle	Trendsetters, conservatives, sophisticates
Personality	Conscientious, agreeable, extrovert
Profile	
Age	Under 12, 12–18, 19–25, 26–35, 36–49, 50–64, 65 and over
Gender	Female, male
Life cycle	Young single, young couples, young parents, middle-aged empty-nesters, retired
Social class	Upper middle, middle, skilled working
Terminal education age	16, 18, 21 years
Income	Income breakdown according to study objectives and income levels per country
Geographic	North vs south, urban vs rural, country
Geodemographic	Upwardly mobile young families living in larger owner-occupied houses, older people living in small houses, European regions based on language, income, age profile and location

variety of benefits, ranging from decay prevention to fresh breath, and great taste to white teeth. Colgate has developed sub-brands that provide each of these benefits, such as Colgate Cavity Protection (decay prevention), Colgate Max Fresh (fresh breath), Colgate Kids (taste), Colgate Sparkling White and Ultrabrite Advanced Whitening (white teeth), and Colgate Sensitive (sensitive teeth). Luxury watch brands like Omega, Hermès and Patek Philippe convey the benefits of status and prestige to their owners as well as being considered to be a good long-term investment (see Exhibit 5.2). Focusing on benefits helps companies to spot business development opportunities.

Purchase behaviour

The degree of brand loyalty in a market is a useful basis for segmenting customers. Some buyers are totally brand loyal, buying only one brand in the product group. For example, a person might invariably buy Fairy washing-up liquid. Most customers, however, practise brand-switching behaviour. Some may have a tendency to buy Fairy Liquid but also buy two or three other brands; others might show no loyalty to any individual brand but switch brands on the basis of special offers (e.g. money-off promotions) or because they are variety seekers who look to buy a different brand each time. A recent trend in retailing is 'biographics'. This is the linking of actual

Exhibit 5.2 This advertisement for Tag Heuer conveys the luxury status of the watch brand.

purchase behaviour to individuals. Initially this practice was pioneered by supermarkets, such Tesco with its Clubcard scheme, which used biographic data to segment and target customers very precisely. For example, it would be easy to identify a group of customers who were ground coffee purchasers and target them through special offers. Analysis of the data allows the supermarkets to stock products in each of their stores that are more relevant to their customers' age, lifestyle and expenditure. Online retailers such as Amazon, Asos and others have taken this to another level, building very accurate profiles of shoppers based on products purchased, items placed in checkout baskets and not purchased, as well as items viewed on their websites.

Usage

Another way of segmenting customers is on the basis of whether they are heavy users, light users or non-users of a selected product category. The profiling of heavy users allows this group to receive the most marketing attention (particularly promotion efforts) on the assumption that creating brand loyalty among these people will pay great dividends. Sometimes the 80:20 rule applies, where about 80 per cent of a product's sales come from 20 per cent of its customers. For example, companies like Netflix may find that the 80:20 rule applies to them – some users frequently bingeing on shows while many others are more occasional users. In some sectors, such as gambling, a focus on heavy users can raise significant social issues. While only 4 per cent of the population in the UK gamble online, almost one-third of heavy-user, at-risk gamblers do. The betting firm 888 was fined a record £7.8m in 2017 after more than 7,000 people who had voluntarily banned themselves from gambling were still able to access their accounts. However, attacking the heavy-user segment can have drawbacks if all of the competition are also following this strategy. Analysing the light and non-user categories may provide insights that permit the development of appeals that are not being mimicked by the competition. The identity of heavy, light and non-user categories, and their accompanying profiles for many consumer goods, can be accomplished by using survey information such as that provided by the Target Group Index (TGI). This is a large-scale annual survey of buying and media habits, and is available in more than 60 countries around the world.

Lifestyle

Lifestyle segmentation aims to categorize people in terms of their way of life, as reflected in their activities, interests and opinions. As we saw in Chapter 3, lifestyle is an important personal factor driving consumer behaviour, and advertisers have identified several different lifestyle groupings. Lifestyle is also a powerful method of segmentation as particular lifestyle groups have fairly predictable media habits (see Marketing in Action 5.1). For example, people who enjoy outdoor activities such as hiking and water sports will be likely to read magazines, watch television programmes, visit websites and join social networks dealing with these topics. Marketers can then use these media to reach their chosen segments.

Marketing in Action 5.1
Lululemon Athletica: serving a global niche

Critical Thinking: Below is a review of the growth and development of the athletic clothing brand Lululemon. Read it and evaluate the segmentation strategy being pursued by the company. What are the strengths and weaknesses of its approach?

After 20 years in the surf, skate and snowboard business in Canada, Chip Wilson took his first yoga class and found the results exhilarating. With a passion for technical athletic fabrics, he considered that the cotton clothing popular at the time was inappropriate for the stretching and sweaty activity that yoga can be. And, anticipating that yoga would grow in popularity, particularly with females, he

(continued)

founded Lululemon in 1998 and opened his first store in Vancouver, Canada, in 2000. The initial idea was that Lululemon would be not just a store but rather a community hub where people could learn about and discuss aspects of healthy living, from yoga to diet and cycling to running. While the ethos of healthy living is still central to the business, it has grown to become a large global retailer of yoga and athletic clothing, with more than 350 stores around the world and sales of $1.8 billion.

In building the business, Lululemon has developed a reputation for some novel marketing practices. Key among them are some of the things that it does not do – it does not use software to gather customer data, it does not use focus groups, it does not build lots of new stores and it does not offer generous discounts on its products. Instead it places a premium on staying close to its customers in the manner that it did when it was a smaller company. Senior management spend hours in stores each week observing how customers shop, listening to their complaints and then using this information to tweak products and stores. Sales staff are also trained to listen to customers, and folding tables are placed near fitting rooms so that customer comments can be heard. Stores have a large chalkboard where customers can write complaints and comments. Scarcity is a second key element of the firm's marketing strategy. A limited supply of many product lines is carried in stock so that demand for these items is high and consequently sold at full price. And a third key element of its marketing is its ambassador programme. Yoga and Pilates teachers are given free merchandise to wear while they teach in return for spreading the word about Lululemon.

The brand is also very active on social media, where it can continue the conversation about healthy living on platforms like Facebook and Instagram. From its inception, Lululemon's target market segment has been yoga practitioners and those females interested in healthy, active lifestyles. Its products were available only up to US size 12 (European size 16), thus effectively excluding many females from its products. When it encountered some quality problems with its yoga pants in 2013, Wilson caused a storm of controversy by arguing that the products simply didn't work for some women's bodies. These comments were later retracted but the incident was generally viewed as a public relations disaster. As the company seeks to grow it has added several new lines such as a men's range and the Ivivva range for girls aged 6–14.

Based on: Berg, 2014;[4] Mattioli, 2012;[5] Wexler, 2012[6]

An interesting example of the successful use of **lifestyle segmentation** is provided by a small US frozen foods firm, the SeaPak Shrimp Company. Although operating in a low-involvement product category that is often dominated by retailer own-brands, it identified two core but completely different lifestyle groups, namely those that 'live to cook' and those that 'cook to live', and set about creating separate brands for each segment. The live-to-cook lifestyle has a passion for cooking, for discovering new recipes and for preparing unique meals. SeaPak surrounded these shoppers with content that enabled their passion, such as access to famous chefs through online events, original seafood recipes and monthly emails. Other elements of the brand offering included higher-end non-breaded seafood products, upscale packaging and placement near the fresh seafood counter in supermarkets where these types of customers shop. For the cook-to-live group, the emphasis was on product quality and ease of preparation, with quick-bake breaded items in the frozen food section of shops. This two-segment approach yielded the firm a 15 per cent sales increase in a declining category.[7]

Age

Age is a factor that has been used in the segmentation of a host of consumer markets.[8] As we saw in Chapter 3 and the Marketing Spotlight, children have become a very important market believed to be worth about US$1 trillion per year and now have their own television programmes, cereals, computer games and confectionery. However, the importance of the baby market is also extremely interesting. A growing and very dynamic baby market exists, with growth expected to reach US$121 billion by 2025. This is an increase at a CAGR (Compound Annual Growth Rate) of 6.9 per cent from 2016 to 2025.[9] The market is attributing this increase to the growth in numbers of working mums, who are seeking the convenience of ready-to-use products. Many of the new businesses in the sector have been founded by working mums themselves such as Helen Wooldridge and Polly Marsh who set up Cuddledry in the UK.[10] The inspiration for the business was the difficulty mums have at bath time with a slippery baby and not enough hands, giving them the idea for the bath towel that parents wear like an apron while keeping both their hands free for lifting babies out of the bath and drying them (see Exhibit 5.3).

The role of children in influencing household purchasing is very significant. The expression 'pester power' is often used by advertisers to describe the process by which children subtly influence, or more overtly nag, their parents into buying a product. Young children are very brand aware. Studies show that more than 80 per cent of children aged between 3 and 6 recognize the Coca-Cola logo.[11] The charity Childwise has estimated that children in the UK spend £4.2 billion annually, demonstrating the size of the potential market.[12] It is also estimated that more than two-thirds of households buying a new car are influenced in the decision by their children. Therefore Toyota in Australia has very successfully included chickens, puppies and kittens in its advertising.[13] Overt efforts by firms to target children continue to be a significant source of controversy, as shown in Critical Marketing Perspective 5.1.

Exhibit 5.3 The Cuddledry Baby Bath Towel a novel innovation aimed at the baby market segment.

Critical Marketing Perspective 5.1
'Junk food' marketing to children

Few issues in marketing generate as much heated debate and discussion as the question of 'junk food' marketing to children. To many it represents the ugly and sinister face of capitalism. They see fast-food companies as deliberately targeting children in their advertising and communications to encourage them to pester their parents to buy products or even to seek products out themselves.[15] These opponents of marketing to children[16] have highlighted the systematic ways in which firms target younger and younger consumers. The skills adopted by 'junk food' marketers have been likened to the manipulative activities of Cambridge Analytical due to the hyper targeting of advertising using profile and behaviour information (see Critical Marketing Perspective 4.1).

But it's exactly what 'junk food' marketers have been doing for years: bombarding children with clever marketing messages that distort their food choices. The causal link between unhealthy food marketing and childhood obesity has been conclusively proved according to the Irish Heart Foundation, and as a result restrictions on broadcast advertising have been put in place to address this. However, this has not been the case for online advertising, as junk food marketers looked to digital marketing providing a more personalized and effective message to target the audience. As a result, 'junk food' brands have achieved a wholly inappropriate proximity to children called the 'brand in hand', targeting children relentlessly in school, at home, and even in their bedrooms through their smartphones.[17]

Marketers have access to volumes of individual information extracted from digital platforms such as Facebook on a child, as to who they are, where they live, how they socialize. They use this

(continued)

information to connect with children on a one-to-one basis, using powerful engagement, emotional and entertainment-based tactics, playing on fun and humour, using sports stars and celebrities, festivals and competitions. The effect is that children associate positive emotions and excitement with junk brands, and as a result they do not realize they are being advertised to. For example, brands get on to children's newsfeeds and interact like real friends, or by tagging friends to the brand's advert, which all happens behind parents' backs on social media. Much of the pester power parents are being subjected to is generated by 'junk food' brands pestering children.

Consequently, many countries have placed restrictions on 'junk food' advertising to children, most notably Australia and the Scandinavian countries, which have placed limits on both the type and amount of advertising that is allowed. For example, the Obesity Policy Commission (OPC) in Australia placed restrictions on advertisers on free-to-air television, with regard to the period of advertising. This was largely based on the broadcast of pre-school and children's programmes from 4p.m. to 5p.m.[18] However, these measures have also come in for criticism. Because of the proliferation of ways in which marketers can reach children, such as through programme and video-game sponsorship, marketing in schools, using cross-national television channels and social media, marketing to children is very hard to police fairly. Others have pointed to the fact that some countries have suffered a reduction in the quality of children's programming when they have banned advertising. And anyway, these critics argue, kids need to be exposed to marketing so that they can understand it and make informed decisions.

While it will continue to generate fierce debate, one thing seems certain and it is that 'junk food' marketers under more and more competitive pressures will continue to experiment with all sorts of ways of reaching and influencing the next generation of consumers.

Suggested reading: World Health Organization, 2016;[19] Barber, 2007[20]

Reflection: In your view, what kinds of restrictions (if any) should be placed on junk food advertising to children?

As we saw in Chapter 2, age distribution changes within the European Union are having a profound effect on the attractiveness of various age segments to marketers, with people over 50 years of age likely to become increasingly important in the future. Labelled the 'grey market', people are now living longer, with life expectancies rising into the eighties in developed countries around the world. Many 'grey consumers' are healthy, active, well educated, financially independent and have a lot of leisure time, making them a very attractive market. For example, in the music business, record companies have been struggling with the fact that the core market (young people) are buying less music, preferring to download it, often for free, from file-sharing websites. Therefore, Universal Music Group brought out a CD of songs for people who grew up in the 1950s named *Dreamboats and Petticoats*. It was so successful, it was followed by a West End musical and three other albums that have sold over 2.3 million copies.[14] Other media companies, such as television stations, radio stations and newspapers, are increasingly realizing that the best potential for their offerings may lie with the grey market.

Geography

At a very basic level, markets can be segmented on the basis of country or regions within a country or on the basis of city size. More popular in recent years has been the combination of geographic and demographic variables into what are called **geodemographics**. In countries that produce population census data, the potential exists for classifying consumers on the combined basis of location and certain demographic (and socio-economic) information. Households are classified into groups according to a wide range of factors, depending on what is asked on census returns. In the UK, variables such as household size, online behaviour, occupation, family size and ethnic background are used to group small geographic areas (known as enumeration districts) into segments that share similar characteristics. Two of the best-known geodemographic systems are ACORN (from its full title – A Classification Of Residential Neighbourhoods), produced by CACI Market Analysis, and MOSAIC, produced by Experian. The main ACORN groupings and their characteristics are shown in Table 5.2. CACI amalgamates a wide variety of open data files and commercial databases, all generally at address level. The result of classifying this data is then matched to many market research surveys and some 500 lifestyle variables to produce a detailed consumer picture of the UK. All 1.9 million postcodes are classified in this way, enabling some very precise targeting of the market. For example, for each of the groups listed in Table 5.2, CACI can provide information on such things as internet usage and social media activity in the past week, brand of smartphone owned, free and paid content downloaded to mobile phone, online purchases in the past 12 months, preferred hobbies and holiday destinations, and so on.

Using a similar classification system, MOSAIC Global classifies 380 million households from countries in Europe, North America and Asia Pacific. Based on the assumption that the world's cities share common patterns of residential segregation, it uses 10 distinct types of residential neighbourhood, each with a characteristic set of values, motivations and consumer preferences, to generate consumer classifications ranging from 'Comfortable Retirement' to 'Metropolitan Strugglers'. Geodemographic information has been used to select recipients of direct mail campaigns, to identify the best locations for stores and to find the best poster sites. This is possible because consumers in each group can be identified by means of their postcodes. Another area where census data are employed is in buying advertising spots on television. Agencies depend on information from viewership panels, which record their viewing habits so that advertisers can get an insight into who watches what. This means that advertisers who wish to reach a particular geodemographic group can discover the type of programme they prefer to watch and buy television spots accordingly. Advertising on social media sites like

Table 5.2 The ACORN targeting classification

Categories	% in UK population	Groups	% in UK population
A: Affluent Achievers	22.5	1 Lavish Lifestyles	1.3
		2 Executive Wealth	12.4
		3 Mature Money	8.8
B: Rising Prosperity	9.1	4 City Sophisticates	3.2
		5 Career Climbers	5.9
C: Comfortable Communities	27.2	6 Countryside Communities	6.4
		7 Successful Suburbs	6.1
		8 Steady Neighbourhoods	8.3
		9 Comfortable Seniors	2.5
		10 Starting Out	4.0
D: Financially Stretched	22.5	11 Student Life	2.5
		12 Modest Means	7.4
		13 Striving Families	8.1
		14 Poorer Pensioners	4.5
E: Urban Adversity	17.7	15 Young Hardship	5.1
		16 Struggling Estates	7.9
		17 Difficult Circumstances	4.7

Source: Neighbourhood Statistics (NISRA 2011 Census) Website: www.nisra.gov.uk/ninis Contains public-sector information licensed under the Open Government Licence v2.0. Sources include: Land Registry; Strategic Statistics Division; www.justice.gov.uk; DWP, 2012 Contains Crown Copyright data produced by Registers of Scotland. © Crown copyright material is reproduced with the permission of Registers of Scotland. Please see the following link for further information about this register of Scotland Crown Copyright data: www.ros.gov.uk/public/publications/crown_copyright1.html Copyright © (2012) Care Quality Commission (CQC); Care Inspectorate for Scotland 2012; CSSIW - Care and Social Services Inspectorate Wales 2012; Regulation and Quality Improvement Authority 2012. © CACI Limited 1979-2014 © Crown Copyright 2013 Adapted from data from the ONS (2011 Census) and National Records of Scotland, licensed under the Open Government Licence v.1.0.

Note: Due to rounding, the percentages total 99.

Facebook can also be targeted very specifically at customer groups based on the profile information submitted by members when they create their accounts, as we saw in Chapter 4.

A major strength of geodemographics is that it can link buyer behaviour to customer groups. Buying habits can be determined by means of large-scale syndicated surveys – for example, the TGI and MORI Financial Services – or from panel data (e.g. the grocery and toiletries markets are covered by AGB's Superpanel). By 'geocoding' respondents, those ACORN groups most likely to purchase a product or brand can be determined. This can be useful for branch location since many service providers use a country-wide branch network and need to match the market segments to which they most appeal to the type of customer in their catchment area. The merchandise mix decisions of retailers can also be affected by customer profile data. Media selections can be made more precise by linking buying habits to geodemographic data.[21]

In short, a wide range of variables can be used to segment consumer markets. Flexibility and creativity are the hallmarks of effective segmentation analysis. Often, a combination of variables (hybrid segmentation) will be used to identify groups of consumers that respond in the same way to marketing mix strategies. For example, Facebook used a combination of demographic, behavioural and attitudinal data to create 14 segments in the US voting population in 2016.[22]

Segmenting organizational markets

As we noted in Chapter 3, organizational markets, in contrast to consumer markets, tend to be characterized by relatively small numbers of buyers. Nevertheless, there are also many cases where it will be appropriate to segment organizational markets.

Organizational segmentation criteria

Some of the most useful bases for segmenting organizational markets are described below.

Organizational size

Market segmentation in this case may be by size of buying organization. Large organizations differ from medium-sized and small organizations in having greater order potential, more formalized buying and management processes, increased specialization of function, and special needs (e.g. quantity discounts). The result is that they may form important target market segments and require tailored marketing mix strategies. For example, the sales force may need to be organized on a key account basis, where a dedicated sales team is used to service important industrial accounts. List pricing of products and services may need to take into account the inevitable demand for volume discounts from large purchasers, and the sales force will need to be well versed in the art of negotiation. In contrast, decision cycles are often much shorter in smaller firms and it was with this in mind that the telecommunications company, T Mobile decided to focus on the small-to-medium business segment in the US market. It marketed its Simple Choice for Business plans to these customers using direct mail and email focusing predictable monthly costs and greater productivity on a faster network.[23]

Industry

Industry sector – sometimes identified by the Standard Industrial Classification (SIC) codes – is another common segmentation variable. Different industries may have unique requirements from products. For example, software applications suppliers like Oracle and SAP can market their products to various sectors, such as banking, manufacturing, healthcare and education, each of which has unique needs in terms of software programs, servicing, price and purchasing practice. By understanding each industry's needs in depth, a more effective marketing mix can be designed. In some instances, further segmentation may be required. For example, the education sector may be further divided into primary, secondary and further education, as the product and service requirements of these sub-sectors may differ. Industry sector is a very popular method for segmenting industrial markets.

Geographic location

The use of geographic location as a basis for differentiating marketing strategies may be suggested by regional variations in purchasing practice and needs. The purchasing practices and expectations of companies in Central and Eastern Europe are likely to differ markedly from those in Western Europe. Their more bureaucratic structures may imply a fundamentally different approach to doing business that needs to be recognized by companies attempting to enter these growing industrial markets. These differences, in effect, suggest the need for regional segments since marketing needs to reflect these variations.

Choice criteria

The factor of choice criteria segments the organizational market on the basis of the key criteria used by buyers when they are evaluating supplier offerings. One group of customers may rate price as the key choice criterion, another segment may favour product performance, while a third may be service orientated. These varying preferences mean that marketing and sales strategies need to be adapted to cater for each segment's needs. Three different marketing mixes would be needed to cover the three segments, and salespeople would have to emphasize different benefits when talking to customers in each segment. Variations in key choice criteria can be powerful predictors of buyer behaviour.

Purchasing organization

Another segmentation variable is that of decentralized versus centralized purchasing, because of its influence on the purchase decision.[24] Centralized purchasing is associated with purchasing specialists who become experts in buying a range of products, and is particularly popular in sectors like grocery retailing. Specialization means that they become more familiar with cost factors, and the strengths and weaknesses of suppliers than do decentralized generalists. Furthermore, the opportunity for volume buying means that their power to demand price concessions from suppliers is enhanced. They have also been found to have greater power within the decision-making unit (DMU – see Chapter 3) than decentralized buyers, who often lack the specialist's expertise and status to counter the view of technical members like designers and engineers. For these reasons, purchasing organization provides a good base for distinguishing between buyer behaviour, and can have implications for marketing activities. For example, the centralized purchasing segment could be served by a national account sales force, whereas the decentralized purchasing segment might be covered by territory representatives.

Interesting opportunities often appear at the intersection of consumer and industrial markets. For example, a small German technology company called Wagner has become the biggest supplier of spray guns for painting in the USA, with an 85 per cent market share. It used its expertise, built up through working with professional painters, to make products that also appeal to DIY painters. Its vast range of 3,000 products enabled it to span both consumer and industrial markets, with prices ranging from $50 up to $2 million for large industrial systems. Though most manufacturers concentrate on industrial segments, two-thirds of Wagner's sales in the USA came from consumer spray guns.

Criteria for successful segmentation

To determine whether a company has properly segmented its market, five criteria are usually considered.

1 *Effective*: the segments identified should consist of customers whose needs are relatively homogeneous within a segment, but significantly different from those in other segments. If buyer needs in different segments are similar, then the segmentation strategy should be revised.
2 *Measurable*: it must be possible to identify customers in the proposed segment, and to understand their characteristics and behaviour patterns. For example, some personality traits, like 'extrovert' or 'conscientious', might be difficult to pin down, whereas variables like age or occupation would be more clear-cut.
3 *Accessible*: the company must be able to formulate effective marketing programmes for the segments that it identifies (see Marketing in Action 5.2). In other words, it must be clear what kinds of promotional campaign might work best for the segment, how the products might best be distributed to reach the segment, and so on.
4 *Actionable*: the company must have the resources to exploit the opportunities identified through the segmentation scheme. Certain segments – for example, in international markets – might be identified as being very attractive but the company may not have the resources or knowledge necessary to serve them.
5 *Profitable*: most importantly, segments must be large enough to be profitable to serve. This is what is meant by the clichéd expression 'Is there a market in the gap?' Very small segments may be unprofitable to serve, though advances in production and distribution technologies mean that, increasingly, micro-segments can be profitable (see the section on customized marketing).

Marketing in Action 5.2
Maltesers' successful 'Look on the Light Side' campaigns

> **Critical Thinking:** Below is an example of a major brand that has identified diversity challenges of underrepresented segments of our society within advertising. Do you think that these advertisements will resonate with the Maltesers target consumer?

The perfectly circular-shaped melt-in-your-mouth chocolate offering by Maltesers does much more than taste good. In fact, it has created a growing campaign that *looks on the light side* in an attempt to shine the spotlight on invisible and misrepresented segments of society within advertising and communications. In 2018, Maltesers 'celebrating similarities' campaign is telling stories of diverse women who are often invisible in advertising, in a follow-up to the brand's successful campaign that aimed to break taboos of people with disabilities.

The first of these campaigns, launched by Maltesers in 2016, is currently the most successful campaign in the brand's history. In the ads people with disabilities recounted everyday situations such as running over a bride's foot with a wheelchair or, in another advert, a woman with cerebral palsy who experiences a mishap while having sex with her new boyfriend. That campaign won Channel 4's Superhumans Wanted competition for the Rio Paralympics, which awarded £1 million in free airtime to the best creative idea about diversity.

This latest effort by Maltesers in 2018 aims to tackle a different diversity problem: the inequality of gender representation in advertising, giving a light-hearted take on awkward or taboo moments. 'Powerpoint' is about women going through menopause, while 'Accountant' is about a lesbian who laments the challenges of dating. This is all done in line with the brand's down-to-earth nature. The source of inspiration for these stories was driven by focus groups with real women, whose stories inspired those depicted in the ads. The adverts were tested on social media, among employees and among new talent, with positive feedback received.

These campaigns are largely in contrast to Maltesers' advertising in the past, which actively focused on the message of 'low' in calories, aimed at young to middle-aged females. However, these latest advertisements centre on social issues. Ultimately the mission of Maltesers owner Mars is to inspire the entire UK market in leading change in increased diversity and inclusion within advertising and communications. This is a big mission, and so far consumers seem to be enjoying looking on the light side!

Based on: Kiefer, 2018;[25] Simpson, 2008[26]

Target marketing

Once the market segments have been identified, the next important activity is the selection of target markets. **Target marketing** refers to the choice of specific segments to serve, and is a key element in marketing strategy. An organization needs to evaluate the segments to decide which ones to serve using the five criteria outlined above. For example, the Coca-Cola brand Powerade conducted research across five European countries with people between the ages of 16 and 40 who practised sports at least two to three times per month. From this research, it identified seven consumer segments whose attitudes and needs varied significantly. The brand chose to focus on the 'true sportsman' segment, which saw participation in sports as a daily activity and way of life. Though a small segment of the market, this group played team sports twice as often as the average consumer and consumed a significant volume of sports drinks.[27]

The aim of evaluating market segments is for a company to arrive at a choice of one or more segments to concentrate on. Target market selection is the choice of what and how many market segments in which to compete. There are four generic target marketing strategies from which to choose: undifferentiated marketing, differentiated marketing, focused marketing and customized marketing (see Figure 5.3). Each option will now be examined.

Figure 5.3 Target marketing strategies

Undifferentiated marketing

Market analysis will occasionally reveal no pronounced differences in customer characteristics that have implications for a marketing strategy. Alternatively, the cost of developing a separate marketing mix for different segments may outweigh the potential gains of meeting customer needs more exactly. Under these circumstances a company may decide to develop a single marketing mix for the whole market. This absence of segmentation is called **undifferentiated marketing**. Unfortunately, this strategy can occur by default. For example, companies that lack a marketing orientation may practise undifferentiated marketing through lack of customer knowledge and focus. Furthermore, undifferentiated marketing is more convenient for managers since they have to develop only a single product/marketing strategy. Finding out that customers have diverse needs, which can be met only by products with different characteristics, means that managers have to go to the trouble and expense of developing new products, designing new promotional campaigns, training the sales force to sell the new products, and developing new distribution channels. Moving into new segments also means that salespeople have to start prospecting for new customers. This is not such a pleasant activity as calling on existing customers who are well known and liked.

Traditionally, undifferentiated marketing has been viewed as a flawed or even failed approach to targeting. However, some recent research suggests that targeting particular segments is overdone and that in mature markets a sophisticated form of mass marketing may be feasible. This involves recognizing market heterogeneity but, rather than try to respond to all differences, focus only on the critical ones in order to develop offerings that appeal to as large a slice of the market as possible.[28]

Differentiated marketing

Specific marketing mixes can be developed to appeal to all or some of the segments when market segmentation reveals several potential targets. This is called **differentiated marketing**; it is a very popular market targeting strategy that can be found in sectors as diverse as cars, hotels and fashion retailing (see Figure 5.4). For example, Arcadia's segmentation of the fashion market revealed distinct customer groups for which specific marketing mixes could be employed. In response, the group has a portfolio of shops that are distinctive in terms of shop name, style of clothing, décor and ambience. In all, the company has nine separate brands, including, for example, Miss Selfridge (aimed at the 18–24 age group), Dorothy Perkins (aimed at women in their twenties and thirties) and Evans (which stocks women's clothes that are size 16+). Similarly, as part of its turnaround strategy, Marks & Spencer sought to move away from one brand (St Michael) with wide market appeal, to a range of sub-brands such as Autograph (an upmarket brand) and Per Una, which is aimed at fashion-conscious women up to the age of 35. A differentiated target marketing strategy exploits the differences between marketing segments by designing a specific marketing mix for each segment.

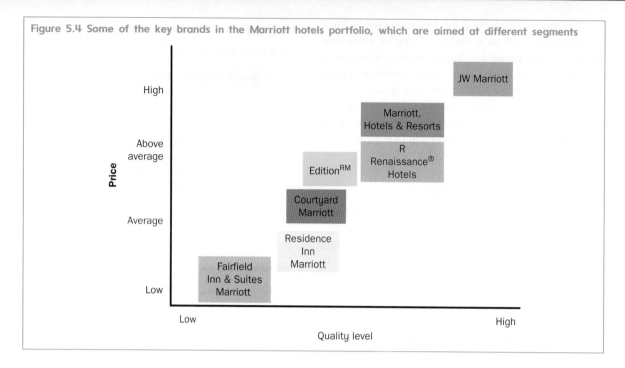

Figure 5.4 Some of the key brands in the Marriott hotels portfolio, which are aimed at different segments

Another significant advantage is that it enables firms to achieve economies of scale and spread costs over a wide range of potential customer groups (see Marketing in Action 5.3). This can be crucial in some industries, like car manufacturing, where complying with more stringent environmental regulations involves major costs. For example in 2013, the German manufacturer Volkswagen announced that it would be spending €84 billion over five years on new vehicles and technology.[29] Challenges and risks do exist for firms in pursuing a differentiated marketing strategy. Two of the risks associated with using a differentiated marketing strategy are creating confusion in the marketplace and spreading the organization's resources too thinly.

Marketing in Action 5.3
Luxor's differentiated marketing has helped it to expand

> **Critical Thinking:** Below is a discussion of the use of a differentiated marketing strategy by global pen manufacturer Luxor. What are the challenges that exist for Luxor in managing multiple brands such as Luxor, Parker and Pilot within India and beyond?

The Luxor group is the leading manufacturer and exporter of writing instruments today. Luxor was founded in 1963 in India, and became a global brand, Luxor International, in 1980, exporting to 85 countries across the globe. The company manufactures and markets pens and writing instruments under the Luxor, Parker and Pilot brands. So how has this company been so successful? Luxor knows how to reach out to different groups in different segments of the market.

The strategy being used is to remain flexible with its media mix and stay true to its brand promise. A smart mix of print and television has worked well for the brand, with some award-winning print campaigns and television commercials, which have established the brand in the minds of consumers. Luxor High-lighter's full-page ads in 2008 used images of the face of a historical character. The product was for students and the ad creative featuring historical figures like Che Guevara became a hit with this segment.

(continued)

Within India, Luxor focused on tapping in to consumers in smaller towns and exploring growth opportunities in the non-metro but rapidly expanding cities of India like Indore and Patna. Luxor's business in these cities needed a different approach using separate marketing strategies for different regions of the country depending on tastes and preferences. Parker focuses on the executive class, while Pilot is perceived as a youthful product trying to engage college students. Luxor carefully designs campaigns for each product, identifying the right media mix. One of its campaigns was focused on student examinations, with an advert stating 'Write more. Score more. Pilot wishes you all the best in your exams'.

In contrast, in 2011, when Luxor wanted to recreate the magic of Parker, it came out with a campaign called 'What the world calls a pen'. The multimedia campaign was targeted to reposition the brand as a pen for the real connoisseur on a global scale (see https://www.youtube.com/watch?v=ERUOmZiQbqQ). The campaign extensively used the print and television media to invigorate the charisma in Parker through various newspapers and niche magazines. The objective behind the campaign was to reach out to the masses, and to be positioned in the minds of millions, but ultimately to be so special as to be owned only by a select consumer base.

As a result of Luxor's different products with varying consumer bases, the business adopts a differentiated strategy. This involves a mix of television, print, digital and outdoor, which all form a very integral part of its media mix and, depending on the product and the target group, this will determine the media plan for that specific campaign. Brand Luxor, which started with writing instruments, has diversified into notebooks and other stationery product categories as well, but the real connect that allows the brand to comfortably expand its portfolio is the use of a differentiated marketing strategy and a strong brand promise.

Based on: Gaurav, 2014[30]

The casual clothing retailer Gap Inc. is a classic case of the former. There are different segments of the market for casual clothes, ranging from those who want to shop in discount outlets to those looking for smart casual garments for work or social events. To meet the needs of these different segments, Gap Inc. acquired both the Old Navy (discount fashions) and Banana Republic chains (smart casual). But a lack of sufficient differentiation between the three brands led to cannibalization of one another's sales, with first Old Navy taking sales from Gap and then Gap taking sales from Banana Republic as it tried to position itself away from the discount retailer.[31] Confusion and reputational damage can also be caused by how a brand owner chooses to differentiate. From example, the leading wine brand Wolf Blass chooses to identify most of its range by the colour of the label, with variants like Yellow Label and Red Label sold in supermarkets, while its more exclusive wines like Gold, Grey and Platinum Label are available only in specialist wine shops. However, because all of these brands share the Wolf Blass name, some consumers may associate the brand only with the low-price (and moderate-quality) wines that they see in supermarkets and not select it when choosing to buy an expensive wine.

Focused marketing

Just because a company has identified several segments in a market does not mean that it should serve them all. Some may be unattractive or out of step with its business strengths. Perhaps the most sensible route would be to serve just one of the market segments. When a company develops a single marketing mix aimed at one target (niche) market, it is practising **focused marketing**. This strategy is particularly appropriate for companies with limited resources. Small companies may stretch their resources too far by competing in more than one segment. Focused marketing allows research and development expenditure to be concentrated on meeting the needs of one set of customers, and managerial activities can thus be devoted to understanding and catering for those needs. Large organizations may not be interested in serving the needs of this one segment, or their energies may be so dissipated across the whole market that they pay insufficient attention to their requirements.

Exhibit 5.4 The FPS video game *Battlefield I* was the 15th instalment of the series and primarily targeted at existing fans of the franchise.

An example of a firm pursuing a focused marketing approach is Bang & Olufsen (B&O), the Danish audio electronics firm; it targets its stylish music systems at upmarket consumers who value self-development, pleasure and open-mindedness. Anders Kwitsen, the company's former chief executive, described its positioning as 'high quality, but we are not Rolls-Royce – more BMW'. Focused targeting and cost control mean that B&O defies the conventional wisdom that a small manufacturer could not make a profit by marketing consumer electronics in Denmark.[32] In sectors like luxury goods and video gaming, focused marketing is the norm (see Exhibit 5.4). For example, when Ferrari brought out its new hybrid car in 2013, it carried a price tag of £1.5 million and was primarily aimed at consumers who already owned at least five Ferraris, estimated to be a total of about 400 people worldwide.[33]

One of the challenges for focused marketers is to evolve their targeting strategy effectively as the market grows. For example, the sports nutrition supplements company Maximuscle traditionally focused on the narrow niche of bodybuilders, but has evolved the brand through its marketing communications to target a broader base of lifestyle gym-goers and those active in sports. To do this, it was necessary to overcome consumer resistance to sports supplements, which has connotations of steroids and other banned substances. Similarly, low-cost airlines that have traditionally focused on budget travellers have expanded their appeal to budget-conscious business travellers by offering some flights to primary airports like London Gatwick and Paris Charles De Gaulle, as well as offering priority boarding and access to frequent-flyer loyalty schemes.[34]

Customized marketing and personalization

The requirements of individual customers in some markets are unique, and their purchasing power sufficient to make viable the design of a discrete marketing mix for each customer. Segmentation at this disaggregated level leads to the use of **customized marketing**. Many service providers, such as advertising and marketing research agencies, architects and solicitors, vary their offerings on a customer-by-customer basis. They will discuss face to face with each customer their requirements, and tailor their services accordingly. Customized marketing is also found within organizational markets because of the high value of orders and the special needs of customers. Locomotive manufacturers will design and build products according to specifications given to them by individual rail transport providers. Similarly, in the machine tools industry, the German company Emag is a global leader in making 'multitasking' machines that cut metals used in industries like aerospace and vehicles. It practises customized marketing by manufacturing basic products at a cost-effective production site in eastern Germany but then finishing off or customizing these products in factories around the world that are located close to the customer.[35] Customized marketing is often associated with close relationships between suppliers and customers in these circumstances because the value of the order justifies a large marketing and sales effort being focused on each buyer.

Recent decades have seen a gradual growth in the potential application of customized marketing in consumer markets. The first stage in the 1980s was the development of flexible production systems, initially pioneered by Japanese companies to deliver customized products such as men's suits, bicycles and golf clubs to private consumers.[36] This was followed in other sectors such as technology where, for example, personal computer companies allowed their customers to configure products from a menu of options available to them. The practice has become ever more widespread. NikeiD enables customers to design their own personal versions of Nike shoes and apparel. Initially only available online, Nike has followed up the success of this service by opening NikeiD studios in Nike Town stores around the world. Consumers create designs in the studio, which can then be delivered either via the Nike Town stores or direct to their homes.

Advances in technology are continuing to facilitate developments in customized marketing in consumer markets (see Exhibit 5.5). This is particularly evident within the cosmetics industry. With all of us having unique skin tones, it is now possible through technology developed by MATCHco to scan your skin through your iPhone camera and blend a product that is 100 per cent customized.[37] The consumption of media and entertainment is also increasingly customized. Services like those offered by Netflix mean that the consumption of television and movies is highly individualistic. Online content aggregators play a similar role. Music streaming services like Spotify and Pandora create an individual listening experience, while news apps like Flipboard and Zite collect stories from around the web and tailor them to user preferences. An interesting feature of these apps is that they use software that tracks the news items that users read, like and share, and then feeds more of these types of content to them, further personalizing the experience. New developments, such as 3D printing, create the potential for a much wider range of customized products. Already this form of manufacturing is being deployed to create body tissues using living cells.[38] Using a process known as additive manufacturing, objects are created first from blueprints that can be adjusted and customized on a computer screen, and are then 'printed' out one layer at a time until the new product is built up. Because this kind of production does not need to happen in a factory, high levels of customization and niche production will be feasible.

Exhibit 5.5 Customizable cosmetics are changing the face of make-up: three custom colour specialists produce high-end make-up for all of their customers' personal beauty needs through their custom blending offering.

Customized marketing is reflective of the contemporary way of thinking about marketing as a value co-creation process based on close relationships between organizations and customers (see the discussion of service dominant logic and relationship marketing in Chapter 7). Research has found that products customized on the basis of expressed user preferences bring about significantly higher benefits for customers in terms of willingness to pay, purchase intention and attitudes toward the product than standard products.[39]

Personalization

The most recent expression of the rise of customized marketing is personalization, or personalized marketing, which has been defined as 'an approach where brands deliver messages, products, experiences and services on a one-to-one basis by leveraging data and technology to meet, or anticipate an individual customer's needs'.[40] Note the two important differences between customization and personalization. Whereas customized marketing involves the co-creation of products with customers, personalization may lead also to the creation of products for new customers and observing, usually through data analytics, that they have a profile similar to some existing customer. Second, personalization is about more than product creation – it also incorporates other elements, such as personalized advertising and experiences (see Exhibit 5.6).

The key enabler of personalized marketing is technology (see Figure 5.5). Consumers, particularly millennials, are increasingly heavy users of data-generating technologies.[41] We socialize online, liking, sharing and commenting on the things that interest us. We record our fitness and leisure activities on wearable devices. An ever increasing amount of our payments for goods and services are being conducted

Exhibit 5.6 Nutella created personalized Nutella jars as part of its Christmas campaigns for the brand.

electronically (see Case 9). And as the Internet of Things (IoT) continues to grow, everything from our cars to our fridges is recording and transmitting information about how we live our lives. Aggregating and mining these data gives marketers very accurate profiles of existing and potential customers. Graze, the British healthy snack food company, is a business built around the idea of personalized marketing. Despite being a food company, it exists almost entirely online and uses its propriety algorithm DARWIN (Decision Algorithm Rating What Ingredient's Next) to decide which of its 500 product lines will go into a snack box containing four or eight items. Graze's algorithms are informed by its customers, who provide more than 15,000 ratings per hour of snack box contents sent to them.

Positioning

So far, we have examined two key aspects of the marketing management process, namely market segmentation (where we look at the different needs and preferences that may exist in a market) and market targeting (where we decide which segment or segments of the market we are going to serve). We now arrive at one of the most important and challenging aspects of marketing: **positioning**. Positioning can be defined as

> *the act of designing the company's offering so that it occupies a meaningful and distinct position in the target customer's mind.*

This is the challenge that faces all organizations. All firms make products or provide services but, as we saw in Chapter 1, consumers buy benefits. Positioning is essentially that act of linking your product or service to the solutions that consumers seek and ensuring that, when they think about those needs, your brand is one of the first that comes to mind. For example, there is a segment of the car-buying market that values safety as one of its key purchasing criteria. Over the years, Swedish car manufacturer Volvo successfully positioned itself as one of the safest cars in the market through a combination of its design and its advertising messages. When asked which car they thought was the safest, Volvo was consistently mentioned by customers, though technical tests showed that it was not significantly safer than other brands in the market. This is the power of effective positioning: ensuring that your brand occupies a meaningful and distinct place in the target customer's mind. The clarity of Volvo's positioning contrasts markedly with that of Saab, another Swedish car brand, whose image

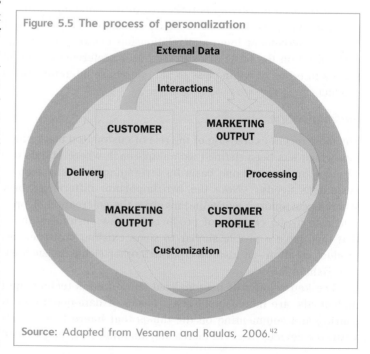

Figure 5.5 The process of personalization

Source: Adapted from Vesanen and Raulas, 2006.[42]

declined so badly that it had to be rescued from bankruptcy by an Asian consortium, NEVS, in 2012.

Colgate Ad Insight: This ad targets a particular audience by showcasing one benefit.

Exhibit 5.7 Kellogg's has positioned its Special K offering for females and its Bran Flakes for males.

An example of effective positioning can be seen in the array of breakfast cereal offerings from Kellogg's, with products for all members of the household (see Exhibit 5.7). Kellogg's offers two healthy options in the form of Special K and Bran Flakes. These products have clearly been positioned as an offering for females (Special K) and for males (Bran Flakes). For example, previous marketing campaigns run by Kellogg's signed up athletes such as Sir Chris Hoy, Olympic cyclist, to be the face of Bran Flakes, giving rise to Bran Flakes becoming known as 'Special K for men'.[43]

Positioning is both important and difficult. It is important because today we live in an over-communicated society.[44] Consumers are constantly exposed to thousands of marketing messages per day and, as we saw in Chapter 3, as few as 5 per cent of these messages may gain the attention of the target audience. To cut through this clutter, a company needs messages that are simple, direct and that resonate with the customer's needs. Failure to gain a position in the customer's mind significantly increases the likelihood of failure in the marketplace.

Developing a positioning strategy

Deciding what position to try to occupy in the market requires consideration of three variables, namely the customers, the competitors and the company itself. In terms of customers we must examine what attributes matter to them – there is little point in seeking a position that is unimportant from the customer's point of view. In many markets, competitors are already well entrenched, so the next challenge is to find some differential advantage that ideally cannot easily be matched. Third, as implied by the resource-based view of the firm, the company should look at building a position based on its unique attributes as this increases the likelihood that advantage can be sustained.[45]

Once the overall positioning strategy is agreed, the next step is to develop a positioning statement. This is a memorable, image-enhancing, written summation of the product's desired stature. The statement can be evaluated using the criteria shown in Figure 5.6. Coca-Cola has become one of the world's most valuable brands through its effective exploitation of catchy positioning slogans like 'You Can't Beat the Real Thing' in the 1990s and 'Open Happiness' in its 2000s advertising. The critical attributes of effective positioning are as follows.

1 *Clarity*: the idea must be perfectly clear, both in terms of target market and differential advantage. Complicated positioning statements are unlikely to be remembered. Simple messages such as 'BMW – The Ultimate Driving Machine', 'Apple – Think Different' and 'L'Oréal – Because I'm Worth it' are clear and memorable (see Figure 5.7).

2 *Consistency*: because people are bombarded with messages daily, a consistent message is

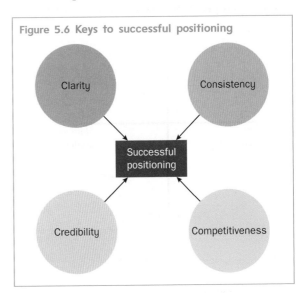

Figure 5.6 Keys to successful positioning

Clarity

Consistency

Successful positioning

Credibility

Competitiveness

required to break through this noise. Confusion will arise if, this year, we position on 'quality of service' and next year change this to 'superior product performance'. For example, Carlsberg built its brand using the positioning statement 'probably the best lager in the world' and then, having switched to 'that calls for a Carlsberg', decided to switch back again to its more established tag-line (see Marketing in Action 6.3).

3 *Credibility*: the selected differential advantage must be credible in the minds of target customers. An attempt to position roll-your-own cigarette tobacco as an upmarket exclusive product failed due to lack of credibility. Similarly, Toyota's lack of credibility as an upmarket brand caused it to use 'Lexus' as the brand name for its top-of-the-range cars.

4 *Competitiveness*: the chosen differential advantage must possess a competitive edge. It should offer something of value to the customer that the competition is failing to supply. For example, the success of the iPod was based on the differential advantage of seamless downloading of music from iTunes, Apple's dedicated music store, to a mobile player producing high-quality sound.

Apple Ad Insight: Apple Watch celebrates the diversity of its users and their passions.

The perceptual map is a useful tool for determining the position of a brand in the marketplace. It is a visual representation of consumer perceptions of a brand and its competitors, using attributes (dimensions) that are important to consumers. The key steps in producing a perceptual map are as follows:

Figure 5.7 Some classic advertising slogans

'We try harder.'	Avis
'Go to work on an egg.'	Egg Marketing Board
'Guinness is good for you.'	Guinness
'Don't be vague. Ask for Haig.'	Haig Scotch Whisky
'Happiness is a cigar called Hamlet.'	Hamlet
'Heineken refreshes the parts other beers cannot reach.'	Heineken
'Beanz Meanz Heinz.'	Heinz
'It is. Are you?'	The Independent
'Just do it.'	Nike
'Think small.'	Volkswagen

Source: www.adslogans.co.uk

1 Identify a set of competing brands.
2 Identify – using qualitative research (e.g. group discussions) – the important attributes consumers use when choosing between brands.
3 Conduct quantitative marketing research where consumers score each brand on all key attributes.
4 Plot brands on a two-dimensional map (or maps).

Figure 5.8 shows a perceptual map for seven supermarket chains. The results show that the supermarkets are grouped into two clusters: the high-price, wide-product-range group; and the low-price, narrow-product-range group. These are indicative of two market segments and show that supermarkets C and D are close rivals, as measured

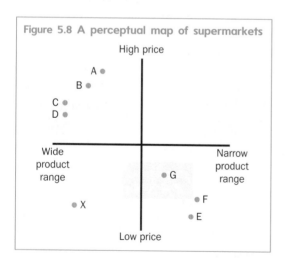

Figure 5.8 A perceptual map of supermarkets

by consumers' perceptions, and have very distinct perceptual positions in the marketplace compared with E, F and G. Perceptual maps are a visually appealing way of presenting a diverse market. They are also useful in considering strategic moves. For example, an opportunity may exist to create a differential advantage based on a combination of wide product range and low prices (as shown by the theoretical position at X).

Repositioning

Frequently, perhaps because of changing customer tastes or poor sales performance, a product or service will need to be repositioned. **Repositioning** involves changing the target market, the differential advantage, or both (see Figure 5.9). The first option is to keep product and target market the same but to change the image of the product. For example, many companies marketing products to older customers are realizing that they need to be very careful in not portraying this group as kindly, slightly doddery souls when many remain reasonably healthy and active into old age. Therefore, the Complan brand of powdered energy drinks has changed its image from one of a caring, sickbed 'meal replacement' drink to a proactive brand with a sense of humour, by using tongue-in-cheek cartoon characters on its packaging and in its advertising, engaged in lively activities like skateboarding and crowd surfing.[46] An alternative approach is to keep the same target market but to modify the product. For example, in the intensely competitive food delivery market, Just Eat has had to constantly improve its ordering and customer service app, and has invested in innovations such as allowing customers to order via Apple TV, Microsoft Xbox and smart TV platforms.[47]

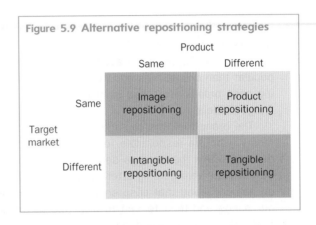

Figure 5.9 Alternative repositioning strategies

	Product	
	Same	Different
Target market — Same	Image repositioning	Product repositioning
Target market — Different	Intangible repositioning	Tangible repositioning

Some repositioning strategies involve retaining the product but changing the market segment it is aimed at (see Marketing in Action 5.4). Lucozade, a carbonated drink, is a famous example of this kind of so-called 'intangible repositioning'. Manufactured by Beechams Foods, it was initially targeted at sick children. Marketing research found that mothers were drinking it as a midday pick-me-up and the brand was consequently repositioned to aim at this new segment. Subsequently the energy-giving attributes of Lucozade have been used to appeal to a wider target market – young adults – by means of advertisements featuring leading athletes and soccer players. The history of Lucozade shows how a combination of repositioning strategies over time has been necessary for successful brand building. Several other brands have sought to repeat what Lucozade has done. For example, Rubex, the vitamin C drink, has transformed its positioning from a cold and flu drink to one that assists young people in overcoming the effects of a hard night's clubbing, while Red Bull has moved from a drink associated with clubbing to a more mainstream energy drink.

When both product and target market are changed, a company is said to be practising 'tangible repositioning'. For example, a company may decide to move up- or downmarket by introducing a new range of products to meet the needs of its new target customers. British Midland found it necessary to use both target and product repositioning in the face of growing competition in the airline business. The company was worried about its local British image and set about transforming itself into a global airline. It joined the Star Alliance led by Lufthansa and United Airlines, and commenced a long-haul service to the USA. It also spent £15 million on a corporate rebranding initiative to change its name from British Midland to bmi to create a more international appeal. The company was subsequently acquired by the Lufthansa Airlines Group in 2012.

Marketing in Action 5.4
Mattesson's Fridge Raiders: from mums to gamers

Critical Thinking: Below is a review of how Mattesson's effectively changed the target market for its Fridge Raiders brand. Read it and consider other examples of intangible repositioning that you have observed. How effective have they been?

Mattesson's Fridge Raiders is a perfect example of how intangible repositioning can turn around the fortunes of a brand that faces market challenges. Mattesson's is a UK-based processed meats company, manufacturing products like sausages, pates and sliced meats. In 2003, it successfully introduced Fridge Raiders, a meat snack, to the marketplace. However, 10 years later, this brand was in decline facing multiple challenges, including competition from own-label brands and the market leader Peperami. In addition, meat snacking was something of a niche activity, much less popular than crisps, nuts and popcorn in the snacking stakes. And, to make matters worse, leading crisp brands often had significantly bigger marketing budgets, whose spend dwarfed that of Fridge Raiders.

The brand took the courageous decision to move its focus away from its traditional target – mums, who are responsible for most of the grocery shopping – and focus instead on creating demand within the teenage segment. By examining teen lifestyles, the company observed that 61 per cent were gaming after school with two-thirds snacking during this time. Further research on gamers found that crisp snacking was a frustrating choice. Crisps rarely fully satisfied hunger pangs and they tended to give rise to greasy fingers, which made game playing difficult. This insight represented an opportunity for Fridge Raiders to create a new meat snacking occasion, while at the same time avoiding direct competition with other meat snack brands. To target the gaming market, Mattesson's enlisted the help of leading gaming vloggers. In a partnership with Syndicate Project and his followers, the company came up with the MMM3000 – the world's first hands-free meat snacking device. This was followed up by a collaboration with Ali A, another leading gamer, with more than 5 million followers, who received a mysterious delivery to his back garden. He and his followers had to crack a series of codes to reveal F.R.H.A.N.K, the world's first artificially intelligent snacking and gaming robot. F.R.H.A.N.K became something of a phenomenon in the gaming community, with content generating almost 14 million views.

Entering the new world of gaming, vloggers and meat helmets proved to be a brave and successful move for Fridge Raiders. By infiltrating the teen gaming culture, it created a new meat snacking occasion. More importantly, it moved from being a brand that was facing the axe to one of the shining stars in the group. It overtook Peperami as the meat snacking market leader, growing the category, and delivering significant sales and profitability growth for Mattesson's.

Based on: Chicourel and Poskett, 2016;[48] McVie, 2017[49]

Summary

This chapter has examined the key activities of market segmentation, market targeting and positioning. The following issues were addressed.

1. The process of market segmentation: not all consumers in the market have the same needs and we can serve them better by segmenting the market into groups with homogeneous needs.

2. A variety of bases are available for segmenting both consumer and industrial markets, and often a combination of bases is used to effectively segment markets. In consumer markets, behavioural variables such as benefits sought and purchase behaviour are particularly powerful bases for segmentation. Choice criteria are a key factor in segmenting organizational markets.

3. The five criteria for successful segmentation: effective, measurable, accessible, actionable and profitable.

4. The four generic target marketing strategies: undifferentiated marketing, differentiated marketing, focused marketing and customized marketing. Differentiated and focused marketing have their unique strengths and weaknesses, while customized marketing continues to grow in popularity.

5. The definition of personalization and the growing role of the personalization strategy for changing consumer demographics.

6. What is meant by the concept of positioning, why it is important, and the need for clarity, consistency, credibility and competitiveness in a positioning statement. Consumers buy benefits, not products or services, and positioning is the key to conveying these benefits.

7. The concept of repositioning and the four repositioning strategies: image repositioning, product repositioning, intangible repositioning and tangible repositioning. Repositioning is challenging and should be undertaken with great care.

Study questions

1. Discuss the advantages and related challenges of segmenting the market.

2. You have been asked by a client company to segment the confectionery market. Use at least three different bases for segmentation and describe the segments that emerge.

3. Many consumer goods companies have recently been experimenting with the possibilities of a customized target marketing strategy. What are the advantages and limitations of such a strategy?

4. Research has emerged that views the targeting of particular segments as overdone. Discuss the merits and weaknesses of the mass marketing approach of appealing to as large a slice of the market as possible.

5. A friend of yours wants to launch a new breakfast cereal on the market but is unsure how to position the product. Develop a perceptual map of the breakfast cereal market, identifying brands that compete in the same space, and also if there are gaps where there are currently no major brands.

6. What is the difference between positioning and repositioning? Choose a brand that has been repositioned in the marketplace and describe both its old positioning and its new positioning. Is its repositioning strategy best described as image, product, intangible or tangible repositioning?

7. Visit Experian.co.uk and review the MOSAIC Global geodemographic system. Select any one MOSAIC group (e.g. Sophisticated Singles) and identify some products that could be targeted at this group and what kind of marketing strategy would be most appropriate for reaching the group.

Suggested reading

Canhoto, A.I., Clark, M. and **Fennemore, P.** (2013) Emerging segmentation practices in the age of the social consumer, *Journal of Strategic Marketing*, 21(5): 413–28.

Diaz, A., Gomez, M., Molina, A. and **Santos, J.** (2018) A segmentation study of cinema consumers based on values and lifestyle, *Journal of Retailing and Consumer Behaviour*, 41: 79–89.

Dibb, S. and **Simkin, L.** (2009) Implementation rules to bridge the theory/practice divide in market segmentation, *Journal of Marketing Management*, 25(3/4): 375–96.

Franke, N., Keinz, P. and **Steger, C.J.** (2009) Testing the value of customization: when do customers really prefer products tailored to their preferences? *Journal of Marketing*, 73(5): 103–21.

Lutz, C. and **Newlands, G.** (2018) Consumer segmentation within the sharing economy: the case of Airbnb, *Journal of Business Research*, 88: 187–96.

Ries, A. and **Trout, J.** (2001) *Positioning: The Battle for Your Mind*. New York: Warner.

Yankelovich, D. and **Meer, D.** (2006) Rediscovering market segmentation, *Harvard Business Review*, 84(2): 122–31.

References

1. **Pasquarelli, A.** (2017) Crayola colors outside the lines. *adage.com*, 31 July.
2. **Aroean, L.** and **Michaelidou, N.** (2014) A taxonomy of mobile phone consumers: insights for marketing managers, *Journal of Strategic Marketing*, 22(1): 73–89.
3. **Van Raaij, W.F.** and **Verhallen, T.M.M.** (1994) Domain-specific market segmentation, *European Journal of Marketing*, 28(10): 49–66.
4. **Berg, M.D.** (2014) Lululemon scrambles to reverse its bad PR, *Adage.com*, 14 January.
5. **Mattioli, D.** (2012) Lululemon's secret sauce, *Wallstreetjournal.com*, 22 March.
6. **Wexler, E.** (2012) Brands of the year: Lululemon takes local to the Next level, *Strategy Online*, 2 September.
7. **Heile, C.** (2009) Brands: taking a narrow view, *Brandchannel.com*, 5 January.
8. **Tynan, A.C.** and **Drayton, J.** (1987) Market segmentation, *Journal of Marketing Management*, 2(3): 301–35.
9. **Grand View Research** (2017) Baby product market size to reach USD121.0 billion by 2025, *grandviewresearch.com*, January.
10. **Anonymous** (2009) Young Enterprise gives Entrepreneur Helen Woodbridge Self Belief to Succeed, *Telegraph.co.uk*, Available at www.telegraph.co.uk/finance/yourbusiness/young-enterprise/5344057/Young-Enterprise-gives-entrepreneur-Helen-Woodbridge-self-belief-to-succeed.html (Accessed 15 August 2018).
11. **Jones, H.** (2002) What are they playing at? *Financial Times*, Creative Business, 17 December, 6.
12. **Pidd, H.** (2007) We are coming for your children, *Guardian.co.uk*, 31 July.
13. **Lindstrom, M.** (2003) The real decision makers, *Brandchannel.com*, 11 August.
14. **Anonymous** (2011) Peggy Sue got old, *The Economist*, 9 April, 67–8.
15. **Bardon, N.** (2018) Junk food marketers targeting Irish children through social media ads – here's how ads find our kids, expand their waists, and shorten their lives, *TheSun.ie*, 18 April.
16. **Shannon, J.** (2018) Junk food marketers bombarding children, *Irishheart.ie*, 18 April.
17. **Pollak, S.** (2018) Irish children being manipulated by marketing of junk food, *irishtimes.com*, 18 April.
18. **OPC** (2018) Food advertising regulations in Australia, *opc.org.au*, January.
19. **World Health Organization** (2016) Tackling food marketing to children in a digital world: transdisciplinary perspective, *euro.who.int*.
20. **Barber, B.** (2007) *Consumed: How Markets Corrupt Children, Infantilize Adults and Swallow Citizens Whole.* London: W.H. Norton & Co.
21. **Mitchell, V.W.** and **McGoldrick, P.J.** (1994) The role of geodemographics in segmenting and targeting consumer markets: a Delphi study, *European Journal of Marketing*, 28(5): 54–72.
22. **Ritson, M.** (2017) Facebook's segmentation abilities are depressingly impressive, *Marketingweek.com*. Available at www.marketingweek.com/2017/11/09/mark-ritson-facebook-segmentation/ (accessed 10 May 2018).
23. **Anonymous** (2014) T Mobile: B2B small business acquisition, *Warc.com*. Available at www.warc.com/content/article/dma/tmobile_b2b_small_business_acquisition/104293 (accessed 10 May 2018).
24. **Corey, R.** (1978) *The Organisational Context of Industrial Buying Behavior.* Cambridge, MA: Marketing Science Institute, 6–12.
25. **Kiefer, B.** (2018) Maltesers shines spotlight on misrepresented women in latest effort to diversify advertising, *campaignlive.co.uk*, 23 April.
26. **Simpson, A.** (2008) Maltesers less than 11 calories was misleading, *telegraph.co.uk*, 14 October.

27. **Anonymous** (2011) Powerade: keep playing, *Warc.com*. Available at www.warc.com/content/article/arfogilvy/powerade_keep_playing/93609 (accessed 31 May 2018).

28. **Ritson, M.** (2016) Ditching targeting for mass marketing is going back to the Dark Ages, *Marketing Week.com*. Available at www.marketingweek.com/2016/04/12/mark-ritson-ditching-targeting-for-mass-marketing-is-going-back-to-the-dark-ages/ (accessed 31 May 2018); **Sharp, B.** (2010) *How Brands Grow: What Marketers Don't Know*. Melbourne, Australia: Oxford University Press.

29. **Anonymous** (2014) Kings of the road, *The Economist*, 11 January, 49–50.

30. **Gaurav, A.** (2014) Luxor's differentiated marketing strategy has helped them expand, *Pitch*, 6 January, 1.

31. **Gayatri, D.** and **Phani Madhav, T.** (2004) Gap and Banana Republic: changing brand strategies with fashion, Case 504-087-1, European Case Clearing House.

32. **Richards, H.** (1996) Discord amid the high notes, *The European*, 16–22 May, 23.

33. **Ritson, M.** (2013) LeFerrari shows LeWay forward, *MarketingWeek.com*, 9 May.

34. **Anonymous** (2011) In the cheap seats, *The Economist*, 29 January, 56.

35. **Marsh, P.** (2004) Mass-produced for individual tastes, *Financial Times*, 22 April, 12.

36. **Westbrook R.** and **Williamson, P.** (1993) Mass customisation: Japan's new frontier, *European Management Journal*, 11(1): 38–45.

37. **Boyd, S.** (2018) Changing the makeup game with customizable cosmetics, *Forbes.com*, 23 February.

38. **Anonymous** (2014) Printing a bit of me, *Economist Technology Quarterly*, 8 March, 15–17.

39. **Franke, N., Keinz, P.** and **Steger, C.J.** (2009) Testing the value of customization: when do customers really prefer products tailored to their preferences? *Journal of Marketing*, 73(5): 103–21.

40. **Vesanen, J.** (2007) What is personalisation? A conceptual framework, *European Journal of Marketing*, 41(5/6): 409–18.

41. **Balta, H.** (2015) Personalisation for millennials, *Public Relations Tactics*. Public Relations Society of America, April.

42. **Vesanen, J.** and **Raulas, M.** (2006) Building bridges for personalization – a process model for marketing, *Journal of Interactive Marketing*, 20(1): 1–16.

43. **Charles, G.** (2008) Kellogg's signs up Olympic cyclist Chris Hoy, *campaignlive.co.uk*, 11 December.

44. **Ries, A.** and **Trout, J.** (2001) *Positioning: The Battle For Your Mind*. New York: Warner.

45. **Fahy, J.** (2001) *The Role of Resources in Global Competition*. London: Routledge.

46. **Dowdy, C.** (2005) Advertisers smoke out images of pipes and slippers, *Financial Times*, 7 November, 30.

47. **Roderick, L.** (2016) Just Eat on why its tech will become a 'permanent feature' in UK living rooms, *MarketingWeek.com*. Available at www.marketingweek.com/2016/06/17/just-eat-on-why-its-tech-will-become-a-permanent-feature-in-uk-living-rooms/ (accessed 31 May 2018).

48. **Chicourel, R.** and **Poskett, W.** (2016) The Mattessonassiance, *Warc.com*. Available at www.warc.com/content/article/ipa/the_mattessonaissance/107998 (accessed 31 July 2018).

49. **McVie, S.** (2017) How Fridge Raiders put influencers at the heart of its brand turnaround, *MarketingWeek.co.uk*. Available at www.marketingweek.com/2017/12/04/fridge-raiders-youtube-influencers/ (accessed 31 July 2018).

Brewdog and segmentation, targeting and positioning

Introducing Brewdog

'In today's interconnected digital world, full of savvy Gen Y consumers, every single thing you do is marketing,' wrote Brewdog co-founder, James Watt. Today, Brewdog is famous for selling a wide range of distinctively tasty and unusually named beers and stouts through its cool, minimalistic urban bars, and in garishly coloured cans through major supermarkets.

Watt and schoolfriend Martin Dickie began brewing beer as 22 year olds in a lock-up garage in Aberdeenshire, Scotland, in 2005. Two years later, they founded Brewdog, currently the fastest-growing food and drinks company in the UK, which is redefining the relationship between consumers and beer. Brewdog makes a wide variety of craft beers, rejecting the bland, gassy, commoditized drinks often produced by multinational brewing conglomerates in favour of quirky, distinctive, inventive and 'authentic' beers, using outlandish marketing and a seemingly 'anti-corporate' business model to engage its audiences.

Brewdog's first bar opened in Aberdeen in 2010, and there are now more than 30 in the UK, 14 in Europe, one in Australia, one in São Paolo, and two (including a craft beer hotel and new brewing facility) in Columbus, Ohio, USA. Breweries in China and Australia are planned and, as the company's market valuation has passed £1 billion, it intends to consign 'big, bland beer' to the history books. While critics of the brand accuse it of pretentious hipsterism, shock tactics and over-promotion, it commands a hugely loyal band of consumers, who consider themselves fans. To fund its rapid expansion, Brewdog regularly sells shares to its fans – 'Equity for Punks'. It now has more than 75,000 shareholders, who have contributed approximately £55 million. Brewdog really can claim that its customers are invested in the brand's success.

The UK's problematic beer market

The UK beer market has declined by a third in the past four decades, and around 20 public houses ('pubs') close for ever each week. This may be attributable to several factors. Traditional working-class industries such as coal mining, steelmaking and shipbuilding – all of which nurtured a male-dominated, beer-drinking culture – have largely disappeared, along with many of the pubs where workers would gather in evenings to ▶

socialize and drink. The UK and other governments have progressively sought to discourage problem drinking within society through alcohol taxation and marketing communications conveying the potentially deleterious health effects of alcohol – a form of 'demarketing', seeking to reduce, rather than increase, consumer demand. Since the Western economic crash of 2008, many consumers have found themselves lacking disposable income for frequent nights out, and have sought alternatives. It is more common nowadays for younger consumers to drink canned or bottled alcohol at home before going to a bar or nightclub, and for older consumers to arrange dinner parties in which guests 'bring a bottle' – usually of wine. In fact, the UK is now Europe's biggest consumer of wine per capita, despite having only a very small domestic wine-making industry, as wine has quickly become a drink of the masses. Moreover, spirits, cocktails, 'mixers' and gin have been resurgent recently, as consumers seek inventive, distinctive and differentiated drinks – reflecting the fact that many people now drink not as a nightly social habit, but as a less frequent indulgence.

Quality and authenticity fight back

The Campaign for Real Ale (CAMRA, founded in 1971) in England seeks to encourage the brewing of 'quality' ales that differ substantially from those of multinational conglomerates. Championing quality beers, pubs and bars, CAMRA defines 'real ale' as beer brewed using water, hops, barley and yeast, free from added carbon dioxide, and literally 'living' or fermenting continuously in the cask (container), bottle or can from which it is served. The UK's thriving 'real ale' industry accounts for more than 11,000 different drinks and around 8 per cent of the beer market but, despite significant efforts to change the demographic, a disproportionately large number of enthusiasts are male, middle aged and middle class. Even among the Baby Boomer and Generation X segments, which form their natural demographic hinterland, 'real ale buffs' (i.e. consumers and enthusiasts of real ale) are often considered unfashionable. The United States also experienced a reaction against bland, commoditized corporate beer offerings, with a flourishing craft beer industry. Craft beer differs from real ale insofar as the qualifying criteria are less stringent. Most craft beers use powerful, bitter-tasting hops from the west coast of America, and are served cold. Brewdog contends that the term 'real ale' is meaningless and anachronistic, considering itself a maker of craft beers, but it helps smaller craft beer and real ale breweries to establish themselves, distribute their products and

challenge the corporates. It enjoys experimenting, often making small, one-off batches of unusually flavoured concoctions – its grapefruit-infused Elvis Juice and the extra-strong Cocoa Psycho Russian Imperial Stout proving surprisingly popular.

Brewdog versus the top dogs

Many beer brands compete in the UK and Europe, and this can lead towards commoditization. Even Stella Artois, which declares itself 'reassuringly expensive', has been deeply discounted in supermarkets such as Asda, potentially distressing its brand. Many household brands are owned by a few multinational conglomerates (e.g. Budweiser, Michelob and Rolling Rock by Anheuser-Busch, Guinness and Harp by Diageo). Some bigger players (e.g. Diageo, Carlsberg, Heineken) are represented in the UK by a self-founded, self-regulating industry watchdog called the Portman Group. Its declared aim is to promote responsible drinking and marketing, but Brewdog founder, James Watt, has called it a 'thinly veiled cartel . . . making sure their member companies entrench their market position' – in other words, the ringfencing and bolstering of their corporate privilege at the cost of consumers and of smaller competitors. The Portman Group often criticizes Brewdog. One instance was when a Brewdog advert used the line, 'Drink fast, live fast, sleep late and rip it up down empty streets', which the Portman Group said encouraged irresponsible drinking. On another occasion, the Portman Group objected to Brewdog using the term 'aggressive' on a label, so Brewdog instead launched a product called SpeedBall, named after a powerful heroin and cocaine-based drug, which was immediately banned by the Portman Group and garnered huge publicity. Brewdog appears to enjoy controversy and fighting establishment figures. An 18 per cent stout – six times stronger than many beers – caused much consternation in the industry, although it was sold in only very small quantities through a controlled channel. Brewdog used the resulting publicity and word-of-mouth communications to launch a 0.5 per cent ABV beer called Nanny State, thus being paradoxical and unpredictable.

Segmentation

In pursuing its stated aims of encouraging people to be passionate about craft beer and challenging the Portman Group members, Brewdog must appeal to a broad demographic. James Watt contends that the company must expand rapidly and constantly to achieve this. Therefore, the market segment that makes up so many real ale enthusiasts – white, middle-class, middle-aged men – would simply be too narrow and unsustainable to fuel Brewdog's business model or mission. In short, it needs younger consumers, belonging to Generation Y, and particularly millennials, and a larger proportion of women. This is achieved through a segmentation strategy that is often behavioural but mainly psychographic. By having a strong brand personality, which suggests the rebel/outlaw archetype, confronting the establishment, appearing subversive and having leaders who publicly personify the brand, the relationship between Brewdog and its customers is built on shared values and a short psychological distance, and is therefore more powerful.

Targeted communications and branding

Brewdog is extremely transparent in its internal communications. Production and retail updates are issued weekly to its teams, and its weekly company newsletter, *DogTales,* is also made available externally. 'Crew Members' at all levels have complete freedom to challenge colleagues, managers and processes, enjoy access to the organization's monthly profit and loss figures, and are fully involved in the recruitment of their colleagues. In its external marketing communications, Brewdog aims to be direct, honest, fresh and uncompromising. It is sufficiently transparent to publish its recipes, allowing fans to brew their own. One video on its website, entitled 'Don't buy the advertising', showed a Brewdog poster strapped across a tower block, which was then demolished. Another video shows one of the co-founders throwing bottles of beer into the air while the other blasts them with a shotgun. In 2015, they dropped stuffed cats on to the City of London (and its 'fat cats') from a helicopter to celebrate crowdfunding £5 million – and these are not even its most outrageous or humorous publicity stunts.

Brewdog utilizes a range of approaches to attract, engage and retain customers. In 2018, it gave away one million beers, prompting customers to spread the word to friends. An *Intergalactic Bar Visa* stamp book (itself a modern variation on a traditional technique used by local chapters of CAMRA) is available to fans, setting out challenges, such as the 'Flying Scotsman', in which customers have at least one drink in all the brand's Scottish bars. The Brewdog Chain Gang is an initiative encouraging cycling clubs to use Brewdog bars as their clubhouses – riders log their ride details in a joint Strava/Brewdog competition table, engendering gamification and community. Equity Punks (shareholders) get ID cards giving discounts, free beers on their birthdays, an invitation to the Annual General Meeting (which is in the form of a music festival) in Aberdeen, a *Craft Beer for the People* book, and certain voting rights. Boosted benefits for high-value shareholders include factory tasting and dinner tours, free trips to the craft beer hotel in Columbus, Ohio, opportunities to distil Lonewolf Whisky and keep cases of one's own-recipe beer, and even installation of a Brewdog bar, with three taps, a keg and fridge, at home.

Positioning through values

Brewdog has very distinctive values – originality, daring, non-conformity, inclusivity and fun – which permeate every aspect of the brand's DNA. In aiming to 'revolutionize the beer industry and completely redefine British beer-drinking culture', its mission is 'to make other people as passionate about great craft beer as we are'. Brewdog has selected its 1,000+ staff very carefully, and treats them exceptionally well, aiming to be the best company to work for, ever. The first 'Living Wage' employer in the sector, it provides staff benefits such as phone counselling services, private healthcare, generous pension contributions, discounts, a monthly beer allowance, early Friday home time, 'beer schools' and support through prestigious training degrees (successful graduates getting significantly boosted salaries), as well as childcare vouchers – which it says are 'not redeemable in Brewdog bars'! It also has a number of unusual employee initiatives: in addition to the enhanced maternity and paternity allowances, it grants one week's paid 'pawternity leave' to owners of new puppies, to allow them to start the housetraining process and bond with their dog; dogs are allowed to accompany office staff to work; a Unicorn Fund donates 10 per cent of all company profits to charities voted for by staff and Equity Punks (shareholders); it shares a further 10 per cent of its profits among all its staff teams, with all ranks benefiting equally; it will match any staff charitable fundraising up to £200 with a donation; and it grants staff four weeks' paid sabbatical every five years, plus an all-expenses Copenhagen Beer Festival trip after ten years.

Conclusion

Brewdog has travelled a huge distance in a very short time without spending heavily on advertising, selling out or becoming corporate. It has enthused customers and fans, crowdsourcing investment from them and generating word-of-mouth communications among them. It offers a broad and varied product range, a highly visionary and democratic ethos, visible and vocal leaders, an engaging and fun experience in its bars or from afar, and – perhaps most important of all – an extremely differentiated brand that appeals to younger adults and intuitively taps in to the anti-establishment Zeitgeist.

Questions

1. What would be the main benefits to Brewdog of its market segmentation strategy?
2. How would you evaluate the success of Brewdog's approach to segmentation?

3. To date, Brewdog has taken a focused approach to its market targeting. Is this still appropriate, or should it now consider a differentiated marketing strategy?
4. Evaluate Brewdog's positioning strategy.

This case was prepared by David Brown, Northumbria University, UK from various published sources as a basis for class discussion rather than to show effective or ineffective management.

Part 2

Creating Customer Value

Chapter 6

Value through Products and Brands

Chapter outline

What is a product?

Product differentiation

Branding

Building brands

Managing brands

Managing product and
brand portfolios

Managing brands and
product lines over time:
the product life cycle

New product development

Learning outcomes

By the end of this chapter you will:

1   Understand what is meant by a product in
    marketing terms

2   Explain the differences between products and brands

3   Analyse the alternative ways of differentiating products

4   Evaluate the key aspects of building and managing a
    successful brand

5   Critique the role of brands in society

6   Analyse how to manage a diverse product or
    brand portfolio

7   Understand how product performance evolves
    over time

8   Explain the importance of innovation and the new
    product development process

Samsung

When we think of any high-end consumer durable like a camera, MP3 player, integrated mobile phone, plasma TV or even a camcorder, Samsung naturally comes to mind. In 2017, Samsung was ranked number six on Interbrand's 'Best Global Brands' list, with a brand value of US$56.2 billion. From being on the verge of bankruptcy during the 1997 Asian financial crisis, Samsung has become a truly world-class business empire.

Samsung is a South Korean multinational conglomerate headquartered in Samsung Town, Seoul. It comprises numerous affiliated businesses, most of them united under the Samsung brand. It was founded by Lee Byung-chul in 1938 as a trading company. Over the next three decades, the group diversified into areas including food processing, textiles, insurance, securities and retail. It entered the electronics industry in the late 1960s and this area of its business would drive its subsequent growth.

Samsung Electronics is the flagship division within the group, and a global leader in semiconductors, telecommunications and digital media technologies. It employs more than 300,000 people worldwide and spends more than US$10 billion on research and development each year. Samsung is the leading smartphone vendor worldwide. In 2016, its market share of the global smartphone market was around 20 per cent, with Apple as its closest competitor in the market. In 2016 alone, the South Korean company sold more than 300 million smartphones worldwide. It also holds a sizeable position in the tablet computer market, with the Android-powered Samsung Galaxy Tab competing against Apple's iPad. In early 2017, Samsung held the position of the second largest tablet vendor in the world, accounting for around 16.5 per cent of all shipments. Aside from having a strong presence in the mobile market, it is also successful in the semiconductor industry and in 2018 surpassed Intel to become the world's biggest semiconductor manufacturer. It has been the world's largest television manufacturer since 2008, and the South Korean giant is also the world's largest producer of LCD panels and has the greatest share of the global market for NAND flash memory.

From the beginning, Samsung had to fight to change customers' perceptions of it as a manufacturer of cheap electronic goods. Starting in 1993, it adopted an aggressive branding and advertising strategy, which has helped reposition the brand from a cheap manufacturer to a brand of class and quality. Samsung's branding philosophy is built on five main pillars: innovation, cutting-edge technology, world-class designs, recruiting the world's best talents, and internal branding. It also uses many different communication channels to convey its brand positioning and personality. Mass media advertising, public relations, event sponsorship, sports sponsorship, product placements, the Samsung experience gallery and Samsung experience retail stores have been its major brand communication channels.

It hasn't all been smooth sailing for the brand. In late summer 2016, it launched the Note 7 smartphone but, within weeks of launch, disaster struck as customer reports starting to come in of the phone catching fire and even exploding. Samsung quickly lost US$26 billion in value on the stock market and the future of the Note 7 and Samsung was in question. This was followed by the arrest of the company's de facto chairman Jay Y. Lee in a bribery scandal that took down the South Korean president. Lee's sentencing confirmed what had long been suspected: links between the nation's most successful and renowned company and the country's government.

However, Samsung seems to have shrugged off this crisis. Its sales have rebounded and, in 2017, the electronics company reported a record US$50 billion profit. Experts say that a mix of factors, including Samsung's crisis response, its position in the global smartphone market and good timing for the worst possible news, helped the brand escape a crisis that could have set it back

(continued)

for years or even have put it under. Samsung Electronics plans to buy up more companies in 2018 and is planning on moving out of its comfort zone and focusing on three new sectors: automotive, digital health (particularly preventative health) and business software. All the evidence shows that Samsung continues to thrive and its future looks bright.[1]

As we saw in Chapter 1, the essence of marketing is the delivery of value to some customer group. Products and brands are the embodiment of that value proposition. For example, until recently, two of the dominant brands in the mobile phone business were Nokia and BlackBerry. In the early part of this century, Nokia was the undisputed global leader in the rapidly growing mobile phone industry. It led the way in consumer markets with innovative designs, the most extensive product range and a strong brand proposition, namely 'connecting people'. In terms of the decade from 2000 to 2009, Nokia accounted for more than one-third of all mobile phones sold globally, far ahead of its nearest rival, Motorola. Canadian brand BlackBerry was more favoured by business professionals as it contained a full QWERTY keyboard and a facility for checking and responding to emails. So powerful was its appeal that it earned itself the nickname 'Crackberry' – a reference to the addictiveness of the drug, crack cocaine. Towards the end of the last decade, these two brands were also the leaders in the then emerging smartphone business, Nokia with 39 per cent and Black-Berry a further 20 per cent of the market in 2009. But their failure to match the innovativeness and market orientation of brands like Apple and Samsung has meant that their decline since then has been swift. In 2017, Nokia's smartphones captured 1 per cent of global market share and BlackBerry's share of the global smart-phone market was 0.01 per cent. That same year, the two former titans of the mobile market staged a comeback in an attempt to resurrect their brands and they launched eight Android phones between them that year. However, to date neither has been able to stage its anticipated triumphant return and it is clear that neither one has turned the tide.[2]

This chapter will deal with all these core marketing issues. First, we will begin by examining what we mean by the term 'product', and then explain the difference between a product and a brand, which is one of the most important distinctions that students of marketing must grasp. Then we will take a comprehensive look at the different aspects of managing modern brands. Many firms, such as global corporations like Diageo or Colgate, can have an extensive range of brands, so we will also examine how to manage these portfolios of brands or products. As the example of brands like Nokia and BlackBerry shows, the demand for products can change very rapidly, so we will look, too, at how to manage products and brands effectively over time. An important element of this is innovation and ensuring a steady supply of new products, which is also discussed.

What is a product?

Conventionally, when thinking about products, people tend to think of tangible items such as a mobile phone, a plasma screen television or a kettle, and so on. These are all products but, in marketing terms, the definition of what comprises a product is much broader. A visit to a theme park like Legoland is a product, so is a sports star like Usain Bolt, so is the running of the bulls in Pamplona, the fundraising efforts of the International Red Cross and the political activities of the Liberal Democratic Party. In marketing terms, any form of value that is offered in exchange for money, votes or time is a product. In recent years, we have seen an increase in the marketing of ideas. For example, **social marketing** has emerged as a field of study due to the increase in marketing efforts behind socially beneficial causes such as the reduction in obesity and alcoholism and the promotion of wilderness protection, human rights and so on.

One of the most effective ways to think about products is in terms of their mix of tangible and intangible components (see Figure 6.1). Some products are high on tangible components and the company's marketing of these products places a great deal of emphasis on these tangible elements. Those at the intangible end of the spectrum are usually referred to as services and in Chapter 7 we will focus more specifically on the types of marketing efforts that are employed when creating value through service, experiences and relationships. But it is important to remember that almost all value offerings combine elements of both tangible and

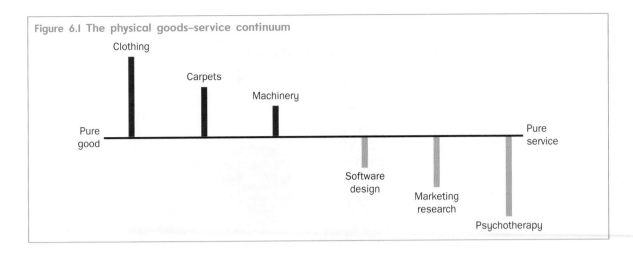

Figure 6.1 The physical goods–service continuum

Clothing

Carpets

Machinery

Pure good

Pure service

Software design

Marketing research

Psychotherapy

intangible components. Apple markets innovative handheld items like smartphones and tablets but the experience of the Apple store is an important part of its offering. A consultation with a psychotherapist is largely an intangible, mental activity but it will take place in a physical setting such as a consultation room (that probably contains a couch!).

The next important distinction that needs to be made is between products and brands. As we saw above, a product can be anything that has the capacity to satisfy customer needs by providing some form of benefit or value. **Brands**, on the other hand, fulfil the very important function of distinguishing the offering of one company from those of others in a competitive environment (see Exhibit 6.1). The word 'brand' is derived from the old Norse word 'brandr', which means 'to burn' as brands were and still are the means by which livestock owners mark their animals to identify ownership.[3] As we shall see, branding has become an ever more important aspect of marketing. This is due to the fact that the technical differences between products are becoming fewer and fewer. For example, the competing brands of many basic consumer electronics like flat-screen TVs may all be made in the same factory on the same production line. The technical features of the product are mainly the same – the key element that differs is the brand name. In these situations, value is derived less from the actual product and more from the brand associations. The power of brands to affect perceptions is particularly noticeable in blind product testing, where customers often fail to distinguish between competing offerings even though they may have a high level of loyalty to one brand. The power of brands over products can also be seen in the way that some products are more commonly known by the brand name than by the product name.

Exhibit 6.1 Years of brand development by Nike means that its 'swoosh' logo has become one of the most recognizable brand logos in the world.

Product differentiation

To understand fully both the nature of the product offering and how it can be best distinguished from those of competitors, it has been customary to think in terms of the different levels of product (see Figure 6.2). At the most basic level, there is the core benefit provided by the product, such as cars that provide transportation

Figure 6.2 The three levels of product

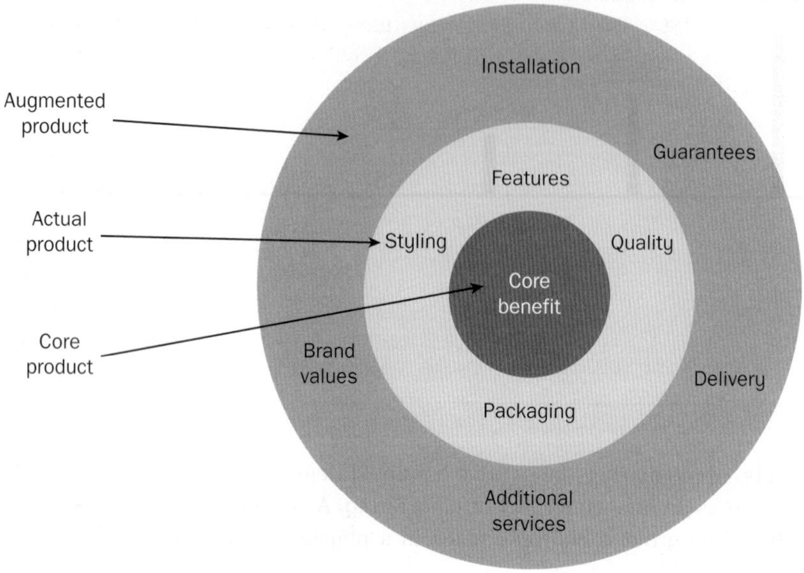

Augmented product →

Actual product →

Core product →

Installation

Guarantees

Features

Styling

Quality

Core benefit

Brand values

Delivery

Packaging

Additional services

or telephones that provide a means of communication. Products will quickly decline if the core benefit can be met most effectively in another way, as we saw in the case of Nokia. Around the basic benefit is the 'actual product' the consumer purchases, which comprises certain features, styling, and so on. For example, a Neff electric oven is an actual product, which is a blend of design, style, features and packaging assembled to meet the needs of the market. There is also a third level of product, namely the 'augmented product'. This is the additional bundle of benefits that are added to a product, and typically include elements like guarantees, additional services and additional **brand values**. For example, the Lexus GS includes extras like a keyless entry system, air-conditioned front seats, Bluetooth connectivity for mobile phones, parking-assist sensors and a rear electric sunshade. Product differentiation can take place at any of these three levels. Product differentiation is important as it has been found to have an impact on a firm's ability to use premium pricing, which in turn can have an impact on profitability.[4]

Core differentiation

The most radical product differentiation takes place at the core level and usually arises when there are significant technological breakthroughs. Therefore, the core benefit of keeping track of our appointments has moved from paper diaries to electronic ones stored on PCs or mobile phones, with significant implications for paper diary manufacturers like Filofax. Similarly, the music industry has been transformed many times as technological changes enabled consumers to switch first from albums to CDs and then from CDs to digital downloading and streaming. The first change meant a significant rise in profits for music companies, the second, a significant fall. Core differentiation also occurs due to shifts in strategic thinking. For example, for years, airlines have been trying to outdo one another by competing on actual differentiation such as expanding menu items on flights. Low-cost carriers have made huge inroads in the business by simply focusing again on the core benefit, namely moving people from one location to another, and by removing – or charging customers for – any extras.

Actual differentiation

Actual differentiation occurs when organizations aim to compete on the basis of elements of the product such as its quality, its design, its features or its packaging. Quality is a key aspect of the product and has long been positively associated with corporate performance. It refers to both the fact that a product is free from defects and that it meets the needs of customers. Around the world, most companies look to the uniform standards of the International Organization for Standardization (ISO) for quality guidelines through its various certifications such as ISO 9001. Operational systems such as total quality management (TQM) are employed to emphasize the relentless pursuit of quality. Problems with quality regularly undermine the marketing efforts of companies. For example, Toyota is one of the most renowned brands in the world but it suffered significant quality problems involving both the acceleration and braking of some of its car brands in 2009 and 2010. Also in 2018, Toyota recalled 645,000 vehicles worldwide to fix an electrical problem that could stop air bags from inflating in a crash.[5] In all, a total of more than 9 million Toyota vehicles have had to be recalled, resulting in damage to the brand as well as potentially expensive legal judgments against it. Product safety is particularly crucial in industries such as food, transport and medicines. How firms deal with these problems is also very important.

Duracell Ad Insight: This ad shows how Duracell aims to differentiate itself through the quality and durability of its products and its link to the Star Wars franchise.

With the increased difficulty of differentiating products based on their features many companies turn to elements like product design. Dyson has long differentiated its vacuum cleaners from others on the market by focusing on providing products that are well designed and function better than their competitors. James Dyson is known as a brilliant engineer and an exceptional designer and his love of product sets him apart. He cares about how a product looks, how it performs and how it can be different. Recent evidence of this can be seen in the launch of the company's latest Dyson Cyclone V10 vacuum. It operates on a powerful digital motor, which spins at 125,000 rpm, and is so advanced that it matches the power of any cylinder or upright cleaner that uses mains power, and has a battery life of 15 years. Dyson is so confident in the design of this product that in 2018 it announced that it would no longer develop vacuum cleaners that plug into the wall, stating that its future lies in cordless vacuums.[6] Other leading firms, like Apple and Sony, are renowned for their design capability. Key to effective design is a deep understanding of customer lifestyles and preferences.

Packaging involves all those decisions on the kind of container or wrapper used for the product. In the past, the primary purpose of packaging was simply to protect the product but in modern marketing it has a much more significant role in terms of attracting attention, carrying information about the product and conveying elements of the product's positioning. For example, the packaging of Apple products is highly distinctive, with a focus on style and minimalism. Organizations frequently change their product packaging as part of their marketing strategy but this is a difficult and risky thing to do. A major packaging change may mean that some existing customers no longer recognize or can find the product. For the Coca-Cola 'Share-a-Coke' campaign, Coke replaced its brand name on the packaging with the top 250 names in a particular country. Debranding its product in this way could have been a risky strategy, but luckily Coca-Cola's stylings and colours were still instantly recognizable.

There are several important ethical dimensions to packaging as well. Slack packaging describes the situation where products are packaged in oversized containers, giving the impression that they contain more than they actually do. The scale of growing plastic packaging waste is also causing huge public concern and has led companies such as Evian to reassess their use of plastic bottles. In response, Evian has recently vowed to use 100 per cent recycled plastic in its bottles by 2025.[7] Accurate labelling is also a significant issue, particularly in the case of food products. For example, in the UK, the 'country of origin' is only the last country where the product was 'significantly changed'. So oil pressed from Greek olives in France can be labelled 'French' and foreign imports that are packed in the UK can be labelled 'produce of the UK'. Consumers should be wary of loose terminology. For example, Batchelors Sugar Free Baked Beans actually contain 1.7g of sugar per 100g, Kerry LowLow Spread, which is marketed as low in fat, contains 42g of fat per 100g and Walkers Lite crisps are a hefty 22 per cent fat. Attempts by consumer groups to have labelling systems that highlight this information have been resisted by leading manufacturers and retailers, who favour a system whereby levels of sugar, fats and salt are given as a percentage of an adult's 'guideline daily amount'.[8] Similarly, EU legislation aims to outlaw vague claims such as 'vitalize your body and mind' (Red Bull) or 'cleanse and refresh your body and soul' (Kombucha).[9]

Augmented differentiation

Finally, organizations may choose to differentiate their offerings on the augmented dimensions. Most differentiation efforts take place at this level (see Marketing in Action 6.1). Firms are constantly looking for new features they can add that will give them an advantage in the marketplace. For example, mobile phone manufacturers are constantly trying to improve dimensions like screen size and resolution, weight and portability, navigation features and reliability. However, these types of advantages are often short-lived, being quickly

Marketing in Action 6.1
Adidas: differentiating the brand in a competitive market

Critical Thinking: Below is an account of Adidas's augmented differentiation strategy. Read it and consider other examples of augmented differentiation that you can think of.

Adidas is a multinational corporation, founded and headquartered in Herzogenaurach, Germany, that designs and manufactures shoes, clothing and accessories. It is the largest sportswear manufacturer in Europe and the second largest in the world after Nike. It is a household brand name, with its three-stripes logo recognized in markets across the world. Just a few years ago, it seemed like the global battle between Nike and Adidas for footwear dominance was all but over, with Nike emerging the clear winner. It was not only the bigger brand of the two, but its shoes were cooler and, simply put, Adidas didn't really seem to have any kind of stylistic or athletic advantage over Nike.

However, despite Nike's dominance, Adidas has given the leader some cause for concern over the past few years. Today the story for Adidas is very different as the brand benefits from its red-hot collaborations with Kanye West and its limited-edition NMD runners that have really resonated with a younger audience. It also has running shoes like the UltraBoost, which have become gym and street staples, and its comfortable Boost shoe soles, make a strong case to Nike Air devotees about making the switch. Meanwhile, Adidas classics like Stan Smiths, Gazelles and Superstars have all become favourites among fashion followers and regular consumers alike.

When you look back through history, Adidas was the only brand in sports that had a very strong connection to culture. In the 1980s, it was with Run-D.M.C. and Madonna, and it was the first brand back in the early 2000s to launch intense collaborations with fashion designers like Stella McCartney and Yohji Yamamoto with Y-3. It has always been a brand that has been looking at outside partners to collaborate with, and this continues to be a key strategy for the brand leading up to 2020. It is open to influencers who are dominant in youth culture, as its recent partnerships with Pharrell Williams, Kanye West and Rita Ora show. Adidas's cultural success is also reflected in its numbers: its overall footwear sales jumped 80 per cent in 2016, according to retail tracker NPD Group, while its stock price jumped 67 per cent between 2016 and 2017. Meanwhile, Nike's stock dropped by 3 per cent over the same period, even if it is still by far the bigger brand, generating US$30 billion of revenue globally in 2015 compared with Adidas's US$19 billion.

According to Arthur Hoeld, the company's senior VP of global brand strategy, Adidas has two advantages over its competitors. First, it is more authentically connected to culture and, second, it is more willing to experiment: 'We give people the freedom to have a creative discussion about what Adidas could look like. We are engaging with other viewpoints on the brand and invite strong conversations.' Nike has been a very strong competitor for Adidas over the last decade, but rather than copy Nike's approach, Adidas is confident in its future direction and differentiation strategy, which it hopes will help further close the gap between the rivals in the coming years.

Based on: Anonymous, 2017;[10] Lenton, 2018;[11] Woolf, 2017[12]

imitated by competitors or becoming standard parts of the offering of all major rivals. As a result, firms are putting greater efforts into intangible changes which cannot be so easily imitated. These intangible elements are captured in the brand and it is to this key decision that we now turn.

Branding

Developing a brand is difficult, expensive and takes time. We have seen that brands enable companies to differentiate their products from competitive offerings, but we must look in more detail at the benefits of brands for both organizations and consumers.

The benefits of brands to organizations

Strong brands deliver the following benefits to organizations.

Company value

The financial value of companies can be greatly enhanced by the possession of strong brands. The concept of **brand equity** is used to measure the strength of the brand in the marketplace and high brand equity generates tangible value for the firm in terms of increased sales and profits. For example, Nestlé paid £2.5 billion (€3.6 billion) for Rowntree, a UK confectionery manufacturer – a sum six times its balance sheet value. However, the acquisition gave Nestlé access to Rowntree's stable of brands, including KitKat, Quality Street, After Eight and Polo (see Exhibit 6.2).

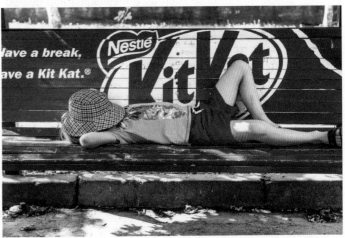

Exhibit 6.2 The Nestlé brand KitKat has used distinctive positioning and branding to build its presence in the competitive confectionery market

Consumer preference and loyalty

Strong brand names can have positive effects on consumer perceptions and preferences. This in turn leads to brand loyalty where satisfied customers continue to purchase a favoured brand. Ensuring a positive brand experience is critical for brand managers opting to maintain consumers' self–brand connection and brand loyalty.[13] Over time, some brands, such as Apple, Harley-Davidson and Virgin, become cult brands: consumers become passionate about the brand and levels of loyalty go beyond reason.[14] Companies are increasingly building online communities to engage consumers and build brand loyalty (see Marketing in Action 6.2). The strength of brand loyalty can be seen when companies try to change brands, such as Coca-Cola's proposed introduction of New Coke, or when the brand is threatened with extinction, such as Bewley's Cafés in Dublin.[15]

Barrier to competition

The impact of the strong, positive perceptions held by consumers about top brands means it is difficult for new brands to compete. Even if the new brand performs well on blind taste tests, this may be insufficient to knock the market leader off the top spot. This may be one of the reasons that Virgin Coke and Lucozade Cola failed to dent Coca-Cola's domination of the cola market.

High profits

Strong, market-leading brands are rarely the cheapest. Brands such as Kellogg's, Coca-Cola, Mercedes, Apple and Intel are all associated with premium prices. This is because their superior brand equity means that consumers receive added value over their less powerful rivals. Strong brands also achieve distribution more readily and

Marketing in Action 6.2
Snapchat and consumer engagement

Critical Thinking: Below is a review of the growth of Snapchat and its increasing use by companies and brands. Read it and evaluate the brands and companies that you currently follow on Snapchat. Why do these appeal to you? Reflect on your level of attachment to the brand or organization.

For all consumer-facing businesses, a prevalent, engaged brand community is the ultimate asset. Research has shown that branded communities not only drive greater reach, but also add value at the other points of the user journey, such as encouraging conversions, or improving existing customer relationships. These brand communities can be developed across many different social media platforms, such as Facebook, Twitter, Instagram or Snapchat.

Snapchat was once seen as a messaging app geared mostly towards teens and pre-teens. But over the last several years, the social network has added features and made changes that make it appealing for brands, celebrities and other influencers to create their own accounts. It is no longer a niche picture-texting service – it has become an established platform valued at more than US$19 billion, with in excess of 161 million daily users. From impressive uses of augmented reality to clever lenses and filters, the company logged more than one trillion snaps in 2017 – that's more than all the pictures taken by smartphones in the world. Recently, the company's CEO, Evan Spiegel, revealed that the photo and video-sharing app now receives 10 million video plays per day, surpassing Facebook's figures and cementing Snapchat's place among the world's most popular social media platforms.

As the number of engaged users grows, both fast-rising companies and established brands are seeking ways to capture the attention of Snapchat's engaged audiences and increase brand awareness by growing their Snapchat channels and creating Snapchat brand communities. An industry report by Social Media Examiner found that more than 90 per cent of businesses use social networking sites to market their brands and products, due to their ability to increase brand exposure, attract website traffic, develop loyal fans and gain marketplace intelligence. Marketers, brands and major publishers have started leveraging Snapchat's most popular features (like Stories, which allows users to stitch Snaps together to create a daily narrative), to promote upcoming events, show behind-the-scenes footage, or partner with top social media influencers for Snapchat takeovers or other influencer marketing collaborations.

One brand that has used Snapchat effectively to build a brand community and engage its followers is WOW Airlines. For example, one initiative used by the brand involved taking a page from the 'Best job in the world' campaign from Tourism Australia. WOW Airlines offered its Snapchat-savvy fans a chance to win the ultimate summer trip to some of the airline's 28 destinations. Dubbed the world's first-ever SnapTraveler programme, the campaign asked applicants to create a Snapchat story in English lasting under two minutes, save the video file and upload it to the company's contest microsite for a chance to win. WOW selected four winners from around the world, who spent the summer creating content for the company's social media channels, including Snapchat. In addition to generating 10 million views across the brand's social media channels, the contest also became WOW Air's most shared news story, with a total of 1.4 million social media shares. In addition to being a dream competition to win for fans, the contest was a great example of how a campaign can build a brand community and give consumers an opportunity to connect and engage with their favoured brands.

Based on: Hong, 2015;[16] Kolowich, 2017;[17] Anonymous, 2015;[18] Anonymous, 2015;[19] Gioglio, 2018[20]

are in a better position to resist retailer demands for price discounts. Research into return on investment for US food brands supports the view that strong brands are more profitable. The number one brand's average return was 18 per cent, number two achieved 6 per cent, number three returned 1 per cent, while the number four position was associated with a minus 6 per cent average return on investment.[21]

Base for brand extensions

A strong brand provides a foundation for leveraging positive perceptions and goodwill from the core brand to brand extensions. Examples include Pepsi Max, Diet Coke Feisty Cherry, Heineken Light and Google Scholar. The new brand benefits from the added value that the brand equity of the core brand bestows on the extension.

The benefits of brands to consumers

Brands also provide consumers with a variety of benefits, as follows.

Communicate features and benefits

In the first instance, brands are a source of information about a product. Through their associated marketing communications, they communicate information about a product and its benefits, which assists consumers in making a buying decision. The associated brand elements also make it easier for consumers to identify products.

Reduce the risk in purchasing

As we saw in Chapter 3, consumers experience a range of potential risks when they are making a purchase, including functional risks (that the product does not perform to expectations), financial risk (that it is not worth the price that is paid) as well as social risk (that the product produces social embarrassment). Brands reduce these risks because consumers can trust the brands they choose based on past experiences (see Exhibit 6.3).

Exhibit 6.3 Purchases such as car tyres carry several risks as this advertisement for one of the leading brands, Continental, demonstrates.

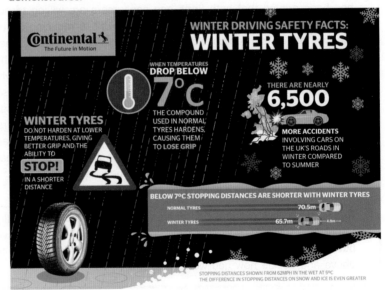

Simplify the purchase decision

As we have seen already, we live in an over-communicated society, where consumers are faced with a proliferation of product choices. To rationally evaluate all these options is impossible, so brands make consumers' lives easier by providing shortcuts for product choices. Trusted and preferred brands are purchased again and again, giving rise to the notion of brand loyalty.

Provide symbolic value

Most importantly of all, brands provide consumers with the opportunity for self-expression. Brands of clothing, music, cars, perfume and so on are powerful indicators of the consumer's personality type. For example, recent research has demonstrated the role of brands in signalling one's desirability to potential mates.[22]

Brands are not just a consumer phenomenon. They are also increasingly important in the worlds of industrial and technology marketing. For example, although many people would not recognize a microprocessor, the chances are that they have heard of Intel, one of the world's leading technology firms, which has invested heavily in branding. But it is not something that is simple, as Microsoft found in its forays into brand building. An advertising campaign featuring its founder Bill Gates and comedian Jerry Seinfeld confused many consumers.[23] The widespread development of brands in politics, popular culture and elsewhere means that the ethical dimensions of branding have taken on even greater importance (see Critical Marketing Perspective 6.1).

Critical Marketing Perspective 6.1
Ethical branding

For the past two decades, the concept of ethics has become increasingly important in the area of branding. There is widespread acceptance of the idea that consumers often take into account ethical considerations when evaluating and choosing between different brands. Marketers have realized that their ethics may constitute a viable and important dimension for differentiating and positioning their brand in the marketplace. By practising ethical marketing and promoting ethical brands, this may provide the company with a competitive edge over its rivals. Brands that take an ethical stance drive brand value and attract conscientious consumers. These consumers are increasingly taking an interest in brands' ethical positioning and ethical values, ahead of price, quality and overall reputation. As a result, when there is a lot of choice and competition in the marketplace, the importance of brand values may determine whether a person will choose one brand over another. A recent Aflac survey into the potential business impact of ethical commerce and corporate philanthropy found that 92 per cent of millennial consumers are more likely to buy products from ethical companies and 82 per cent of those consumers believe ethical brands outperform similar companies that lack a commitment to ethical principles. Companies that have been successful due to their ethical branding include Ben & Jerry's and The Body Shop (now owned by global giant L'Oréal).[24]

However, the incorporation of ethics into brand building can be a complex and tricky matter. It has been argued that both firms and consumers are willing to act ethically only as long as it can be aligned with a capitalist logic of making profit or reducing costs. When forced to decide between the two, ethics is often considered to be the least important. One of the risks of employing ethical branding is that there are multi-faceted meanings attributed to the concept by both marketers and consumers. This makes it difficult for consumers to establish which brands are genuinely ethical. It may also be unclear for firms what they need to do to be considered ethical brands. In addition, nurturing a brand image that is not mirrored by a firm's business practices involves an element of deception, which may generate a cynical attitude among consumers. Unfortunately, some companies have worked to create an ethical brand image but may fail to engage in ethical conduct. Truly ethical companies are those that embrace it not as a cheap gimmick that can be exploited to drive sales, but as a core part of their mission and values as organizations.[25]

Suggested reading: Bertilsson, 2014; Alwi et al., 2017

Reflection: Critics of marketing argue that ethics or acting ethically should become a matter of duty rather than free choice when selling brands. It should not just be viewed as a tool for differentiation, but rather something that people take for granted and expect from brands. Consider the points above and decide how you would respond.

Building brands

Building brands involves making decisions about the brand name and how the brand is developed and positioned in the marketplace.

Naming brands

Three brand name strategies can be identified: family, individual and combination.

A **family brand name** is used for all products – for example, Philips, Heinz and Google. The goodwill attached to the family brand name benefits all brands, and the use of the name in advertising helps the promotion of all of the brands carrying the family name. The risk is that if one of the brands receives unfavourable publicity or is unsuccessful, the reputation of the whole range of brands can be tarnished. This is also known as 'umbrella branding'. Some companies create umbrella brands for part of their brand portfolios to give coherence to their range of products. For example, Sony has created PlayStation for its range of video game consoles.

The **individual brand name** does not identify a brand with a particular company – for example, Procter & Gamble does not use its company name on its brands Always, Head & Shoulders, Pampers, Febreze, and so on (see Table 6.4). This may be necessary when it is believed that each brand requires a separate, unrelated identity. In some instances, the use of a family brand name when moving into a new market segment may harm the image of the new product line. One famous example is the decision to use the Levi's family brand name on a new product line – Levi's Tailored Classics – despite marketing research information which showed that target customers associated the name Levi's with casual clothes, thus making it incompatible with the smart suits the company was launching. This mistake was not repeated by Toyota, which abandoned its family brand name when it launched its upmarket executive car, the Lexus.

In the case of combination brand names, family and individual brand names are combined. This capitalizes on the reputation of the company while allowing the individual brands to be distinguished and identified (e.g. Kellogg's All Bran, Volkswagen Polo, Microsoft Windows 10).

Much careful thought should be given to the choice of brand name since names convey images. For example, Renault chose the brand name Safrane for one of its executive saloons because research showed that this brand name conveyed an image of luxury, exotica, high technology and style. The brand name Pepsi Max was chosen for the diet cola from Pepsi targeted at men as it conveyed a masculine image in a product category that was associated with women. So, one criterion for deciding on a good brand name is that it evokes positive associations.

Another important criterion is that the brand name should be memorable and easy to pronounce. Short names such as Esso, Shell, Daz, Ariel, Swatch and Mini fall into this category. Interesting examples of name shortening are taking place online. Facebook has used the domain name for Montenegro – .me – for fb.me. There are exceptions to this general rule, as in the case of Häagen-Dazs, which was designed to sound European in the USA where it was first launched. A brand name may suggest product benefits – as in the case of Right Guard (deodorant), Alpine Glade (air and fabric freshener) and Head & Shoulders (anti-dandruff shampoo) – or express what the brand is offering in a distinctive way, such as Furniture Village. Technological products may benefit from numerical brand naming (e.g. Audi A4, Airbus A380, Yamaha YZF R125). This also overcomes the need to change brand names when marketing in different countries.

Some specialist companies have been established to act as brand-name consultants. Market research is used to test associations, memorability, pronunciation and preferences. The value of a good brand name can be seen in the prices paid for some of the top domain names in the world, such as diamond.com (US$7.5 million), vodka. com (US$3 million) and cameras.com (US$1.5 million).[26] Even for an established brand entity, the brand name continues to be of importance over time and can have a long-term effect on a brand's equity.[27] It is important to seek legal advice to ensure that a brand name does not infringe an existing brand name. Interesting controversies can arise relating to brand names and trademarks such as Victoria Beckham's efforts to stop Peterborough United Football Club trademarking its decades-old nickname 'Posh'. More controversially, some companies are also trying to obtain the legal rights to slogans – such as Nestlé for the KitKat slogan 'Have a Break'.

Legal protection for a brand name, brand mark or trade character is provided through the registration of **trademarks**. As brands assume greater importance so too does their legal protection. The Nike swoosh, the Starbuck's mermaid and the Apple icon are all highly valuable to their owners, and these registered trademarks can be legally protected from copying by rivals. For example, Apple Computers won a court case against Apple Corporation – the owners of the Beatles Music company – which had sued against its use of the apple logo. Trademarks also need to be protected online. Search advertising regulations allow firms to use trademarks as keywords and in display ads, increasing the costs of trademark protection for brand owners.[28]

Table 6.1 summarizes those issues that are important when choosing a brand name, while Table 6.2 shows how brand names can be categorized.

Table 6.1 Brand name considerations

A good brand name should:	
1	evoke positive associations
2	be easy to pronounce and remember
3	suggest product benefits
4	be distinctive
5	use numerals when emphasizing technology
6	not infringe an existing registered brand name

Developing brands

Building successful brands is an extremely challenging marketing task. In fact, of Britain's top 50 brands, only 18 per cent have been developed since 1975.[29] This also implies that, when a brand becomes established, it tends to endure for a very long time. Table 6.3 lists the world's leading brands, some of which are more than 100 years old, so we can see that brand building is a long-term activity. There are many demands on people's attention; generating awareness, communicating brand values and building customer loyalty usually takes many years, which is why the rapid rise to prominence of brands like Amazon and Google is so admirable. As was highlighted in the Marketing Spotlight at the beginning of this chapter, Samsung has moved from being seen as a company that produced cheap televisions and microwave ovens to a leading global premium brand in sectors like mobile phones, memory chips and flat panels. This was achieved through doubling its marketing spend to US$3 billion, advertising that showed the company's prowess in technology, product placement in futuristic films like *Matrix Reloaded* and sponsorship of the Athens Olympics, which increased general awareness of the brand.[30] The value of the Samsung brand is now greater than that of the once dominant Sony. League tables like those presented in Table 6.3 are also illustrative in charting both the demise of venerable brands like Gap, BlackBerry and Hewlett-Packard,

Table 6.2 Brand name categories

Descriptive:	General Motors, The Body Shop, Shredded Wheat
Evocative:	Amazon, Virgin, Nike
Invented:	Exxon, Kodak, Xerox
Lexical:	Dunkin' Donuts, PayPal, Flickr
Acronym:	IBM, HP, GE
Geographical:	American Express, Halifax, Air France
Founder:	Ben & Jerry's, Ralph Lauren, Cadbury

Source: adapted from Lischer, B. (2018) *7 Popular Types of Brand Names.* San Diego, CA: Ignyte.

Table 6.3 The top 20 most valuable brands worldwide, 2017

Company	2017 brand value (US$ billions)	Country of origin	% change from 2012
Apple	184,154	USA	3
Google	141,703	USA	6
Microsoft	79,999	USA	10
Coca-Cola	69,733	USA	−5
Amazon	64,796	USA	29
Samsung	56,249	South Korea	9
Toyota	50,291	Japan	−6
Facebook	48,188	USA	48
Mercedes	47,829	Germany	10
IBM	46,829	USA	−11
General Electric	44,208	USA	3
McDonald's	41,533	USA	5
BMW	41,521	Germany	0
Disney	40,772	USA	5
Intel	39,459	USA	7
Cisco	31,930	USA	3
Oracle	27,466	UK	3
Nike	27,021	USA	8
Louis Vuitton	22,919	France	−4
Honda	22,696	Japan	3

Source: Interbrand.

and the rise of powerful new brands like Cisco, Amazon and Facebook. Management must be prepared to provide a consistently high level of brand investment to establish and maintain the position of a brand in the marketplace. Unfortunately, it can be tempting to cut back on expenditure in the short term, particularly when there is a downturn in the economy. Such cutbacks need to be resisted in order for the brand to be supported, as it is one of the key drivers of shareholder value.[31]

Figure 6.3 is an analytical framework that can be used to dissect the current position of a brand in the marketplace, and to form the basis of a new brand positioning strategy. The strength of a brand's position in the marketplace is built on six elements: brand domain, brand heritage, brand values, brand assets, brand personality and brand reflection. The first of these, brand domain, corresponds to the choice of target market (where the brand competes); the other five elements provide avenues for creating a clear differential advantage with these target consumers. These elements are expanded on briefly below.

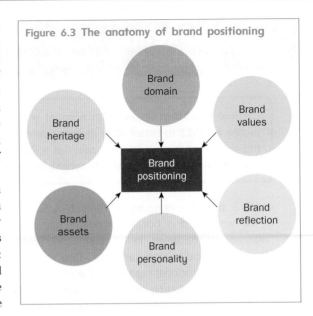

Figure 6.3 The anatomy of brand positioning

1 *Brand domain*: the brand's target market, i.e. where it competes in the marketplace.
2 *Brand heritage*: the background to the brand and its culture. How it has achieved success (and failure) over its life (see Exhibit 6.4). Hellman's is a brand that has a strong brand heritage. It has been around for more than 100 years and has obtained iconic status due to its ability to offer consistent quality to consumers over the years.
3 *Brand value*: the core values and characteristics of the brand.
4 *Brand assets*: what makes the brand distinctive from other competing brands (symbols, features, images and relationships, etc.).
5 *Brand personality*: the character of the brand described in terms of other entities, such as people, animals or objects. Celebrity endorsement of brands gives them personality. Sales of Cocoa Brown, a small Irish tanning brand, were significantly boosted when Kylie Jenner revealed her love for the product on Instagram. This helped raise the profile of the brand among a younger audience and helped the brand to move from being a niche brand to one with global appeal.[32]
6 *Brand reflection*: how the brand relates to self-identity; how the customer perceives him/herself as a result of buying/using the brand.

Brand managers can form an accurate portrait of how brands are positioned in the marketplace by analysing each of the elements listed above. Brand building is expensive and great care needs to be taken with brand investment decisions. A classic case in point has been the decision by Carlsberg to change its tagline, although some would argue unsuccessfully (see Marketing in Action 6.3).

Exhibit 6.4 This Hovis Bread advertisment focuses on the brand's heritage.

Siri Ad Insight: Apple has successfully used 'The Rock' in its Siri viral advertising campaign, which has helped raise the profile of the brand.

Marketing in Action 6.3
Carlsberg: 'Probably the best tagline in the world'

Critical Thinking: Below is an account of Carlsberg's efforts to change its iconic 'Probably' tagline in 2011 to better align its brand internationally. Read it and discuss the extent to which the change of tagline to 'That calls for a Carlsberg' was a good move for the brand. Are there any dangers associated with its recent decision to revert to the original 'Probably' tagline?

In 1973, the advertising agency Saatchi & Saatchi gave Carlsberg the tagline 'Probably the best lager in the world' and it became synonymous with the brand. That is, until the brand underwent an 'international makeover' in 2011 and the 'Probably' tagline was pushed aside for the brand's new slogan, 'That calls for a Carlsberg'. One reason for this change of tagline was Carlsberg's desire to engage in international expansion. Carlsberg wished to establish the brand as a global icon, with unity of image and marketing message across the globe. The 'That calls for a Carlsberg' tagline was aimed to add a greater sense of essence to the brand, to appeal to a new generation of drinkers. However, many questioned Carlsberg's bold move to replace its iconic 'Probably' tagline, and some speculated that this was a major risk for the brand. While the benefits of being successful in international markets were improved as a result of the tagline change, Carlsberg was running the risk of upsetting the UK market – a market that represents 40 per cent of the brand's profits.

For four years, Carlsberg launched a series of ads containing the 'That calls for a Carlsberg' tagline. However, in 2015, the brand made a surprising U-turn and decided to revert to its original 'Probably the best lager in the world' tagline. In 2015 it launched a TV and online ad, 'Probably the best supermarket in the world', and more recently, in 2017, introduced a £15 million advertising campaign featuring Danish star Mads Mikkelsen incorporating the 'Probably' slogan and focusing on the brand's Danish heritage. For the beer giant's marketing controller, Lynsey Woods, the creative marked a 'back to basics' approach for the brand.

Changing a tagline can be a powerful strategy for brand renewal or revitalization. However, Carlsberg's change of tagline on two occasions risks confusing customers. By reverting to the original 'Probably' tagline, there is a risk that it may be extremely difficult for the brand to emulate its previous successes. Some wonder if the process of revitalizing previous concepts is a good idea or will it just result in a tired and half-hearted advertising idea that will be considered overdone by consumers. In addition, some argue that reviving a previous idea/tagline displays a lack of imagination in times of uncertainty.

Based on: Wegert, 2016;[33] Millington, 2015;[34] Clark, 2011;[35] Gwynn, 2017;[36] Anonymous, 2015[37]

Managing brands

Once brands have been established, several important management decisions need to be made. The first of these is whether or not to extend or stretch the brand. A **brand extension** is the use of an established brand name on a new brand within the same broad market. For example, the Anadin brand name has been extended to related brands: Anadin Extra, Ultra, Soluble, Paracetamol and Ibuprofen. **Brand stretching** is when an established brand name is used for brands in unrelated markets. Among the most famous examples of brand stretching is the Virgin brand, which began life as Virgin Music (music publishing) and Megastores (music retailing) but grew to encompass more than 200 businesses in everything from financial services to modelling to rail travel (see Marketing in Action 3.2).

The question of whether or not the same brand can be marketed in the same way across geographic boundaries is an important decision facing brand managers when an organization internationalizes. The expansion of economic unions and the growing globalization of business are forces that seem to favour the use of standardized or **global branding** strategies, which help to reduce campaign costs and generate global uniformity for brands. Major multinational corporations adopt different approaches to the global/local choice. Unilever has cut its brand portfolio from over 1600 down to just 400 big brands that are marketed across international boundaries. Similarly, P&G has narrowed its brand portfolio, focusing the business on its 60–70 most important brands and cutting another 100 brands, selling some and shifting resources away from others.[38] Other companies have spent heavily on renaming local brands, such as Mars' decision to rename Marathon as Snickers, and P&G's decision to rename its popular Fairy laundry detergent as Dawn, with the aim of giving these brands global consistency.

In contrast, the German consumer group Henkel is going in the opposite direction. Like Unilever, Henkel has grown through the acquisition of local companies, but rather than focus on global leaders it maintains a portfolio of national and international brands. Persil, its premium brand in the laundry detergent business, is not suitable for the US market where washing machines on average use more water at lower temperatures than in Europe, so for this reason it paid US$2.9 billion for the Dial group in 2003 to acquire the US washing powder Purex. After the failure of Fa, its range of personal care products, in the USA, it acquired the deodorants Right Guard, Soft & Dri and Dry Idea from P&G for US$275 million. In the company's view, Americans tend to prefer to suppress sweating, while continental Europeans want to conceal any odour without blocking perspiration, illustrating the kinds of differences that can exist between markets.

Finally, a popular strategy for some companies today is co-branding, where two brands are combined. This may take the form of **product-based co-branding** or **communications-based co-branding**. Product-based co-branding involves the linking of two or more existing brands from different companies to form a product in which both brand names are visible to the consumer. There are two variants of this approach. **Parallel co-branding** occurs when two independent brands join forces to form a combined brand, such as HP and Apple iPod to form the HP iPod. **Ingredient co-branding** is where one supplier explicitly chooses to position its brand as an ingredient of a product. Intel is one of the best-known ingredient brands through its popular slogan 'Intel inside', seen on PCs worldwide.

There are a number of advantages to product-based co-branding. First, the co-branding alliance can capture multiple sources of brand equity, and therefore add value and provide a point of differentiation. Combining Häagen-Dazs ice cream and Baileys liqueur creates a brand that adds value through distinctive flavouring that is different from competitive offerings. Second, a co-brand can position a product for a particular target market. For example, Volkswagen teamed up with Trek mountain bikes to develop the Jetta Trek, a special edition of the Volkswagen Jetta. The car was equipped with a bike rack and a Trek mounted on top, and appealed to some 15 million mountain bikers. Finally, co-branding can reduce the cost of product introduction since two well-known brands are combined, accelerating awareness, acceptance and adoption.[39]

Communications-based co-branding involves the linking of two or more existing brands from different companies or business units for the purpose of joint communications. For example, one brand can recommend another, such as Whirlpool's endorsement of Ariel washing powder.[40] Also the alliance can be used to stimulate interest or provide promotional opportunities, such as the deal between McDonald's and Disney, which gives the former exclusive global rights to display and promote material relating to new Disney movies in its outlets. Communications alliances are very popular in sponsorship deals, such as Shell's brand name appearing on Ferrari cars.

Whatever basis is used to differentiate products in a market, three important product management issues remain – namely, managing large portfolios of products and brands, managing products over time and developing new products. We now turn to address each of these.

Managing product and brand portfolios

Some companies have a large portfolio of products or brands (see Table 6.4). They can be described in terms of a company's product line and mix. A **product line** is a group of products that are closely related in terms of their functions and the benefits they provide (e.g. Dell's range of personal computers or Samsung's line of television sets). The *depth* of the product line refers to the number of variants offered within the product line. A 'product mix' is the total set of brands or products marketed in a company. It is the sum of the product lines offered. Thus, the *width* of the product mix can be gauged by the number of product lines an organization offers. Philips, for example, offers a wide product mix comprising the brands found within its product lines of televisions, audio equipment, irons, vacuum cleaners, and so on. Coca-Cola, for example, is deemed to be more

Table 6.4 Sample brand portfolios of leading companies

Johnson & Johnson	Procter & Gamble	Nestlé	Unilever	L'Oréal	Diageo
Band-Aid	Always	Nescafé	Persil	Vichy	Guinness
Neutrogena	Bounce	Perrier	Surf	Garnier	Baileys
Regaine	Ambi-Pur	Maggi	Marmite	La Roche-Posay	Smirnoff
Sudafed	Pantene	KitKat	Domestos	Maybelline	J&B
Compeed	Pampers	Stouffer's	Cif	Lancôme	Bundaberg
Clean & Clear	Tampax	Purina	Dove	Ralph Lauren perfumes	Captain Morgan
Aveeno	Crest	Milo	Bovril	Helena Rubinstein	Pimm's
Acuvue	Vicks	Nespresso	Pot Noodle	Giorgio Armani perfumes	Ciroc
Pepcid	Head & Shoulders	Carnation	Knorr	Cacherel	Tanqueray
Tylenol	Gillette Fusion	Lean Cuisine	PG Tips	Shu Uemura	Johnnie Walker
Imodium	Braun	Buitoni	Lipton	Biolage	Archers
Visine	Olay	Nesquik	Vaseline	Diesel	Haig Club
Splenda	Tide	Häagen-Dazs	TRESemme	Redken	Ketel One
Benylin	Old Spice	Chef	Magnum		Smithwicks
Listerine	Herbal Essences	Smarties	Axe		Bells
	Oral B	Friskies	Slimfast		
	Febreze	Dreyer's	Brylcreem		
	Flash	Poland Spring	Bertolli		

vulnerable to market trends than its rival Pepsi because of its greater dependence on sales of sugary drinks, whereas Pepsi has a broader portfolio of drinks and food.

The process of managing groups of brands and product lines is called **portfolio planning**. This can be a very complex and important task. Some product lines will be strong, others weak. Some will require investment to finance their growth, others will generate more cash than they need. Somehow companies must decide how to distribute their limited resources among the competing needs of products so as to achieve the best performance for the company as a whole. Specifically, management needs to decide which products to invest in, hold or withdraw support from.

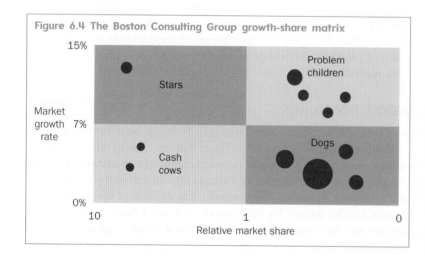

Figure 6.4 The Boston Consulting Group growth-share matrix

The Boston Consulting Group's (BCG's) growth-share matrix is a technique borrowed from strategic management that has proved useful in helping companies to make product mix and/or product line decisions (see Figure 6.4). The matrix allows portfolios of products to be depicted in a 2×2 box, the axes of which are based on market growth rate and relative market share. The size of the circles reflects the proportion of revenue generated by each product line. Market growth rate forms the vertical axis and indicates the annual growth rate of the market in which each product line operates; in Figure 6.4 this is shown as 0–15 per cent although a different range could be used depending on economic conditions. Market growth rate is used as a proxy for market attractiveness.

Relative market share refers to the market share of each product relative to its largest competitor, and is shown on the horizontal axis. This acts as a proxy for competitive strength. The division between high and low market share is 1. Above this figure a product line has a market share greater than its main competitor. For example, if our product had a market share of 40 per cent and our main competitor's share was 30 per cent this would be indicated as 1.33 on the horizontal axis. Having plotted the position of each product on the matrix, a company can begin to think about setting the appropriate strategic objective for each line.

The market leaders in high-growth markets are known as *stars*. They are already successful and the prospects for further growth are good. Resources should be invested to maintain/increase the leadership position. Competitive challenges should be repelled. These are the cash cows of the future and need to be protected.

Problem children (also known as *question marks*) are cash drains because they have low profitability and require investment to enable them to keep up with market growth. They are so called because management has to consider whether it is sensible to continue the required investment. The company faces a fundamental choice: to increase investment (build) to attempt to turn the problem child into a star, or to withdraw support, either by harvesting (raising the price while lowering marketing expenditure) or divesting (dropping or selling it). In a few cases a third option may be viable: to find a small market segment (niche) where dominance can be achieved.

The high profitability and low investment associated with high market share in low-growth markets mean that *cash cows* should be defended. Consequently, the appropriate strategic objective is to hold sales and market share. The excess cash that is generated should be used to fund stars, problem children that are being built, and research and development for new products. For example, the C&C group sold its soft drinks business (a cash cow) to Britvic for €249 million, a deal aimed to fund its star division: cider.[41]

Dogs are weak products that compete in low-growth markets. They are the also-rans that have failed to achieve market dominance during the growth phase and are floundering in maturity. For those products that achieve second or third position in the marketplace (*cash dogs*) a small positive cash flow may result and, for a few others, it may be possible to reposition the product into a defendable niche. For the bulk of dogs, however, the appropriate strategic objective is to *harvest* – that is, to generate a positive cash flow for a time – or to *divest*, which allows resources and managerial time to be focused elsewhere.

The strength of BCG's growth-share matrix is its simplicity. Once all of the company's products have been plotted it is easy to see how many stars, problem children, cash cows and dogs there are in the portfolio. Cash can be allocated as necessary to the different product lines to ensure that a balanced portfolio is maintained. For example, the world's biggest maker of alcoholic drinks, Diageo, sold off its food businesses such as Burger King in order to focus on its global brands in whisky, vodka and stout. However, the tool has also attracted a litany of criticism.[42] Some of the key problems with using the technique are as follows.

1 The matrix was based on cash flow but perhaps profitability (e.g. return on investment) is a better criterion for allocating resources.
2 Since the position of a product on the matrix depends on market share, this can lead to an unhealthy preoccupation with market share gain. In addition, market definition (which determines market share) can be very difficult.
3 The matrix ignores interdependencies between products. For example, a dog may need to be marketed because it complements a star or a cash cow (it may be a spare part or an accessory, for example). Alternatively, customers and distributors may value dealing with a company that supplies a full product line. For these reasons dropping products because they fall into a particular box may be naive.
4 Treating market growth rate as a proxy for market attractiveness, and market share as an indicator of competitive strength, is to oversimplify matters.

Despite these problems, the BCG matrix is still viewed as an important corporate portfolio planning technique.[43] However, there are many other factors that have to be taken into account when measuring market attractiveness (e.g. market size, the strengths and weaknesses of competitors) and competitive strengths (e.g. exploitable marketing assets, potential cost advantages) besides market growth rates and market share. This led to the introduction of more complex portfolio matrices such as the McKinsey/GE market attractiveness–competitive position matrix, which used a variety of measures of market attractiveness and competitive strength.

Marketing in Action 6.4
Dell's product lines

Critical Thinking: Below is an overview of some of the leading product lines in Dell Technologies' portfolio. Read it, plot along the lines mentioned on a BCG matrix and advise Dell on what it should do.

Dell Technologies is an American multinational computer technology company based in Texas, which develops, sells, repairs and supports computers and related products and services. Dell's revenue comes from selling a diverse portfolio of products including personal computers (PCs), servers, data storage devices, software, HDTVs, cameras, printers and MP3 players. The company was a pure hardware vendor for much of its existence, but in 2009 it entered the market for IT services and has since made additional acquisitions in storage and networking systems, with the aim of expanding its portfolio from offering computers only to delivering complete solutions for its customers.

Dell is operating in several market segments, some of which are more attractive than others. It is operating in some markets experiencing high market growth rates where substantial revenue can be earned, but is also involved in selling in other markets where market growth is less favourable. When it comes to Dell's PC business, worldwide the demand for PCs has decreased sharply as we move into the post-PC era and this has prompted Dell to decrease its reliance on PC sales and attempt to refashion itself more as a full-service technology company offering software and services. However, despite this slump in PC sales, about 60 per cent of Dell's revenue still comes from its PC sales, showing that Dell's PC business is still the backbone of the company. Dell has been able to continue to obtain substantial revenue through its PC business and this has helped the computer giant to maintain its strong position in the market, while using the profits generated by this segment to grow other areas of its business.

At present, Dell's monitor and laptop business is generating significant amounts of revenue for the company. Its ultra-thin monitor is operating in a growing industry that allows firms to create new product designs and use the innovative ideas to make the products profitable. Another notable example that has generated a significant amount of revenues for the company is its laptops, primarily the XPS 13, which is marked by a high degree of flexibility and offers users a 360-degree hinge, along with the ease of portability. It also has key features including wireless monitor connections, single-cable docking stations, WiGig (802.11ad gigabit wireless internet), and the ability to charge smartphones, all of which are relevant to changing consumer needs.

Dell's acquisition of EMC in 2016 facilitated its move into cloud computing. Although this has been an important move for the company, the future of cloud computing platforms under the management of Dell is still in an emerging phase. It can become a profitable venture for Dell as the rising trend of cloud computing can bring higher revenues and profitability to the company. However, the future progress of this product segment is still uncertain. Not all of Dell's diversification moves have been positive. Dell has launched its own brand of cell phones to cater for the needs of smartphone users across the globe. However, as yet these have not become a major revenue source for the technology leader.

Dell is a company that has business strength and high market share in certain segments in which it operates. Its global PC market share is on the increase and it lies in third place, after HP and Lenovo. When it comes to Dell's laptop business, it is the third largest laptop manufacturer in the world, commanding a 15 per cent market share. However, Dell EMC was late to enter the cloud computing market and this has left it lagging behind pioneers such as Amazon and Salesforce, IBM, Microsoft, Oracle and Fujitsu in terms of market share. In addition, contrary to company expectations, its entry into the smartphone market was challenging as it continues to struggle to compete against market leaders such as Samsung, Apple, Huawei, Xiaomi and OPPO.

Based on: Fallon, 2016;[44] Kasi, 2017;[45] Holden, 2016[46]

The main contribution of the portfolio matrices generally has been to demonstrate that *different products should have different roles* in the product portfolio (see Marketing in Action 6.4). For example, to ask for a 20 per cent return on investment (ROI) for a star may result in underinvestment in an attempt to meet the profit requirement. On the other hand, 20 per cent ROI for a cash cow or a harvested product may be too low. However, the models should be used only as an aid to managerial judgement, and other factors that are not adequately covered by the models should be considered when making product mix decisions.

Managing brands and product lines over time: the product life cycle

Both individual brands and product lines need to be managed over time. A useful tool for conceptualizing the changes that may take place during the time that a product is on the market is called the **product life cycle**. The classic product life cycle (PLC) has four stages (see Figure 6.5): introduction, growth, maturity and decline.

The PLC emphasizes the fact that nothing lasts for ever. For example, the drop in demand for elaborate tea services has seen dramatic declines at the makers of porcelain and fine bone china products, like Royal Worcester and Royal Doulton. Portable data storage devices like floppy disks, zip disks and USB sticks have all rapidly become popular and then faded out of popularity just as quickly. There is a danger that management may fall in love with certain products, as in the case of a company that is founded on the success of a particular product. Sony persisted with developing new iterations of its

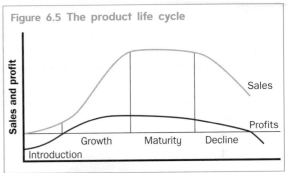

Figure 6.5 The product life cycle

PlayStation video games console even though many consumers switched to playing games on smartphone apps. The PLC underlines the fact that companies have to accept that products need to be terminated and new products developed to replace them. Without this sequence, a company may find itself with a group of products all in the decline stage of their PLC. A nicely balanced product array would see the company marketing some products in the mature stage of the PLC, a number at the growth stage and the prospect of new product introductions in the near future.

The PLC emphasizes the need to review marketing objectives and strategies as products pass through the various stages. Changes in market and competitive conditions between the PLC stages suggest that marketing strategies should be adapted to meet them. Table 6.5 shows a set of stylized marketing responses to each stage. Note that these are broad generalizations rather than exact prescriptions, but they do serve to emphasize the need to review marketing objectives and strategies in the light of environmental change.

Table 6.5 Marketing objectives and strategies over the product life cycle

	Introduction	Growth	Maturity	Decline
Strategic marketing objective	Build	Build	Hold	Harvest/manage for cash
Strategic focus	Expand market	Penetration	Protect share	Productivity
Brand objective	Product awareness/trial	Brand preference	Brand loyalty	Brand exploitation
Products	Basic	Differentiated	Differentiated	Rationalized
Promotion	Creating awareness/trial	Creating awareness/ trial repeat purchase	Maintaining awareness/ repeat purchase	Cut/eliminated
Price	High	Lower	Lowest	Rising
Distribution	Patchy	Wider	Intensive	Selective

Introduction

When a product is first introduced on to the market its sales growth is typically low and losses are incurred as a result of heavy development and initial promotional costs. Companies will be monitoring the speed of product adoption and, if it is disappointing, may terminate the product at this stage.

The strategic marketing objective is to build sales by expanding the market for the product. The brand objective will be to create awareness so that customers will become familiar with generic product benefits. The product is likely to be fairly basic, with an emphasis on reliability and functionality rather than special features to appeal to different customer groups. Promotion will support the brand objectives by gaining awareness for the brand and product type, and stimulating trial. Advertising has been found to be more effective at the start of the life of a product than in later stages.[47] Typically, price will be high because of the heavy development costs and the low level of competition. Distribution will be patchy as some dealers will be wary of stocking the new product until it has proved successful in the marketplace.

Growth

This second stage is marked by a period of faster sales and profit growth (see Exhibit 6.5). Sales growth is fuelled by rapid market acceptance and, for many products, repeat purchasing. Profits may begin to decline towards the latter stages of growth as new rivals enter the market attracted by the twin magnets of fast sales growth and high profit potential. For example, the internet search engine business grew rapidly and delivered very high profits for some incumbent firms like Google, but the profitability of this sector attracted a range of new entrants, such as 360daily.com, dogpile.com and duckduckgo.com, all of which provided new and innovative search solutions. However, not only did each of these new entrants fail to dislodge Google from its dominant position, they all subsequently withdrew from the search engine business. Similarly, in developed countries, the growth in pet ownership has given rise to a rapidly growing pet products and pet services sector. The end of the growth period is often associated with 'competitive shake-out', whereby weaker suppliers cease production.

Exhibit 6.5 Virtual and augmented reality headsets and glasses continue to be a growing industry; they will reach sales of 22 million units in 2018 and will grow fivefold to 121 million in 2022.

The strategic marketing objective during the growth phase is to build sales and market share. The strategic focus will be to penetrate the market by building brand preference. To accomplish this task the product will be redesigned to create differentiation, and promotion will stress the functional and/or psychological benefits that accrue from the differentiation. Awareness and trial are still important, but promotion will begin to focus on repeat purchasers. As development costs are defrayed and competition increases, prices will fall. Rising consumer demand and increased sales-force effort will widen distribution.

Maturity

Sales will eventually peak and stabilize as saturation occurs, hastening competitive shake-out. Mobile phone adoption rates, for example, have surpassed 100 per cent in most European countries. The survivors now battle for market share by introducing product improvements, using advertising and sales promotional offers, dealer discounting and price cutting; the result is strain on profit margins, particularly for follower brands. The need for effective brand building is felt most acutely during maturity and brand leaders are in the strongest position to resist pressure on profit margins.[48] Careful strategic decisions are very important in mature markets. For example, the falling profitability of Starbucks in 2007 was attributed to decisions that sought to grow the business too rapidly (it now has more than 17,000 outlets worldwide) in a mature market, which has led to market saturation and poor control over cafés.[49]

Decline

During the decline stages – when new technology or changes in consumer tastes work to reduce demand for the product – sales and profits fall. Suppliers may decide to cease production completely or reduce product depth. Promotional and product development budgets may be slashed and marginal distributors dropped as suppliers seek to maintain (or increase) profit margins. Products like cathode ray tube (CRT) televisions have fallen out of favour as consumers have switched to HD and 4K Ultra HD televisions. In 2014, a consumer would have spent €17,000 for one of the few 4K Ultra HD sets available at the time. In 2018, consumers could get one that plays HDR video – the new hot feature that makes things look more colourful and realistic – for less than €500.[50]

A key ethical consideration is the speed with which many products move through the product life cycle. For example, mobile phone models and computer software quickly become outdated. Fast fashion retailers like Zara aim to change the range of clothing in their retail outlets every two weeks. This 'planned obsolescence' is a significant boon for organizations as consumers need to repurchase updates or new models and discard old ones. Critics argue that this kind of consumption is not only expensive from the consumer's point of view but significantly wasteful from society's viewpoint. Clothes or computers that are perfectly 'fit for purpose' are being discarded simply because newer models are available.

Like BCG's growth-share matrix, the PLC theory has been the subject of a significant amount of criticism. First, not all products follow the classic S-shaped curve. The sales of some products 'rise like a rocket then fall like a stone'. This is normal for fad products such as fidget spinners, which in 2017 saw phenomenal sales growth (they accounted for 17 per cent of all online toy sales in May that year), followed by a rapid sales collapse as the youth market moved on to another craze.[51] Blockbuster movies have a similarly short life cycle. For example, *X-Men, The Last Stand* grossed US$123 million in its first four days in cinemas, which was more than it earned for the remaining four months of its run.[52] Second, the duration of the PLC stages is unpredictable. The PLC outlines the four stages a product passes through without defining their duration. For example, e-books languished in the introduction stage of the product life cycle for longer than anticipated before finally taking off. Clearly this limits its use as a forecasting tool since it is not possible to predict when maturity or decline will begin. Finally, and perhaps most worryingly, it has been argued that the PLC is the *result* of marketing activities, not the cause. Clearly, sales of a product may flatten out or fall simply because it has not received enough marketing attention, or because there has been insufficient product redesign or promotional support. Using the PLC, argue its critics, may lead to inappropriate action (e.g. harvesting or dropping the product) when the correct response should be increased marketing support (e.g. product replacement, positioning reinforcement or repositioning). Like many marketing tools, the PLC should not be viewed as a panacea to marketing thinking and decision-making, but as an aid to managerial judgement.

Nevertheless, the dynamic nature of brands and product lines focuses attention on the key marketing challenge of developing new products and services. It is to this issue that we turn next.

New product development

The introduction of new products to the marketplace is the lifeblood of corporate success. But new product development is inherently risky. Pharmaceutical companies research hundreds of molecular groups before coming up with a marketable drug and less than 2 per cent of films account for 80 per cent of box office returns.[53] However, failure has to be tolerated; it is endemic in the whole process of developing new products. One of the outcomes of the innovative process is the large number of interesting product ideas that do not stand the test of time and never go on to be commercially successful in the long term (see Table 6.6).

Table 6.6 Top 10 products that no longer exist

1. Jolt Cola
2. Crystal Pepsi
3. Trump: The Game
4. Nintendo Virtual Boy
5. Google Glass
6. New Coke
7. Surge
8. Pepsi Blue
9. Amazon Firephone
10. Microsoft Zune

Source: *Newsday*.

Some new products reshape markets and competition by virtue of the fact that they are so fundamentally different from products that already exist. However, a shampoo that is different from existing products only by means of its brand name, fragrance, packaging and colour is also a new product. In fact, four broad categories of new product exist:[54]

1   *Product replacements*: these account for about 45 per cent of all new product launches, and include revisions and improvements to existing products (e.g. the Ford Focus replacing the Fiesta), repositioning (existing products such as Lucozade being targeted at new market segments) and cost reductions (existing products being reformulated or redesigned so that they cost less to produce).

2   *Additions to existing lines*: these account for about 25 per cent of new product launches and take the form of new products that add to a company's existing product lines. This produces greater product depth. An example is the launch by Weetabix of a brand extension, Oatibix, to compete with other oat-based cereals.

3   *New product lines*: these total around 20 per cent of new product launches and represent a move into a new market. For example, in Europe, Mars has launched a number of ice cream brands, which made up a new product line for this company. This strategy widens a company's product mix.

4   *New-to-the-world products*: these total around 10 per cent of new product launches and create entirely new markets. For example, the video games console, the MP3 player and the 3D printer have created new markets because of the highly valued customer benefits they provided.

Ultimaker 2 3D Printer Ad Insight: This ad is for a new-to-the-world product that is serving a growing market segment.

Of course, the degree of risk and reward involved will vary according to the new product category. New-to-the-world products normally carry the highest risk since it is often difficult to predict consumer reaction. Often, market research will be unreliable in predicting demand as people do not really understand the full benefits of a product until it is on the market and they get the chance to experience it. For example, initial market testing yielded very negative results for products like Red Bull and Nespresso coffee machines, which went on to become global leaders. At the other extreme, adding a brand variation to an existing product line lacks significant risk but is also unlikely to proffer significant returns (see Table 6.7 for a list of the world's most innovative companies).

Table 6.7 The world's most innovative companies 2017

Company	Business
1. Amazon	Online shopping
2. Google	Internet software, computer hardware
3. Uber	Transportation, delivery/commerce
4. Apple	Computer hardware, software, consumer electronics, etc.
5. Snap	Hardware, social media
6. Facebook	Internet
7. Netflix	Entertainment
8. Twilio	Communications
9. Chobani	Food processing
10. Spotify	Streaming, on-demand media

Source: Fast Company.

Managing the new product development process

New product development is expensive, risky and time consuming – these are three inescapable facts. A seven-step new product development process is shown in Figure 6.6. Although the reality of new product development may resemble organizational chaos, the discipline imposed by the activities carried out at each stage leads to a greater likelihood of developing a product that not only works, but also confers customer benefits. We should note, however, that new products pass through each stage at varying speeds: some may dwell at a stage for a long period while others may pass through very quickly.[55]

Idea generation

The sources of new product ideas can be internal to the company: scientists, engineers, marketers, salespeople and designers, for example. Some companies use the **brainstorming** technique to stimulate the creation of ideas, use financial incentives to persuade people to put forward ideas or invest in innovation programmes. Autodesk, the US multinational software corporation, is a leader in 3D design and engineering software. It has built a strong culture of innovation, and a reputation as an employer that values both innovation and employees' ideas. It brings its employees through a series of innovation workshops where they are taught not only how to come up with new ideas but also what to do with the good ideas they come up with. Autodesk employees are given both the training and resources to create business pitches that highlight the value of their ideas and demonstrate why Autodesk is uniquely positioned to implement the solutions.[56]

Sources of new product ideas can also be external to the company and the turnaround at P&G was largely attributable to its chief executive officer (CEO) A.G. Lafley setting a goal that 50 per cent of innovation in the company should come from external sources.[57] Examining competitors' products may provide clues to product improvements. Distributors can also be a source of new product ideas directly, since they deal with customers and have an interest in selling improved products. A major source of good ideas is the customers themselves. Their needs may not be satisfied with existing products and

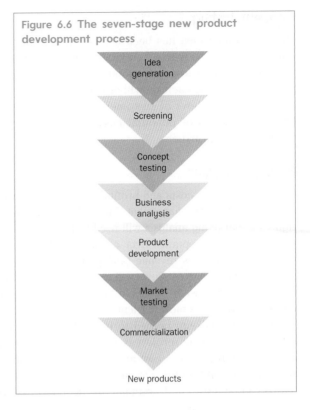

Figure 6.6 The seven-stage new product development process

Idea generation

Screening

Concept testing

Business analysis

Product development

Market testing

Commercialization

New products

they may be genuinely interested in providing ideas that lead to product improvement. For example, the Dutch electronics group Philips employs anthropologists and cognitive psychologists to gather insights into the desires and needs of people around the world, to enable it to compete more effectively with Asian rivals.[58] Internet-based social communities are a powerful source of innovation, with like-minded individuals willing to share ideas and innovations for the common good. Companies like Lego and Walkers have worked with consumers to generate new products, and the open source software movement is one of the most powerful examples of consumer-led innovation.

In organizational markets, keeping in close contact with customers who are innovators and market leaders in their own marketplaces is likely to be a fruitful source of new product ideas. These 'lead customers' are likely to recognize required improvements ahead of other customers as they have advanced needs and are likely to face problems before other product users. Some innovations, such as GE's Light Speed VCT, which provides a three-dimensional image of a beating heart, and Staples' Wordlock, a padlock that uses words instead of numbers, have been developed in co-operation with lead customers.

A 2017 *Harvard Business Review* (HBR) study found that, although innovative companies seek to tap the potential of 'open innovation' by encouraging their employees to scout for ideas among external partners (universities, research institutes, competitors and customers), the most common sources of inspiration for new ideas continue to be employees inside the organization, rather than players outside the firm.[59]

Screening

Once new product ideas have been developed they need to be screened in order to evaluate their commercial value. Some companies use formal checklists to help them judge whether the product idea should be rejected or accepted for further evaluation. This ensures that no important criterion is overlooked. Criteria may be used that measure the attractiveness of the market for the proposed product, the fit between the product and company objectives, and the capability of the company to produce and market the product. Other companies may use a less systematic approach, preferring more flexible open discussion among members of the new product development committee to gauge likely success.

Concept testing

Once a product idea has been deemed worthy of further investigation, it can be framed into a specific concept for testing with potential customers. The concept may be described verbally or pictorially so that the major features are understood. In many instances the basic product idea will be expanded into several product concepts, each of which can be compared by testing with target customers. **Concept testing** thus allows the views of customers to enter the new product development process at an early stage. The buying intentions of potential customers are a key factor in judging whether any of the concepts are worth pursuing further.

Business analysis

Estimates of sales, costs and profits will be made, based on the results of the concept test, as well as on considerable managerial judgement. This is known as the **business analysis** stage. In order to produce sensible figures a marketing analysis will need to be undertaken. This will identify the target market, its size and projected product acceptance over a number of years. Consideration will be given to various prices and the implications for sales revenue (and profits) discussed. By setting a tentative price this analysis will provide sales revenue estimates. Costs will also need to be estimated. If the new product is similar to existing products (e.g. a brand extension) it should be fairly easy to produce accurate cost estimates. For radical product concepts, the process is more difficult.

When the quantity needed to be sold to cover costs is calculated, *break-even analysis* may be used to establish whether the project is financially feasible. *Sensitivity analysis*, in which variations from given assumptions about price, cost and customer acceptance, for example, are checked to see how they impact on sales revenue and profits, can also prove useful at this stage. 'Optimistic', 'most likely' and 'pessimistic' scenarios can be drawn up to estimate the degree of risk attached to a project.

Product development

This stage involves the development of the actual product. It is usually necessary to integrate the skills of designers, engineers, production, finance and marketing specialists so that product development is quicker, less costly and results in a high-quality product that delights customers. Costs are controlled by a method called target costing. Target costs are worked out on the basis of target prices in the marketplace, and given as engineering/design and production targets.

A key marketing factor in many industries is the ability to cut time to market by reducing the length of the product development stage. There are two reasons why product development is being accelerated. First, markets such as those for personal computers, consumer electronics and cars change so fast that to be slow means running the risk of being out of date before the product is launched. Second, cutting time to market can lead to competitive advantage. For example, Zara's ability to reduce time to market for new styles gave it a competitive advantage in the fashion industry.

Product testing concentrates on the functional aspects of a product, as well as on consumer acceptance. Functional tests are carried out in the laboratory and in the field to check such aspects as safety, performance and shelf-life. Products also need to be tested with consumers to check their acceptability in use. Care at this stage can avoid expensive product recalls, as we saw earlier in the case of Toyota. 'Paired companion tests' are used when the new product is used alongside a rival so that respondents have a benchmark against which to judge the new offerings. Alternatively, two (or more) new product variants may be tested alongside one another.

Market testing

Up to this point in the development process, although potential customers have been asked if they intend to buy the product, they have not been placed in the position of having to pay for it. **Market testing** takes measurement of customer acceptance one crucial step further than product testing, by forcing consumers to put their money where their mouth is, so to speak. The basic idea is to launch the new product in a limited way so that consumer response in the marketplace can be assessed. There are two major methods: the simulated market test and **test marketing**.

Simulated market tests take a number of forms, but the main idea behind them is to set up a realistic market situation in which a sample of consumers choose to buy goods from a range provided by the organizing company (usually a market research organization). For example, a sample of consumers may be recruited to buy their groceries from a mobile supermarket that visits them once a week. Simulated market tests are useful as a preliminary to test marketing by spotting problems, such as in packaging and product formulation, that can be rectified before test market launch. They can also be useful in eliminating new products that perform so badly compared with the competition in the marketplace that test marketing is not justified.

When the new product is launched in one, or a few, geographical areas chosen to be representative of its intended market, this is known as test marketing. Towns or television areas are chosen in which the new product is sold into distribution outlets so that performance can be gauged face to face with rival products. Test marketing is the acid test of new product development since the product is being promoted as it would be in a national launch, and consumers are being asked to choose it against competitor products as they would if the new product went national. It is a more realistic test than the simulated market test, and therefore gives more accurate sales penetration and repeat purchasing estimates.

However, test marketing does have a number of potential problems. Test towns and areas may not be representative of the national market, and thus sales projections may be inaccurate. Competitors may invalidate the test market by giving distributors incentives to stock their product, thereby denying the new product shelf space. Also, test markets need to run for long enough to enable the measurement of repeat purchase rates for a product since this is a crucial indicator of success. One of the main advantages of test marketing is that the information it provides facilitates the 'go/no go' national launch decision.

Commercialization

The final stage of this rigorous process is the launch of the product in the marketplace. As an indication of the scale of the process, Hewlett-Packard generates 1,800 raw ideas per year with the goal of examining 200 in detail and then commercializing two.[60] An effective commercialization strategy relies on marketing management making clear choices regarding the target market (*where* it wishes to compete), and the development of a marketing strategy that provides a differential advantage (*how* it wishes to compete). These two factors define the new product positioning strategy, as discussed in Chapter 5.

 Dyson Supersonic Hairdryer Ad Insight: Dyson has recently launched its Supersonic Hairdryer on the market. With a price tag of €399.99 the product is not for everyone, but as the ad shows, it has a clear differential advantage over competitors' offerings.

An understanding of the **diffusion of innovation** process is a useful starting point for choosing a target market (see Figure 3.5).[61] Particularly important is the notion that not all people or organizations that comprise a market will be in the same state of readiness to buy a new product when it is launched. For example, some consumers will be much quicker to adopt a new technology like a smartphone than others. Firms launching new products initially aim to target innovators and early adopters. For example, innovators are often adventurous and like to be different; they are willing to take a chance with an untried product. In consumer markets they tend to be younger, better educated, more confident and more financially affluent, and consequently can afford to take a chance on buying something new. In organizational markets, they tend to be larger and more profitable companies if the innovation is costly, and have more progressive, better-educated management.

In summary, bringing out new products and services is the key to long-term corporate success. It is a risky activity, but a systematic approach is likely to improve the chances of success.

Summary

In this chapter we have explored a number of issues involved in the marketing of products and brands. The following key issues were addressed.

1. In marketing terms, products are anything that delivers benefits and value to a consumer, and all products contain some tangible and some intangible elements.

2. The important distinction between products and brands. A product is anything that is capable of satisfying customer needs. Brands are the means by which companies differentiate their offerings from those of their competitors.

3. The three different levels of product – namely the core, the actual and the augmented product – and how differentiation can take place at any of these levels.

4. The key aspects involved in building brands, including decisions regarding the brand name, and developing and positioning brands. Firms can choose from family, individual and combination brand names, and developing the brand requires key decisions regarding its customer value proposition.

5. The challenge of managing a diverse group of products and brands, and the role of portfolio planning in assisting with this process. Many firms own significant portfolios of products and ongoing decisions need to be made regarding which ones should be invested in and which should be wound down.

6. The challenge of managing products and brands over time and the role of the product life cycle concept in assisting with this process. Products at different stages of growth require different marketing strategies and, despite its weaknesses, the product life cycle offers a helpful way of thinking about these decisions.

7. The importance of new product development and the process by which products are taken from the idea stage through to commercialization. Careful management is required during all the main stages, including idea generation, screening, concept testing, business analysis, product development, market testing and commercialization.

Study questions

1. Explain the difference between a product and a brand.

2. Think of five brand names. To what extent do they meet the criteria of good brand naming as laid out in Table 6.1? Do any of the names legitimately break these guidelines?

3. Examine a product like bottled water through the lens of the core, actual and augmented product. What types of differentiation strategies are being used by brands in this sector? Can you suggest any new sources of differentiation?

4. The product life cycle is more likely to mislead marketing management than provide useful insights. Discuss.

5. Many companies comprise a complex group of business units, which in turn often have wide product lines. Discuss the techniques available to the marketer for managing this complexity.

6. Outline the main stages in the new product development process, identifying the potential sources of failure at each stage.

7. Visit www.readersdigest.ca. Review the 2018 Reader's Digest Trusted Brand Winners. How do these brands go about building this trust?

8. What is portfolio planning? Describe the use of the BCG matrix in portfolio planning, referring to the characteristics of the four types of products identified in the matrix.

Suggested reading

Alwi, S., Ali, S. and **Nguyen, B.** (2017) The importance of ethics in branding, mediating effects of ethical branding on company reputation and brand loyalty, *Business Ethics Quarterly*, 27(3), 393–422.

Batra, R., Ahuvia, A. and **Bagozzi, R.** (2012) Brand love, *Journal of Marketing*, 7 (March), 1–16.

Davcik, N. and **Sharma, D.** (2015) Impact of product differentiation, marketing investments and brand equity on pricing strategies, *European Journal of Marketing*, 49(5/6), 760–81.

Gladwell, M. (2000) *The Tipping Point: How Little Things Can Make a Big Difference*. London: Abacus.

Holman, R., Kaas, H. and **Keeling, D.** (2003) The future of product development, *McKinsey Quarterly*, 3, 28–40.

Ind, N., Iglesias, O. and **Schultz, M.** (2013) Building brands together: emergence and outcomes of co-creation, *California Management Review*, 55(3), 5–26.

Madsen, D.O. (2017) Not dead yet: the rise, fall and persistence of the BCG Matrix, *Problems and Perspectives in Management*, 15(1), 19–34.

Moon, Y. (2005) Break free from the product life cycle, *Harvard Business Review*, 83(5), 86–95.

Round, G. and **Roper, S.** (2017) When and why does the name of a brand still matter? *European Journal of Marketing*, 51(11/12), 2118–37.

van der Westhuizen, L.-M. (2018) Brand loyalty: exploring self-brand connection and brand experience, *Journal of Product and Brand Management*, 27(2), 172–84.

References

1. **Amman, J.** (2017) Samsung Electronics rises to no. 6 in Interbrand's best global brands 2017, *Samsung*, 2 October; **Hutton, L.** (2016) AIB featured business – Samsung, *Australian Institute of Business*, 25 May; **Anonymous** (2018) Samsung Electronics – statistics and facts. Available at https://www.statista.com/topics/985/samsung-electronics/ (accessed 4 May 2018); **Anonymous** (2017) Samsung – the global Asian brand. Available at https://martinroll.com/resources/articles/marketing/samsung-global-asian-brand/ (accessed 4 May 2018); **Tsukayama, H.** (2018) How Samsung moved beyond its exploding phones, *Washington Post*, 23 February; **Kwack, J.** (2017) Samsung's de-facto chief denies wrongdoing in first trial appearance, *New York Times*, 7 April; **Premack, R.** (2017) Why Samsung thinks the key to its future (and profits) could be in the auto sector, *Forbes*, 7 December.

2. **Dolcourt, J.** (2018) Blackberry and Nokia still struggling to make a comeback, *CNET*, 22 February.

3. **Keller, K.** (2003) *Strategic Brand Management*. Upper Saddle River, NJ: Pearson.

4. **Davcik, N.** and **Sharma, D.** (2015) Impact of product differentiation, marketing investments and brand equity on pricing strategies, *European Journal of Marketing*, 49(5/6), 760–81.

5. **Associated Press** (2018) Toyota recalls 645,000 vehicles globally, including in Canada; airbags may not inflate, *Global News*, 31 January.

6. **Phelan, D.** (2018) Dyson Cyclone V10 cordless vacuum is 'the future', Dyson stops developing corded cleaners, *Forbes*, 6 March.

7. **Anonymous** (2018) Danone's Evian vows to use 100% recycled plastic in their bottles by 2.25, *CNBC*, 18 January.

8. **Pope, C.** (2007) New labels hit a red light, *Irish Times*, 15 January, 13.

9. **Hegarty, S.** (2003) You are what you think you eat, *Irish Times*, Weekend Review, 19 July, 1.

10. **Anonymous** (2017) Adidas – statistics and facts, *Statista*.

11. **Lenton, J.** (2018) Is Adidas finally cooler than Nike? Available at https://www.apetogentleman.com/heart-and-sole-is-adidas-finally-cooler-than-nike/ (accessed 4 May 2018).

12. **Woolf, J.** (2017) Adidas tells us how it plans to catch Nike, *GQ*, 27 April.

13. **van der Westhuizen, L.-M.** (2018) Brand loyalty: exploring self-brand connection and brand experience, *Journal of Product and Brand Management*, 27(2), 172–84.

14. **Roberts, K.** (2004) *The Future Beyond Brands: Lovemarks*. New York: Powerhouse Books.

15. **Healy, A.** (2004) Campaigners appeal for cafes to be rescued, *Irish Times*, 25 November, 6.

16. **Hong, P.** (2015) 10 exceptional examples of brand communities, *Lindex*, 15 January.

17. **Kolowich, L.** (2017) 14 of the best Snapchat accounts to follow for inspiration, *Hubspot*, 18 April.

18. **Anonymous** (2015) 10 top Snapchat influencers to follow. Available at http://mediakix.com/2015/06/10-top-snapchat-influencers-to-follow/ (accessed 4 May 2018).

19. **Anonymous** (2015) 25 best Snapchat marketing tips. Available at http://mediakix.com/2015/11/best-snapchat-marketing-tips/#gs.Ex4megI (accessed 4 May 2018).

20. **Gioglio, J.** (2018) 10 creative ways companies are using Snapchat, http://www.convinceandconvert.com/social-media-case-studies/5-creative-ways-brands-are-using-snapchat/ (accessed 4 May 2018).

21. **Reyner, M.** (1996) Is advertising the answer? *Admap*, September, 23–6.

22. **Anonymous** (2011) I've got you labelled, *The Economist*, 2 April, 74.

23. **Waters, R.** (2008) Microsoft says 'We're human too', *Financial Times*, 9 September, 16; **Anonymous** (2008) Postmodern wriggle, *The Economist*, 13 September, 72.

24. **Shewan, D.** (2017) Ethical marketing: 5 examples of companies with a conscience, *Wordstream*, 21 December.

25. **Bertilsson, J.** (2014) The slippery relationship between brand ethic and profit, *Ephemera*, 14(1), 125–36.

26. **Palmer, M.** (2007) What's in a name? A lot if it's your domain, *Financial Times*, 14 March, 24.

27. **Round, G.** and **Roper, S.** (2017) When and why does the name of a brand still matter? *European Journal of Marketing*, 51(11/12), 2118–37.

28. **O'Connor, R.** (2010) Question marks over trademarks, *Marketing Age*, 4(1), 49–51.

29. **Brady, J.** and **Davis, I.** (1993) Marketing's mid-life crisis, *McKinsey Quarterly*, 2, 17–28.

30. **Anonymous** (2005) As good as it gets, *The Economist*, 15 January, 60–2.

31. **Doyle, P.** (2000) *Value-based Marketing*. Chichester: John Wiley & Sons.

32. **Mulcahy, S.** (2016) Irish tanning brand Cocoa Brown is the latest must have celebrity obsession. Available at https://evoke.ie/2016/08/27/style/beauty-buzz/cocoa-brown-tan (accessed 6 May 2018).

33. **Wegert, T.** (2016) How Carlsberg produces probably the best beer content in the world, *The Content Strategist*, 25 August.

34. **Millington, A.** (2015) Why Carlsberg is bringing back 'If Carlsberg did' after 4 years, *Marketing Week*, 16 February.

35. **Clark, N.** (2011) Carlsberg: probably a risky rebrand, *Campaign*, 13 April.

36. **Gwynn, S.** (2017) Carlsberg reinvented as icon of Danish lifestyle in Mads Mikkelsen campaign, *Campaign*, 20 April.

37. **Anonymous** (2015) If Carlsberg did adverts … they would probably be the best in the world, *PicPR*, 20 February.

38. **Calkins, T.** (2016) The great brand portfolio debate: Unilever vs P&G, *Strong Brands*, 28 September.

39. **Brech, P.** (2002) Ford Focus targets women with *Elle* tie, *Marketing*, 8 August, 7.

40. **Keller, K.** (2003) *Strategic Brand Management*. Upper Saddle River, NJ: Pearson.

41. **Brown, J.M.** (2007) Soft drinks sale to Britvic enables C&C to concentrate on high margin alcohol, *Financial Times*, 15 May, 22.

42. See, e.g., **Day, G.S.** and **Wensley, R.** (1983) Marketing theory with a strategic orientation, *Journal of Marketing*, Fall, 79–89; **Haspslagh, P.** (1982) Portfolio planning: uses and limits, *Harvard Business Review*, January/February, 58–73; **Wensley, R.** (1981) Strategic marketing: betas, boxes and basics, *Journal of Marketing*, Summer, 173–83.

43. **Madsen, D.O.** (2017) Not dead yet: the rise, fall and persistence of the BCG Matrix, *Problems and Perspectives in Management*, 15(1), 19–34.

44. **Fallon, P.** (2016) Amid need to diversify, Dell's PC business continues to grow. Available at https://www.bizjournals.com/austin/blog/techflash/2016/04/amid-need-to-diversify-dells-pc-business-continues.html (accessed 9 May 2018).

45. **Kasi, A.** (2017) BCG Matrix of Dell. Available at http://bcgmatrixanalysis.com/bcg-matrix-of-dell/ (accessed 9 May 2018).

46. **Holden, J.** (2016) Dell EMC World a mix of merger celebrations and cost cutting anxiety, *Irish Times*, 20 October.

47. **Vakratsas, D.** and **Ambler, T.** (1999) How advertising works: what do we really know? *Journal of Marketing*, 63, January, 26–43.

48. **Doyle, P.** (1989) Building successful brands: the strategic options, *Journal of Marketing Management*, 5(1), 77–95.

49. **Anonymous** (2008) Starbucks v McDonald's: coffee wars, *The Economist*, 12 January, 54–5.

50. **Moynihan, T.** (2017) As 4K TVs approach perfection, cheap sets go on the attack, *Wired*, 13 January.

51. **Fu, L.** (2017) The fidget spinner trend is ending and you missed it, *Fortune*, 13 June.

52. **Anonymous** (2007) Endless summer, *The Economist*, 28 April, 69–70.

53. **Anonymous** (2011) Fail often, fail well, *The Economist*, 16 April, 66.

54. **Booz, Allen & Hamilton** (1982) *New Product Management for the 1980s*. New York: Booz, Allen & Hamilton.

55. **Cooper, R.G.** and **Kleinschmidt, E.J.** (1986) An investigation into the new product process: steps, deficiencies and impact, *Journal of Product Innovation Management*, June, 71–85.

56. **Wunker, S.** (2015) 5 strategies big businesses use to build a culture of innovation, *Forbes*, 29 July.

57. **O'Dea, A.** (2008) Open for Innovation, *Marketing Age*, September/October, 22–6.

58. **Tomkins, R.** (2005) Products that aim straight for your heart, *Financial Times*, 29 April, 13.

59. **Dahlander, L.** and **O'Mahony, S.** (2017) A study shows how to find new ideas inside and outside the company, *Harvard Business Review Digital Edition*, 18 July, 2–5.

60. **Lillington, K.** (2008) Taking invention out of the lab, *Innovation*, May, 32–4.

61. **Rogers, E.M.** (1983) *Diffusion of Innovations*. New York: Free Press.

'The Notorious' Conor McGregor

Born in Dublin, Ireland, Conor McGregor's rise to stardom has been one of sport's biggest success stories. He took up boxing at the age of 12, but was unemployed and surviving on benefits by the time he began training in mixed martial arts (MMA) in 2006. He signed a contract with the Ultimate Fighting Championship (UFC) in 2013, and his talent and dedication to the sport became obvious immediately. As well as his success in the ring, which has earned him the name 'The Notorious', he draws big crowds for trash-talking his opponents. In 2016, he became the first UFC fighter to hold two belts after taking the lightweight title while he was still reigning featherweight champion. In the summer of 2017, he made history and dominated headlines for months after tempting US boxer Floyd Mayweather out of retirement for a crossover fight in Las Vegas, which netted him a reported US$100 million (€81 million).

The McGregor brand

Conor McGregor is one of the most bankable stars in the UFC and his rags-to-riches story has inspired millions around the world. Before Conor McGregor's rise to fame, MMA occupied a similar position in TV sports rosters and most viewers' minds as sumo wrestling or World's Strongest Man contests. It was viewed as an oddity and had a very small and dedicated fan base, often viewed as too violent for the mainstream. That is until Conor McGregor came on to the scene and literally changed the game. He burst into the mainstream, landing on magazine covers and luring many to a sport they might never have even considered. He has gone from being a name that only hard-core MMA fans recognized, to being one of the UFC's biggest names.

McGregor has an abundance of confidence and charisma, a sharp wit and a flamboyant style inside and outside the octagon. Ambition is everything to McGregor and he is willing to take risks and achieve his goals. He has always been ambitious; since coming to the UFC, even as an unknown featherweight, he always predicted his fighting success and financial ambitions, and he has always had his eye on the end prize. Conor McGregor is a social media powerhouse and this has played a key role in developing his personal brand. His Instagram account has been well curated since day one and he has amassed 23 million followers. He also has a presence on Twitter, where he has 7.1 million followers, and on Facebook, where he has 7.6 million followers.

Leveraging the McGregor brand

McGregor has been actively involved in developing his personal brand, seeking to protect what he believes is his intellectual property, in conjunction with launching new products and licensing opportunities. In recent years, he has extended his brand in a number of ways. In late 2017, he made his mark in the fashion industry when he teamed up with his tailor David August Heil, CEO and creative director for clothing company David August, to work on a new menswear label. This new label, which was the first apparel venture for McGregor, offers modern suiting, sportswear and accessories inspired by McGregor's colourful style. Designed and priced to appeal to millennial males, who follow McGregor's sartorial swagger, the August McGregor line offers complete suiting options, including shirts and accessories.

The fighter launched his own movie, *Notorious*, in November 2017. Filmed over the course of four years, it is a gripping access-all-areas account of McGregor's personal and professional journey from claiming benefits and living in his mum's spare room with his girlfriend to claiming multiple championship belts and nine-figure pay packets. Featuring exclusive interviews, unprecedented access and fight footage, it was promoted as 'the ultimate behind-the-scenes look at a sporting icon and his meteoric rise'. The movie enjoyed the biggest opening weekend of any Irish film that year at the Irish box office, with *Notorious* hitting the number-four spot for Irish cinema takings after it grossed €103,000 (€172,000 including previews).

Not all of Conor's brand extensions have been successful though. In August 2017, the fighter revealed his plan to cash in on his name by launching a whiskey brand using his moniker 'Notorious'. However, Seamus O'Hara of Carlow Brewing Company is attempting to block McGregor's attempts to register 'Notorious', complaining that McGregor's trademark is identical to his 'Notorious Red IPA Pale Ale', covers identical product categories and is likely to confuse the public.

McGregor has also been trying to trademark several words and phrases associated with his personal brand, as part of a strategy to capitalize on his global commercial appeal as one of the world's best-known sports stars. However, he has been faced with legal opposition from a number of multinational consumer brands. In September 2017, he applied for a European trademark for 'Mystic Mac', a nickname he acquired for predicting the outcome of his fights. However, this was opposed by Make Up Cosmetics (MAC), Inc., the New York-based make-up giant, which argued that it could be confused with its products if McGregor used his proposed brand to sell men's toiletries. McGregor's 'Mystic Mac' application was also opposed by the German company that owns the Mac Jeans brand, which claims it would confuse its customers if applied to clothing.

The fighter's application to register his name, 'Conor McGregor', was opposed in the EU by a Dutch fashion company that already holds the trademark McGregor for clothing and accessories. McGregor is also seeking a European trademark for 'Champ-Champ', a moniker he publicly bestowed upon himself as the holder of world belts in two different weight divisions in MMA. That application was opposed by the Irish division of the global company behind the Champion sportswear brand. It has also been opposed by Cleats LLC, a US company that makes the Champ brand of sports footwear studs. In addition, McGregor is seeking a European trademark for the phrase 'I am Boxing', which was opposed by the Swiss retailer Migros, which sells the 'I Am' brand across several product classes of cosmetics and clothing.

McGregor's worldwide success has allowed him to exploit his publicity rights beyond the octagon (and boxing ring). He has signed endorsement deals with many brands, including Beats by Dre, Monster Energy, Reebok and Bud Light. In early 2018, he also signed a deal with Burger King and appeared in its advertising campaign promoting its products. It is estimated that all his endorsement deals round up to approximately US$8 million.

Controversy

Since he exploded on to the world stage, McGregor has found himself embroiled in extremely controversial moments, whether it's on social media, in press conferences or in the ring itself. He has been slammed for apparent homophobic slurs, when he was caught on camera calling Andre Fili a 'f***ot' after his defeat of training partner Artem Lobov at UFC Gdansk. He was at the centre of multiple controversial racist moments during the build-up to his mega-fight with Floyd Mayweather, including telling his opponent to 'Dance for me boy!' In his press conference with Nate Diaz in the lead-up to the UFC 202 fight, a slanging match between the fighters occurred that descended into bottles being thrown across the room.

In a more recent controversy, an arrest warrant was issued by the state of New York following a major disturbance at the Barclays Centre in April 2018 after a media event ahead of UFC 223. The fighter was caught on video attacking a bus full of fighters with metal railings and chairs, with two fighters injured. McGregor eventually handed himself into authorities and was charged with three counts of assault and one count of criminal mischief.

The future

UFC president Dana White has worked hard to polish the image of the organization, which resulted in a US$4 billion sale to WME-IMG in 2017. The modern UFC is a huge corporate identity desperate to appeal to the mainstream. However, UFC executives have been frustrated with McGregor ever since he knocked out Jose Aldo in 13 seconds back in UFC 194. The win propelled McGregor to new fame, making him almost bigger than the organization itself. It has been argued that this is something he has exploited and that has made him more difficult to control. The UFC may have put up with his behaviour because, for a time, it made it money. However, some would argue that McGregor's antics, particularly his arrest in April 2018, have crossed a line and that he's nothing like the McGregor who became the UFC's greatest star.

There is a belief that, in his early career, McGregor was a humble and introspective man and that was what made him relatable. His success story was one of a common man striving after his passions. However, has he been corrupted by money and power? Some wonder how McGregor can expect to be taken seriously when he can't control his actions or his mouth. Furthermore, how could the UFC feel comfortable and secure continuing its relationship with him when McGregor continues to cause compromising and indefensible public relations incidents through impulse? For those in the Conor McGregor camp, there is also a fear that the McGregor brand will be damaged. Sponsors may be turned off due to the fighter's controversial behaviour and there may be potential damage to the McGregor brand that will impact his future sponsorship earnings.

However, McGregor's commercial reality is different to that of other athletes, as he makes the vast majority of his money from in-ring competition rather than sponsorship deals. According to sponsorship expert Rob Pearson, associate director of Teneo PSG, 'While many athletes need to supplement their income with endorsement deals, McGregor's reality is very different. He is worth more than €140 million according to the Sunday Independent Rich list and makes on average US$15–20 million per fight in the UFC. In 2017, he made an estimated US$8 million in sponsorship endorsements – small fry considering he makes that in five minutes in the octagon!'

Questions

1. Outline the key factors that have led to the growth of the McGregor brand. Comment on the importance of social media in building this brand. Do you think the controversies surrounding McGregor will cause long-term damage to his brand?
2. Identify the six key elements that influence a brand positioning in the marketplace and discuss how these apply to the McGregor brand.
3. What is the difference between a brand and a trademark? Will Conor McGregor's failure to acquire his desired trademarks have an effect on the future of his brand?
4. How has the McGregor brand been leveraged through brand extension and endorsements? What are the risks associated with using a celebrity such as Conor McGregor to endorse your brand?

This case was prepared by Marie O'Dwyer, Waterford Institute of Technology, Ireland, from various published sources as a basis for class discussion rather than to show effective or ineffective management.

Chapter 7

Value through Services, Relationships and Experiences

Learning outcomes

By the end of this chapter you will:

1 Understand the special characteristics of services

2 Analyse the key issues in managing services enterprises

3 Explain the nature of service quality

4 Understand the nature of relationship marketing

5 Analyse the role of customer relationship management (CRM) systems in relationship marketing

6 Critique the role of marketing relationships in society

7 Explain the role of experiential marketing

8 Analyse the nature and characteristics of not-for-profit marketing

N26: the changing face of banking

Banking is one of the oldest industries in the world. Its origins can be found in Ancient Greece and during the Roman Empire, when lenders based in temples made loans while accepting deposits and performing the change of money. It has grown exponentially with the rise of commerce and enterprise, and is frequently associated with the ugly face of capitalism, such as during the global financial crisis of 2008 when banks in many countries that had made huge losses through reckless lending had to be bailed out at the expense of the taxpayer. But, despite its longevity, it is not immune to change, and the phrase 'fintech' has been coined to capture the myriad ways in which technology could disrupt the banking industry.

For most consumers, their experience of banking is to visit their local branch, where a variety of services, such as cash withdrawals, lodgements, loans and mortgages, currency exchange and so on, are provided. Despite the introduction of automated services, for many people a visit to branch is a frustrating experience characterized by long waiting times and slow service. For younger consumers such as millennials, the idea of visiting a bank branch is increasingly something of an anathema. Indeed one study of millennials found that 71 per cent of respondents would rather visit the dentist than go to their local bank branch. Yet banking is an essential feature of daily life. If you want to buy something, go on holiday or plan for your future you need access to banking services. However, the solutions to these customer needs that are being provided by established banks throughout the world are seen as increasingly inadequate, particularly by younger customers who have grown up with technology. It is this emerging opportunity that start-ups like N26 are exploiting.

N26 is a German bank based in Berlin. It began life as a company called Number 26 and was rebranded as N26 in 2016 after receiving its banking licence. The business was started by an Austrian, Valentin Stalf, who along with his co-founders felt that traditional banking models were outdated and instead wanted to create a 'Spotify of banking'. The core of their business idea is a single, seamless online platform where consumers can manage all aspects of their financial lives. N26 has no bank branches, but customers can get cash at any ATM or at any of 7,000 affiliated retailers. It has partnerships with Mastercard (for cash and payments), Clark (for insurance), Transferwise (for money transfers) and Auxmoney (for credit). The idea is that customers will be able to combine all the complexity of their financial lives on one seamless, easy-to-use platform. In 2018, the bank had in the region of 550,000 customers across Germany, Austria, France, Spain and Italy, with plans to open business in the USA and UK. While its customer base is a fraction of that held by established banks, it is growing at a rate of 2,000 customers per day.

The centrepiece of N26's business is its smartphone app. As a start-up, it had many advantages over mainstream banks whose legacy business models often meant that their technology offerings were not customer friendly or easy to use. For example, setting up online access to an account may still require a visit to a bank branch and the completion of paper forms. The N26 app is designed to enable customers to organize their financial lives easily and to do most things, such as payments, in one or two clicks. The app is also designed so that customers can submit ideas or request a feature or product, leading to user-generated innovation. Again, traditional banks tend to review such requests from a legal and technical perspective, whereas N26 approaches them from an experiential one.

N26 is not the only fintech start-up looking to revolutionize banking as we know it. For example, Monese is a digital banking service that lets users open a UK banking account in minutes on their smartphones regardless of their citizenship. Users get a current account and a Visa debit card with a snapshot of their passport and a selfie. Fidor Bank, based in Munich, offers virtual accounts to customers and special services like peer-to-peer lending and crowdsourcing. Imaginbank, based in Spain, allows customers to do basic banking activities on a smartphone app, which can be accessed

(continued)

from their social networks. Future developments are likely to see more radical changes in how banks operate. The use of Big Data and analytics is likely to mean that customers will receive an increasingly personalized experience that takes account of their changing financial situation. And the blurring of the boundaries between banking and other aspects of people's lives is also likely to increase. Already, in China, WeChat has integrated social media, payments and broader financial services.[1]

In Chapter 6, we saw that almost all goods that are offered in a marketplace contain elements that are both tangible and intangible (see Figure 6.1). Those that are high on tangible elements we tend to think of as products and those that are high on intangible elements we think of as services. A wide variety of activities, such as going on holiday, visiting the dentist, receiving an education and getting legal advice, are all generally thought of as service activities because of their high levels of intangibility. Online education, global legal services and IT consultancy mean that many business and consumer services are extensively traded internationally. In 2016, the World Bank estimated that the services sector accounted for almost 66 per cent of global gross domestic product (GDP). Similarly, research conducted by the Macquaire Research Group estimated that employment in the services sector rose from 34 per cent in 1991 to 46 per cent in 2016, while levels in the industrial sector had remained relatively stagnant.[2] Therefore, while most goods can be thought of as a combination of products and services, the high importance of services means that it is a key area of study.

The growth of services has also been accompanied by increased attention in the marketing literature. Early work on services in the 1980s highlighted the unique nature of services enterprises and we will explore these characteristics. This was followed by more detailed work on services marketing and the emergence of the relationship marketing concept, which we also explore in this chapter. More recently, the concept of the service-dominant (S-D) logic was proposed to try to shift the focus of research from the production of goods to the trading of services.[3] The foundational premises of the service-dominant logic are summarized in Table 7.1. Four key propositions have emerged from this initial list. The first is that the fundamental unit of exchange is not goods but service, and that goods are merely an embodiment of service. The second is that value is co-created between the producer and user, placing the concept of value-in-use at the forefront of thinking about innovation and marketing. Third is the idea that exchange is not taking place between just two parties (a producer and consumer, for example) but rather a variety of actors in a network can be involved in value creation. Finally, value is always uniquely determined by each beneficiary. The main contribution of the S-D logic has been to propose a more holistic and integrative way of thinking about marketing activity that captures the highly networked way in which enterprises currently operate.

Table 7.1 The service-dominant (S-D) logic

Key premise	Explanation
1	Service is the fundamental basis of exchange
2	The service basis of exchange is not always apparent as it is masked by goods, money, institutions, etc.
3	Goods are a distribution mechanism for service provision
4	Resources such as knowledge and skills are the primary source of competitive advantage
5	All economies are service economies
6	The customer is always a co-creator of value
7	The enterprise cannot deliver value but only offer value propositions
8	A service-centred view is inherently customer-oriented and relational
9	All social and economic actors are resource integrators
10	Value is always uniquely determined by the beneficiary

Source: Based on Vargo, S.L. and Lusch, R.F. (2008) Service-dominant logic: continuing the evolution, *Journal of the Academy of Marketing Science*, 36, 1–10.

The unique characteristics of services

There are four key distinguishing characteristics of services, namely, intangibility, inseparability, variability and perishability (see Figure 7.1).

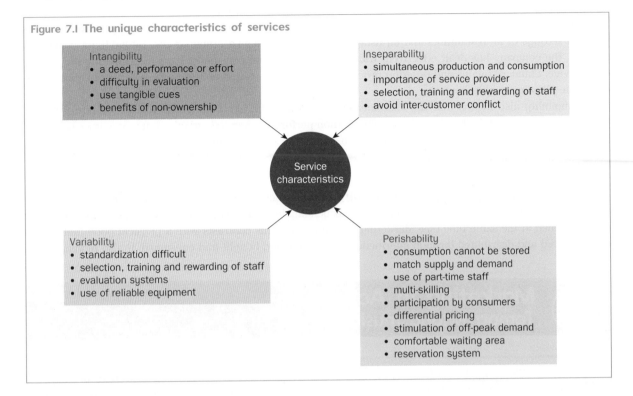

Figure 7.1 The unique characteristics of services

Intangibility
- a deed, performance or effort
- difficulty in evaluation
- use tangible cues
- benefits of non-ownership

Inseparability
- simultaneous production and consumption
- importance of service provider
- selection, training and rewarding of staff
- avoid inter-customer conflict

Service characteristics

Variability
- standardization difficult
- selection, training and rewarding of staff
- evaluation systems
- use of reliable equipment

Perishability
- consumption cannot be stored
- match supply and demand
- use of part-time staff
- multi-skilling
- participation by consumers
- differential pricing
- stimulation of off-peak demand
- comfortable waiting area
- reservation system

Intangibility

Services can be thought of as a deed, performance or effort, not an object, device or thing, and are therefore intangible.[4] This **intangibility** may mean that a customer may find difficulty in evaluating a service before purchase. For example, it is virtually impossible to judge how enjoyable a holiday will be before taking it because the holiday cannot be shown to a customer before consumption. This contrasts with physical products where, at a minimum, the customer has an opportunity to pick up a new product like a smartphone and examine how it looks and feels. Therefore products are characterized by *search* properties (they can be examined in advance) while services exhibit *experience* properties (they can be assessed only after they have been experienced) with the result that service choices are often riskier. Some services, such as a medical operation or a car service, possess *credence* properties – that is, it is not possible to evaluate them even after they have been consumed, which means that these types of choices are particularly difficult for consumers.[5]

The challenge for the service provider is to use tangible cues to service quality (see Exhibit 7.1). For example, a holiday firm may

Exhibit 7.1 AIG Japan's #Tackle the Risk campaign used the All Blacks rugby team to effectively 'tangibilize' how insurance helps to protect people from risks.

show pictures of the holiday destination, display testimonials from satisfied holidaymakers and provide details in a brochure of the kind of entertainment available. The staff of US-based computer services company the Geek Squad are clearly distinguishable through their short-sleeved white shirts, black ties and badges, and their colourful 'Geek Mobiles' in which they drive to house calls.[6] Service companies, like hotels, invest heavily in tangibles such as the décor of rooms and staff uniforms.

The task is to provide an indication of likely service quality. McDonald's does this by controlling the physical settings of its restaurants and by using the golden arches as a branding cue. By having a consistent offering, the company has dealt effectively with the difficulties that consumers have in evaluating the quality of a service. Standard menus and ordering procedures have also ensured uniform and easy access for customers, while allowing quality control.[7]

Intangibility also means that the customer cannot own a service. Payment is for use or performance. For example, a car may be hired or a medical operation performed. Service organizations sometimes stress the benefits of non-ownership such as lower capital costs and the spreading of payment charges.

Inseparability

Unlike physical goods, services have **inseparability** – that is, they have simultaneous production and consumption. For example, a haircut, a medical operation, psychoanalysis, a holiday and a pop concert are produced and consumed at the same time (see Marketing in Action 7.1). This contrasts with a physical good that is produced, stored and distributed through intermediaries before being bought and consumed. It also highlights the

Marketing in Action 7.1
Tomorrowland music festival

> **Critical Thinking:** Below is a review of the marketing of the Tomorrowland music festival in Belgium. Read it and reflect on which of the unique characteristics of services are important in this context and how this impacts upon the marketing used by the festival.

Tomorrowland is one of the many successful boutique music festivals that characterize the European summer. Started in 2005, the electronic music festival takes place in a small town, aptly named Boom, in Belgium. It has since quickly grown into global stardom. For example, the 2012 version of the event included more than 400 DJs and attracted 185,000 music fans from 75 countries. To celebrate its tenth anniversary in 2014, the event was held over two weekends and sold out its 400,000 tickets even before the line-up was announced.

Some key aspects of how the festival is marketed have been critical to its success. First, it clearly targeted a market segment of young, trendy party lovers from Belgium and around the world who have a shared passion for electronic dance music. This is a segment that differs from the more typical rock audience that characterizes summer festival-goers. Second, the event is positioned as a magical journey that takes its audience into a world where anything is possible and reminds them that they are young and free. Finally, the tangible elements of the festival are designed to reflect this magical journey. For example, the theme of the 2013 festival was 'the arising of life' so the main stage was designed as a massive volcano, 140 metres wide and 35 metres high. Entry wristbands were changed from plastic to nicely designed bracelets, while the pathways leading from the festival featured fire-spitting dragons and the recorded sounds of singing birds.

As is the case with services generally, the customer journey begins long before the event itself and also provides opportunities for enhancing the experience. For example, in 2012, the festival partnered with Brussels Airlines to offer travel packages to the festival under the brand Global Journey. Aircraft were customized with the Tomorrowland livery and equipped with grass floors and DJ booths. When guests arrived they were welcomed at a Tomorrowland desk and transferred to their hotels or the festival campsite, DreamVille. Promotion tends to be heavily oriented to social

(continued)

media. For example, the 2016 edition generated 600,000 new Facebook followers, bringing the total to more than 9 million. There were more than 13.7 million live streams of the event on Facebook and in excess of 24 million views of the after movie. This combined with coverage on Twitter, Instagram and Snapchat helped drive more than 175 million unique visits to the official website.

importance of the service provider, who is an integral part of the satisfaction gained by the consumer. How service providers conduct themselves may have a crucial bearing on repeat business over and above the technical efficiency of the service task. For example, how courteous and friendly the service provider is may play a large part in the customer's perception of the service experience. The service must be provided not only at the right time and in the right place but also in the right way.[8]

Often, in the customer's eyes, the photocopier service engineer or the insurance representative *is* the company. Consequently, the selection, training and rewarding of staff who are the front-line service people is of fundamental importance in the achievement of high standards of service quality. This notion of the inseparability of production and consumption means that both internal marketing and relationship marketing are important in services, as we shall see later. In such circumstances, managing buyer–seller interaction is central to effective marketing and can be fulfilled only in a relationship with the customer.[9]

Furthermore, the consumption of the service may take place in the presence of other consumers. This is apparent with restaurant meals, air, rail or coach travel, and many forms of entertainment, for example. Consequently, enjoyment of the service is dependent not only on the service provided, but also on other consumers (see Exhibit 7.2). Therefore service providers need to identify possible sources of nuisance (e.g. noise, smoke, queue jumping) and make adequate provision to avoid inter-customer conflict. For example, a restaurant layout should provide reasonable space between tables so that the potential for conflict is minimized.

Marketing managers should not underestimate the role played by customers in aiding other customers in their decision-making. A study into service interactions in IKEA stores found that almost all customer–employee exchanges related to customer concerns about 'place' (e.g. 'Can you direct me to the pick-up point?') and 'function' (e.g. 'How does this chair work?'). However, interactions between customers took the form of opinions on the quality of materials used in products, advice on bed sizes and how to move around the in-store restaurant. Many customers appeared to display a degree of product knowledge or expertise bordering on that of contact personnel.[10]

Exhibit 7.2 Holidays are a service that illustrate the inseparability of the production and consumption.

Variability

Service quality may be subject to considerable **variability**, which makes standardization difficult. Two restaurants within the same chain may have variable service owing to the capabilities of their respective managers and staff. Two marketing courses at the same university may vary considerably in terms of quality, depending on the lecturer. Quality variations among physical products may be subject to tighter controls through centralized production, automation and quality checking before dispatch. Services, however, are often conducted at multiple locations, by people who may vary in their attitudes (and tiredness), and are subject to simultaneous production and consumption. The last characteristic means that a service fault (e.g. rudeness) cannot be quality checked and corrected between production and consumption, unlike a physical product such as misaligned car windscreen wipers.

The potential for variability in service quality emphasizes the need for rigorous selection, training and rewarding of staff in service organizations. Training should emphasize the standards expected of personnel when dealing with customers. *Evaluation systems* should be developed that allow customers to report on their experiences with staff: for example, many service organizations invite feedback from customers through comment cards, online surveys and social media. Some service organizations may tie reward systems to customer satisfaction surveys, which are based, in part, on the service quality provided by their staff.

Service standardization is a related method of tackling the variability problem. For example, a university department could agree to use the same software platform when developing course delivery. The use of reliable equipment rather than people can also help in standardization – for instance, the supply of drinks via vending machines or cash through bank machines. However, great care needs to be taken regarding equipment reliability and efficiency. For example, the perceived security of smartphone banking apps impacts upon consumers' willingness to use this medium for financial transactions.

Perishability

The fourth characteristic of services is their **perishability** in the sense that consumption cannot be stored for the future. A hotel room or an airline seat that is not occupied today represents lost income that cannot be gained tomorrow. If a physical good is not sold, it can be stored for sale later. Therefore it is important to match supply and demand for services. For example, if a hotel has high weekday occupancy but is virtually empty at weekends, a key marketing task is to provide incentives for weekend use. This might involve offering weekend discounts, or linking hotel use with leisure activities such as golf, fishing or hiking.

Service providers also have the problem of catering for peak demand when supply may be insufficient. A physical goods provider may build up inventory in slack periods for sale during peak demand. Service providers do not have this option. Consequently, alternative methods need to be considered. For example, supply flexibility can be varied through the use of part-time staff during peak periods. Multi-skilling means that employees may be trained in many tasks. Supermarket staff can be trained to fill shelves and work at the checkout in peak periods. Participation by consumers may be encouraged in production (e.g. self-service breakfasts in hotels). Demand may be smoothed through differential pricing to encourage customers to visit during off-peak periods (for example, lower-priced cinema and theatre seats for afternoon performances). If delay is unavoidable then another option is to make it more acceptable, for example, by providing effective queuing systems or a comfortable waiting area with seating and free refreshments. Finally, a reservation system as commonly used in restaurants, hair salons and theatres can be used to control peak demand and assist time substitution.

In summary, intangibility, inseparability, variability and perishability combine to distinguish services from products. As we noted at the outset, products and services are not completely distinct and, in most instances, it is a matter of degree. For example, a marketing research study would provide a report (physical good) that represents the outcome of a number of service activities (discussions with client, designing the research strategy, interviewing respondents and analysing the results). As many firms are finding it increasingly difficult to differentiate themselves on the basis of the products, opportunities for adding value are provided by the service components (see the discussion on augmented differentiation in Chapter 6). For example, staff at a Niketown store may do much more than just assist customers with finding a running shoe that fits correctly. These stores also provide additional services such as gait analysis and advice on training and running techniques – as well as selling Nike products of course!

Managing services enterprises

Because of the unique characteristics described above, managing services enterprises involves some special challenges. Four key issues are physical evidence, people, process and branding. We will now examine each of these in detail.

Physical evidence

As we saw above, customers look for clues to the likely quality of a service by inspecting the tangible evidence or the **servicescape**. For example, prospective customers may look through a restaurant window to check the appearance of the waiters, the décor and furnishings. The ambience of a retail store is highly dependent on décor, and colour can play an important role in establishing mood because colour has meaning. For example, the reception area of the Petshotel chain in the USA is typically furnished with floral soft furnishings, armchairs, a wide-screen television and stainless-steel bowls filled with doggie biscuits. This and its slogan, 'All the comforts of home', is designed to put pet owners at ease that their dogs will be well looked after while they are away.[11]

Changes in the physical evidence are often part of a marketer's effort to reposition a brand. For example, the desire by McDonald's to improve the image of its brand has seen it begin a process of completely revamping the look of its restaurants throughout the world. Out is going the cheap cafeteria look, characterized by orange and yellow colours, fluorescent lighting and cheap chairs and tables, to be replaced with neutral-tone materials such as metal and wood, mood lighting and kitchens that have been turned into an exposed cooking area. This moves the brand much closer to a company like Wagamama rather than its traditional competitors such as Burger King.

People

Because of the simultaneity of production and consumption in services, the firm's personnel occupy a key position in influencing customer perceptions of product quality.[12] The term **service encounter** is used to describe an interaction between a service provider and a customer (see Exhibit 7.3). These encounters may be short and quick, such as when a customer picks up a newspaper at a newsstand, or long and protracted involving multiple encounters, such as receiving a university education. Jan Carlzon, head of the airline SAS, called these interactions 'moments of truth'. He explained that SAS faced 65,000 moments of truth per day (that is, the number of interactions between company personnel and people outside the company) and that the outcome of these interactions determined the success of the company. Research on customer loyalty in service industries has shown that only 14 per cent of customers who stopped patronizing service businesses did so because they were dissatisfied with the quality of what they had bought. More than two-thirds stopped buying because they found service staff indifferent or unhelpful.[13]

Exhibit 7.3 Service providers like Emirates frequently use images of their staff in their advertising.

In order for service employees to be in the frame of mind to treat customers well, they need to feel that their company is treating them well. This has given rise to the idea of the *service profit chain* whereby having a happy workforce leads to having happy customers and, ultimately, superior profitability – a maxim that has been adopted by many leading companies such as the Virgin Group. The evidence to support the existence of a service profit chain is mixed, with some findings showing a correlation between happy staff and happy customers while others have found that having a happy workforce is more important than having happy customers in terms of profitability.[14] An important marketing task, then, is **internal marketing** – that is, selecting, training and motivating staff members to provide customer satisfaction. Without this type of support, employees tend to be variable in their performance, leading to variable service quality.

The selection of suitable people is the starting point of the process as the nature of the job requires appropriate personality characteristics. Once selected, training is required to familiarize recruits to the job requirements and the culture of the organization. Socialization then allows recruits to experience the culture and tasks of the organization. Service quality may also be affected by the degree to which staff are empowered or given the authority to satisfy customers and deal with their problems. For example, each member of staff of Marriott Hotels is allowed to spend up to £1,000 on their own initiative to solve customer problems.[15] Maintaining a motivated workforce in the face of irate customers, faulty support systems and the boredom that accompanies some service jobs is a demanding task. Some service companies give employee-of-the-month awards in recognition of outstanding service. Reward and remuneration are also important. For example, the US retailer Costco competes against Walmart in the discount warehouse sector, but its pay and conditions are far superior to those of its main rival and it has a staff turnover rate of 17 per cent annually compared with 70 per cent for the sector.[16]

Process

The service process refers to the procedures, mechanisms and flow of activities by which a service is acquired. The service process usually contains two elements, namely, that which is visible to the customer and where the service encounter takes place and that which is invisible to the customer but is still critical to service delivery. For example, waiting staff in a restaurant are a key part of the service encounter and they need to be well selected and well trained. How they treat customers is a key element of the service experience. But what happens in the kitchen, even though it is invisible to the customer, is also critical to the service experience. Both parts of the service process need to be carefully managed.

Service process decisions usually involve some trade-off between levels of service quality (effectiveness) and service productivity (efficiency). Productivity is a measure of the relationship between an input and an output. For instance, if more people can be served (output) using the same number of staff (input), productivity per employee has risen. For example, a doctor who reduces consultation time per patient, or a university that increases tutorial group size, raises productivity at the risk of lowering service quality. Clearly, a balance must be struck between productivity and service quality. There are ways of improving productivity without compromising quality. As we saw earlier, customers can be involved in the service delivery process, such as in self-service restaurants and petrol stations, and supply and demand for services can be balanced through either capacity expansion or demand management techniques.

The service process will also be significantly influenced by the service provider's attitude towards investments in technology. Owing to some of the challenges involved in delivering services through people that we discussed above, firms have begun to look at technological solutions. As we saw in the marketing spotlight at the beginning of this chapter, new banks are heavy users of technological processes for managing the day-to-day banking requirements of customers. For many this means that the service encounter is no longer with a banking representative but rather a piece of technology. This may be advantageous in terms of service consistency but it also removes the opportunity to build a personal relationship with the customer. The potential offered by technology has caused some service providers to focus more on productivity rather than on service quality. Significant investments have been made in outsourcing customer service to call centres, from which levels of service quality are often variable, leading to customer frustration and dissatisfaction.

Exhibit 7.4 Starbucks' brand imagery has become so strong that the actual brand name is no longer required to identify the company.

Service branding

Because of the intangible nature of services, branding is of crucial importance. As we saw earlier in the chapter, service decisions are difficult to make because services may be high on experience and credence properties. The reputation of the service provider becomes ever more important as a result and trust is an important factor in the customer buying decision. One way for service providers to differentiate themselves is through the strength of their brand equity (see Exhibit 7.4). The brand name of a service influences the perception of that service. Like product brand names, service brand names should aim for features like distinctiveness, relevance, memorability and flexibility.

Premier Inn Ad Insight: The 'Good Night Guarantee' campaign featuring Lenny Henry conveys the hotel chain's brand proposition.

Wagamama, the successful Japanese noodle chain, literally translates as 'wilful naughty child', but the distinctiveness of its name and service has proven to be attractive in foreign markets. Credit cards provide examples of effective brand names: Visa suggests internationality and Mastercard emphasizes top quality. Obviously, the success of the brand name is heavily dependent on the service organization's ability to deliver on the promise it implies. Sometimes service brand names are changed, such as the decision by Aviva, the UK's biggest insurer group, to drop its Norwich Union brand, which had existed for more than 200 years, and by Eagle Star to change its name to that of its parent, Zurich.

Dimensions of the service brand may also be difficult to communicate. For example, it may be difficult to represent courtesy, hard work and customer care in an advertisement. Once again the answer is to use tangible cues that will help customers understand and judge the service (see Marketing in Action 7.2). A hotel, for

Marketing in Action 7.2
Spies Travel: Do it for Denmark

Critical Thinking: Below is a review of a successful advertising campaign run by Spies Travel. Read it and reflect on the emotional benefits of other types of service experiences such as restaurants meals, a visit to the hairdressers and a pop concert, for example.

Denmark's number-one travel company Spies, was founded in 1956 and built itself a reputation for the traditional package holiday, the kind of two-week holiday in the sun typically taken, or aspired to, by those living in northern European countries. But significant changes in consumer holiday patterns posed important threats to Spies' business. While Danes were taking 33 per cent more flights in 2015 than in 2005, the traditional package holiday business had seen no growth in this time. The reasons for this were twofold. First, Scandinavian countries are now well served by low-cost airlines such as Norwegian Air and easyJet, and this, combined with the growth of price-comparison and aggregator sites like Trivago, meant that younger consumers in particular were creating their own holiday packages, often at cheaper prices. While Spies offered other products such as weekend breaks, its strong association with package holidays meant that it was often not top of mind when it came to these new types of recreational breaks.

Spies needed to respond and did so with its highly acclaimed 'Do it for Denmark' campaign, which was subsequently followed by another themed campaign, 'Do it for Mom'. The genesis for these campaigns was in the simple question 'Why do people go on holidays and breaks?' Aside from the obvious reasons like wanting to see new cities or countries, Spies' researchers wanted to get under the skin of consumers to find the deeper emotional reasons for travel. In the case of city breaks in particular, it emerged that these were mainly taken by couples and one of the underlying reasons was to help restore some of the passion in the relationship. This insight, combined with the fact that the Danish population was in decline due to low birth rates, triggered the provocative and attention-grabbing 'Do it for Denmark' headline.

With a limited promotional budget, Spies was restricted to using public relations (PR) and online video to promote its city breaks offerings. It seeded the Danish media with its research findings on the kinds of holidays most likely to lead to romance and created an online video about a Danish girl, Emma, who was conceived in a Paris hotel room. Elements of the video included a 'make a baby competition' where if couples could prove that they conceived on holiday they would win a three-year supply of baby products and a family getaway. The campaign was hugely successful. It featured on every one of Denmark's top 10 news sites and eight of the top 10 print titles. The campaign was also picked up internationally by global news organizations such as the BBC and the *Washington Post*. Similarly the online video was the eighth most shared on YouTube within three months of its launch. Bookings of city breaks and activity holidays were well ahead of target in 2014 and 2015, generating an additional €10 million in revenues for Spies.

Based on: Carlstrom, 2016;[17] Christensen and Lundgren, 2016;[18] Natividad, 2016[19]

Exhibit 7.5 Using the services of an online dating agency is perceived as risky for many consumers; therefore Match.com used real testimonials in its advertising.

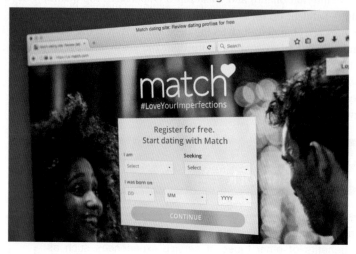

example, can show the buildings, swimming pool, friendly staff and happy customers; an investment company can provide tangible evidence of past performance; testimonials from satisfied customers can also be used to communicate services benefits. Netto, the Danish-based supermarket chain, used testimonials from six customers in its UK advertising to explain the advantages of shopping there. External communications that depict service quality can also influence internal staff if they include employees and show how they take exceptional care of their customers.

Word of mouth is critical to success for services because of their experiential nature (see Exhibit 7.5). For example, reading reviews written by people who have visited a resort or hotel is more convincing than reading holiday brochures. It is estimated that word of mouth can be the primary factor behind anything from 25 to 50 per cent of all consumer decisions.[20] The growth in digital and social media has significantly amplified the word-of-mouth effect, leading to the emergence of the term electronic word of mouth, or eWOM (see Chapter 11). The strength of the word-of-mouth effect is a function of what is said, who says it and where it is said. Content that relates directly to consumer decisions and that comes from trusted sources is likely to have a more powerful effect. However, the existence of a strong brand has been shown to moderate the strength of online customer reviews, implying that service brand building remains an important activity.[21]

Managing service quality

One of the core means of providing value to customers is to focus on the issue of service quality and how it can be improved. All kinds of organizations are making increasing use of customer satisfaction research to guide their marketing activity. This type of research may range from customer comment cards, to mystery shoppers, to online customer satisfaction studies, to social listening. Research has shown that companies that are rated higher on service quality perform better in terms of market share growth and profitability.[22] Yet, for many companies, high standards of service quality remain elusive.

A key to providing service quality is the understanding and meeting of customer expectations. To do so requires a clear picture of the criteria used to form these expectations, recognizing that consumers of services value not only the outcome of the service encounter but also the experience of taking part in it. For example, an evaluation of a haircut depends not only on the quality of the cut but also the experience of having a haircut. Clearly, a hairdresser needs not only technical skills but also the ability to communicate in an interesting and polite manner. Consequently, five core dimensions of service quality have been identified:[23]

1 *Reliability*: is the service consistent and dependable?
2 *Assurance*: that customers can trust the service company and its staff.
3 *Responsiveness*: how quickly do service staff respond to customer problems, requests and questions?
4 *Empathy*: that service staff act in a friendly and polite manner and care for their customers.
5 *Tangibles*: how well managed is the tangible evidence of the service (e.g. staff appearance, décor, layout)?

Improving service quality delivery requires an understanding of both customer expectations and the barriers that cause a difference between expected and perceived service levels. One approach has emphasized the closing of four gaps that are the main cause of service quality problems.[24]

Gap 1

This is the gap between what customers expect from a service provider and what the senior management team in the service organization thinks that customers expect. The gap is caused by senior managers being too far removed from customers – a problem that arises particularly in large organizations. Effective research into customers' expectations can be used to close this gap.

Gap 2

This is the gap between senior management perceptions and the service-level criteria that they set for the organization. All organizations have some service-level criteria, such as the speed with which phones should be answered or the number of breakdowns that should be fixed within a day, and so on. This gap can be closed by ensuring that customer service goals are an important part of the organization's targets for the planning period.

Gap 3

This is the gap between the service-level targets set by the organization and the actual level of service that is delivered by front-line staff. This gap can arise due to there being inadequate resources committed to service delivery, or poor selection, training and motivation of staff. Good internal marketing practices can assist in closing this gap.

Gap 4

Finally, this is the gap between what firms tell their customers to expect in their external communications and what they actually deliver. Therefore, service promises need to be managed very carefully. Over-promising causes customer expectations to rise and failure to deliver on these promises leads to dissatisfaction.

In summary, delivering service quality requires constant attention to the four potential gaps in the service delivery system. This is why consistently high levels of service are so difficult and why only very few firms, such as service leaders like Singapore Airlines and Marriott Hotels, manage to achieve them.

 Singapore Airlines Ad Insight: The 'Across the World' campaign illustrates the company's reputation for outstanding service quality.

Service recovery

Because services involve people, mistakes will inevitably occur even in the best-managed service systems. Service recovery strategies should be designed to solve the problem and restore the customer's trust in the firm, as well as improve the service system so that the problem does not recur in the future.[25] They are crucial because an inability to recover service failures and mistakes loses customers directly as well as through their tendency to tell other actual and potential customers about their negative experiences. This is particularly the case where consumers have paid a great deal for a service, such as first-class airline passengers.

The first ingredient in a service recovery strategy is to set up a tracking system to identify system failures. Customers should be encouraged to report service problems since it is those customers that do not complain that are least likely to purchase again. Second, staff should be trained and empowered to respond to service complaints. This is important because research has shown that the successful resolution of a complaint can cause customers to feel more positive about the firm than before the service failure. For example, when P&O had to cancel a round-the-world cruise because of problems with its ship, the *Aurora*, it reportedly offered passengers their money back plus a discount on their next booking. Many passengers said they planned to travel on a P&O cruise in the future.[26]

Finally, a service recovery strategy should encourage learning so that service recovery problems are identified and corrected. Service staff should be motivated to report problems and solutions so that recurrent failures are identified and fixed. In this way, an effective service recovery system can lead to improved customer service, satisfaction and higher customer retention levels.

Relationship marketing

The intangible nature of services means that customers may also value having a close relationship with a service provider. For example, if a customer finds an organization that she can trust, she may want to go back to this provider again and again as this saves her having to conduct a new information search each time a purchase is made. The relationship may also benefit the service provider as it is generally believed that it is cheaper for the organization to retain its existing customers than it is to gain new ones. These elements have underpinned the concept of **relationship marketing**.

The idea of relationship marketing can be applied to many industries. It is particularly important in services since there is often direct contact between service provider and consumer – for example, doctor and patient, hotel staff and guests (see Exhibit 7.6). The quality of the relationship that develops will often determine its length. Not all service encounters have the potential for a long-term relationship, however. For example, a passenger at an international airport who needs road transportation will probably never meet the taxi driver again, and the choice of taxi supplier will be dependent on the passenger's position in the queue rather than free choice. In this case the exchange – cash for journey – is a pure transaction: the driver knows that it is unlikely that there will ever be a repeat purchase. Organizations therefore need to decide when the practice of relationship marketing is most applicable. The following conditions suggest the use of relationship marketing activities.[27]

Exhibit 7.6 The NHS Blood and Transplant's innovative campaign #Missing Type featured partnerships with a number of iconic brands such as Microsoft and Coca-Cola to raise awareness of the importance of blood donations and to encourage more people to give blood.

- There is an ongoing or periodic desire for the service by the customer, e.g. insurance or theatre service versus funeral service.
- The customer controls the selection of a service provider, e.g. selecting a hotel versus entering the first taxi in an airport waiting line.
- The customer has alternatives from which to choose, e.g. selecting a restaurant versus buying water from the only utility company service in a community.

The existence of strong customer relationships brings benefits both for organizations and customers. There are six benefits to service organizations in developing and maintaining strong customer relationships.[28] The first is *increased purchases*. Customers tend to spend more because, as the relationship develops, trust grows between the partners. Second is *lower costs*. The start-up costs associated with attracting new customers are likely to be far higher than the cost of retaining existing customers. Third, loyal customers generate a significant *lifetime value*. If a customer spends €80 in a supermarket per week, resulting in €8 profit, and uses the supermarket 45 times a year over 30 years, the lifetime value of that customer is almost €11,000. Fourth, the intangible aspects of a relationship are not easily copied by the competition, generating a *sustainable competitive advantage*. Fifth, satisfied customers generate additional business due to the importance of *word-of-mouth* promotion in services industries. Finally, satisfied, loyal customers raise *employees' job satisfaction* and decrease staff turnover.

The net result of these six benefits of developing customer relationships is high profits. A study across a variety of service industries has shown that profits climb steeply when a firm lowers its customer defection rate.[29] Firms can improve profits from 25 to 85 per cent (depending on industry) by reducing customer defections by just 5 per cent. The reasons are that loyal customers generate more revenue for more years and the costs of maintaining existing customers are lower than the costs of acquiring new ones.

Entering into a long-term relationship can also reap benefits for the customer. First, since the intangible nature of services makes them difficult to evaluate beforehand, purchase relationships can help to reduce the risk and stress involved in making choices. Second, strong relationships allow the service provider to deliver a higher-quality service, which can be customized to particular needs. Maintaining a relationship reduces the customer's switching costs and, finally, customers can reap social and status benefits from the relationship, such as when restaurant managers get to know them personally.

Relationship marketing strategies vary in the degree to which they bond the parties together. One framework that illustrates this idea distinguishes between three levels of retention strategy based on the types of bond used to cement the relationship.[30]

1   *Level 1*: at this level the bond is primarily through financial incentives – for example, higher discounts on prices for larger-volume purchases, or frequent-flyer or loyalty points resulting in lower future prices. The problem is that the potential for a sustainable competitive advantage is low because price incentives are easy for competitors to copy even if they take the guise of frequent flyer or loyalty points. However, innovative approaches even at this level can yield significant successes, as shown in Marketing in Action 7.3.

2   *Level 2*: this higher level of bonding relies on more than just price incentives and consequently raises the potential for a sustainable competitive advantage. Level 2 retention strategies build long-term relationships through social as well as financial bonds, capitalizing on the fact that many service encounters are also social encounters. Customers become clients, the relationship becomes personalized and the service customized. Characteristics of this type of relationship include frequent communication with customers, providing personal treatment like sending cards, and enhancing the core service with educational or entertainment activities such as seminars or visits to sporting events. Some hotels keep records of their guests' personal preferences such as their favourite newspaper and alcoholic drink.

3   *Level 3*: this top level of bonding is formed by financial, social and structural bonds. Structural bonds tie service providers to their customers through providing solutions to customers' problems that are designed into the service delivery system. For example, logistics companies often supply their clients with equipment that ties them into their systems.

Marketing in Action 7.3
Tigerair: the Infrequent Flyer's Club

Critical Thinking: Below is a review of Tigerair's highly successful Infrequent Flyer's Club campaign. Read it and critically reflect on the level of value provided by other loyalty and relationship marketing programmes.

Tigerair is an Australian low-cost airline owned by Virgin Australia. Originally known as Tiger Airways, the company began operations in 2007 providing low-cost travel on routes within Australia such as Melbourne to Sydney and Melbourne to the Gold Coast. However, its early years were not without incident. In 2011, the Civil Aviation Authority in Australia grounded the airline over safety concerns. Flights resumed again in 2012, but the company was plagued with problems. Only four in every ten flights arrived on time and the airline had a customer satisfaction rating of just 37 per cent. However, by 2016, it had got its punctuality levels up to 85 per cent and its customer satisfaction levels began to outstrip its main low-cost rival, Jetstar, for the first time. It was also the first year that the company reported a profit from operations.

Contributing to its turnaround was a change in the company's marketing and the launch of its Infrequent Flyer's Club campaign. The key insight behind the campaign was that 77 per cent of Australians fly fewer than three times per year due to the cost of air travel and that these

(continued)

customers were largely ignored by Tigerair's rivals, which focused on higher-value, more frequent travellers. Creatively, the brand wanted to shine a light on the poor value of frequent-flyer programmes, which often created unattainable milestones, and instead speak to passengers who had never seen the inside of a airport lounge. The campaign's tagline was 'The Infrequent Flyer's Club: Don't fly much? Join the club'. With a limited budget of AU$150,000, Tigerair focused on creating awareness of the campaign using online video, promoted Facebook posts and targeted posters in airport terminals. Travellers were invited to sign up to Tigerair's club, which is essentially a CRM platform giving them access to flight deals tailored to their interests and favourite destinations. Shareable content was also created for the brand's social channels, which was also successful in attracting user-generated content. Overall the tone of the campaign was humorous. For example, the club had 18 membership levels but none was better than the other, poking fun at the status attached to gold and platinum levels in the frequent-flyer programmes of rivals. One of its most popular airport posters proclaimed that Tigerair does not have a lounge because 'you have one of those at home'.

The campaign was highly successful. It captured the attention of the mainstream media, generating significant PR value beyond the cost of the campaign, and meant that Tigerair was in the news for positive reasons. The company had set a target of getting 50,000 subscribers to its club. Within a year, this had been exceeded by 1,000 per cent with more than 500,000 club members joining, something that was unprecedented given the previously poor reputation of the airline. Within six months of the campaign commencing, revenues had increased by 18 per cent and sales of AU$15 million, which were directly related to the formation of the club, were achieved within two years.

Based on: Anonymous, 2016;[31] Hatch, 2016[32]

Customer relationship management (CRM) systems

In most cases, customer relationships are managed using **customer relationship management (CRM) systems** where a single database is created from customer information to inform all staff who deal with customers. CRM is a term for the methodologies, technologies and e-commerce capabilities used by companies to manage customer relationships.[33] The basic principle behind CRM is that company staff have a single-customer point of view of each client. Interactions between a customer and an organization may take place across a variety of channels, such as the sales force, call centres, websites, email and social media. All these interactions need to be recorded, kept up to date and shared effectively across the organization. Frequently problems arise as different elements of marketing activity, such as sales and customer service, are automated at different times, leading to issues of incompatibility between systems and frustrations for customers.

The main benefit of a CRM system is that it is based on the knowledge of the customer's previous history and known product preferences. In addition to this, customer information such as buying trends, interests, average spending, location and even gender can be captured and used to manage individual customer relationships and provide a consistent interface to the customer.[34] Good CRM systems throw up all sorts of unusual patterns in consumer behaviour, such as when Tesco found that one segment of its customers were buying beer and nappies during the same shopping trip and it was then able to target these young fathers more carefully.

The effective use of CRM allows organizations to conduct a rigorous analysis of their customers. Businesses frequently find that they are subject to the Pareto Principle, or 80/20 rule – that is, that 80 per cent of their profits may come from 20 per cent of their customers. At a very simple level what this means is that some customers may be more important than others and that, from a marketing point of view, perhaps the company should invest more in those valuable customers. Other researchers have recommended classifying customers on the basis of their value to the organization using labels such as platinum, gold, silver and lead.[35]

Silver and gold customers need to be moved up the scale, while lead customers are gradually 'fired'. Customer relationship management allows firms to measure the following:

1 *Customer retention*: What proportion of customers are staying with the firm, and are these the customers it wants to retain?
2 *Customer defection*: What proportion of customers are leaving the firm? Are these the customers that the firm would want to 'fire' or the ones it would rather retain?
3 *Customer acquisition*: What proportion of new customers are arriving on to the firm's books as a result of its marketing activities?

CRM systems are becoming progressively more complex as the number of potential touchpoints where a customer can interact with a company increases. All these interactions, whether offline or through online and social channels, need to be recorded, monitored and responded to. Touchpoints with customers can occur at all stages of the customer journey (see Chapter 3) and have given rise to the emerging concept of omni-channel management (see Chapter 9). However, research evidence on the effectiveness of CRM is mixed, suggesting that it is not the presence of the technology per se but rather how it is managed that is important. For example, one study has found that marketing orientation (rather than customer orientation) and knowledge management, as well as organizational factors such as employees and leadership, may be key to CRM effectiveness.[36] Similarly a study on the role of social media in CRM failed to find support for these technologies in enhancing customer relationship performance.[37]

Customer loyalty and retention

Relationship marketing strategies focus attention on the important issue of customer loyalty. At the most basic level, it has been suggested that a potential ladder of loyalty exists and that customers progress up or down this ladder (see Figure 7.2). The firm's marketing activity may revolve around trying to move customers up this ladder until they become advocates or partners of the organization. Advocates are an important group because they not only purchase an organization's products but also actively recommend it to their friends and colleagues. At the top of the ladder are partners who trust and support the organization and actively work with it.

The ladder of loyalty also helps organizations to reflect on the different types of loyalty that may exist. For example, some customers may continue to engage in high levels of repeat business with an organization but this may happen for reasons of inertia rather than true loyalty. This has occurred in sectors like retail

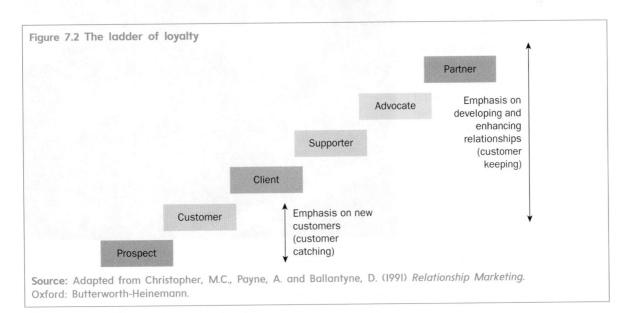

Figure 7.2 The ladder of loyalty

Partner

Advocate

Supporter

Client

Customer

Prospect

Emphasis on developing and enhancing relationships (customer keeping)

Emphasis on new customers (customer catching)

Source: Adapted from Christopher, M.C., Payne, A. and Ballantyne, D. (1991) *Relationship Marketing*. Oxford: Butterworth-Heinemann.

banking, where consumers have demonstrated a reluctance to switch. Similarly, many of the loyalty schemes run by organizations aim to attract and retain customers on a purely financial basis. Again, this is not true loyalty, with customers tending to engage in repeat business only for as long as the financial incentives remain. A much greater understanding of customers' needs and a willingness to meet those needs on an ongoing basis is required for true loyalty to occur.

Recent years have seen the emergence of the important concept of **customer brand engagement**, given the multiplicity of ways in which customers now interact with organizations ranging from becoming fans or followers on social media to posting online reviews to generating new product ideas. Customer brand engagement has been defined as the level of a customer's cognitive, emotional and behavioural investment in specific brand interactions.[38] Not only are customers satisfied with brand or service experiences but they are also emotionally connected (expressing love or passion for a brand). Customer engagement has been found to have a positive effect on a firm's performance, and this effect is stronger in B2B (versus B2C) firms and in services rather than manufacturing firms.[39] Aside from having possible tangible benefits such as increased revenues, some of the intangible benefits of engagement may include a willingness to opt in to the firm's marketing programmes, provide access to personal information and enable the firm to provide relevant marketing information.[40] Therefore it is recommended that firms develop and execute a customer engagement strategy.[41]

Finally, the link between customer loyalty and profitability is a very important one in marketing. Associations between a small increase in customer retention and a large increase in profitability have been identified.[42] This has been explained by the propensity of loyal customers to spend more with the organization and the decreased cost of serving such customers. However, other research has highlighted that this relationship may be more complex. For example, in some instances it has been found that long-standing customers are only marginally profitable, while some short-term customers have been highly profitable.[43] This reaffirms that it is the nature of loyalty rather than the length of time customers have been with a firm that is most important. In keeping with developments in the engagement literature, distinctions have been drawn between attitudinal and behavioural loyalty, with the latter more important in terms of a firm performance.[44]

Experiential marketing

Allied to the provision of service quality and relationships, the creation of customer experiences is another avenue for organizations to deliver value for customers (see Exhibit 7.7). It aims to capitalize on consumer trends in the Western world, where experiences are perceived by many as being more important than the ownership of goods. Through **experiential marketing**, organizations recognize the important role of emotions in consumer decision-making (see Chapter 3). Five different types of experiences have been identified, namely, sensory experiences (SENSE), affective experiences (FEEL), creative cognitive experiences (THINK), physical experiences, behaviours and lifestyles (ACT), and social identity experiences (RELATE).[45] In leveraging experiential opportunities, organizations either partner with existing events or create entirely new ones.

Exhibit 7.7 The Ribena 'Colouring Cafe' was a one-day experiential event in London organized by the drinks brand and Brass Agency, aimed at people who 'wanted to grab life by the felt tip'.

For example, Nike created the 'Nike Air Max Day' in 2016 with the aim of celebrating the brand's heritage and also fostering a sense of community among the brand's fans. The highlight of the day was Air Max Con, a multi-day convention held in New York, Hong Kong and Tokyo. The exhibitions were all significant in the context of the brand. Attendees first entered the 'Nike Air Max Vault', where 100 of the most iconic Air Max styles were displayed, along with a brief written history of each. The next exhibition paid homage to iconic Air Max designers, detailing their personal Air Max stories. These exhibitions served to educate consumers and raise their appreciation of the brand. Esteemed collectors exhibited some of their extensive collections and educated other visitors through Q&A sessions. The conventions made extensive use of stimuli such as sound, provided by local DJs performing music congruent with the Air Max image, visuals from local artists, and touch, where participants were invited to customize Air Max shoes using tablets, all enhancing the sensory experience. Participants were also invited to participate in a 'VoteBack' to decide which Air Max styles should be brought back for 2017, and encouraged to use the hashtag #AirMax on all their social media activity relating to the day.[46]

Experiential marketing has also become very popular within the retail trade as stores and locations seek to find new ways to appeal to potential customers (see Chapter 9). The focus has moved from being a venue where products are sold to one where consumers can have a shopping experience or where they can shop as part of other activities. Many major shopping malls now have cinemas attached, others have leisure facilities such as gymnasiums and swimming pools, while some have theatres and galleries. Luxury store Prada, New York, has a cultural performance space, Louis Vuitton's Paris flagship store has an art gallery and a bookstore, while Gucci's Ginza store in Tokyo also has an art gallery as well as an event space. Nespresso has opened a number of Nespresso Boutiques to create the 'ultimate coffee experience'.

The ideal experiential marketing effort is an ownable, sensory brand experience that makes customers feel like the product or service is theirs. These motivated customers then become product advocates, who influence family, friends and co-workers to try the product. For example, Delta Airlines has developed its SKY360 lounge in New York to create a customer experience. Visitors to the lounge are met by actual flight attendants and ticket agents. They sample food items available on Delta and are asked to try new entertainment systems that are built in to the backs of seats. The lounge has WiFi connections and computer terminals for anyone who wants to book a flight with Delta.[47]

Marketing in non-profit organizations

Non-profit organizations attempt to achieve some other objective than profit. This does not mean that they are uninterested in income as they have to generate cash to survive. However, their primary goal is non-economic – for example, to provide cultural enrichment (an orchestra), to protect birds and animals (Royal Society for the Protection of Birds, Royal Society for the Prevention of Cruelty to Animals), to alleviate hunger (Oxfam), to provide education (schools and universities), to foster community activities (community associations), and to supply healthcare (hospitals) and public services (local authorities) (see Exhibit 7.8). Their worth and standing is not dependent on the profits they generate. They are discussed in this chapter as most non-profit organizations operate in the services sector. Indeed, non-profit organizations account for more than half of all service provision in most European countries.

Marketing is of growing importance to many non-profit organizations because they need to generate funds in an increasingly competitive arena. Even organizations that rely on government-sponsored grants need to show how their work is of benefit to society; they must meet the needs of their customers. Many non-profit organizations rely on membership fees and

Exhibit 7.8 This Unicef campaign, the 'Face of Children of Rohinyga', highlights the importance of education for refugee children.

donations, which means that communication to individuals and organizations is required, and they must be persuaded to join or make a donation. This requires marketing skills, which are increasingly being applied. As we saw in Chapter 1, political parties, universities, hospitals and aid agencies are now frequent users of marketing.

Characteristics of non-profit marketing

There are a number of characteristics of non-profit marketing that distinguish it from that conducted in profit-orientated organizations.[48]

Education vs meeting current needs

Some non-profit organizations see their role not only as meeting the current needs of their customers but also educating them in terms of new ideas and issues, cultural developments and social awareness. **Social marketing** is the term that is used to describe efforts, mainly by public-sector organizations, to encourage positive social change, such as healthy eating, reduced cigarette and alcohol consumption, safe sex, safe driving, human rights and racial equality. Commercial marketing techniques, such as consumer research, segmentation and marketing mix development, are frequently used to achieve these types of goals.

Multiple publics

Most non-profit organizations serve several groups, or publics. The two broad groups are *donors*, who may be individuals, trusts, companies or government bodies, and *clients*, who include audiences, patients and beneficiaries.[49] The need to satisfy both donors and clients is a complicated marketing task. For example, a community association may be partly funded by the local authority and partly by the users (clients) of the association's buildings and facilities. To succeed, both groups have to be satisfied. The BBC has to satisfy not only its viewers and listeners, but also the government, which decides the size of the licence fee that funds its activities. Non-profit organizations need to adopt marketing as a coherent philosophy for managing multiple public relationships.[50]

Measurement of success and conflicting objectives

For profit-orientated organizations success is ultimately measured in terms of profitability. For non-profit organizations, measuring success is not so easy. In universities, for example, is success measured in terms of research output, number of students taught, the range of qualifications or the quality of teaching? The answer is that it is a combination of these factors, which can lead to conflict – more students and a larger range of courses may reduce the time available for research. Decision-making is therefore complex in non-profit-orientated organizations.

Public scrutiny

While all organizations are subject to public scrutiny, public-sector non-profit organizations are never far from the public's attention. The reason is that they are publicly funded from taxes. This gives them extra newsworthiness and they have to be particularly careful not to become involved in controversy. For example, some charitable organizations in Ireland suffered a collapse in funding in 2013 when it emerged that donations were being diverted to top up the salaries of senior executives.

Marketing procedures for non-profit organizations

Despite these differences, the marketing procedures relevant to profit-orientated organizations can also be applied to non-profit organizations. Target marketing, differentiation and tactical marketing decisions need to be made. We will now discuss these issues with reference to the special characteristics of non-profit organizations.

Target marketing and differentiation

As we have already discussed, non-profit organizations can usefully segment their target publics into donors and clients (customers). Within each group, sub-segments of individuals and organizations need to be identified.

These will be the targets for persuasive communications and the development of services. The needs of each group must be understood. For example, donors may judge which charity to give to on the basis of awareness and reputation, the confidence that funds will not be wasted on excessive administration, and the perceived worthiness of the cause (see Marketing in Action 7.4). The charity needs, therefore, not only to promote itself but also to gain publicity for its cause. Its level of donor funding will depend upon both these factors. The brand name of the charity is also important. 'Oxfam' suggests the type of work the organization is mainly concerned with – relief of famine – and so is instantly recognizable. 'Women's Aid' is also suggestive of its type of work.

Marketing in Action 7.4
Women's Aid: innovative, low-cost advertising

> **Critical Thinking:** Below is a review of some of the low-cost advertising campaigns undertaken by the UK domestic abuse charity Women's Aid. Read it and reflect on other innovative campaigns that you have seen from not-for-profit organizations.

Domestic abuse is a highly emotive and often misunderstood issue. Research indicates that one in four women experience abuse in the course of their lifetime and, in the UK, domestic abuse occurs every six to twenty seconds. Women's Aid is a charity organization set up to help people affected by domestic abuse. Like many charities, it has a very limited marketing budget, yet marketing is critically important both in terms of generating funding and creating public awareness of this important issue. As a result, it has had to be very innovative in its marketing activities.

One of its most famous campaigns in 2007 – Valentine's Day: Saying it With Roses, was run on a budget of just over £40,000, yet received national coverage in the mainstream media. By focusing all of its marketing on the one day that is associated with love, it cleverly juxtaposed images of abuse with symbols of romance – such as its press advert, which used the visual of a red rose with a message of abuse. Its powerful tagline reminded everyone that 'for women who suffer domestic abuse, Valentine's Day is just another day'.

More recently, Women's Aid has focused on using technology to overcome its budget limitations. Its famous 2013 cinema campaign exploited the power of 3D technology. 3D glasses contain one vertically and one horizontally aligned lens, altering the image slightly differently for each eye. The brain creates a single image by combining these two images. A short film was created that, viewed through one eye, showed a woman preparing dinner but, viewed through the other, showed the presence of her abusive husband. It fitted perfectly with the advert's tagline of 'Don't turn a blind eye to domestic abuse.'

In 2016, the charity received further plaudits for a very innovative billboard campaign, which relied on the fact that some modern digital billboards have facial recognition cameras to monitor how many people are looking at them. It designed a billboard depicting a beaten and bruised woman. As long as people ignored the screen, the face would stay the, same, but it would take only one person to stop and look at the billboard for the woman's bruises to begin to heal. The more people who stopped to look, the more the woman's face would return to normal and the copy read that 'If you can see it, you can change it.' Twelve sites were chosen in busy locations throughout the UK and again the campaign achieved huge coverage in both mainstream and social media, reaching an estimated 300 million people in total and generating more than 85 million impressions on Twitter alone. The impact of the campaign could also be seen in the fact that the number of people stopping to look at the billboards increased by 2,500 per cent compared with previously.

Based on: Simpson, 2016;[51] Willifer and Hurst, 2013[52]

Market segmentation and targeting are key ingredients in the marketing of political parties. Potential voters are segmented according to their propensity to vote (obtainable from electoral registers) and their likelihood of voting for a particular party (obtainable from door-to-door canvassing returns). Resources can then be channelled to the segments most likely to switch votes in the forthcoming election, via direct mail and doorstep visits. Focus groups provide a feedback mechanism for testing the attractiveness of alternative policy options and gauging voters' opinions on key policy areas such as health, education and taxation. By keeping in touch with public opinion, political parties have the information to differentiate themselves from their competitors on issues that are important to voters. While such marketing research is unlikely to affect the underlying beliefs and principles on which a political party is based, it is a necessary basis for the policy adaptations required to keep in touch with a changing electorate.[53]

Developing a marketing mix

The pricing of services provided by non-profit organizations may not follow the guidelines applicable to profit-orientated pricing. For example, the price of a nursery school place organized by a community association may be held low to encourage poor families to take advantage of the opportunity. Some non-profit organizations exist to provide free access to services – for example, the National Health Service in the UK. In other situations, the price of a service provided by a non-profit organization may come from a membership or licence fee. For example, the Royal Society for the Protection of Birds (RSPB) charges an annual membership fee; in return, members receive a quarterly magazine and free entry to RSPB bird watching sites. The BBC receives income from a licence fee, which all television owners have to pay. The level of this fee is set by government, making relations with political figures an important marketing consideration.

Like most services, distribution systems for many non-profit organizations are short, with production and consumption simultaneous. This is the case for hospital operations, consultations with medical practitioners, education, nursery provision, cultural entertainment and many more services provided by non-profit organizations. Such organizations have to think carefully about how to deliver their services with the convenience that customers require. For example, Oxfam has 750 shops around the UK that sell second-hand clothing, books, music and household items that have been donated to it. It has also formed alliances with online retailers such as abebooks.co.uk to list and sell second-hand books, from which Oxfam receives a commission.

Many non-profit organizations are adept at using promotion to further their needs (see Exhibit 7.9). The print media are popular with organizations seeking donations for worthy causes such as famine in Africa. Direct mail is also used to raise funds. Mailing lists of past donors are useful here, and some organizations use lifestyle geodemographic analyses to identify the type of person who is more likely to respond to a direct mailing. Non-profit organizations also need to be aware of publicity opportunities that may arise because of their activities. Many editors are sympathetic to such

Exhibit 7.9 Misereor is a German not-for-profit organization that is assisting in the fight against hunger and poverty in the world. It developed an innovate campaign whereby consumers can make a donation by swiping their credit/debit cards at interactive billboards and posters.

publicity attempts because of their general interest to the public. Sponsorship is also a vital income source for many non-profit organizations.

Public relations has an important role to play in generating positive word-of-mouth communications and establishing the identity of the non-profit organization (e.g. a charity). Attractive fundraising settings (e.g. sponsored lunches) can be organized to ensure that the exchange proves to be satisfactory to donors. A key objective of communications efforts should be to produce a positive assessment of the fundraising transaction and to reduce the perceived risk of the donation so that donors develop trust and confidence in the organization and become committed to the cause.[54]

Summary

In this chapter, we examined the particular issues that arise when marketing services businesses. The following key issues were addressed.

1. There are four unique characteristics of services, namely, intangibility, inseparability, variability and perishability. As a result marketers must find ways to 'tangibilize' services, must pay attention to service quality, must find ways to ensure service consistency, and must find ways to balance supply and demand for services.

2. The four key elements of managing services enterprises, namely, physical evidence, people, process and service branding.

3. Internal marketing to frontline employees is critical to the success of a service organization, and great attention needs to be paid to their selection, training and motivation. Employee empowerment is a key element of service quality and service recovery.

4. Service quality is an important source of value creation. Essentially, it involves measuring how service perceptions match up against the expectations that customers have of the service provider and taking the types of remedial action necessary to close any service delivery gaps.

5. Relationship marketing is another important source of value creation. Organizations can engage in marketing activities that raise levels of attitudinal loyalty.

6. Value can also be created through the provision of customer experiences, which can be used to improve the consumer's relationship with the organization.

7. Non-profit organizations attempt to achieve some objectives other than profit. Their two key publics are donors and clients; the needs of these two groups often conflict. In managing this complexity, non-profit organizations use conventional services marketing techniques.

Study questions

1. Discuss the implications of the unique characteristics of services for the marketing activities of services enterprises.

2. What are the barriers that can separate expected from perceived service? What must service providers do to eliminate these barriers?

3. Discuss the role of service staff in the creation of a quality service. Can you give examples from your own experiences of good and bad service encounters?

4. Discuss the benefits to organizations and customers of developing and maintaining strong customer relationships.

5. Select any three music, sport or cultural events that you have attended in the past year. What industry partners were involved in the events and what role did they play in each one?

6. How does marketing in non-profit organizations differ from that in profit-orientated companies? Choose a non-profit organization and discuss the extent to which marketing principles can be applied.

7. Visit yelp.com and tripadvisor.com. Discuss the impact of the existence of these websites on organizations that provide good and poor levels of service.

Suggested reading

Ahmed, P.K. and **Mohammed, R.** (2003) Internal marketing: issues and challenges, *European Journal of Marketing*, 37(9), 1177–87.

Choudhury, M.M. and **Harrigan, P.** (2014) CRM to social CRM: the integration of new technologies into customer relationship management, *Journal of Strategic Marketing*, 22(2), 149–76.

Dixon, M., Freeman, K. and **Toman, N.** (2010) Stop trying to delight your customers, *Harvard Business Review*, 88(7/8), 116–22.

Grönroos, C. and **Vioma, P.** (2013) Critical service logic: making sense of value creation and co-creation, *Journal of the Academy of Marketing Science*, 41, 133–50.

McDermott, L., Steed, M. and **Hastings, G.** (2005) What is and what is not social marketing: the challenge of

reviewing the evidence, *Journal of Marketing Management*, 21(5/6), 545–53.

Moeller, S. (2010) Characteristics of services – a new approach uncovers their value, *Journal of Services Marketing*, 24(5), 359–68.

Kumar, V. and **Pansari, A.** (2016) Competitive advantage through engagement, *Journal of Marketing Research*, 53(August), 497–514.

Thakur, R. and **Workman, L.** (2016) Customer portfolio management (CPM) for improved relationship management (CRM): are your customers platinum, gold, silver or bronze? *Journal of Business Research*, 69, 4095–102.

Vargo, S.L. and **Lusch, R.F.** (2008) Service-dominant logic: continuing the evolution, *Journal of the Academy of Marketing Science*, 36, 1–10.

References

1. **Anonymous** (2018) How can a Fintech company win 20 million customers? *Strategy-Business.com*. Available at www.strategy-business.com/article/How-Can-a-Fintech-Company-Win-20-Million-Customers?gko=03727&utm_source=itw&utm_medium=20180320&utm_campaign=resp (accessed 20 March 2018); **Mesoropyan, E.** (2016) Fintech companies that have ended the monopoly on bank account, *Gomedici.com*. Available at www.gomedici.com/fintech-companies-that-have-ended-the-monopoly-on-bank-account/ (accessed 14 June 2016).

2. **Holodny, E.** (2016) There's a new driver of the global economy and it changes how we should look at the world, *Business-Insider.com*. Available at www.uk.businessinsider.com/new-global-economic-order-services-versus-infrastructure-2016-5?r=US&IR=T (accessed 18 June 2018).

3. **Vargo, S.L.** and **Lusch, R.F.** (2004) Evolving a new dominant logic for marketing, *Journal of Marketing*, 68(1), 1–17; **Vargo, S.L.** and **Lusch, R.F.** (2008) Service-dominant logic: continuing the evolution, *Journal of the Academy of Marketing Science*, 36, 1–10.

4. **Berry, L.L.** (1980) Services marketing is different, *Business Horizons*, May–June, 24–9.

5. **Zeithaml, V.** (1984) How consumer evaluation processes differ between goods and services, in C.H.

Lovelock (ed.) *Services Marketing*. Engelwood Cliffs, NJ., Prentice-Hall, 191–9.

6. **Foster, L.** (2004) The march of the geek squad, *Financial Times*, 24 November, 13.

7. **Edgett, S.** and **Parkinson, S.** (1993) Marketing for services industries: a review, *Service Industries Journal*, 13(3), 19–39.

8. **Berry, L.L.** (1980) Services marketing is different, *Business Horizons*, May–June, 24–9.

9. **Aijo, T.S.** (1996) The theoretical and philosophical underpinnings of relationship marketing, *European Journal of Marketing*, 30(2), 8–18; **Grönoos, C.** (1990) *Services Management and Marketing: Managing the Moments of Truth in Service Competition*. Lexington, MA: Lexington Books.

10. **Baron, S., Harris, K.** and **Davies, B.J.** (1996) Oral participation in retail service delivery: a comparison of the roles of contact personnel and customers, *European Journal of Marketing*, 30(9), 75–90.

11. **Birchall, J.** (2005) Top dogs lead the way as pet market grooms and booms, *Financial Times*, 3 August, 28.

12. **Rafiq, M.** and **Ahmed, P.K.** (1992) The marketing mix reconsidered, *Proceedings of the Annual Conference of the Marketing Education Group*, Salford, 439–51.

13. **Schlesinger, L.A.** and **Heskett, J.L.** (1991) The service-driven service company, *Harvard Business Review*, September–October, 71–81.

14. **Anonymous** (2007) Doing well by being rather nice, *The Economist*, 1 December, 74; **Mitchell, A.** (2007) In the pursuit of happiness, *Financial Times*, 14 June, 14.

15. **Bowen, D.E.** and **Lawler, L.L.** (1992) Empowerment: why, what, how and when, *Sloan Management Review*, Spring, 31–9.

16. **Birchall, J.** (2005) Pile high, sell cheap and pay well, *Financial Times*, 11 July, 12.

17. **Carlstrom, V.** (2016) After saving Denmark with sex, this travel agency is back with a hilarious new campaign and a clever price discrimination model, *Nordic.BusinessInsider.com*. Available at www.nordic.businessinsider.com/after-saving-denmark-with-sex-spies-rejser-have-stepped-it-up-with-a-hilarious-new-campaign-and-a-perfect-price-discrimination-model-2016-11/ (accessed 15 March 2017).

18. **Christensen, S.** and **Lundgren, E.** (2016) Spies travel: do it for Denmark and do it for mom, *Warc.com*. Available at www.warc.com/content/article/ipa/spies_travel_do_it_for_denmark_and_do_it_for_mom/108011 (accessed 15 March 2017).

19. **Natividad, A.** (2016) This Danish travel agency dreamed up a fun way to get parents to have more sex, *Adweek*. Available at www.adweek.com/creativity/danish-travel-agency-dreamed-fun-way-get-parents-have-more-sex-174680/ (accessed 15 March 2017).

20. **Bughin, J.**, **Doogan, J.** and **Vetvik, O.J.** (2010) A new way to measure word of mouth marketing, *McKinsey Quarterly*, April.

21. **Nga, N.H.**, **Carson, S.** and **Moore, W.** (2013) The effect of positive and negative online customer reviews: do brand strength and category maturity matter? *Journal of Marketing*, 77(6), 37–53.

22. **Buzzell, R.D.** and **Gale, B.T.** (1987) *The PIMS Principles: Linking Strategy to Performance*. New York: Free Press, 103–34.

23. **Parasuraman, A.**, **Zeithaml, V.A.** and **Berry, L.L.** (1985) A conceptual model of service quality and its implications for future research, *Journal of Marketing*, Fall, 41–50.

24. **Berry, L.L.**, **Parasuraman, A.** and **Zeithaml, V.A.** (1988) The service-quality puzzle, *Business Horizons*, 31(5), 35–44.

25. **Reichheld, F.F.** and **Sasser Jr, W.E.** (1990) Zero defections: quality comes to services, *Harvard Business Review*, September–October, 105–11.

26. **Reinartz, W.J.** and **Kumar, V.** (2002) The mismanagement of customer loyalty, *Harvard Business Review*, 80(7), 86–94.

27. **Berry, L.L.** (1995) Relationship marketing, in A. Payne, M. Christopher, M. Clark and H. Peck (eds) *Relationship Marketing for Competitive Advantage*. Oxford: Butterworth-Heinemann, 65–74.

28. **Zeithaml, V.A.** and **Bitner, M.J.** (2002) *Services Marketing*. New York: McGraw-Hill, 174–8.

29. **Reichheld, F.F.** and **Sasser Jr, W.E.** (1990) Zero defections: quality comes to services, *Harvard Business Review*, September–October, 105–11.

30. **Berry, L.L.** and **Parasuraman, A.** (1991) *Managing Services*. New York: Free Press, 136–42.

31. **Anonymous** (2016) Tigerair Australia: Infrequent Flyer's Club, *Warc.com*. Available at www.warc.com/content/article/cannes/tigerair_australia_infrequent_flyers_club/107601 (accessed 14 June 2016).

32. **Hatch, P.** (2016) How Tigerair, once Australia's worst airline, has turned itself around, *Sydney Morning Herald*. Available at www.smh.com.au/business/companies/how-tigerair-once-australias-worst-airline-has-turned-itself-around-20160805-gqlk8h.html (accessed 14 June 2016).

33. **Foss, B.** and **Stone, M.** (2001) *Successful Customer Relationship Marketing*. London: Kogan Page.

34. **Wynn, M.**, **Turner, P.**, **Banik, A.** and **Duckworth, G.** (2016) The impact of customer relationship management systems in small business enterprises. *Strategic Change*, 25, 659–74.

35. **Zeithaml, V.**, **Rust, R.** and **Lemon, K.** (2001) The customer pyramid: creating and serving profitable customers, *California Management Review*, 43(4), 118–42.

36. **Cambra-Fierro, J.J.**, **Centeno, E.**, **Olavarria, A.** and **Vasquez-Carrasco, R.** (2017) Success factors in a CRM strategy: technology is not all, *Journal of Strategic Marketing*, 25(4), 316–33.

37. **Choudhury, M.M.** and **Harrigan, P.** (2014) CRM to social CRM: the integration of new technologies into customer relationship management, *Journal of Strategic Marketing*, 22(2), 149–76.

38. **Hollebeek, L.** (2011) Exploring customer brand engagement: definition and themes, *Journal of Strategic Marketing*, 19(7), 555–73.

39. **Kumar, V.** and **Pansari, A.** (2016) Competitive advantage through engagement, *Journal of Marketing Research*, 53(August), 497–514.

40. **Pansari, A.** and **Kumar, V.** (2017) Customer engagement: the construct, antecedents and consequences, *Journal of the Academy of Marketing Science*, 45, 294–311.

41. **Venkatesan, R.** (2017) Executing on a customer engagement strategy, *Journal of the Academy of Marketing Science*, 45, 289–93.

42. **Kasper, H.**, **van Helsdingen, P.** and **de Vries Jr, W.** (1999) *Services Marketing Management*. Chichester: Wiley, 528.

43. **Witzel, M.** (2005) Keep your relationship with clients afloat, *Financial Times*, 31 January, 13.

44. **Watson, G.F.**, **Beck, J.T.**, **Henderson, C.M.** and **Palmatier, R.W.** (2015) Building, measuring and profiting from customer loyalty, *Journal of the Academy of Marketing Science*, 43, 790–825.

45. **Schmitt, B.** (1999) Experiential marketing, *Journal of Marketing Management*, 15, 53–67.

46. **Wolf, C.** (2016) Air Max Con NYC is a tour through sneaker heaven, *Racked New York*. Available at www.ny.racked.com/2016/3/24/11299010/air-max-con-nyc (accessed 22 June 2018).

47. **Borden, J.** (2008) Experiential marketing takes the industry by storm in 2008, *Marketing Week*, 15 January, 23–6.

48. **Bennett, P.D.** (1988) *Marketing*. New York: McGraw-Hill, 690–2.

49. **Shapiro, B.** (1992) Marketing for non-profit organisations, *Harvard Business Review*, September–October, 123–32.

50. **Balabanis, G., Stables, R.E.** and **Philips, H.C.** (1997) Market orientation in the top 200 British charity organisations and its impact on their performance, *European Journal of Marketing*, 31(8), 583–603.

51. **Simpson, J.** (2016) How women's aid used digital OOH ads to make 327m people stop & look [blog], *Econsultancy*. Available at www.econsultancy. com/blog/67393-how-women-s-aid-used-digital-ooh-ads-to-make-327m-people-stop-look (accessed 14 June 2018).

52. **Willifer, M.** and **Hurst, E.** (2013) Women's aid: the power of starting in a different place, *Warc.com*. Available at www.warc.com/content/article/apg/womens_aid_the_power_of_starting_in_a_different_place/101277 (accessed 14 June 2018).

53. **Butler, P.** and **Collins, N.** (1994) Political marketing: structure and process, *European Journal of Marketing*, 28(1), 19–34.

54. **Hibbert, S.** (1995) The market positioning of British medical charities, *European Journal of Marketing*, 29(10), 6–26.

Introduction

An essential part of delivering high-quality customer service in the retail sector is the ability to meet and go beyond customer expectations. The retail sector in recent years has become increasingly competitive. It has become harder to attract customers to both online and bricks-and-mortar stores.

Background

Abercrombie & Fitch was established by David T. Abercrombie in 1892, when the company was best known for selling outdoor merchandise. In 1900, part of the company was sold to Ezra Fitch; hence the name Abercrombie & Fitch. During the 1930s Abercrombie & Fitch become known for selling sporting goods, and some of its more famous customers included Theodore Roosevelt and Ernest Hemingway. Abercrombie & Fitch encountered some financial difficulties in 1977 and was acquired by Oshman's Sporting Goods. In 1988 Abercrombie & Fitch was acquired by The Limited. During the 1990s the image of Abercrombie & Fitch brand was associated with racy, sexualized advertisements as opposed to its now well-known preppy image. Today, Abercrombie & Fitch has a range of products geared towards men, women and children.

Hollister was established in 2000 by Abercrombie & Fitch to sell a range of clothing, personal care and accessories to both male and female customers in an attempt to reach out to a younger target audience that it found difficult to attract. The Hollister brand is well recognized for its seagull logo, which was highly visible in the early days on all of its clothing and merchandise. For many years after its launch, Hollister was known as a 'cool' brand with a laid-back Californian vibe. It has managed to maintain a consistent image since its establishment with the brand is very much positioned as a lifestyle brand for consumers at a certain stage in their life. It's main target audience is considered to be Generation Z customers, mainly from teenagers to those in their early twenties. In order to attract this target market, Hollister has to ensure that its brand is perceived as being 'cool' and 'in fashion'. In 2011, sales at the company reached a high of US$2 billion. To date it has 397 stores in the United States and 145 stores internationally. In addition to Hollister, Abercrombie & Fitch launched Gilly Hicks in 2007. This brand was well known for its range of underwear and loungewear clothing. From 2007 to 2013, Gilly Hicks had 23 stand-alone stores. Due to turbulent times in the fashion industry, Abercrombie & Fitch decided to close all of its Gilly Hicks stores in 2013. However, in 2017, Hollister relaunched the Gilly Hicks brand and today it can be found in its retail stores and on its website.

In-store experience

The first Hollister store was opened in Columbus, Ohio. From the beginning, the brand adopted an experiential marketing strategy. It aimed to provide a sensory experience of the laid-back Hollister brand in its stores. Therefore, the in-store experience emphasized the Californian surf culture. To give it the authentic vibe, a beach hut exterior was part of the store experience; some stores also had a porch and steps. Along with the large American flags, large surf boards and palm trees, there were large screens in-store displaying videos of surfers. To continue the Californian vibe, the model-like store assistants were scantily dressed, similar to the models that appeared in Hollister advertisements. The idea behind the store experience was to transport the customer to a time where they were carefree and happy (providing a nostalgic experience). However, the store was dimly lit and customers found it hard to read clothing labels. There was a distinct lack of mirrors, loud music played throughout the store and the air was filled with a thick smell of perfume. In 2014, Hollister changed the look of its stores. This may have been partly due to a ruling in the USA against it for having store entrances featuring steps, which were not wheelchair accessible. The new store fronts have entrances that are easily accessible and large shop front windows, making it easier for customers passing by to view samples of the merchandise. In addition, the music has been toned down and the interior of the store has been redesigned so that it is easier for customers and store assistants to interact. There is still some evidence of the Californian vibe in-store with surf boards and palm trees.

Positioning of the Hollister brand

Up to 2015, Hollister's advertising strategy was to use scantily dressed male and female models to draw attention to the brand. The main focus of these adverts was on the models as opposed to the clothing. In 2015, it changed its advertising strategy to focus more on showcasing the range of clothing products that it has on offer. It was viewed at this time that the sexualization of the brand was not what the brand wanted to portray in its advertising. In addition to this, Abercrombie & Fitch decided to turn Hollister into a 'fast fashion' brand. Fast fashion is a concept whereby products have a limited life span. The idea is to draw customers into the store or on to the website on a regular basis to view, and hopefully purchase, trendy products. This was mainly in response to competitors such as H&M, Zara and Forever 21, which were attracting many of Hollister's potential customers to their stores.

The loyalty programme has become a staple for many retailers as a way of rewarding consumers. In 2016, Hollister launched its Club Cali programme. To date the loyalty programme has attracted more than six million members. Some of the benefits of Club Cali membership include: (1) customers can collect points, which can be converted into money-off vouchers for future purchases in-store or online – for example, for 12,500 points the customers receives €5, or €10 for 25,000; (2) members receive a surprise on their birthday; and (3) members receive special discounts and rewards throughout the year. The loyalty programme, according to Fran Horowitz, the company's chief executive, has resulted in customers purchasing more often than they would have done prior to its introduction.

Social media

As well as having bricks-and-mortar stores, Hollister has a website presence. The online store offers a large range of male and female merchandise. To cater for a more global audience the site is available in six languages. The company currently ships to 31 countries in Europe alone. Customers are often given online exclusive merchandise, thereby rewarding customers for shopping online. The site also provides the customer with sale merchandise discounted up to 60 per cent off the recommended retail price. Customers can also agree to sign up for notification of exclusive offers from the company. Shipping is often provided free of charge if the customer spends €50 in one transaction. From time to time, Hollister offers free delivery to customers with no fixed sale amount. Orders can also be tracked online after the order has been confirmed.

For many years Hollister rarely engaged in an active manner with its target audience. The closest engagement was via traditional advertising methods. However, the company adopted a new targeting strategy in 2016 to engage Generation Z customers. The Generation Z target audience are notoriously difficult to engage and interact with. They tend to skip through adverts on TV and utilize ad-blocking software when online. This makes it very difficult for marketers to get a message to this target audience. Generation Z consumers use a number of different social media platforms for different activities. For example, if they want to showcase the aspirational sides of themselves, they tend to use Instagram. Snapchat is used to show their 'real selves' and they use Facebook to obtain information. It has become essential for companies such as Hollister to embrace social media and their promotional messages should be tailored to suit the different social media platforms. The brand has built up a following of 4 million fans on Instagram and over 11 million followers on Facebook.

Posts on these platforms feature both male and female models wearing Hollister merchandise in social settings such as in the park and at the beach. The carefree vibe of their posts tie in with the overall brand image. It is not enough just to have a social media presence; brands also need to involve the customer in their message in order to attract their attention. Hence, there is now a focus on creating original series around a brand. For fashion companies such as Hollister, there is a need to start a conversation around the brand and create a link between the brand and a particular set of values that Generation Z customers can relate to. However, the content needs to be entertaining in order to attract the attention of these potential customers.

Hollister did this very successfully through its use of Snapchat. It adopted the sponsored Snapchat geo-filter function. Geo-filters are an additional feature introduced in 2014. The user turns on their location on their mobile phone, which enables Snapchat to identify their location. If there is a geo-filter available for their location the user can layer it on to their own snaps. This Snapchat feature is useful for Hollister in that customers can take snaps of themselves trying on clothing in the dressing rooms of the store. This feature can also encourage potential customers to engage with the brand and share their experiences with their friends. However, Hollister was following in the footsteps of McDonald's, which was the first company to adopt sponsored geo-filters.

In 2017, Hollister teamed up with Awesomeness TV in an effort to attract new Generation Z customers to the brand. Awesomeness TV launched in 2012 and at one point was part owned by Dreamworks Animation. In 2016, Verizon acquired a 24.5 per cent stake in the company. Awesomeness TV is a multi-channel network that features on YouTube. Its main target audience is pre-teens and teenagers. In the first year after its launch, Awesomeness TV attracted in excess of one billion viewers and to date has attracted in excess of 47.6 million YouTube subscribers. Taking advantage of the significant numbers of viewers and subscribers, Hollister teamed up with it to launch an original documentary series titled *This is Summer*. This documentary series comprised 24 episodes, which focused on a number of higher-school students and their day-to-day experiences. Each episode aired for between eight and ten minutes. The characters in each series wore Hollister clothing. This aimed to create a link between the brand experience and the target audience. The music from the episodes was streamed on Spotify and, in addition to this, the soundtracks were also played in stores. Hollister is continuing its relationship with Awesomeness TV in 2018 with another original series, titled *Carpe Life*. Hollister is not the only company to use branded-content original series for social media platforms such as YouTube. In 2016, Nike launched its own branded original series titled *Margot vs. Lily*.

Gaming

In addition to using social media, the brand adopted a new strategy to target Generation Z customers in 2017. With the help of Rovio Entertainment (creator of the *Angry Birds* video franchise) and TreSensa, a surf game was devised. The aim of the game is to enable users to surf and collect points. The game was designed for mobile phones as this is where Generation Z consumers spend most of their time. The game was similar to the very popular *Subway Surfers* game, where players collect points and avoid obstacles throughout the game. The game was promoted through social media sites such as Snapchat, Facebook and Instagram. It was also promoted in selected Hollister retail stores. During the first quarter of 2017, the game attracted 27 million impressions across a range of social media platforms.

In July 2017, another game was developed to promote Hollister's denim line. This time the focus was on skateboarding. The two characters in the game have to skate and navigate around obstacles to collect points. Once the player had completed the game they could share their score on social media platforms, where they could then be entered into a competition to win prizes. In addition to this, players can also sign up for the Club Cali programme for discounts and click through to the company website.

In today's environment the traditional perspective of a consumer has changed. The one-way method of communication between a retailer and a consumer is no longer effective. Retailers have to develop innovative ways to interact with and engage customers in order to attract them to both online and physical stores if they want to survive in this very cluttered and competitive sector.

Questions

1. Examine Hollister's business from the perspective of the unique characteristics of services. Assess the relative importance of each of the four characteristics in this case
2. How does Hollister reward and retain its customers?
3. How important is experiential marketing for Hollister? What techniques does it use to enhance the customer experience?

This case was prepared by Valerie McGrath, Institute of Technology Tralee, from various published sources as a basis for class discussion rather than to show effective or ineffective management.

Chapter 8

Value through Pricing

Chapter outline

Key considerations when setting prices

Other factors influencing price-setting decisions

Managing price changes

Customer value through pricing

Learning outcomes

By the end of this chapter you will:

1 Understand the key considerations when setting an initial price

2 Understand how consumers respond to pricing cues

3 Explain how several key factors influence price-setting decisions

4 Critique the impact of pricing on consumers and society

5 Describe the major issues involved in managing pricing decisions over time

6 Understand the strategic role of pricing

Dollar Shave Club

As we have seen throughout this book, products and services are bundles of value that are offered to customers with a certain positioning and associated price points. One of the key trends in the past three decades has been for businesses to strip out some of the value elements in exchange for significantly reduced prices. For example, low-cost airlines removed many value elements that would have been standard in the industry, such as generous baggage allowances, pre-booked seating and free on-board meals, in exchange for lower ticket prices. In the male grooming industry, the US start-up Dollar Shave Club has similarly revolutionized the sector.

Dollar Shave Club came to public attention with the launch of its now famous 'Our Blades are F***king Great' viral video in 2012. As a start-up with very little in the way of resources to spend on marketing, the company decided to shoot a home video to help publicize the company and its value proposition. Company founder Mike Dubin had studied comedy improvization, and he scripted and starred in the shoot, which was set in the company's original warehouse. In it he pokes fun at what he perceives to be the excessive innovation and high prices of existing products, offering his customers instead a powerful proposition of razors for just US$1 per month delivered direct to their homes. Though the video cost the company a mere US$4,500 to produce, its use of humour, combined with a strong value offering, made it an immediate viral hit. More than 12,000 orders were generated on the first day, causing the website to crash and resulting in the company running out of stock in the first six hours.

Surviving that early surge of consumer interest, the company continued to grow quickly, generating revenues of US$6 million in 2012. It refined its price plans, offering US$3/month (the Humble Twin), US$6/month (the 4X) and US$9/month (the Executive) options to increase revenues and profit margins. It also began to leverage the club concept through providing additional customer care, such as advice on grooming, through email, text, online chat and social media. Market research became a big part of the company's growth strategy, initially through talking to 'regular' guys at festivals like the Gilroy Garlic Festival and the Maine Lobster Festival, followed by the use of consumer panels to research new product ideas. The club's product range expanded quickly to offer many of these consumer-led ideas, such as its One Wipe Charlies – a moist, flushable cloth to respond to consumer comments about rough toilet paper. Other products added to the range have included hair gels, skincare and oral care products. In 2016, the company formed an invitation-only panel of 500 long-standing customers who tested new product concepts and gave instant feedback, helping Dollar Shave to decide which new products to launch or abandon.

The initial quirky sense of humour of its launch video has become the hallmark of Dollar Shave Club's marketing communications ever since. Hundreds of other funny videos for TV, YouTube and the company's website have been made, featuring not just Dubin but other members of staff too. Extensive use has been made of content marketing as well. Writers and editors were hired to create *MEL*, an online men's lifestyle magazine, a funny pamphlet called *Bathroom Minutes*, which accompanies every delivery, and a podcast that tackles a range of funny and zany topics such as 'Which body parts can you actually grow back?'

When Dollar Shave Club was launched in 2012, Gillette had 72 per cent of the US razor market. However, its unique strategy of building an online price-leading brand was to disrupt the traditional industry in ways that few could have foreseen. Dubin's early success spawned several new online rivals, such as Harry's and ShaveSOB. By 2015, web sales of shaving gear had doubled to US$263 million and Dollar Shave Club was the number one brand with more than 50 per cent of the market. Industry giant Gillette recognized that it needed to respond too and launched the Gillette Shave Club in that year. The ultimate vindication of Dubin's concept and his execution of it was to come in 2016 when another consumer goods giant, Unilever, made him an offer he could

(continued)

not refuse. So, after five years in existence, with just 205 employees, more than 3 million online subscribers and yet to make a profit, Dollar Shave Club became part of the Unilever Group for an arguably very expensive price tag of US$1 billion.[1]

Setting prices and managing prices over time is another set of important decisions that must be made by the organization. Several factors are likely to have an influence in these decisions. If input costs, such as the price of energy in the form of electricity or oil, are rising, then these input costs may need to be passed on to the customer in terms of increased prices. But if customers are struggling because of an economic downturn, they may be unwilling to accept these increased prices and therefore decide to consume less, thereby reducing organizational sales. And then there is also the role played by competitors. Pricing decisions need to take account of the prices being offered by competitors for alternative products or potential substitutes. Some of these firms may also be seeking to differentiate themselves based on the prices that they charge and will therefore tend to defend their price positions very aggressively.

All these dimensions need to be considered in terms of the principal relationship between price and the ultimate goal of the business, which is profit.[2] This was starkly illustrated by the example of the Harry Potter series of books, which have been the best-selling books of all time. But such was the demand for the books that each of the different sales channels, such as major chains like Tesco and KwikSave, online retailers like Amazon and specialist book stores like Waterstones, competed aggressively to get as big a share of the market as possible. The major competitive tool used was special price reductions on the books, with the result that some retailers made very little overall profit on the sales of this successful series. The importance of the price–profit relationship is also illustrated by the launch of the Mercedes A-Class model in Germany. Initially, the company had chosen a price tag of DM29,500, based on the belief that the DM30,000 mark was psychologically important. However, after further market research that examined the value offered to customers in comparison with competitor brands such as the BMW 3 series and the VW Golf, the price was set at DM31,000. Mercedes still hit its sales target of 200,000, but the higher price increased its income by DM300 million per year.[3]

In many businesses, greater price competition is becoming a fact of life, with the use of technology helping to drive down costs, greater levels of globalization and retail competition helping to depress price levels, and developments like the internet and the introduction of the euro giving rise to greater levels of price transparency (see Exhibit 8.1). Economic downturns focus further attention on price levels and increase demands for greater price transparency so that consumers can understand the true cost of goods such as personal loans or telephone services. As a result, firms must think carefully when setting prices initially and when adjusting them to changing circumstances.

Exhibit 8.1 camelcamelcamel is a company that provides a price-tracking service on products sold on Amazon, showing customers how prices have changed and providing price drop alerts.

Key considerations when setting prices

Shapiro and Jackson[4] identified three methods used by managers to set prices (see Figure 8.1). The first of these – cost-based pricing – reflects a strong internal orientation and, as its name suggests, is based on costs. The second is competitor-orientated pricing, where the major emphasis is on the price levels set by competitors and how our prices compare with those. The final approach is market-led pricing, so called because it focuses on the value that customers place on a product in the marketplace and the nature of the marketing strategy used to support the product. In this section, we will examine each of these approaches, and draw out their strengths and limitations.

Cost-based pricing

Cost-based pricing is a useful approach to price setting in that it can give an indication of the minimum price that needs to be charged in order to break even. Cost-based pricing can best be explained by using a simple example (see Table 8.1). Imagine that you are given the task of pricing a new product and the cost figures given in Table 8.1 apply. Direct costs such as labour and materials work out at €2 per unit. As output increases, more people and materials will be needed and so total costs increase. Fixed costs (or overheads) per year are calculated at €200,000. These costs (such as office and manufacturing facilities) do not change as output increases. They have to be paid whether 1 or 200,000 units are produced.

Once we have calculated the relevant costs, it is necessary to estimate how many units we are likely to sell. We believe that we produce a good-quality product and therefore sales should be 100,000 in the first year. Therefore total (full) cost per unit is €4 and, using the company's traditional 10 per cent mark-up, a price of €4.40 is set.

So that we may understand the problems associated with using **full cost pricing**, we should assume that the sales estimate of 100,000 is not reached by the end of the year. Because of poor economic conditions, or as a result of setting the price too high, only 50,000 units are sold. The company believes that this level of sales is likely to be achieved next year. What happens to price? Table 8.1 gives the answer: it is raised because cost per unit goes up. This is because fixed costs (€200,000) are divided by a smaller expected sales volume (50,000). The result is a price rise in response to poor sales figures. This is clearly nonsense and yet can happen if full cost pricing is followed blindly. A major UK engineering company priced one of its main product lines in this way and suffered a downward spiral of sales as prices were raised each year, with disastrous consequences.

So, the first problem with cost-based pricing is that it leads to an increase in the price as sales fall. Second, the procedure is illogical because a sales estimate is made *before* the price is set. Third, it focuses on internal costs rather than the customer's willingness to pay. And, finally, there may be a technical problem in allocating overheads in multi-product firms. Nevertheless the cost-based approach is popular in practice (see Marketing in Action 8.1). For example, Apple aims to cover costs plus receive a 40 per cent margin on all its new product launches, and leading brands such as Hugo Boss and Nike have only recently switched away from a cost-based approach.

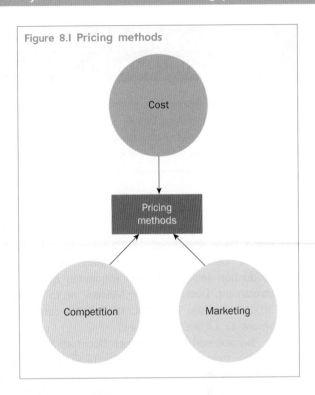

Figure 8.1 Pricing methods

Table 8.1 Cost-based pricing

Year 1	
Direct costs (per unit)	= €2
Fixed costs	= €200,000
Expected sales	= 100,000
Cost per unit	
Direct costs	= €2
Fixed costs (200,000 ÷ 100,000)	= €2
Full costs	= €4
Mark-up (10 per cent)	= €0.40
Price (cost plus mark-up)	= €4.40
Year 2	
Expected sales	= 50,000
Cost per unit	
Direct costs	= €2
Fixed costs (200,000 ÷ 50,000)	= €4
Full costs	= €6
Mark-up (10 per cent)	= €0.60
Price (cost plus mark-up)	= €6.60

Marketing in Action 8.1
Dacia: Europe's best-selling car brand

Critical Thinking: Below is a review of the successful growth of the Dacia car brand. Read it and evaluate how cost-based pricing has been central to its success. Why have competitors been so slow to follow the Dacia lead?

Dacia, a low-cost car brand owned by the French motoring group Renault, has been one of the most successful new car launches in Europe in the past two decades. Its origins began in Renault's failed bid to buy Skoda after the fall of the Iron Curtain in 1989. In its place, it selected the Romanian brand, Dacia and invested €2.2 billion updating its facilities and product line. Like many East European brands, Dacia cars had a reputation for poor quality and frequent breakdowns. Renault's superior production technology and efficiency quickly changed all that. For example, before Renault's investment, Dacia's plant in Mioveni, north of Bucharest, was producing 110,000 cars per year with 30,000 workers. By 2014, this plant's output had risen to 340,000 units while its workforce had shrunk to 14,000 employees.

Renault had originally seen Dacia as a brand that could be used to serve the Romanian and the broader Central and Eastern European markets. But it also became apparent that there could be a market for a low-cost car brand in more affluent Western European markets, which it began targeting in 2005. A key element of its production strategy is what it termed 'design to cost'. A price target for a certain part is set, and designers, engineers and suppliers work together to meet that price. For example, one of Dacia's most popular brands is the Duster, its compact SUV, which has a base price of €11,990 in France. To reach this price, the car's designers had to work directly with suppliers to see if parts could be manufactured differently and therefore more cheaply. Exterior colour options are limited to just five shades, identical door panels are used on multiple models and Dacia windscreens are built at a steeper angle to reduce production and installation costs. In some instances, particular features or technologies were eliminated altogether as they were too costly.

The main appeal of the Dacia is that it gives price-conscious car buyers an option. Instead of buying a second-hand car, as many traditionally would have done, they can now buy a new car with a three-year guarantee at the same price. This low price positioning has been highly successful. Beginning with the launch of the Logan, its first brand in 2004, the Dacia range has expanded to include the Sandero in 2008, which has become Europe's best-selling car, the Duster in 2010, and more recently the Lodgy and Dokker brands. In total, Dacia has sold more than 5 million units since its launch, giving it a 3 per cent share of the European market. In addition, it is estimated that its operating margins, derived from its focus on production efficiencies, are in the region of 9 per cent – very favourable when compared with mainstream car brands. What has been somewhat surprising is the slow pace of response from rivals to the market opportunity identified by Dacia, and it still has relatively few rivals in this market segment. However, it works hard to keep its cost base low. Demand for increased wages at its Romanian plants has seen some production shifted to lower-cost centres such as its operations in Morocco, and the increased use of technology as a substitute for labour.

Based on: Foy, 2013;[5] Gillet, 2014;[6] Sigal, 2018[7]

The real value of this approach is that it gives an indication of the minimum price necessary to make a profit. Once direct and fixed costs have been measured, 'break-even analysis' can be used to estimate the sales volume needed to balance revenue and costs at different price levels. Therefore, the procedure of calculating full costs is useful when other pricing methods are used since full costs may act as a constraint. If they cannot be covered then it may not be worthwhile launching the product. In practice, some companies will set prices below full costs (known as direct cost pricing, or **marginal cost pricing**). As we saw in Chapter 7 this is a popular strategy for services companies. For example, where seats on an aircraft or rooms in hotels are unused at any time, that revenue is lost. In such situations, pricing to cover direct costs plus a contribution to overheads is sensible to reduce the impact of excess capacity, although this approach is not sustainable in the long term.

Competitor-orientated pricing

Competitor-orientated pricing may take any one of three forms:

1 Where firms follow the prices charged by leading competitors
2 Where producers take the going-rate price
3 Where contracts are awarded through a **competitive bidding** process.

Some firms are happy simply to benchmark themselves against their major competitors, setting their prices at levels either above, the same as or below them (see Exhibit 8.2). This is very popular in the financial services area where, for example, the price of a loan (that is, the interest rate) is often very similar across a wide range of competitors. It can be a risky approach to take, particularly if the firm's cost position is not as good as that of its competitors (see 'Cost-based pricing' above).

In other circumstances, all competitors receive the same price because it is the going rate for the product. **Going-rate prices** are most typically found in the case of undifferentiated commodities such as coffee beans or cattle meat. The challenge for the marketer in this situation is to find some creative ways of differentiating the product in order to charge a different price.

In addition, many contracts are won or lost on the basis of competitive bidding. The most usual process is the drawing up of detailed specifications for a product and putting the contract out to tender. Potential suppliers may quote a price, which is known only to themselves and the buyer (known as a 'sealed bid'), or the bidding may take place in a public auction where all competitors see what prices are being bid. All other things being equal, the buyer will select the supplier that quotes the lowest price. A major focus for suppliers, therefore, is the likely bid price of competitors. Increasing price pressures, European competition legislation and the growing use of technology have resulted in more and more supply contracts being subject to competitive bidding. For example, traditionally, many hospital supply companies sold directly to doctors and nurses in hospitals, which meant that suppliers invested in developing selling skills and building relationships with these customers. Now, the norm is that supply contracts are put out to tender, with the winning bidder often securing the contract for a period of three to five years. Thus supply firms have had to develop skills in different areas, such as tender preparation and pricing. Online auctions present suppliers with a whole new set of demands (see Chapter 3).

The main advantage of the competitor-orientated pricing approach is that it is simple and easy to use, except in the case of competitive bidding, where it may be difficult to guess what prices competitive bids will come in at. Increased price transparency in Europe, brought about by the introduction of the euro and the growing use of the internet as a tool for comparing prices, will perhaps increase the level of attention being given to competitor-orientated pricing. It also suffers, however, from two significant flaws. First, it does not take account of any differential advantages the firm may

Exhibit 8.2 The launch price of the PlayStation 4 much more closely matched that of competitors than did its predecessor the PlayStation 3, which was priced significantly above the competition and did not reach sales targets as a result.

have, which may justify its charging a higher price than the competition. As we have seen, the creation of a differential advantage is a fundamental marketing activity, and firms should seek to reap the rewards of this investment. Second, as noted above, competitor-orientated pricing is risky where a firm's cost position is weaker than that of its competitors.

Market-led pricing

A key marketing consideration when setting prices is estimating a product's value to the customer. In brief, the more value a product gives compared with the competition, the higher the price that can be charged (see Exhibit 8.3). Simply because one product costs less to make than another does not imply that its price should be less. The logic of this position is borne out by Glaxo's approach when it launched Zantac, an ulcer treatment drug. It set the price for the drug at 50 per cent more than that of SmithKline

Exhibit 8.3 The Hermès Matte Crocodile Birkin bag is priced at roughly US$120,000.

Beecham's Tagamet, which was then the world's best-selling drug. Thanks to its fewer side effects, Zantac overtook Tagamet and the resulting superior revenues transformed Glaxo from a mid-sized UK company to a global powerhouse.[8]

In this section, we shall explore a number of ways of estimating value to the customer. Marketers have at their disposal three useful techniques for uncovering customers' value perceptions: **trade-off analysis**, experimentation and **economic value to the customer (EVC)** analysis.

Trade-off analysis

Measurement of the trade-off between price and other product features – known as trade-off analysis, or conjoint analysis – enables their effects on product preference to be established.[9] Respondents are not asked direct questions about price but instead product profiles consisting of product features and price are described, and respondents are asked to name their preferred profile. From their answers, the effect of price and other product features can be measured using a computer model. For example, respondents are shown different combinations of features, such as speed, petrol consumption, brand and price in the case of a car, and asked which combinations they prefer. This exercise enables one to measure the impact on preferences of increasing or reducing the price. Companies like 3M, which are renowned for their product innovation, use trade-off analysis at the test marketing stage for new products. Different combinations of variables, such as the brand, packaging, product features and price, are tested to establish the price level that customers are prepared to pay.[10]

Experimentation

A limitation of trade-off analysis is that respondents are not asked to back up their preferences with cash expenditure. Consequently, there can be some doubt whether what they say they prefer would be reflected in an actual purchase when they are asked to part with money. 'Experimental pricing research' attempts to overcome this drawback by placing a product on sale at different locations with varying prices. Test marketing (see Chapter 6) is often used to compare the effectiveness of varying prices. For example, the same product could be sold in two areas using an identical promotional campaign, but with different prices between areas. The areas would need to be matched (or differences allowed for) in terms of target customer profile so that the result would be comparable. The test needs to be long enough so that trial and repeat purchase at each price can be measured. This is likely to be between 6 and 12 months for products whose purchase cycle lasts more than a few weeks.

EVC analysis

Experimentation is more usual when pricing consumer products. However, industrial markets have a powerful tool at their disposal when setting the price of their products: economic value to the customer (EVC) analysis. Many organizational purchases are motivated by economic value considerations since reducing costs and increasing revenue are prime objectives for many companies. If a company can produce an offering that has a high EVC, it can set a high price and yet still offer superior value compared with the competition. A high EVC may be because the product generates more revenue for the buyer than the competition or because its operating costs (such as maintenance, operation or start-up costs) are lower over its lifetime. EVC analysis is usually particularly revealing when applied to products whose purchase price represents a small proportion of the lifetime costs to the customer.[11]

For example, assume that a manufacturer is buying a robot to use on its production line. The robot costs €100,000 but this represents only one-third of the customer's total life-cycle costs. An additional €50,000 is required for start-up costs such as installation and operator training, while a further €150,000 needs to be budgeted for post-purchase costs such as maintenance, power, etc. Assume also that a new product comes on the market that, due to technological advances, reduces start-up costs by €20,000 and post-purchase costs by €50,000. Total costs then have been reduced by €70,000 and the EVC that the new product offers is €170,000 (€300,000 − €130,000). Thus the EVC figure is the total amount that the customer would have to pay to make the total life-cycle costs of the new and existing robot the same. If the new robot were priced at €170,000 this would be the case – any price below that level would create an economic incentive for the buyer to purchase the new robot.

The main advantage of market-led pricing is that it keeps customer perceptions and needs at the forefront of the pricing decision. However, in practice, it is sensible for a company to adopt an integrated approach to pricing, paying attention not only to customer needs but also to cost levels (cost-based pricing) and competitor prices (competitor-orientated pricing).

Other factors influencing price-setting decisions

Aside from the basic dimensions of cost, competitive prices and customer value, various aspects of the firm's marketing strategy will also affect price-setting decisions. In particular, marketing decisions such as positioning strategies, new product launch strategies, product-line strategies, competitive marketing strategies, distribution channel strategies and international marketing strategies will have an impact on price levels.

Positioning strategy

As we saw in Chapter 5, a key decision that marketing managers face is positioning strategy, which involves the choice of target market and the creation of a differential advantage (see Exhibit 8.4). Each of these factors can have an enormous impact on price. Price can be used to convey a differential advantage and to appeal to a certain market segment.

Exhibit 8.4 Transavia, Air France/KLM's low-cost operator, developed an award-winning direct marketing campaign, 'Snack Holidays', using the slogan 'plane tickets so cheap you buy them like a snack'.

www.transavia.com

Craquez.

Barcelone

35€

transavia
parais, volez, souriez

Les 1ers snacks avec des billets d'avion dedans.
#SnackHolidays¹ en vente dans les Carrefour City², distributeurs Selecta et cinéma MK2 participants.
Plus de destinations sur transavia.com

POUR VOTRE SANTÉ, MANGEZ AU MOINS CINQ FRUITS ET LÉGUMES PAR JOUR. WWW.MANGERBOUGER.FR

Leading European retail chains such as Aldi and Lidl target cost-conscious grocery shoppers through a policy of lowest prices on a range of frequently purchased household goods. At the other end of the spectrum, many firms will charge very high prices in order to appeal to individuals with a high net worth. Products such as yachts, luxury cars, golf club memberships, luxury holidays, and so on, are sold in this way. Massimo Dutti, the fashion brand that is part of the Inditex group, is targeted at the 25–50-year-old age group and is priced higher than sister companies like Zara but lower than the luxury fashion brands, leading to it being labelled 'credit-crunch fashion'.

Price is a powerful positioning tool because, for many people, it is an indicator of quality. But recent research in the field of behavioural economics has demonstrated that consumers experience significant difficulties when they attempt to judge price and quality in an objective way. For example, one experimental study involved participants being subjected to electric shocks. During the course of the treatment, one part of the sample were administered a pill that costs US$2.50 per dose while another subset received a pill that cost 10 cents. In the former case, all participants experienced pain relief compared with only half of the 10 cent group. In reality, both groups had simply received a vitamin C capsule, but clearly the higher price had influenced participants' perception of the product.[12] In short, this demonstrates that a higher price can lead to a perception of higher quality, although that may not actually be the case.

 Rimmel Ad Insight: The London Glam'Eyes campaign reflects the company's new positioning.

Because price perceptions are so important to customers, many companies engage in what is called **psychological pricing** – that is, the careful manipulation of the reference prices that consumers carry in their heads. Consequently, the price of most grocery products ends in '.99' because the psychological difference between €2.99 and €3.00 is much greater than the actual difference.

New product launch strategy

When launching new products, price should be carefully aligned with promotional strategy. Figure 8.2 shows four marketing strategies based on combinations of price and promotion. Similar matrices could also be developed for product and distribution, but, for illustrative purposes, promotion will be used here. A combination of high price and high promotion expenditure is called a 'rapid skimming strategy'. The high price provides high-margin returns on investment and the heavy promotion creates high levels of product awareness and knowledge. The launches of Microsoft's Xbox and Apple's iPod and iPhone are examples of a rapid skimming strategy (see Exhibit 8.5). A 'slow skimming strategy' combines high price with low levels

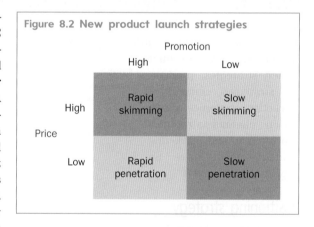

Figure 8.2 New product launch strategies

	Promotion	
	High	**Low**
Price **High**	Rapid skimming	Slow skimming
Low	Rapid penetration	Slow penetration

of promotional expenditure. High prices mean big profit margins, but high levels of promotion are believed to be unnecessary, perhaps because word of mouth is more important and the product is already well known, or because heavy promotion is thought to be incompatible with product image, as with cult products. One company that used a skimming pricing policy effectively is German car components supplier Bosch. It applied an extremely profitable skimming strategy, supported by patents, to its launch of fuel injection and anti-lock brake systems.[13] Companies that combine low prices with heavy promotional expenditure are practising a 'rapid penetration strategy'. In a break with its traditional policy of rapid skimming, Apple changed to a rapid penetration strategy with its launch of the iPad due to intense competition with rival tablet makers. Finally, a 'slow penetration strategy' combines low price with low promotional expenditure. Own-label brands use this strategy: promotion is not necessary to gain distribution and low promotional expenditure helps to maintain high profit margins for these brands. This price/promotion framework is useful when thinking about marketing strategies at launch.

Exhibit 8.5 The original Apple iPhone was launched using a rapid skimming strategy.

 Kindle Ad Insight: This ad clearly conveys Kindle's benefits and price proposition.

Rapid skimming strategies are particularly popular in sectors like consumer electronics, such as with popular phones and gaming devices. Because of the speed of imitation by competitors, innovator firms use rapid skimming to try to recoup the high costs of research and development before competitors erode margins. High price (skimming) strategies and low price (penetration) strategies may be appropriate in different situations. A skimming strategy is most suitable in situations where customers are less price sensitive, such as where the product provides high value, where customers have a high ability to pay and where they are under high pressure to buy. However, setting the price too high can lead to problems in generating sales. For example, when Nissan launched its 350Z sports car, it was priced at levels similar to top sports cars like the Porsche Boxster and BMW Z4. However, poor sales levels forced it to cut its retail price by €10,000, a move that brought it closer to the next level of sports cars such as the Mazda RX-8. Penetration pricing strategies are more likely to be driven by circumstances where the company is seeking to dominate the market, where it is comfortable to establish a position in the market initially and make money later, and/or where it seeks to create a barrier to entry for competitors.

Product-line strategy

Marketing-orientated companies also need to take account of where the price of a new product fits into its existing product line. Where multiple segments appear attractive, modified versions of the product should be designed, and priced differently, not according to differences in costs, but in line with the respective values that each target market places on a product. All the major car manufacturing companies have products priced at levels that are attractive to different market segments, namely, economy cars, family saloons, executive cars, and so on. In 2009, iTunes abandoned its long-standing strategy of charging a flat fee of 99 cents per song download in favour of a three-tier structure with songs priced at 69 cents, 99 cents and US$1.29 to appeal to different market segments. However its competitor, Spotify has been criticized for having just two pricing plans, namely, US$9.99 per month for an individual user and US$14.99 per month for a family plan. Consumer propensity to pay for music varies from US$5–$15 per month, suggesting that several price segments may exist in this market and that Spotify is leaving money on the table by having a one-size-fits-all price plan.[14]

Some companies prefer to extend their product lines rather than reduce the price of existing brands in the face of price competition (see Exhibit 8.6). They launch cut-price 'fighter brands' to compete with the low-price rivals. This has the advantage of maintaining the image and profit margins of existing brands. For example, the department store John Lewis launched its value range to compete with the lower-price offerings of retailers like Tesco. Intel, a global leader in the semiconductor industry, brought out the Celeron, a cheaper version of its better-known Pentium chips, to meet the growing demand from low-cost personal computer manufacturers.[15] By producing a range of brands at different price points, companies can cover the varying price sensitivities of customers and encourage them to trade up to the more expensive, higher-margin brands. However, this strategy must be pursued carefully as they also risk cannibalizing the sales of their existing brands (see Chapter 5).

Exhibit 8.6 US-based upmarket grocery store Whole Foods launched a 'fighter brand', Whole Foods 365, featuring the company's own-label items, to compete with lower-priced rivals.

Competitive marketing strategy

The pricing of products should also be set within the context of the firm's competitive strategy. Four strategic objectives are relevant to pricing: build, hold, harvest and reposition.

Build objective

For price-sensitive markets, a build objective for a product implies a price lower than that of the competition. If the competition raise their prices we would be slow to match them. For price-insensitive markets, the best pricing strategy becomes less clear-cut. Price in these circumstances will be dependent on the overall positioning strategy thought appropriate for the product.

Hold objective

Where the strategic objective is to hold sales and/or market share, the appropriate pricing strategy is to maintain or match the price relative to the competition. This has implications for price changes: if the competition reduces prices, then our prices would match this price fall.

Harvest objective

A harvest objective implies the maintenance or raising of profit margins, even though sales and/or market share are falling. The implication for pricing strategy would be to set premium prices. For products that are being harvested, there would be much greater reluctance to match price cuts than for products that were being built or held. On the other hand, price increases would swiftly be matched.

Reposition objective

Changing market circumstances and product fortunes may necessitate the repositioning of an existing product. This may involve a price change, the direction and magnitude of which will be dependent on the new positioning strategy for the product.

The above examples show how developing clear strategic objectives helps the setting of price and clarifies the appropriate reaction to competitive price changes. Price setting, then, is much more sophisticated than simply asking 'How much can I get for this product?' The process starts by asking more fundamental questions like 'How is this product going to be positioned in the marketplace?' and 'What is the appropriate strategic objective for this product?' Answering these questions is an essential aspect of effective price management.

Channel management strategy

When products are sold through intermediaries such as distributors or retailers, the list price to the customer must reflect the margins required by them. Some products, such as cars, carry margins of typically less than 10 per cent, therefore car dealers must rely on sales of spare parts and future servicing of new cars to generate returns. Other products, such as jewellery, may carry a margin of several hundred per cent. When Müller yoghurt was first launched in the UK, a major factor in gaining distribution in a mature market was the fact that its high price allowed attractive profit margins for the supermarket chains. Conversely, the implementation of a penetration pricing strategy may be hampered if distributors refuse to stock a product because the profit per unit is less than that available on competitive products.

The implication is that pricing strategy is dependent on understanding not only the ultimate customer but also the needs of distributors and retailers who form the link between them and the manufacturer. If their needs cannot be accommodated, product launch may not be viable or a different distribution system (such as direct selling) might be required (see Chapter 9). Greater levels of price transparency have meant that many luxury brands are now forward integrating and taking control of their distribution channels in order to maintain control of price and to prevent discounting. In many instances, this means the reduction or elimination of sales through department stores in favour of wholly owned retailers.

International marketing strategy

The firm's international marketing strategy will also have a significant impact on its pricing decisions. The first challenge that managers have to deal with is that of **price escalation**. This means that a number of factors can combine to put pressure on the firm to increase the prices it charges in other countries. These include the additional costs of shipping and transporting costs to a foreign market, margins paid to local distributors, customs duties or tariffs that may be charged on imported products, differing rates of sales taxes and changes to the price that may be driven by exchange rates and differing inflation rates. All of these factors combine to mean that the price charged in a foreign market is often very different to that charged on the home market. For example, a 16GB Apple iPhone 5s in Brazil cost the equivalent of the average monthly income in the country's major cosmopolitan areas, or just over 2,000 reals, which made it the most expensive place in the world to buy this phone brand. This was largely due to tariffs and state and federal taxes on imports.

While international prices are often higher, they can also be lower if circumstances dictate that low prices are necessary to gain sales, as would be the case in countries where levels of disposable income are low. In such instances, it is important for firms to guard against **parallel importing** – this is when products destined for an international market are re-imported back into the home market and sold through unauthorized channels at levels lower than the company wishes to charge. For example, the online music company CD Wow was fined £41 million when it was charged with selling cut-price CDs in the UK that it had imported from Hong Kong. But trading of products across borders within the European Union is legal, so companies like Chemilines have been able to build a successful business importing pharmaceuticals from EU accession states for sale in the UK, where prices can be up to 30 per cent higher.[16]

While most firms seek to standardize as many elements of the marketing mix as possible when operating internationally, pricing is one of the most difficult to standardize, for the reasons outlined above. Sometimes the price differences are driven by cost variations, but sometimes they are also due to the absence of competitors or different customer value perceptions, which can lead to accusations of ripping off customers. Now that international prices are much easier to compare through, for example, the introduction of the euro, price differences across markets have become much more controversial (see Critical Marketing Perspective 8.1).

Critical Marketing Perspective 8.1
What is a fair price?

Price is one of the most hotly debated aspects of marketing. News reports regularly present stories of price variations for products and services across Europe, leading to claims that some consumers are being unfairly ripped off by companies charging inflated prices. A particular case in point has been the sale of theatre and concert tickets. Tickets for such events are available usually directly

(continued)

from the venue or from primary ticket sites such as Ticketmaster. That should be straightforward, except it is not. Tickets for popular events typically sell out in minutes and then begin appearing at vastly inflated prices on secondary sites such as Get Me In! and Viagogo. Genuine fans face two major problems. First, primary sites own some of the secondary sites and the latter are users of 'botnets' – software programmes that harvest swathes of tickets the second they go on sale.[17] Politicians in Ireland brought forward legislation in 2018 to ban the practice of ticket touting or the above-face-value resale of tickets for entertainment events.

There are several ways in which organizations can exploit consumers by overcharging for goods and services. One of the most common is price fixing, which is illegal and banned throughout Europe. Rather than compete on price, companies collude with one another to ensure that everyone charges the same or similar prices. For example, 14 retailers in Germany, including leading chains like Metro, Edeka and Rewe, were investigated in 2010 on suspicion of working with manufacturers of products like confectionery, pet food and coffee to fix minimum price levels. It is the job of regulatory authorities like the Competition Authority of Ireland and the Office of Fair Trading (OFT) in the UK to identify and investigate possible price collusion. For example, in 2008, the OFT investigated possible collusion between British supermarkets and their suppliers. The 'big four' supermarkets – Tesco, Asda, Sainsbury's and Morrisons – along with suppliers like Britvic, Coca-Cola, Mars, Nestlé, Procter & Gamble, Reckitt Benckiser and Unilever, were asked to hand over documents. Price fixing is most likely to be found in industries where brand differentiation is difficult, such as oil, paper, glass and chemicals.

Equally controversial is the practice of deceptive pricing – in other words, where prices are not the same as they may first appear. Low-cost airlines have been significant users of deceptive pricing. For example, quoted fares may be as low as 99 cents but when all additional items, such as taxes, baggage charges, fuel surcharges, seat charges and credit card charges, are added in, fares may end up being well in excess of €70. These companies are also users of opt-outs. That is, unless consumers specifically opt out of additional items like travel insurance they will be charged for these as well. Furthermore, many of the headline low-fares offers are very limited in their availability, often restricted to just a few seats. EU regulators have targeted the industry to clean up its act on pricing. Airlines must now give a clear indication of the total price and extra charges have to be indicated at the start rather than the end of the booking. Yet another tool in the armoury of marketers is decoy pricing – that is, having pricing options that make more expensive items looker cheaper. For example, Apple uses this strategy for its iPad and iPhone ranges. Typically an iPad might include four variants based on storage capacity but as the gigabyte storage doubles the model price rises by a lower amount making the more expensive model look like it is better value.

All of this means that consumers need to be very careful when judging the price of a good or service. Ultimately, this debate rests on the issue of price and value. Consumers can vote with their feet. If they feel that a price is excessive, in most cases they can switch to substitute products or to other vendors. Consumers need to inform themselves and companies need to take great care in setting price levels. As this chapter shows, pricing must be an integral part of a company's marketing strategy.

Reflection: Consider the points made above and discuss the contention that firms will always charge as much as they possibly can unless forced to do otherwise.

Managing price changes

So far, our discussion has concentrated on those factors that affect pricing strategy but, in a highly competitive world, managers need to know when and how to raise or lower prices, and whether or not to react to competitors' price moves. First, we will discuss initiating price changes, before analysing how to react to competitors' price changes.

Three key issues associated with initiating price changes are: the circumstances that may lead a company to raise or lower prices, the tactics that can be used, and estimating competitor reaction. Table 8.2 illustrates the major points relevant to each of these considerations.

Table 8.2 Initiating price changes

	Increases	Cuts
Circumstances	Value greater than price Rising costs Excess demand Harvest objective	Value less than price Excess supply Build objective Price war unlikely Preempt competitive entry
Tactics	Price jump Staged price increases Escalator clauses Price unbundling Lower discounts	Price fall Staged price reductions Fighter brands Price bundling Higher discounts
Estimating competitor reaction	Strategic objectives Self-interest Competitive situation Past experience	

Circumstances

Marketing research (for example, trade-off analysis or experimentation) which reveals that customers place a higher value on the product than is reflected in its price could mean that a price increase is justified. Rising costs, and hence reduced profit margins, may also stimulate price rises. Another factor that leads to price increases is excess demand. This regularly happens, for example, in the residential property market where the demand for houses can often grow at a faster pace than houses can be built by construction companies, resulting in house price inflation. A company that cannot supply the demand created by its customers may choose to raise prices in an effort to balance demand and supply. This can be an attractive option as profit margins are automatically widened. The final circumstance when companies may decide to raise prices is when embarking on a harvest objective. Prices are raised to increase margins even though sales may fall.

In the same way, price cuts may be provoked by the discovery that a price is high compared with the value that customers place on a product, by falling costs and by excess supply leading to excess capacity. A further circumstance that may lead to price falls is the adoption of a build objective. When customers are thought to be price sensitive, price cutting may be used to build sales and market share, though doing so involves the risk of provoking a price war (see Marketing in Action 8.2).

Marketing in Action 8.2
Is 'Black Friday' the real deal?

> Critical Thinking: Below is a review of 'Black Friday'. Read it and critically evaluate the pros and cons of this annual promotional event. Do you think the idea or concept of Black Friday deals in store will diminish over time?

'Black Friday' is the term used to describe the phenomenon that takes place in the USA on the day after Thanksgiving Thursday, when millions of consumers get the day off work or school to

(continued)

crowd into stores for what is traditionally considered as the beginning of the Christmas shopping season. Black Friday is one of the biggest shopping promotional events of the calendar year as retailers offer deals galore across product categories such as technology, entertainment, travel and holidays. It is often seen as a frantic day of driving to the store at the crack of dawn to fight off other shoppers for great deals. There have been reports of stampedes of customer mobs breaking barricades, injuring other customers, injuring workers and even causing deadly situations. All of this just for discounted goods! Until 2010, Black Friday was an American phenomenon, but it has spread to more and more retailers across the world and has become synonymous with amazing money-saving deals.

With the growth of e-commerce, Black Friday has now moved into cyberspace. This has resulted in the sales bonanza that is Black Friday moving to a four-day long event culminating in so-called 'Cyber Monday'. While Black Friday is the top shopping day of the year for bricks-and-mortar stores, Cyber Monday offers consumers many great deals online. The Black Friday season is crucial for the economy as around 30 per cent of annual retail sales tend to occur between Black Friday and Christmas. In the UK alone, in 2016 £1.74 million was spent online every minute of Black Friday, £3 billion over the four days from Black Friday to Cyber Monday and more than £10 billion over the entire week.

In recent years, shoppers have been warned that Black Friday deals don't always live up to the hype. A year-long investigation by consumer experts Which? tracked the prices of 35 of the most popular technology, home and personal care products on sale on Black Friday 2016 and their results throw the entire validity of the Black Friday deal into question. They found that six out of ten Black Friday deals in 2016 were for products that had, in fact, been cheaper or at the same price at other times of the year. This may be seen as misleading on the part of retailers, who often hype up the size of Black Friday discounts, and it may cast a cloud over the whole Black Friday experience.

The build-up to Black Friday has already been diluted by the fact that so many retailers are now discounting goods for the weeks before and after the day. With online shopping, consumers are increasingly realizing they don't need to do all their shopping on one day and retailers are responding by stretching out their holiday deals to respond to when and where consumers actually want to shop. Added to this, in the UK there is concern that discounts are not as high as those in other countries. While online prices were cut by an average of 12 per cent in the UK in 2016, they were down 29 per cent in the USA, and 20 per cent and 33 per cent in Germany and France respectively, which may dampen its appeal in the UK market. Finally, some consumers avoid Black Friday altogether as it is often viewed as the most stressful time of the year to do your shopping. All of this calls into question what this extravagant promotional event will look like in the future.

Based on: Butler, 2017;[18] Segran, 2017;[19] Smellie, 2017;[20] Wood, 2016[21]

Tactics

There are many ways in which price increases and cuts may be implemented. The most direct is the 'price jump', or fall, which increases or decreases the price by the full amount in one go (see Exhibit 8.7). A price jump avoids prolonging the pain of a price increase over a long period, but may raise the visibility of the price increase to customers. This happened in India, where Hindustan Lever, the local subsidiary of Unilever, used its market power to raise the prices of its key brands at a time when raw materials were getting cheaper. As a result, operating margins grew from 13 per cent in 1999 to 21 per cent in 2003. Subsequently, though, sales fell sharply due to competition from P&G and Nirma, a local brand, as well as creating consumer disaffection.[22] Using staged price increases might make the price rise more palatable but may elicit accusations of 'always raising your prices'. This frequently happens in sectors like utilities and broadband services.

Exhibit 8.7 Austrian pharmacy retailer BIPA's 'Permanent Price Proof' campaign set a Guinness World Record for one man reading the new prices of 15,000 products.

A one-stage price fall can have a high-impact dramatic effect that can be heavily promoted but also has an immediate impact on profit margins. When the demand for hotel beds fell globally after the terrorist attacks on New York in 2001, the industry reacted by slashing hotel rates to try to generate business. One of the effects was that it proved to be difficult to raise rates again when the recovery took place.[23] As a result, the hospitality industry has been less willing to make big rate cuts as a result of the global economic downturn. Staged price reductions have a less dramatic effect but may be used when a price cut is believed to be necessary, although the amount needed to stimulate sales is unclear. Small cuts may be initiated as a learning process that proceeds until the desired effect on sales is achieved.

'Escalator clauses' can also be used to raise prices. The contracts for some organizational purchases are drawn up before the product is made. Constructing the product – for example, a new defence system or motorway – may take a number of years. An escalator clause in the contract allows the supplier to stipulate price increases in line with a specified index (for example, increases in industry wage rates or the cost of living).

Another tactic that effectively raises prices is **price unbundling**. Many product offerings actually consist of a set of products for which an overall price is set (for example, computer hardware and software, or an airline flight). Price unbundling allows each element in the offering to be priced separately in such a way that the total price is raised. A variant on this process is charging for services that were previously included in the product's price. For example, manufacturers of mainframe computers have the option of unbundling installation and training services, and charging for them separately, while low-fares airlines charge for baggage, check-in, etc. separately. Alibaba.com, the world's largest online platform for trade between businesses, moved from a uniform membership package to a new structure that involved a basic membership fee, and charges for additional services such as factory audits and keyword searching – a move that significantly raised the company's profits.[24]

Yet another approach is to maintain the list price but lower discounts to customers. In periods of heavy demand for new cars, dealers lower the cash discount given to customers, for example. Similarly, if demand is slack, customers can be given greater discounts as an incentive to buy. However, there are risks if this strategy is pursued for too long a period of time. For example, owing to poor sales of its car models, GM pursued a four-year price discounting strategy in the US market, with disastrous effects. The net effect of this strategy was to take the total in incentives available to the buyer to more than US$7,000, or over 20 per cent off the suggested retail price of the car.[25] The resulting price war with Ford and Chrysler, which followed with similar schemes, hurt profits. But, more worryingly, the effect of the campaign seemed to be that GM customers simply brought forward purchases that they were going to make anyway to avail themselves of the discounts, and customer attention switched to price rather than the value offered by the product.[26]

Quantity discounts can also be manipulated to raise the transaction price to customers. The percentage discount per quantity can be lowered, or the quantity that qualifies for a particular percentage discount can be raised.

Those companies contemplating a price cut have three choices in addition to a direct price fall.

1 A company defending a premium-priced brand that is under attack from a cut-price competitor may choose to maintain its price while introducing a fighter brand. The established brand keeps its premium-price position while the fighter brand competes with the rival for price-sensitive customers.
2 Where a number of products and services that tend to be bought together are priced separately, price bundling can be used to effectively lower the price. For example, televisions can be offered with 'free three-year repair warranties' or cars with 'free service for three years'.
3 Finally, discount terms can be made more attractive by increasing the percentage or lowering the qualifying levels.

Reacting to competitors' price changes

Companies need to analyse their appropriate reactions when their competitors initiate price changes.[27] Three issues are relevant here: when to follow, what to ignore and the tactics to use if the price change is to be followed. Table 8.3 summarizes the main considerations.

Table 8.3 Reacting to competitors' price changes

	Increases	Cuts
When to follow	Rising costs Excess demand Price-insensitive customers Price rise compatible with brand image Harvest or hold objective	Falling costs Excess supply Price-sensitive customers Price fall compatible with brand image Build or hold objective
When to ignore	Stable or falling costs Excess supply Price-sensitive customers Price rise incompatible with brand image Build objective	Rising costs Excess demand Price-insensitive customers Price fall incompatible with brand image Harvest objective
Tactics Quick response Slow response	Margin improvement urgent Gains to be made by being customers' friend	Offset competitive threat High customer loyalty

When to follow

When competitive price increases are due to general rising cost levels or industry-wide excess demand, they are more likely to be followed. In these circumstances the initial pressure to raise prices is the same on all parties. Following a price rise is also more likely when customers are relatively price insensitive, which means that the follower will not gain much advantage by resisting the price increase. Where brand image is consistent with high prices, a company is more likely to follow a competitor's price rise as to do so would be consistent with the brand's positioning strategy. Finally, a price rise is more likely to be followed when a company is pursuing a harvest or hold objective because, in both cases, the emphasis is more on profit margin than sales/market share gain.

When they are stimulated by general falling costs or excess supply, price cuts are likely to be followed. Falling costs allow all companies to cut prices while maintaining margins, and excess supply means that a company is unlikely to allow a rival to make sales gains at its expense. Price cuts will also be followed in price-sensitive markets since allowing one company to cut price without retaliation would mean large sales gains for the price cutter. This has happened in the UK toiletries market, where Boots has failed to follow Tesco in aggressive price cutting on products like shampoo and skin cream, suffering significant sales losses as a result. The image of the company can also affect reaction to price cuts. Some companies position themselves as low-price manufacturers or retail outlets. In such circumstances, they would be less likely to allow a price reduction by a competitor to go unchallenged for to do so would be incompatible with their brand image. Finally, price cuts are likely to be followed when the company has a build or hold strategic objective.

In such circumstances, an aggressive price move by a competitor would be followed to prevent sales/market share loss. For example, Amazon dropped the price of its Kindle e-reader from US$350 in 2009 to under US$150 in 2011, in response to price competition from other e-readers such as Barnes & Noble's Nook. In the case of a build objective, the response may be more dramatic, with a price fall exceeding the initial competitive move. For example, Vodafone halved the monthly tariff for wireless datacards from £30 to £15, which put it on a par with 3, the industry leader, in a bid to grow its share of the mobile data services market.

When to ignore

In most cases, the circumstances associated with companies not reacting to a competitive price move are simply the opposite of the above. Price increases are likely to be ignored when costs are stable or falling, which means that there are no cost pressures forcing a general price rise. In the situation of excess supply, companies may view a price rise as making the initiator less competitive and therefore allow the rise to take place unchallenged, particularly when customers are price sensitive. Companies occupying low-price positions may regard a price rise in response to a price increase from a rival to be incompatible with their brand image. Finally, companies pursuing a build objective may allow a competitor's price rise to go unmatched in order to gain sales and market share.

Price cuts are likely to be ignored in conditions of rising costs, excess demand and when servicing price-insensitive customers. Premium-price positioners may be reluctant to follow competitors' price cuts, for to do so would be incompatible with their brand image (see Exhibit 8.8). For example, some luxury brands, such as Lacoste, have suffered heavily because of pursuing a strategy of discounting when faced with excess capacity while competitors chose not to follow.[28] Finally, price cuts may be resisted by companies using a harvest objective.

Tactics

If a company decides to follow a price change, it can do this quickly or slowly. A quick price reaction is likely when there is an urgent need to improve profit margins. Here, the competitor's price increase will be welcomed as an opportunity to achieve this objective.

In contrast, a slow reaction may be the best approach when a company is pursuing the image of customers' friend. The first company to announce a price increase is often seen as the high-price supplier. Some companies have mastered the art of playing low-cost supplier by never initiating price increases and following competitors' increases slowly.[29] The key to this tactic is timing the response: too quick and customers do not notice; too slow and profit is foregone. The optimum period can be found only by experience but, during it, salespeople should be told to stress to customers that the company is doing everything it can to hold prices for as long as possible.

If a firm wishes to ward off a competitive threat, a quick response to a competitor's price fall is called for. In the face of undesirable sales/market share erosion, fast action is needed to nullify potential competitor gains. However, reaction will be slow when a company has a loyal customer base willing to accept higher prices for a period as long as they can rely on price parity over the longer term.

Exhibit 8.8 Market leader P&O Cruises decided to move away from the price competition that was rampant in its business and focus instead on the value of a cruise holiday through its 'This is the life' campaign.

Customer value through pricing

Price leadership has become the central value proposition for firms in a wide variety of industries (see Exhibit 8.9). For example, in grocery retailing, the German hard discounters Aldi and Lidl have led the way. Similar strategies have been pursued by the likes of Primark and TK Maxx in apparel retailing, Ryanair and easyJet in air travel, Lenovo in personal computers, and so on. Because these firms aim to continually offer the best prices in the marketplace, the various issues described in this chapter take on particular importance. Offering low prices means that profit margins may be tight unless firms can find ways to drive their cost base down or find additional product/service elements for which they can charge handsomely. The three tools that firms have at their disposal to assist in this challenge are cost management, **yield management** and **dynamic pricing**.

Cost management

Cost control is critical for firms that attempt to lead on price as their success in controlling costs has a direct impact on profit margins. For example, retailers like Walmart and airlines like Ryanair have a reputation for being fanatical in their search for ways of reducing cost. One of the first costs to be removed by some airlines was the practice of selling seats through travel agents and paying them a margin of up to 10 per cent, which was incorporated into the price. Most airline seats are now booked directly by customers online. Services like catering and check-in are outsourced, flights go to small regional airports where landing charges are low and, in extreme instances like Ryanair, flight crews buy their own uniforms and pay for their training. The Norwegian low-cost carrier, NAS, bases its planes and hires staff in Spain, has its back office in Latvia and its IT department in Ukraine.[30] Along with this type of aggressive cost management, low price operators seek as much scale as possible in order that fixed costs can be spread over a larger number of units and are thus reduced.

Yield management

Another tool in the armoury of low price competitors is yield management, which is the monitoring of demand or potential demand patterns. It is very popular in services businesses like travel and hotel accommodation. Levels of demand are tracked electronically on a daily basis. Therefore, over the course of a year, this information can be stored and used to set prices for rooms or flights, which vary from day to day, for the next year. It is also possible to track enquiries and use this information to make decisions regarding potential demand levels.

Exhibit 8.9 Foxconn is a world-leading consumer electronics contract manufacturer headquartered in Taiwan, providing low-cost components for companies like Apple, Amazon, Nokia and Sony.

Dynamic pricing

An interesting aspect of many low-price companies is their level of profitability. For example, despite its reputation for low prices, Ryanair is the most profitable airline in Europe. Aside from its attention to costs, a key reason for its success is its flexible approach to pricing, which is known as dynamic pricing. This means that prices are adjusted continually, based on demand and potential demand. Therefore, while prices on some flights may be cheap, on others they may be high if these flights coincide with peak holiday periods or major sporting events. Also, if demand for particular flights were to rise quickly for any reason, prices are quickly adjusted upwards. The practice of dynamic pricing is extending beyond air travel to a variety of other sectors such as entertainment venues, car parks, theme parks and sports events; indeed anywhere that demand levels fluctuate. Rapid price adjustments that traditionally were only available online are also coming to bricks-and-mortar stores. For example, 'smart shelves' allow grocery retailers to adjust their prices several times per day. This allows retailers to experiment with different price points and monitor how this affects demand. Customers too can be notified of price changes and deals directly on their phones. An even more precise form of flexible pricing, known as personalized pricing, is also being tested in several markets (see Marketing in Action 8.3).

Marketing in Action 8.3
Personalized pricing

> **Critical Thinking:** Below is a review of the recent rise in personalized pricing. Read it and consider the ethical implications of this trend. What steps can consumers take to protect themselves from exploitation by companies in this way?

The combined growth in online shopping and data capture is giving rise to the new phenomenon of personalized pricing, in other words, prices that vary based upon who is shopping. This can manifest itself in many different ways. For example, in 2012, the travel site Orbitz was found to be adjusting its prices for Apple Mac users after it emerged that they were prepared to pay over 30 per cent more for hotel rooms than other users. In other words, consumers logging on to the site using Apple products were shown different, and often more expensive, options than those shown to PC users. In the same year, Staples, a US office supplies company, was found to be offering different prices to consumers based on their proximity to the stores of competitors. The website was using the IP address of the customer to check their location and charge those who lived within a 20-mile radius of a competitor's store a lower price for products than those who lived further away.

The implications of these developments are clear. Online companies increasingly have the capability to monitor the browsing history of customers and use this information to develop the profiles of shoppers. Once these profiles are developed, offerings and their prices can be adjusted accordingly. For example, one research study created two personas on different computers – one that resembled a wealthy customer and another that resembled a budget-conscious one (these personas were based on the cookies and internet-browsing histories of the two 'users'). While the study did not reveal price differences when these 'customers' shopped online, they did reveal different search results. Headphones and hotels suggested to the 'affluent buyer' were more expensive than those suggested to the 'budget-conscious buyer'. Personalized pricing may be at a rudimentary level today but the potential for it to increase is obvious. For example, Avantcard is an Irish credit card and loan company that offers online loans up to €75,000 but with interest rates that reflect the borrower's credit history. The company currently has just three categories of borrower – Great, Good and OK – with the latter paying more for its loans than the others. It is easy to see how the number of customer categories could be increased, as well as how the prices of other financial products such as insurance could be personalized in this way.

(continued)

Of course, personalized pricing is not entirely new. In the offline world of markets and car dealerships, prices will vary from customer to customer depending on the shopper's ability to haggle and/or the salesperson's ability to judge how much a customer will pay. Indeed, salespeople in car showrooms are trained to observe how customers speak, dress and the kinds of cars they currently drive in order to determine their price potential. The biggest difference in the online sphere is one of information – it is difficult for you as a customer to know what information a retail site has about you and how it is using it to decide what to offer you. It is also possible to argue that these developments are not always negative. Retail sites may provide customers with better and more suitable offers based on the information they have. But the profit motive driving commercial enterprises is likely to leave many consumers worried that once again they will be at the mercy of companies looking to extract as much of their hard-earned cash as possible.

Based on: Fletcher, 2017;[31] McMullin, 2018;[32] Walker, 2017;[33] White, 2012[34]

Dynamic pricing has been shown to positively impact on organizational performance. For example, a study in the hotel sector found that firms employing dynamic pricing techniques had significantly higher revenues per room than those using standardized pricing.[35] With technologies enabling much closer monitoring of demand and tracking of consumer behaviour, flexibility in the price points offered to customers is likely to increase. The challenge for consumers will be to monitor and compare the prices of different vendors in this environment.

Summary

Price is a key aspect of the organization's marketing strategy and is also the core value proposition for some businesses. In this chapter, the following key issues were addressed.

1. There are three bases upon which prices are set, namely, cost, competition and market value. We noted that all three should be taken into account when setting prices. Costs represent a floor above which prices must be set to build a viable business, while competition and customers will influence the overall height of prices.

2. That the pricing levels set may also be influenced by a number of other marketing strategy variables, namely, positioning strategy, new product launch strategy, product line strategy, competitive strategy, channel management strategy and international marketing strategy.

3. That marketers need to make decisions relating to initiating price changes or responding to the price changes made by competitors. Whether prices are rising or falling, various factors need to be taken into account; these are important decisions as they affect the overall profitability of the firm.

4. That there are key issues surrounding the ethics of price setting. Price fixing is illegal, and other unethical practices such as deceptive pricing and product dumping are frequently targeted by regulators. Greater levels of price transparency are assisting consumers to avoid being exploited by unscrupulous companies.

5. Price may be the core value proposition offered by some businesses. In these cases, organizations employ a combination of cost management, yield management and dynamic pricing to generate high profitability levels.

Study questions

1. Accountants are always interested in profit margins; sales managers want low prices to help push sales; and marketing managers are interested in high prices to establish premium positions in the marketplace. To what extent do you agree with this statement in relation to the setting of prices?

2. Why is value to the customer a more logical approach to setting prices than cost of production? What role can costs play in the setting of prices?

3. To what extent do you use price to judge the potential quality of an item that you are considering purchasing? Critically reflect on the pros and cons of using price as a decision cue in this way.

4. Discuss how a company pursuing a build strategy is likely to react to both price rises and price cuts by competitors.

5. Discuss the specific issues that arise when pricing products for international markets.

6. Visit vodafone.co.uk, o2.co.uk, ee.co.uk and three.co.uk and compare the prices these companies charge for their products. How difficult is it to make an accurate comparison of the cost of a mobile phone package? Why do you think this is so?

7. What is meant by personalized pricing? Evaluate the reasons for the growth in personalized pricing and critically reflect on its implications for society.

Suggested reading

Baker, W., Marn, M. and **Zawada, C.** (2010) Do you have a long-term pricing strategy? *McKinsey Quarterly*, October, 1–7.

Bertini, M. and **Gourville, J.** (2012) Pricing to create shared value, *Harvard Business Review*, 90(6), 96–104.

Bryce, D., Dyer, J. and **Hatch, N.** (2011) Competing against free, *Harvard Business Review*, 89(6), 104–11.

Hinterhuber, A. (2016) The six pricing myths that kill profits, *Business Horizons*, 59, 71–83.

Mohammed, R. (2005) *The Art of Pricing: How to Find the Hidden Profits to Grow Your Business*. London: Crown Business.

Sahay, A. (2007) How dynamic pricing leads to higher profits, *Sloan Management Review*, 48(4), 53–60.

References

1. **Chakravorti, B.** (2016) Unilever's big strategic bet on the Dollar Shave Club, *HBR.org*. Available at www.hbr.org/2016/07/unilevers-big-strategic-bet-on-the-dollar-shave-club (accessed 4 July 2018); **Daneshkhu, S.** (2016) How Michael Dubin built Dollar Shave Club into a $1 billion company, *Ft.com*. Available at www.ft.com/content/2aca7c08-4e69-11e6-8172-e39ecd3b86fc (accessed 4. July 2018); **Lashinky, A.** (2015) How Dollar Shave Club got started, *Fortune.com*. Available at www.fortune.com/2015/03/10/dollar-shave-club-founding/ (accessed 4 July 2018); **Trop, J.** (2017) How Dollar Shave Club's founder built a $1 billion company that changed the industry, *Entrepreneur.com*. Available at www.entrepreneur.com/article/290539 (accessed 4 July 2018).

2. **Hinterhuber, A.** (2016) The six pricing myths that kill profits, *Business Horizons*, 59, 71–83.

3. **Lester, T.** (2002) How to ensure that the price is exactly right, *Financial Times*, 30 January, 15.

4. **Shapiro, B.P.** and **Jackson, B.B.** (1978) Industrial pricing to meet customer needs, *Harvard Business Review*, November–December, 119–27.

5. **Foy, H.** (2013) Dacia leads charge of emerging market cars in Europe, *FT.com*. Available at www.ft.com/content/5b7d14b8-feb3-11e2-97dc-00144feabdc0 (accessed 24 July 2018).

6. **Gillet, K.** (2014) Dawn of the Dacia: how Romania's no thrills car maker raced ahead, *Theguardian.com*. Available at www.theguardian.com/business/2014/oct/21/dacia-romania-car-maker-europe-sales (accessed 24 July 2018).

7. **Sigal, P.** (2018) How Renault's budget brand Dacia keeps down costs, *Europe.automotivenews.com*. Available at www.http://europe.autonews.com/article/20180113/ANE/180109871/how-renaults-budget-brand-dacia-keeps-down-costs (accessed 24 July 2018).

8. **London, S.** (2003) The real value in setting the right price, *Financial Times*, 11 September, 15.

9. **Kucher, E.** and **Simon, H.** (1987) Durchbruch bei der Preisentscheidung: conjoint-measurement, eine neue Technik zur Gewinnoptimierung, *Harvard Manager*, 3, 36–60.

10. **Lester, T.** (2002) How to ensure that the price is exactly right, *Financial Times*, 30 January, 15.

11. **Forbis, J.L.** and **Mehta, N.T.** (1979) Economic value to the customer, McKinsey Staff Paper. Chicago, IL: McKinsey and Co., February, 1–10.

12. **Ariely, D.** (2008) *Predictably Irrational*. London: HarperCollins Publishers.

13. **Simon, H.** (1992) Pricing opportunities – and how to exploit them, *Sloan Management Review*, Winter, 55–65.

14. **Campbell, P.** (2018) Tearing down Spotify's pricing, *Priceintelligently.com*. Available at www.priceintelligently.com/blog/spotify-pricing-strategy (accessed 25 July 2018).

15. **Ritson, M.** (2009) Should you launch a fighter brand? *Harvard Business Review*, 87(10), 86–94.

16. **Jack, A.** (2005) Drugs groups seek cure for irritation of parallel trading, *Financial Times*, 10 August, 18.

17. **Cavaglieri, C.** (2015) The 1000% ticket mark-up scandal, *Which?*, December, 46–8.

18. **Butler, S.** (2017) UK shoppers forecast to spend £10 billion in Black Friday sales, *The Guardian*, 17 November.

19. **Segran, E.** (2017) Black Friday is dying, *Fast Company*, 14 November.

20. **Smellie, A.** (2017) Why Black Friday is a fake: Thought it was the day to bag a bargain? In fact six out of ten of last year's deals were cheaper at other times of the year, *Daily Mail*, 19 November.

21. **Wood, Z.** (2016) Black Friday worry as report finds only half of offers are real deals, *The Guardian*, 16 November.

22. **Anonymous** (2004) Slow moving: can Unilever's Indian arm recover from some self-inflicted wounds? *The Economist*, 6 November, 67–8.

23. **Blitz, R.** (2008) Hotels keep door shut to big rate cuts, *Financial Times*, 27 November, 28.

24. **Hille, K.** (2010) Alibaba marketing push brings results, *Financial Times*, 11 August, 18.

25. **Simon, B.** (2005) GM's price cuts drive record sales, *Financial Times*, 5 July, 28.

26. **Simon, B.** (2005) Detroit Giants count cost of four-year price war, *Financial Times*, 19 March, 29.

27. **Hinterhuber, A.** (2016) The six pricing myths that kill profits, *Business Horizons*, 59, 71–83.

28. **Dowdy, C.** (2003) Wealth, taste and cachet at bargain prices, *Financial Times*, 9 October, 17.

29. **Ross, E.B.** (1984) Making money with proactive pricing, *Harvard Business Review*, November–December, 145–55.

30. **Anonymous** (2013) Here come the Vikings, *Economist*, 27 April, 53–4.

31. **Fletcher, V.** (2017) Are you falling foul of price discrimination? *Which?*, April, 38–41.

32. **McMullin, S.** (2018) What is personalised pricing? Here's how you can get a great rate on personal loans – that is perfect for your situation, *Irishmirror.ie*. Available at www.irishmirror.ie/sponsored/what-personalised-pricing-heres-how-12666233 (accessed 13 July 2018).

33. **Walker, T.** (2017) How much? ... The rise of dynamic and personalised pricing, *Theguardian.com*. Available at www.theguardian.com/global/2017/nov/20/dynamic-personalised-pricing (accessed 13 July 2018).

34. **White, M.** (2012) Orbitz shows higher prices to Mac users, *Time.com*. Available at www.http://business.time.com/2012/06/26/orbitz-shows-higher-prices-to-mac-users/ (accessed 13 July 2018).

35. **Al-Shakhsheer, A., Habiballah, M., Ababne, M. and Alhelalat, J.** (2107) Improving hotel revenue through the implementation of a comprehensive dynamic pricing strategy: A conceptual framework and empirical investigation of Jordanian hotels, *Business Management Dynamics*, 7, 19–33.

Primark: faster, cheaper fashion

Introduction

Primark (known as Penneys in the Republic of Ireland) is an Irish clothing and accessories company, which is owned by Associated British Foods (ABF).[1] The first Penneys store was opened in June 1969 on Mary Street, Dublin, with this original store still in operation to this day.[2]

Since its inception in 1969, Primark has grown considerably over the years, engaging in international expansion. It now has more than 350 stores in 11 different countries worldwide.[3] It opened its first UK store in 1974 but was forced to change its name to Primark because the US company JC Penney had trademarked the name in the UK. The company's major expansion into the UK really happened in the mid-2000s, leading it to become a staple on Britain's high streets. In 2005, it bought the Littlewoods retail stores for £409 million, retaining 40 out of the 199 stores and selling the rest.[4] In May 2006, the first Primark store outside Ireland and the UK opened in Madrid, Spain.[5] Since then, it has marched steadily across the continent, opening stores in the Netherlands, followed by Portugal, Germany, Belgium and Austria.

It expanded into France in 2013 and its first Italian store opened in 2014.[6, 7] This expansion saw Primark's sales rise by 150 per cent between 2009 and 2014, making it a new force in the global rag trade.[8]

However, the company had its sights on further expansion and in 2015 made a bold move, opening its first US store in Boston, followed shortly by the establishment of eight other stores in the United States.[8] Taking on the US market worth US$200 billion was a big challenge for Primark, demanding an initial capital investment of US$340 million.[9] In 2017, further plans for expansion were revealed when it opened 29 additional stores, mainly outside the UK, in an attempt to gain an even deeper presence in Europe and the USA. This expansion plan came after the business tripled its floorspace to about 13 million square feet (1.2 million square metres) over the previous decade.[10]

A recipe for success

Primark has increasingly made its mark on global retailing and many have tried to identify its 'recipe for success'. Some have argued that Primark is to fashion what Ryanair is to aviation, an Irish success story spreading affordable fashion across the globe.[9] Primark's success is built on selling trendy clothes at astonishingly low prices. Appealing to the 16–24-year-old market, especially women, Primark has shown that, no matter what your budget, it has a great range of fashion and home accessories at affordable prices.[11] Maureen Hinton of Conlumino, a retail consultant, argues that Primark has a winning combination: cool clothes, attractive stores and – most importantly – rock-bottom prices. It targets budget-conscious shoppers with catwalk styles and has the ability to react to trends quickly, identify and promote seasonal and novelty items, and offer value for money. According to Sanford C. Berstein, in Britain in 2015 the average selling price of women's clothes in H&M was £10.69, compared with £3.87 in Primark.[8] Along with retailers such as Zara and H&M, Primark has helped to contribute to the contemporary fast fashion trend. This sees consumers buy lots of items at very low prices, discard them after a few wears and then come back for another batch of outfits.[8]

Primark adheres to cost-based pricing and is a price leader. Its business model focuses on high turnover and low profit margins.[12] The company withstands tiny margins, making its money on volume. It believes demand for clothes is elastic and that, the cheaper they are, the more shoppers buy of them. This seems to ring true according to recent research, which has shown that H&M sells on average £3,400-worth of clothes per square metre in Britain, whereas Primark sells £5,300-worth. People are buying cheap clothes in Primark and in large quantities. John Bason, ABF's finance director, says Primark achieves its low prices thanks to sleek logistics, a meagre marketing budget and its scale, which helps win bargains from suppliers.[8] It tries to be as efficient as possible when transporting products from factories to stores, keeping logistics costs down – for example, it asks its suppliers to pack T-shirts so that they are ready to go straight on to store shelves. It spends very little on advertising and chooses to use social media to promote its brand, rather than expensive celebrity fashion advertising campaigns. It designs clothes that offer the latest trends, but doesn't use expensive hangers, tags or labels. It also sells a lot of items across all of its stores worldwide, which allows it to make savings from buying in bulk for all of its stores. These decisions mean that it makes savings from buying at every stage of its supply chain.[11]

The cost of low prices

With its business model focused on offering the lowest prices on the high street, Primark is constantly questioned over its commitment to a range of ethical and environmental issues.[13] It has been struggling to overcome the consumer's pre-fixed notion that fast fashion is not sustainable and certainly not ethically made.[14] In the past, there have been concerns about the conditions in which cheap clothing is made. In 2013, more than 1,100 people were crushed when a factory complex collapsed in Bangladesh. The victims included workers stitching clothes for Primark.[8] In 2014, a £10 dress bought in a Primark branch in Swansea contained a cry-for-help label sewn with the message 'forced to work for exhausting hours', while a cheap top from the same store read 'degrading sweatshop conditions'. Another woman, who purchased a pair of trousers from Primark in Belfast in 2011, claimed to have found a handwritten note from China pleading for help from the international community for alleged human rights violations.[15] In addition, Primark's culture of disposable fashion doesn't always sit well with environmentalists. Concerns have been raised about the impact its products have on the environment 'from the cradle to the grave'.[8]

Primark claims that, although its prices are low, the standards it expects from members of its supply chain are high. It does not own its own factories but is very selective about who it works with, claiming that the welfare of the people making its products matters to it.[14] Primark works directly with suppliers and their factories to ensure that internationally recognized standards are being met. It also works with NGOs and other organizations to improve ethical and environmental standards in the industry. It is a member of the Sustainable Apparel Coalition, committed to Greenpeace's Detox Campaign in 2014 and is a founding member of the ACT initiative on wages. It has also been a member of the Ethical Trading Initiative since 2006 and has achieved top-level 'leadership' status since 2011.[11]

Primark has been accused in the past of lacking transparency about its ethical standards. However, it recently developed a new online tool, 'The Global Sourcing Map', which allows consumers to access information about the 1,071 factories and suppliers that make up the company's supply chain. This is a positive move for Primark as it builds on its previous efforts to promote social and environmental sustainability in its supply chain.[16]

Challenges ahead

In recent years, Primark has faced a number of different challenges that have the potential to impact on its business. First, unlike most clothing retailers,

Primark relies entirely on old-fashioned bricks-and-mortar stores and has shunned an e-commerce offering.[10] Its lack of an online store may be viewed as a challenge going forward. Consumers are increasingly shifting their spending online and there is a fear that Primark may struggle to compete with online retailers offering low prices.[12] If consumers switch in large numbers to buying clothes online, through social networks and messaging services, Primark may get left behind.[8] Second, as Primark expands globally and makes inroads into the US market, it is aware that not all foreign retailers have found this move easy. Tesco has struggled with its transatlantic venture and underestimated the costs of breaking into such a large and highly competitive market. A market that appears so similar can have unexpected differences and challenges.[8]

In 2017, sales at the fast-fashion chain were more than 19 per cent ahead of 2016 figures. Primark has achieved the highest market share gains of all players in the sector, outperforming online giants ASOS and sportswear specialist JD Sports. Primark is also on track to overtake Next as the UK's second-biggest clothing retailer. The clothing chain is said to have benefited when some of its competitors have suffered, because it kept its prices steady. Many rivals had increased prices in response to rising costs, caused by the fall in the value of the pound since the Brexit vote. However, Primark has been adept at capitalizing on shoppers trading down.[17]

Primark's website and social media activity play a key role in tempting shoppers into stores. A huge part of the Primark website is 'Primania', a hub of user-generated content. It's an online platform that invites customers from all over the world to share photos and images of their Primark outfits to Instagram with the hashtag #Primania, which are subsequently shown in its LED store displays across Europe and the USA.[18] In its first year, 'Primania' notched up 300,000 visitors a week. Primark has also been clever in harnessing the power of social media. The company has 11 million followers across a number of social media platforms, nearly half of whom are on Instagram. Primark's social media following is rising rapidly as young people increasingly use their mobile phones to browse fashions before heading into stores. Despite the challenges that Primark faces – global differences, lack of an e-commerce site, ethical and environmental concerns – the evidence shows that the retailer continues to thrive as it has been able to generate significant sales growth. The future for the low-price retailer looks bright.[19]

Questions

1. What factors have allowed Primark to sustain its price leadership position? How has it used price to convey a differential advantage and appeal to a certain market segment?

2. Highlight the main ethical concerns associated with Primark's pricing approach. What evidence is there that Primark has taken these ethical concerns seriously and has shown commitment to a range of ethical and environmental issues?

3. What are the strategic options open to Primark? Should it move in to online retailing and develop an e-commerce website? Why, or why not?

4. Why do you think Primark made the decision to move into the US market? What are the opportunities and challenges associated with this decision?

This case was prepared by Marie O'Dwyer, Waterford Institute of Technology, Ireland, from various published sources as a basis for class discussion rather than to show effective or ineffective management.

References

1. **Anonymous** (2018) Primark Holdings, *SoloCheck. ie.* Available at www.solocheck.ie/Irish-Company/Primark-Holdings-19672 (accessed 21 December 2018).

2. **Anonymous** (2015) A household Irish name built from humble beginnings: The Penneys story, *the-Journal.ie*, 1 March. Available at www.thejournal.ie/penneys-business-1957209-Mar2015/?utm_source=businessetc (accessed 21 December 2018).

3. **Primark** (n.d.) Our stores, *Primark.com*. Available at www.primark.com/en/our-stores (accessed 21 December 2018).

4. **Finch, J.** (2005) M&S to cash in as Littlewoods disappears, *Guardian.com*, 8 August. Available at www.theguardian.com/business/2005/aug/08/highstreetretailers.marksspencer?INTCMP=ILCNETTXT3487 (accessed 21 December 2018).

5. **O'Leary, E.** (2015) Penney's opens its second biggest store in the world in Spain, *Independent.ie*, 15 October. Available at www.independent.ie/business/penneys-opens-its-second-biggest-store-in-the-world-in-spain-34114143.html (accessed 21 December 2018).

6. **Ruddick, G.** (2013) Primark targets chic French shoppers as it opens in Marseille, *Telegraph.co.uk*, 16 December. Available at www.telegraph.co.uk/finance/newsbysector/retailandconsumer/10520533/Primark-targets-chic-French-shoppers-as-it-opens-in-Marseille.html (accessed 21 December 2018).

7. **Anonymous** (2014) Primark, la catena di shopping low cost arriva in Italia, *VelvetStyle.it*, 31 August. Available at velvetstyle.it/2014/08/31/primark-shopping-in-italia-le-novita/ (accessed 21 December 2018).

8. **Anonymous** (2015) Faster, cheaper fashion, *Economist.com*, 5 September. Available at www.economist.com/news/business/21663221-rapidly-rising-super-cheap-irish-clothes-retailer-prepares-conquer-america-rivals-should (accessed 21 December 2018).

9. **McQuillan, D.** (2016) Thanks, Penneys. The rise and rise of Primark, *IrishTimes.com*, 8 April. Available at www.irishtimes.com/life-and-style/fashion/thanks-penneys-the-rise-and-rise-of-primark-1.2602124 (accessed 21 December 2018).

10. **Bloomberg** (2017) Primark plans biggest expansion in a decade as sales soar, *BusinessofFashion.com*, 19 April. Available at www.businessoffashion.com/articles/news-analysis/primark-plans-biggest-expansion-in-a-decade-as-sales-soar (accessed 21 December 2018).

11. **Anonymous** (n.d.) How we do it, *Primark.com*. Available at m.primark.com/en/our-ethics/how-primark-keeps-prices-low (accessed 21 December 2018).

12. **Sills, L.** (2017) Primania: why knowing your audience is crucial to retail marketing, 256media.ie, 3 May. Available at www.256media.ie/2017/05/primark-case-study-retail-marketing/ (accessed 21 December 2018).

13. **Russell, M.** (2017) Why Primark is working to do 'the right thing' – interview, *Just-Style.com*, 31 October. Available at www.just-style.com/interview/why-primark-is-working-to-do-the-right-thing-interview_id130303.aspx (accessed 21 December 2018).

14. **Hendriksz, V.** (2017) A closer look at Primark's stance on responsible fashion, *FashionUnited.uk*, 20 April. Available at fashionunited.uk/primark-sustainability (accessed 21 December 2018).

15. **Maltwood, H.** (2017) Concerns that Primark's cheap prices could be compromising its ethics: the heavily criticised chain stands by its practices, *CornwallLive.com*, 9 November. Available at www.cornwalllive.com/news/cornwall-news/concerns-primarks-cheap-prices-could-753997 (accessed 21 December 2018).

16. **Sustainable Brands** (2018) Primark sheds light on supply chain with global sourcing map tool, *SustainableBrands.com*, 16 February. Available at www.sustainablebrands.com/news_and_views/supply_chain/sustainable_brands/primark_sheds_light_supply_chain_global_sourcing_map_ (accessed 21 December 2018).

17. **Anonymous** (n.d.) *FT.com*. Available at www.ft.com/content/c307085f-373f-33f1-8125-9f104f949631 (accessed 21 December 2018).

18. **Hendriksz, V.** (2016) Can 'Primania' satisfy Primark's lack of e-commerce? *FashionUnited.uk*, 4 February. Available at fashionunited.uk/news/fashion/can-primania-satisfy-primark-s-lack-of-e-commerce/2016020419285 (accessed 21 December 2018).

19. **Butler, S.** (2018) Primark primed to overtake Next as UK's No 2 clothing retailer, *Guardian.com*, 18 January. Available at www.theguardian.com/business/2018/jan/18/primark-primed-overtake-next-uk-no-2-clothing-retailer (accessed 21 December 2018).

Part 3

Delivering and Managing Customer Value

Chapter 9

Distribution: Delivering Customer Value

Chapter outline

Types of distribution channel

Channel integration

Retailing

Key retail marketing decisions

Physical distribution

Personal selling

Sales management

Learning outcomes

By the end of this chapter you will:

1   Understand the different types of distribution channel for consumer goods, industrial products and services

2   Analyse the three components of channel strategy – channel selection, intensity and integration

3   Analyse the five key channel management issues – member selection, motivation, training, evaluation and conflict management

4   Explain the different kinds of retail store format

5   Critique the changing face of offline and online retailing

6   Explain the key issues in managing the physical distribution system

7   Explain the main stages in the personal selling process

8   Understand the key activities involved in sales management

Domino's: appealing to new breed of digital-age consumers

Domino's Pizza is a pizza delivery and take-out restaurant chain headquartered in Ann Arbor, Michigan, in the United States. The company was founded as a one-store operation in 1960 by brothers Tom and James Monaghan when they purchased a pizza store named DomiNick's located in Ypsilanti, Michigan. In 1965, the company was renamed Domino's Pizza. The company went public in 2004 and is now traded on the New York Stock Exchange. As well as pizza, the chain offers a range of other dishes, including pasta, oven-baked sandwiches, fried chicken, side dishes and desserts. Today, the company is the largest pizza chain worldwide with almost US$3 billion in revenue as well as a franchise network of 15,000 stores.

Domino's has transformed itself from a pizza maker into a technology-driven company. By 2010, the competition was catching up and Domino's needed to appeal to a new generation of technologically savvy and social media-oriented customers who demand ultra-fast service, online and off. So the company developed a powerfully simple strategy: harness technology to make Domino's the easiest pizza chain to do business with. Domino's also wanted to differentiate through data. This meant creating the capability to collect and analyse all kinds of information about customers, from their names and phone numbers to their online ordering habits.

Digital ordering now makes up 60 per cent of Domino's business. In partnership with the technology company, Cisco, Domino's has looked at its ordering processes as a way to differentiate itself in a competitive marketplace. For instance, Domino's Tracker, allows customers to digitally follow their order from prep table to doorstep. Building on the emerging Internet of Things (IoT), this technology can even trigger devices to mark each step of your pizza's journey, including setting your music device to play when the pizza is in the oven, or having your home-automation system switch on your porch light or even turn off your front-yard sprinkler. Domino's is harnessing ordering data from its worldwide network to improve the customer experience. 'Customers' expectations are so much higher today,' executive vice president J. Kevin Vasconi explains. 'They have zero patience for downtime and latency.' Moreover, with large volumes of credit card and other personal information exchanging hands over the internet, security had to be super tight. Today Domino's.com ranks as one of the top 10 US e-commerce sites in dollar volume and has met the challenge of appealing to a new breed of digital-age consumers. As a result, technology innovations have helped to drive a 2,000 per cent increase in stock price over 10 years, as digital ordering, data insights and richer in-store experience drove more sales.

Domino's also wants people to be able to get a pizza at any time – even if they are somewhere without a traditional street address, like the beach. The pizza chain announced in April 2018 that it will now deliver orders to more than 150,000 US outdoor locations. These so-called 'Domino's Hotspots' are currently available only for prepaid online orders. When customers place their orders, they can give additional information, like what colour shirt they're wearing, so the Domino's delivery car can more easily locate them. Domino's does not stop innovating the distribution process and has recently been trying to up its delivery game by making it easy to order a pizza through tweets, smart TVs and Amazon's Alexa. Other pizza companies, like Pizza Hut, still require traditional addresses for deliveries.

The next iteration could see technology actually replace the pizza delivery person. More than a year after unveiling its DRU (Domino's Robotic Unit) prototype in Brisbane in 2016, the fast-food chain has successfully transported its first meal to an actual customer. The DRU was tested successfully in Hamburg in 2017 and proved the company is serious about its investment in technology to manage pizza delivery. Through the DRU, pizzas are packed into a locked compartment that can

(continued)

be opened only by using the Domino's app. The robot delivers the package by rolling along the footpath. A two-way audio system and alarm system, along with multiple cameras, enables the robot to navigate city streets. The obstacle-detection system allows the robots to build a picture of the area they are travelling through, with sensors to let them avoid people and to cross roads when it's safe to do so. The company has also been examining the use of drones as delivery vehicles.[1]

Dominos Ad Insight: Introducing Hot-Spots B-Roll

As we have seen throughout the book, several activities need to be conducted in order for organizations to market themselves effectively. These activities do not only include generating customer insights, developing differential products and services, pricing them correctly and communicating with customers, but also making them available to the customers. Delivering products or services to customers also requires important decisions to be made. For example, in consumer markets significant shifts in buying habits are taking place, such as online purchasing and the increased proportion of expenditure on foods being absorbed by supermarkets. In general, products need to be available in adequate quantities, in convenient locations and at times when customers want to buy them. In this chapter we will examine the functions and types of distribution channel, the key decisions that determine channel strategy, how to manage channels, the nature of retailing, and issues relating to the physical flow of goods through distribution channels (physical distribution management).

Producers need to consider the requirements of **channel intermediaries** – those organizations that facilitate the distribution of products to customers – as well as the needs of their ultimate customers. For example, success for Müller yoghurt in the UK was dependent on convincing a powerful retail group (Tesco) to stock the brand. The high margins that the brand supported were a key influence in Tesco's decision. Without retailer support, Müller may have found it uneconomic to supply consumers with its brand. Clearly, establishing a supply chain that is efficient and meets customers' needs is vital to marketing success. This supply chain is termed a **channel of distribution** and is the means by which products are moved from the producer to the ultimate customer. Gaining access to distribution outlets is not necessarily easy. For example, in the consumer food products sector, many brands vie with one another for prime positions on supermarket shelves (see Exhibit 9.1).

An important aspect of marketing strategy is choosing the most effective channel of distribution. The development of supermarkets effectively shortened the distribution channel between producer and consumer by eliminating the wholesaler. Prior to their introduction, the typical distribution channel for products like food, drink, tobacco and toiletries was producer to wholesaler to retailer. The wholesaler

Exhibit 9.1 Eye level is the best position to have in a shopping aisle and brands will compete aggressively to gain and hold these positions. Eye-tracking technology is increasingly used by researchers to understand what captures the attention of customers.

would buy in bulk from the producer and sell smaller quantities to the retailer (typically a small grocery shop). By building up buying power, supermarkets could shorten this chain by buying direct from producers. This meant lower costs to the supermarket chain and lower prices to the consumer. The competitive effect of this was to drastically reduce the numbers of small grocers and wholesalers in this market. By being more efficient and better at meeting customers' needs, supermarkets had created a competitive advantage for themselves, which they have been able to retain for many years. Similarly, the rapid development of the internet has given rise to a process called **disintermediation**, which occurs when a company decides to reduce or eliminate intermediaries in the distribution process. For example, intermediaries like travel agents were largely eliminated from many aspects of the travel industry when airlines allowed their customers to book directly on their websites. Major holiday companies such as Dream Holidays and Holidays4UK ceased trading, and established distributors like Thomas Cook were forced to undertake dramatic restructuring programmes. The rise of virtual marketplaces is further eliminating the need for channels. For example, on platforms like Amazon and Alibaba, buyers and sellers are brought together and can trade directly with one another, eliminating the need for channel intermediaries.

We will now explore the different types of channel that manufacturers use to supply their products to customers, and the types of function provided by these channel intermediaries.

Types of distribution channel

Whether they be consumer goods, industrial goods or services, all products require a channel of distribution. Industrial channels tend to be shorter than consumer channels because of the small number of ultimate customers, the greater geographic concentration of industrial customers and the greater complexity of the products that require close producer/customer liaison. Service channels also tend to be short because of the inseparability of the production and consumption of many services.

Consumer channels

Figure 9.1 shows four alternative consumer channels. We will look briefly at each one in turn.

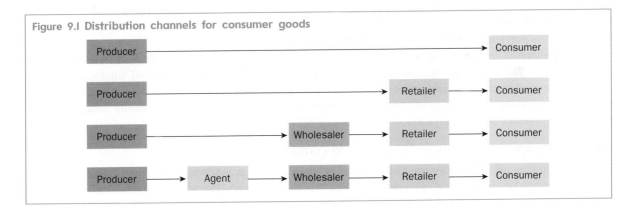

Figure 9.1 Distribution channels for consumer goods

Producer direct to consumer

This option may be attractive to producers because it cuts out distributors' profit margins. Direct selling between producer and consumer has long been a feature of the marketing of many products, ranging from the sale of fruit in local markets to the sale of cosmetics produced by Avon or Mary Kay. It is a form of distribution that is starting to grow rapidly again (see Exhibit 9.2). Concerns over food quality in supermarkets and a growing market for organic foods have seen a rapid rise in farmers' markets in Europe. And, in the past 20 years or so, the internet has been the great new direct distribution medium for products ranging from books to air travel to clothing, and so on. This has had huge implications for traditional retailers like bookshops, travel agents and clothing shops, many of whom have suffered falling sales or have ceased trading. In the UK in 2017, 37 retail businesses ceased trading, including such well-known names as Agent Provocateur (underwear), Jaeger (men's and ladies' wear) and Brantano (footwear).[2]

Producer to retailer to consumer

For a variety of reasons, a producer may choose to distribute products via a retailer to consumers. Retailers provide the basic service of enabling consumers to view a wide assortment of products under one roof, while manufacturers continue to gain economies of scale from the bulk production of a limited number of items. For many people, retailing is the public face of marketing, and large in-city and out-of-town shopping centres have become popular venues for consumers to spend their leisure time. For example, the Mall of the Emirates in Dubai features an indoor ski

Exhibit 9.2 Dutch company Jumbo's Pick Up Points Service offers customers the convenience of ordering online and collecting groceries at a time that suits them.

resort, providing a host of winter activities, a Magic Planet family entertainment centre, a shark-filled aquarium and cinemas. As we shall see later in the chapter, retailers have become increasingly sophisticated in their operations and dominate many distribution channels. For example, in 2018, Sainsbury's and Asda, the number two and three supermarket retailers in the UK, announced a merger that would give them a combined network of 2,800 Sainsbury's, Asda and Argos stores, and a market share of over 31 per cent.[3]

The use of wholesalers makes economic sense for small retailers (e.g. small grocery or furniture shops) with limited order quantities. Wholesalers can buy in bulk from producers, and sell smaller quantities to numerous retailers (this is known as 'breaking bulk'). The danger is that large retailers in the same market have the power to buy directly from producers and thus cut out the wholesaler. In certain cases, the buying power of large retailers has meant that they can sell products to their customers more cheaply than a small retailer can buy from the wholesaler. Consolidation in distribution channels has seen larger retailers buy up wholesalers, such as Tesco's purchase of Booker in the UK in 2017.

Longer channels tend to occur where retail oligopolies do not dominate the distribution system. In some Asian countries, like Japan, distribution channels can involve up to two and three tiers of wholesalers, which supply the myriad small shops and outlets that serve Japanese customers.[4] Many of these wholesalers provide additional services to their customers (the retailers) such as collecting and analysing customer data, which can be used to get better deals from producers.[5]

Producer to agent to wholesaler to retailer to consumer

This is a long channel, sometimes used by companies entering foreign markets, which may delegate the task of selling the product to an agent (who does not take title to the goods). The agent contacts local wholesalers (or retailers) and receives a commission on sales. Companies entering new export markets often organize their distribution systems in this way.

Business-to-business channels

Common business-to-business distribution channels are illustrated in Figure 9.2. A maximum of one channel intermediary is used under normal circumstances.

Producer to business customer

Supplying business customers direct is common practice for expensive business-to-business products such as gas turbines, diesel locomotives and aero-engines. There needs to be close liaison between supplier and customer to co-create products and solve technical problems, and the size of the order makes direct selling and distribution economic.

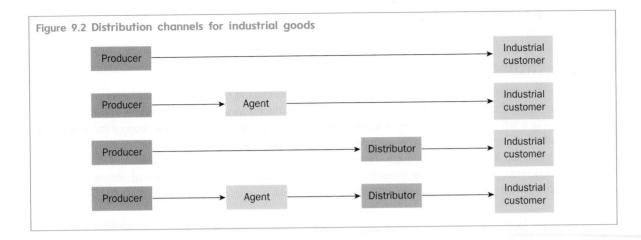

Figure 9.2 Distribution channels for industrial goods

Producer to agent to business customer

Instead of selling to business customers using their own sales force, a business-to-business goods company could employ the services of an agent, who may sell a range of goods from several suppliers (on a commission basis). This spreads selling costs and may be attractive to those companies that lack the reserves to set up their own sales operations. The disadvantage is that there is little control over the agent, who is unlikely to devote the same amount of time to selling these products as a dedicated sales team.

Producer to distributor to business customer

For less expensive, more frequently bought business-to-business products, distributors are used; these may have both internal and field sales staff.[6] Internal staff deal with customer-generated enquiries and order placing, order follow-up (often using the telephone) and check inventory levels. Outside sales staff are more proactive; their practical responsibilities are to find new customers, get products specified, distribute catalogues and gather market information. The advantage to customers of using distributors is that they can buy small quantities locally.

Producer to agent to distributor to business customer

Where business customers prefer to call upon distributors, the agent's job will require selling into these intermediaries. The reason why a producer may employ an agent rather than a dedicated sales force is usually cost-based (as previously discussed).

Services channels

Distribution channels for services are usually short, either direct or via an agent (see Figure 9.3). Since stocks are not held, the role of the wholesaler, retailer or industrial distributor does not apply.

Service provider to consumer or business customer

The close personal relationships between service providers and customers often means that service supply is direct. Examples include healthcare, office cleaning, accountancy, marketing research and law.

Service provider to agent to consumer or business customer

A channel intermediary for a service company usually takes the form of an agent. Agents are used when the service provider is geographically distant from customers, and where it is not economical for

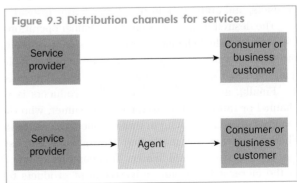

Figure 9.3 Distribution channels for services

the provider to establish its own local sales team. Examples include insurance, travel, secretarial and theatrical agents.

Channel strategy and management

The design of the distribution channel is an important strategic decision that needs to be integrated with other marketing decisions. For example, products that are being positioned as upmarket, premium items are usually available only in a select number of stores. **Channel strategy** decisions involve the selection of the most effective distribution channel, the most appropriate level of distribution intensity and the degree of channel integration. Once the key channel strategy decisions have been made, effective implementation is required. Channel management decisions involve the selection, motivation, training and evaluation of channel members, and managing conflict between producers and channel members.

Channel selection

Ask yourself why Procter & Gamble sells its brands through supermarkets rather than selling direct. Why does Mitsui sell its locomotives direct to train operating companies rather than use a distributor? The answers are to be found by examining the following factors that influence channel selection. These influences can be grouped under the headings of market, producer, product and competitive factors.

Market factors

Buyer behaviour is an important market factor; buyer expectations may dictate that a product be sold in a certain way. Buyers may prefer to buy locally or online. Failure to match these expectations can have catastrophic consequences, as illustrated by the experience of entertainment retailers, which continue to struggle as more and more consumers switch to digital downloading. Similarly, innovative technologies are changing the way consumers obtain their news. Platforms like Flipboard and Buzzfeed scan the internet and aggregate content in a magazine-style format based on each individual user's interests. These types of developments have implications for both magazine and newspaper publishers, as well as the retail outlets through which these print editions are sold.

The geographical concentration and location of customers also affects channel selection. The more local and clustered the customer base, the more likely it is that direct distribution will be feasible. Direct distribution is also more prevalent when buyers are few in number and buy large quantities, such as in many industrial markets. A large number of small customers may mean that using channel intermediaries is the only economical way of reaching them (e.g. department stores). Buyers' needs regarding product information, installation and technical assistance also have to be considered. For example, products that require facilities for local servicing, such as cars, often use intermediaries to carry out the task.

Producer factors

When a producer lacks adequate resources to perform the functions of the channel, this places a constraint on the channel decision. Producers may lack the financial and managerial resources to take on channel operations. Lack of financial resources may mean that a sales force cannot be recruited and sales agents and/or distributors are used instead. Producers may feel that they do not possess the customer-based skills to distribute their products, and prefer to rely on intermediaries instead.

The desired degree of control of channel operations also influences the selection of channel members. The use of independent channel intermediaries reduces producer control. For example, by distributing their products through supermarkets, manufacturers lose control of the price charged to consumers. Furthermore, there is no guarantee that new products will be stocked. Direct distribution gives producers control over such issues.

Finally, an important decision for producers is whether they want to push their product through the channel or rather market to the end consumer, who then 'pulls' the product through the channel. The former requires investing heavily in trade support to ensure that products are carried and given desired shelf space. The latter means that marketing is targeted at end users, who through their demand for the product ensure that it is carried by middlemen. This has raised important ethical issues in the medical profession because of the increased consumer advertising of products by pharmaceutical companies. By building well-known brands like Viagra, Prozac and Vioxx, pharmaceutical companies have been accused of driving consumers to demand products that are not always necessary, in effect pulling them through the channel despite possible objections by medical practitioners. For example, the US drug firms Merck and Schering-Plough have been embroiled in controversy since a study concluded that their joint cholesterol drug, Vytorin, is no more effective than generic versions costing a third of its price. The drug had been aggressively marketed by these two companies.[7]

Product factors

Large and/or complex products are often supplied direct to the customer. The need for close personal contact between producer and customer, and the high prices charged, mean that direct distribution and selling is both necessary and feasible. Perishable products, such as fruit, meat and bread, require relatively short channels to supply the customer with fresh stock. Bulky or difficult-to-handle products may require direct distribution because distributors may refuse to carry them if storage or display problems arise.[8] A significant proportion of products that can be digitized, such as books, music, video, software and education, are distributed through online channels.

Competitive factors

An innovative approach to distribution may be required if competitors control traditional channels of distribution – for example, through franchise or exclusive dealing arrangements. Two available alternatives are to recruit a sales force to sell direct, or to set up a producer-owned distribution network (see the information about administered vertical marketing systems, a topic discussed later under the heading 'Conventional marketing channels'). Producers should not accept that the channels of distribution used by competitors are the only ways to reach target customers. Direct marketing provides opportunities to supply products in new ways, as many online companies have shown. For example, shaving equipment was traditionally sold through retailers in supermarkets and department stores, but companies like DollarShave Club and Harry's changed this business model by selling direct to consumers online.

Distribution intensity

The choice of distribution intensity is the second channel strategy decision. The three broad options are intensive, selective and exclusive distribution. We will look at each of these now.

Intensive distribution

By using all available outlets, **intensive distribution** aims to provide saturation coverage of the market. With many mass-market products, such as snacks, foods, toiletries, beer and newspapers, sales are a direct function of the number of outlets penetrated (see Exhibit 9.3). This is because consumers have a range of acceptable brands from which they choose and, very often, the decision to purchase is made on impulse. If a brand is not available in an outlet, an alternative is bought. The convenience aspect of purchase is paramount. New outlets may be sought that hitherto had not stocked the products, such as the sale of alcoholic drinks and grocery items at petrol stations.

Exhibit 9.3 The use of vending machines, meaning that its products are available everywhere, has been a big part of the Coca-Cola success story. Its innovative 'happiness machine' campaign, which involves machines giving out a range of free gifts, has been a strong source of viral promotion and positive social media coverage.

Selective distribution

Selective distribution also enables market coverage to be achieved. In this case, a producer uses a limited number of outlets in a geographical area to sell its products. The advantages to the producer are: the opportunity to select only the best outlets to focus its efforts on building close working relationships; having to train distributor staff on fewer outlets than with intensive distribution; and, if selling and distribution are direct, reducing costs. Upmarket, aspirational brands like Hugo Boss and Raymond Weil are often sold in carefully selected outlets. Retail outlets and industrial distributors like this arrangement since it reduces competition. Selective distribution is more likely to be used when buyers are willing to shop around when choosing products. This means that it is not necessary for a company to have its products available in all outlets. Products such as audio and video equipment, cameras, clothing and cosmetics may be sold in this way (see Marketing in Action 9.1).

Marketing in Action 9.1
Lush: a fresh approach to cosmetics retailing

Critical Thinking: Below is a review of the growth of the ethical brand Lush Cosmetics. Read it and reflect on the reasons why this brand has been successful in the market place. What role has its channel strategy played in its success?

Lush Cosmetics, which was founded in the UK in 1995, is a global speciality beauty retailer marketing a range of creams, soaps, shampoos, shower gels, lotions, moisturizers and other cosmetics for the face, hair and body, using only vegetarian and vegan recipes. The company's founder, Mark Constantine, had previously been a main supplier of products to the Body Shop, another cosmetics retailer founded on ethical principles. Constantine's first venture into consumer marketing was a mail order business, Cosmetics To Go (CTG), selling natural, handmade beauty products and perfumes. This idea proved highly successful, but its customer base grew so fast that problems in inventory management and distribution meant that it was unable to fulfil orders swiftly enough and the business failed after four years. Eventually, this led to a move into retail through the Lush Cosmetics brand, which has proved to be much more successful. The business currently has more than 930 stores around the world, generating revenues in excess of £720 million in 2016.

The unique selling proposition for Lush is that its products are fresh and about 70 per cent contain no preservatives. All of its products, and their ingredients, have never been tested on animals and are suitable for vegetarians, with about 80 per cent suitable for vegans. The products are handmade with ingredients from around the world, ranging from fresh produce purchased from local farms to shea butter sourced from women's co-operatives in Ghana. Lush uses ingredients that are not normally associated with the manufacture of cosmetics. In 2016, the company purchased over one ton of lemons, five tons of limes, 220 tons of cocoa butter, nine tons of bananas, 137,000 pounds of honey, 41,000 pounds of olive oil, one ton of vanilla beans, 352 pounds of dark vegan chocolate and more than 1,400 pounds of various seaweeds. The resulting products are colourful and designed in shapes and sizes resembling ice creams and desserts, leading many to mistake them as being edible! In that year, it produced 41 million products, of which 13.3 million were Bath Bombs, its most popular line.

In contrast to most players in the cosmetics industry, Lush also believes in minimal packaging. Aside from the cost savings and environmental benefits, this means that customers have the full sensory experience of seeing, smelling and touching the products. In keeping with its green principles, Lush has also given more than US$17 million to 1,400 charities, to support the environment. For example, all earnings from its Charity Pot body lotion go to environmental, animal protection and human rights organizations, enabling it to become a brand associated with a strong ethical and environmental stance, which appeals to both its employees, who may share the same values, and as its customers.

(continued)

Lush stores are typically found in select locations in major cities around the world usually on main shopping thoroughfares next to other outlets that sell high-end items. The design and layout of a Lush store is based on the company's principle that it is a 'cosmetics grocer' – in other words, it draws inspiration from how fruit and vegetables are displayed. Inside, colourful heaps of soaps and bubble bars are arranged, giving off a powerful, attractive fragrance. Bowls of water are available where employees can demonstrate the products and customers can try them out. There is a strong focus on customer service and the creation of a relaxed atmosphere in store, with the result that Lush was ranked number one for 'fun' in the *Sunday Times* 100 Best Companies in 2005. Finally, the company has managed to grow a strong global brand with minimal spend on mainstream advertising, relying instead on advocacy by its employees, content marketing on its website and social media channels, and powerful word-of-mouth effects from having been adopted by influencers like Zoella and Tanya Burr.

Based on: Leob, 2017;[9] Purkayastha and Fernando, 2007[10]

Problems can arise when a retailer demands distribution rights but is refused by producers. This happened in the case of Superdrug, a UK discount store chain, which requested the right to sell expensive perfume but was denied by manufacturers, which claimed that its stores did not have the right ambience for the sale of luxury products. Superdrug maintained that its application was refused solely because it wanted to sell perfumes for less than their recommended prices. A Monopolies and Mergers Commission investigation supported current practice. European rules allow perfume companies to confine distribution to retailers who measure up in terms of décor and staff training. Manufacturers are not permitted to refuse distribution rights on the grounds that the retailer will sell for less than the list price.[11]

Exclusive distribution

Exclusive distribution is an extreme form of selective distribution in which only one wholesaler, retailer or business-to-business distributor is used in a particular geographic area. Cars are often sold on this basis, with only one dealer operating in each town or city. This reduces a purchaser's power to negotiate prices for the same model between dealers, since to buy in a neighbouring town may be inconvenient when servicing or repairs are required. It also allows very close co-operation between producer and retailer over servicing, pricing and promotion. The right to exclusive distribution may be demanded by distributors as a condition for stocking a manufacturer's product line. Similarly, producers may wish for exclusive dealing where the distributor agrees not to stock competing lines.

Exclusive distribution arrangements can restrict competition in a way that may be detrimental to consumer interests. As an example, top woman's apparel brand, Gucci, had licensed its products to many retailers, some of which discounted Gucci's products. This tarnished the brand's image. As a result, Gucci cancelled contracts with its resellers and controlled distribution of its products, as well as opening its own stores to sell its products.

Channel integration

Channel integration can range from conventional marketing channels – comprising an independent producer and channel intermediaries – through a franchise operation, to channel ownership by a producer. Producers need to consider the strengths and weaknesses of each system when selecting a channel strategy.

Conventional marketing channels

The producer has little or no control over channel intermediaries because of their independence. Arrangements such as exclusive dealing may provide a degree of control, but separation of ownership means that each party will look after its own interests. Conventional marketing channels are characterized by hard bargaining and, occasionally, conflict. For example, a retailer may believe that cutting the price of a brand is necessary to move stock, even though the producer objects because of brand image considerations.

A manufacturer that, through its size and strong brands, dominates a market may exercise considerable power over intermediaries even though they are independent. This power may result in an **administered vertical marketing system** where the manufacturer can command considerable co-operation from wholesalers and retailers. For example, Pfizer created some controversy when it sought to change its drug distribution arrangements in the UK, which would see all its products distributed through one company, UniChem. Other wholesalers sought to have the action deemed anti-competitive, while retailers were also concerned about the possible emergence of a single, powerful wholesaler.[12]

In recent years, retailers have exerted significant control in an administered vertical marketing system. For example, grocery retailers have been particularly strong in their channels, with firms like Tesco, Carrefour and Walmart achieving positions of significant dominance. A key way in which these retailers hurt other channel members is through the development of their own retailer brands or private labels. Outlets like Aldi, Lidl and Marks & Spencer sell primarily their own branded products rather than manufacturer brands. In relatively undifferentiated product categories like milk, pasta, ready meals, refuse bags and aluminium foil, private-label penetration levels have been very high, posing particular problems for manufacturers. However, manufacturers have done a much better job of holding their dominant positions in sectors like beer, toothpaste and cosmetics.

Franchising

A legal contract in which a producer and channel intermediaries agree each member's rights and obligations is called a **franchise**. Usually, the intermediary receives marketing, managerial, technical and financial services in return for a fee. Franchise organizations such as McDonald's, Domino's Pizza, Hertz and The Body Shop combine the strengths of a large sophisticated marketing-oriented organization with the energy and motivation of a locally owned outlet, and hence have been highly successful in building global businesses. Although a franchise operation gives a degree of producer control, there are still areas of potential conflict. For example, the producer may be dissatisfied with the standards of service provided by the outlet, or the franchisee may believe that the franchising organization provides inadequate promotional support. Goal conflict can also arise.[13] A franchise agreement provides a **contractual vertical marketing system** through the formal co-ordination and integration of marketing and distribution activities.

Three economic explanations have been proposed to explain why a producer might choose franchising as a means of distribution.[14] Franchising may be a means of overcoming resource constraints whereby the cost of distribution is shared with the franchisee. It may also be an efficient system for overcoming producer/distributor management problems, because producers may value the notion of the owner-manager who has a vested interest in the success of the business. Finally, franchising may be a way for a producer to access the local knowledge of the franchisee. Franchising may therefore be attractive when a producer is expanding into new international markets. The biggest franchises operating in Europe are listed in Table 9.1.

Table 9.1 Leading franchises in Europe in 2017, by number of units

Rank	Franchise	Number of units	Business	Country of origin
1	7 Eleven	55,944	Convenience stores	USA
2	Subway	44,589	Food: sandwich bars	USA
3	McDonald's	30,197	Restaurants	USA
4	Kumon Institute of Education	25,800	Children's education	Japan
5	Burger King	14,927	Restaurants	USA
6	KFC	14,631	Restaurants	USA
7	Pizza Hut	13,507	Restaurants	USA
8	Domino's Pizza	12,530	Restaurants	USA
9	Spar	12,176	Convenience stores	Netherlands
10	Dunkin' Donuts	11,941	Coffee and baked goods chain	USA

Source: www.statista.com

Franchising can occur at four levels of the distribution chain.

1 *Manufacturer and retailer*: the car industry is dominated by this arrangement. The manufacturer gains retail outlets for its cars and repair facilities without the capital outlay required with ownership.

2 *Manufacturer and wholesaler*: this is commonly used in the soft drinks industry. Manufacturers such as Schweppes, Coca-Cola and Pepsi grant wholesalers the right to make up and bottle their concentrate in line with their instructions, and to distribute the products within a defined geographic area.

3 *Wholesaler and retailer*: this is not as common as other franchising arrangements, but is found with car products and hardware stores. It allows wholesalers to secure distribution of their product to consumers.

4 *Retailer and retailer*: a frequently used method that often has its roots in a successful retailing operation seeking to expand geographically by means of a franchise operation, often with great success. Examples include Subway, Best Western, Pizza Hut and KFC (see Exhibit 9.4).

Exhibit 9.4 The global food service business has been a fertile ground for franchise arrangements.

Channel ownership

Channel ownership brings with it total control over distributor activities. This establishes a **corporate vertical marketing system**. By purchasing retail outlets, producers control their purchasing, production and marketing activities. In particular, control over purchasing means a captive outlet for the manufacturer's products. For example, the purchase of Pizza Hut and KFC by Pepsi has tied these outlets to the company's soft drinks brands.

The benefits of control have to be balanced against the high price of acquisition and the danger that the move into retailing will spread managerial activities too widely. Nevertheless, corporate vertical marketing systems have operated successfully for many years in the oil industry, where companies such as Shell, Texaco and Statoil own not only considerable numbers of petrol stations but also the means of production.

Channel management

Channels need to be managed on an ongoing basis once the key channel strategy decisions have been made. This involves the selection, motivation, training and evaluation of channel members, and the resolution of any channel conflict that arises.

Selection

The selection of channel members involves two main activities: first, the identification of potential channel members and, second, development of selection criteria. A variety of potential sources can be used to identify candidates, including trade sources, such as trade associations and participation at exhibitions, talking to existing customers and/or to the field sales force, and taking enquiries from interested resellers.[15] Common selection criteria include market, product and customer knowledge, market coverage, quality and size of sales force (if applicable), reputation among customers, financial standing, the extent to which competitive and complementary products are carried, managerial competence and hunger for success, and the degree of enthusiasm for handling the producer's lines. In practice, selection may be complex because large, well-established distributors may carry many competing lines and lack enthusiasm for more. Smaller distributors, on the other hand, may be less financially secure and have a smaller sales force, but be more enthusiastic and hungry for success.

Motivation

Once they have been chosen, channel members need to be motivated to agree to act as a distributor, and allocate adequate commitment and resources to the producer's lines. The key to effective motivation is to understand the needs and problems of distributors, since needs and motivators are linked. For example, a distributor who values financial incentives may respond more readily to high commission than one that is more concerned with having an exclusive territory. Possible motivators include financial rewards, territorial exclusivity, providing resource support (e.g. sales training, field sales assistance, provision of marketing research information, advertising and promotion support, financial assistance and management training) and developing strong work relationships (e.g. joint planning, assurance of long-term commitment, appreciation of effort and success, frequent interchange of views and arranging distributor conferences). In short, the management of independent distributors is best conducted in the context of informal partnerships.[16]

Training

Channel members' training requirements obviously depend on their internal competencies. Many smaller distributors have been found to be weak on sales management, marketing, financial management, stock control and personnel management, and may welcome producer initiatives on training.[17] From the producer's perspective, training can provide the necessary technical knowledge about a supplier company and its products, and help to build a spirit of partnership and commitment.

Evaluation

Channel member evaluation has an important impact on distributor retention, training and motivation decisions. Evaluation provides the information necessary to decide which channel members to retain and which to drop. Shortfalls in distributor skills and competencies may be identified through evaluation, and appropriate training programmes organized by producers. Where a lack of motivation is recognized as a problem, producers can implement plans designed to deal with the root causes of demotivation (e.g. financial incentives and/or fostering a partnership approach to business).[18] It needs to be understood, however, that the scope and frequency of evaluation may be limited where power lies with the channel member. If producers have relatively little power because they are more dependent on channel members for distribution, then in-depth evaluation and remedial action will be restricted. Where manufacturer power is high through having strong brands and many distributors from which to choose, evaluation may be more frequent and wider in scope. Evaluation criteria include sales volume and value, profitability, level of stocks, quality and position of display, new accounts opened, selling and marketing capabilities, quality of service provided to customers, market information feedback, ability and willingness to keep commitments, attitudes and personal capability.

Managing conflict

First, given that producers and channel members are independent, conflict will inevitably occur from time to time (see Marketing in Action 9.2). First, such discord may arise because of differences in goals – for example, an increase in the proportion of profits allocated to retailers means a reduction in the amount going to manufacturers. For instance, when Irish tour operator Budget Travel cut the commissions it paid to travel agents for selling its holidays from 10 to 5 per cent, its subsequent research found that many agents were omitting Budget from the list of choices being presented to customers. Its response was to reach out directly to the end consumer through a €1 million multimedia campaign, urging consumers to consider Budget as one of their potential travel choices.[19] However, this campaign was unsuccessful and the firm subsequently ceased trading.

Second, in seeking to expand their businesses many resellers add additional product lines. For example, UK retailer WHSmith originally specialized in books, magazines and newspapers, but has grown as it has added new product lines such as computer disks, DVDs and software supplies. This can cause resentment among its

Marketing in Action 9.2
Marmite: caught in the crossfire

Critical Thinking: Below is an example of a conflict over pricing between Unilever and Tesco in the UK. Read it and consider the arguments from both sides. As a consumer who do you support?

Channel conflict is commonplace in a variety of industries, and frequently arises due to the conflicting goals of channel members. A typical example of the type of conflict that can arise occurred in 2016 and featured two of Europe's biggest consumer goods companies, Unilever and Tesco. The row was sparked by Britain's vote to leave the European Union, commonly referred to as Brexit (see Marketing in Action 2.2). This controversial decision had an immediate effect on Britain's currency, the pound, causing it to lose some of its value relative to the euro as investors feared for the future of the British economy after it left the European zone. The weaker pound meant an increase in the costs of importing goods into Britain, so Unilever, which is based in the Netherlands, asked its channel members – the major supermarkets – to raise their prices on a range of popular brands such as Ben & Jerry's, Lynx and Marmite by 10 per cent to offset this increase to its cost base.

Not surprisingly such a request caused much concern in the channel given the hyper-competitive nature of supermarket retailing. The stakes rose significantly when the leading player, Tesco, defied Unilever and refused to raise its prices. As a result, Unilever stopped the delivery of certain brands, resulting in a shortage of several leading brands such as Persil, Dove, Comfort, Ben & Jerry's and Marmite in Tesco stores and on Tesco.com. Disputes about pricing are not unusual among manufacturers and retailers but what was surprising in this case was that the dispute went so far. Clearly each of these two big players thought it could win. For example, it is estimated that Unilever brands have almost 40 per cent of the ice cream market in the UK, while in other categories particular brands like Marmite hold an 85 per cent market share. Given that consumer loyalty may be more with particular brands rather than where they shop, it would appear to put Unilever in a strong position. Tesco ran a big risk in not stocking popular brands, particularly at a time when consumers typically do their weekly shop across more than one supermarket. But clearly it also believed that it had an opportunity to be perceived as a consumer champion by resisting a price rise from a large multinational company.

Equally unusual was the speed with which both parties resolved the dispute. The issue was resolved within 24 hours of it becoming public without any revelations regarding whether one company caved in or whether a compromise was reached. Either way, 'Marmitegate', as it was dubbed, illustrated the speed at which disagreements between channel members can escalate. And, as if to illustrate how controversies can sometimes have unexpected side effects, Marmite sales rose 61 per cent following all the coverage it received as part of the pricing controversy.

Based on: Butler, 2016;[20] Roderick, 2016[21]

primary suppliers, who perceive the reseller as devoting too much effort to selling secondary lines. This problem can also work in reverse. Small newsagents in Ireland asked the Competition Authority to review the system whereby wholesalers insisted that they carry a full range of magazine titles, with the result that many were left unsold, increasing the costs to the retailer.[22]

Third, in trying to grow their business, producers can use multiple distribution channels, such as selling direct to key accounts or other distributors, which may irritate existing dealers. For example, Alanis Morissette's record company, Maverick Records, created a significant amount of channel conflict in North America when it granted exclusive rights for the sale of her album *Jagged Little Pill* to Starbucks, which was allowed to sell the album for six weeks in its then 4,800 stores before it became available elsewhere. HMV, one of the leading record stores at the time, reacted by removing all of the artist's music from the shelves of its Canadian stores.[23] For digitized products such as music and software, online distribution is significantly cheaper, making it very difficult for physical stores to compete with this channel, which is often a source of conflict.

Finally, an obvious source of conflict is when parties in the supply chain do not perform to expectations. For example, Dixon's Carphone, the owner of the PC World and Currys retail chains, claimed that its poor financial performance in 2007 was partly attributable to a lack of promotional support by Microsoft for its new Vista operating system, which left it with thousands of unsold computers that had to be heavily discounted. This type of conflict is also very common in the telecommunications business, where mobile and fixed-line operators buy bundles of time on networks for resale to their customers. Any increase or reduction in these wholesale prices can have a significant impact on their profitability.

There are several ways of managing conflict. Developing a partnership approach calls for frequent interaction between producer and resellers to develop a spirit of mutual understanding and co-operation. First, sales targets can be mutually agreed, and training and promotional support provided. Second, staff may need some training in conflict handling to ensure that situations are dealt with calmly and that possibilities for win/win outcomes are identified. Third, where the conflict arises from multiple distribution channels, producers can try to partition markets. For example, Hallmark sells its premium greetings cards under its Hallmark brand name to upmarket department stores and its standard cards under the Ambassador name to discount retailers.[24] Fourth, where poor performance is the problem, the most effective solution is to improve performance so that the source of conflict disappears. Finally, in some cases, the conflict might be eliminated through the purchase of the other party or through coercion, where one party gains compliance through the use of force, such as where a large retailer threatens to delist a manufacturer. The merger between Procter & Gamble and Gillette was seen by many as a move to put these two manufacturers on an equal footing with giant retailers like Walmart.

Retailing

Retailing is conducted primarily in stores such as supermarkets and department stores, and increasingly through online retailers. Many large retailers exert enormous power in the distribution chain because of the vast quantities of goods they buy from manufacturers (see Critical Marketing Perspective 9.1). This power is reflected in their ability to extract 'guarantee of margins' from manufacturers. This is a clause inserted in a contract that ensures a certain profit margin for the retailer, irrespective of the retail price being charged to the customer. One manufacturer is played against another, and own-label brands are used to extract more profit.[25]

Critical Marketing Perspective 9.1
How millennials are driving brands to practise ethical distribution

The overall demographic trends, discussed in Chapter 2, show significant developments that impact marketing of products and services. The Financial Times reported in 2017 that younger consumers are shifting to ethical products, and that the demand for sustainable goods, from free-range meat to vegan haircare, is rising. In addition, YouGov data showed that, in 2016 alone, the proportion of 18 to 24 year olds turning to vegetarianism for environmental or welfare reasons increased from 9 to 19 per cent. And it is not just about their consumer habits. 'We know that millennials want to work for companies that take this stuff seriously,' says Rob Harrison, director of Ethical Consumer. 'Lots of new start-ups have an ethical mission and it translates across into buying patterns.'

The overall trends in ethical consumption translate into the higher level of consciousness of customers with the aspects of distribution. For example, the platform Conscious Consumers provides retailers with data about customers' ethical preferences, while shoppers sign up online and link their credit or debit card to the app. Whenever the customers spend money at businesses registered with Conscious Consumers, data entered on their profile – from whether they would prioritize buying organic to whether they are interested in climate change or workers' welfare – is sent to the retailer.

(continued)

Following these developments, distribution of products and services requires adjustments as well, as millennial consumers are more likely to buy products from ethical companies, and are concerned about ethical distribution too. Ethical distribution refers to the process by which companies deliver their goods and services by focusing not only on how their products benefit customers, but also how they benefit socially responsible or environmental causes. To put it another way, ethical distribution isn't a strategy, it's a philosophy. It includes everything from ensuring advertisements are honest and trustworthy, to building strong relationships with consumers through a set of shared values. There's no arguing that millennials are the future of the workforce and their influence on making distribution decisions for businesses will only increase. It's important for distributors to devise strategies that cater to their preferences and behaviours.

The millennial generation is the first to grow up fully online – they are 'digital natives.' They research online before making a purchasing decision and many prefer to use self-service sales channels, a fact that makes having a B2B e-commerce platform a non-negotiable component for wholesale distribution. B2B wholesale distributors need to understand this shift in purchasing behaviour, so they can make sure their distribution channels are set up to serve this market.

Table 9.2 gives an overview of how millennials are changing the wholesale distribution channel and how the company can address it and adapt their marketing strategies to stay competitive.

Table 9.2 Trends in millennials' behaviour that affect companies' distribution policies and required actions

Trend in millennials behaviour	Required action by the company
Online research	Ensure feasibility in search engines and website optimization
Lead nurturing	Devise a lead capture mechanism and a lead nurturing sequence
Online transaction	Use a robust eCommerce platform to support quick and seamless product search, account management, checkout, order management and re-ordering.
B2C user experience	Pay attention to the user experience design (UX): relevant and informative content, interactive tools, and distinctive brand identity
Omnichannel customer experience	Guarantee consistent brand experience across all channels and customer touch points.

Source: Apruve: Five ways millennials are changing the wholesale distribution channel

Suggested reading: Weber and Urick, 2017[26]

Reflection: Do you think that ethical brands will outperform similar companies that lack a commitment to ethical principles? Consider the arguments for and against ethical distribution. Put forward your own point of view. Evaluate your statements and support your argumentation by three recent examples, indicating the primary company and the competitor activities.

Major retail store types

A wide variety of different retailer types can be observed in the marketplace, as described below.

Supermarkets are large self-service stores, which traditionally sell food, drinks and toiletries, but the broadening of their ranges by some supermarket chains means that such items as non-prescription pharmaceuticals, cosmetics and clothing are also being sold. Carrefour, Europe's biggest retailer, is renowned for its huge hypermarkets. In 2018, its average store size was 10,000 square metres, stocking a vast array of food and non-food items. The main attractions of supermarkets are their convenient locations, wide product ranges and competitive prices. Supermarket operators are skilled marketers who use a variety of techniques, such as psychological research, sensory experiences and loyalty schemes to capture a significant share of the market.

Department stores are titled thus because related product lines are sold in separate departments, such as men's and women's clothing, jewellery, cosmetics, toys and home furnishings. In recent years such stores have been under increasing pressure from discount houses, speciality stores and the move to out-of-town shopping. Nevertheless, many continue to perform well in this competitive arena through a strategy of becoming one-stop shops for a variety of leading manufacturer brands, which are allocated significant store space.

Convenience stores, true to their name, offer customers the convenience of a close location and long opening hours every day of the week. Because they are small they may pay higher prices for their merchandise than supermarkets, and therefore have to charge higher prices to their customers. Some of these stores, such as Spar, join buying groups to gain some purchasing power and lower prices. The main customer need they fulfil is that of top-up buying – for example, when a customer is short of a carton of milk or loaf of bread. Societal changes, such as rising divorce rates, decreasing family sizes, long commuting times and time-poor consumers, have all combined to help revitalize the convenience store sector. Consumers are once again favouring quick, convenient purchases, as offered by convenience stores, over a big weekly shop at a supermarket. Consequently, major retailers like Tesco and Sainsbury's have been aggressively buying in to this sector.

Speciality stores, as their name suggests, specialize in a narrow product line and can be observed in a variety of industries, such as food (butchers, bakers), clothing (ladies' wear) and giftware (jewellery). Speciality shops usually focus on high product quality and product knowledge as well as providing good service. Because of their expertise in particular sectors, speciality shops are sometimes described as 'category killers', where they come to dominate (see Exhibit 9.5). Examples might include Nevada Bob's Discount Golf Warehouses (golf equipment), Woodies (DIY) and Halfords (bicycles and auto accessories). However, speciality shops can be vulnerable to rapidly changing tastes. The sports retailer JJB Sports collapsed as the blend-

Exhibit 9.5 One of the original 'category killers', Toys 'R' Us ceased trading in 2018 due to competition, particularly from online rivals.

ing of sportswear and fashion, giving rise to the phrase 'athleisurewear', opened up the market to a host of competitors such as fashion shops and supermarkets. And, in 2018, one of the original 'category killers', Toys 'R' Us, ceased trading. The company was founded in 1957 and was known globally for its huge out-of-town stores filled from floor to ceiling with children's toys. But competition from other offline and online rivals, changing consumer tastes and a failure to respond quickly enough to market developments all combined to overwhelm the business.

Finally, **discount houses** sell products at low prices by accepting low margins, selling high volumes and bulk buying. For example, 'pound shops' sell a wide range of items, such as fashion accessories, toys, stationery and tools for £1, and operate on low margins of 2–3 per cent. Good location and rapid product turnover are the keys to success. Low prices, sometimes promoted as sale prices, are offered throughout the year. Many discounters operate from out-of-town retail warehouses with the capacity to stock a wide range of merchandise. The UK pound shop Poundland is Europe's biggest discount house. The company was founded in 1990 and, by 2018, had more than 700 outlets throughout the UK, many in high-street locations, and more than 60 in the Republic of Ireland. A growing form of discount retailing is factory outlet stores. These are usually out-of-town shopping locations comprising a wide range of manufacturer-owned retail shops that carry out-of-season stock or unsold products from department stores that are heavily discounted. Some of these outlet malls are repositioning themselves as premium outlets (rather than factory outlets) and feature prestigious brand names such as Versace, Gucci, Dolce & Gabbana, Ralph Lauren, Yves Saint Laurent, and so on.

Online retailing

Online retailing is one of the fastest-growing forms of distribution, and is proving particularly popular for products like electrical goods, groceries, clothing/footwear and music/video. It can take any of three major forms. First, in pure online retailing scenarios, the product is ordered, paid for and received online in a completely electronic transaction. Any product that can be digitized can be retailed in this way. Second, products can be ordered online and then distributed either through the postal system or through the use of local distribution companies in the case of groceries or wine, for example. Finally, most leading retailers have an online presence. For example, the top retailers that have a significant presence both online and offline include Tesco, Marks & Spencer, Argos, Next, Carrefour and Aldi.

Online retailers possess several advantages that help to explain their rapid rise. Online stores are open 24 hours per day, every day of the year, offering customer convenience, and they offer a much wider product range than possible in a physical location. For instance, physical bookstores, video game shops and so on are limited by the number of titles they can carry, making supply choices very important. The same applies to clothing outlets, where the range of size, colour or even design is more limited than the stock available online. Online retailers have relatively unlimited carrying capacity as their products are stored in huge warehouses, with other online affiliates, or in digital formats such as e-books, with the result that they can potentially offer almost any niche product a consumer may be looking for. Second, the cost of doing business is relatively lower for an online retailer. Small players can establish a web presence relatively cheaply, while offline retailers have to invest in store locations, shop fittings, sales personnel and so on. Finally, online businesses have access to a global market where one of the key marketing challenges is finding ways of driving customers from all over the world to your web store.

From multi-channel to omni-channel retailing

The past two decades have witnessed dramatic changes in the nature of retailing and distribution, giving rise to successive phases of growth that have been labelled **multi-channel** and **omni-channel** retailing. The growth of the internet and e-commerce, in particular, brought the issue of multi-channel management into focus. Firms were challenged with the task of how to manage the combination of both offline and online channels. For example, when supermarket Tesco decided to begin its e-commerce business, Tesco.com, it was faced with decisions like whether online orders would be fulfilled from local Tesco stores or from dedicated Tesco distribution centres. Multi-channel retailing typically refers to a combination of channels, which includes physical stores, direct distribution such as mail order and catalogues, as well as online stores. Decisions with regard to this set of channels might include which products are available through the different routes, what level of integration there is between the channels, whether price points across channels should vary to take account of different distribution costs, and how channel conflict might be resolved. Multi-channel customer management has been formally defined as

> the design, deployment, coordination, and evaluation of channels to enhance customer value through effective customer acquisition, retention, and development.[27]

However, as technology continues to impact further on distribution and the customer experience, the concept of omni-channel retailing has emerged to capture more fully the marketing challenges involved.[28] For example, customers in a physical store may use their mobile phones or tablets to search the company's online store, compare prices using a price comparison website, look up product reviews and communicate with their friends on social media. Consequently, search engines, referral websites, social media and company apps can all be considered channels. Different channels and touchpoints are being used constantly, interchangeably and simultaneously by firms and customers to facilitate the customer's retail experience. Omni-channel management, therefore, has been defined as the

> synergetic management of the numerous available channels and customer touchpoints, in such a way that the customer experience across channels and the performance of channels is optimized.[29]

The main differences between multi-channel and omni-channel management are summarized in Table 9.3.

Table 9.3 Multi-channel versus omni-channel management

	Multi-channel management	Omni-channel management
Channel focus	Interactive channels only	Interactive and mass-communication channels
Channel scope	Retail channels: store, online and direct marketing (catalogue)	Retail channels: store, online website, direct marketing, mobile channels (smartphones, tablets, apps), social media Customer touchpoints (including mass communication channels–TV, radio)
Separation of channels	Separate channels with no overlap	Integrated channels providing seamless retail experiences
Brand versus channel customer relationship focus	Customer-retail channel focus	Customer-retail channel-brand focus
Channel management	Per channel	Cross-channel objectives (e.g. overall retail experience, total sales over channels)

Source: Verhoef et al., 2015.[30]

Companies like the UK clothing and household goods firm Next have been managing the transition from multi-channel to omni-channel retailing (see Exhibit 9.6). Next provides a catalogue, the *Next Directory*, to customers, which can be browsed in the comfort of their own homes, containing product codes that are easily entered on the company's website or app. Purchases are then delivered direct to the customer's home or to their nearest store. If in-store delivery is being used, customers receive a text message to say their items have arrived, and stores also provide a point where unsuitable items are easily returned. However, trying to create seamless customer experiences is not without its challenges and companies will continue to invest in areas like data analytics and machine intelligence in order to try to make this happen.

Key retail marketing decisions

A retail outlet needs to be thought of as a brand involving the same set of decisions we discussed when we looked at branding in Chapter 6. Retailers need to anticipate and adapt to changing environmental circumstances, such as the growing role of information technology and changing customer tastes. However, there are a number of specific issues that relate to retailing, and are worthy of separate discussion.

Exhibit 9.6 Next combines its distribution channels and technology to provide a seamless experience for its customers.

Retail positioning

Retail positioning – as with all marketing decisions – involves the choice of target market and differential advantage. Targeting allows retailers to tailor their marketing mix (which includes product assortment, service levels, store location, prices and promotion) to the needs of their chosen customer segment. Differentiation provides a reason to shop at one outlet rather than another. A useful framework for creating a differential advantage has been proposed by Davies, who suggests that innovation in retailing can only come from novelty in the process offered to the shopper, or from novelty in the product or product assortment offered.[31] Discount supermarkets like Aldi and Lidl have been growing their market share by focusing on a limited assortment of own-label items sold at competitive prices (product innovation). The growth in e-commerce has changed the process of retailing, with many consumers choosing to do a significant proportion of their shopping from the comfort of their homes rather than visiting a retail outlet. The changing face of retail has also led to significant challenges for our cities, as illustrated in Critical Marketing Perspective 9.2.

Critical Marketing Perspective 9.2
Repositioning: the death and rebirth of the high street

Traditionally, the 'high street', or main streets in the centres of our towns and cities, were the heartbeat of urban spaces, filled with shopping outlets, leisure outlets such as cafés and bars, and most importantly of all, people. But the changing face of retailing has meant that this is no longer always the case. First, the growth of large, out-of-town shopping centres with a wide range of stores in one location and easy parking has meant less frequent visits to the high streets. The recent growth in online shopping has given rise to further pressure on high-street retailers faced with the dual challenge of meeting high rental costs at the same time as sales decline.

As a result, high streets have had to change and engage in repositioning strategies to enable them to identify potential competitive advantages. To do this, clear understanding is required of the current and future needs of the catchment population in order to recover their original vitality and viability. This may require a fundamental shift away from retailing to other functions and services that might thrive in the town centre.

Research across 10 UK towns that participated in the HSUK2020 project identified a strategy for repositioning that will involve shifting from external to internal objectives, to focus on: (1) liveability (repositioning centres as places to live); (2) town centre activity (repositioning offer, services and activities, anchors, e.g. markets, multi-functional); (3) connectivity (repositioning links, transport accessibility, integration of transport into place, infrastructure); and (4) demographic change (repositioning to meet the needs of a changing catchment of younger families, older generations).

Ultimately, the repositioning of a high street is no different from that of a brand, with insight required into understanding how people engage with the centres, as well as creating a fit between the competencies of the town and the needs and benefits sought by customers. With change can come challenges, but if managed efficiently, change can bring great opportunities.

Suggested reading: Millington and Ntouris, 2017[32]

Reflection: Reflect on how and where you shop. Can you think of a high street that has positioned itself as a 'must go to' place? Think of what this place has created to attract the consumer.

Store location

Conventional wisdom has it that the three factors critical to the success of a retailer are location, location and location. Convenience is an important issue for many shoppers, and so store location can have a major bearing on sales performance. Retailers have to decide on regional coverage, the towns and cities to target within regions, and the precise location to select within a given town or city. The choice of town or city will depend on such factors as correspondence with the retailer's chosen target market, the level of disposable income in the catchment area, the availability of suitable sites and the level of competition. The choice of a particular site may depend on the level of existing traffic (pedestrian and/or vehicular) passing the site, parking provision, access to the outlet for delivery vehicles, the presence of competition, planning restrictions and whether there is an opportunity to form new retailing centres with other outlets. For example, Starbucks has sought to locate its coffee shops on the side of the street most favoured by commuters going to work, based on the notion that consumers would not cross a busy street for a coffee. Also, two or more non-competing retailers (e.g. Sainsbury's and Boots) may agree to locate outlets together in an out-of-town centre to generate more pulling power than each could achieve individually. Having made that decision, the partners will look for suitable sites near their chosen town or city.

Product assortment

Retailers have to make a decision on the breadth and depth of their product assortment. Leading supermarkets typically carry in the region of 20,000 products and many have continued to widen their assortments to include everything from pet food products to clothing. Where retailers carry a diverse product assortment this is called 'scrambled merchandising'. Similarly, department stores offer a broad range of products, including toys, cosmetics, jewellery, clothes, electrical goods and household accessories. Other retailers begin with one product line and gradually broaden their product assortment to maximize revenue per customer. For example, petrol stations broadened their product range to include motor accessories and, more recently, confectionery, drinks, flowers and newspapers. Services like hot food and car washes offer much greater profit margins than the sale of petrol. A by-product of this may be to reduce customers' price sensitivity since selection of petrol station may be based on the availability of other products there rather than the fact that it offers the lowest price.

Own-label branding gives rise to another product decision. Major retailers may decide to sell a range of own-label products to complement national brands. Often the purchasing power of these large retail chains means that prices can be lower and yet profit margins higher than for competing national brands. This makes the activity an attractive proposition for many retailers. For example, the electrical retailer DGSi, which owns retail brands like Currys and PC World, has developed a range of own brands with the launch of Essentials, Logik, Advent and Sandstrom. As the name suggests, Essentials offers entry-level household items such as kettles and fridges, while Sandstrom is a premium range of TVs and other electrical goods.[33]

Price

Price is a key factor in store choice for some market segments. Consequently, some retailers major on price as their differential advantage. This requires vigilant cost control and massive buying power. A recent trend is towards the 'everyday low prices' favoured by retailers, rather than the higher prices supplemented by promotions that are supported by manufacturers. Retailers such as B&Q, the do-it-yourself discounter, maintain that customers prefer predictable low prices rather than occasional money-off deals, three-for-the-price-of-two offers and free gifts. Supermarket chains are also pressurizing suppliers to provide consistently low prices rather than temporary promotions. This action is consistent with the desire to position themselves on a low price platform. For example, in France, Carrefour has introduced a system whereby the bonuses of store managers are linked to whether prices are lower than those of comparable retailers. The importance of price competitiveness is reflected in an alliance of European food retailers called Associated Marketing Services (AMS). Based in the Netherlands, the group includes retailers such as Morrisons (UK), Ahold Delhaize (the Netherlands), Hagar (Iceland), Kesko (Finland), Migros (Switzerland), Musgrave Group (Ireland) and others, which have joined forces to foster co-operation in the areas of purchasing and marketing of brands. Their range of activities includes own branding, joint buying, the development of joint brands and services, as well as the exchange of information and skills.

Store atmosphere

Atmosphere is created by a combination of the design, colour and layout of a store. Both exterior and interior design affect atmosphere. External factors include architectural design, signs, window displays and use of colour, which create an identity for a retailer and attract customers. As we saw in Marketing in Action 9.1, Lush Cosmetics, for example, projects its environmentally caring image through the exterior design of its shops and through window displays that focus on environmental issues. Interior design also has a major impact on atmosphere. Store lighting, fixtures and fittings, and layout are important considerations (see Exhibit 9.7). Colour, sound and smell can affect mood. Department stores often place perfume counters near the entrance, supermarkets use the smell of freshly baked bread to attract customers, and upmarket shirt companies like Thomas Pink even pump the smell of freshly laundered linen around their stores. Clothing brands in particular often aim to have their own signature scent – Abercrombie & Fitch, for example. In addition, supermarkets often use music to create a relaxed atmosphere, whereas some boutiques use loud pop music to draw in their target customers. Sensory cues can have a powerful effect on behaviour. For example, the playing of French music has boosted sales of French wines in a wine shop, while fast-tempo music makes people eat and drink faster.

Multi-sensory marketing describes an approach adopted by retailers to appeal to as many senses as possible and is an important marketing tool in the battle with online retailers. There are challenges in ensuring that multi-sensory overload does not happen and that the combination of sensory cues is appropriate for the target market.[34]

As we saw in Chapter 7, the rise of experiential marketing has placed a significant focus on store atmospherics as retailers strive to create a shopping experience for consumers. Shoppers are considered to have three attention zones.[35] The first of these operates at a distance of 30 feet from the shopper, and requires the retailer to use a combination of sound, colour, scent and motion to attract potential buyers. At 10 feet,

Exhibit 9.7 Clothing retailer Thomas Pink is renowned for its use of multi-sensory marketing.

what is important is placement on a shelf and an ability to stand out from competitors, placing a premium on how well manufacturers influence the distribution process. And, at 3 feet, the consumer is already holding a potential choice or reaching out for it, so it is the look and feel of the product or its packaging that is important.

Physical distribution

Earlier in this chapter we examined channel strategy and management decisions that concern the choice of the correct outlets to provide product availability to customers in a cost-effective manner. Physical distribution decisions focus on the efficient movement of goods from producer to intermediaries and the consumer. Clearly, channel and physical distribution decisions are interrelated, although channel decisions tend to be made earlier. Physical distribution is defined as a set of activities concerned with the physical flows of materials, components and finished goods from producer to channel intermediaries and consumers. It is a business that has become increasingly complex as customers such as Walmart, Tesco and others extend their global reach. Allied to this is the huge growth in online retailing. According to Statista, in 2017, retail e-commerce sales worldwide amounted to US$2.3 trillion and are projected to grow to US$4.88 trillion in 2021. All of these products need to be stored, processed and delivered, creating a boom for companies involved in the physical distribution business. It has given rise to mergers between logistics companies such as that involving Exel and Tibbet & Britten, as companies seek to provide integrated solutions for their clients, ranging from warehouse management to home delivery.[36]

Distribution aims to provide intermediaries and customers with the right products, in the right quantities, in the right locations, at the right time. Distribution problems caused by, for example, a move to a new warehouse frequently impact on corporate performance. Physical distribution activities have been the subject of managerial attention for some time because of the potential for cost savings and improving customer service levels. Cost savings can be achieved by reducing inventory levels, using cheaper forms of transport and shipping in bulk rather than small quantities. For example, Benetton's blueprint for reviving its fortunes has been predicated on getting clothes from the factory to the shop rail faster, to enable it to compete with fast-fashion retailers like Zara and H&M.[37] Customer service levels can be improved by fast and reliable delivery, including just-in-time (JIT) delivery, holding high inventory levels so that customers have a wide choice and the chances of stock-outs are reduced, fast order processing, and ensuring that products arrive in the right quantities and quality. Physical distribution management concerns the balance between cost reduction and meeting customer service requirements. Trade-offs are often necessary. For example, low inventory and slow, cheaper transportation methods reduce costs but lower customer service levels and satisfaction.

As well as the trade-offs between physical distribution costs and customer service levels, there is the potential for conflict between elements of the physical distribution system itself. For example, low-cost containers may lower packaging costs but raise the cost of goods damaged in transit. This fact, and the need to co-ordinate order processing, inventory and transportation decisions, means that physical distribution needs to be managed as a system, with a manager overseeing the whole process.

The key elements of the physical distribution system are customer service, order processing, inventory control, warehousing, transportation and materials handling.

Customer service

It is essential to set customer service standards. For example, a customer service standard might be that 90 per cent of orders are delivered within 48 hours of receipt and 100 per cent are delivered within 72 hours. Higher customer service standards normally mean higher costs as inventory levels need to be higher. In some cases, customers value consistency in delivery time rather than speed. For example, a customer service standard of guaranteed delivery within five working days may be valued more than 60 per cent within two and 100 per cent within seven days. Customer service standards should be given considerable attention for they may be the differentiating factor between suppliers: they may be used as a key customer choice criterion. Methods of improving customer service standards include improving product availability, improving order cycle time, raising information levels and improving flexibility. An example of raising information levels is the kind of service now being provided online by courier companies like Federal Express and UPS, which offer their customers a facility whereby they can log on and get immediate updates on delivery status. However, in modern global supply chains, the outsourcing of activities means a lack of control, which can impact on customer service. For example, clothing companies that have outsourced production to countries in Southeast Asia, such as Bangladesh, have supplies frequently interrupted by monsoon flooding there.

 DHL Ad Insight: The 'Speed of Yellow' campaign illustrates the value the logistics company creates for its customers.

Order processing

This relates to the question of how orders are handled. A reduction in the time between a customer placing an order and receiving the goods may be achieved through careful analysis of the components that make up the order processing time. A computer link between the salesperson and the order department may be effective. Electronic data interchange can also speed order processing time by checking the customer's credit rating, and whether the goods are in stock, issuing an order to the warehouse, invoicing the customer and updating the inventory records. The grocery sector illustrates the challenge of order processing. An order to Tesco.com might comprise 60–80 items across three temperature regimes from a total range of around 25,000 products within 12–24 hours for delivery to customers within one- to two-hour time slots.

Inventory control

Inventory control deals with the question of how much inventory should be held. A balance has to be found between the need to have products in stock to meet customer demand and the costs incurred in holding large inventories. Having in stock every conceivable item a customer might order would normally be prohibitively expensive for companies marketing many items. Decisions also need to be taken about when to order new stocks. These order points are normally before stock levels reach zero because of the lead time between ordering and receiving inventory. The JIT inventory system is designed to reduce lead times so that the order point (the stock level at which re-ordering takes place), and overall inventory levels for production items, are low. The more variable the lead time between ordering and receiving stocks and the greater the fluctuation in customer demand, the higher the order point. This is because of the uncertainty caused by the variability, leading to the need for **safety (buffer) stocks** in case lead times are unpredictably long or customer demand unusually high. How much to order depends on the cost of holding stock and order-processing costs. Orders can be small and frequent, or large and infrequent. Small, frequent orders raise order-processing costs but reduce inventory carrying costs; large, infrequent orders raise inventory costs but lower order-processing expenditure.

Warehousing

This part of the distribution chain involves all the activities required in the storing of goods between the time they are produced and the time they are transported to the customer. These activities include breaking bulk, making up product assortments for delivery to customers, storage and loading. Storage warehouses hold goods for moderate or long time periods, whereas distribution centres operate as central locations for the fast movement of goods. Retailing organizations use regional distribution centres where suppliers deliver products in bulk. These shipments are broken down into loads that are then quickly transported to retail outlets. Distribution centres are usually highly automated, with computer-controlled machinery facilitating the movement of goods (see Marketing in Action 9.3). A computer reads orders and controls the fork-lift trucks that gather goods and move them to loading bays. Further technological advances are likely to have a significant impact on warehousing and the movement of goods through the supply chain. Warehousing strategy involves the determination of the location and the number of warehouses or distribution centres to be used. The trend is towards a smaller number of ever larger warehouses. For example, the UK retailer Boots closed its 17 regional distribution centres in favour of a £70 million automated warehouse in Nottingham. The Amazon fulfilment centre in Scotland is the largest warehouse in the UK measuring 1 million square feet. At the extreme, some retailers are seeking single distribution centres for the whole of Europe, with locations such as Moissy-Cramayel in France measuring the size of 350 football pitches.[38]

Marketing in Action 9.3
Wehkamp: physical distribution in an online world

Critical Thinking: Below is an overview of the activities related to the distribution practices of Wehkamp, one of the leading Dutch e-commerce platforms. Read it, and review the physical distribution system of one of your favourite online stores.

Wehkamp is a Dutch mail-order company and online department store owned by Apax Partners. The company has approximately 2 million regular customers and ships 10 million products per year. It carries a product assortment of 400,000 items across fashion, living and sleeping, garden and DIY, consumer electronics, sports and leisure, and heath and beauty. It has as its mission to 'make the lives of all families in the Netherlands more beautiful and easier'.

Mechanization has always been central to the growth of the business, whether this has been in the management of its warehouses or its customer databases, which have been built up over the years. In 2015, it opened a new, state-of-the-art distribution centre in Zwolle in the presence of Dutch King Willem Alexander. The new building is a fully automated e-commerce centre, creating a multi-functional and flexible distribution site measuring more than 60,000 m^2. The new building places an emphasis on environmental considerations, partly using sustainable materials as well as 100 per cent LED lighting. In addition, charging stations were installed for electric cars, along with 17,000 solar panels on the roof, generating the energy to run the centre.

Fast customer service is central to the Wehkamp proposition. Within 30 minutes of placing an order the package is ready for shipment. The new distribution centre is equipped with the latest technologies to make ordering and fulfilling customer requests better, faster and more accurate. The company's CEO Gert van de Weerdhof had said that, 'Same-day delivery is one of the most important elements that we will offer to all our customers. In addition, the handling of return shipments is faster and easier. Thanks to the latest automation in the distribution centre, we can offer our customers a state-of-the-art service and the chance of errors is reduced to almost zero.'

Combining the desire to provide a high level of service with a concern for the environmental impact of physical distribution, Wehkamp delivers on Sundays as well as fulfilling some orders by bicycle.

Transportation

This refers to the means by which products will be transported; the five major modes are rail, road, air, water and pipeline. Railways are efficient at transporting large, bulky freight on land over long distances, and are often used to transport coal, chemicals, oil, aggregates and nuclear flasks. Rail is more environmentally friendly than road, but the major problem with it is lack of flexibility. Motorized transport by road has the advantage of flexibility because of direct access to companies and warehouses. This means that lorries can transport goods from supplier to receiver without unloading en route. However, the growth of road transport in Europe, and particularly the UK, has received considerable criticism because of increased traffic congestion, damage done to roads by heavy juggernauts and the impact on the environment. The key advantages of air freight are its speed and long-distance capabilities. Its speed means that it is often used to transport perishable goods and emergency deliveries. Its major disadvantages are high cost, and the need to transport goods by road to and from air terminals. Water transportation is slow but inexpensive. Inland transportation is usually associated with bulky, low-value, non-perishable goods such as coal, ore, grain, steel and petroleum. Ocean-going ships carry a wider range of products. When the cost benefits of international sea transportation outweigh the speed advantage of air freight, water shipments may be chosen. But some industries, such as fashion retailing, have seen production move from low-cost countries like China to Eastern Europe and Turkey because it takes 22 days by water to reach the UK from China compared with five days from Turkey. So, although the cost of production is lower in China, the fast turnaround of fashion items makes sea transportation unappealing. Finally, pipelines are a dependable and low-maintenance form of transportation for liquids and gases such as crude petroleum, water and natural gas.

Materials handling

Materials handling involves the activities related to the movement of products in the producer's plant, warehouses and transportation depots. Modern storage facilities tend to be of just one storey, allowing a high level of automation. In some cases robots are used to conduct materials-handling tasks. Lowering the human element in locating inventory and assembling orders has reduced error and increased the speed of these operations. For example, the pharmaceuticals distributor Cahill May Roberts has replaced a paper-based system with Vocollect voice technology, whereby material handlers speak to computers to confirm the products that they have collected rather than making paper records. It distributes in the region of 180,000 product units per day to pharmacies in Ireland and accurate records are critical because of the nature of the products being dealt with.[39] Two key developments in materials handling are unit handling and containerization. Unit handling achieves efficiency by combining multiple packages on pallets that can be moved by fork-lift trucks. Containerization involves the combination of large quantities of goods (e.g. car components) in a single large container. Once sealed, such containers can easily be transferred from one form of transport to another.

Personal selling

As we noted earlier in the chapter, direct distribution is a very common feature of business-to-business and service industries. A key stage in these distribution channels is the interaction between the company's salespeople and the customer. In industrial marketing, more than 70 per cent of the marketing budget is usually spent on the sales force. This generally involves face-to-face contact with a customer, permitting a direct interaction between buyer and seller. This two-way communication means that the seller can identify the specific needs and problems of the buyer and tailor the sales presentation in the light of this knowledge. The particular concerns of the buyer can also be dealt with on a one-to-one basis.

The make-up of the personal selling function is changing, however. Organizations are reducing the size of their sales forces in the face of greater buyer concentration, moves towards centralized buying, and in recognition of the high costs of maintaining a field sales team. The concentration of buying power into fewer hands has also fuelled the move towards relationship management, often through key account selling, whereby a sales team may be responsible for a lead customer, such as a large supermarket chain for example. This involves the use of a small number of dedicated sales teams, which service the accounts of major buyers as opposed to having a large number of salespeople. Instead of sending salespeople out on the road, many companies now collect a large proportion of their sales through inbound and outbound sales, either online or via telephone.

The three main types of salespeople are order-takers, order-creators and order-getters. Order-takers respond to already committed customers such as a sales assistant in a convenience store or a delivery salesperson. Order-creators have traditionally been found in industries like healthcare, where the sales task is not to close the sale but to persuade the medical representative to prescribe or specify the seller's products. Order-getters are those in selling jobs where the major objective is to persuade the customer to make a direct purchase. They include consumer salespeople such as those selling utilities like broadband or electricity, through to organizational salespeople, who often work in teams where products may be highly technical and negotiations complex.

Personal selling skills

While the primary responsibility of a salesperson is to increase sales, there are a number of additional enabling activities carried out by many salespeople, including **prospecting**, maintaining customer records, providing service, handling complaints, relationship management and self-management. Prospecting involves searching for and calling on potential customers. Prospects can be identified from several sources, including talking to existing customers and searching trade directories and the business press. Customer record-keeping is an important activity for all repeat-call salespeople because customer information is one of the keys to improving service and generating loyalty. Salespeople should be encouraged and rewarded for gathering and inputting customer information into CRM systems. Providing service to customers – including, for example, advice on ways of improving productivity and handling customer complaints – can also be a key sales force activity. In general, there has been a rise in the number of salespeople involved in relationship management roles with large organizational customers. Trust is an important part of relationship development and is achieved through a high frequency of contact, ensuring promises are kept and reacting quickly and effectively to problems (see Marketing in Action 9.4). Finally, given the flexibility of the salesperson's job, many are

Marketing in Action 9.4
Cisco's brave new world

Critical Thinking: Below is a review of some of Cisco's marketing efforts in the Middle East. Read it and critically reflect on the nature of modern personal selling.

Cisco Systems, the networking giant, sees a major part of its future growth coming from massive construction projects in the Middle East. One example is the creation of King Abdullah Economic City (KAEC) in Saudi Arabia. By 2020, the Saudis expect 2 million people to be living in a future metropolis supported by some of the most advanced technology that money can buy. All told, King Abdullah plans to build four brand-new cities and upgrade the country's infrastructure at a cost of US$6 billion over the coming years.

To tap in to this vast potential, Cisco hired a well-connected local person to head the business in the country. He, in turn, hired salespeople and engineers and got Cisco involved in major government projects. For the KAEC project, senior Cisco executives played host to the king for a demonstration of Cisco technology that allowed a person elsewhere to appear on stage as a holographic image. They realize, though, that Cisco is not just selling technology (a product feature). The real benefit is that it can help countries such as Saudi Arabia modernize their economies and become leaders in the internet age. The company argues that, by investing in the internet infrastructure that Cisco sells, these governments can better educate their people, improve healthcare and boost national productivity.

To achieve this, Cisco provides consulting services to help government officials work out how best to use the internet, and pays for training centres to produce the technicians to implement such plans. Cisco is helping the leaders of countries like Saudi Arabia imagine the future, to bring about 'country transformations' and brainstorm big ideas. One example was the call to Cisco to help with

(continued)

a new broadband network for Sudair City, but a Cisco executive saw the potential of the city as a hub for vast computer data centres, based on its cheap electricity rates. The electricity bill is often the biggest expense in running such centres, which are increasingly important for internet companies like Google and Amazon. The idea was well received and helped Cisco secure a U$280-million contract to create the underlying fibre-optic network for Sudair City.

Based on: Burrows, 2008[40]

required to practise self-management, including decisions on call frequencies and journey routing, for example. In order to develop personal selling skills it is useful to distinguish seven phases of the selling process (see Figure 9.4). We will now discuss each of these in turn.

Preparation

The preparation carried out prior to a sales visit can reap dividends by enhancing confidence and performance when the salesperson is face to face with the customer. Some situations cannot be prepared for: the unexpected question or unusual objection, for example. But many customers face similar situations, and certain questions and objections will be raised repeatedly. Preparation can help the salesperson respond to these recurring situations. Salespeople will benefit from gaining knowledge of their own and competitors' products, by understanding buyer behaviour, by having clear sales call objectives and by having planned their sales presentation.

The opening

It is important for salespeople to consider how to create a favourable initial impression with customers as this can often affect later perceptions. Good first impressions can be gained by adopting a businesslike approach, being friendly, but not overly familiar, being attentive to detail, observing common courtesies like waiting to be asked to sit down and by showing the customer appreciation for having taken the time to see you.

Need and problem identification

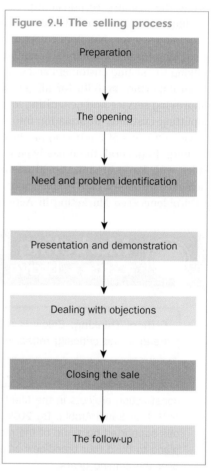

Figure 9.4 The selling process

- Preparation
- The opening
- Need and problem identification
- Presentation and demonstration
- Dealing with objections
- Closing the sale
- The follow-up

Consumers will buy a product because they have a 'problem' that gives rise to a 'need'. Therefore the first task is to identify the needs and problems of each customer. Only by doing this can a salesperson connect with each customer's situation. Effective need and problem identification requires the development of questioning and listening skills. The hallmark of inexperienced salespeople is that they do all the talking; successful salespeople know how to get the *customer* to do most of the talking.

Presentation and demonstration

It is the presentation and demonstration that offers the opportunity for the salesperson to convince customers that they can supply the solution to their problem. It should focus on **customer benefits** rather than **product features**. The salesperson should continue to ask questions during the presentation to ensure that the customer has understood what he or she has said, and to check that what the salesperson has talked about really is of importance to the customer. This can be achieved by asking questions like 'Is that the kind of thing you are looking for?'

Dealing with objections

Salespeople rarely close a sale without first having to overcome customer objections. Although objections can cause problems, they should not be regarded negatively since they highlight issues that are important to the buyer. The secret of dealing with objections is to handle both the substantive and emotional aspects. The substantive part is to do with the objection itself. If the customer objects to the product's price, the salesperson needs to use convincing arguments to show that the price is not too high. But it is a fact of human personality that the argument that is supported by the greater weight of evidence does not always win since people resent being proven wrong. Therefore, salespeople need to recognize the emotional aspects of objection handling. Under no circumstances should the buyer be caused to lose face or be antagonized during this process. Two ways of minimizing this risk are to listen to the objection without interruption and to employ the 'agree and counter' technique, where the salesperson agrees with the buyer but then puts forward an alternative point of view.

Closing the sale

The inexperienced salesperson will sometimes imagine that an effective presentation followed by the convincing handling of any objections should guarantee that the buyer will ask for the product without the seller needing to work to close the sale. This does occasionally happen but, more often, it is necessary for the salesperson to take the initiative. This is because many buyers still have doubts in their minds that may cause them to wish to delay the decision to purchase. Closing techniques include simply asking for the order, summarizing the key points and asking for the order, or offering a special deal to close the sale (the concession close).

The follow-up

Once an order has been placed there may be a temptation for the salesperson to move on to other customers, neglecting the follow-up visit. However, this can be a great mistake since most companies rely on repeat business. If problems arise, customers have every right to believe that the salesperson was interested only in the order and not their complete satisfaction. By checking that there are no problems with delivery, installation, product use and training (where applicable), the follow-up can show that the salesperson really does care about the customer.

Sales management

Because of the unique nature of the selling job, sales management is a challenging activity. For example, many salespeople spend a great deal of their time in the field, separated from their managers, while others may suffer repeated rejections in trying to close sales, causing them to lose confidence. Therefore, the two main aspects of the sales manager's job are designing the sales force and managing the sales force.

Designing the sales force

The critical design decisions are determining sales force size and organizing the sales force. The most practical method for deciding the number of salespeople required is called the 'workload approach'. It is based on the calculation of the total annual calls required per year divided by the average calls per year that can be expected from one salesperson.[41]

There are three alternative approaches to organizing the sales force. A *geographic* structure is where the sales area is broken down into territories based on workload and potential, and a salesperson is assigned to each one to sell all of the product range. This provides a simple, unambiguous definition of each salesperson's sales territory, and the proximity to customers encourages the development of personal relationships. A *product* structure might be effective where a company has a diverse product range selling to different customers (or at least different people within a given organization). A *customer-based* structure is where sales forces are organized on the basis of market segments, account sizes or new versus existing account lines. This structure enables salespeople to acquire in-depth knowledge of particular customer groups.

A growing form of customer-based sales force organization is **key account management**, which reflects the increasing concentration of buying power into fewer but larger customers. These are serviced by a key account sales force comprising senior salespeople, who develop close personal relationships with customers, can handle sophisticated sales arguments and are skilled in the art of negotiation. A number of advantages are claimed for a key account structure, including that it enables close working relationships with customers, improved communication and co-ordination, better follow-up on sales and service, more in-depth penetration of the DMU, higher sales and the provision of an opportunity for advancement for career salespeople.

Managing the sales force

The following elements are involved in sales force management: setting specific salesperson objectives; recruitment and selection; training; **sales force motivation** and compensation; and **sales force evaluation**. These activities have been shown to improve salesperson performance, indicating the key role that sales managers play as facilitators, helping salespeople to perform better. Sales objectives are usually set in sales terms (sales quotas) but, increasingly, profit targets are being used, reflecting the need to guard against sales being bought cheaply by excessive discounting. The importance of recruiting high-calibre salespeople cannot be overestimated. A study of sales force practice asked sales managers the following question: 'If you were to put your most successful salesperson into the territory of one of your average salespeople and made no other changes, what increase in sales would you expect after, say, two years?'[42] The most commonly stated increase was 16–20 per cent, and one-fifth of all sales managers said they would expect an increase of more than 30 per cent.

Sales training should include not only product knowledge, but also skills development. Training programmes typically include providing knowledge about the company, its products and competitors, as well as sales techniques and relationship management, and work organisation. A deep understanding of salespeople as individuals, their personalities and value systems, is the basis for effective motivation. Managers can motivate their sales staff by getting to know what each salesperson values and what they are striving for, increasing the responsibility given to salespeople in mundane jobs, providing targets that are attainable and challenging, and recognizing that rewards can be both financial and non-financial (e.g. praise). In terms of financial rewards, sales staff can be paid either a fixed salary, commission only or on a salary-plus commission basis. Salaries provide security while commissions are an incentive to sell more as they are tied directly to sales levels. Great care must be taken in designing commission and bonus structures. For example, a Chrysler car dealership in the USA found that monthly sales for April were significantly down because salespeople who knew that they would not hit their targets for that month were encouraging customers to delay sales until May in hope of getting the May bonus.[43]

Sales force evaluation gathers the information required to check whether targets are being achieved, and provides raw information that will help guide training and motivation. By identifying the strengths and weaknesses of individual salespeople, training can be focused on the areas in need of development, and incentives can be aimed at weak spots such as poor prospecting performance. Often, performance will be measured on the basis of quantitative criteria such as sales revenues, profits generated or number of calls. However, it is also important to use qualitative criteria such as sales skills acquired, customer relationships, product knowledge and self-management.

Summary

In this chapter we have examined the key issue of delivering products and services to customers. In particular, the following aspects were addressed.

1. There are important differences in the structure of consumer, industrial and service channels. Consumer channels tend to be longer and involve more channel partners (intermediaries), while many industrial and service channels are direct to the customer.

2. Channel strategy involves three key decisions, namely channel selection, choice about the distribution intensity and channel integration. These decisions must be aligned with the firm's overall marketing strategy. For example, positioning decisions may drive the number and type of channel members selected to distribute a product and the extent to which they are controlled.

3. The key channel management issues are the selection and motivation of middlemen (intermediaries), providing them with training, evaluating their performance and resolving any channel conflict issues that may arise. Digitalization that reduces the number of intermediaries may increase the chance of channel conflict. Effective support for channel members is often necessary to achieve marketing objectives.

4. There is a diverse range of retail types, including supermarkets, department stores, speciality shops, discount houses, convenience stores and finally online (e-commerce) retailing, which has grown rapidly in recent years.

5. The key retail marketing decisions include retail positioning, store location, product assortment, price and store atmosphere. Many retailers are strong brands in their own right and need to be managed as such.

6. Physical distribution concerns decisions relating to customer service, order processing, inventory control, warehousing, transportation and materials handling, which impact on the efficiency and effectiveness of the supply chain. Technology has changed the distribution process, leading to enhanced performance, increased flexibility and productivity, better warehouse management, and improved traffic management and delivery.

7. Personal selling is an important activity and salespeople are required to develop a range of selling skills, including preparation for the sale, opening the sale, identifying customer needs and problems, presenting and demonstrating, dealing with objections, closing the sale and following up. Sales management involves designing and managing the sales team.

Study questions

1. A friend of yours who has been pursuing pottery as a hobby has just formed a business selling a range of gift items. Advise the founder on her options for distributing the company's products.

2. Evaluate the three distribution intensity options that are available to an organization. In what kinds of circumstances might each be used?

3. Describe situations that can lead to conflict between channel members. What can be done to avoid and resolve conflict?

4. Discuss the impact of the growth of online retailing on other retail formats.

5. Discuss the reasons why more and more distribution channels are being characterized by a small number of large central distribution centres rather than by a large number of relatively small outlets.

6. Visit www.starbucks.co.uk and www.costa.co.uk. Compare and contrast these two coffee chains in terms of the major retail marketing decisions such as retail positioning, product assortment, store location and store atmospherics.

7. Discuss the differences between multi-channel and omni-channel marketing.

8. Imagine you are working as a salesperson for a household goods company selling items such as fridge freezers, furniture and bedding, and televisions, for example. Pick one product category and write down five objections to purchase and how you would respond to them.

Suggested reading

Anderson, C. (2006) *The Long Tail: The New Economics of Culture and Commerce*. London: Random House Books.

Chevas, J.M. (2018) The transformation of professional selling: implications for leading the modern sales organization, *Industrial Marketing Management*, 69: 198–208.

Jerath, K. and Zhang, J. (2010) Store within a store, *Journal of Marketing Research*, 47(4): 748–63.

Kumar, V., Anand, A. and Song, H. (2017) Future of retailer profitability: an organising framework, *Journal of Retailing*, 93(1): 96–119.

Morschett, D. (2011) Disintermediation in distribution channels: a transaction cost-based analysis of wholesalers, *European Retail Research*, 25(11): 93–112.

Rigby, D. (2011) The future of shopping, *Harvard Business Review*, 89(12): 64–75.

Spence, C., Puccinelli, N.M., Grewal, D. and Roggeveen, A.L. (2014) Store atmospherics: a multisensory perspective, *Psychology and Marketing*, 31(7): 472–88.

Verhoef, P., Kannan, P.K. and Inman, J. (2015) From multi-channel retailing to omni-channel retailing: introduction to the Special Issue on Multi-Channel Retailing, *Journal of Retailing*, 91(2): 174–81.

References

1. **Domino's company website** (2018) DRU – Domino's Robotic Unit. Available at https://www.dominos.com.au/inside-dominos/technology/dru (accessed 15 May 2018); **Newsy** (2018) Domino's to deliver to even more locations like the beach. Available at https://www.newsy.com/stories/domino-s-to-deliver-to-even-more-locations-like-the-beach/ (accessed 25 May 2018); **Statista** (2018) Domino's Pizza – Statistics & Facts. Available at https://www.statista.com/topics/1688/dominos-pizza/ (accessed 10 May 2018).

2. **Hobbs, T.** (2017) Trends for 2018: retailers will face a tougher test as big brands dominate, *MarketingWeek.com*. Available at www.marketingweek.com/2017/12/11/trends-2018-retail-consolidation/ (accessed 31 May 2018).

3. **Hammett, E.** (2018) Sainsbury's and Asda to operate 'dual brand strategy' in merger that creates new market leader, *MarketingWeek.com*. Available at www.marketingweek.com/2018/04/30/sainsburys-and-asda-agree-merger/ (accessed 6 June 2018).

4. **Fahy, J.** and **Taguchi, F.** (1995) Reassessing the Japanese distribution system, *Sloan Management Review*, Winter.

5. **Anonymous** (2011) The Co-op strikes back, *The Economist*, 29 January, 58.

6. **Narus, J.A.** and **Anderson, J.C.** (1986) Industrial distributor selling: the roles of outside and inside sales, *Industrial Marketing Management*, 15: 55–62.

7. **Anonymous** (2008) Shock to the system, *The Economist*, 2 February, 67–8.

8. **Rosenbloom, B.** (1987) *Marketing Channels: A Management View*. Hinsdale, IL: Dryden, 160.

9. **Leob, W.** (2017) Lush beauty: taking the industry by storm thanks to young love, *Forbes.com*. Available at www.forbes.com/sites/walterloeb/2017/04/07/lush-beauty-taking-the-industry-by-storm-thanks-to-young-love/#3adf81d011c5 (accessed 12 May 2018).

10. **Purkayastha, D.** and **Fernando, R.** (2007) Innovative marketing strategies of Lush Fresh Handmade Cosmetics, *ICMR Centre for Management Research*, Case Number 507-072-1.

11. **Laurance, B.** (1993) MMC in bad odour over Superdrug ruling, *Guardian*, 12 November, 18.

12. **Jack, A.** (2007) Wholesalers to seek injunction on Pfizer's drug distribution plan, *Financial Times*, 1 March, 4.

13. **Helmore, E.** (1997) Restaurant kings, or just silly burgers? *Observer*, 8 June, 5.

14. **Hopkinson, G.C.** and **Hogarth Scott, S.** (1999) Franchise relationship quality: microeconomic explanations, *European Journal of Marketing*, 33(9/10): 827–43.

15. **Rosenbloom, B.** (1987) *Marketing Channels: A Management View*. Hinsdale, IL: Dryden, 160.

16. **Shipley, D.D., Cook, D.** and **Barnett, E.** (1989) Recruitment, motivation, training and evaluation of overseas distributors, *European Journal of Marketing*, 23(2): 79–93.

17. **Shipley, D.D.** and **Prinja, S.** (1988) The services and supplier choice influences of industrial distributors, *Service Industries Journal*, 8(2): 176–87; **Webster, F.E.** (1976) The role of the industrial distributor in marketing strategy, *Journal of Marketing*, 40, 10–16.

18. **Pegram, R.** (1965) *Selecting and Evaluating Distributors*. New York: National Industrial Conference Board, 109–25; **Shipley, D.D., Cook, D.** and **Barnett, E.** (1989) Recruitment, motivation, training and evaluation of overseas distributors, *European Journal of Marketing*, 23(2): 79–93.

19. **Coyle, D.** (2004) Budget Travel accuses agents of blacklisting, *Irish Times*, 16 November, 16; **Coyle, D.** (2005) Challenges circle overhead for tour operator, *Irish Times Business*, 7 January, 22.

20. **Butler, S.** (2016) Tesco runs short on Marmite and household brands in price row with Unilever, *Guardian.com*. Available at www.theguardian.com/business/2016/oct/12/tesco-running-low-key-unilever-brands-price-row-supplier-supermarket-falling-pound (accessed 11 June 2016).

21. **Roderick, L.** (2016) Tesco versus Unilever: who won the Marmite price row? *MarketingWeek.com*. Available at www.marketingweek.com/2016/10/13/tesco-versus-unilever-who-will-win-the-marmite-row/ (accessed 9 June 2016).

22. **Slattery, L.** (2007) Concern at merger plan for distributor Eason, *Irish Times*, 29 January, 18.

23. **Sexton, P.** (2005) A music sales storm is brewing in a coffee shop, *Financial Times*, 21 June, 14.

24. **Hardy, K.G.** and **Magrath, A.J.** (1988) Ten ways for manufacturers to improve distribution management, *Business Horizons*, November–December, 68.

25. **Krishnan, T.V.** and **Soni, H.** (1997) Guaranteed profit margins: a demonstration of retailer power, *International Journal of Research in Marketing*, 14: 35–56.

26. **Weber, J.** and **Urick, M.** (2017) Examining the millennials' ethical profile: assessing demographic variations in their personal value orientations. *Business and Society Review*, 122, 469–506.

27. **Neslin, S. A., Grewal, D., Leghorn, R., Shankar, V., Teerling, M.L., Thomas, J.S.** and **Verhoef, P.C.** (2006) Challenges and opportunities in multichannel customer management, *Journal of Service Research*, 9(2): 95–112.

28. **Brynjolfsson, E., Hu, Y.J.** and **Rahman, M.S.** (2013) Competing in the age of omnichannel retailing, *Sloan Management Review*, 54(4): 23–39.

29. **Verhoef, P.C., Kannan, P.K.** and **Inman, J.J.** (2015) From multi-channel retailing to omni-channel retailing: introduction to the Special Issue on Multi-Channel Retailing, *Journal of Retailing*, 91(2): 174–81.

30. **Verhoef, P.C., Kannan, P.K.** and **Inman, J.J.** (2015) From multi-channel retailing to omni-channel retailing: introduction to the Special Issue on Multi-Channel Retailing, *Journal of Retailing*, 91(2): 174–81.

31. **Davies, G.** (1992) Innovation in retailing, *Creativity and Innovation Management*, 1(4): 230.

32. **Millington, S.** and **Ntouris, N.** (2017) Repositioning the high street: evidence and reflection from the UK, *Journal of Place Management and Development*, 10(4): 364–379.

33. **Baker, R.** (2010) DSGi ready to do battle with consumer brands, *MarketingWeek.co.uk*, 3 August.

34. **Spence, C., Puccinelli, N.M., Grewal, D.** and **Roggeveen, A.E.** (2014) Store atmospherics: a multisensory perspective, *Psychology & Marketing*, 31(7): 472–88.

35. **Roberts, K.** (2006) *The Lovemarks Effect: Winning in the Consumer Revolution*. New York: Powerhouse Books.

36. **Felsted, A.** and **Goff, S.** (2004) Going global is crucial to deliver goods, *Financial Times*, 17 June, 27.

37. **Anonymous** (2003) Benetton starts 'Dring' drive, *Financial Times*, 10 December, 33.

38. **Pickard, J.** (2005) Growing trend sees warehouses swell, *Financial Times*, 17 August, 25.

39. **Lillington, K.** (2008) Giving voice to new technology, *Irish Times Health Supplement*, 29 January, 4.

40. **Burrows, P.** (2008) Cisco's brave new world, *Business Week*, 24 November, 57–68.

41. **Talley, W.J.** (1961) How to design sales territories, *Journal of Marketing*, 25(3): 16–28.

42. **PA Consultants** (1979) *Sales Force Practice Today: A Basis for Improving Performance*. Cookham: Institute of Marketing.

43. **Griffith, V.** (2001) Targets that distort a company's aim, *Financial Times*, 21 November, 18.

Omni-channel marketing at Danske Bank: using technology to provide great customer service

Danske Bank is a Danish-based banking group whose customer service roots go back almost 150 years. Although it is the largest bank in Denmark, and has operations in 16 countries, Danske likes to keep things simple. Its headquarters have been located at the same address in Copenhagen since 1871, and its name literally translates into 'Danish bank' in English.

Still struggling with the aftermath of the great financial crisis of 2008, the bank went through a turbulent period in 2012 and 2013. With a highly publicized row with the Danish Financial Supervisory Authority, and customers complaining about newly instituted current account fees (the bank would lose almost 120,000 customers in the year after instituting a new pricing structure), the company needed to act fast. In an attempt to regain its balance, Danske Bank announced in 2013 that it would pay more attention to strategy execution, as well as become more customer focused.

Setting priorities

A key element of that renewed customer focus was upper management's realization that people wanted banking to be fast and simple, with the expectation that they should be able to perform, from start to finish, any kind of transaction they wanted on any device or platform they wanted. More challenging for Danske was the conclusion that it would have to adapt its products and services to the way people used technology in their everyday lives, and not the other way around. Furthermore, any solution that the company came up with would have to perform seamlessly across all of the different ways in which people access banking services. Fortunately, this task was not as daunting as it sounded. Danske has a long history of being an innovator, having been the first bank in Europe to introduce the concept of safety deposit boxes in 1881, as well as being the first in Denmark to connect all of its branches digitally by computers in 1973.

Senior managers at Danske talked in terms of wanting to optimize the customer's financial journey. And the solution they arrived at was an omni-channel marketing strategy that would let people bank how, when and where they wanted, allowing them to use whatever digital (or physical) platform they desired. Danske's renewed effort at customer satisfaction was helped in large part by software and technology provided by SAS Institute. Thanks to a co-ordinated initiative, Danske's customers would be able to do their banking by post, internet, mobile phone app, a telephone conversation with a customer representative or a face-to-face meeting at one of the bank's physical branches. This allows almost 5 million retail customers to get the service they need in the fashion they want it.

Omni-channel + technology = great customer service!

Early initiatives of this new omni-channel strategy were features that allowed people to do banking on their mobile phones and tablets. But one of the most successful strategic actions was the introduction of 'Mobilepay', a mobile phone app designed to make transferring money as easy as sending a text message. Since its introduction in May 2013 it has gained almost 4 million subscribers in Denmark alone. Originally designed for P2P (person to person) payments, the app is now ubiquitous, with more than half a billion money transfers being made since its activation. It has been estimated that, in its first year, Mobilepay was able to achieve the same number of users that previously, before the invention of the smartphone, would have taken the bank 10 years to acquire. In fact, the success of Mobilepay came as such a shock to the company that management created a team to travel the world looking for the latest trends in technology and consumer behaviour (lest a competitor beat them to it).

But Danske also realized that it needed to get back to customer service basics if it wanted to turn around its operations. In the same year that it rolled out Mobilepay it also introduced a traditional customer loyalty programme that provided improved pricing and interest rates based on a customer's volume of business with the bank. For Danske Bank to provide the best levels of customer service possible, it would apparently require something old and something new.

Senior management says that its omni-channel marketing strategy is 'designed to travel across borders, giving us a competitive edge in new markets because of synergies and a strong, agile organization'. Danske Bank has an advantageous position in its home market of Denmark, as well as in Finland and Northern Ireland. But it would be seen as an underdog in neighbouring Norway and Sweden. Will its customer-centric multi-platform banking approach help it to successfully expand in competing markets? Danske believes the answer is 'yes'.

In a constant effort to improve the customer service experience, Danske Bank announced in April 2018 that it was forming a partnership with Swedish FinTech developer Minna Technologies. This new arrangement will give Danske's customers access to a 'Subscription Manager' solution that will be integrated into a new mobile banking app. This new service will allow customers to manage all of their online bills, making it easier to cancel and change service providers, as well as negotiate better deals to save money on their monthly bills. Lars Malmberg, global head of business development at Danske Bank, says 'This is a good example of an innovative, digital solution that we believe can make a difference for our customers, and which is closely aligned with our ambition of giving customers full control and overview of their finances.' Not content to stop there, Danske Bank has also announced plans to provide a new function to its mobile banking app that will allow customers to check on all of their accounts at different banks using the bank's app. This is on top of a 'pocket money' app that the bank released in 2017, a digital feature specifically designed for parents with children between 8 and 12 years old. The app allows parents to transfer money to an ATM card that their children can then use to withdraw pocket money for small purchases.

Head of personal banking, Thomas Mitchell, says, 'Many of our customers have requested an easier way of handling pocket money. Parents want to transfer money digitally and to monitor their children's spending. Many also look for a tool that allows their children to check their pocket money in the bank and to spend the money in the real world. We have developed a user-friendly app and a pocket money card, so that children can safely practise managing their finances, with the parents watching from the sidelines.'

Perhaps even more ambitious (some might say frightening) is the bank's decision to use artificial intelligence (AI) to better understand its customers' needs through its own in-house start-up called Advanced Analytics. This internal unit, created in 2015, uses machine learning techniques and predictive models to analyze customer behaviour at the individual level. The bank says that, by studying massive amounts of data, it can find out how customers wish to be contacted (by telephone, post, email, etc.), thus improving the effectiveness of its omni-channel marketing initiatives by up to a factor of four. AI also allows Danske to anticipate a customer's needs. For instance, if someone's personal situation changes (e.g. they take a new job) the bank's technology will now know to contact that person and offer them tailored financial services.

An example of these advanced analytics in action was when Danske successfully identified unmarried customers with high incomes who were at an age when people usually start families. These customers are extremely attractive because they are at a point where their financial needs can suddenly increase (i.e. they might be getting ready to buy a house, furniture, a car, etc.). Traditionally, the bank did not have much contact with these people – being single and wealthy, they most likely had more exciting things to do than talk to a bank manager. By analysing data such as their financial transactions, age, salary, credit history, etc., the bank was able to zero in on this lucrative cohort and reach out to them. Not only that, Danske also had the capability to do it by whatever banking platform or channel the customer preferred. The results were incredible: 9 per cent of the targeted group (a very successful response rate in marketing terms) actually met with a financial adviser. This performance was far more effective than that usually seen using more traditional marketing methods.

Danske's analytical models can also predict when a customer is getting ready to close an account (a phenomenon in the industry known as 'churn'). By analysing data relating to events associated with churn, the bank can create a profile of an 'at risk customer'. This then prompts Danske to reach out to the client, once more on one of the many channels and platforms available, and make a genuine effort to find a solution to the customer's lack of satisfaction with the bank. In the first three months after launching the customer retention initiative, 20,000 contacts were made, reducing churn by 70 per cent.

Machine learning has also improved Danske's anti-fraud efforts. The bank used to get 1,200 false indications a day for fraud when monitoring transactions. Usually, it would take only a few minutes to resolve each problem, but over time it added up to a huge cost and inconvenience. Thanks to advanced machine learning techniques, the bank was able to reduce the incidences of false positives by roughly 60 per cent, and improve the rate at which it detected real cases of fraud by about 50 per cent. Now, with a reduction in the number of false positives, investigators have more time to focus on more serious incidents of fraud (and don't bother customers with false alarms).

AI is also offering the potential for new revenue streams and new ways to service customers. In 2017, Danske introduced a wealth management robot called June. Aimed primarily at retail and small business customers looking for advice on how to invest their idle cash (no small feat in a country that has had negative interest rates since early 2015), the service was able to attract 11,500 clients a little more than six months after introduction.

Leaving behind the bricks and mortar?

It is clear that technology will continue to be at the heart of Danske's omni-channel marketing strategy. It had better be. Tech giants such as Facebook and Apple both supposedly have plans to enter the digital payments arena. And while they haven't entered the Scandinavian market yet, there is no assurance that they won't in the near future. To stay ahead of the competition, Danske says that it plans on working with more advanced FinTechs in order to achieve a strategic marketing advantage by providing innovative digital solutions that provide real value to customers. Some hard-core technophiles, however, might be disappointed. In March 2018 the bank announced that it would in no way be involved with the use or promotion of cryptocurrencies. It appears that, for the moment, there are still some high-tech frontiers that Danske Bank doesn't wish to explore.

Danske's focus on using technology to provide customers with products and services in the digital world is not without its consequences in the physical world. As consumer behavior changes, and with the increasing adoption of 'e-wallets' and distaste for using cash, the need for a bank branch in every neighbourhood is obsolete. This phenomenon is nothing new. Danske says that since 2011 it has closed well over 100 branches. But at the same time, thanks to its omni-channel marketing, service and distribution capabilities, it has increased the number of customer contacts by well over 100%.

Questions

1. What are some of the innovative ways in which Danske Bank provides its customers with a seamless service experience?
2. How does Danske Bank identify and cater to the needs of its different private banking customer groups?
3. How does Danske Bank use machine learning and artificial intelligence in its customer-centric marketing strategy?
4. What impact has the digitalization of retail banking had on physical distribution channels, especially at the branch level?

This case was prepared by Tom McNamara and Irena Descubes, Rennes Business School, France from various published sources as a basis for class discussion rather than to show effective or ineffective management.

Sources

Andersen, T. (2014) Danske Bank embraces digital future with omni-channel business model, *World Finance*, 2 December. Available at https://www .worldfinance.com/banking/danske-bank-embraces-digital-future-with-omni-channel-business-model (accessed 21 April 2018).

Andersen, T. (2016) How to capitalize on digital disruption? Danske Bank Investor Day, 9 February. Available at https://www.google.com/url?sa=t&rct=j&q=&esrc=s&source=web&cd=1&cad=rja&uact=8&ved=0ahUKEwix27C6l8vaAhXRMewKHfJ1Ag4QFggpMAA&url=https%3A%2F%2Fdanskebank.com%2F-%2Fmedia%2Fdanske-bank-com%2Ffile-cloud%2F2016%2F2%2Fdanske-bank-investor-day---new-york.pdf&usg=AOvVaw0fJ7eAcEV1ZdtHM6zpxE7j (accessed 21 April 2018).

Baskin, S.J. (2016) A bank that wants to disrupt itself, *Forbes*, 23 May. Available at https://www.forbes.com/sites/jonathansalembaskin/2016/05/23/a-bank-that-wants-to-disrupt-itself/#3a37a7c82f95 (accessed 21 April 2018).

Benita, J. (2017) Danske Bank is closing physical branches according to customer behaviour, *International Finance*, April–June. Available at http://www .internationalfinance.com/magazine/danske-bank-is-closing-physical-branches-according-to-customer-behaviour/ (accessed 19 May 2018).

Brogger, T.H. (2017) Danske Bank's wealth management robot now has 11,500 clients, *Bloomberg*, 10 December. Available at https://www.bloomberg.com/news/articles/2017-12-10/danske-bank-s-wealth-management-robot-now-has-11-500-clients (accessed 21 April 2018).

Büchmann-Slorup, B. (2016) Customer retention at Danske Bank, *Comex Implement*, 29 April. Available at https://www.google.com/url?sa=t&rct=j&q=&esrc=s&source=web&cd=2&ved=0ahUKEwjq36nr1cvaAhXDVRQKHRD-BTUQFggvMAE&url=http%3A%2F%2Fimplementconsultinggroup.com%2Fmedia%2F2635%2Fcustomer_retention_comex_160429-danske-bank-praesentation.pdf&usg=AOvVaw2x8ROjD0matqxB0Ly0z45w (accessed 21 April 2018).

Business Insider Nordic (2018) Cryptocurrencies were just banned by the largest bank in Denmark, 27 March. Available at https://nordic.businessinsider .com/cryptocurrencies-were-just-banned-by-the-largest-bank-in-denmark-danskebank.com (accessed 21 April 2018).

CGI, Inc. (2014) Understanding financial consumers in the digital era: a survey and perspective on emerging financial consumer trends. Available at https://www.cgi.com/sites/default/files/pdf/br_fs_consumersurveyreport_final_july_2014.pdf (accessed 19 May 2018).

Finextra (2017) Danske Bank develops pocket money app, 30 June. Available at https://www.finextra.com/newsarticle/30768/danske-bank-develops-pocket-money-app (accessed 21 April 2018).

Fowell, M. (2016) Nordics focus: how Danske Bank optimised their customer experience strategy, *CX Network*, 1 May. Available at https://www.cxnetwork.com/cx-financial-services/interviews/nordics-focus-how-danske-bank-optimised-their-cust (accessed 21 April 2018).

Groenfeldt, T. (2017) Danske Bank uses tech to prevent digital fraud, *Forbes*, 30 October. Available at https://www.forbes.com/sites/tomgroenfeldt/2017/10/30/danske-bank-uses-tech-to-prevent-digital-fraud/#aed9aae193ae (accessed 21 April 2018).

Hõbe, L. and **Alas, R.** (2015) Management challenges for the financial services sector. In *International Conference on Management, Leadership & Governance* (p. 103), February. Academic Conferences International Limited.

Løck, S. (2017) Denmark's largest bank is using AI and machine learning to 'tear everything apart' – and it's starting to pay off, *Business Insider Nordic*, 1 November. Available at https://nordic.businessinsider.com/denmarks-largest-bank-is-using-machine-learning-to-predict-the-customers-behavior--and-they-like-it-2017-11/ (accessed 21 April 2018).

Milne, R. (2013) Danske Bank ousts chief executive Eivind Kolding, *Financial Times*, 16 September. Available at https://www.ft.com/content/6c2d7822-1ea5-11e3-b80b-00144feab7de (accessed 19 April 2018).

Mobile Pay (n.d.) The story of mobile pay, plus a few facts. Available at https://www.mobilepay.dk/da-dk/Pages/The-story-in-English.aspx (accessed 19 April 2018).

SAS (n.d.) Omni-channel marketing and insights gives Danske Bank an improved customer service. Available at https://www.sas.com/fi_fi/customers/ omni-channel-marketing-and-insights-gives-danske-bank-an-improve.html (accessed 19 April 2018).

Treanor, J. (2014) Digital revolution presents banks with more change in 10 years than in last 200, *Guardian*, 26 October. Available at https://www.theguardian .com/business/2014/oct/26/banks-digital-revolution-change-regulation-job-losses (accessed 19 May 2018).

Chapter 10

Integrated Marketing Communications I: Offline Communications Techniques

Chapter outline

Integrated marketing communications

Advertising

Sales promotion

Public relations and publicity

Sponsorship

Direct marketing techniques

Other promotional techniques

Learning outcomes

By the end of this chapter you will:

1   Explain the concept of integrated marketing communications (IMC) and understand the stages involved in developing and conducting an integrated marketing communications campaign

2   Analyse the nature and role of advertising in the IMC mix

3   Analyse the roles played by sales promotion, public relations and sponsorship as promotional tools

4   Understand the role of direct marketing in the IMC mix and analyse the main direct marketing techniques

5   Explain the roles played by exhibitions, product placement, ambient advertising and guerrilla marketing in the IMC mix

KFC's plucky approach to a chicken crisis

In February 2018, KFC went through a highly publicized, and somewhat bizarre, PR crisis in the UK, when the fast food chain, known for its fried chicken, actually ran out of chicken. KFC was brief and somewhat sheepish in the statements posted in its shops, saying that there had been a 'few hiccups with delivery today'. The crisis soon spread, leading the company to claim that the shortage stemmed from 'operational issues' with KFC's new delivery provider DHL. Hundreds of KFC stores were forced to close temporarily and disappointed fans took to social media to vent their frustration, leading to the hashtag #KFCCrisis trending on Twitter. Some customers even called the police, and no fewer than three police forces issued statements asking the public not to contact them about the closures. KFC even set up a website to let fans know where their closest open store was located.

Such a basic error might seem unforgivable on the surface, but the response from Meghan Farren, KFC's cool-headed UK chief marketing officer (CMO), and the company's agency Mother has many stating that KFC may have avoided any perceptual damage to its reputation due to its management of this PR crisis. Recognizing that an apology was in order, KFC ran a full-page colour newspaper advertisement in the *Sun* and *Metro*, apologizing for the ordeal. The newspaper ad featured an empty chicken bucket, with the letters of the company's name rearranged to spell FCK. Text below the image read 'We're sorry. A chicken restaurant without any chicken. It's not ideal.' The statement continued to apologize to inconvenienced customers and thanked KFC employees, stating 'It's been one hell of a week, but we're making progress.' The newspaper advertisement's honest and apologetic tone, and its use of self-deprecating humour resonated with the general public.

The fast-food chain's chosen platform to communicate during this PR crisis wasn't an elaborate social media post, video or infographic. It was a traditional full-page colour newspaper advertisement in two of the UK's most popular newspapers. The *Sun* and *Metro* are two of the UK's highest-circulation newspapers. Taking out a full-page ad in each of these newspapers guaranteed the brand huge exposure and allowed KFC to take advantage of newspaper advertising's targeted, timely and flexible nature. In addition, it allowed the brand to leverage the strength of traditional advertising media to directly address readers in a newsworthy and trusted space. The fact that the newspaper advertisement could then be transferred effectively to social media sharing was also key to it having the impact it had.

KFC's apology appeared to strike the right tone, resulting in an immediate positive response from fans of the fast-food chain on social media. Its willingness to address the issue head on, take ownership of its error and hold up its hands without looking to lay the blame elsewhere, was praised by many. Founder and group managing director at Frank PR, Andrew Bloch, tweeted that the apology was 'a masterclass in PR crisis management', while other marketers and fans alike tweeted in praise of the brand's apology. The fast-food chain proved that honesty and a sense of humour can help a brand weather a crisis and even come out on top.[1]

As well as deciding what form of value an organization is proposing to offer its customers, it is also important to make a series of decisions regarding how this value is going to be communicated in the marketplace. As we saw in Chapters 3 and 5 in particular, these are very important decisions owing to the sheer volume of marketing messages that are currently aimed at consumers and there is the likelihood that many of these messages will not even be attended to, not to mention affect recipients in the ways that might be intended. This makes the study of marketing communications one of the most fascinating aspects of marketing as we seek to answer questions regarding what kinds of messages we should create and how we should communicate them. There are two major classes of tools available to the marketer. Marketers can use offline communications techniques such as television advertising, direct marketing, public relations or sponsorship, and these kinds of techniques will be the focus of this chapter. In addition, many organizations use online communications techniques such as display advertising, email marketing and social media advertising, which will be examined in Chapter 11.

The overall range of techniques available to the marketer is usually known as the 'promotional mix'. Offline promotional mix elements include advertising, sales promotion, PR and publicity, sponsorship and direct marketing. In addition to these key promotional tools, the marketer can also use a wide range of other techniques, such as exhibitions, events, product placement in movies, music videos or video games, and more recent techniques like ambient marketing and guerrilla marketing. Given the potentially wide menu of communications choices that the organization has, it is important that these decisions are consistent with all other elements of marketing, such as branding, pricing and distribution, in order to ensure a consistent positioning in the marketplace. It is also important to consider that each of the major offline promotional tools has its own strengths and limitations. Marketers will carefully weigh these factors against promotional objectives to decide the amount of resources they should channel into each tool.

Usually, the following five considerations will have a major impact on the choice and mix of promotional tools a company will use.

1   *Resource availability and the cost of promotional tools*: to conduct a national advertising campaign may require several million euros. If resources are not available, cheaper tools, such as direct marketing or publicity, may have to be used.
2   *Market size and concentration*: if a market is small and concentrated then personal selling (see Chapter 9) may be feasible, but for mass markets that are geographically dispersed, selling to the ultimate customer would not be cost-effective. In such circumstances advertising or direct marketing may be the correct choice.
3   *Customer information needs*: if an organization wants to correct consumer misconceptions, public relations may be preferred. If what is required is the development of brand image, a well-chosen sponsorship may be more appropriate.
4   *Product characteristics*: industrial goods companies tend to spend more on personal selling than advertising (see Chapter 9), whereas consumer goods companies tend to do the reverse.
5   *Push versus pull strategies*: a **distribution push** strategy involves an attempt to sell into channel intermediaries (e.g. retailers), and may be dependent on industrial exhibitions and trade promotions. A **consumer pull** strategy bypasses intermediaries to communicate to consumers direct. The resultant consumer demand persuades intermediaries to stock a product. Advertising and consumer promotions are more likely to be used.

If several different communications tools are being used, it is also important that they are consistent with and complement one another. This is what is meant by the concept of integrated marketing communications (IMC).

Integrated marketing communications

The traditional model of the communication process is shown in Figure 10.1. The source (or communicator) encodes a message by translating the idea to be communicated into a symbol consisting of words or pictures, such as an advertisement. The message is transmitted through media, such as television or the internet, which are selected for their ability to reach the desired target audience in the desired way. 'Noise' – distractions and distortions during the communication process – may prevent transmission to some of the target audience. The vast amount of promotional messages a consumer receives daily makes it a challenge for marketers to cut through this noise. When a receiver sees or hears the message, it is decoded. This is the process by which the receiver interprets the symbols transmitted by the source. Communicators need to understand their targets before encoding messages so that they are credible, otherwise the response may be disbelief and rejection. In a **personal selling** situation, feedback from buyer to salesperson may be immediate, as when objections are raised or a sale is concluded. For other types of promotion, such as advertising and sales promotion, feedback may rely on marketing research to estimate reactions to commercials, and increases in sales due to incentives.

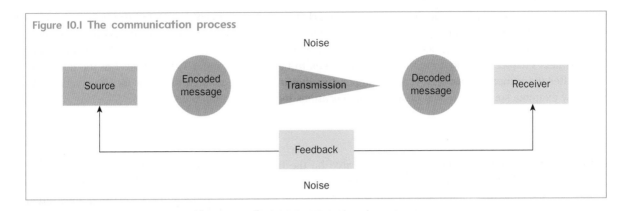

Figure 10.1 The communication process

If several different communications tools are being used, it is important that they are consistent with and complement one another. This is what is meant by the concept of integrated marketing communications (IMC). As the range of promotional techniques expands, there is an increasing need to co-ordinate the messages and their execution. This problem is often exacerbated by the fact that, for example, advertising is controlled by the advertising department, whereas personal selling strategies are controlled by the sales department, leading to a lack of co-ordination. This has led to the adoption of **integrated marketing communications** by an increasing number of companies. Integrated marketing communications is the system by which companies co-ordinate their marketing communications tools to deliver a clear, consistent, credible and competitive message about the organization and its products. While digital marketing is a significant area of growth, most companies aim to create campaigns that have both online and offline dimensions. For example, one of the best examples of a successful integrated marketing communications campaign is Compare the Market's classic 'Compare the Meerkat' campaign, which has been running for more than nine years. It integrates TV advertising, outdoor advertising, social media marketing and search engine marketing, while using real meerkat toys as gifts to keep Compare the Market's brand awareness high.[2] The application of this concept of integrated marketing communications can lead to improved consistency and clearer positioning of companies and their brands in the minds of consumers.

Stages in developing an integrated communications campaign

For many small and medium-sized firms, marketing communications planning involves little more than assessing how much the firm can afford to spend, allocating it across some media and, in due course, looking at whether sales levels have increased or not. It is clear that, to avoid wasting valuable organizational resources, marketing communications should be planned and evaluated carefully. The various stages involved in doing this are outlined in Figure 10.2.

The process begins by looking at the firm's overall marketing strategy, its positioning strategy and its intended **target audience**. What is the firm trying to achieve in the marketplace and what role can marketing communications play? If, for example, the firm is trying to reposition a brand or change consumer attitudes, then advertising is likely to play an important role in this, but it must be integrated with the other marketing mix elements. Objectives need to be set for the IMC campaign and they should be quantifiable. For example, the objective is to increase sales by a given

Figure 10.2 A framework for implementing integrated marketing communications

amount or to increase awareness among the youth market by a given percentage. Only after these stages are complete should the company begin thinking about what it is going to say (the message decisions) and where it is going to say it (the media decisions). These are complex decisions, which are discussed in detail in this and the next chapter. A budget for the campaign needs to be agreed, usually at board level in the company. Then, after the campaign has been run, it is imperative that it is fully evaluated to assess its effectiveness. We will now examine some of the key offline communications techniques in more detail.

Advertising

Advertising is very big business. This is illustrated by the fact that, in 2017, global advertising expenditure was estimated at US$559 billion. That year[3] represented a major turning point in the advertising industry as it was the first time that digital advertising spend worldwide exceeded traditional TV advertising, illustrating advertisers' growing move towards the use of digital communication tools.[4] There has long been considerable debate as to how advertising works. The consensus is that there can be no single all-embracing theory that explains how all advertising works because it has varied tasks. For example, advertising that attempts to make an instant sale by incorporating a return coupon that can be used to order a product is very different from corporate image advertising that is designed to reinforce attitudes. Advertising is likely to have different roles depending on the nature of the product and the degree of involvement of the customer.

More recent perspectives from consumer culture theory (see Chapter 3) interpret consumer advertising more in terms of the transfer of meaning. In other words, advertising acts as a source of meanings through which we express ourselves and communicate with others. For example, marketing communications may have social meaning and consumers differentiate themselves from others by consuming particular products (see Exhibit 10.1). Research has found that the brands of clothes worn by people have an impact on co-operation from others, job recommendations and even collecting money when soliciting for a charity.[5] However one chooses to explain it, one should not underestimate the power of advertising. When Oprah Winfrey appeared in Weight Watchers advertising endorsing the brand, revenue rose by 10.3 per cent to US$341.7 million, while profits soared 48.1 per cent to US$45.2 million.[6]

Exhibit 10.1 Consumers may choose to differentiate themselves through their choice of car brands; a high-end luxury car will affect the impression they make on others.

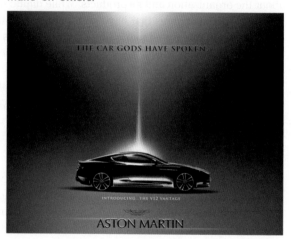

Developing advertising strategy

Each of the steps identified in Figure 10.2 is appropriate irrespective of whether the firm is conducting an advertising campaign, a **direct marketing** or **sales promotion** campaign; all that changes is the detail involved. Here we examine some specific advertising issues.

Defining advertising objectives

Although, ultimately, advertising is a means of stimulating sales and increasing profits, a clear understanding of its communication objectives is of more operational value. Advertising can have a number of communications objectives. First, it can be used to *create awareness* of a brand or a solution to a company's problem. Awareness creation is critical when a new product is being launched or when the firm is entering a new market. For example, Heineken used advertising extensively to raise awareness of its new zero-alcohol variant Heineken 0.0, using TV advertising, digital advertising and experiential activity.[7] Second, advertising can be used to *stimulate trial*, such as car advertising encouraging motorists to take a test drive. Third, and as we saw in Chapter 5, advertising is used to help *position products* in the minds of consumers, such as L'Oréal's repeated use of the slogan 'Because I'm worth it' or Ronseal's 'It does exactly what it says on the tin.' Other objectives of advertising include the *correction of misconceptions* about a product or service, *reminding* customers of sales or special offers, and *providing support* for the company's sales force.

Setting the advertising budget

The amount that is spent on advertising governs the achievement of communication objectives. There are four methods of setting advertising budgets. A simple method is the *percentage of sales* method, whereby the amount allocated to advertising is based on current or expected revenue. However, this method is weak because it encourages a decline in advertising expenditure when sales decline, a move that may encourage a further downward spiral of sales. Furthermore, it ignores market opportunities, which may suggest the need to spend more (not less) on advertising. Major consumer brands typically spend in the region of 10–15 per cent of sales on marketing.

Alternatively, companies may set their advertising budgets based upon matching competitors' expenditures, or using a similar percentage of sales figure as their major competitor. This is known as the *competitive parity* method. Again this method is weak because it assumes that the competition has arrived at the optimum level of expenditure, and ignores market opportunities and communication objectives. Sometimes firms make a decision on the basis of what they think they can afford (the *affordability* method). While affordability needs to be taken into account when considering any corporate expenditure, its use as the sole criterion for budget setting neglects the communication objectives that are relevant for a company's products, and the market opportunities that may exist, to grow sales and profits.

The most effective method of setting advertising budgets is the *objective and task* method. This has the virtue of being logical since the advertising budget depends upon communication objectives and the costs of the tasks required to achieve them. It forces management to think about objectives, media exposure levels and the resulting costs. In practice, the advertising budgeting decision is a highly political process.[8] Finance may argue for monetary caution, whereas marketing personnel, who view advertising as a method of long-term brand building, are more likely to support higher advertising spend. During times of economic slowdown, advertising budgets are among the first to be cut, although this can be the time when advertising expenditure is most effective. However, research has shown that maintaining or increasing promotional expenditures during a recession can have a positive impact on sales, market share and profitability.[9]

Message decisions

The **advertising message** translates an organization's basic value proposition into an **advertising platform**– that is, the words, symbols and illustrations that are attractive and meaningful to the target audience. In the 1980s, IBM realized that many customers bought its computers because of the reassurance they felt when dealing with a well-known supplier. The company used this knowledge to develop an advertising campaign based on the advertising platform of reassurance/low risk. This platform was translated into the advertising message 'No one ever got fired for buying IBM.' As we shall see, the choice of media available to the advertiser is vast, therefore one of the challenges of message formulation is to keep the message succinct and adaptable across various media. For example, Nike's slogan 'Just Do It', which has been used for more than 30 years, allows the brand to communicate its message clearly, and its iconic slogan resonates across different cultures, experiences and media.[10]

Most of those who look at a press advertisement read the headline but not the body copy. Because of this, some advertisers suggest that the company or brand name should appear in the headline otherwise the reader may not know the source of the advertisement. For example, the headlines 'Good food costs less at Sainsbury's' and 'United Colors of Benetton' score highly because, in one phrase or sentence, they link a customer benefit or attribute with the name of the company. Even if no more copy is read, the advertiser has got one message across by means of a strong headline.

Messages broadcast via television also need to be built on a strong advertising platform. Because television commercials are usually of a duration of 30 seconds or less, most communicate only one major selling appeal, which is the single most motivating and differentiating thing that can be said about the brand. A variety of creative treatments can be used, from *lifestyle*, to *humour*, to *shock* advertising. Cosmetics brands like Estée

Lauder have traditionally favoured the lifestyle approach to advertising (showing the brand as being part of an attractive lifestyle) though many have now moved to using top models and celebrities in their advertising (*testimonials*) (see Exhibit 10.2). *Sexual imagery* remains a popular attention-getting tactic in advertising, though recent research casts doubt on its effectiveness (see Marketing in Action 10.1).[11] *Comparative advertising* is another popular approach frequently used by companies like low-cost airlines, supermarkets and banks to demonstrate relative price

Exhibit 10.2 Rihanna's association with Puma gave its sales a significant boost in 2017.

advantages. It can be a risky approach as it often leads to the banning of adverts and possibly legal battles over claims made. For example, in 2016, the Advertising Standards Authority (ASA) in the UK banned three adverts from Aldi due to misleading claims that its prices were cheaper that those of the other four big UK retailers (Tesco, Asda, Morrisons and Sainsbury's).[12]

Marketing in Action 10.1
Tom Ford: does sex sell?

Critical Thinking: Below is a review of the use of sexual appeals in Tom Ford advertising. Critically evaluate the pros and cons of this advertising tactic. Is the use of sexual appeals in advertising more acceptable for certain products or services?

Tom Ford is an American fashion designer whose career in fashion has spanned more than two and a half decades. He previously served as creative director at Gucci and Yves St Laurent (YSL), helping to turn Gucci from a dying fashion house into a billion-dollar brand. In 2006, he launched his own eponymous luxury brand, specializing in menswear, eyewear, cosmetics, fragrances and accessories. However, Ford's journey through the world of fashion has by no means been a smooth one. His use of sexually suggestive advertising campaigns and controversial designs have earned him a reputation for sleaze and perversion. In the past, notorious adverts featuring a naked Sophie Dahl for YSL Opium, Gucci branding shaved into a model's pubic hair for a magazine advertisement and full-frontal nudity for YSL's fragrance M7, have earned him the title 'King of Sex'.

When he launched his own Tom Ford label, scandal continued to follow him. His frequent use of overtly sexual imagery in his advertising campaigns has been described as vulgar and sexist, and he has frequently been accused of objectifying women. Responding to his critics,

(continued)

Ford comments: 'I get the criticism … about the objectification. I've objectified men as much in my career … but few would accept that, because our culture is more comfortable with the objectification of men to sell products. I'm for equal opportunity objectification.' In the past, Ford has teamed up with controversial photographer Terry Richardson to create a number of sexually explicit advertisements. One of these ads shows a reclining nude model, her legs spread wide towards the camera, with a bottle of Tom Ford men's fragrance strategically placed to cover her genitalia, while yet another shows a bottle wedged between a model's breasts. The advertisements are aimed squarely 'for men' and the images are so explicit that they were banned in several countries. More recently, a Tom Ford fragrance advert starring Cara Delevingne lying naked in a bath of orchids was the subject of criticism, and was described as 'inappropriate' and 'degrading to women'.

Ford is not the only brand to use sex in advertising. Many other fashion brands, such as Miu Miu, American Apparel, Prada and Calvin Klein, have used sexually provocative or erotic imagery in advertising to arouse interest in their brand. According to the book *Sex in Advertising: Perspective on the Erotic Appeal*, around 20 per cent of all ads use some form of sexual appeal. Brands have long used these sexual appeals in the belief that 'sex sells', and that advertisements that have a sexual element draw more attention. However, some question whether we have outgrown the age of sexy advertising altogether. University of Illinois researcher John Wirtz recently reviewed nearly 80 advertising studies and concluded that sex appeals had zero correlation with propensity to buy products, thereby suggesting that, in fact, sex doesn't sell! But maybe we shouldn't be too quick to sound the death knell for sex in advertising. A racy spring 2017 advertising campaign for fashion brand Eckhaus Latta showed couples in a variety of sex acts, and the public's interest in viewing these ads was so great that it actually caused its website to crash under a barrage of clicks. Perhaps this shows that our penchant for the provocative in advertising still remains.

Based on: Allwood, 2015;[13] Adams, 2017;[14] Reichert, 2008;[15] Shepherd, 2017;[16] Suggetti, 2018;[17] Winick, 2015[18]

Television advertising is often used to build a brand personality. The brand personality is the message the advertisement seeks to convey. Lannon suggests that people use brand personalities in different ways, such as acting as a form of self-expression, reassurance, a communicator of the brand's function and an indicator of trustworthiness.[19] The value of the brand personality to consumers will differ by product category and this will depend on the purpose served by the brand imagery. In 'self-expressive' product categories, such as perfumes, cigarettes, alcoholic drinks and clothing, brands act as 'badges' for making public an aspect of personality ('I choose this brand [e.g. Michael Kors] to say this about myself').

Television advertising has long been the staple method of promoting consumer brands, although it now faces many challenges. Technologies like digital recorders enable viewers to avoid watching the commercial breaks and the multiplicity of channels available means that it is harder for advertisers to reach large audiences. The growing trend towards multitasking may well mean that consumers are also online at the same time as they are watching television, further reducing attention. Advertisers have responded to these trends in a number of ways. First they have moved towards the use of live TV adverts. For example, Virgin Holidays launched its first ever global live-streamed ad in 2016 from 18 global locations in a bid to convince people to take long-haul holidays with Virgin Holidays.[20] Similarly, Snickers used the 2017 Super Bowl to premiere its live TV commercial in which things intentionally went awry, to achieve reach and engagement, generating 1.5 billion organic impressions.[21] Second, there is the growth of **consumer-generated advertising**, where brands hold competitions inviting consumers to submit adverts or to participate in the creation of adverts. For example, the Doritos 'Crash the Super Bowl' contest, which ran between 2006 and 2016, invited consumers to create their own Doritos ad each year, with at least one being aired during the Super Bowl.[22] Finally, some television advertising invites consumers to go to websites to avail themselves of special offers, to take account of consumer trends towards multi-tasking.

 Paddy Power Ad Insight: This World Cup 2018 Paddy Power advertisement uses humour as an effective creative treatment.

Media decisions

Because of the proliferation of media now available to an advertiser, such as hundreds of television channels or radio stations, the media selection decision has become a very important one. Choice of media class (e.g. television versus press) and media vehicle (e.g. a particular newspaper or magazine) are two key decisions. Both of these will be examined next.

Table 10.1 lists the major media class and vehicle options (the media mix). The media planner faces the choice of using television, press, cinema, outdoor, radio, the internet and so on, or a combination of media classes. Creative factors have a major bearing on the choice of media class. For example, if the *objective* is to position the brand as having a high-status, aspirational personality, television or product placement would be better than outdoor advertising. However, if the communication objective is to remind the target audience of a brand's existence, an outdoor or an ambient campaign may suffice.

Table 10.1 Media choices

Media class	Media vehicle
Television	Channel 4 News; Eurosport
Radio	Classic FM; Star FM
Newspapers	The Guardian; El Mundo
Magazines – consumer	Hello!; Glamour
Magazines – business	Marketing Week; Construction News
Outdoor	Billboards; bus shelters; London Underground
Internet	Google Adwords; YouTube videos; Facebook advertising
Cinema	Particular movies
Exhibitions	Motor Show; Ideal Home
Product placement	TV programmes; music videos; video games
Ambient	Street pavements; buildings

Each medium possesses its own set of creative qualities and limitations. Television can be used to demonstrate the product in action, or to use colour and sound to build an atmosphere around the product, and thus enhance its image. Although television was traditionally one of the most powerful advertising mediums, concerns about fragmentation of the television audience have led many leading advertisers to move away from it. Furthermore, there is concern about whether viewers are actually watching advertisements when they are on. Many brands have responded by reducing the amount of advertising they place on television, switching instead to outdoor and internet advertising. Despite these developments, television is still an important advertising medium (see Figure 10.3) and some research shows it plays a significant role in brand building.[23]

Press advertising is useful for providing factual information and offers an opportunity for consumers to re-examine the advertisement at a later stage. Advertisers are increasingly using colour print ads to ensure that their brands stand out. Magazines can

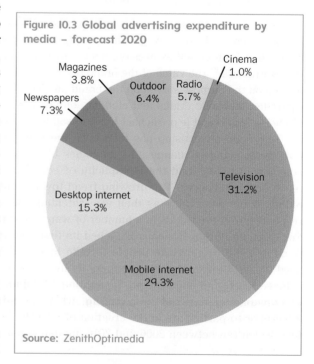

Figure 10.3 Global advertising expenditure by media – forecast 2020

- Cinema 1.0%
- Magazines 3.8%
- Outdoor 6.4%
- Radio 5.7%
- Newspapers 7.3%
- Television 31.2%
- Desktop internet 15.3%
- Mobile internet 29.3%

Source: ZenithOptimedia

be used to target particular markets and one growing sector is customer magazines, whereby leading brands such as BMW and Mercedes produce colour magazines of pictures and editorial about their products. Posters are a very good support medium, as their message has to be short and succinct because consumers such as motorists will normally have time only to glance at the content. Outdoor advertising continues to be favoured as the growth of cities, metros and long commuting times make the medium appealing. Technology is increasingly being used in outdoor advertisements to catch the attention of busy consumers. For example, Guinness devised a creative campaign in London that allowed the brand to direct RBS 6 Nations fans to nearby pubs to watch the tournament. The dynamic creative alerted people to an upcoming match and its kick-off time, as well as the distance to the local pub. Participating pubs then used sensors to capture footfall data and, if they got too full, would trigger a change in creative to direct fans to alternative venues.[24] Radio is limited to the use of sound and is therefore more likely to be useful in communicating factual information rather than building image, while cinema benefits from colour, movement and sound, as well as the presence of a captive audience. Cinema is a particularly good medium for brands trying to reach young audiences, as is internet advertising. Companies are becoming more creative in their use and placement of advertising to grab consumers' attention (see Exhibit 10.3).

A number of other factors also affect the **media class decision**. An important consideration is the size of the *advertising budget*. Some media are naturally more expensive than others. For example, €500,000 may be sufficient for a national poster campaign but woefully inadequate for television. The relative cost per opportunity to see (OTS) is also relevant. The target audience may be reached much more cheaply using one medium rather than another. However, the calculation of OTS differs according to media class, making comparisons difficult. For example, in the UK,

Exhibit 10.3 Immersive advertising inside a London tube station.

an OTS for the press is defined as 'read or looked at any issue of the publication for at least two minutes', whereas for posters it is 'traffic past site'. A further consideration is *competitive activity*. A company may decide to compete in the same medium as a competitor or seek to dominate an alternative medium. For example, if a major competitor is using television, a firm may choose posters, where it could dominate, and thus achieve a greater impact. Finally, for many consumer goods producers, the views of the *retail trade* (for example, supermarket buyers) may influence the choice of media class. Advertising expenditure is often used by salespeople to convince the retail trade to increase the shelf space allocated to existing brands and to stock new brands.

The choice of a particular newspaper, magazine, television spot, poster site, etc., is called the **media vehicle decision**. Although creative considerations still play a part, the cost per thousand calculation is the dominant influence. This requires readership and viewership figures. In the UK, readership figures are produced by the National Readership Survey, based on 36,000 interviews per year. Television viewership is measured by the Broadcasters' Audience Research Board (BARB), which produces weekly reports based on a panel of 5,100 households equipped with metered television sets (people meters). Traffic past poster sites is assessed by considering poster visibility, competition (one or more posters per site), angle of vision, height above ground, illumination and weekly traffic past site. Cinema audiences are monitored by Film Audience Measurement and Evaluation (FAME) and radio audiences are measured by Radio Joint Audience Research (RAJAR). When it comes to online advertising, Google Adwords are sold in online auctions where the price of the word is determined by its popularity.

Media buying is a specialist area and a great deal of money can be saved on rate card prices by powerful media buyers. Media buying is generally done by specialist media-buying agencies, which may be owned by a full-service advertising agency or part of a communications group. Specialist media-buying agencies have significant buying power as well as established relationships with media vehicles.

Executing the campaign

When an advertisement has been produced and the media selected, it is sent to the chosen media vehicle for publication or transmission. A key organizational issue is to ensure that the right advertisements reach the right media at the right time. Each media vehicle has its own deadlines after which publication or transmission may not be possible.

Evaluating advertising effectiveness

Measurement can take place before, during and after campaign execution. *Pre-testing* takes place before the campaign is run and is part of the creative process. In television advertising, rough advertisements are created and tested with target consumers. This is usually done with a focus group, which is shown perhaps three alternative commercials, and the group members are asked to discuss their likes, dislikes and understanding of each one. The results provide important input from the target consumers themselves rather than relying solely on **advertising agency** views. Such research is not without its critics, however. They suggest that the impact of a commercial that is repeated many times cannot be captured in a two-hour group discussion. They point to the highly successful Heineken campaign – 'Refreshes the parts other beers cannot reach' – which was rejected by target consumers in the pre-test.[25] Despite this kind of criticism, advertising research is a booming business because of the uncertainty surrounding the effectiveness of new advertising campaigns.

Post-testing can be used to assess a campaign's effectiveness once it has run. Sometimes formal post-testing is ignored through laziness, fear or lack of funds. However, checking how well an advertising campaign has performed can provide the information necessary to plan future campaigns. The top three measures used in post-test television advertising research are image/attitude change, actual sales and usage, although other financial measures, such as cash flow, shareholder value and return on investment, are increasingly being used. Image/attitude change is believed to be a sensitive measure, which is a good predictor of behavioural change. Those favouring the actual sales measure argue that, despite difficulties in establishing cause and effect, sales change is the ultimate objective of advertising and therefore the only meaningful measure. Testing recall of advertisements is also popular. Despite the evidence suggesting that recall may not be a valid measure of advertising effectiveness, those favouring recall believe that, because the advertising is seen and remembered, it is effective.

Heineken Ad Insight: As part of its drink driving programme, Heineken has created an ad featuring Formula 1 champion Nico Rosberg.

Organizing for campaign development

There are four options open to an advertiser when organizing for campaign development. First, small companies may develop the advertising in *co-operation with people from the media*. For example, advertising copy may be written by someone from the company, but the artwork and final layout of the advertisement may be done by the newspaper or magazine. Second, the advertising function may be conducted *in-house* by creating an advertising department staffed with copy writers, media buyers and production personnel. This form of organization locates total control of the advertising function within the company, but since media buying is on behalf of only one company, buying power is low. Third, because of the specialist skills that are required for developing an advertising campaign, many advertisers opt to work with an *advertising agency*. Larger agencies offer a full service, comprising creative work, media planning and buying, planning and strategy development, market research and production. Because agencies work for many clients, they have a wide range of experience and can provide an objective outsider's view of what is required and how problems can be solved. A fourth alternative is to use in-house staff (or their full-service agency) for some advertising functions, but to use *specialist agencies* for others. The attraction of the specialist stems in part from the large volume of business that each controls. This means that they have enormous buying power when negotiating media prices, for example. Alternatively, an advertiser could employ the services of a 'creative hot-shop' to supplement its own or its full service agency's skills.

The traditional system of agency payment was by commission from the media owners. Under the commission system, media owners traditionally offered a 15 per cent discount on the rate card (list) price to agencies. For example, a €1 million television advertising campaign would result in a charge to the agency of €1 million minus 15 per cent (€850,000). The agency invoiced the client at the full rate-card price (€1 million). The agency commission therefore totalled €150,000.

Large advertisers have the power to demand some of this 15 per cent in the form of a rebate. For example, companies like Unilever and P&G have reduced the amount of commission they allow their agencies. The second method of paying agencies is by fee. For smaller clients, commission alone may not be sufficient to cover agency costs. Also, some larger clients are advocating fees rather than commission, on the basis that this removes a possible source of agency bias towards media that pay commission rather than a medium like direct mail or online for which no commission is payable.

Payment by results is the third method of remuneration. This involves measuring the effectiveness of the advertising campaign using marketing research, and basing payment on how well communication objectives have been met. For example, payment might be based on how awareness levels have increased, brand image improved or intentions-to-buy have risen. Procter & Gamble uses the payment-by-results method to pay its advertising agencies. Remuneration is tied to global brand sales, so aligning its income more closely with the success (or otherwise) of its advertising.[26]

Sales promotion

Sales promotions are incentives to consumers or the trade that are designed to stimulate purchase. Examples include money off and free gifts (consumer promotions), and discounts and sales-force competitions (trade promotions). A vast amount of money is spent on sales promotion and many companies engage in joint promotions. Some of the key reasons for the popularity of sales promotion include the following.

- *Increased impulse purchasing*: the rise in impulse purchasing favours promotions that take place at the point of purchase.
- *The rising cost of advertising and advertising clutter*: these factors erode advertising's cost-effectiveness.
- *Shortening time horizons*: the attraction of the fast sales boost of a sales promotion is raised by greater rivalry and shortening product life cycles.
- *Competitor activities*: in some markets, sales promotions are used so often that all competitors are forced to follow suit.
- *Measurability*: measuring the sales impact of sales promotions is easier than for advertising since its effect is more direct and, usually, short term.

If sales require a 'short, sharp shock', sales promotion is often used to achieve this. In this sense it may be regarded as a short-term tactical device. The long-term sales effect of a promotion could be positive, neutral or negative. If the promotion has attracted new buyers who find that they like the brand, repeat purchases from them may give rise to a positive long-term effect.[27] Alternatively, if the promotion (e.g. money off) has devalued the brand in the eyes of consumers, the effect may be negative.[28] Where the promotion has caused consumers to buy the brand only because of its incentive value, with no effect on underlying preferences, the long-term effect may be neutral.[29] A 2016 study of the long- and short-term effects of sales promotion on consumer behaviour showed a significant relationship between sales promotion and both purchase intentions and sales volume, and also identified a significant and positive connection between sales promotion and brand loyalty, consumer attitudes and switching costs for consumers.[30]

Sales promotion strategy

As with advertising, a systematic approach should be taken to the management of sales promotions involving the specification of objectives for the promotion, decisions on which techniques are most suitable and an evaluation of the effectiveness of the promotion.

Sales promotions can have a number of objectives. The most usual goal is to *boost sales* over the short term. Short-term sales increases may be required for a number of reasons, including the need to reduce inventories or meet budgets prior to the end of the financial year, moving stocks of an old model prior to a replacement, or to increase stock-holding by consumers and distributors in advance of the launch of a competitor's product. A highly successful method of sales promotion involves *encouraging trial*. Home sampling and home couponing are particularly effective methods of inducing trial. Certain promotions, by their nature, *encourage repeat purchasing* of a brand over a period of time. Any promotion that requires the collection of packet tops or labels (e.g. free mail-ins and promotions such as bingo games) attempts to increase the frequency of repeat purchasing during the promotional period. Some promotions are designed to encourage customers to *purchase larger pack sizes*. Finally, trade promotions are usually designed to *gain distribution and shelf space*. Discounts, free gifts and joint promotions are methods used to encourage distributors to stock brands.

Selecting the type of sales promotion to use

There is a very wide variety of promotional techniques that a marketer can consider using (see Figure 10.4). Major consumer sales promotion types are money off, bonus packs, premiums, free samples, coupons and prize promotions. A sizeable proportion of sales promotions are directed at the trade, including price discounts, free goods, competitions and allowances.

Consumer promotion techniques

Money-off promotions provide direct value to the customer and therefore an unambiguous incentive to purchase. They have a proven track record of stimulating short-term sales increases but need to be carefully

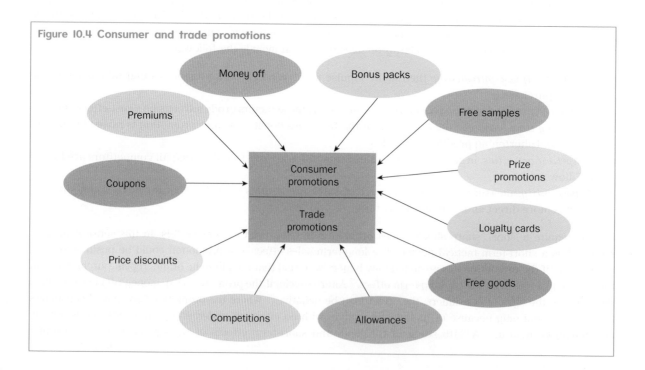

Figure 10.4 Consumer and trade promotions

planned (see Marketing in Action 10.2). However, price reductions can easily be matched by competitors and if used frequently can devalue brand image. **Bonus packs** give added value by giving consumers extra quantity at no additional cost; they are often used in the drinks, confectionery and detergent markets. The promotion might be along the lines of 'Buy 10 and get 2 free'. Because the price is not lowered, this form of promotion runs less risk of devaluing the brand image. When two or more items are banded together the promotion is called a multi-buy. These are frequently used to protect market share by encouraging consumers to stock up on a particular brand when two or more items of the same brand are banded together, such as a shampoo and conditioner. Multi-buys can also generate range trial when, for example, a jar of coffee is banded with samples of other coffee varieties such as lattes and mochas. **Premiums** are any merchandise offered free or at low cost as an incentive to purchase a brand; they can come in three forms: free in-pack or on-pack gifts, free in-the-mail offers and self-liquidating offers, where consumers are asked to pay a sum of money to cover the costs of the merchandise. For example, Kellogg's ran an on-pack promotion that offered consumers the chance to claim a personalized breakfast spoon. Consumers had to buy three promotional packs of Kellogg's cereal brands, collect the unique codes printed inside, choose their favourite Kellogg's character they wished to have engraved on the spoon and select a name/message (up to 10 characters long) to put on the spoon. The main role of premiums is in encouraging bulk purchasing and maintaining share. A behavioural argument for the inclusion of a free gift is that it is a powerful tool in reducing buyer risk and therefore likely to lead to desired purchases or product choices.[31]

Free samples of a brand may be delivered to the home or given out in a store and are used to encourage trial. For new brands or brand extensions this is an effective, if sometimes expensive, way of generating trial. Coupons can be delivered to the home, appear in magazines or newspapers, or appear on packs, and are used to encourage trial or repeat purchase. Increasingly, online coupons are being used. Daily deal websites like Groupon, Wowcher and LivingSocial have become very popular online destinations for bargain hunters. Coupons are a popular form of sales promotion, although they are usually less effective in raising initial sales than money-off promotions because there is no immediate saving and the appeal is almost exclusively to existing consumers.[32]

Marketing in Action 10.2
Build-A-Bear: 'Pay Your Age Day' woes

> **Critical Thinking:** Below is a review of Build-A-Bear's 'Pay Your Age Day' promotion. Read it and consider the reasons why this promotion caused so much difficulty in its stores. Reflect on the challenges involved in the getting the levels of promotional offers 'just right'.

One of the interesting challenges surrounding sales promotional activity is finding new and innovative ways to construct a promotion that will engage a customer base that is perhaps jaded from a surfeit of conventional offers such as 'two for one' or '15 per cent off'. Such thinking may well have been behind Build-A-Bear's decision to run a 'Pay Your Age Day' promotion in July 2018. The offer, which was limited to the company's stores in the USA, UK and Canada, meant that customers could avail themselves of any cuddly toy in the store for just the price of the age of the child purchasing it. These toys would normally cost in the region of US$20–35. However, what Build-A-Bear failed to foresee was just how popular this promotion would be with its customers. Long queues formed at its stores, with people lining up as early as 6 a.m. at its Mall of America store in Bloomington, Minnesota. As the crowds grew and stocks began to run out, frustration and anger levels increased for customers and, in many instances, local police had to be called. Eventually, the company had no option but to close all its stores for security and safety reasons bringing a promotion that was described as 'madness' by many, to an abrupt end.

(continued)

Not surprisingly, consumer reaction to the debacle was swift and furious. Shoppers took to social media to vent their frustrations. Tweets such as 'thank you @buildabear for ruining my 8 and 2 year old's day' and 'you guys stressed out a lot of already stressed out moms and made a lot of kids cry' were typical of the kind of social media reaction that this event garnered. The company responded by offering a US$15 voucher to all those who had queued, which was valid until the end of August 2018, while the Pay Your Age Day offer was extended and could be redeemed in the month of the child's birthday for all Build-A-Bear loyalty programme members.

Despite all the negative publicity surrounding the event, and the distress and frustration it caused for many of those attending it, the promotion appears to have had an overall positive impact on the company's business. Company revenues for the third quarter of 2018 were up more than 6 per cent on the same period in the previous year, although profits were down. Company representatives said that sales for the quarter had been falling but that the Pay Your Age event had led to a surge in store visits causing sales to 'sky-rocket' thereafter. It would appear that the sales promotion had a silver lining after all!

Based on: Kelly, 2018;[33] Rushe, 2018;[34] Sung, 2018;[35] Taylor, 2018[36]

There are three main types of prize promotion: competitions, draws and games. These are often used to attract attention or stimulate interest in a brand. Competitions require participants to exercise a certain degree of skill and judgement, and entry is usually dependent on purchase, whereas draws make no demand on skill and judgement, as the result simply depends on chance. Sometimes competitions can land companies in hot water, as was witnessed by Burger King's promotion run during the 2018 World Cup in Russia, offering a lifetime supply of Whoppers to Russian women who got pregnant by World Cup players. Critics assailed the promotion, which was announced on Russian social media, as sexist and demeaning. Shortly after announcing the campaign, it was pulled due to the extensive public backlash.[37]

Trade promotion techniques

The trade may be offered (or may demand) discounts in return for purchase, which may be part of a joint promotion whereby the retailer agrees to devote extra shelf space, buy larger quantities, engage in a joint competition and/or allow in-store demonstrations. An alternative to a price discount is to offer more merchandise at the same price (free goods); for example, the 'baker's dozen' technique involves offering 13 items (or cases) for the price of 12. Manufacturers may use competitions, such as providing prizes for a distributor's sales force, in return for achieving sales targets for their products. Finally, a manufacturer may offer an allowance (a sum of money) in return for retailers providing promotional facilities in store (display allowance). For example, allowances would be needed to persuade a supermarket to display cards on its shelves indicating that a brand was being sold at a special low price.

The pharmaceutical industry is one of the biggest users of trade promotion. Trade promotions involve gifts, samples and industry-sponsored training courses. Research by Global Data has shown that 9 out of 10 big pharmaceutical companies in the USA spend more on marketing than on research. It is estimated that, in the USA in 2012, pharmaceutical companies such as Johnson & Johnson, Novartis and Pfizer collectively spent US$24 billion on marketing directly to healthcare professionals.[38] Drug companies often pay specialized medical communications agencies to recruit and train leading doctors, specialists and academics as 'key opinion leaders' (KOIs). These people are paid to promote certain drugs to other doctors through presentations, research papers, discussions and debate.[39]

The final stage in a sales promotion campaign involves testing the promotion. As with advertising, both pre-testing and post-testing approaches are available. The major pre-testing techniques include **group discussions** (testing ideas on groups of potential targets), **hall tests** (bringing a sample of customers to a room where alternative promotions are tested) and **experimentation** (where, for example, two groups of stores are selected and alternative promotions run in each). After the sales promotion has been implemented, the effects must be monitored carefully. Care should be taken to check sales both during and after the promotion so that post-promotional sales dips can be taken into account (a lagged effect). In certain situations, a sales fall can precede a promotion (a lead effect). If consumers believe a promotion to be imminent, they may hold back purchases until it takes place. Alternatively, if a retail sales promotion of consumer durables (e.g. gas fires, refrigerators, televisions) is accompanied by higher commission rates for salespeople, they may delay sales until the promotional period.[40] If a lead effect is possible, sales prior to the promotion should also be monitored.

 Harvey Norman Ad Insight: This ad highlights some of the promotional offers available in Harvey Norman stores for Black Friday.

Public relations and publicity

All organizations have a variety of stakeholders (such as employees, shareholders, the local community, the media, government and pressure groups) whose needs they must take into account (see Figure 10.5). **Public relations** is concerned with all of these groups, and public relations activities include **publicity**, corporate advertising, seminars, publications, lobbying and charitable donations. PR can accomplish many objectives:[41] it can foster prestige and reputation, which can help companies to sell products, attract and keep good employees, and promote favourable community and government relations; it can promote products by creating the desire to buy a product through unobtrusive material that people read or see in the press, or on radio and television; awareness and interest in products and companies can be generated; it can be used to deal with issues or opportunities, or to overcome misconceptions about a company that may have been generated by bad publicity; and it can have a key role to play in fostering goodwill among customers, employees, suppliers, distributors and the government. For example, in March 2018 CALM (Campaign Against Living Miserably) and ad agency Adam & Eve/DDB teamed up to run a PR and publicity campaign to raise awareness of male suicide. The campaign (called Project 84) involved a stunt that placed 84 lifelike mannequins on the ledges of London's ITV Southbank buildings. They wanted to raise awareness of the fact that, every two hours, a man takes his own life, making about 84 deaths per week. The stunt was supported by broadcast coverage on ITV's *This Morning*, online communications, posters and volunteers on the ground raising awareness of male suicide, the signs to look out for and how to support people who are suicidal. The campaign generated huge publicity for the issue and Project 84 has had more than 150 million social impressions and more than 32,000 uses of the campaign's hashtag #project84.[42, 43]

Three major reasons for the growth in public relations are a recognition by marketing teams of the power and value of public relations, increased advertising costs leading to an exploration of more cost-effective communication routes, and improved understanding of the role of public relations. The dramatic growth of social media has further revolutionized the public relations business.

Publicity is a major element of public relations. It is defined as the communication of information about a product or organization by the placing of news about it in the media without paying for the time or space directly. The three key tasks of a publicity department are responding to requests for information from the media, supplying the media with information on important events in the organization, and stimulating the media to carry the information and viewpoint of the organization.[44] Information dissemination may be through news releases, news conferences, interviews, feature articles, photocalls and public speaking (at conferences

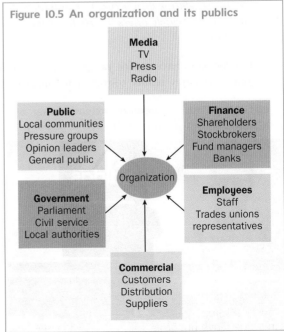

Figure 10.5 An organization and its publics

Media
TV
Press
Radio

Public
Local communities
Pressure groups
Opinion leaders
General public

Finance
Shareholders
Stockbrokers
Fund managers
Banks

Organization

Government
Parliament
Civil service
Local authorities

Employees
Staff
Trades unions
representatives

Commercial
Customers
Distribution
Suppliers

and seminars, for example). No matter which of these means is used to carry the information, publicity has three important characteristics.

1 *The message has high credibility*: the message has greater credibility than advertising because it appears to the reader to have been written independently (by a media person) rather than by an advertiser. Because of this enhanced credibility it can be argued that it is more persuasive than a similar message used in an advertisement.

2 *No direct media costs*: since space or time in the media does not have to be bought there is no direct media cost. However, this is not to say that it is cost free. Someone has to write the news release, take part in the interview or organize the news conference. This may be organized internally by a press officer or publicity department, or externally by a public relations agency.

3 *No control over publication*: unlike advertising, there is no guarantee that the news item will be published. This decision is taken out of the control of the organization and into the hands of an editor.

Table 10.2 Potentially newsworthy topics

Being or doing something first	
Marketing issues	**Financial issues**
New products	Financial statements
Research breakthroughs:	Acquisitions
future new products	Sales/profit
Large orders/contracts	achievements
Sponsorships	
Price changes	**Personal issues**
Service changes	Training awards
New logos	Winners of company
Export success	contests
Production issues	Promotions/new
Productivity	appointments
achievements	Success stories
Employment changes	Visits by famous people
Capital investments	Reports of interviews
	General issues
	Conferences/seminars/
	exhibitions
	Anniversaries of
	significant events

A key factor in this decision is whether the item is judged to be newsworthy. Newsworthy items include where a company does something first, such as a new product or research breakthrough, new employees or company expansions, sponsorships, etc. A list of potentially newsworthy topics is provided in Table 10.2. Equally there is no guarantee that the content of the news release will be published in the way that the news supplier had intended or that the publicity will occur when the company wants it to.

Sponsorship

Sponsorship has been defined by Sleight as:[45]

a business relationship between a provider of funds, resources or services and an individual, event or organization which offers in return some rights and association that may be used for commercial advantage.

Potential sponsors have a wide range of entities and activities from which to choose, including sports, arts, community activities, teams, tournaments, individual personalities or events, competitions, fairs and shows.

Exhibit 10.4 Adidas has been an extensive user of sports sponsorship in building its brand globally.

Sports sponsorship is by far the most popular sponsorship medium as it offers high visibility through extensive television coverage, the ability to attract a broad cross-section of the community and to service specific niches, and the capacity to break down cultural barriers (see Exhibit 10.4). For example, the 2016 Olympics Games in Rio was the richest games in 120 years of Olympic history, attracting an estimated US$4.1 billion in TV broadcasting revenue (combined Summer and Winter Olympics), US$900 million in worldwide marketing and sponsorship revenue, US$300 million from other rights and licensing, US$1.3 billion in domestic sponsorship deals and US$250 million from other revenues.[46] Such is the scramble for sponsorship opportunities that even a football team's pre-season tour can be sponsored; Chevrolet, Aon and Gulf Oil have all acted as pre-season sponsors for Manchester United.[47]

Sponsorship can be very expensive. For example, being one of only seven worldwide partners for the 2018 Soccer World Cup in Russia was estimated to cost between US$19 million and US$38 million annually.[48] Similarly, companies hoping to become leading partners of the Tokyo 2020 Olympics and Paralympic Games will reportedly have to pay around US$128 million.[49] Brand activation or spending associated with the sponsorship is usually at a ratio of 1:1 with the amount committed to the sponsored property.[50] A recent study of the influence of sports sponsorship on brand equity and purchase behaviour has shown that a sponsorship agreement is not enough for brand equity building or sales augmentation. Sponsors need to truly leverage activities to promote their quality and to motivate fans to engage with their brand in order to see results.[51] Therefore organizations need to have a carefully thought-out and well-planned sponsorship strategy. The five principal objectives of sponsorship are to gain publicity, create entertainment opportunities, foster favourable brand and company associations, improve community relations, and create promotional opportunities.

 Mastercard Ad Insight: Mastercard's long-running sponsorship of the Brit Music Awards is highlighted in this advertisement showing music artists such as Jessie J and Emeli Sandé creating priceless moments for their fans.

Gaining publicity

Sponsorship provides ample opportunity to create publicity in the news media. Worldwide events such as major golf, football and tennis tournaments supply the platform for global media coverage. Such **event sponsorship** can provide exposure to millions of people, and the publicity opportunities of such global sponsorship deals can provide major awareness shifts. For example, in an effort to increase brand awareness in China, Renault Sport Formula One team and Alibaba's Tmall partnered for the 2018 FIFA Formula One Championship in an effort to improve brand awareness and opinion of the French car manufacturer in China.[52] Similarly, in an effort to get globalized, the Wanda Group, one of FIFA's partners for the 2018 World Cup in Russia, used its sponsorship deal as an opportunity to raise awareness of the company on a global platform.[53]

Creating entertainment opportunities

A major objective of much sponsorship is to create entertainment opportunities for customers and the trade. Sponsorship of music, the arts and sports events can be particularly effective. For example, Etihad Airways' sponsorship of London Fashion Week provides the company with an opportunity to entertain its clients. It invites some of its clients to this sponsored event, where key personalities from the fashion world may also be present to join the sponsor's guests and to further add to its attractiveness.[54] Similarly, sponsors of the Volvo Ocean Race, such as Musto and Brunel, use the event to entertain their best clients on board sponsored boats in desirable locations like Hong Kong and Melbourne.

Fostering favourable brand and company associations

A third objective of sponsorship is to create favourable associations for the brand, company person or destination (see Marketing in Action 10.3). For example, sponsorship of athletes by the Lucozade Sport brand reinforces its market position and its energy associations. Red Bull has built a global brand on the back of sponsorship of everything from Formula 1 motor racing to extreme sports such as cliff diving. Both the sponsor and the sponsored activity become involved in a relationship with a transfer of values from activity to sponsor. The audience, finding the sponsor's name, logo and other symbols threaded through the event, learns to associate sponsor and activity with each other. For example, as Special Olympics technology partner, Microsoft has been collaborating with the Special Olympics since 2004, when the two organizations launched a multi-year global partnership with the goal of empowering programmes and athletes through technology. This sponsorship deal has helped foster favourable brand and company associations for Microsoft, which has now long been associated with such a positive cause.[55]

Marketing in Action 10.3
Rwanda and Arsenal FC: when the poor sponsor the rich

Critical Thinking: Below is a review of Rwanda's recent controversial sponsorship deal with Arsenal Football Club. Read it and critically evaluate whether you think this sponsorship deal is appropriate. Do you think it carries any risks for Arsenal? Do you think this investment will help boost tourism in Rwanda?

Rwanda's President Paul Kagame is an avid Arsenal fan, who regularly shares his views on club matters. Kagame is a former army commander who emerged victorious at the end of the Rwandan civil war and has been president of the country since 2000. He recently changed the country's constitution to allow him to run for a third election, amid accusations of dirty tricks against those who dared stand against him. Since 2000, Kagame has attempted to transform the country into a prosperous nation and much of the development work there has been assisted by aid from Western nations. In 2018, it was announced that the Rwandan Development Board had struck a sponsorship deal with English soccer club Arsenal for £30 million. The deal will see the slogan 'Visit Rwanda' emblazoned on the sleeves of Arsenal players' shirts for three years, in an effort to promote tourism in Rwanda. Players from the men's and women's teams will also visit the country for training camps, and the country's logo will appear at the side of the pitch at the Emirates Stadium and on the backdrop for post-match interviews.

However, the sponsorship deal has drawn criticism at home and abroad for a number of reasons. First, because of President Kagame's well-known love of Arsenal FC, some question how much of a personal interest was at play when the deal was made. There is also the fact that Rwanda, more than two decades after a devastating civil war, remains one of the poorest countries in the world, with 63 per cent of the population still living in extreme poverty. Then there is also the issue of the millions of pounds in development aid per year that Rwanda gets from abroad – £62 million of this foreign aid comes from the UK alone. To critics, the deal is an example of one of the poorest countries in the world indulging a passion while subsidizing one of the richest clubs in the world of football. Some British journalists have referred to the deal as 'obscene' and have used the term 'the shirt of shame' to refer to the proposed 'Visit Rwanda' slogan on the players' shirts. Politicians have spoken out and questioned why a country that is supported by huge handouts from the UK is in turn pumping millions into an obviously rich football club in London. Finally, there are also questions about why the money spent on the sponsorship deal is not redirected to solve the many economic challenges Rwandan citizens face, or to improve the country's infrastructure.

However, the sponsorship deal is viewed by its supporters as a canny move that is getting people thinking about the impoverished country's tourism industry, which offers lakeside resorts and walks with mountain gorillas. The hope is that this sponsorship deal will help provide Rwanda with brand recognition and shift the image of Rwanda from being a civil war country in the past, to being an attractive location for both tourists and investors. Rwanda is getting the endorsement of one of the world's most recognizable football clubs, and another stage in its subtle repositioning as a feel-good tale and high-end wildlife tourism destination. For the Rwandan government, it is part of a broader strategy to develop tourism, which in 2017 accounted for about 12.7 per cent of GDP and £300 million in revenue. It has been estimated that the country's £30 million deal with Arsenal FC may help bring in £225 million in revenue. The next three years will show how this sponsorship deal works out and just how many jobs 'Visit Rwanda' slogans printed on Arsenal jerseys have helped to create.

Based on: Kaschel, 2018;[56] Liew, 2018;[57] Morris, 2018;[58] Reyntjens, 2018;[59] Waterson, 2018[60]

Improving community relations

Sponsorship of schools – for example, by providing low-cost personal computers as Tesco has done – and supporting community programmes can foster a socially responsible, caring reputation for a company. Many multinational companies get involved in community initiatives in local markets. For example, Lidl has supported communities in meaningful ways through a number of initiatives. These include its partnership with CLIC Sargent, one of the UK's leading cancer charities, its sponsorship of the Pride of Britain Awards and its partnership with the STV Appeal, which provides support to Scotland's most vulnerable young people in a sustainable long-term way.[61] Similarly, Virgin Money helps foster favourable brand and company associations through its sponsorship of the London Marathon, an event that raises a huge amount of money for charity. Since it began sponsoring the event in 2010, Virgin Money has broken the fundraising record every year and has raised more than £435.5 million in the last eight years. Its sponsorship of this iconic event and its link to fundraising reflects very positively on the brand.[62]

Creating promotional opportunities

Sponsorship events provide an ideal opportunity to promote company brands. Sweatshirts, bags, pens, and so on, carrying the company logo and name of the event, can be sold to a captive audience. One of the attractions of O2's sponsorship of the former Millennium Dome (now known as the O2 Arena) was to showcase the latest in mobile phone technology and WiFi services as part of improving the overall visitor experience at the Dome.[63] For example, O2 customers can avoid having to get a paper ticket and instead receive a barcode on their phones that allows them access to an event. By doing so, O2 is hoping to both win new customers and persuade existing customers to buy new services. Similarly, EE, the UK's largest mobile network operator, has managed to successfully promote its brand by providing Glastonbury Festival attendees with the official Glastonbury app, 4G WiFi and phone-charging tents on site, including wireless charging. Customers using the app can get up-to-the-minute news on festival events, and can drop location pins to ensure they don't lose their friends and can find their way back to their tent or car.[64]

New developments in sponsorship

Sponsorship has experienced major growth in the past 30 years. Some of the factors driving the rise in sponsorship expenditure include the escalating costs of media advertising, restrictive government policies on tobacco and alcohol advertising, the fragmentation of traditional mass media, the proven record of sponsorship and greater media coverage of sponsored events.[65] Accompanying the growth of event sponsorship has been the phenomenon of **ambush marketing**. Originally, the term referred to the activities of companies that tried to associate themselves with an event without paying any fee to the event owner. Nike has been a particularly successful ambush marketer at various Olympic Games in the past.[66] The activity is legal as long as no attempt is made to use an event symbol, logo or mascot. For example, during the 2014 World Cup in Brazil, Beats by Dr. Dre ran a number of campaigns that referred to 'The Game Before the Game', featuring World Cup players wearing the headphones while conducting their pre-game rituals. Despite no official connection to the World Cup, this positioned Beats by Dr. Dre at the heart of the event, which saw the brand experience a growth of 130 per cent in headphone sales and receive more than 26 million views on YouTube for its advertisements.[67] Regulations are catching up with ambush marketers, however, as event organizers are anxious to protect sponsors' rights given their enormous commercial investment, and to prevent any types of free advertising prevailing during a sponsored event.

The selection of an event or individual to sponsor requires consideration to be given to a number of key questions. These include the firm's communication objectives, its target market, the promotional opportunities presented, the costs involved and the risks associated with the sponsorship. As with all communications initiatives, the sponsorship should be carefully evaluated against the initial objectives to assess whether it was successful or not. Nike's lifetime deal with global soccer icon Cristiano Ronaldo, which is reportedly worth US$1 billion, may seem like a huge investment. However, as one of the top influencers on the planet, he has leveraged his 262 million global social media following and engagement into a media powerhouse to drive tremendous value for his sponsorship. It is estimated that Ronaldo's social media presence alone generated US$474 million in media value for Nike in 2016, indicating a good return on investment for the brand from this deal.[68] Timico has also seen a good return on investment from its sponsorship of the Cheltenham Gold Cup horse racing event. Cheltenham plays host to more than 70,000 visitors on Gold Cup day, with 1.5 million-plus tuning in to watch live on ITV. Also, as sponsor of the day's feature race, it allows Timico to take centre stage and showcase its brand at prominent positions around the racecourse, parade ring and public enclosures. This has really helped increase exposure for the brand.[69] However, a recent McKinsey study has found that many brands still don't have a decision-making process in place to decide on sponsorship. This may reflect the fact that there is insufficient evidence on how to measure sponsorship's effectiveness well.[70]

Direct marketing

Direct marketing is the term that is used to describe the distribution of products, information and promotional benefits to target consumers through interactive communication in a way that allows response to be measured. The origins of direct marketing lie in direct mail and mail-order catalogues and, as a result, direct marketing is sometimes seen as synonymous with 'junk mail'. However, today's direct marketers use a wide range of media, such as telemarketing, direct response advertising and email, to interact with people. Also, unlike many other forms of communication, direct marketing usually requires an immediate response, which means that the effectiveness of most direct marketing campaigns can be assessed quantitatively.

A direct marketing campaign is not necessarily a short-term response-driven activity. More and more companies are using direct marketing to develop ongoing relationships with customers. Some estimates consider that the cost of attracting a new customer is five times that of retaining existing customers. Direct marketing activity can be one tool in the armoury of marketers in their attempt to keep current customers satisfied and spending money. Once a customer has been acquired, there is the opportunity to sell that customer other products marketed by the company. Direct Line, the UK's first direct car insurance company, became market leader in motor insurance by bypassing the insurance broker to reach the consumer directly through direct-response television advertisements using a freephone number and financial appeals to encourage car drivers to contact it. Once it has sold customers motor insurance, trained telesales people offer substantial discounts on other insurance products, including buildings and contents insurance. In this way, Direct Line has built a major business through using a combination of direct marketing methods.

Direct marketing covers a wide array of methods, including:

- direct mail
- telemarketing (both in-bound and out-bound)
- direct response advertising (coupon response or 'phone now')
- catalogue marketing
- inserts (leaflets in magazines)
- door-to-door leafleting.

The proportion of the promotional budget being devoted to direct marketing has been increasing steadily in recent decades. Direct marketing expenditure in Europe alone is estimated at US$118 billion.[71] The significant growth in direct marketing activity has been explained by five factors.

1   The growing *fragmentation of media and markets*. The growth of specialist magazines and television channels means that traditional mass advertising is less effective. Similarly, mass markets are disappearing as more and more companies seek to customize their offerings to target groups (see Chapter 5).
2   *Developments in technology*, such as databases, and software that generates personalized letters, have eased the task for direct marketers. Recent developments, like variable data printing (VDP), have enabled different elements within direct mail documents, including text, pricing, offers, images and graphics, to be uniquely personalized.
3   *Increased supply of mailing lists*. List brokers act as an intermediaries in the supply of lists from list owners (often either companies that have built lists through transactions with their customers, or organizations that have compiled lists specifically for the purpose of renting them). List brokers thus aid the process of finding a suitable list for targeting purposes.

4 *Sophisticated analytical techniques* such as geodemographic analysis (see Chapter 5) can be used to pin-point targets for mailing purposes.

5 The *high costs* of other techniques, such as **personal selling**, have led an increasing number of companies to take advantage of direct marketing techniques, such as direct response advertising and telemarketing, to make sales forces more cost-effective.

A wide range of EU legislation impacts on the direct marketing sector. Compliance requirements are stiffest for marketing and sales to private consumers. Companies need to focus, in particular, on the clarity and completeness of the information they provide to consumers prior to purchase, and on their approaches to collecting and using consumer data[72] (see Critical Marketing Perspective 10.1).

Critical Marketing Perspective 10.1
GDPR and direct marketing

The General Data Protection Regulation (GDPR) is a legal framework that sets guidelines for the collection, storage, use and deletion of personal information of individuals within the EU. The regulation, which came into effect on 25 May 2018, supersedes an earlier law called the Data Protection Directive and is aimed at standardizing the rules across the entire EU region. GDPR is the biggest overhaul of data protection legislation for more than 25 years and affects all companies that deal with the data of EU citizens, so it is a critical regulation for corporate compliance.

Some of the main conditions of the GDPR legislation that impact on individuals and companies include:

- *The 'right to be forgotten'*: When an individual no longer wants her/his data to be processed, and if there are no legitimate grounds for retaining it, the data should be deleted in order to protect the privacy of individuals.
- *Easier access to one's data*: Individuals are entitled to more information on how their data is processed, and this information should be available in a clear and understandable way. A *right to data portability* will make it easier for individuals to transmit personal data between service providers.
- *The right to know when one's data has been hacked*: Companies and organizations must notify the national supervisory authority of data breaches that put individuals at risk, and communicate to the data subject all high-risk breaches as soon as possible so that users can take appropriate measures.
- *Data protection by design and by default*: The GDPR guidelines state that data protection safeguards will be built into products and services from the earliest stage of development, and privacy-friendly default settings will be the norm – for example, on social networks or mobile apps.
- *Stronger enforcement of the rules*: Data protection authorities will be able to fine companies that do not comply with EU rules up to 4 per cent of their global annual turnover.
- *Data transfers outside the EU*: Under GDPR regulations, any country processing or interacting with the personal data of an EU citizen will have to comply with the data protection laws.[73]

GDPR has major implications for companies using any form of direct marketing where the company holds confidential data on an individual. Direct marketers now must be able to prove that they have obtained an individual's consent (consent must be given and not assumed) and, if they cannot, the likelihood is that they will be fined. There must be clarity around the purpose of collecting the data and, for GDPR purposes, this explanation must be unambiguous, clear and simple. If it is not, then it will not be accepted. The collection of an individual's data must be relevant to the purpose. This

(continued)

means that if a company has run a direct marketing campaign or competition, then it can use the information only for that purpose. Creating another purpose to use that information will need further consent from the data subject. This poses a challenge for direct marketers as they will need to clean and review their databases to ensure that their organization can identify whether consent has been granted lawfully and fairly, whether it is being used for explicit and legitimate purposes, what data has been collected and the accuracy of that information.[74]

While it is easy for many direct marketers to view GDPR negatively, it is, in fact, driving many good practices in direct marketing and improving the stewardship of personal data. A lot of companies aspire to implementing a truly customer-focused approach to business and GDPR makes this a necessity. It forces direct marketers to think about how to improve the perception of their marketing among their customers, it helps companies become more customer-focused and may lead to an overall improvement in the quality of individual marketing.[75] This is a view supported by Alan Coleman, CEO of Wolfgang Digital, who believes that GDPR may force brands to be more creative in how they deliver brand experiences and may also increase the focus on existing customers, who are more likely to give permission to be marketed to.[76] Although it has caused a significant shift in how companies carry out personalized marketing, for savvy direct marketers it may represent an opportunity to significantly improve customer engagement. Adhering to GDPR will be of paramount importance when it comes to moving forward with direct marketing, and it will be interesting to see how direct marketers will continue to use their ingenuity and creativity to deliver a personalized user experience and at the same time comply with GDPR.

Suggested reading: Anonymous, 2018;[77] Neville, 2018[78]

Reflection: What are the pros and cons of GDPR for both individual consumers and companies engaged in direct marketing?

Managing a direct marketing campaign

Direct marketing, as with all promotional campaigns, should be fully integrated to provide a coherent marketing strategy. Direct marketers need to understand how the product is being positioned in the marketplace as it is crucial that messages sent out as part of a direct marketing campaign do not conflict with those communicated by other channels such as advertising or the sales force.

The stages involved in conducting a direct mail campaign are similar to those for mass communications techniques described earlier in this chapter (see Figure 10.6). The first step is the identification of the target audience, and one of the advantages of direct mail is that audience targeting can be very precise. For example, Tesco's loyalty card programme enabled it to build up very accurate profiles of its customers. By monitoring purchasing patterns and products selected, Tesco's loyalty card scheme has consistently provided an excellent marketing return-on-investment and importantly provides Tesco with a fine-grained analysis of its shoppers. Tesco

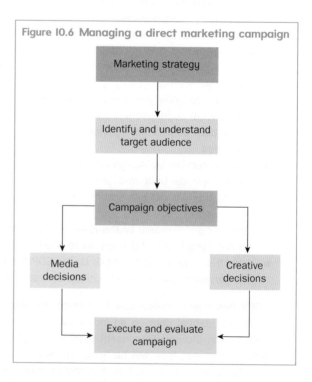

Figure 10.6 Managing a direct marketing campaign

Marketing strategy

Identify and understand target audience

Campaign objectives

Media decisions

Creative decisions

Execute and evaluate campaign

has more than two decades' worth of data on its 16 million UK Clubcard holders, making this one of the supermarket's most valuable assets.[79] Tesco can use the data collected through its loyalty card to provide

Clubcard members with an 'individual experience' through the use of a variety of marketing techniques such as personalized coupons, deep discounts delivered by email on birthdays, and print campaigns delivered directly to the door, to customize its approach.[80]

The objectives of direct marketing campaigns can be the same as those of other forms of promotion: to improve sales and profits, to acquire or retain customers, or to create awareness. However, one of the benefits of direct marketing is that it usually has clearly defined short-term objectives against which performance can be measured, which makes the evaluation of effectiveness relatively easy. For example, in 2017 Marmite (a yeast extract spread) created the Gene Project (Exhibit 10.5), a study commissioned by the brand to give weight to its legitimate marketing slogan 'Love it or hate it'. A scientific study had shown that people's taste preferences for Marmite is in their genes and this project was aimed at testing this hypothesis. A multimedia campaign was used to make the public aware of the project and direct mail was used to send Gene Test Kits to 250 adults for genetic analysis. As well as generating huge publicity for the brand, the campaign resulted in a 14 per cent increase in Marmite sales.[81]

Exhibit 10.5 The Marmite Gene Project is an example of a very effective direct marketing campaign by a consumer brand.

The next major decision involves the media to be used for conducting the direct marketing campaign. Each of the major alternatives available to the marketer is discussed below. Once the media have been selected, the creative decisions must be made. The creative brief usually contains details of the communications objectives, the product benefits, the target market analysis, the offer being made, the communication of the message and the action plan (i.e. how the campaign will be run). As direct marketing is more orientated to immediate action than advertising, recipients will need to see a clear benefit before responding.

Finally, the campaign needs to be executed and evaluated. Execution can be in-house or through the use of a specialist agency. As we noted earlier, direct marketing does lend itself to quantitative measurement. Some of the most frequently used measures are response rate (the proportion of contacts responding), total sales, sales rate (percentage of contacts purchasing), enquiry rate, cost per contact, enquiry or sale, and repeat purchase rate.

Direct mail

Material sent through the postal service to the recipient's home or business address, with the purpose of promoting a product and/or maintaining an ongoing relationship, is known as direct mail. Sainsbury's successfully used direct mail to boost loyalty and improve customers' perception of its home delivery shopping service, by creating a series of colourful and personalized postcards focused on food products, getting right to the heart of the Sainsbury's brand – quality. The result was a fantastic response rate of between 14 and 33 per cent. Customer retention also increased by 10 per cent, with customers buying 5% per cent more produce from the retailer.[82] Similarly, Nestlé sent out a mailer that was made to look like the card left by postmen when they are unable to deliver a parcel. Instead of saying that a package couldn't be delivered, however, the mailer claimed that the package (KitKat Chunky) was unable to be posted as it was 'too chunky for your letterbox'. The lucky recipients were able to exchange their card at their local newsagency for a free KitKat Chunky chocolate bar.[83] A major advantage of direct mail is its cost. For example, in business-to-business marketing, it might cost €50 to visit potential customers, €5 to telephone them but less than €1 to send out a mailing.[84] The advantages of direct mail were also highlighted in a recent research report published by InfoTrends, which showed that 66 per cent of direct mail is opened, 82 per cent is read for a minute or more, 56 per cent of consumers who responded to direct mail went online or visited the physical store, 62 per cent of consumers who responded to direct mail in the past three months made a purchase, and more than 84 per cent reported that personalization made them more likely to open a direct mail piece.[85]

A key factor in the effectiveness of a direct mail campaign is the quality of the mailing list. For example, in one year in the UK, 100 million items were sent back marked 'return to sender'. So the effectiveness of direct mail relies heavily on the quality of the list being used. Poor lists raise costs and can contribute to the growing negative perception of 'junk mail'. As a result, it is often preferable to rent lists from list houses rather than purchase them.

Telemarketing

Telemarketing refers to the use of telecommunications in marketing and sales activities. It can be a most cost-efficient, flexible and accountable medium.[86] The telephone permits two-way dialogue that is instantaneous, personal and flexible.

Technological advances have significantly assisted the growth of telemarketing. For example, integrated telephony systems allow for callers to be easily identified. The caller's telephone number is relayed into the computer database and his/her details and account information appear on the screen even before the call is picked up. Technology has also greatly improved the effectiveness and efficiency of out-bound telemarketing. For example, predictive dialling enables multiple out-bound calls to be made from a call centre. Calls are delivered to agents only when the customer answers, cutting out wasted calls to answering machines, engaged signals, fax machines and unanswered calls. In addition, scripts can be created and stored on the computer so that operators have ready and convenient access to them on-screen.

Telemarketing can be used in a number of roles, and this versatility has also assisted in its growth. It can be used for direct selling when the sales potential of a customer does not justify a face-to-face call or, alternatively, an incoming telephone call may be the means of placing an order in response to a direct mail or television advertising campaign. Second, it can be used to support the field sales force, for example, in situations where salespeople may find contacting their customers difficult given the nature of their job. Third, telemarketing can be used to generate leads through establishing contact with prospective customers and arranging a sales visit. Finally, an additional role of telemarketing is to maintain and update the firm's marketing database.

Telemarketing has a number of advantages.

- It has *lower costs* per contact than a face-to-face salesperson visit. But such has been the success of telemarketing that calls to businesses are growing significantly, with many companies moving call centre operations to low-cost countries.
- It is *less time consuming* than personal visits.
- The increasing *sophistication of telecommunications technology* has encouraged companies to employ telemarketing techniques. For example, digital networks allow the seamless transfer of calls between organizations.
- Despite the reduced costs compared with a personal visit, the telephone retains the advantage of *two-way communication*.

However, telephone selling is often considered intrusive, leading to consumers objecting to receiving unsolicited telephone calls. For example, under current UK law, companies can be fined up to £500,000 for plaguing UK householders with unwanted cold calls. In 2018, proposals were introduced to extend this to include the bosses of those offending companies, who now may also face personal fines of up to £500,000.[87]

Direct response advertising

Although direct response advertising appears in prime media, such as television, newspapers and magazines, it differs from standard advertising in that it is designed to elicit a direct response such as an order, enquiry or a request for a visit. Often, a freephone telephone number is included in the advertisement or, for the print media, a coupon response mechanism may be used. This combines the ability of broadcast media to reach large sections of the population with direct marketing techniques that allow a swift response on behalf of both prospect and company. For example, direct response advertising is used very regularly by not-for-profit organizations such as the National Society for the Prevention of Cruelty to Children (NSPCC) in order to increase the number of volunteers and donors.

Direct response television has experienced fast growth. It is an industry worth £3 billion globally and comes in many formats. The most basic is the standard advertisement with telephone number; 60-, 90- or 120-second advertisements are sometimes used to provide the necessary information to persuade viewers to use the freephone number for ordering. Other variants are the 25-minute product demonstration (these are generally referred to as 'infomercials') and live home shopping programmes. Home shopping has a very loyal customer base and many of the major shopping channels, such as QVC and HSN, broadcast live 24/7. A popular misconception regarding direct response television (DRTV) is that it is suitable only for products such as music compilations and cut-price jewellery. In Europe, a wide range of products, such as leisure and fitness products, motoring and household goods, books and beauty care products, are marketed in this way through pan-European channels such as Eurosport, Super Channel and NBC.

 AIG Ad Insight: This direct response ad for AIG Home Insurance highlights the company's freephone number, which consumers can call, allowing response to be measured.

As with many other forms of direct marketing, the effectiveness of campaigns is highly measurable, which is attractive to advertisers, who are also able to avail themselves of the multiplicity of digital channels in order to target adverts more carefully.

Catalogue marketing

The sale of products through catalogues distributed to agents and customers, usually by mail or at stores if the catalogue marketer is a store owner, is known as **catalogue marketing**. This method is popular in Europe with organizations such as Germany's Otto, the Next Directory in the UK, La Redoute in France and IKEA in Sweden. Catalogue marketing is popular in some countries where, for example, legislation restricts retail opening hours. A common form of catalogue marketing is mail order, where catalogues are distributed and, traditionally, orders received by mail. Some enterprising companies, notably Next, saw catalogue marketing as an opportunity to reach a new target market: busy, affluent, middle-class people who value the convenience of choosing products at home.

Used effectively, catalogue marketing to consumers offers a convenient way of selecting products that allows discussion between family members in a relaxed atmosphere away from crowded shops and the high street. Often, credit facilities are available, too. Catalogue marketing was originally popular with consumers living in remote rural locations, obviating the need to travel long distances to town-based shopping centres. For catalogue marketers, the expense of high-street locations is removed and there is an opportunity to display a wider range of products than could feasibly be achieved in a shop. Distribution can be centralized, lowering costs. Nevertheless, catalogues are expensive to produce (hence the need for some retailers to charge for them) and they require regular updating, particularly when selling fashion items. They do not allow goods to be tried (e.g. a vacuum cleaner) or tried on (e.g. clothing) before purchase. Although products can be seen in a catalogue, variations in colour printing can mean that the curtains or suite that are delivered do not have exactly the same colour tones as those appearing on the printed page. Catalogue marketing is big business. IKEA distributes 210 million copies of its catalogue in 44 countries and in 32 languages. Increasingly, catalogues are being made available online, which reduces the costs of production and distribution, and means that they can easily be updated.

Other promotional techniques

Because of the fragmentation of traditional audiences such as press and television, a variety of other promotional techniques are becoming more commonplace. Four popular offline communications tools are exhibitions and product placement, as well as ambient advertising and guerrilla marketing. These are examined below.

Exhibitions

Exhibitions are unique in that, of all the promotional tools available, they are the only one that brings buyers, sellers and competitors together in a commercial setting. Two-thirds of the world's leading trade exhibitions/trade fairs take place in Germany, such as the Frankfurt Book Fair, the Düsseldorf Boat Show and the Berlin Tourism Fair. All told, Germany hosts some 150 international trade fairs each year for 180,000 exhibitors and 10 million visitors.[88] One of these trade fairs, the Anuga food and drinks exhibition, brings together more than 7,400 international exhibitors with 165,000 buyers. Exhibitions are a particularly important part of the industrial promotional mix, and can be a key source of information on buyers' needs and preferences.

Exhibitions are growing in their number and variety. Aside from the major industry exhibitions such as motor shows and property shows, more specialized lifestyle exhibitions are emerging in niche markets. For example, the International Beauty Show held in New York every year is one of the world's leading trade fairs, attracting more than 500 exhibitors and around 62,500 professionals. Salon professionals flock to this event to see and buy beauty and salon products, and to avail themselves of free educational sessions with top industry experts.[89]

Exhibitions can have a variety of objectives, including identifying prospects and determining their needs, building relationships, providing product demonstrations, making sales, gathering competitive intelligence and fostering the image of the company. They require careful planning and management to ensure that they run smoothly; and post-show evaluation needs to take place to determine their effectiveness. Fortunately, there are a variety of variables that can easily be quantified, and this can be used to measure success. These include number of visitors to the stand, number of leads generated, number of orders received and their value, and so on. Following up the trade show through contact with prospects and customers is also important.

Product placement

Product placement is the deliberate placing of products and/or their logos in movies, television, songs and video games, usually in return for money. While it has been big business in some countries, like the USA, for some time, restrictions preventing product placement have only recently been relaxed in Europe. Product placement has become very important in financing movies. *Smurfs 2* actually managed to cover the entire cost of its US$105 million budget with US$150 million worth of product placement deals.[90] However, not all movies have a perfectly smooth experience regarding product placement. For example, Paramount Studios was sued for US$27.7 million by a Chinese tourism company for failing to place its logo in the *Transformers 4* movie (which had an amazing 55 product placements), even though it had paid US$750,000 for a product placement.[91] Corporate tie-ins with movies are also big business. For example, *Star Wars: The Last Jedi* received promotional help from corporate tie-ins with six major brands, including General Mills, Nissan, Verizon and Vizio. Nissan teamed up with Lucas Films to develop a marketing campaign to promote Nissan's Intelligent Mobility Strategy, General Mills introduced a range of *Star Wars*-themed food and snacks, and the elite fashion brand Christian Louboutin partnered with *Star Wars* to create shoes inspired by iconic *Star Wars* characters.[92] Similarly in the music business, when the hip-hop artist Busta Rhymes had a smash hit with 'Pass the Courvoisier', US sales of the cognac rose by 14 per cent in volume and 11 per cent in value.[93] Product placement spending in the USA was estimated at US$4.75 billion in 2012 and is forecast to reach US$11.44 million by 2019.[94]

Product placement has grown significantly in recent years for the following reasons: media fragmentation means it is increasingly hard to reach mass markets; the brand can benefit from the positive associations it gains from being in a film or television show; many consumers do not realize that the brand has been product-placed; repetition of the movie or television show means that the brand is seen again and again; careful choice of movie or television show means that certain segments can be targeted; and promotional and merchandising opportunities can be generated on the show's website. For example, the clothes and accessories worn by actresses in popular television shows like *The Big Bang Theory*, *Pretty Little Liars* and *Scandal* have been in great demand from viewers, and some have quickly sold out. There are now a number of different apps, such as Shop Your TV, Pradux, Worn on TV, The Take and Spotern, which allow viewers to find exactly the same outfit they have seen on TV.[95] Show producers are increasingly looking at the merchandising opportunities their shows can present. Technological developments in the online gaming sector allow for different products to be placed in games at different times of the day or in different geographic locations, expanding the marketing possibilities available to companies. Product placement is significantly more restricted in Europe than it is in the USA, although the Audiovisual Media Services Directive adopted by the EU in 2007 permits greater levels of placement on EU television programmes, but not news, current affairs, sport or children's programming.

While product placement is becoming very popular, it is important to remember that there are risks involved. If the movie or television show fails to take off it can tarnish the image of the brand and reduce its potential exposure. Audiences can become annoyed by blatant product placement, damaging the image, and brand owners may not have complete control over how their brand is portrayed. Also, the popularity of product placement is fast giving rise to claims that it constitutes deceptive advertising. Lobby groups in the USA claim that one of the difficulties with product placement is that it can't be controlled by the consumer, in the way the traditional advertising breaks can, through zapping, and they want it restricted.

Product placement is subject to the same kinds of analysis as all the other promotional techniques described in this chapter. For example, the new Lexus luxury LC Coupe featured prominently in the 2018 blockbuster Marvel superhero movie *Black Panther*. In addition, in the lead-up to the movie's release, Lexus commissioned an original graphic novel, *Black Panther: Soul of a Machine*, featuring the LC500 and a Lexus takumi master craftsman as heroes. It also released a *Black Panther*-themed Super Bowl ad for the Lexus LS 500. This integrated campaign resulted in an explosion of ad impressions across TV, social media and movie theatres due to the film and the product tie-ins. In the week following *Black Panther*'s premiere in the USA, online searches for Lexus on shopping site Auto Trader were up 15 per cent on the previous week. Likewise, Auto Trader revealed that online traffic for the LC500 specifically was up 10 per cent.[96]

Ambient advertising and guerrilla marketing

Two increasingly popular mass communications techniques are **ambient advertising** and **guerrilla marketing**. Ambient advertising generally refers to advertising carried on outdoor media that does not fall into the established outdoor categories such as billboards and bus signs. Therefore advertising that appears on shopping bags, on petrol pump nozzles, on balloons or on banners towed by aeroplanes, on street pavements, on overhead lockers on aircraft, and so on, are classed as ambient (see Exhibit 10.6). Ambient media is limited only by advertiser imagination.

Closely related to ambient advertising is guerrilla marketing. In essence, the latter is the delivery of advertising messages through unexpected means and in ways that almost 'ambush' the consumer to gain attention. One example of an effective guerrilla marketing campaign was that developed by UNICEF Finland to raise awareness of children's rights. To provoke and create discussion, it placed baby strollers across major cities in Finland that played the sound of a crying baby. It placed the following message inside each stroller: 'Thank you for caring. We hope there are more people like you. UNICEF Be a Mom for a Moment.' The campaign generated a huge response, it was reported on all media channels and reached more than 80 per cent of the population within two days.[97]

Ambient and guerrilla tactics tend to be used by advertisers with limited budgets or to complement a bigger budget campaign. The main strength of these techniques lies in their ability to capture audience attention, although they also come in for criticism for adding to the proliferation of advertising messages in society.

Exhibit 10.6 This very clever piece of guerrilla marketing demonstrates the possibilities of this communications tool.

Summary

This chapter has provided an overview of offline promotional techniques. The following key issues were addressed.

1. The promotional mix comprises the offline and online communication tools available to the marketer. Decisions regarding which combination of communication tools to use will be driven by the nature of the product, resource availability, the nature of the market and the kind of strategies being pursued by the company.

2. Because of the breadth of promotional techniques available, it is necessary to adopt an integrated approach to marketing communications. This means that companies carefully blend the promotional mix elements to deliver a clear, consistent, credible and competitive message in the marketplace.

3. It is important to take a systematic approach to communications planning. The various steps involved include consideration of the company's marketing and positioning strategy, identifying the target audience, setting communications objectives, creating the message, selecting the promotional mix, setting the promotional budget, executing the strategy and evaluating the strategy.

4. Advertising is a highly visible component of marketing, but it is only one element of the promotional mix. Advertising strategy involves an analysis of the target audience, setting objectives, budgeting decisions, message and media decisions, and evaluating advertising effectiveness. Advertising is undergoing many changes due to developments in technology.

5. Sales promotions are a powerful technique for giving a short-term boost to sales or for encouraging trial. Some of the most popular consumer promotion techniques include premiums, coupons, loyalty cards and money-offs, while discounts and allowances are popular trade promotion techniques.

6. Publicity plays a very important role in the promotional mix. It is the mechanism through which organizations communicate with their various publics. It has more credibility than advertising and incurs no direct media costs, but firms cannot control the content or timing of publication.

7. Sponsorship is a popular form of promotion. The most common types of sponsorship include sports, the arts, community activities and celebrities. Its principal objectives are to generate publicity for the sponsor, create entertainment opportunities and foster favourable brand and company associations.

8. Direct marketing is where consumers are precisely targeted through a variety of different techniques including direct mail, telemarketing, direct response advertising and catalogue marketing. Direct marketing provides many advantages to companies, such as the ability to target customers directly, to run cost-effective campaigns and to allow the effectiveness of campaigns to be easily measurable.

9. Other important offline communications techniques include exhibitions, product placement, ambient marketing and guerrilla marketing, all of which play different roles in the promotional mix.

Study questions

1. What is meant by integrated marketing communications? Explain the advantages of taking an integrated approach to marketing communications.
2. Select three recent advertising campaigns with which you are familiar. Discuss the target audience, objectives and message executions adopted in each case.
3. Discuss the role of sponsorship in the promotional mix.

4. There is no such thing as bad publicity. Discuss.

5. Discuss the reasons why ambient and guerrilla marketing have become such popular promotional techniques for some product categories. What are the ethical issues surrounding the growth of these mass communications techniques?

6. Companies now have a variety of direct marketing media that they can consider when planning a direct marketing campaign. Compare and contrast any two direct marketing media. In your answer, give examples of the kinds of markets in which the media you have chosen might be useful.

Suggested reading

Chen, J., Yang, X. and **Smith, R.** (2016) The effects of creativity on advertising wear-in and wear-out, *Journal of the Academy of Marketing Science*, 44(3), 334–49.

Dinh, T.D. and **Mai, K.N.** (2016) Guerrilla marketing's effects on Gen Y's word-of-mouth intention – a mediation of credibility, *Asia Pacific Journal of Marketing and Logistics*, 28(1), 4–22.

Ilhem, A. and **Breslow, H.** (2016) Social media for public relations: lessons from four effective cases, *Public Relations Review*, 42(1), 20–30.

Juska, J. (2018) *Integrated Marketing Communication.* New York: Taylor & Francis.

Ots, M. and **Nyilasy, G.** (2017) Just doing it: theorizing IMC practices, *European Journal of Marketing*, 51(3), 490–510.

Ryan, A. and **Fahy, J.** (2012) Evolving priorities in sponsorship: from media management to network management, *Journal of Marketing Management*, 28(9/10), 1132–58.

Schultz, E., Don, P. and **Block, M.** (2014) Sales promotion influencing consumer brand preferences/purchases, *Journal of Consumer Marketing*, 31(3), 212–17.

Tsordia, C., Papadimitriou, D. and **Parganas, P.** (2017) The influence of sports sponsorship on brand equity and purchase behaviour, *Journal of Strategic Marketing*, 26(1), 85–105.

References

1. **Jardine, A.** (2018) KFC says 'FCK' in UK apology ad, *Ad Age*, 23 February; **Matheson, J.** (2018) Why exactly was KFC's crisis PR response so FCK-ing good? *Grayling*, 28 February; **Glenday, J.** (2018) KFC says 'FCK' in responsive print ad after restaurants kick the bucket, *The Drum*, 23 February; **Topping, A.** (2018) 'People have gone chicken crazy'. What the KFC crisis means for the brand, *Guardian*, 24 February; **Kiefer, B.** (2018) Pick of the week: KFC comes out on top with witty apology ad, *Campaign*, 1 March; **Oster, E.** (2018) KFC responds to UK chicken shortage scandal with a timely 'FCK, we're sorry', *Adweek*, 23 February.

2. **Allen, R.** (2017) What is integrated marketing? *Insights*, 22 June.

3. **Barnard, J.** (2017) *Advertising expenditure forecast June 2017.* Zenith.

4. **Kafka, P.** (2017) 2017 was the year digital ad spend finally beat TV, *Recode*, 4 December.

5. **Anonymous** (2011) I've got you labelled, *The Economist*, 2 April, 74.

6. **Wohl, J.** (2017) Weight Watchers keeps gaining (because, well, Oprah), *Ad Age*, 3 August.

7. **Roderick, L.** (2017) Four challenges Heineken needs to overcome to make its non-alcoholic beer a success, *Marketing Week*, 19 May.

8. **Piercy, N.** (1987) The marketing budgeting process: marketing management implications, *Journal of Marketing*, 51(4), 45–59.

9. **Tellis, G.** and **Tellis, K.** (2009) Research on advertising in a recession: a critical review and synthesis, *Journal of Advertising Research*, 39(3), 304–27.

10. **O'Neill, S.** (2017) How Nike tells its brand strategy across multiple channels, *Skyword*, 8 November.

11. **Anonymous** (2004) Sex doesn't sell, *The Economist*, 30 October, 46–7.

12. **Rodionova, Z.** (2016) Aldi sale adverts banned for being misleading after Morrisons complaint, ASA rules, *Independent*, 29 June.

13. **Allwood, E.H.** (2015) Fashion vs censorship: a history of banned ads, *dazedigital.com*, 13 May.

14. **Adams, B.** (2017) Tom Ford talks sex, disruption and spring '18, *crfashionbook.com*, 14 August.

15. **Reichert, T.** (2008) *Sex in Advertising: Perspectives on the Erotic Appeal.* Taylor & Francis.

16. **Shepherd, L.** (2017) Sex, scandal and screenplays: Tom Ford and his controversial career, *mybag.com*. Available at https://www.mybag.com/blog/fashion/sex-scandal-screenplays-tom-ford-controversial-career/ (accessed 26 October 2018).

17. **Suggetti, P.** (2018) Does sex really sell in advertising? *The Balance Career*, 3 January.

18. **Winick, K.** (2015) Cara Delevingne's Tom Ford ad gets banned, *Elle*, 30 April.

19. **Lannon, J.** (1991) Developing brand strategies across borders, *Marketing and Research Today*, August, 160–7.

20. **Roderick, L.** (2016) Why live TV ads won't work for every brand, *Marketing Week*, 13 September.

21. **Tode, C.** (2017) How Snickers' Super Bowl 'mistake' generated 1.5 billion organic impressions, *Marketing Dive*, 21 February.

22. **Snyder, B.** (2016) Here's why Doritos is ending its 'Crash the Super Bowl' contest, *Fortune*, 29 January.

23. **Terazono, E.** (2005) TV fights for its 30 seconds of fame, *Financial Times*, 20 September, 13.

24. **Davis, B.** (2017) Six clever examples of what dynamic outdoor advertising can do, *Econsultancy*, 23 May.

25. **Bell, E.** (1992) Lies, damned lies and research, *Observer*, 28 June, 46.

26. See **Tomkins, R.** (1999) Getting a bigger bang for the advertising buck, *Financial Times*, 24 September, 17; **Waters, R.** (1999) P&G ties advertising agency fees to sales, *Marketing Week*, 16 September, 1.

27. **Rothschild, M.L.** and **Gaidis, W.C.** (1981) Behavioral learning theory: its relevance to marketing and promotions, *Journal of Marketing*, 45(Spring), 70–8.

28. **Tuck, R.T.J.** and **Harvey, W.G.B.** (1972) Do promotions undermine the brand? *Admap*, January, 30–3.

29. **Brown, R.G.** (1974) Sales response to promotions and advertising, *Journal of Advertising Research*, 14(4), 33–9.

30. **Santini, F., Vieira, V., Sampaio, C.** and **Perin, M.** (2016) Meta analysis of the long- and short-term effects of sales promotion on consumer behaviour, *Journal of Promotion Management*, May/June, 22(3), 425–42.

31. **Ariely, D.** (2008) *Predictably Irrational*. London: HarperCollins Publishers, 54.

32. **Davidson, J.H.** (1998) *Offensive Marketing*. Harmondsworth: Penguin, 249–71.

33. **Kelly, L.** (2018) Build-A-Bear's stores forced to close as 'Pay Your Age' day leads to 'extreme crowds and safety concerns', *independent.ie*. Available at www.independent.ie/business/world/buildabear-stores-forced-to-close-as-pay-your-age-day-leads-to-extreme-crowds-and-safety-concerns-37111413.html (accessed 1 October 2018).

34. **Rushe, D.** (2018) Build-A-Bear Boss apologizes after Pay-Your-Age sale causes chaos, *theguardian.com*. Available at www.theguardian.com/business/2018/jul/13/build-a-bear-sale-pay-your-age-chaos-apology (accessed 1 October 2018).

35. **Sung, M.** (2018) Build-A-Bear's 'Pay Your Age Day' was an absolute disaster, *mashable.com*. Available at www.mashable.com/article/build-a-bear-pay-your-age-day-disaster/?europe=true#nW07uGc6DOqP (accessed 1 October 2018).

36. **Taylor, K.** (2018) Build-A-Bear's 'Pay Your Age Day' promotion Ended in chaos, but it transformed a failing quarter into a success for the company, *ukbusinessinsider.com*. Available at www.ukbusinessinsider.com/build-a-bears-pay-your-age-day-deal-pays-off-despite-chaos-2018-9?r=US&IR=T (accessed 1 October 2018).

37. **Mahdawi, A.** (2018) Get impregnated by World Cup stars and win free Whoppers says Burger King, *Guardian*, 20 June.

38. **Swanson, A.** (2015) Big pharma companies are spending far more on marketing than research, *Washington Post*, 11 February.

39. **Bulik, B.S.** (2017) Who's influential? Key opinion leaders, again and still, *Fierce Pharma*, 26 September.

40. **Doyle, P.** and **Saunders, J.** (1985) The lead effect of marketing decisions, *Journal of Marketing Research*, 22(1), 54–65.

41. **Lesly, P.** (1991) *The Handbook of Public Relations and Communications*. Maidenhead: McGraw-Hill, 13–19.

42. **Page, J.** (2018) Why CALM installed suicide statues on top of the ITV tower, *Campaign Live*, 29 March.

43. **Bennett, B.** (2018) Ad of the day: Adam & Eve/DDB and CALM 84 sculptures on the ledge to help curb males suicide, *The Drum*, 27 March.

44. **Lesly, P.** (1991) *The Handbook of Public Relations and Communications*. Maidenhead: McGraw-Hill, 13–19.

45. **Sleight, S.** (1989) *Sponsorship: What it is and How to Use it*. Maidenhead, McGraw-Hill, 4.

46. **Anonymous** (2015) How Rio Olympics 2016 total revenue to reach $4 billion, *TotalSportek2*, 27 February.

47. **Ogden, M.** (2016) Sponsors milk their cash cow on pre-season tour of China, *Independent*, 20 July.

48. **Rains, B.** (2018) Here's how FIFA's World Cup sponsors have performed on the stock market, *Nasdaq*, 7 June.

49. **Osborne, P.** (2015) Sponsors to pay $128 million for leading package at Tokyo 2020, *Inside the Games*, 19 January.

50. **Papadimitriou, D.** and **Apostolopoulou, A.** (2009), Olympic sponsorship activation and the creation of competitive advantage, *Journal of Promotion Management*, 15(1/2), 90–117.

51. **Tsordia, C., Papadimitriou, D.** and **Parganas, P.** (2017) The influence of sports sponsorship on brand equity and purchase behaviour, *Journal of Strategic Marketing*, 26(1), 85–105.

52. **Hammett, E.** (2018) Renault looking to boost brand awareness in China with new Alibaba deal, *Marketing Week*, 19 February.

53. **Xinhua** (2018) Chinese brands shine at Russia World Cup to promote globalization, *Xinhuanet*, 14 June.

54. **Anonymous** (2017) London Fashion Week sponsors and suppliers, *www.londonfashionweek.co.uk*.

55. **Microsoft** (2018) Special Olympics, *www.microsoft.com*.

56. **Kaschel, H.** (2018) Rwanda's Arsenal sponsorship deal sparks outrage, *www.dw.com*, 31 May.

57. **Liew, J.** (2018) Rwanda's deal with Arsenal yet another example of dubious regimes banking on the moral apathy poisoning football, *Independent*, 25 May.

58. **Morris, H.** (2018) Rwanda, fresh from its deal with Arsenal, announces surge in UK visitors, *Telegraph*, 29 May.

59. **Reyntjens, F.** (2018) When the poor sponsor the rich: Rwanda and Arsenal FC, *The Conversation*, 28 May.

60. **Waterson, J.** (2018) Rwanda's £30m Arsenal sponsorship divides opinion, *The Guardian*, 29 May.

61. **Lidl** (2018) Community and social responsibility, *www.lidl.co.uk*.

62. **Virgin Money** (2018) Using our expertise to do some good, *https://uk.virginmoney.com*.

63. **Carter, M.** (2007) Sponsorship branding takes on new name, *Financial Times*, 12 March.

64. **Darbyshire, R.** (2017) EE set to connect campers with 4G smart tent at Glastonbury Festival, *The Drum*, 19 June.

65. **Miles, L.** (1995) Sporting chancers, *Marketing Director International*, 6(2), 50–2.

66. **Bowman, J.** (2004) Swoosh rules over official Olympic brands, *Media Asia*, 10 September, 22.

67. **Anonymous** (2015) Case study: Beats by Dre/'The Game Before the Game', *Campaign*, 12 October.

68. **Gallagher, K.** (2017) Ronaldo's $1 billion Nike deal could be the future of social media marketing, *Business Insider UK*, 8 March.

69. **Ruthven, H.** (2017) Why sports sponsorship worked for these three businesses, *Real Business*, 3 January.

70. **Jacobs, J., Pallau, J.** and **Surana, K.** (2014) Is sports sponsorship worth it? *McKinsey*, June.

71. **Statista** (2018) Spending on direct marketing in Europe from 2007 to 2018, *www.statista.com*.

72. **Anonymous** (2017) European Union – direct marketing, *www.export.gov*, 19 August.

73. **Anonymous** (2018) What is GDPR? *Asystec.ie*.

74. **Anonymous** (2018) Implications of GDPR for marketing in the UK and Europe, *Smart Insights*.

75. **Neville, T.** (2018) GDPR leveraging the marketing opportunity, *Gain Theory*.

76. **Kennedy, J.** (2018) Privacy by default: GDPR will change the rules of marketing forever, *Silicon Republic*, 13 March.

77. **Anonymous** (2018) Implications of GDPR for marketing in the UK and Europe, *Smart Insights*.

78. **Neville, T.** (2018) GDPR leveraging the marketing opportunity, *Gain Theory*.

79. **Hammett, E.** (2018) Tesco 'absolutely concerned' about the impact of GDPR on Clubcard, *Marketing Week*, 29 May.

80. **Anonymous** (2017) How Tesco refreshed their marketing strategy to get back on track, *Smart Insights*, 10 October.

81. **Marmite** (2017) Gene project, *www.marmite.co.uk*.

82. **Cerna, N.** (2018) Five successful postcard direct mail campaigns, *Romax*, 27 March.

83. **Royal Mail Market Research** (2018) Kit Kat grabbed attention by spoofing an everyday mailing, *www.getmedia.com*.

84. **Benady, D.** (2001) If undelivered, *Marketing Week*, 20 December, 31–3.

85. **Gould, S.** (2017) Five ways to spice up your direct mail marketing in 2017, *Forbes*, 10 January.

86. **McHatton, N.R.** (1988) *Total Telemarketing*. New York: Wiley, 269.

87. **Little, A.** (2018) Cold call crackdown: huge fines for company bosses could finally put an end to nuisance calls, *Sunday Express*, 30 May.

88. **Delamaide, D.** (2018) Why Germany dominates the global trade show business, *Handelsblatt Global*, 6 March.

89. **McKelvey, M.** (2018) Save the date: International Beauty Show New York, *American Salon*, 6 February.

90. **McFarland, K.** (2013) *The Smurfs 2* already covered its production budget with product placement, *AvNews*, 5 August.

91. **Lee, B.** (2016) Paramount sued by Chinese company for failed Transformers product placement, *The Guardian*, 27 April.

92. **McCarthy, J.** (2017) How the Disney empire rallied brands for yet another Star Wars with the *Last Jedi*, *The Drum*, 14 December.

93. **Tomkins, R.** (2003) The hidden message: life's a pitch, and then you die, *Financial Times*, 24 October, 14.

94. **Anonymous** (2018) Product placement spending worldwide in select countries 2012, 2014 and 2019 (in million US dollars), *www.statista.com*.

95. **Rivet, D.** (2017) You can now Shazam your favourite outfits from TV, *www.konbini.com*.

96. **Anonymous** (2018) Lexus' genius product placement in Marvel's *Black Panther* movie highlights growing influence of African American buying power, *PRNewsWire*, 9 March.

97. **Anonymous** (2017) Five fantastic guerrilla marketing examples, *Marketing Logic*, 7 March.

Introduction

Guinness is an Irish dry stout that originated in the brewery of Arthur Guinness at St James's Gate Brewery in Dublin, Ireland. It is owned by the beverage company Diageo and has become one of the most successful beer brands worldwide. The brand is now brewed in almost 50 countries and is available in more than 120.[1] Every day, more than 10 million glasses of Guinness are being enjoyed around the world and, every year, more than 1.8 billion pints are sold.[2]

The evolution of Guinness advertising

Although founded in 1759, Guinness didn't publish its first advertisement until 1794 and it soon set the standard for beer advertising, with engaging ads that have helped create arguably the best-known beer worldwide.[3] Its advertising has traditionally focused on dramatizing the product. For example, the first ever Guinness ad used the advertising slogan 'Guinness is Good For You', based on the perceived medicinal benefits of the drink. Over the years, it has produced a diverse collection of ads, for its different product variants and different markets. However, there has often been little connection between these ads and its campaigns have lacked a global unified approach.[4]

Challenges facing the Guinness brand

In 2011, Guinness was a global brand in terms of its footprint and had a reputation for producing a high-quality product, but it had never really developed an advertising campaign that united all of its products across the globe. The brand faced a number of complex challenges that had an impact on the brand and how it was advertised globally.[4]

First, it was operating in vastly different territories with different audiences, meaning that the drink needed to appeal to a wide range of nationalities, age groups, characteristics and needs. Marketing to so many different audiences was therefore expensive and time consuming. Second, it had vastly different products and formats across the world, from premium draught in Asia, to the bottles of stronger foreign Extra Stout in Africa, to the iconic Guinness black-and-white pint most often seen in Ireland and the UK.[4]

Third, Guinness had more than 15 global taglines stemming from five different positionings in its marketing worldwide. For example, in Ireland, it was 'There's More Life in the Dark', which positioned Guinness to younger, more social and lively drinkers. In the UK, it was about how the product comes to life in front

Exhibit C10.1 Early Guinness advertising.

of your eyes. In the USA, it was 'Genius', in Africa it was 'Greatness', and in Asia it was split between 'Inner Strength' for bottled stout and 'Rise Together' for draught. The final challenge was that each of the many markets in which Guinness operated presented a unique set of challenges for the brand.[4] For example, it was facing the rise of craft beers in Western markets, price premiums in developing markets and an ageing consumer base in its Asian markets.[5] In addition, global recession in some of its markets was creating a desire to create economies of scale.[6]

Faced with these challenges, Guinness wanted to elevate the brand above other competing beers and, in the process, recruit the next generation of drinkers. It saw the need to develop a marketing strategy that would speak to a global audience and support all of Guinness product formats.

The birth of the 'Made of More' campaign

In order to achieve this, Guinness wanted to move the focus of its future advertising away from just focusing on the drink and instead focus on developing a shared attitude between the brand and the drinker. It wanted to create emotional, feel-good advertising that would illustrate the brand's values and attract a new community of Guinness drinkers.[7] This led to the birth of the Guinness 'Made of More' advertising platform, which was built on the premise that Guinness is a beer with more to it, for those who have more to them.[4] This new campaign heralded the start of another chapter in the Guinness advertising legacy, championing 'a life made of more' and celebrating the attitude shared by Guinness brewers and drinkers alike.[8] Since 2012, Guinness has worked very closely with the advertising agency Abbott Mead Vickers (AMV) BBDO to bring the 'Made of More' platform to life across multiple forms of promotion and advertising media.[9]

Guinness launched the 'Made of More' platform with two films called 'Cloud' and 'Clock'. These were stories that followed inanimate objects that choose to break the constraints of what is expected of them.[5] Released in 2012, the 'Cloud' ad followed the extraordinary journey of an unusual cloud that drifts alone through a city. The ad uses the cloud as a metaphor to show how amazing things happen to people if they make the most of themselves.[10] The advertisement was aired on TV, and was supported with outdoor and press activities.[11]

'Clock', the second ad in the 'Made of More' campaign, was launched in 2013 and helped to further cement the 'Made of More' platform via the metaphor of a clock that chooses not to settle for the ordinary,

but to do more and be more. The ad tells the story of a town's clock that changes time to enhance the well-being of the public – either by speeding up time for a boring task to go faster, reversing time to avoid an unfortunate event, or pausing time to allow a precious moment to last longer. Going live on the brand's social media channels, the ad subsequently aired on TV and in cinemas. The ad was supported by a significant £5.5 million media spend in Great Britain and €4 million in Ireland.[12]

However, research showed that, although people found both of these ads interesting, most were unclear as to why Guinness had chosen to talk about being 'Made of More'. Both the 'Cloud' and 'Clock' ads had used inanimate objects and metaphors to explain the 'Made of More' idea, but Guinness's research found that these metaphors were bereft of certain Guinness characteristics that its audience had come to expect – humanity, character and communion.[5]

To ensure that its work was more character-filled and less distant, Guinness wanted its next creative work to celebrate people who shared its brand philosophy. It wanted to find global stories of people in life who were truly 'Made of More'. To take its work from good to great, its next iteration of 'Made of More' would need a greater injection of Guinness soul and spirit.[5] The result was the third instalment in the 'Made of More' series, titled 'Basketball', which appeared in 2014. This TV ad told the real story of a group of wheelchair basketball players, with an unexpected twist at the end. It is revealed that actually only one of the players is wheelchair bound and the others are playing out of loyalty and dedication to their friend. The friends show that they are 'made of more', and carve their own path by choosing the less-trodden path of character and integrity.[4]

In 2014, Guinness also launched the 'Sapeurs' 'Made of More' campaign that shone a light on the Society of Elegant Persons of the Congo, better known as Sapeurs. These blue-collar workers dedicate their lives to colourful fashion and transform themselves into vibrant icons of the local nightlife.[13] Through their attitude and style, they demonstrate that, no matter the circumstances, you can always choose who you are and carve your own path.[4] Both the 'Basketball' and 'Sapeurs' ads were creatively hugely successful, with 'Sapeurs' alone winning more than 70 creative awards. Culturally, both ads were a viral success, with 'Basketball' gaining 7 million YouTube views in its first weekend alone.[5]

Guinness continued its 'Made of More' ad series that featured ordinary people achieving extraordinary things. In 2015, it introduced a campaign featuring John Hammond, who in his search for great music brought black and white musicians together, overcoming divides, and creating a fantastic music and social legacy.[14] The film was launched online and on TV, and was later reinforced through the use of cinema and online advertising on YouTube, Facebook, Twitter and Instagram.[15]

More recently, in 2017, Guinness launched the 'Compton Cowboys' advertising campaign. The ad tells the story of a group of men, living in Compton, LA, a city known for its gangs and violence. By following their true passion and caring for horses, they have made an unusual but brave choice to take a different path to that of the gang life they grew up with. The ad aired for the first time on TV, with supporting social and digital content on YouTube, Facebook, Instagram and Snapchat.[16]

Guinness and AMV BBDO have created many different 'Made of More' ads since their collaboration began in 2012. Initially these ads used the slogan 'Made of More' as a metaphor for the brand's unique characteristics and personality. However, over time these ads have evolved and the focus of more recent 'Made of More' ads has been to champion real people who have shown unexpected character to enrich the world around them. These people are made of more, just like Guinness is a brand that is made of more; a brand with more to it.[3]

Sponsorship

Guinness has been keen to extend its 'Made of More' platform to create communications that could leverage its sponsorship of rugby. The brand is a long-standing sponsor of rugby, having sponsored various teams and tournaments over the past three decades. Currently, it is one of the official sponsors of the NatWest 6 Nations and, at a provincial level, has been involved in sponsoring some of Europe's elite teams, including Leinster, Munster and London Irish. It is also title sponsor of the Guinness Pro14 rugby championship, a partnership that began back in 2014.[17, 18]

In 2015, Guinness struck a chord with rugby fans by releasing a series of beautifully made, emotive short films and TV advertisements. These were part of its overarching 'Made of More' campaign. Debuted ahead of the 2015 Rugby World Cup, they tell the tale of attitude and achievements of rugby legends. One of these features rugby legend Gareth Thomas, the former Wales captain, who came out as gay in 2009. Others featured Ashwin Willemse, who escaped the deadly gang life in South Africa, Bill McLaren's recovery from tuberculosis to become the 'voice of rugby', Welsh rugby player Shane Williams, who was told that he was 'too small to play rugby', and the Munster team's against-all-odds defeat of New Zealand in 1978.[19]

Their stories speak to the transformative power of sport in an immensely powerful way and, by extension, elevate Guinness, simply because the brand is willing to give the athletes a forum to tell their gripping tales. The videos helped reinforce the 'Made of More' platform among a global audience, and ensured that the campaign extended its reach and appeal.[18]

Conclusion

The Guinness 'Made of More' platform has gone through several iterations since its initial development in 2012. In building a long-term strategy and developing its global creative platform over the last several years, Guinness has been able to deliver strong returns and increase the efficiency of its return on investment. Since the launch of 'Made of More', Guinness has spent £35.6 million on the campaign in the UK and Ireland alone. The total retail revenue (money taken at the tills in pubs and bars) across both markets during the period of the campaign was £700 million, implying a revenue return on investment (ROI) of £19.90 for every £1 spent, with a total gross profit margin ROI of £3.88 (almost twice the category norm).

In addition, there is considerable evidence of the campaign's global success. In Western Europe, Guinness has seen the first sales growth in Ireland in six years and reversed the decline in fortunes in the UK. In North America, it has seen a 47 per cent increase in positive feeling towards the brand along with a 23 per cent increase in trial. In Africa, outside Nigeria, which has been under macroeconomic pressure, it is also seeing double-digit volume growth in every other market where 'Made of More' has been implemented. In Asia, while it has not rolled out the idea across all markets, it has seen huge growth in Korea where 'Made of More' has been implemented (+39 per cent in the seven periods of the current financial year). This has given it confidence that it will see success as it rolls out the platform throughout Asia.[4]

It has also won more than 100 creative awards for the 'Made of More' campaign and has built widespread cultural traction for the brand.[5] By committing long term to a brand idea, 'Made of More', Guinness defied significant challenges in its global markets and created an effective global communications platform that effectively communicated the brand's distinctiveness and salience.[20]

Questions

1. Comment on the main challenges facing Guinness in 2011, which led to the development of the 'Made of More' campaign. What are the objectives of the campaign?

2. What is an advertising platform? Discuss the advertising platform that formed the basis of the 'Made of More' advertising campaign. Why do you think this platform has had such longevity? Do you think this is a platform that Guinness can continue to use in its future advertising campaigns?

3. Why did Guinness use rugby sponsorship to extend the 'Made of More' platform? What do you think are the principal objectives of a sponsorship arrangement?

4. Evaluate the effectiveness of the 'Made of More' campaign. What metrics would you use to assess its effectiveness?

This case was written by Marie O'Dwyer, Waterford Institute of Technology, Ireland, as a basis for class discussion rather than to illustrate either effective or ineffective management.

References

1. **Anonymous** (2011) Famous brewer expands with national launch of Guinness Black Lager, *Prnewswire.com*, 24 August. Available at https://www.prnewswire.com/news-releases/famous-brewer-expands-with-national-launch-of-guinness-black-lager-128316313.html (accessed 19 December 2011).

2. **C.R.** (2014) Why Guinness is less Irish than you think, *The Economist*, 16 March. Available at https://www.economist.com/the-economist-explains/2014/03/16/why-guinness-is-less-irish-than-you-think (accessed 7 April 2018).

3. **Anonymous** (2012) 250 years of genius: the evolution of Guinness advertising, *TheJournal.ie*, 18 March. Available at http://www.thejournal.ie/250-years-of-genius-the-evolution-of-guinness-advertising-382849-Mar2012/ (accessed 7 April 2018).

4. **Marketing Society** (2015) Available at https://www.marketingsociety.com/sites/default/files/the-library/Winner%202015%20Guinness%20Global%20Marketing%20-%20Full%20case%20study%20Redacted.pdf (accessed 7 April 2018).

5. **Anonymous** (2015) Jay Chiat Awards – Guinness: 'Made of More', *WARC.com*. Available at https://www.warc.com/content/article/guinness_made_of_more/105600 (accessed 7 April 2018).

6. **Anonymous** (n.d.) *FT.com*. Available at https://www.ft.com/content/a6b77284-9ca3-11e6-8324-be63473ce146 (accessed 7 April 2018).

7. **Anonymous** (2014) ARF Ogilvy Awards – Guinness: 'Score!' with Basketball, *WARC.com*. Available at https://www.warc.com/content/article/A101535_Guinness_Score_with_Basketball/101535 (accessed 7 April 2018).

8. **Guinness** (n.d.) Guinness advertising, *Guinness.com*. Available at https://www.guinness.com/en-ie/advertising/ (accessed 7 April 2018).

9. **Campaign staff** (2016) World's most creative partnerships: Guinness & AMV BBDO, *Campaignlive.co.uk*, 21 June. Available at https://www.campaignlive.co.uk/article/worlds-creative-partnerships-guinness-amv-bbdo/1399167 (accessed 7 April 2018).

10. **Kimberley, S.** (2012) Guinness launches 'Cloud' TV campaign, *Campaignlive.co.uk*, 2 October. Available at https://www.campaignlive.co.uk/article/guinness-launches-cloud-tv-campaign/1152779 (accessed 7 April 2018).

11. **Kevin Hanrahan** (KH) (2015) Guinness Made of More, *kevinhanrahan.com*. Available at http://www.kevinhanrahan.com/portfolio/pine-woods/ (accessed 7 April 2018).

12. **AMV BBDO** (2013) Guinness 'Clock' ad in 'Made of More' campaign, *LLBOnline.com*. Available at https://lbbonline.com/news/guinness-clock-ad-in-made-of-more-campaign/ (accessed 7 April 2018).

13. **Griner, D.** (2014) Ad of the day: Congo's Sapeurs star in the best-dressed Guinness commercial ever, *Adweek*, 5 January. Available at http://www.adweek.com/brand-marketing/ad-day-clothes-make-men-stylish-guinness-spot-congos-sapeurs-154995/ (accessed 7 April 2018).

14. **Winstanley, B.** (2016) Video: Guinness launches new 'Made of More' advertising campaign, *Morning Advertiser*, 3 February. Available at https://www.morningadvertiser.co.uk/Article/2016/02/03/Guinness-TV-advert-Made-of-More-John-Hammond (accessed 7 April 2018).

15. **Anonymous** (2016) New Guinness ad celebrates John Hammond, 'Intolerant Champion of Tolerance', *LLBOnline.com*. Available at https://lbbonline.com/news/new-guinness-ad-celebrates-john-hammond-intolerant-champion-of-tolerance/ (accessed 7 April).

16. **Anonymous** (2016) Ad of the Week: Guinness – The Compton Cowboys, *Adworld.ie*. Available at https://www.adworld.ie/2017/09/20/guinness-reveals-latest-advert-in-the-made-of-more-series-the-compton-cowboys/ (accessed 7 April 2018).

17. **Six Nations** (n.d.) Guinness, *sixnationsrugby.com*. Available at https://www.sixnationsrugby.com/en/championship/partners_guinness.php (accessed 7 April 2018).

18. **Guinness PRO12 Editor** (2016) PRO12 Rugby announces four year Guinness sponsorship extension, *pro14rugby.org*, 23 August. Available at https://www.pro14rugby.org/2016/08/23/pro12-rugby-announces-four-year-guinness-sponsorship-extension/ (accessed 7 April 2018).

19. **Gianatasio, D.** (2015) Ad of the day: Guinness tells athletes' dark stories in gripping ads for Rugby's World Cup, *Adweek*, 8 September. Available at http://www.adweek.com/brand-marketing/ad-day-guinness-tells-athletes-dark-stories-gripping-ads-rugbys-world-cup-166759/ (accessed 7 April 2018).

20. **Anonymous** (2016) IPA Effectiveness Awards case study – Guinness: an effectiveness story made of more, *IPA.co.uk*. Available at https://ipa.co.uk/knowledge/case-studies/guinness-an-effectiveness-story-made-of-more (accessed 7 April 2018).

Chapter 11

Integrated Marketing Communications II: Online Communications Techniques

Learning outcomes

By the end of this chapter you will:

1   Understand the reasons for the growth in online communications techniques

2   Understand the principles of effective website design and search engine optimization

3   Evaluate the role of mobile marketing in online communications

4   Explain the concept of content marketing and how it is used

5   Understand the different techniques that are used in online advertising

6   Understand the principles of effective email advertising

7   Evaluate the effectiveness of online communications campaigns

Always girl emojis: #LikeAGirl

In 2014, the feminine hygiene brand Always was looking for a way to appeal to the next generation of consumers in the face of growing competition from rival brands. Its award-winning response was to launch the #LikeAGirl campaign, which aimed to turn the phrase 'Like A Girl', which had become an insult, into an empowering message. The campaign's main objective was to stop the drop in confidence girls experience at puberty and to tackle the many stereotypes that exist in society about girls that can affect their self-perceptions and behaviour. The campaign was hugely successful and turned #LikeAGirl into a huge movement to promote confidence among young women.

Building on previous iterations, in 2016 Always decided to continue its focus on gender equality by shining a light on how women and men are portrayed differently in emojis. Male emojis are often shown cycling, surfing, playing basketball or doing jobs like being a police officer. Women meanwhile are often portrayed in emojis wearing pink, dancing, having their nails painted, shopping or getting their hair cut. Female emojis often fail to celebrate female achievement and instead reinforce the societal limitations faced by girls in real life. Always believed that these emojis were subtly reinforcing society's prejudices towards girls and it set about designing an integrated marketing campaign that would challenge this.

Always teamed up with advertising agency Leo Burnett to tap into the current buzz around emoji-speak. Its research had shown that 70 per cent of young women would like to see female emojis portrayed more progressively, depicting such professions as lawyers, or partaking in activities like wrestling and weight lifting. The result was the creation of a two-and-a-half-minute-long video interviewing girls and asking them how they felt about the existing emojis. The video used these interviews to highlight the fact that 81 per cent of females aged 16 to 24 use emojis on a daily basis, and called for one of the world's fastest-growing 'languages' to stop reducing them to stereotypes and start making icons that are as 'unstoppable as the girls they represent'. The online video rallied girls in 22 markets globally to share the video, and invited them to take a picture, shoot a video or tweet the girl emojis they wanted, using the hashtag #LikeAGirl, to show girls everywhere that anything and everything is possible. Always wanted to use the campaign to empower girls and give them a voice, so the campaign's focus was about more than just driving awareness of the issue, it was about encouraging widescale participation.

Social media platforms such as YouTube and Facebook were central to this campaign, and were used to promote the video and invite girls to share what emojis they would like to see used. Always responded by creating girl emojis on request, including a girl coder, a girl palaeontologist, a girl lawyer and more. Public relations also played an important role, and was used to leverage digital and cultural influencers, such as Emma Watson and Michele Obama, on YouTube and Twitter. For example, when Michelle Obama asked to be part of the #LikeAGirl conversation, Always fuelled the discussion and amplified the message across Twitter, which drove even further engagement. It partnered with Michelle Obama's 'Let Girls Learn' initiative for an experiential event to empower girls on International Women's Day in Washington, DC. The three-month integrated campaign resulted in more than 30 million video views worldwide and 44 inspiring new emojis, 11 of which were approved and included on several digital platforms. For Always the integrated campaign resulted in a growth in the brand's equity and saw sales increase by 16 per cent in the three months after the campaign's launch. Even more importantly, it challenged the way the world perceived what girls are capable of. The powerful combination of emojis, girl empowerment and brand message was rolled into this perfect socially relevant campaign for its target consumer.[1]

The growth in online communications

The marketing landscape has been transformed by the growth in internet and social media usage. Web browsing opens up a world of purchasing and sales opportunities for consumers and businesses. Search engines have become a key vehicle for consumers to find the products and services they want, giving rise to new industries like search engine optimization services and search engine marketing. As an increasing amount of social activities by consumers are conducted online, websites like Facebook and Snapchat make changes to their platforms to try to capture greater shares of this online time. This, in turn, makes them more attractive to advertisers, with the result that a greater proportion of marketing budgets are being allocated to digital and social platforms.

Internet usage throughout the world continues to rise (see Table 11.1). Unsurprisingly, the highest penetration levels are in North America and Europe. However, internet usage is now a global phenomenon. The majority of users are in Asia, while the most dramatic growth rates are happening in Africa and the Middle East. Internet technologies have become a force that has effectively brought the world closer together, fostering global business and cross-border commerce.

Table II.I World internet usage

World regions	Internet users	Penetration (%)	% growth 2000–18	% of total users
Africa	453,329,534	35.2	9,941	10.9
Asia	2,023,630,194	48.1	1,670	48.7
Europe	704,833,752	85.2	570	17.0
Middle East	164,037,259	64.5	4,893	3.9
North America	345,660,847	95.0	219	8.3
Latin America/Caribbean	437,001,277	67.0	2,318	10.5
Oceania/Australia	28,439,277	68.9	273	0.7
World total	4,156,932,140	54.4	1,052	100.0

Source: Data from InternetWorldStats (2018) World internet usage statistics – the internet big picture. Available at http://www.internetworldstats.com/stats.htm (accessed August 2018).

In just a four-year period, from 2014 to 2018, the proportion of the world's population that is using the internet has grown from one-third to just over one-half. This mirrors the recent patterns that have been seen in the diffusion of technology. For example, in the USA, it took 65 years for telephones to reach a 40 per cent penetration level of the population, but just 10 years for smartphones to achieve the same level of usage. Similarly, the design cycle for new cars has fallen from 60 months to 24–36 months in just five years.[2] The net impact of these changes is that firms have to move more quickly than ever to take advantage of new opportunities. The growth in smartphone usage is important for another reason, which is its growing importance as a medium through which people connect to the internet. In 2010, just 3 per cent of the world's population went online using a mobile but, by 2018, this figure had exceeded 52 per cent.[3] The impact of this trend is discussed in the section on **mobile marketing**.

Now that a greater number of consumers than ever are online, two questions are of particular interest to marketers, namely what are consumers doing online and how much business is being transacted through this medium (see Critical Marketing Perspective 11.1). Figure 11.1 shows the most popular daily online activities of adult users of the internet in 2017. As we can see, the most popular activities were sending and reading emails, using a search engine to find information and using a social networking site. Internet activity also varies by age and gender. Consumers aged under 30 are the biggest users of the internet to engage in social networking, send instant messages and watch videos. Those in the 30–60 age range are the most likely to use search engines to find information and to get their news online. Females are bigger users of social networking sites than males and are more likely to shop online, while males are bigger users of the internet to access news and information.[4]

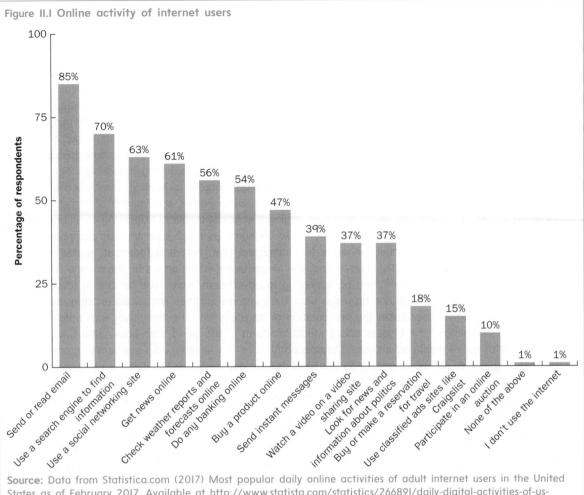

Figure II.I Online activity of internet users

Source: Data from Statistica.com (2017) Most popular daily online activities of adult internet users in the United States as of February 2017. Available at http://www.statista.com/statistics/266891/daily-digital-activities-of-us-internet-users/ (accessed August 2018).

Critical Marketing Perspective II.I
Engagement or addiction?

The internet has had a transformative impact on the world. In the space of a decade, internet usage has become pervasive in developed countries and is growing rapidly elsewhere, as seen in Table 11.1. It has become essential for our work lives and arguably the dominant activity in our non-work lives. For many, the two have blurred to such an extent that it is difficult to say where work stops and leisure begins. But internet-enabled devices are never too far away from us. Whether it is checking emails in the evening to scrolling through social media feeds to playing video games, more and more of our time is devoted to looking at screens. Inevitably, questions are raised regarding whether all of this activity is good for our health.

Have you ever wondered why it is so difficult to resist checking your phone? Or to stop playing a video game? If you find either of these difficult you are not alone, and it is now estimated that teenagers in Britain are spending an average of 18 hours per week on their phones. The media is replete with stories of individuals who cannot separate themselves from technology, such as a tabloid headline in 2018 that read 'Game over: Girl 9 in rehab after getting hooked playing Fortnite for 10 hours a day and wets herself to avoid switching off.' This has led many to claim that video

(continued)

games and social media sites are 'engineered for addiction'. For example, an investigation by the BBC's *Panorama* programme found evidence of design for addiction by technology companies.[5] Some of the elements of Facebook that were found to be particularly addictive include the infinite scroll feature and the 'Like' button. Infinite scroll has been found to keep users looking at their phones far longer than necessary. The Facebook 'Like' feature has been likened to a shot of dopamine (the brain's pleasure chemical) as it not only keeps users coming back to check on how many Likes their posts are receiving but, more worryingly, it is also linked to levels of self-worth in some. Similarly, the Snapstreaks feature on Snapchat, which tells how many consecutive days two people have sent snaps to each other on the platform, is equally designed to keep users coming back but has also been criticized because it is used by teens as a way of quantifying friendships. Features on Twitter, like the 'spinning wheel' which shows that more content is loading, are based on the same principle as casino slot machines. Industry insider, Sean Parker, the founder of Napster and founding president of Facebook, is on record as saying that social media is 'exploiting a vulnerability in human psychology' and that Facebook set out to consume as much user time as possible.

Fundamentally, it is essential for users to understand that, first and foremost, social media sites are businesses and advertising platforms. The longer users spend on a site, the more attractive it is to investors as the site will then be appealing to advertisers, which can be crucial to getting the necessary funding to build and grow the site. The platform will then attract advertising revenue through the size of its user base, the composition of its users and the frequency with which they use it. Not surprisingly, the biggest social media platform in the world, Facebook, also takes the lion's share of social media advertising. Consequently, it is in a social media platform's commercial interest to make its site as engaging as possible. But, in doing so, the line between engaging and compulsively addictive becomes difficult to define.

Is scrolling through endless social media feeds or playing video games for hours really all that bad? It may well be more of an issue than we realize. For example, it is estimated that, in the USA, nine people are killed and more than 1,000 are injured every day due to distracted driving.[6] A wide variety of medical problems, such as obesity, depression and anxiety, have been associated with excessive use of technology. Social media sites also stand accused of contributing to cyberbullying, unrealistic expectations, negative body image and unhealthy sleep patterns. Social media has even given rise to new terms, such as FOMO (fear of missing out), which describes the anxiety felt by users that they are missing out on the positive experiences or emotions that others are having. Faced with this growing backlash, technology companies have begun rolling out a wide variety of 'digital well-being tools'. These tools allow users to track the amount of time they spend online, such as the TimeWatched feature on YouTube, or to limit notifications from apps. Apple's Screen Time feature monitors how often users pick up their iPhone or iPad during the day and also helps them to manage notifications. However, many critics see this as a cynical exercise by tech companies to set up a new industry to help us with our technological addictions.

Suggested reading: Alter, 2018;[7] Eyal, 2014[8]

Reflection: Have technology companies put revenues and profits ahead of the interests of their users?

The most popular social networking sites in the world are shown in Figure 11.2. The dominance of Facebook in this space is very apparent. Aside from the fact that it has more than 2 billion monthly active users, it is also the owner of WhatsApp, Facebook Messenger and Instagram, all of which have more than 1 billion active users. WeChat and QQ are the dominant social media platforms in China. Due to their popularity with consumers, social media have become ever important platforms for communications between businesses and consumers.

The level of business being transacted online has also grown dramatically. Global e-commerce sales reached US$2.3 trillion in 2017, with an estimated 1.66 billion people purchasing goods online.[9] This growth is predicted to continue and the share of total global retail sales accounted for by e-commerce is expected to reach 17.5 per cent

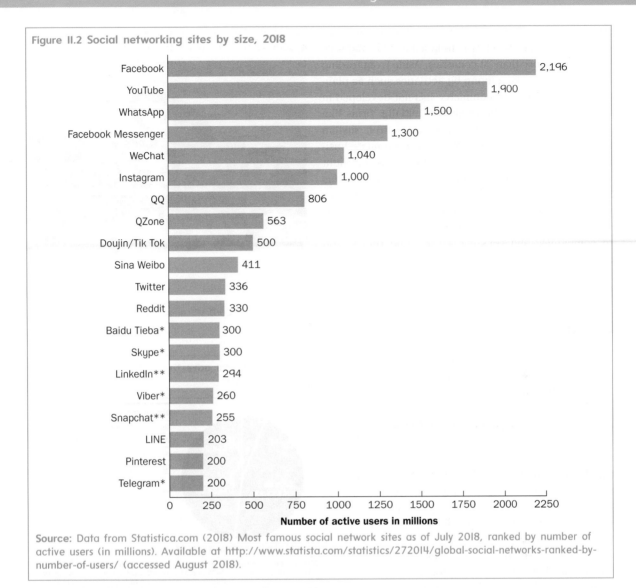

Figure 11.2 Social networking sites by size, 2018

Platform	Number of active users in millions
Facebook	2,196
YouTube	1,900
WhatsApp	1,500
Facebook Messenger	1,300
WeChat	1,040
Instagram	1,000
QQ	806
QZone	563
Doujin/Tik Tok	500
Sina Weibo	411
Twitter	336
Reddit	330
Baidu Tieba*	300
Skype*	300
LinkedIn**	294
Viber*	260
Snapchat**	255
LINE	203
Pinterest	200
Telegram*	200

Number of active users in millions

Source: Data from Statistica.com (2018) Most famous social network sites as of July 2018, ranked by number of active users (in millions). Available at http://www.statista.com/statistics/272014/global-social-networks-ranked-by-number-of-users/ (accessed August 2018).

by 2021.[10] Not surprisingly, the two largest e-commerce markets are China and the USA, with the UK, despite its small size, taking third position with annual e-commerce sales of US$99 billion representing 14.5 per cent of total retail sales.[11] Some of the most popular product categories transacted online include, books, music and stationery, travel, fashion, and personal care and beauty. Business-to-business (B2B) e-commerce is substantially larger than business-to-consumer (B2C) trade, estimated to be worth over US$7.7 trillion in 2017.[12]

One of the significant features of the digital environment was that it changed the interactions between businesses and consumers. Traditionally this had been a somewhat one-way communication, whereby businesses developed products and services that they marketed to consumers. However, the internet has changed all that, facilitating not just B2B and B2C commerce but also C2C and C2B interactions. As noted above, in terms of market value, B2B trade is the largest. Companies either manage their procurement of parts and supplies through dedicated electronic platforms or through B2B exchanges where there are numerous buyers and suppliers. For example, one of the biggest e-commerce firms in the world is the Chinese company, Alibaba (see Exhibit 11.1). It connects Chinese companies with overseas buyers and foreign companies with customers in China. It has an estimated 18 million buyers and suppliers residing in more than 240 countries and trading in 40 industry categories. B2C commerce is facilitated by both 'pure play' e-commerce businesses like Amazon, as well as traditional retailers like Tesco and Edeka. The internet also provides the opportunity for private individuals to trade with one another, with an estimated one in five individuals in the UK using it to sell goods and services in 2016.[13] The best-known C2C company is eBay, which was founded in 1995 and now operates in more than 30 countries. Aside from trading goods, others make a living by activities such as playing poker online. C2B commerce has not developed in a way that was initially predicted. Initially, firms like Priceline sought to create a *reverse auction* system whereby companies would bid for a customer's business, such as when a consumer wanted to book a flight or some accommodation, for example. However, this has not proved popular. Nowadays, C2B activity takes a variety of forms such as influencers offering their services to brands, freelancers providing their services to companies, and consumers providing reviews on sites like Amazon and TripAdvisor.

Exhibit II.I Alibaba is one of the largest e-commerce companies in the world.

eBay Ad Insight: This campaign puts across the company's core value in an online world.

Inevitably, all of this online activity has forced marketers to reassess how they allocate their marketing budgets. It raises questions such as, if consumers are spending more time on social media and doing their shopping online, should we still be spending money on traditional media such as radio and newspapers, for example. The year 2017 was significant in that it was the first time that expenditure on digital advertising exceeded that on television. Worldwide digital ad spending reached US$209 billion, or 41 per cent of the market, while television spend was US$178 billion (35 per cent of the market). At current levels of growth, it is estimated that digital will account for more than half of all global ad spend by 2020.[14] Digital ad spend is accounted for by two major formats: search and display (see Figure 11.3). Search advertising refers to advertising on search engines, such as using Google Adwords, while display advertising refers to everything from banner ads on websites to advertising on social media like Facebook.

Figure II.3 US digital advertising spend by format, 2016 (US$ billions)

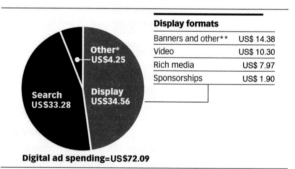

Display formats	
Banners and other**	US$ 14.38
Video	US$ 10.30
Rich media	US$ 7.97
Sponsorships	US$ 1.90

Search US$33.28 · Other* US$4.25 · Display US$34.56

Digital ad spending=US$72.09

Note: includes advertising that appears on desktop and laptop computers as well as mobile phones, tablets and other internet-connected devices on all formats mentioned; numbers may not add up to total due to rounding; *includes classifieds and directories, email, lead generation and mobile messaging; **includes ads such as Facebook's News Feed Ads and Twitter's Promoted Tweets

Source: eMarketer.com (2018) US digital ad spending, by format, 2016 (billions). Available at www.emarketer.com/Chart/US-Digital-Ad-Spending-by-Format-2016-billions/196615/ (accessed August 2018).

Objectives of online communications

As with any form of marketing communications, organizations should carefully consider the purpose of the campaign and what they are hoping to achieve before commencing. Critics of digital marketing argue that many firms are currently investing money in this space without clear commercial objectives and are perhaps guilty of following a fashion by having online elements to their communications.[15] Chaffey and Smith developed the 5S framework to demonstrate the overall goals of digital marketing.[16]

| *Sell*: Grow sales through wider distribution. A new online channel allows marketers to reach customers that couldn't previously be reached offline. There is no limit to store space online; a wider variety of products may be displayed and offered to customers, therefore increasing sales.

2   *Serve*: Add value through extra benefits for customers online. Give them better customer service, or a discount for buying products online. Customers online may also be offered gift wrapping of products, free delivery, etc. as part of their online experience.

3   *Speak*: Get closer to customers through creating a dialogue with them. Listen to their suggestions or ask for their opinion on a variety of aspects like products, design of the website, etc. Engaging in a dialogue with customers makes them feel important and has a positive influence on their brand loyalty.

4   *Save*: Save money through limiting print, store and rental costs. There are many options here: emailing customers will reduce print and postage costs; there's no need to open, equip and staff another bricks-and-mortar store, etc. These savings may then be redirected into enhancing customers' experience or adding extra services.

5   *Sizzle*: Extend the brand online through enhancing the online experience using interactivity with customers. Ensure confidentiality and safety of customers to gain their trust and loyalty.

This 5S model is the basis of all the digital activity marketers may undertake. At the level of marketing communications specifically, four core objectives can be identified, as follows.

1   *Awareness*: Online communications can be an effective means of helping consumers become aware of a particular product or service. In a digital marketplace where suppliers are competing with providers from anywhere in the world, getting heard in this crowded space and creating awareness are crucial objectives. So, for example, companies might enlist the help of a well-known influencer who introduces their brands to his/her followers (see Exhibit 11.2). Similarly, brands might invest in search engine marketing campaigns so that their offerings appear early on in the list of results presented to consumers searching for goods and services.

Exhibit 11.2 Cara Delevingne is a leading UK influencer who has had commercial arrangements with brands like Jimmy Choo, Chanel and Sephora.

2   *Engagement*: Whether working with potential or existing customers, companies might use online communications to try to build levels of engagement with those customers. Engagement is a central aspect of much digital marketing communications such as material posted by brands on social media sites or viral video campaigns run through platforms like YouTube. The field of **content marketing** discussed later in this chapter has grown rapidly as brands look for new and innovative ways to engage consumers online. However, building engagement levels through the likes of social media continues to be very challenging for brands, as we shall see.

3   *Conversion*: While high levels of awareness and engagement are great, the ultimate aim of marketing activities in commercial firms is to generate a sale. Online communications techniques are also useful in attempting to close sales. For example, email campaigns can feature limited-time offers designed to drive immediate purchases. Similarly, internet technology has enabled firms to engage in the controversial practice of **retargeting**. Consumers rarely buy on a first visit to a website, opting instead to browse several sites or postpone purchases until later. However, it is likely that, when a site was visited initially, the customer, perhaps unknowingly, accepted a **cookie** from that site. Cookies are pieces of computer code that websites use to help them recognize returning visitors, but they also help to identify customers as they travel around the web. So customers that may have considered a purchase on one website will frequently find that they see adverts for the same product as they visit other sites. From a marketer's point of view this is appealing as adverts are served only to those customers who are clearly considering a purchase, improving the chances of conversion.

4 *Retention*: Finally, online communications may be designed to assist with retaining customers through interacting with them post-purchase or helping to assist with customer service issues. Social media can be a quicker and more efficient way to interact with businesses than attempting to contact them through a call centre, for example. One of the novel features of digital marketing has been the unboxing phenomenon (see Exhibit 11.3). Unboxing refers to the process by which consumers record and upload videos of themselves unpacking their recent online purchases. This has proved to be particularly popular for the purchase of technology and fashion items.

Exhibit II.3 Unboxing has seen fans of brands post videos of their latest purchases online.

It is also useful to think about the objectives of online communications in the context of the consumer journey (see Chapter 3) and omni-channel marketing (see Chapter 9). The consumer decision process is no longer linear, and the number of potential touchpoints between the customer, other customers and organizations has changed greatly (see Figure 11.4). Marketers need to consider the relevant points on the customer journey, and how they can apply digital technologies and communications to assist customers and enhance their experience.[17] For example, in the tourism sector, new technologies like augmented reality (AR) and virtual reality (VR) can help to enhance the tourism experience. Augmented reality refers to the addition of digital elements to a live view, usually on a smartphone. So, for example, a tourist could examine enhanced videos of a particular destination at an early stage of the customer decision journey such as at the consideration

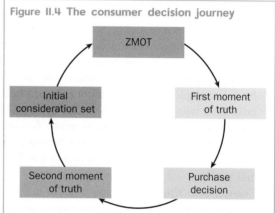

Figure II.4 The consumer decision journey

Source: Based on Chaffey, D. and Ellis-Chadwick, F. (2016) *Digital Marketing: Strategy, Implementation and Practice.* London: Pearson Education.

phase. Then, having reviewed the video, the person may decide to visit the actual destination. Arriving at the destination site, the experience can then be enhanced by virtual reality, whereby the visitor is equipped with a headset that blocks out the physical world and perhaps transports the guest back in time if the site is a historical monument.

Figure 11.4 illustrates the importance of the idea of 'moments of truth' in marketing. The term was first coined by Jan Carlzon, the then chief executive of Scandinavian Airlines, who was referring to every touchpoint between a customer and a representative of his company and how it was necessary to make this a positive experience.[18] Later, CEO of Proctor & Gamble, A.G. Lafley, identified two specific moments of truth, namely, when the consumer selects a brand in a store and then uses it for the first time at home. Then, taking account of changes in consumer behaviour, Google introduced the concept of Zero Moment of Truth in 2011, to describe all the online research activity that goes on before a brand is selected either online or in-store. What these key moments help to illustrate is that there are critical points in the consumer decision journey, some or all of which could be the focus of online communications activity.

Web design

As we saw in the previous section, a key objective of online communications is to drive traffic to an organization's online presence such as a website or Facebook page. Before looking at online communications in detail, let us first focus on the basic principles of online presence design. We will also focus on web design, bearing in mind that the principles discussed may also be applied to the design of mobile sites, apps and social media sites. The design of an online presence needs to be directed by two key elements: business objectives derived from current situation analysis, and target audience requirements (customers, suppliers, staff and other stakeholders).

Building the website based solely on the creative skills of designers or marketers is ineffective. Online design is an iterative process and is rarely done right the first time. To achieve user-centred design and effective ways to communicate with the audience, online research into their needs, as well as reviews and testing, should be factored into management of the website. The target audience of the designed website influences the structural and interactive elements. Needs and behaviours of different segments such as adults and teenagers may vary. Therefore factors such as interactivity, topics and content style need to be designed specifically for the target audience of the website.

Another important factor to be considered for the online design process is the intended access device. Websites designed for mobile devices, such as mobile phones or tablets, will differ from those intended for desktop computers. This need comes mainly from the time required to load a page on such devices and the size of the screen. The initial solution used by web designers focused on duplicating the content and creating a separate website for each single device. This is a less common practice now, however, and has been replaced by responsive web design (RWD). RWD is 'a combination of fluid grids and images with media queries to change layout based on the size of a device viewport. It uses feature detection to determine available screen capabilities and adapt accordingly.'[19] With the introduction of responsive web design, marketers can focus on the development of a single web place, rather than ensuring consistency of information presented on sites created for various devices.

An effective web presence is important as at any point on the customer journey, a potential customer may cease their interactions with a website. Various metrics can be used to measure website effectiveness. First is the **bounce rate**, which is the percentage of visitors to a particular website who navigate away after viewing just one page. Anything under 40 per cent is considered excellent, 41–55 per cent is average, 56–69 per cent is high but may not be a cause for concern, depending on the website, and anything above 70 per cent is considered problematic for everything outside the likes of blogs, news and events. **Dwell time** measures the length of time a visitor spends on a webpage before moving back to a search results page. It can be used as an indicator of the quality and relevance of web design and content.

Basic elements of effective web design

Presentation

As with any other communication tool: make it professional and clear. Steve Krug[20] demonstrated that users online act instinctively and they don't want to spend time learning how to use a new website. With this in mind, marketers shouldn't be afraid to follow the standards (fonts, consistency in colour scheme, presentation of links, position of logo, use of breadcrumbs, etc.). Users are goal-oriented and have little patience with websites that they can't use. With the amount of information online, if they can't find it in one place, they will move to another. Standardization of certain aspects of design gives them a feeling of mastery and empowerment, leading to successful completion of the task.[21, 22]

Page width and length need to be considered as important factors of design. Some pages will be printed by users, therefore designers need to consider the amount of content on such pages. Printers work with a maximum width of 750 pixels, and any content outside this will be chopped. As for the length, users shouldn't have to scroll down the page to find vital information. Pictures, graphics and video clips should complement the website rather than be the main element. It's not good for search engine optimization (SEO) to overload the website with visual elements.

Usability

Usability focuses on assessing how easily the user can complete their task online. Tasks may differ from finding information (address of the store, particular product, etc.) to completing a purchase or contacting the author of the page. In simple terms, usability deals with user friendliness online or user experience (UX). Usability of a website's user interfaces was defined by ISO 9241-151 as follows.

The effectiveness, efficiency and satisfaction with which specified users achieve specified goals in particular environments:

■ *effectiveness: the accuracy and completeness with which specified users can achieve specified goals in particular environments;*
■ *efficiency: the resources expended in relation to the accuracy and completeness of goals achieved;*
■ *satisfaction: the comfort and acceptability of the work system to its users and other people affected by its use.*[23]

Usability was considered by computer engineers much earlier than by marketers. However, what they described informs successful marketing endeavours. Two usability experts, Jakob Nielsen and Bruce Tognazzini, focus on ensuring that a well-designed website should concentrate on the user (the customer). Each element of the website should be relevant, up to date, accessible and clear for the user. Both of them are also strong advocates of simplicity and consistency of design.[24, 25]

Consistency for marketers refers not only to the website itself but reaches further. Websites should serve as part of an offline campaign and agree with branding in general. This way, the online presence of the company is part of IMC. Also, ensuring consistency between online and offline channels gives the customer a sense of familiarity and recognition while online, and enhances their satisfaction (see Exhibit 11.4).

Exhibit II.4 The UK clothing brand Oasis is a recognized leader in omni-channel retailing, blending its offline and online presence.

Navigation

Navigation on the website is not there to be pretty, but to allow visitors to find their way around. Think about a dictionary: an A–Z order is not pretty or inventive, but it works perfectly. The same applies to websites, so the navigation (menus, breadcrumbs, links, footer) needs to be familiar and easy to use. Good navigation will help customers to find what they need, navigate back if they make a mistake and reduce the number of times when disappointed customers leave the website because they got lost.

Testing

Before launching a website online, it needs to be tested for errors and performance. Due to the multiplicity of web browsers and devices used, companies need to ensure that every visitor to their website will see it exactly as intended. Rushing through this process is not advisable as premature launch may lead to lost transactions, errors on the page and, ultimately, unsatisfied customers.

Reviews and maintenance

As mentioned before, the design process doesn't finish once the website is online. At this stage, customers become testers, so their opinions need to be heard, and marketers need to react to them and their suggestions. Errors and non-working parts need to be fixed immediately; suggestions for improvement should be considered and addressed if appropriate. Constant dialogue with customers will lead to customer satisfaction and loyalty.

Therefore, according to Vila and Kuster[26] a well-designed website will increase customers' confidence, attitude and satisfaction, lowering perceived risk and, ultimately, leading to increased purchase intention (see Figure 11.5).

Content and copywriting

We need to remember that writing for the web differs significantly from the writing we are used to. The reason for this is simple: people don't read on the web: '79% of people scan the new page and only 16% read it word by word'.[27]

Pulizzi and Barrett[28] recommend that companies need to change their mind-sets to implement a successful content strategy. They recommend using the BEST principles for creating content for online media:

- **B**ehavioural – is there a purpose in the content? What action do you want to trigger in customers?
- **E**ssential – don't publish content that will become just space filler. If your customers visit a page that is about nothing, they will leave and never come back.

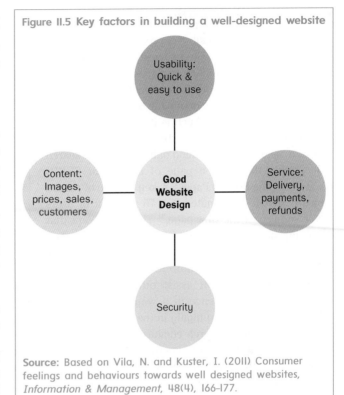

Figure 11.5 Key factors in building a well-designed website

Usability: Quick & easy to use

Content: Images, prices, sales, customers

Good Website Design

Service: Delivery, payments, refunds

Security

Source: Based on Vila, N. and Kuster, I. (2011) Consumer feelings and behaviours towards well designed websites, *Information & Management*, 48(4), 166–177.

- **S**trategic – your content delivered online needs to support your overall business objectives and be an integral part of your marketing activity.
- **T**argeted – don't use the same content across a variety of platforms. Each platform attracts different people for a reason, so make sure your content is always relevant for them.

Writing for the web therefore is difficult, and writing for mobile devices is even more challenging. Marketers need to understand how to write to engage with users. General consumers don't like business jargon and convoluted words. Focusing on the benefits of the product or service in simple words (but avoiding being patronizing) will work much better. Users rarely read the full content of a website; they prefer to scan it.[29, 30] Eye-tracking studies have determined that users scan web pages in an 'F' pattern: they scan/read through upper sections of the content, then they go through the left side of the content in a vertical movement. See Exhibit 11.5 for an example of a heat map – the most read parts of the websites are in red, followed by yellow, and the least-viewed areas are blue. Grey areas didn't attract any users.

The last crucial aspect of good content writing is making sure that it is grammatically correct and has been spell checked. Grammar and spelling mistakes negatively affect the credibility and reputation of the business. Knowledge of basic HTML coding can speed up the process of removing such errors from the website.

Exhibit 11.5 Eye-tracking research results for webpages.

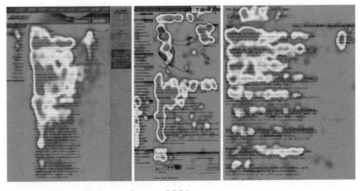

Source: Nielsen Norman Group, 2006

Search engine optimization

So you have gone through the process of developing and finalizing your website or social media presence. Now you want to be found! And, yes, the first port of call for most people looking for something online is a search engine, the most dominant of which by far is Google (see Table 11.2). Such is its dominance that it has given rise to the new verb: to google – in other words, to search for something online. A Google search will quickly throw up a page of results, or SERPs (Search Engine Results Pages). A key feature of results pages is that it is estimated that 75 per cent of users never scroll past the first page.[31] This has meant that achieving one of those coveted positions on the first page has become all important. And this has given rise to the search engine optimization (SEO) industry, namely, businesses that assist other businesses to design their web presence in a way that maximizes their chances of scoring highly in the search rankings.

Table II.2 Search engines by global market share, 2016

Search engine	% of global market
Google	72.48
Excite	0.01
AOL	0.15
Ask	0.22
Baidu	7.14
Yahoo!	7.78
Bing	10.39
Other	1.82

Source: Search Engine Watch (2018) What are the top 10 most popular search engines? Available at www.searchenginewatch.com/2016/08/08/what-are-the-top-10-most-popular-search-engines/ (accessed 28 August 2018).

The key aim for search engines like Google and Bing is to provide relevant search results for their users who have entered a search query. Therefore, results are ranked using a complex algorithm that will determine the position given to each individual webpage. Google's algorithm has been undergoing a process of constant revision and refinement ever since the company began conducting business in 1998. It is estimated that it is made up of approximately 200 components whose relative importance changes over time. Google makes in the region of 500 changes to its algorithm each year. Most of these changes are made without any fanfare, but from time to time Google announces significant changes that provide insights into what criteria influence a webpage's position on the rankings (see Exhibit 11.6).

Some of Google's major updates are described below.

Exhibit II.6 Google's major algorithm updates.

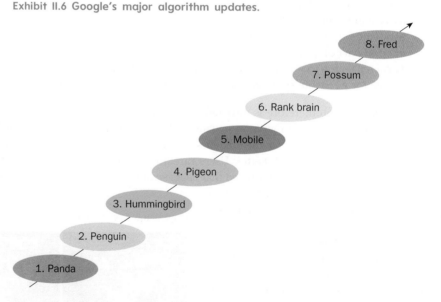

1 *Panda*: Launched in 2011, this update focused on website content, downgrading sites assessed as having poor or spammy content, plagiarized content or having engaged in keyword stuffing (a practice whereby keywords are repeated many times on webpages in order to improve their chances of being found).

2 *Penguin*: Launched in 2012, this update targeted manipulative links tactics. Because inward links to a website improve its position in the rankings, some businesses had created fake links or paid links and were penalized for this.

3 *Hummingbird*: Launched in 2013 with the goal of producing more relevant results by understanding the meaning behind queries. Matching searcher intent increased the focus on webpage content.

4 *Pigeon*: Launched in 2014 with the goal of providing high-quality, local search results. This update used location and distance as key factors influencing results ranking.

5 *Mobile*: Launched in 2015, this update gave a ranking boost to websites optimized for mobile devices and lowered the rankings of those that were not. Mobile rankings were done at page level rather than website level.

6 *RankBrain*: Launched in 2015, this update aimed to deliver better search results based on relevance and machine learning. It took account of metrics such as bounce rates.

7 *Possum*: Launched in 2016, this update further improved results based on location.

8 *Fred*: Launched in 2017, this update penalized websites that were set up primarily to generate advertising and affiliate revenue, such as blogs.

Search engine optimization describes the range of tools and techniques employed to try to ensure that a webpage ranks as high on the SERPs as possible. If a website consists of multiple pages, each must be optimized individually as engines search pages not websites. Taking account of the various updates to the Google algorithm discussed above, a number of practices that have been found to improve search rankings are discussed below. The importance of these criteria changes as algorithms change and search engine optimization (SEO) consultants assist businesses to optimize their websites for search.

1 *Keywords*: Consumers search for something using keywords such as 'hotels in London' or 'content marketing'. Keywords are essential, therefore, in helping Google to establish what a page is about and whether or not to include it in the results for a particular query. An important marketing decision concerns which keywords to use. Various companies provide tools that demonstrate the most popular keywords that people are searching, or the keywords that might be driving business to competitor websites. Keyword selection will also involve choices regarding short-tail and long-tail keywords such as 'hotels' and 'hotels in Murcia with pool and gym', the latter being more precise and specific and likely to reduce the number of results presented. Each page needs to optimized for relevant keywords and, as we have seen, it is important to avoid the practice of keyword stuffing, which is penalized by the Google algorithm.

2 *Content*: Throughout the various algorithm updates, the importance of content has risen. Google has built its business on providing relevant search results to users. The better the content on the page, the more likely searchers will find it useful. This has helped give rise to another new industry, namely, content marketing, which we shall examine in greater detail below.

3 *Links*: The quality and relevance of a site can also be reflected in the number and quality of other sites linking to it (inbound links). Links from authoritative sites such as the BBC or CNN will improve a website's position in the rankings. In the past, many sites tried to exploit this by creating links, either by encouraging or paying others to link to their sites. As we have seen, Google used its Penguin update to tackle such manipulative link tactics. Nowadays, it is recognized that the best way to generate links is to provide high-quality content and to market the website effectively so that potential users are aware of it.

4 *Localization*: Many businesses, such as offline retailers or service companies, draw most of their consumers from a nearby radius of their outlets. Registering with Google Places is a free and effective way of boosting SEO as Google has sought to customize results based on the location of the searcher since its Pigeon update in 2014. Positive customer reviews left on the Google Places page also help to boost rankings.

5 *Design features*: Search engines trawl through millions of webpages using automated programmes called 'bots' or 'spiders' that capture the page details and store them in a database called an index, which is optimized to deliver instant results when search queries come through. Websites need to be designed so that they are easy to crawl. As a result, they have become increasingly clear and simple, and have reduced their dependence on technical programming languages like Flash, JavaScript and webpage elements like Frames.

In summary, the purpose of SEO activity is to ensure that a website achieves and maintains the highest possible position in the search rankings. As we can see, this is difficult given the number of variables that determine ranking position and also due to the competitive activity of rival sites. Providing high-quality, relevant content is one of the most important factors and we shall now look at this issue in more detail.

Content marketing

Traditional marketing communications, such as television advertising, radio advertising, sponsorship and so on, are frequently described as forms of *out-bound* marketing – in other words, companies invest in a one-way effort of pushing their marketing messages out to an audience of potential customers. In contrast, a key feature of online marketing communications is that it is *in-bound*, meaning that it is designed to attract an audience to visit a website or social media page. One of the ways to do this is to create great content that consumers will not only seek out and find but may also share on their own social media profiles, thereby amplifying the effect. Content marketing has been defined as:

> *a strategic marketing approach focused on creating valuable, relevant and consistent content to attract and retain a clearly defined audience – and ultimately to drive profitable customer action.*[32]

The dynamic, two-way nature of content is worthy of note. The creation of content, such as the posting of a YouTube video, enables organizations to initiate conversations with customers who can like, share and comment on the content. Consumers themselves can also create content, known as **user-generated content**, which, in turn, may be used by organizations in their marketing activities.

Content marketing has been with us as long as marketing has existed. For example, the first issue of *The Furrow*, an agricultural magazine produced by tractor manufacturer John Deere, was published in 1895. It had a circulation of more than four million readers in the USA and Canada by 1912.[33] Similarly, the *Red Bulletin*, a lifestyle magazine by the Red Bull brand, began publishing in 2005. With the advent of the internet, content marketing has exploded for a number of reasons. First, as we saw earlier, content is a key variable in search rankings which has been a major boost to the industry. Second, the two-way nature of internet communications has meant that users can interact with content, commenting on it and sharing it. Third, in contrast to traditional forms of content, the cost of distribution of online content is virtually nil. While there may be costs incurred in the production of a video, it can be distributed free of charge via a website or social media channels. Physical content like a magazine must be distributed through the postal service or combined with other media like newspapers. Finally, the consumer's appetite for content for both information and entertainment purposes has increased. As we saw in Chapter 3, consumers are heavy users of online research in order to assist them with making purchase decisions, while social media channels, in particular, are relied on for entertainment.

Content marketing campaigns

A vast array of content types have been identified. Some of the most popular include website articles, blogs, news stories, case studies, testimonials, annual reports, research papers, white papers, e-books, podcasts, video, presentations, images and infographics. With such a wide range of options available, it is clear that, like any aspect of marketing communications, content marketing needs to be carefully planned. Attention needs to be paid to the objectives of the campaign, to the content that will be created, to the channels through which it will be distributed and, finally, to how its effectiveness will be measured. In addition, decisions will need to be made regarding who is responsible for content marketing in-house and whether or not the services of a content marketing agency will be employed.

Strategy and objectives

In the same way that a television advertising campaign might be used to build a company's brand, online content can play a similar role. Therefore careful thought needs to be given to brand positioning and strategy. All forms of content produced need to reflect and communicate these brand values. Second, it will not be possible to assess the effectiveness of a content campaign without some clearly defined objectives. Content might be used to create awareness, to engage consumers, to inform decision-making or help consumers solve problems, and so on. A good knowledge of the target audience will also help to clarify objectives (see Exhibit 11.7). The objectives of content marketing might be linked to stages in the consumer decision journey. For example, in a B2B context, a detailed white paper might help a consumer to evaluate the different alternatives available. Technical papers or instructional videos might help the consumer to solve problems.

Exhibit II.7 Booking.com's 'Love Stories' campaign was a video content campaign focusing on millennials' passion for travel.

Content type

Different types of content can play different roles in an organization's content marketing strategy. For example, *news stories* and *blog content* can address topical issues and keep an online presence current and up to date, which will also help to boost its search rankings. *White papers* and *e-books* are more detailed forms of content that might be used to indicate expertise in a particular field. *Infographics* and *slideshows* are a graphical representation of some material and are designed to be highly shareable and used to drive traffic to a website. Similarly, *images* and *videos* can also be highly shareable. A number of characteristics of great content have been identified, including credibility, shareability, usefulness or fun, interesting, relevant, different and on brand.[34] However, the relative importance of these characteristics will be contingent on the objectives of the content. For example, content designed to try to generate awareness should be highly shareable and on brand (see Exhibit 11.8).

Exhibit 11.8 The video content campaign by pet brand Whiskas reflected the fact that cats are the most searched item on YouTube.

Distribution platforms

The next set of decisions is concerned with how content will be distributed, which will also be influenced by campaign objectives and content type. Short- and long-form content such as blogs and white papers might be carried on the organization's website or on certain social sites such as LinkedIn. More visual or entertaining content might be reserved for social channels such as YouTube, Facebook and Twitter. Good-quality content might also be seeded with or picked up by both online and offline channels such as bloggers, influencers and journalists, greatly amplifying its effect. This is known as **earned media**. Finally, decisions need to be made about the timing of content. This should be a carefully planned rather than a haphazard activity. An active organization will be producing a vast amount of content, which is planned and scheduled using a content calendar.

Assessment of effectiveness

While the distribution of content may be free, its production certainly is not, potentially involving high levels of staff time and some direct costs in the case of video, for example. Therefore it is essential to assess the return on investment associated with content marketing. Depending on the objectives of the campaign, effectiveness might be measured in terms of metrics such as reach, engagement levels, website visits, and so on. A more complete review of the mechanisms for assessing online communications campaigns is presented later in this chapter.

The role of content marketing

Content marketing is playing a growing role in the integrated marketing communications mix. This is partly due to the recognition of the importance of storytelling in marketing (see Marketing in Action 11.1).[35] Humans largely understand the world through stories. This process begins very early in life, with exposure to children's stories, and continues on through the consumption of media such as movies as well as social interactions.

Marketing in Action II.I
ONLY: 'The Liberation'

> **Critical Thinking:** Below is a review of ONLY's use of storytelling to revitalize its fashion catalogue. Read it and think of examples of other brands that have used storytelling in their content creation.

ONLY is a Danish fashion brand that was founded in 1995. Selling primarily denim, T-shirts and tops, its target market is younger females. The company initially sold its products through company-owned stores before expanding through other retail outlets to currently have a presence in 23 countries around the world. In the post-global financial crisis world after 2008, ONLY was struggling in the face of competition from fast-fashion rivals such as Zara and H&M, whose products were perceived as better and cheaper. Something needed to be done, and quickly, to prevent the brand from slipping into decline.

The fashion catalogue is one of the mainstays of the industry. Brands allocate a significant portion of their marketing budgets to the production of these booklets, which illustrate the currents season's trends and looks. But differentiating the brand is difficult given that many of these catalogues look alike. And, more importantly, an opportunity that appeared to be missed by many fashion brands is that the catalogue does not fit well with the media habits of younger consumers. ONLY sought to exploit this opportunity through the development of an interactive digital 'catalogue' called 'The Liberation', made up of specially shot film and other content. Critically, the film also told the story of a girl in a sleepy town who was fascinated by three rebellious newcomers. Viewers get to follow the story of the three heroines (who are all wearing ONLY clothes), interact with the movie – such as helping the girls to get out of town – and after watching the content could then visit their own personal store in the catalogue to share content and purchase the clothes they had viewed.

A carefully planned marketing campaign accompanied the launch of the film. Top European fashion bloggers and journalists were invited to the shoot to report live from the production. Journalists were also invited to pre-launch events and the 'catalogue' was announced through an online banner-advertising campaign. The launch itself coincided with a collaboration with supergroup Swedish House Mafia and the screening of a full-length movie in Danish cinemas. In total, more than 15 million users interacted with and engaged with 'The Liberation' online. The campaign was significant in improving engagement. Play-to-end rate is one important metric for video projects. Good-performing film trailers average about 60 per cent, whereas 'The Liberation' hit an average of 68 per cent, unprecedented for a commercial project. Dwell time on the company's website also increased significantly. The campaign also had a significant sales effect. During the promotion, the proportion of site visitors buying clothes almost doubled, while basket size increased by over 50 per cent compared with 'normal' buyers at the web store. The sell-through rates of products featured in the film also rose strongly in ONLY's physical stores. Overall, the company estimated that the successful campaign delivered a return-on-investment of €53 for every euro spent and helped to turn the brand's declining sales fortunes around.

Based on: Samuelsen, Prosager and Gladstone, 2014[36]

People relate to one another through stories, and brands often play both central and peripheral roles in these stories.[37] Critical to stories are the characters, such as the rebel, the hero, the villain, the innocent, and so on. The essence of brand building is the absorption of these characters into the brand story, for example the winner (Nike), the outlaw (Marlboro) and the creator (Lego). Content marketing provides a platform for brands to both tell their story and to invite consumers to be part of the story. Aside from big brands, storytelling is also central to the growth of start-up businesses, social enterprises and personal brands online.[38] Individuals use storytelling to highlight their positive attributes that are of value while at the same time differentiating themselves from other individuals in the marketplace.[39]

In essence, the creation of content is not entirely dissimilar to what a newspaper or a television news service does. In fact, some leading brands have formally adopted the structures and processes of the 'newsroom' in order to assist them in creating and delivering relevant, current and engaging content. In particular, sports brands like Adidas and Puma have adopted the newsroom concept in order to be able to quickly tap into trending sporting events while at the same time achieving consistency across online communications.[40] This means employing journalists and responding quickly to stories that the brand's audience might care about. Speed of response is critical to the effectiveness of this type of content, sometimes resulting in it being labelled **real-time marketing**. When something happens in the world of sport, the brand associated with that team or personality will want to be the first to produce online content about it (see Exhibit 11.9).

Exhibit 11.9 Businesses like Adidas are extensive users of real-time marketing.

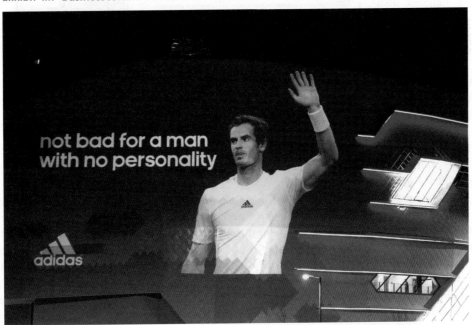

With content being relatively easy to produce, and with so many brands producing it, the sector has exploded. It is estimated that every day there are 1 million pieces of content shared on Facebook, 500,000 tweets on Twitter and 100,000 hours of video uploaded on YouTube.[41] Therefore one of the biggest challenges to be faced is that of consumer engagement. For example, it is estimated that 5 per cent of the content is generating 90 per cent of the engagement.[42] Distinctions have been drawn in the literature between passive/active engagement and positive/negative engagement.[43] Simply viewing a post or a video is a relatively passive activity, while commenting on/sharing the post or uploading content constitutes active engagement. Similarly, the consumer response can be positive in terms of liking the post or negative in terms of posting a critical comment, for example. Some of the factors that have been found to increase engagement levels include emotional or experiential messages and incentives to share content.[44]

Online advertising

As we have seen, some of the primary online activities include using search engines, visiting websites and visiting social media sites. As a result, all of these activities also represent an opportunity for marketers to advertise to consumers. Therefore while users may see Google as a search engine or Facebook as a social media site to enable them to interact with friends, these are actually advertising platforms that generate the bulk of their revenues in this way. Indeed, such is their dominance of the online advertising business that they are frequently referred to as the digital duopoly commanding more than half of all global digital advertising revenues. In contrast, other well-known social media sites, such as Snapchat and Twitter, account for less than 1 per cent each of global ad revenues.[45]

Search engine advertising

Earlier in this chapter, we examined the tools and techniques that organizations use to try to achieve and maintain a high position in the search rankings. However, search engines also offer users the opportunity to advertise on the search results page (SERPs). Search ads are given priority, appearing before the organic results or on a side bar, as shown in Exhibit 11.10.

There are a number of reasons why organizations might advertise on a search results page. First, search

Exhibit II.IO Examples of search engine advertising.

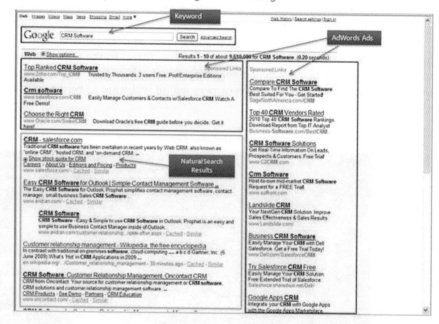

advertising might be used to drive traffic to a website while waiting for the effects of search engine optimization to kick in. SEO tactics such as the use of keywords and generating good content take time to achieve their effects, meaning that businesses work their way up through the rankings slowly. Paid search advertising gives these businesses priority as they are returned first on a SERPs page. Second, search advertising is attractive because it is highly targeted. Ads will be shown only to people who have entered particular keywords, meaning that they are interested in the product or service and have effectively pre-qualified themselves. Third, search ads are flexible and measurable. Different versions of the advert can be employed and tested in the marketplace – known as **A/B testing**. Response levels to the different adverts are immediately observable, allowing advertisers to change, delete or continue with adverts easily and quickly. Finally, a unique advantage of search advertising (along with some other forms of digital advertising) is that the advertiser is not paying for the ad to be displayed (as one would when using a billboard or advertising on television, for example) but only when a user clicks on the actual ad. This is known as **PPC**, or 'pay per click', and represents an efficient form of advertising.

Search advertising campaigns

Search advertising may comprise all or part of an integrated marketing communications campaign. Either way, like all forms of marketing communications, it requires careful planning to ensure that organizational resources are invested wisely. The key stages involved in running a search advertising campaign are outlined below.

- *Target audience*: The target audience for the campaign will require careful consideration. Search queries, almost by definition, are quite specific. Therefore organizations need to carefully consider who their campaign is being aimed at.

- *Objectives*: Like all communications campaigns, clarification of objectives is critical at the outset. Typical objectives of a search advertising campaign might be to drive traffic to a website or to promote special offers, for example.
- *Keywords*: In our earlier section on **search engine optimization**, we noted the importance of the keyword. This takes on even greater relevance in search advertising as keywords are bid for through an auction system. The difference between short- and long-tail keywords is important here as the former are likely to be more generic, such as 'hotels in London', and hence more expensive, having a high cost per click but relatively low conversion rates. When selecting keywords, advertisers have the flexibility to specify exact matches (your ad appears only if the exact keywords are entered) or broad matches (your ad appears if the exact or related keywords are entered). Broad matching generates more traffic but is less targeted.
- *Budgets*: Generally, multiple search advertising campaigns are run simultaneously; therefore decisions need to be made regarding the overall budget size and its allocation across the various campaigns. Advertisers are free to set monthly limits on an account-wide or individual-campaign basis and to specify the maximum amount per click that they are willing to pay for each ad. This will determine how frequently an ad appears and its position in the rankings.
- *Advertising copy*: Writing the advertising copy is a challenging exercise as search ads are limited to 130 characters, which includes the headline (keywords), body copy of the advert (which should say something compelling) and the destination URL (your website or social media page). Companies like Google attribute a quality score to search ads, which takes account of the keyword's click-through rate, the ad text relevance and landing page relevance, among other variables, and this, in combination with the bid level, will determine the ranking of the ad. Therefore great care should be taken in writing ad copy.
- *A/B testing*: Creating effective search advertising campaigns takes time and practice. Different combinations of keywords, ad copy and landing pages should be trialled to determine which work best.
- *Measuring effectiveness*: Search engine advertising companies provide users with a suite of metrics that can be used to test effectiveness. Some of the most critical include *click-through rate* (percentage of users that clicked on the ad), *cost per click* (average amount paid per click), *ad position* (average position the ad appears in on the rankings) and *conversion rate* (ratio of orders or leads to the number of clicks).

Display advertising

Display advertising is the oldest form of online advertising and refers to the placement of adverts on webpages. In fact, many of the initial web businesses were set up on the basis that offering advertising space would allow them to generate a revenue stream. Display adverts take a number of forms, as follows.

- *Banner advertising*: Banner adverts are the original and most popular form of digital display advertising. They are static adverts that come in a variety of sizes and shapes, frequently appearing across the top or on the side bar of a webpage (see Exhibit 11.11).
- *Pop-up advertising*: Though still very common, pop-up adverts are among the least popular forms of display advertising as they are interruptive of the browsing experience. Their use has helped to fuel the growth in the use of the ad-blocking software, which grew by an estimated 30 per cent in 2016.[46]
- *Rich-media advertising*: Rich-media adverts refer to all forms of display that have some active features, such as video, skippable video (popular on YouTube), ads containing live information or adverts that interact with the viewer, such as requiring the input of an email address.

With online display, every website (known as a publisher) is conceivably a potential advertising outlet if it welcomes ad content. This makes the publisher choice dizzyingly complex, forcing the advertiser to reflect on the size of the website audience, the nature of that audience, which webpage to advertise on, as well as the format and timing of the advert. **Programmatic advertising** has grown in response to the complexity of online display.

Exhibit 11.11 Banner adverts are the most popular form of online display advertising.

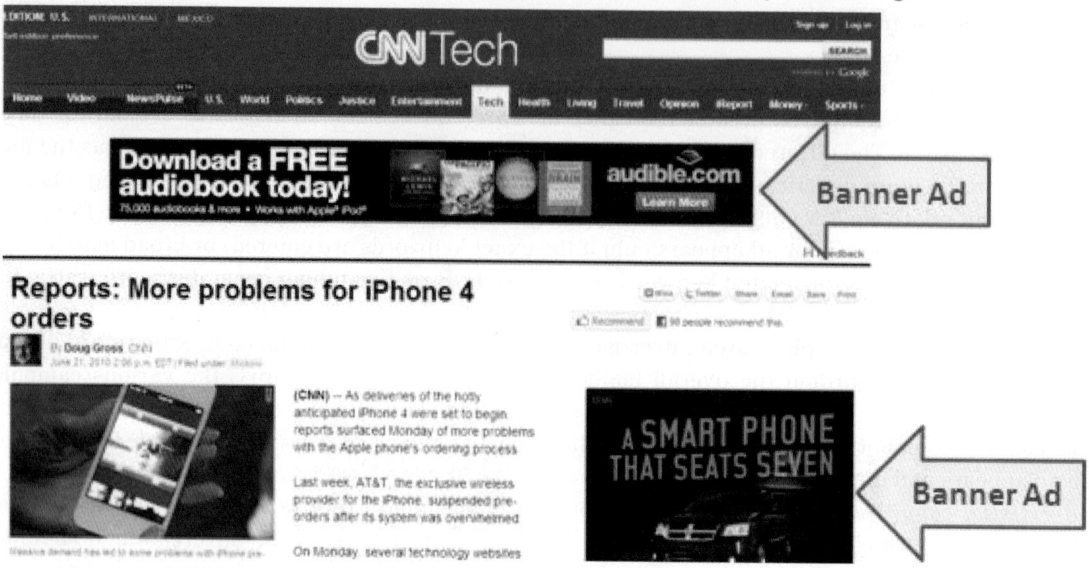

Programmatic advertising

Programmatic advertising is defined as an automated system for the buying and selling of online display adverts. Several players may be involved in this process. On the one side, there are advertisers looking to spend money on display while, on the other, there are websites and social media platforms willing to carry adverts; these, as noted above, are known as *publishers*. Transactions between them can be facilitated by a variety of players, most notably *ad brokers*, who bring buyers and sellers together, *demand-side platforms (DSPs)* that allow buyers to buy on many different platforms through a single interface, and *ad exchanges*, where adverts are bought and sold.

A key development that illustrates the strengths of the automated process is **real-time bidding (RTB)**. Simply put, when a user clicks on a weblink, in the micro-seconds it takes the webpage to load, this impression is auctioned to a potential advertiser through an automated system. If the advertiser's bid wins, then an advert is displayed (or served) on the page when it loads. RTB has played a big role in the growth of **retargeting**, where adverts are served specifically to prospects that have already been identified through their online behaviour. In the USA, approximately 44 per cent of ad buying was through the RTB system in 2017.[47] The remainder was through direct marketplaces where advertisers and agencies buy impressions in bulk, on a cost-per-thousand basis, giving them greater certainty about the audiences they are targeting and allowing them the flexibility to use rich-media formats.

As with search advertising, discussed earlier, display advertising campaigns need to be planned carefully, taking account of the target audience, objectives, budgets, advertising message and assessment of effectiveness. Equally, many of the advantages of online display are similar to those of search. The effectiveness of campaigns can be measured accurately through click-through rates on display ads or the number of views of a rich-media video. Ad content can be A/B tested to determine which visuals or copy are most effective. Through activities like retargeting, precise audiences can be targeted. One of the interesting outcomes of targeting efforts has been the growth in **contextual targeting**, which is a process by which webpages or social media sites are scanned for keywords and ads are served that relate to this content. However, this is a process that does not always operate as accurately as it should, as described in Marketing in Action 11.2.

Marketing in Action II.2
Advertising on YouTube

> **Critical Thinking:** Below is a review of the controversy surrounding the placement of advertising next to controversial content on YouTube. Read it and critically reflect on the strengths and weaknesses of programmatic advertising.

One of the benefits of programmatic advertising is speed – ads can be auctioned and served in the length of time it takes a webpage to load. But removing the human element from ad placement has its risks. A classic case in point was the difficulties faced by YouTube in 2017. The video giant had been the subject of criticism for a number of years for allowing extremist and explicit content to appear on its platform. But a further investigation by *The Times* newspaper in the UK revealed that some of these videos were also advertising-enabled, meaning that adverts would play either before the video began or appear as a banner ad while the video was playing. For example, in one instance, adverts from the Argos retail store and from Marie Curie, a hospice charity, appeared in videos promoting Combat 18, a violent pro-Nazi group. In other instances identified by journalists, T-Mobile ads appeared on videos about abortion, *Minecraft* banners were on videos about snorting cocaine and Novartis heart medication ads ran on videos entitled 'feminism is cancer'. To make matters worse, the YouTube advertising model generally operates on a 55:45 split, with 55 per cent of the advertising income going to the publisher. Inadvertently, some of the world's leading brands may be helping to fund the activities of extremist organizations.

Not surprisingly, the business community reacted quickly to the revelations. A range of global brands, including GSK, Pepsi, Walmart, Starbucks and Johnson & Johnson, all pulled their advertising from YouTube until they received assurances that their ads would not appear next to controversial content. But the black box that is programmatic advertising makes giving such assurances difficult. When an ad appears against a piece of content, it is not always clear whether it is on the basis of the browser's search history and interests or whether the brand is affiliated with a particular content creator such as a YouTube star. Ad placement that is being done by an algorithm is never likely to be as effective as a human's ability to identify particular nuances. YouTube provides 'brand safety' controls for advertisers, allowing them to pick what kinds of videos they are happy to be associated with based on keywords – but with an average of 400 hours of video being uploaded each minute, it is difficult to keeping paying customers and controversial content apart.

The YouTube ad controversy revealed a number of important issues. First, the controls put in place by social media sites like YouTube and Facebook to prevent the uploading of unpalatable content or to have it removed quickly do not always work as effectively as they should. Second, these platforms need to improve their algorithms so that the placement of brand advertising is done better. Third, and perhaps most interesting from a marketing point of view, is the revelation that many brands do not always know where their advertising is appearing on online platforms. It was estimated that the controversy could cost YouTube in the region of US$750 million in lost advertising despite its promise to address the problem. And it looks like an issue that is not going to go away quickly. In 2018, Under Armour pulled its advertising from the platform after it appeared alongside white nationalist content from the channel 'Wife with a Purpose'.

Based on: Field, 2018;[48] Ingram, 2017;[49] Mostrous, 2017;[50] Solon, 2017[51]

Social and native advertising

The newest and fastest-growing forms of online advertising are social and native advertising. **Social advertising** refers to adverts placed on social media platforms like Facebook, Instagram, Twitter, YouTube and Snapchat (see Exhibit 11.12). The value of the global social media advertising market was estimated to be worth more than US$67 billion in 2018 and, with growth levels of almost 30 per cent per year, it was forecast to overtake TV ad revenues by 2020.[52, 53] The rapid growth in social media advertising is commensurate with the increased use of these platforms for news, leisure and socializing with friends and family, as well as the increased use of mobile devices to access the internet (see the following section on mobile marketing). In addition, it is their potential for targeting niche audiences that makes them particularly attractive to advertisers. By far the biggest player is Facebook, which allows advertisers to very precisely target audiences based on the information that Facebook knows about them, such as age, marital status, location, hobbies/interests and behaviours, such as posts that users have liked, shared and commented on. This allows advertisers to specify the audiences to which they wish to serve ads. As with other forms of digital advertising, direct purchasing or real-time bidding may be used, and advertisers pay on a pay-per-click (PPC) basis. On Facebook, mobile ads are significantly more expensive than those appearing on desktops, so the increased use of mobile has significantly boosted its revenues.

Exhibit 11.12 Wilkinson Sword's Facebook Couples campaign was effective in driving demand for its Hydro 5 Groomer Razor in the 18–30-year-old demographic.

Another rapidly growing form of online advertising is known as **native advertising**, which the Native Advertising Institute defines as paid advertising that matches the form, feel and function of the content of the media on which it appears. Native advertising is particularly popular on social media and can take many forms, such as sponsored Facebook posts, Twitter-promoted tweets, BuzzFeed-branded articles, advertiser-funded videos or web TV. It can also be found in the offline world in the form of advertorials in newspapers and magazines. Some estimates put native advertising as accounting for more than half of all digital display revenues in 2016, and this percentage is expected to grow rapidly.[54] One of the key reasons for this is that native advertising, by definition, attempts to fit seamlessly into its surrounding content. For example, before becoming a public company in 2012, Facebook allowed advertising to appear only on a sidebar and not in the user's newsfeed, meaning that advertising was relatively easy to avoid and did not interrupt the browsing experience. However, after it became a publicly quoted business, one of its key decisions to grow its advertising revenues was the introduction of sponsored posts – that is, paid-for posts appearing in user newsfeeds. Because native ads look more like actual content, click-through rates are better than for display ads and they therefore prove more popular with advertisers. There is a legal requirement that native campaigns be clearly labelled as 'sponsored', 'promoted' or as 'advertising', though many users may miss this and think it is a bona fide post from an independent third party.[55] The blurring of the boundaries between content and advertising is a growing challenge for web users. Also, as more internet users move to mobile, native ads are more appealing than display ads, which do not work as effectively in that format.

Mobile marketing

As we have seen throughout this chapter, the increasing use of mobile devices to access the internet has had an impact on many aspects of online marketing communications, from the growth of social media power-houses like Facebook to the rise of native advertising. Globally, mobile devices such as smartphones and tablets overtook desktops and notebooks as the most popular means of accessing the internet for the first time in 2016. In some regions, like Asia and Africa, mobile access accounted for almost two-thirds of all web traffic in 2018.[56] Traditionally, mobile phones were a key tool for direct marketing where companies sent SMS (short messages) or MMS (multimedia messages) to customers on their mailing lists. However, the advent of the smartphone gave rise to two new forms of marketing, namely, proximity marketing and mobile applications, which we will discuss now.

Proximity marketing

Location is one of the most useful of the many features on a smartphone. By enabling it, users are able to identify where they are and plot routes to destinations that they might be looking for. But, by downloading software applications (apps) that ask for your location, this means that marketers also know where you are, which enables them to reach out to you with marketing messages. This is known as **proximity marketing**, which is defined as the use of wireless devices to distribute marketing messages to specific locations. It has applications in many areas. For example, retailers or consumer service businesses can send messages to people who are physically near their premises. This is another form of real-time marketing in that, for example, if a restaurant is quiet it can provide special offers to nearby customers who visit within a given, specified time period (see Exhibit 11.13). Proximity marketing has also been used extensively at destinations where large groups of people gather, such as festivals and sporting events.

Exhibit II.13 The German food brand Knorr used a proximity marketing campaign for its Naturally Tasty range, targeting busy mums near or in supermarkets.

Mobile applications (apps)

As we saw in Chapter 2, software applications, or apps, are computer programs that allow a user to perform a single or several related tasks. In recent years, the growth in apps has exploded. For example, in 2018, it was estimated that there were almost 4 million apps available to Android users and 2 million available on Apple's App Store.[57] In most markets, the average smartphone user has more than 80 apps on their phone and uses close to 40 of them per month.[58] As well as social activity, apps are used for news, games, entertainment and sporting information. Marketers have used apps in innovative ways to interact with customers and boost revenues. For example, shoppers can use apps to scan a barcode and compare product prices in another store.

Apps have been developed that allow consumers to pay bills, make insurance claims and buy products. Branded mobile apps, which are apps that display a brand's identity in the name of the app, or through a logo or other brand marks, have become increasingly popular (see Marketing in Action 11.3). For example, Colgate's MaxWhite Photo Recharger app features a photo-editing tool that allows users to brighten their teeth in photos with a virtual Colgate toothbrush. A content analysis of the branded apps being used by 106 global brands found that they used enhanced user navigation and control features in order to improve customer engagement with the app. Other features that improved engagement levels included vivid graphics and customized user interfaces.[59] Other research has found that branded apps attract more users and obtain stronger brand images if they are made available to consumers at no cost.[60]

Marketing in Action 11.3
L'Oréal Paris: Makeup Genius

Critical Thinking: Below is a review of the L'Oréal Paris Makeup Genius app. Read it and consider the manufacturer and consumer problems that it helps solve. What other commercial apps do you use and why?

Marketing is at its most effective when it solves a specific problem faced by customers. A case in point was the launch of the Makeup Genius app by L'Oréal Paris. Cosmetics users face an almost endless variety of choice in terms of shades, colours and tones. However, they are also usually very reluctant to buy a new product without first trying it out. Consequently, sampling new looks at department stores and retail outlets is big business but, even here, many products like lipsticks cannot be tried before purchase. L'Oréal Paris set out to tackle this problem using augmented reality and in the process reinvent makeup sampling.

The company invented a mobile app to allow women to try on makeup anytime, anywhere and turn product trial into a fun, creative experience. The app scans your face and allows you to virtually try on different products. It used facial mapping technology so that, even if you moved, smiled or pouted, the makeup stayed in the correct place, enhancing the experience. It gave women the opportunity to sample hundreds of products in the privacy of their own homes, as well as providing suggested looks and the options of sharing looks and purchasing these products directly from their smartphones. The app was launched with a global campaign that emphasized the way that the service empowered women to become designers and creators of their own looks, using the tagline, 'don't just apply makeup, design your beauty'.

The development of the app had many strategic and commercial benefits. First, as sampling has traditionally taken place in retail stores, retailers controlled the interaction with customers. However, Makeup Genius enabled L'Oréal Paris to connect directly with its users. Second, as smartphone usage was higher among younger consumers, it enabled the brand to reach the more digitally savvy customer. And, third, the app was an instant commercial success. By 2016, it had been downloaded more than 16 million times and the cumulative number of products tried had exceeded 270 million worldwide. The app proved to be particularly popular in Asian countries. For example, almost one-third of total downloads were in China, a country where girls are renowned for being shy about trying on makeup at a sampling counter or when going out with friends. It also proved popular in Japan, another country with high levels of smartphone usage. Launching Makeup Genius helped L'Oréal Paris become the number-three makeup brand globally in 2016.

Based on: Anonymous, 2016;[61] Daneshkhu, 2014;[62] Doland, 2015[63]

Email marketing

Email marketing is essentially the online equivalent of direct mail, which was discussed in Chapter 10. Simply defined, it is the act of sending a commercial message to a group of people via email. Therefore, the nature and structure of email campaigns are very similar to those of direct mail. They require the development or purchase of email lists, the setting of campaign objectives, the creation and delivery of content, and the assessment of effectiveness. However, great care needs to be taken with the development of email campaigns. Research studies have identified that consumers find unsolicited emails more intrusive and irritating than postal direct mail.[64] Furthermore, estimates frequently put the level of spam (or unsolicited emails) at close to half of all emails received, and this despite the presence of anti-spam software and spam filters. Therefore, email marketers should restrict their communications to only those customers who have opted to receive communications. This is known as **permission marketing**, which is a practice whereby consumers are given the option of receiving marketing messages or not and have chosen the former.

Email marketing campaigns

Email marketing campaigns begin with the development of mailing lists. One of the most common ways in which email lists are built is through the provision of specialized content on websites, where access to such content requires the entry of an email address. Calls to action to sign up for emails frequently appear as pop-up windows on websites, and incentives may also be provided to encourage subscriptions. Email lists may also be supplemented from lists of names on the organization's CRM (customer relationship management) systems (see Chapter 7). Marketers may also have the option to rent lists from specialized marketing companies. Only lists provided by reputable organizations should be selected, where those on the list have opted to receive messages from third-party vendors or partners, to avoid the problem of spam.

The next set of decisions involves consideration of the target audience and objectives for the campaign. Distinctions have been drawn between out-bound and in-bound email marketing.[65] Out-bound campaigns are a form of direct marketing to encourage trial or purchase, while in-bound email marketing refers to the receipt of email from customers, typically to deal with problems or service issues. Therefore, in terms of the overall objectives of online communications that we identified earlier in the chapter, out-bound campaigns can seek to create awareness or achieve conversion, while in-bound campaigns are more focused on customer retention.

Critical to the success of a campaign will be the design and content of the email message. Design is key in order to catch the consumer's attention and to communicate the important aspects of the message, as many emails are scanned quickly. The look of an email message may also be enhanced through the use of rich media, but care needs to be taken here regarding how well such enhancements load with different browsers and email platforms. In terms of email, perhaps the most critical element is the subject line, which needs to be engaging enough to encourage the consumer to open the message rather than simply delete it. The copy itself should be written in the consumer's language and the key elements of the message should be clearly communicated at the outset. Great care should be taken with the words used in the body copy as spam filters use keywords in determining which emails to block. The message should also include a clear call to action.

A variety of commercial organizations, known as email service providers (ESPs), such as Mailchimp (see Exhibit 11.14), provide platforms through which email campaigns can be executed. Consideration needs to be given to a number of variables, such as the day of the week and time of the day that messages arrive in the consumer's inbox. As with many aspects of online communications, A/B testing can be used to establish which practices work best. Finally, a wide variety of metrics can be used to assess the effectiveness of a campaign. Some of the most important include:

- *bounce rate* (emails will bounce if the address is no longer valid or the email is caught by a spam filter)
- *open rate* – what percentage of emails were opened
- *click-through rate* – the percentage of recipients who clicked on email content
- *conversion rate* – the percentage of emails leading to a sale
- *unsubscribe rate* – the number of consumers unsubscribing from the mailing list.

Exhibit 11.14 Email service providers like Mailchimp provide marketers with platforms for managing their email campaigns.

Managing and evaluating online campaigns

Digital marketing is no different from traditional marketing and companies need to measure the profitability of their activities. The digital footprint left by every person online is a source of important data. The amount of data that can be captured by online systems is almost infinite, but it's important to identify metrics that are a source of vital data for overall campaign performance.

Measurement of a company's online presence is an area, next to web design, where marketers need to work closely with IT experts. The task for marketers is to identify relevant metrics, and then analyse data, while IT experts need to implement and retrieve data from the analytics system. Companies can get data about how many website visits they have had, how many fans or followers they have on social media channels and how many times an app was downloaded. These basic measures are available to us by default and there's no need to set up anything special, but for more complex data like bounce rates, visit duration, new/returning visitors, conversion rates, etc. (see Table 11.3) additional software may be required.

There are many solutions available, both free and licensed, like Google Analytics, Web Trends, Adobe Site Catalyst and Coremetrics. A careful evaluation is required before the decision to purchase new software is made. Analytics tools are not cheap, as many of them need to be customized (the licensed or hosted ones), and therefore the cost is higher. Additionally, the decision to purchase analytics software should be driven by the linked profitability of the business, and specific business decisions should be informed by newly obtained data.

Analytics software may analyse a company's online presence overall (website, app, social media) and produce reports on valuable metrics (see also Chapter 1).

If a company can't afford to purchase expensive software, it can always go for open-source analytics solutions. These may have more limited functionality compared with expensive products, but can deliver enough information to provide some metrics on digital marketing.

Table II.3 Some main metrics and dimensions used online

Metrics and dimensions	Definition
Bounce rate	The percentage of visitors to a website who leave the site after viewing only one page
Conversion rate (goal conversion rate)	The percentage of sessions that resulted in a conversion to at least one of your goals
Average session duration	The average duration of user sessions, represented in total seconds
Ad clicks	The total number of times users have clicked on an ad to reach your property
Cost per click	Cost to advertiser per click; applies for paid advertising
Click-through rate	The click-through rate for the ad; this is equal to the number of clicks divided by the number of impressions for the ad (e.g. how many times users clicked on one of the ads where that ad appeared)
Cost per conversion	The cost per conversion (including e-commerce and goal conversions) for the site
Return on investment (ROI)	Overall transaction profit divided by derived advertising cost
Page views per session	The average number of pages viewed during a session on your site; repeated views of a single page are counted
Average search depth	The average number of pages people viewed after performing a search on your site
Time on page	How long a user spent on a particular page in seconds, calculated by subtracting the initial view time for a particular page from the initial view time for a subsequent page; thus this metric does not apply to exit pages for your site
Dimension	'A descriptive attribute or characteristic of an object that can be given different values. For example, a geographic location could have dimensions called Latitude, Longitude or City Name. Values for the City Name dimension could be San Francisco, London or Singapore'
Metrics	'Individual elements of a dimension which can be measured as a sum or a ratio. For example, the dimension City can be associated with a metric like Population, which would have a sum value of all the residents of the specific city'[66]

Source: Most definitions provided by Google Analytics.[67]

For measuring social media activity, certain platforms provide built-in analytics tools (e.g. Facebook Insights – see Figure 11.6). Social media metrics can be divided into three main categories, as follows.[68]

1 *Activity (input) metrics*: these metrics show how much input the company has into the social media activity (e.g. number of posts, frequency, type of posts).
2 *Interaction (response) metrics*: these metrics show how our target audience engages with our social media content, such as number of fans/likes/followers, comments, shares, virality, tags, mentions, etc.
3 *Performance (outcome) metrics*: these metrics focus on outcomes of our activity, such as financial, satisfaction, etc.

For a quick list of how many things you can measure on social media, visit David Berkowitz's 'The who, what, where, when, why, and how of the 100 ways to measure social media'.[69]

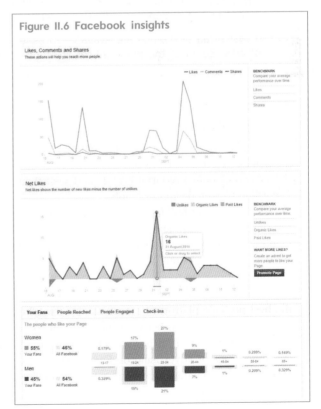

Figure II.6 Facebook insights

Summary

In this chapter, we have examined the important issues of digital marketing. The following key issues were addressed.

1. Digital marketing is a dynamic area of marketing that is constantly changing and giving marketers new ways to communicate with consumers. Digital marketing revolutionized communication from monologue to dialogue, where customers are empowered to express their opinions.

2. More consumers than ever are online and are spending a greater proportion of their time online. E-commerce is increasing and the proportion of advertising budgets being allocated to digital platforms is growing.

3. Online communications can assist with the marketing objectives of awareness, engagement, conversion and retention, and can be concentrated on some or all aspects of the customer decision journey.

4. Effective website design requires consideration of key variables such as presentation, usability and the user experience, navigation and testing the site on different devices and browsers.

5. Search engine optimization describes the range of tools and techniques employed to try to ensure that a webpage ranks as high on the SERPs as possible. Some of the key variables that have an impact on search rankings include keywords, content and links.

6. The creation of relevant and valuable content that is distributed through websites and social media channels has become one of the most popular online communications tools, and companies and brands try to increase consumer engagement levels.

7. The three major forms of online advertising are search advertising, display advertising and social advertising. Native advertising is a further form, where the advertising or branded content fits in seamlessly with the form and function of the other content surrounding it.

8. Two of the unique ways in which marketers exploit the growing use of mobile devices to access the internet are through the use of proximity marketing and branded mobile apps.

9. Email marketing campaigns are the online equivalent of direct mail and can be used to enhance customer conversion and retention levels.

10. A vast array of metrics are available to assess the effectiveness of digital and online marketing efforts. Some of the most critical are those that measure traffic, engagement and conversion.

Study questions

1. Discuss changes in the digital environment that you have noticed in the past 5–10 years. What is your opinion about current trends in the field?

2. Select two of your favourite brands and visit their websites. Evaluate the content of the websites according to web design principles.

3. Search for 'student holidays' (or anything else) using a search engine (Google, Bing, Yahoo!). Go to the third results page and select one of the links. Evaluate the content of this website and recommend changes to improve its search engine position.

4. What is meant by content marketing? Explain the reasons for its growth and its role in an online communications strategy.

5. For the company of your choice, analyse and discuss its current social media presence. Did it select the best possible platform to meet its objectives? Can you suggest a better solution?

6. Explain the differences between the different forms of online advertising, namely, search, display, social and native. Visit https://www.facebook.com/business/products/ads and learn about the different dimensions of advertising on Facebook.

7. Discuss how companies may integrate their online and offline campaigns. What are the benefits of such an approach?

Suggested reading

Chaffey, D. and **Ellis-Chadwick, F.** (2016) *Digital Marketing: Strategy, Implementation and Practice* (6th ed.). Harlow: Pearson Education Limited.

Dessart, L. (2017) Social media engagement: a model of antecedents and relational outcomes, *Journal of Marketing Management*, 33, 375–99.

Grewal, D., Bart, Y., Spann, M. and **Zubcsek, P.** (2016) Mobile advertising: a review and research agenda, *Journal of Interactive Marketing*, 34, 3–14.

Kannan, P. and **Li, H.** (2017) Digital marketing, a framework, review and research agenda, *International Journal of Research in Marketing*, 34, 22–45.

Killian, G. and **McManus, K.** (2015) A marketing communications approach for the digital era: managerial guidelines for social media integration, *Business Horizons*, 58, 539–49.

Lemon, K. and **Verhoef, P.** (2016) Understanding customer experience throughout the customer journey, *Journal of Marketing*, 80, 69–96.

Puluzzi, J. (2012) The rise of storytelling as the new marketing, *Public Research Quarterly*, 28, 116–23.

Ryan, D. (2017) *Understanding Digital Marketing.* London: Kogan Page.

References

1. **Anonymous** (2015) Always: Procter & Gamble and Leo Burnett's #LikeAGirl, *Campaign*, 12 October; **O'Reilly, L.** (2016) The latest Always #LikeAGirl ad claims emojis are sexist, *Business Insider UK*, 3 March; **Effies** (2017) Always: Like a Girl emojis. Available at www.warc.com/content/paywall/article/effies/always_like_a_girl_emojis/112255 (accessed 26 October 2018); **Cardenas, L.** and **Perrin, J.** (2017) Always: Girl emojis #LikeAGirl. Available at www.warc.com/content/paywall/article/warc-awards/always_girl_emojis_likeagirl/110967 (accessed 26 October 2018); **Nudd, T.** (2016) Not every brand loves emojis. Always 'Like A Girl' says the female ones are terrible, *Adweek*, 2 March; **Stewart, R.** (2016) Latest Always #LikeAGirl ad says emojis are limiting girls and calls for 'unstoppable' representation, *The Drum*, 2 March.

2. **Gunther-McGrath, R.** (2013) The pace of technology adoption is speeding up, *Harvard Business Review*. Available at www.hbr.org/2013/11/the-pace-of-technology-adoption-is-speeding-up (accessed 21 August 2018).

3. **Statistica.com** (2018) Percentage of all global web pages served to mobile phones from 2009 to 2018. Available at www.statista.com/statistics/241462/global-mobile-phone-website-traffic-share/ (accessed 21 August 2018).

4. **Statistica.com** (2017) Most popular daily online activities of adult internet users in the United States as of February 2017, by age group. Available at www.statista.com/statistics/184541/typical-daily-online-activities-of-adult-internet-users-in-the-us/ (accessed 21 August 2018); **Statistica.com** (2017), Most popular daily online activities of adult internet users in the United States as of February 2017, by gender. Available at www.statista.com/statistics/184557/typical-daily-online-activities-of-adult-internet-users-in-the-us-by-gender/ (accessed 21 August 2018).

5. **Andersson, H.** (2018) Social media apps are deliberatively 'addictive' to users, *Bbc.com*. Available at www.bbc.com/news/technology-44640959 (accessed 8 October 2018).

6. **Dillard-Wright, D.** (2018) Technology designed for addiction, *Psycologytoday.com*. Available at www.psychologytoday.com/us/blog/boundless/201801/technology-designed-addiction (accessed 8 October 2018).

7. **Alter, A.** (2018) *Irresistible: The Rise of Addictive Technology and the Business of Keeping Us Hooked.* London: Penguin Books.

8. **Eyal, N.** (2014) *Hooked: How To Build Habit-Forming Products.* London: Portfolio Penguin.

9. **Statistica.com** (2018) Online shopping and e-commerce worldwide: statistics and facts. Available at www.statista.com/topics/871/online-shopping/ (accessed 22 August 2018).

10. **Statistica.com** (2018) Online shopping and e-commerce worldwide: statistics and facts. Available at www.statista.com/topics/871/online-shopping/ (accessed 22 August 2018).

11. **Edquid, R.** (2017) 10 of the largest ecommerce markets in the world by country, *Business.com*. Available at www.business.com/articles/10-of-the-largest-ecommerce-markets-in-the-world-b/ (accessed 22 August 2018).

12. **Orendorff, A.** (2017) Global ecommerce: statistics and international growth trends (infographic), *Shopify.com*. Available at www.shopify.com/enterprise/global-ecommerce-statistics (accessed 18 August 2018).

13. **Statistica.com** (2017) Share of individuals using the internet to sell goods and services in the United Kingdom (UK) from 2005 to 2016. Available at www.statista.com/statistics/381336/online-c2c-commerce-penetration-in-the-uk/ (accessed 22 August 2018).

14. **Kafka, P.** and **Molla, R.** (2017) 2017 was the year that digital ad spending finally beat TV, *Recode.net*. Available at www.recode.net/2017/12/4/16733460/2017-digital-ad-spend-advertising-beat-tv (accessed 22 August 2018).

15. **Roderick, L.** (2017) L'Oreal's new CMO on why brands shouldn't have a digital strategy, *Marketingweek.com*. Available at www.marketingweek.com/2017/11/13/loreal-new-cmo-brands-shouldnt-digital-strategy/ (accessed 28 August 2018).

16. **Chaffey, D.** and **Smith, P.R.** (2013) *E-marketing Excellence: Planning and Optimizing Your Digital Marketing* (4th ed.). Oxon: Routledge.

17. **Lemon, K.** and **Verhoef, P.** (2016), Understanding customer experience throughout the customer journey, *Journal of Marketing*, 80, 69–96.

18. **Carlzon, J.** (2001) *Moments of Truth*. London: HarperBusiness.

19. **Wroblewski, L.** (2011) Multi-device design: an evolution. Available at www.lukew.com/ff/entry.asp?1436 (accessed August 2014).

20. **Krug, S.** (2006) *Don't Make Me Think! A Common Sense Approach to Web Usability*. Berkeley, CA: New Riders.

21. **Nielsen, J.** (2004) The need for web design standards. Available at www.nngroup.com/articles/the-need-for-web-design-standards/ (accessed June 2014).

22. **Nielsen, J.** (2004) Mastery, mystery and misery: the ideologies of web design. Available at www.nngroup.com/articles/ideologies-of-web-design/ (accessed July 2014).

23. **ISO** (2008) Ergonomics of human–system interaction. guidance on world wide web user interfaces. Available at www.iso.org/obp/ui/#iso:std:iso:9241:-151:ed-1:v1:en (accessed June 2014).

24. **Nielsen, J.** (1995) 10 usability heuristics for user interface design. Available at www.nngroup.com/articles/ten-usability-heuristics/ (accessed June 2014).

25. **Tognazzini, B.** (2014) First principles of interaction design (revised and expanded). Available at http://asktog.com/atc/principles-of-interaction-design/ (accessed 30 October 2018).

26. **Vila, N.** and **Kuster, I.** (2011) Consumer feelings and behaviours towards well designed websites, *Information and Management*, 48(4–5), 166–77.

27. **Nielsen, J.** (1997) How users read on the web. Available at www.nngroup.com/articles/how-users-read-on-the-web/ (accessed June 2014).

28. **Pulizzi, J.** and **Barrett, T.** (2010) *Get Content. Get Customers*. Columbus, OH: McGraw-Hill.

29. **Estes, J.** (2013) User-centric vs maker-centric language: 3 essential guidelines. Available at www.nngroup.com/articles/user-centric-language/ (accessed July 2014).

30. **Nielsen, J.** (2013) Website reading: it (sometimes) does happen. Available at www.nngroup.com/articles/website-reading/ (accessed July 2014).

31. **Ryan, D.** (2017) *Understanding Digital Marketing: Marketing Strategies for Engaging the Digital Generation*. London: Kogan Page.

32. **Content Marketing Institute** (2018) Getting started. Available at www.contentmarketinginstitute.com/getting-started/ (accessed 2 February 2018).

33. **Gardiner, K.** (2013) The story behind 'The Furrow', the world's oldest content marketing, *Contently.com*. Available at www.contently.com/strategist/2013/10/03/the-story-behind-the-furrow-2/ (accessed 29 August 2018).

34. **Kingsnorth, S.** (2016) *Digital Marketing Strategy: An Integrated Approach to Online Marketing*. London: Kogan Page.

35. **Pulizzi, J.** (2012) The rise of storytelling as the new marketing, *Public Research Quarterly*, 28, 116–23.

36. **Samuelsen, L., Porsager, C.** and **Gladstone, M.** (2014) ONLY: our basket is full – how emotional storytelling in the digital space drove commercial success, *Warc.com*. Available at www.warc.com/content/article/ipa/only_our_basket_is_full_how_emotional_storytelling_in_the_digital_space_drove_commercial_success/102460 (accessed 8 March 2017).

37. **Woodside, A., Sood, S.** and **Miller, K.** (2008) When consumers and brands talk: storytelling theory and research in psychology and marketing, *Psychology and Marketing*, 25, 97–145.

38. **Pera, R., Viglia, G.** and **Furlan, R.** (2016) Who am I? How compelling storytelling builds digital personal reputation, *Journal of Interactive Marketing*, 35, 44–55.

39. **Labrecque, L., Markos, E.** and **Milne, G.** (2011) Online personal branding: processes, challenges and implications, *Journal of Interactive Marketing*, 76, 109–25.

40. **Joseph, S.** (2014) Adidas details 'digital newsroom' strategy for brands, *Marketingweek.com*. Available at www.marketingweek.com/2014/03/03/adidas-details-digital-newsroom-strategy-for-brands/ (accessed 4 September 2018).

41. **Ritson, M.** (2016) Ritson on content: clutter means that you are now a proper, grown-up marketing tool, *Marketingmag.com.au*. Available at www.marketingmag.com.au/hubs-c/mark-ritson-content-marketing-clutter (accessed 4 September 2018).

42. **Ritson, M**. (2016) Is content marketing a load of bollocks? *marketingweek.com*. Available at www.marketingweek.com/2016/10/11/is-content-marketing-a-load-of-bullsht/ (accessed 4 September 2018).

43. **Dolan, R., Conduit, J., Fahy, J.** and **Goodman, S.** (2016) Social media engagement behaviour: a uses and gratifications perspective, *Journal of Strategic Marketing*, 24, 261–77.

44. **Ashley, C.** and **Tuten, T.** (2015) Creative strategies in social media marketing: an exploratory study of branded social content and consumer engagement, *Psychology and Marketing*, 24, 15–27.

45. **Statistica.com** (2018) Net digital advertising revenue share by major ad-selling companies worldwide from 2016 to 2019. Available at www.statista.com/statistics/290629/digital-ad-revenue-share-of-major-ad-selling-companies-worldwide/ (accessed 4 September 2018).

46. **O'Reilly, L.** (2017) Ad blocker usage is up 30% – and a popular methods publishers use to thwart it isn't working, *Businessinsider.com.* Available at www.businessinsider.com/pagefair-2017-ad-blocking-report-2017-1?r=US&IR=T (accessed 4 September 2018).

47. **Marvin, G.** (2017) Nearly 80 percent of US ad spend will be programmatic in 2017, *Marketingland.com.* Available at www.marketingland.com/80-percent-us-display-ad-spend-programmatic-212780 (accessed 5 September 2018).

48. **Field, M.** (2018) Under Armour pulls youtube ads in fresh extremist video controversy, *Telegraph.co.uk,* Available at www.telegraph.co.uk/technology/2018/04/20/youtube-accused-still-airing-adverts-extremist-videos/ (accessed 8 October 2018).

49. **Ingram, M.** (2017) Why the YouTube ad boycott could cost Google €750 million, *Fortune.com.* Available at www.fortune.com/2017/03/27/google-youtube-ad-boycott/ (accessed 8 October 2018).

50. **Mostrous, A.** (2017) Google faces questions over videos on YouTube, *Thetimes.co.uk.* Available at www.thetimes.co.uk/article/google-faces-questions-over-videos-on-youtube-3km257v8d?t=ie (accessed 8 October 2018).

51. **Solon, L.** (2017) Google's bad week: YouTube loses millions as advertising row reaches the US, *Theguardian.com.* Available at www.theguardian.com/technology/2017/mar/25/google-youtube-advertising-extremist-content-att-verizon (accessed 8 October 2018).

52. **Statistica.com** (2018) social media advertising worldwide. Available at www.statista.com/outlook/220/100/social-media-advertising/worldwide (accessed 5 September 2018).

53. **Sweney, M.** (2018) Social media ad spend to overtake TV's in spite of Facebook woes, *Theguardian.com.* Available at www.theguardian.com/media/2018/apr/02/social-media-ad-spend-to-overtake-tvs-in-spite-of-facebook-woes (accessed 5 September 2018).

54. **Boland, M.** (2016) Native ads will drive 74% of all ad revenue by 2021, *Businessinsider.com.* Available at www.businessinsider.com/the-native-ad-report-forecasts-2016-5?r=US&IR=T&IR=T (accessed 5 September 2016).

55. **DeMers, J.** (2018) Is native advertising sustainable for the long haul? *Forbes.com.* Available at www.forbes.com/sites/jaysondemers/2018/03/01/is-native-advertising-sustainable-for-the-long-haul/#74f63b263733 (accessed 5 September 2018).

56. **Statistica.com** (2018) mobile internet traffic as a percentage of total web traffic in April 2018, by region. Available at www.statista.com/statistics/306528/share-of-mobile-internet-traffic-in-global-regions/ (accessed 5 September 2018).

57. **Statistica.com** (2018) Number of apps available in leading app stores as of 1st quarter 2018. Available at www.statista.com/statistics/276623/number-of-apps-available-in-leading-app-stores/ (accessed 5 September 2016).

58. **Appannie.com** (2018) The average smartphone user accessed close to 40 apps per month in 2017. Available at www.appannie.com/en/insights/market-data/apps-used-2017/ (accessed 6 September 2018).

59. **Kim, E., Lin, J.** and **Sung, Y.** (2013) To app or not to app: engaging customers via branded mobile apps, *Journal of Interactive Advertising*, 13, 53–65.

60. **Stocchi, L., Guerini, C.** and **Michaelidou, N.** (2017) When are mobile apps worth paying for? How marketers can analyze the performance of mobile apps, *Journal of Advertising Research*, 57, 260–71.

61. **Anonymous** (2016) L'Oréal: Makeup Genius, *Warc.com.* Available at www.warc.com/content/article/cannes/loreal_makeup_genius/107868 (accessed 6 February 2017).

62. **Daneshkhu, S.** (2014) L'Oréal make-up goes virtual for the selfie age, *Ft.com.* Available at www.ft.com/content/e980243e-13ee-11e4-8485-00144feabdc0?segmentId=9b41d47b-8acb-fadb-7c70-37ee589b60ab (accessed 6 February 2017).

63. **Doland, A.** (2015) Why millions in China downloaded L'Oreal's Makeup Genius app, *Adage.com.* Available at www.adage.com/article/special-report-women-to-watch-china-2015/4-7-million-chinese-women-downloaded-l-oreal-s-makeup-app/299878/ (accessed 6 February 2017).

64. **Morimoto, M.** and **Chang, S.** (2006) Consumers' attitudes towards unsolicited commercial e-mail and postal direct mail marketing methods: intrusiveness, perceived loss of control, and irritation, *Journal of Interactive Advertising*, 7, 1–11.

65. **Chaffey, D.** and **Ellis-Chadwick, F.** (2016) *Digital Marketing: Strategy, Implementation and Practice.* Harlow: Pearson Education Limited.

66. **Google Support** (2014) Dimensions and metrics. Available at https://support.google.com/analytics/answer/1033861?hl=en-GB (accessed July 2014).

67. **Google Analytics** (2014) Dimensions and metrics reference. Available at https://developers.google.com/analytics/devguides/reporting/core/dimsmets (accessed July 2014).

68. **Tuten, T.** and **Solomon, M.** (2014) *Social Media Marketing.* Harlow: Pearson.

69. **Berkowitz, D.** (2009) The who, what, where, when, why, and how of the 100 ways to measure social media. Available at www.marketersstudio.com/2009/11/the-who-what-where-when-why-and-how-of-the-100-ways-to-measure-social-media.html#more (accessed July 2014).

Introduction

Luxury fashion brands are often renowned more for their innovative designs than for their communication campaigns. There have, of course, been creative and at times provocative advertising campaigns that have caused headlines for the right or wrong reasons. However, there has been a quiet revolution in the domain of how the fast-changing world of fashion has embraced the world of digital. Marketing communication campaigns were traditionally confined to the glossy pages of *Vogue* and other leading fashion print titles. As a result, media budgets were dominated by magazine advertising. Traditional media still play an important role, but there is no doubt that the new competitive battlefield lies within the digital arena. According to McKinsey & Co., nearly 80 per cent of luxury sales today are 'digitally influenced'.[1] If fashionistas want to get close to the latest collections, or check out the views and opinions of leading fashion experts, they are just a tap or swipe away. In an era of digital content, luxury brands need to rethink how best to communicate with a digital-savvy audience.

Dashingly digital

According to the UK Luxury Benchmark Study, on average, 20 per cent of respondents' marketing budget is allocated to digital purchases.[2] However, some luxury brands are evidently more oriented towards digital marketing than others. For example, media reports suggest that Burberry spends 60 per cent of its marketing budget on digital. It is an investment that, for a company founded in 1856, has arguably led the digital democratization of luxury. Burberry has set out to leverage social media to engage and interact with customers that would otherwise be difficult or more costly to reach. It is ranked as one of the most engaging luxury brands on social media.[3] It is therefore no surprise that Burberry is actually the most popular British brand on Instagram, with more than 10.4 million followers.[4] Its iconic tartan check has become one of the most recognizable patterns in the world. The result is a £2.8 billion global business through its quintessentially British appeal, which has extended beyond fashion to accessories, sunglasses, beauty and fragrances.

Burberry's digital success was not an overnight phenomenon. The fashion label crafted a strategy to be at the forefront of digital innovation. The brand is considered as a first mover and pioneer in many new digital channels which has struck a chord with a new generation of customers. It was, for example, the first luxury fashion brand to use Snapchat's Snapcode feature, launch a campaign on Snapchat Discover and develop a dedicated Apple Music channel. However, Burberry's digital approach is less about gimmicky campaigns and more about how to maximize a seamless and holistic digital experience.

Pre-purchase

Burberry has developed digital content with the objective to influence and inspire customers to consider buying the brand. Its website is essentially the brand's shop window, which helps to facilitate a virtual browsing experience. It also uses online advertising to increase awareness of new collections and special promotions. However, Burberry's use of key opinion leaders (KOLs) allows the brand to target aspirational consumers and gain credibility among a fashion-conscious audience. Interestingly, McKinsey & Co. found that half of Chinese digital consumers surveyed use social media to conduct product research or get recommendations.[5] This is among the reasons why Burberry partnered with one of China's leading fashion bloggers, Mr Bags, for the launch of its leather DK88 handbag.

Purchase

Burberry's quest to integrate the digital medium within a retail environment is showcased at its flagship store, which reopened on London's Regent Street in 2012. A range of technological initiatives is able to gently nudge a customer from consideration of a brand to purchasing it. For instance, sales staff are equipped with a 'clientelling' app, which gives them a digital profile of customers' past choices and preferences. If, for example, a customer had recently bought a Burberry trench coat, the sales assistant could show an appropriate handbag. This enables sales staff to provide a personalized service, which certainly matters given that two-thirds of affluent consumers expect a highly customized experience when shopping for luxury goods.[6] Embedded RFID (radio frequency identification) tags are also able to transform mirrors into screens that display video content such as details of the craftsmanship that was used to manufacture the garment. This is not restricted to the London flagship store. Products fitted with RFID tags that can communicate with shopper's smartphones provide extra content, such as recommendations on how the item can be worn.

Post-purchase

Many of Burberry's digital activities are leveraged after the sale, with the aim to help maximize the brand experience. Exclusive social media content has helped to build a stronger brand relationship with its customer base. For example, if it wasn't possible to receive a front-row seat invitation to Burberry's London Fashion Week 2018 and join the high-calibre guest list, with Naomi Campbell, Kate Moss and Cara Delevingne, not all was lost. The show was streamed in real time on various social media platforms including Facebook and YouTube, and on the Chinese messaging service WeChat. However, the emphasis on creating a bespoke digital relationship has remained a critical aspect of the post-purchase experience. Customers who share their personal information, including social media activity, enable Burberry to provide a more personalized experience including personalized recommendations.

Virtually in first place

In a 2015 Digital IQ Index study conducted by L2, Burberry was ranked first out of 83 global fashion brands in terms of digital competence. But competitors are learning fast. In the latest 2017 study, it is Gucci that now heads the ranking, while Burberry has slipped to fourth place.[7] Could Burberry be losing its digital shine? This could have serious implications for the luxury brand given that millennials, with their Generation Z cohorts, are expected to be luxury's largest group of consumers by 2030.[8] These are essentially digital natives who have not only been brought up with technology, but consider the use of social media and other applications as being integral to their daily lives.

Burberry will therefore need to continue to adopt and adapt new platforms as it reaches new audiences. This will also make the brand more attractive to younger shoppers. There are already signs that the brand is taking steps to regain the digital initiative as it seeks to differentiate itself versus other luxury competitors. For example, in 2016 Burberry launched a chatbot through Facebook Messenger, which allowed fans to get updates and see behind-the-scenes content as part of London Fashion Week. The brand is also currently experimenting with augmented reality for its mobile app, which allows users to virtually add 'Burberry-inspired' drawings by artist Danny Sangra, which can then be shared on social media.

Social selling

A future challenge for luxury brands is to align digital communications with the growing appetite for luxury e-commerce. By 2025, nearly a fifth of all luxury sales will be online.[9] Customers expect more than just an online transactional relationship. For example, Burberry Bespoke allows its clientele to customize their own Burberry trench coat online, right down to the choice of buttons. Similarly, the Burberry Scarf Bar enables customers to preview their personalized scarf in real time.

However, the biggest challenge is to leverage the opportunities of social selling. In China, social media has evolved as an online purchasing platform. Although Western luxury brand executives may be familiar with Instagram's 'shop now' and Pinterest's 'buy it' features, it is China that is leading the way in social selling. Burberry has recently set up a store on WeChat. The potential success of the social selling model was demonstrated when Dior used WeChat to sell a limited-edition Lady Dior handbag. The collection sold out almost immediately.

Burberry has demonstrated that it is indeed possible to integrate tradition with technology. Digital luxury is not for the faint-hearted, however. Luxury brands need to be aware that the powerful blade of technology cuts two ways when developing the online component of their techno-marketing strategy. This is a dilemma facing luxury brand executives. For instance, luxury is about outstanding customer service, which questions – despite technological advancements – whether human personal service really is replaceable. Luxury is also about maintaining exclusiveness and, conversely, digital media is democratic. Overexposure could have negative consequences on brand image and desirability. This raises the question of whether luxury brands such as Burberry can strike a balance between exclusivity and accessibility in an increasing digital marketplace.

Questions

1. Discuss the benefits of Burberry using digital communications.
2. Discuss how Burberry can use digital communications to influence the consumer decision-making process.
3. Advise Burberry on how to develop a digital communications strategy without losing exclusivity.

This case was prepared by Glyn Atwal, Burgundy School of Business, and Douglas Bryson, Rennes School of Business, from various published sources as a basis for class discussion rather than to show effective or ineffective management.

References

1. **Achille, A., Marchessou, S.** and **Remy, N.** (2018) Luxury in the age of digital Darwinism, McKinsey & Company Report, February. Available at https://www.mckinsey.com/industries/retail/our-insights/luxury-in-the-age-of-digital-darwinism (accessed 8 March 2018).
2. **Anonymous** (2016) Wealth-X and Walpole present: luxury in the UK, *wealthx.com*, 3 March. Available at https://www.wealthx.com/featured/2016/wealth-x-walpole-uk-luxury (accessed 22 November 2017).
3. **Anonymous** (2018) A deep dive into the social media habits and performance of Burberry, *unmetric.com*. Available at https://unmetric.com/brands/burberry (accessed 13 November 2018).
4. **Marfil, L.** (2017) Burberry named most popular British brand on Instagram, *WWD.com*, 24 November. Available at http://wwd.com/fashion-news/fashion-scoops/burberry-named-most-popular-british-brand-instagram-11056077 (accessed 5 March 2018).
5. **Wang, K.W., Lau, A.** and **Gong, F.** (2016) How savvy, social shoppers are transforming Chinese e-commerce, McKinsey & Company Survey, April. Available at https://www.mckinsey.com/industries/retail/our-insights/how-savvy-social-shoppers-are-transforming-chinese-e-commerce (accessed 20 November 2017).
6. **Rosen, E.** (2015) Burberry gets personal, *L2Inc.com*, 1 December. Available at https://www.l2inc.com/daily-insights/burberry-gets-personal (accessed 18 December 2017).
7. **L2** (2017) Gartner L2 Digital IQ Index – Fashion 2016, *L2Inc.com*, 28 November. Available at https://www.l2inc.com/research/fashion-2016 (accessed 18 December 2017).
8. **Agnew, H.** and **Sanderson, R.** (2018) Gucci aims to step into Louis Vuitton's shoes, *Financial Times*, 5/6 May, p. 14.
9. **Achille, A., Marchessou, S.** and **Remy, N.** (2018) Luxury in the age of digital Darwinism, McKinsey & Company Report, February. Available at https://www.mckinsey.com/industries/retail/our-insights/luxury-in-the-age-of-digital-darwinism (accessed 8 March 2018).

Chapter 12

Marketing Planning and Strategy

Chapter outline

The process of marketing planning

Situation analysis

Marketing objectives

Marketing strategies

Executing marketing strategies

Assessing marketing strategies

Effective marketing planning

Learning outcomes

By the end of this chapter you will understand:

1   The role of marketing planning within businesses

2   The process of marketing planning

3   The rewards and problems associated with marketing planning

4   The roles of external and internal analysis in planning and strategy

5   The different marketing strategies, and the sources of competitive advantage

6   How to assess the effectiveness of marketing efforts

President Trump: defying the odds

Across any competitive context, be it business, sporting or political, the most unprecedented out-come was the election of businessman Donald Trump as the 45th President of the United States in 2016. When he began his campaign, he was given very little chance of getting the Republican nomination against a field of 16 other candidates let alone being seen as a credible contender for President. In fact, at the start of the campaign in August 2015, the odds being offered on Trump were in the region of 25 to 1, confirming his status as a rank outsider in the race for the White House. And when a man with no political experience defied those odds to become President of the most powerful nation in the world, attention turned to how he had managed to do it, and particularly to the role that marketing might have played in his success.

The starting point of this analysis is the environmental context within which Trump developed his campaign. The USA was a country facing many challenges. Coming off the back of the Great Recession of 2008, the economy was recovering, but that recovery was not equally distributed, and the gap between rich and poor continued to widen. Added to this were concerns about illegal immigration and the threat of terrorism. The promise of the Obama years had faded somewhat and voters were increasingly disenfranchised by the political process. For someone with a business and celebrity background rather than a political one, this represented an opportunity, and soon Trump was busy exploiting that opportunity.

Core to his strategy was to focus on a specific target audience. Trump did not try to appeal to all voters but instead aimed his messaging at one segment, namely white, middle-class males, a group that had suffered significantly as a result of the Great Recession. Having no political experience was a weakness but he cleverly turned this around by claiming that the woes this segment were suffering were down to the establishment politicians, both Republican and Democrat, and to the bad trade deals they had made with other countries. He even went so far as to turn this weakness into a core element of his brand – voters should vote for him precisely because he was *not* a politician. But he also used his strengths as a businessman, real estate deal maker and TV celebrity as elements of his brand too. Because he was a self-made billionaire, he alone of the candidates had the skills to help 'make America great again' and, by implication, improve the lives of those white, middle-class voters. He took these ideas of differentiation further by also 'branding' his opponents, such as 'Lyin' Ted' Cruz (Republican opponent) and 'Crooked Hillary' Clinton (Democratic Presidential nominee). By doing this he sought to undermine the brands of his opponents while also emphasizing the strengths of his.

As we have seen throughout this book, marketing is not just about creating brand values but also about communicating them, and again this is something that Trump, with his TV background, excelled at. Both in medium and content, Trump, once again, took a different approach to his rivals. For example, one of the remarkable features of his campaign was how relatively little he spent on traditional media advertising. His Republican rival, Jeb Bush, is estimated to have outspent him by a factor of eight, yet had to drop out of the race after securing only a couple of percentage points of the Republican vote. Similarly, in the presidential race, the Clinton campaign spent far more on TV and direct mail, following the pattern of previous elections. Yet what set Trump apart was the amount of 'earned media' he received – that is, free publicity on TV, in print and on social media. Trump dominated the headlines through his controversial and provocative comments on everything from race to gender, his brusque, offensive manner, as well as his carefully orchestrated 'big announcements'. For example, in a two-month period in the run-up to the 2016 election, Trump was receiving 40 million mentions on Twitter compared with 26 million for his rival, Clinton.

Of course, aside from Trump himself, the Trump electoral campaign has not been without its controversy. The Cambridge Analytica scandal (see Critical Marketing Perspective 4.1), where a UK company used a fake account to breach Facebook data, became associated with the campaign

(continued)

when it emerged that these data were used to target messaging in favour of Trump. There have also been many allegations of Russian interference in the election. Yet Trump's approach to the campaign followed patterns that would be familiar to students of marketing. He identified, understood and carefully focused on his target audience. He built his brand and carefully differentiated it from those of his competitors. And he spent his marketing money wisely, generating a much higher return on investment than his rivals.[1]

In Chapter 1 we introduced the notion of marketing planning. Then, throughout the book, we have examined the nature of customers and markets, and the environmental context within which organizations operate. We have also examined the variety of decisions that need to be taken by marketers. Given the challenging competitive environment in which firms operate, it is important that these decisions are not taken in an ad hoc way but rather in a systematic and rational manner. The process by which businesses analyse the environment and their capabilities, decide upon courses of marketing action and implement those decisions is called **marketing planning**, and it is this that will be the focus of this chapter. Equally, it is important to remember that there must be a strategic element to marketing plans – that is, they must map out a direction for the organization over the medium to long term. In this chapter, we will also examine some of the popular frameworks used by organizations to help them to answer key strategic questions, such as where and how to compete, and how to grow. Answers to these questions will be central aspects of any marketing plan.

Marketing planning forms part of the broader concept known as 'strategic planning'; this involves not only marketing but also the fit between production, finance and personnel strategies, and the environment. The aim of strategic planning is to shape and reshape an organization so that its business and products continue to meet corporate objectives (e.g. profit or sales growth). Because marketing management is charged with the responsibility of managing the interface between the company and its environment, it has a key role to play in strategic planning. As we saw in the Marketing Spotlight, strategic and marketing planning is not restricted solely to commercial organizations but is equally relevant in political and not-for-profit organizations.

A firm may be composed of a number of businesses (often equating to divisions), each of which serves distinct groups of customers and has a distinct set of competitors (see Chapter 6). Each business may be strategically autonomous and thus form a **strategic business unit** (SBU). A major component of a corporate plan will be the allocation of resources to each SBU. Strategic decisions at the corporate level are normally concerned with acquisition, divestment and diversification. Here, too, marketing can play a role through the identification of opportunities and threats in the environment as they relate to current and prospective businesses. Therefore, as Varadarajan puts it, strategic marketing research can best be thought of in terms of strategic marketing issues, decisions and problems at *all levels in a firm* rather than as *firm-level* issues, decisions and problems.[2]

As we saw in Chapter 1, the following essential questions need to be asked when thinking about marketing planning decisions:

■ Where are we now?
■ Where would we like to be?
■ How do we get there?

While these may seem relatively simple questions, they can be difficult to answer in practice. Organizations comprise individuals who may have very different views on the answers to these questions. Furthermore, the outcome of the planning process may have fundamental implications for their jobs. Planning is therefore a political activity, and those with a vested interest may view it from a narrow departmental, rather than business-wide, perspective. A key issue in getting planning systems to work is tackling such behavioural problems.[3] However, at this point in the chapter it is important to understand the process of marketing planning.

The process of marketing planning

The process of marketing planning is outlined in Figure 12.1. The process provides a well-defined path from generating a **business mission** to implementing and controlling the resultant plans. It provides a framework that shows how all the key elements of marketing discussed so far relate to one another.

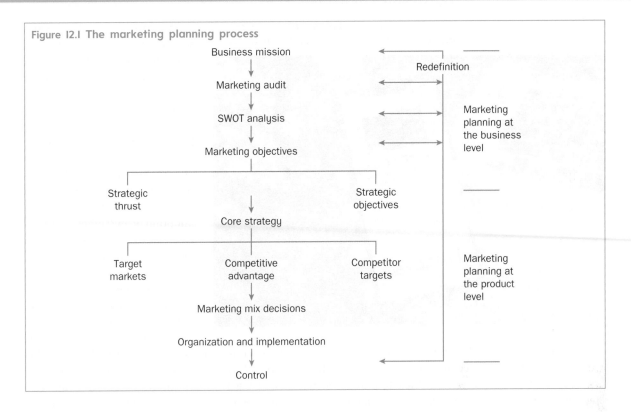

Figure 12.1 The marketing planning process

In real life, planning is rarely as straightforward and logical. In a rapidly changing business environment, a high level of flexibility is required to take account of significant changes such as the adoption of a new technology.[4]

Business mission

Ackoff defined the business mission as:

> *a broadly defined, enduring statement of purpose that distinguishes a business from others of its type.*[5]

This definition captures two essential ingredients in mission statements: they are enduring and specific to the individual organization.[6] Two fundamental questions that need to be addressed are: 'What business are we in?' and 'What business do we want to be in?' In a global, highly competitive marketplace, where industry boundaries are constantly blurring, the answers to these questions may not be as obvious as they might at first appear. The answers also define the scope and activities of the company, and will be determined by an assessment of the needs of the market, the competencies of the firm and background of the company, plus the personalities of its senior management. As we saw in the Marketing Spotlight at the beginning of Chapter 7, banks may traditionally have seen themselves as the dominant players in the business of retail payments. However, as technological changes open up the sector, telecommunications companies and technology businesses such as Apple and Google have decisions to make regarding whether or not this is a business that they want to be in (see Exhibit 12.1).

Including the market and needs factors ensures that the business definition is market focused rather than product based. For example, humans are social creatures so one of our most innate needs is for connection. Leaders in the telephone industry have used the idea of connecting people – indeed, Nokia even used 'connecting people' as its slogan. However, with the development of even better platforms for connection by companies such as Facebook and Snapchat, Nokia lost its leadership to smartphone manufacturers like Apple and Samsung. This shows the importance of ensuring that a business definition is market focused as products are transient, while basic needs such as transportation, entertainment and

Exhibit 12.1 Apple Pay is a mobile payment and digital wallet service that allows users to make payments in person, online and in iOS apps.

eating are lasting. For example, Philips' vision statement declares that it strives to make the world healthier and more sustainable through innovation, with a goal of improving the lives of 3 billion people by 2025 (see Exhibit 12.2). Thus, Levitt argued that a business should be viewed as a customer-satisfying process not a goods-producing process.[7] By adopting a customer perspective, new opportunities are more likely to be seen.

Management must be wary of business definitions that are either too narrow or too wide. Levitt suggested that railway companies would have survived had they defined their business as transportation and moved into the airline business. However, this ignores the limits of business competency of the railways. Did they possess the necessary skills and resources to run an airline? Clearly a key constraint on a business definition can be the competencies (both actual and potential) of management, and the resources at their disposal. Conversely, competencies can act as the motivator for widening a business mission. Asda (Associated Dairies) redefined its business mission as a producer and distributor of milk to a retailer of fast-moving consumer goods (fmcg) partly on the basis of its distribution skills, which it rightly believed could be extended to products beyond milk.

The background of the company and the personalities of its senior management are the final determinants of the business mission. Businesses that have established themselves in the marketplace over many years and have a clear position in the minds of the customer may ignore opportunities that are at variance with that position. The personalities and beliefs of the people who run businesses also shape the business mission. This last factor emphasizes the judgemental nature of business definition. There is no right or wrong business mission in abstract. The mission should be based on the vision that top management and their staff have of the future of the business. This vision is a coherent and powerful statement of what the business should aim to become.[8] The business mission will serve as an overriding influence on the nature of the marketing plan and should also serve to motivate all staff to attain the targets set out in the plan.

Situation analysis

Information is required to develop an effective marketing plan. Therefore, one of the starting points of planning is an analysis of the organization's current situation, or what is known as a **marketing audit**. This is a systematic examination of a firm's marketing environment, objectives, strategies and activities, which aims to identify key strategic issues, problem areas and opportunities. An internal audit concentrates on those areas that are under the control of marketing management, whereas an external audit focuses on those forces over which management has no control. The

Exhibit 12.2 Vision statements, such as that of Dutch healthcare company Philips, aim to inspire both employees and customers.

results of the marketing audit are a key determinant of the future direction of the business and may give rise to a redefined business mission statement. A checklist of those areas that are likely to be examined in a marketing audit is given in Tables 12.1 and 12.2. Aspects of the external marketing audit were addressed in detail in Chapters 2 and 3.

Table 12.1 External marketing audit checklist

Macroenvironment
Economic: inflation, interest rates, unemployment
Social/cultural: age distribution, lifestyle changes, values, attitudes
Technological: new product and process technologies, materials
Political/legal: monopoly control, new laws, regulations
Ecological: conservation, pollution, energy
The market
Market: size, growth rates, trends and developments
Customers: who are they, their choice criteria, how, when, where do they buy, how do they rate us vis-à-vis competition on product, promotion, price, distribution
Market segmentation: how do customers group, what benefits does each group seek
Distribution: power changes, channel attractiveness, growth potential, physical distribution methods, decision-makers and influencers
Suppliers: who and where they are, their competencies and shortcomings, trends affecting them, future outlook
Competition
Who are the major competitors: actual and potential
What are their objectives and strategies
What are their strengths (distinctive competencies) and weaknesses (vulnerability analysis)
Market shares and size of competitors
Profitability analysis
Entry barriers

Table 12.2 Internal marketing audit checklist

Operating results (by product, customer, geographic region)
Sales
Market share
Profit margins
Costs
Strategic issues analysis
Marketing objectives
Market segmentation
Competitive advantage
Core competencies
Positioning
Portfolio analysis
Marketing operations effectiveness
Product
Price
Promotion
Distribution
Marketing structures
Marketing organization
Marketing training
Intra- and interdepartmental communication
Marketing systems
Marketing information system
Marketing planning system
Marketing control system

External analysis

External analysis covers the macroenvironment, the market and the competition. The macroenvironment consists of broad environmental issues that may impinge on the business. These include the economy, social/cultural issues, technological changes, political/legal factors and ecological concerns (as we saw in Chapter 2). These factors are outside of the control of the business but can have a significant impact on performance, as we have seen, for example, with the impact of Brexit (a political factor) or the global financial crisis (an economic factor).

Market analysis consists of a statistical analysis of market size, growth and trends, and **customer analysis** (including who they are, what choice criteria they use, how they rate competitive offerings and market segmentation bases). Next, **distribution analysis** covers significant movement in power bases, channel attractiveness studies, the potential impact of the growth in online channels, changes in physical distribution methods, and understanding the role and interests of decision-makers within distribution.

The remaining two levels of external analysis are the industry and competitors. As we saw in Chapter 2, the popular Porter 'five forces' model is a useful tool for assessing trends in the industry and understanding the drivers of industry profitability. **Competitor analysis** examines the nature of actual and potential competitors, and their objectives and strategies. It would also seek to identify their strengths (distinctive competencies), weaknesses (vulnerability analysis), market share and size. For example, firms considering entering the cloud computing business might conduct an analysis of both existing competitors and potential opportunities in this space (see Table 12.3).

Internal analysis

An internal audit permits the performance and activities of a business to be assessed in the light of environmental developments. Operating results form the basis of assessment through analysis of sales, market share, profit margins and costs. **Strategic issues analysis** examines the suitability of marketing objectives and segmentation bases in the light of changes in the marketplace. Competitive advantages and the core competencies on which they are based would be reassessed and the positioning of products in the market critically reviewed. Finally, product portfolios should be analysed to determine future strategic objectives.

Each aspect of the marketing mix is reviewed in the light of changing customer requirements and competitor activity. The **marketing structures** on which marketing activities are based should be analysed. Marketing structure consists of the marketing organization, training, and the intra-departmental and interdepartmental communication that takes place within an organization. Marketing organization is reviewed to determine fit with strategy and the market, and marketing training requirements are examined. Finally, communications and relationships within the marketing department, and between marketing and other functions (e.g. R&D, engineering, production), need to be appraised.

Table 12.3 Competitors in the cloud computing industry.

Operating results (by product, customer, geographic region)
Amazon Web Services
Sun Microsystems
Google
Intel
Apple
HP INVENT
DELL
OpenD
EMC2
VMWARE
Force.com
Microsoft
salesforce.com
BUNGEEconnect
Azure Services Platform
3tera
IBM
ORACLE
MOSSO
NETSUITE
Sun Grid Compute Utility
ACROBAT.COM
YAHOO! DEVELOPER NETWORK
Joyent Accelerators

Marketing systems are audited to check their effectiveness. This covers the marketing information, planning and **control** systems that support marketing activities. Shortfalls in information provision are analysed; the marketing planning system is critically appraised for cost-effectiveness, and the marketing control system is assessed in the light of accuracy, timeliness (whether it provides evaluations when managers require them) and coverage (whether the system evaluates the key variables affecting company performance).

The checklists in Tables 12.1 and 12.2 provide the basis for deciding on the topics to be included in the marketing audit. However, to give the same amount of attention and detailed analysis to every item would cause the audit to grind to a halt under the weight of data and issues. In practice, the judgement of those conducting the audit is critical in deciding the key items to focus upon. Those factors that are considered of crucial importance to the company's performance will merit most attention. One by-product of the marketing audit may be a realization that information about key environmental issues is lacking.

All assumptions should be made explicit as an ongoing part of the marketing audit. For example, key assumptions might be:

- inflation will average 2 per cent during the planning period
- VAT levels will not be changed
- worldwide overcapacity will remain at 150 per cent
- no new entrants into the market will emerge.

The marketing audit should not be a desperate attempt to turn around an ailing business, but an ongoing activity. Some companies conduct an annual audit as part of their annual planning system; others, operating in less turbulent environments, may consider two or three years an adequate period between audits. Some companies may feel that the use of an outside consultant to co-ordinate activities and provide an objective, outside view is beneficial, while others may believe that their own managers are best equipped to conduct such analyses. Clearly, there is no set formula for deciding when and by whom the audit is conducted. The decision ultimately rests on the preferences and situation facing the management team.

SWOT analysis

A structured approach to evaluating the strategic position of a business by identifying its strengths, weaknesses, opportunities and threats is known as a **SWOT analysis**. This provides a simple method of synthesizing the results of the marketing audit. Internal strengths and weaknesses are summarized as they relate to external opportunities and threats (see Figure 12.2).

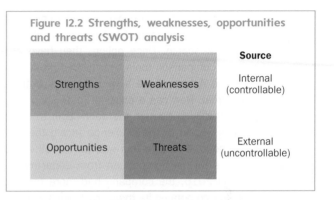

Figure 12.2 Strengths, weaknesses, opportunities and threats (SWOT) analysis

For a SWOT analysis to be useful a number of guidelines must be followed. First, not only absolute, but also relative strengths and weaknesses should be identified. Relative strengths focus on strengths and weaknesses as compared with the competition. Thus, if everyone produces quality products, this is not identified as a relative strength. Unique resources and capabilities that a firm has may provide it with a relative strength.[9] Two lists should be drawn up based on absolute and relative strengths and weaknesses. Strengths that can be exploited can be both absolute and relative, but how they are exploited and the degree to which they can be used depends on whether the competition also possesses them. Relative strengths provide the distinctive competencies of a business (see Exhibit 12.3). But strengths need to be looked at objectively as they can sometimes turn into weaknesses. A case in point is Sony, one of whose strengths has been its product innovation capabilities. Such was the

Exhibit 12.3 Dyson's design and engineering capabilities have enabled it to build sustainable advantages in product areas like vacuum cleaners.

success of its products that it took its eye off the market and technological trends. For example, the Walkman was supplanted by the Apple iPod in the portable audio business and, similarly, its dominance of cathode ray tube television technology caused it to initially miss the trend towards flat-screen televisions, although it subsequently introduced its own models in this product category.[10]

An absolute weakness that competitors also possess should be identified because it can clearly become a source of relative strength if overcome. If all businesses in an industry are poor at after-sales service, this should be noted as a weakness, as it provides the potential for gaining competitive advantage. Relative weaknesses should also be listed because these may be the sources of competitive disadvantage on which managerial attention should be focused. For example, internal analysis by the Dixons Carphone group, which owns Currys PC World and Carphone Warehouse, found that customer service, the internal layout of stores and product presentation were significant weaknesses (see Marketing in Action 12.1).[11]

Second, only those resources or capabilities that would be valued by the customer should be included when evaluating strengths and weaknesses.[12] Thus, strengths such as 'We are an old established firm', 'We are a large supplier' and 'We are technologically advanced' should be questioned for their impact on customer satisfaction. It is conceivable that such bland generalizations confer as many weaknesses as strengths.

Marketing in Action 12.1
Dixons Carphone: meeting the online challenge

Critical Thinking: Below is a review of the competitive challenges facing the consumer electronics retailer Dixons Carphone. Read it and critically review the company's responses. Discuss whether you believe physical consumer electronics retailers have a future in the industry or not.

Any analysis of the future of consumer electronics retailing has to take account of the growing impact of the internet. It is estimated that nine out of ten customers start their shopping journey online, usually through search. Once online, they have access to many useful tools, such as customer reviews, price comparison tools and tailored product preferences based on previous purchases. Online specialists like Amazon have a vast range of both products and third-party vendors that customers can choose from. How can a physical retail shop with a limited product range and little knowledge of the customer walking through the door begin to compete in this environment?

This is the scale of the challenge facing the UK's last remaining consumer electronics retailer, Dixons Carphone. Added to this was an overall steady decline in the sales of consumer electronics products, plus further competition from department stores like John Lewis and catalogue retailers like Argos. In 2016, the company had more than 1,000 stores in the UK and Ireland, about one-third of which incorporated its three key brands, Currys, PC World and Carphone Warehouse, all formerly independent brands that have been merged to enable them to compete in the new environment. Its plan was to consolidate its stores into three sizes: megastores (greater than 30,000 square feet), superstores (16,000–30,000 square feet) and regular stores (5,000–16,000 square feet). While about 25 per cent of its sales, and growing, are online, Dixons Carphone believes the physical store still has a key role to play. Its focus has been to emphasize display, interactivity and service. For example, the vacuum cleaner section has three types of flooring so that customers can try out a device. Noise-cancelling headphones can be tested against ambient sounds that might be encountered every day, while mirrors are provided to enable customers to assess how they look as well as sound. The overall strategy has been to create an immersive emporium of electronics where customers can explore, interact and engage with products and staff.

A focus on its frontline sales staff and the role that they play in assisting customers was central to differentiating it from online competitors. This customer service element was the theme to its 2014/15 advertising campaign, which used the tagline 'We start with you' (see Exhibit 12.4). The essential message in the campaign was that store staff were trained to assist customers to find the right products from the wide and often confusing ranges available. Executions of the campaign included a focus on large-screen TVs for the 2014 football World Cup; *simplification*, which dramatized the assisted shopping experience for Christmas of that year, and a focus on how technology could fit into customers' lives for 2015. The campaign ran across various media, including television, press, outdoor and social content. In addition,

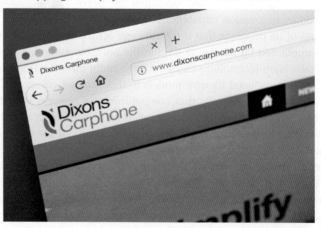

Exhibit 12.4 Dixons Carphone's 'We start with you' campaign aimed to demonstrate the service benefits of shopping in a physical store rather than online.

(continued)

product content such as buying guides and how-to videos were rewritten and reproduced to reflect customer needs rather than technical product specifications. The impact of the campaign was that positive perceptions of the Dixons Carphone in-store staff rose significantly, along with its key financial metrics such as sales and profitability.

Based on: Claridge, Edwards and Sellars, 2016;[13] Davidson, 2016;[14] Joseph, 2014[15]

Third, opportunities and threats should be listed as anticipated events or trends *outside* the business that have implications for performance. They should not be couched in terms of strategies. For example, 'To enter market segment X' is not an opportunity but a strategic objective that may result from a perceived opportunity arising from the emergence of market segment X as attractive because of its growth potential and lack of competition. The ability to spot and exploit an opportunity can lead to success that dramatically exceeds expectations, as demonstrated by the rapid growth of companies like Facebook, Amazon and PayPal.

Marketing objectives

The definition of **marketing objectives** may be derived from the results of the marketing audit and the SWOT analysis. Two types of objective need to be considered: strategic thrust and strategic objectives.

Strategic thrust

Objectives should be set in terms of which products to sell in which markets. This describes the **strategic thrust** of the business. The strategic thrust defines the future direction of the business, and the basic alternatives are summarized in the Ansoff growth matrix, as shown in Figure 12.3. These are:

- existing products in existing markets (market penetration or expansion)
- new products for existing markets (product development)
- existing products in new markets (market development)
- new products for new markets (diversification).

Figure 12.3 Product growth strategies: the Ansoff matrix

	Product	
	Existing	New
Existing Markets	Market penetration or expansion	Product development
New	Market development	Diversification

We will now look at each of these in turn.

1 *Market penetration*: this strategy involves taking the existing product in the existing market and attempting to increase penetration. Existing customers may become more brand loyal (i.e. brand switch less often) and/or new customers in the same market may begin to buy the brand. Other tactics to increase penetration include getting existing customers to use the brand more often (e.g. eat breakfast cereals as daytime snacks) and to use a greater quantity when they use it (e.g. two teaspoons of coffee instead of one). The latter tactic would also have the effect of expanding the market. Market penetration is usually achieved by more effective use of promotion or distribution, or by cutting prices.

2 *Product development*: this strategy involves increasing sales by improving current products or developing new products for current markets (see Exhibit 12.5). For example, many companies provide additional services to their customers. Faced with pressure on their margins for product sales, drugstores in the USA have started providing walk-in clinics where patients are examined by nurse practitioners who conduct basic procedures such as vaccinations for lower prices than doctors charge. Global accounting firms like KPMG and Deloitte provide management consulting services to clients.

3 *Market development*: this strategy is used when current products are sold in new markets. This may involve moving into new international markets or moving into new market segments. For example, Nestlé, the world's biggest food group, has been able to grow sales of its brands such as Kit Kat confectionery and Nescafé instant coffee by more than 10 per cent in emerging markets such as Africa, Asia and Oceania compared with relatively stagnant sales growth in Western Europe.[16]

4 *Diversification*: this strategy occurs when new products are developed for new markets. This is the most risky strategy but may be necessary when a company's current products and markets offer few prospects of future growth. There have been many celebrated examples of companies that took this decision only for their efforts to fail. For example, the fashion brand Diesel ventured into the wine business with a range of boutique wines that ultimately were unsuccessful. Similarly, US restaurant chain Hooters' entry into the airline business was unsuccessful as were Colgate's efforts to enter the ready-to-eat meals business. When there is synergy between the existing and new products this strategy is more likely to work, as illustrated by Ryanair's move into the accommodation business with Ryanair Rooms. A further potential diversification that has been mooted is Ryanair Holidays – an all-inclusive low-cost breaks service.[17]

Exhibit 12.5 Breakfast cereal manufacturers have moved into the snack food business with products like these.

Strategic objectives

Alongside objectives for product/market direction, **strategic objectives** for each product also need to be agreed. This begins the process of planning at the product level. There are four alternatives:

1 build
2 hold
3 harvest
4 divest.

For new products, the strategic objective will inevitably be to build sales and market share. For existing products, the appropriate strategic objective will depend on the particular situation associated with the product. This will be determined in the market audit, SWOT analysis and evaluation of the strategic options outlined earlier. In particular, product portfolio planning tools such as the Boston Consulting Group's growth-share matrix (as outlined in Chapter 6) may be used to aid this analysis.

The important point to remember at this stage is that *building* sales and market share is not the only sensible strategic objective for a product. *Holding* sales and market share may make commercial sense under certain conditions; *harvesting*, where sales and market share are allowed to fall but profit margins are maximized, may also be preferable to building; finally, *divestment*, where the product is dropped or sold, can be the logical outcome of the situation analysis.

Together, strategic thrust and strategic objectives define where the business and its products intend to go in the future. For any given planning period, the objectives should meet the SMART criteria, namely, that they are stated in specific, measurable, attainable, realistic and time-specific terms. So, for example, to state that our objectives are to grow brand awareness or increase sales of brand X are weak, whereas writing our objectives in terms such as 'to expand the customer base by adding 100 new customers per month for the next year' is much better as we can easily check whether or not we have achieved this objective at the end of the planning period.

Marketing strategies

When thinking about marketing strategy, our two key decisions are which markets to target and how we aim to compete in those markets. Target market selection will be informed by our market segmentation analysis (see Chapter 5) and the strategic thrust decisions that we have made. Following this, how we compete has been conventionally thought of in terms of a choice between differentiation and cost leadership. When combined with the competitive scope of activities (broad vs narrow) these two means of competitive advantage result in four generic strategies: differentiation, cost leadership, differentiation focus and cost focus. The differentiation and cost leadership strategies seek competitive advantage in a broad range of market or industry segments, whereas differentiation focus and cost focus strategies are confined to a narrow segment. Seeking one of these positions of advantage is critical to survival. For example, the only players remaining in the fashion business are either megabrands with a billion dollars in sales, such as Gucci, Louis Vuitton, Burberry, Prada and others, or niche brands with sales of between US$1 million and US$100 million, such as Rochas and Balenciaga.

Differentiation

Differentiation strategy involves the choice of one or more choice criteria that are used by many buyers in an industry. A firm then uniquely positions itself to meet these criteria. For example, firms might seek to be better (i.e. have superior quality), be faster (i.e. respond more quickly) or be closer (i.e. build better relationships with customers).[18] The aim is to differentiate in a way that leads to a price premium in excess of the cost of differentiating. Differentiation gives customers a reason to prefer one product over another and thus is central to strategic marketing thinking. For example, semiconductors (products that many people will not even have heard of) are at the centre of our modern society, powering our smartphones, tablets and computers. Today, most semiconductors made from silicon, which has given rise to labels like 'Silicon Valley' and the 'silicon economy'. It is a huge industry, estimated to have been worth almost US$500 billion in 2017, and dominated by large firms like Samsung, Intel and Qualcomm (see Exhibit 12.6). The key to success in this industry has always been about differentiation through innovation. In the past, this was about building ever faster, smaller and powerful chips to drive products like smartphones. With the emerging opportunities provided by the Internet of Things (IoT), the innovation race has changed again as manufacturers now require chips with data capture and communications capabilities.

Exhibit 12.6 This 2017 advert from the semiconductor company, Qualcomm celebrates its role in smartphone technology.

Cost leadership

The cost leadership approach involves the achievement of the lowest cost position in an industry. Many segments in an industry are served and great importance is placed on minimizing costs on all fronts. As long as the price achievable for its products is around the industry average, cost leadership should result in superior performance. Thus, cost leaders often market standard products that are believed to be acceptable to customers. Ryanair is a cost leader in aviation and Lenovo a cost leader in personal computers. They market acceptable products at reasonable prices, which means that their low costs result in above average profits. Amazon has built a dominant position in e-commerce through pursuing a cost leadership strategy. Some cost leaders need to discount prices in order to achieve high sales levels. The aim here is to achieve superior performance by ensuring that the cost advantage over the competition is not offset by the price discount. No-frills supermarket discounters like Costco, KwikSave and Aldi fall into this category.

Differentiation focus

By taking a differentiation focus approach, a firm aims to differentiate within one or a small number of target market segments (see Marketing in Action 12.2). The special needs of the segment mean that there is an opportunity to differentiate the product offering from those of competitors who may be targeting a broader group of customers. For example, some small speciality chemical companies thrive on taking orders that are too small or specialized to be of interest to their larger competitors. Similarly, Domino's Pizza has built the world's biggest home-delivery pizza company on the back of a strategy of fast service and consistent quality (see the Marketing Spotlight at the beginning of Chapter 9). Microbreweries have been on the rise around the world to meet niche tastes not catered for by the big brewers. Those firms adopting a differentiation focus must be clear that the needs of their target group differ from those of the broader market (otherwise there will be no basis for differentiation) and that existing competitors are underperforming.

Marketing in Action 12.2
Emirates Airlines: bringing luxury back into air travel

> **Critical Thinking:** Below is a review of some marketing innovations by Emirates Airlines. Read it and critically reflect on how the company seeks to differentiate itself in a crowded marketplace.

It is estimated that there are more than 5,000 airlines operating in the global aviation industry, giving consumers lots of options in terms of how they travel to different parts of the world. One company that has successfully found its niche in this crowded marketplace is the Dubai airline, Emirates. There was a time when air travel was primarily available only to the relatively well off, so competitors focused on trying to replicate the comforts of home, providing quality meals accompanied by good service. The rise of the low-fares airlines changed all that with the emphasis on price effectively equating air travel to a 'bus in the sky'. However, in its strategy, Emirates has aimed to restore air travel to its more glorious past.

Long-haul travel is characterized by the three main pricing options of first class, business class and economy class. In a bid to boost their revenues, many carriers have been reducing or phasing out their first-class spaces and expanding the number of business-class seats that they offer instead. Emirates has taken the opposite route, growing its first-class section and putting an emphasis on maximizing luxury. Its first-class cabins offer 40 square feet of private space and are fully enclosed with floor-to-ceiling sliding doors. They include a fully flat bed offering a 'zero-gravity position', which aims to simulate the feeling of weightlessness that astronauts experience on board spacecraft. Several other elements of the design are inspired by the luxury German car brand Mercedes-Benz, including leather seating, a high-tech control system and mood lighting. The cabins also include 'virtual windows', which project real-time live footage of views captured by cameras installed outside the plane. Other luxuries include noise-cancelling headphones, seats with a massage function and a video link to communicate with cabin crew. To replicate all the comforts of a luxury hotel, passengers are served high-quality meals, have access to shower facilities and can

(continued)

go to the bar to enjoy some cocktails if they wish. Despite a premium price tag, demand for its 14 first-class seats generally outstrips that of all its other offerings.

As we saw in Chapter 7, tangibles are a key element of services marketing, so Emirates flight attendants with their red hats, white veils and tan suits are a big part of the marketing strategy. In recent years, the company has been at or close to the top of the customer satisfaction charts, along with competitors like Qatar Airways and Singapore Airlines. Relative to its competitors, it spends less on television advertising, focusing instead on sponsorship, such as its association with the football World Cup. However, it did achieve global recognition for its series of ad campaigns featuring the actress Jennifer Aniston (see Exhibit 12.7). All of these activities have combined to build Emirates' brand equity, making it the most valuable airline brand in the world in 2017. The company has become a force in global aviation in recent years but it would appear that it will not have things all its own way. Competition remains intense, with rivals like Etihad challenging its leadership in luxury by offering first-class three-room apartments, dubbed 'Residence' class, in its planes. It would appear that the bar for luxury will just soar ever higher in the airline world.

Exhibit 12.7 Emirates has used popular US actress Jennifer Aniston to front its advertising campaigns.

Based on: Kim, 2017;[19] Voight, 2014[20]

Cost focus

By adopting a cost focus strategy, a firm seeks a cost advantage with one or a small number of target market segments. By dedicating itself to a segment, the cost focuser can seek economies that may be ignored or missed by broadly targeted competitors. In some instances, the competition, by trying to achieve wide market acceptance, may be over-performing (for example, by providing unwanted services) to one segment of customers. By providing a basic product offering, a cost advantage will be gained that may exceed the price discount necessary to sell it. For example, Kiwibank is a low-cost domestic bank that was set up by the New Zealand Government as an alternative to the foreign-owned banks dominating the market. It has proved particularly attractive to low-income customers because of its low fee structure.[21]

Choosing a competitive strategy

So it seems that the essence of corporate success is to choose a generic strategy and pursue it enthusiastically. Below-average performance is associated with failure to achieve any of these generic strategies. The result is no competitive advantage: a stuck-in-the-middle position that results in lower performance than that of the cost leaders, differentiators or focusers in any market segment. An example of a company that struggled to maintain its initial advantage was Starbucks. Throughout its early phase of growth in the 1980s and 1990s, Starbucks had carved out a differentiated position for itself as being more than just a coffee shop chain but rather a 'third place' between home and work, complete with comfortable seating, quality coffee facilities for downloading music, and so on. But, as it expanded, it added drive-through facilities, food items and pre-ground coffee, which brought it more into competition with low-cost operators such as McDonald's and Dunkin' Donuts. The company's sales and share price dropped dramatically and it brought back its founder, Howard Schultz, as chief executive in order to try to recover the ground it had lost by becoming 'stuck in the middle' between low cost and differentiated. Schultz successfully turned the company around, restoring it to its dominant position in the global coffee business.

Firms need to understand the generic basis for their success and resist the temptation to blur strategy by making inconsistent moves. For example, a no-frills cost leader or focuser should beware of the pitfalls of moving to a higher cost base (perhaps by adding on expensive services). A focus strategy involves limiting sales volume. Once domination of the target segment has been achieved, there may be a temptation to move into other segments in order to achieve growth with the same competitive advantage. This can be a mistake if the new segments do not value the firm's competitive advantage in the same way.

Differentiation and cost leadership strategies are incompatible in most situations: differentiation is achieved through higher costs. However, there are circumstances when both can be achieved simultaneously. For example, a differentiation strategy may lead to market share domination that lowers costs through economies of scale and learning effects; or a highly differentiated firm may pioneer a major process innovation that significantly reduces manufacturing costs, leading to a cost leadership position. When differentiation and cost leadership coincide, performance is exceptional since a premium price can be charged for a low-cost product.

Sources of competitive advantage

In order to create a differentiated or lowest cost position, a firm needs to understand the nature and location of the potential sources of competitive advantage. The nature of these sources are the superior skills and resources of a firm. Management benefits by analysing the superior skills and resources that offer, or could contribute to, competitive advantage (i.e. differentiation or lowest cost position).

Superior skills

These are the distinctive capabilities of key personnel, which set them apart from the personnel of competing firms. The benefit of superior skills is the resulting ability to perform functions more effectively than other firms. For example, superior selling skills may result in closer relationships with customers than competing firms can achieve. Superior quality assurance skills can result in improved and more consistent product quality.

Superior resources

The tangible requirements for advantage that enable a firm to exercise its skills are known as superior resources (see Exhibit 12.8). Superior resources may include:

- the number of salespeople in a market
- expenditure on advertising and sales promotion
- distribution coverage (the number of retailers who stock the product)
- expenditure on r&d
- scale of and type of production facilities
- financial resources
- brand equity
- knowledge.

Specifically, within the domain of marketing, key resources and capabilities that have been identified

Exhibit 12.8 Roche, the Swiss-based global pharmaceutical giant, is one of the leading spenders on research and development (R&D) in its industry, ploughing an estimated 20 per cent of revenues back into research.

by researchers include market sensing and knowledge management capabilities, relational capabilities such as customer relationship management processes, brand assets and functional marketing mix capabilities.[22]

Value chain

The value chain provides a useful method for locating superior skills and resources. Many firms consist of a set of activities that are conducted to design, manufacture, market, distribute and service their products. The value chain of primarily service businesses may be shorter and involve fewer stages. The value chain categorizes actions into primary and support activities (see Figure 12.4). This enables the sources of costs and differentiation to be understood and located.

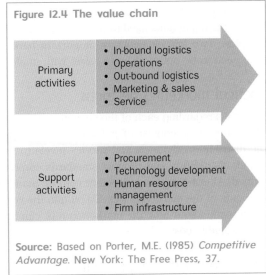

Figure 12.4 The value chain

Primary activities
- In-bound logistics
- Operations
- Out-bound logistics
- Marketing & sales
- Service

Support activities
- Procurement
- Technology development
- Human resource management
- Firm infrastructure

Source: Based on Porter, M.E. (1985) *Competitive Advantage*. New York: The Free Press, 37.

1 *Primary activities* include in-bound physical distribution (e.g. materials handling, warehousing, inventory control), operations (e.g. manufacturing, packaging), out-bound physical distribution (e.g. delivery, order processing), marketing (e.g. advertising, selling, channel management) and service (e.g. installation, repair, customer training).

2 *Support activities* are found within all of these primary activities, and consist of purchased inputs, technology, human resource management and the firm's infrastructure. These are not defined within a given primary activity because they can be found in all of them. Purchasing can take place within each primary activity, not just in the purchasing department; technology is relevant to all primary activities, as is human resource management; and the firm's infrastructure – which consists of general management, planning, finance, accounting and quality management – supports the entire value chain.

If management examines each value-creating activity, it can pinpoint the skills and resources that may form the basis of low cost or differentiated positions. To the extent that skills and resources exceed or could be developed to exceed the competition, they form the key sources of competitive advantage. Not only should the skills and resources within value-creating activities be examined but so also should the *linkages* between them. For example, greater co-ordination between operations and in-bound physical distribution may give rise to reduced costs through lower inventory levels.

Tests of an effective marketing strategy

The six tests of an effective marketing strategy are detailed in Figure 12.5. First, the strategy must be based upon a clear definition of target customers and their needs. Second, an understanding of competitors is required so that the strategy can be based on a competitive advantage. Third, the strategy must incur acceptable risk. Challenging a strong competitor with a weak competitive advantage and a low resource base would not incur acceptable risk. Fourth, the strategy should be resource and managerially supportable. It should match the resource capabilities and managerial competencies of the business. Fifth, core strategy should be derived from the product and marketing objectives established as part of the planning process. A strategy (e.g. heavy promotion) that makes commercial logic when following a build

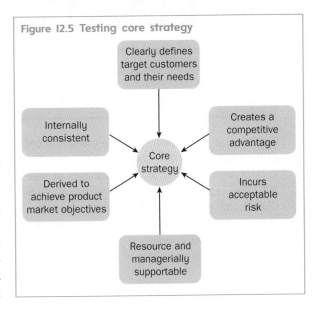

Figure 12.5 Testing core strategy

- Clearly defines target customers and their needs
- Creates a competitive advantage
- Internally consistent
- Core strategy
- Incurs acceptable risk
- Derived to achieve product market objectives
- Resource and managerially supportable

objective may make no sense when a harvesting objective has been decided. Finally, the strategy should be internally consistent. The elements should blend to form a coherent whole.

Executing marketing strategies

Taking great care with a situation analysis and formulating carefully thought-out strategies is all well and good, but eventually actions need to be taken and decisions made regarding how to effectively implement the marketing plan. Two key elements are important here, namely, the tactical actions required and the structures that may need to be put in place to assist with implementation.

Tactical marketing decisions

Decisions regarding each of the elements of the marketing mix make up the next stage of the planning process. These decisions consist of judgements about price levels, the blend of promotional techniques to employ, the distribution channels and service levels to use, and the types of products to manufacture. Where promotional, distribution and product standards surpass those of the competition, a competitive advantage may be gained. Alternatively, a judgement may be made only to match, or even undershoot, the competition on some elements of the marketing mix. To outgun the competition on everything is not normally feasible. Choices have to be made about how the marketing mix can be manipulated to provide a superior offering to the customer at reasonable cost.

Organization and implementation

It is said that no marketing plan will succeed unless it 'degenerates into work'.[23] Consequently, the business must design an organization that has the capabilities necessary to implement the plan. Indeed, organizational weaknesses discovered as part of the SWOT analysis may restrict the feasible range of strategic options. Reorganization could mean changes to the marketing organization or department in the business (see Marketing in Action 12.3). Environmental change may cause strategic change, and this may imply a reorganization of marketing and sales. The growth of large corporate customers with enormous buying power has resulted in businesses focusing their resources more firmly on meeting their needs (strategy change), which has led, in turn, to dedicated marketing and sales teams being organized to service these accounts (reorganization). A strong, well-developed marketing organization is important as it has been found to contribute significantly to customer relationship performance levels, overall firm performance levels and longer-term shareholder value.[24]

Marketing in Action 12.3
The death of the marketing department!

Critical Thinking: Below is a review of some of the innovations taking place in the structure of marketing departments around the world. Read and critically reflect on the environmental changes that are driving these innovations.

One thing is for certain – life in a marketing department is never boring! The rapidly changing nature of the field means that changes in the structure and organization of marketing activity are frequent. In large organizations, the core activities of sales, customer service, insights and brand management are often organized into their own separate sub-departments, all overseen by a marketing director or CMO (chief marketing officer). Even within the brand management function there may be a large number of brand managers all running their own brand teams. But can this kind of rigid, bureaucratic structure still be effective in a competitive environment that is changing very rapidly, and is being disrupted by developments in digital marketing and technology generally? The answer would appear to be no!

(continued)

For example, one of the companies that frequently innovates in the area of marketing organization is Proctor & Gamble, the venerable owner of many of the world's best-known brands, which employs almost 100,000 people. In 2014, it abolished the term 'marketing director', which had existed in the company since 1993, and 'marketing department'. Instead these were renamed as 'brand director' and 'brand management', respectively. The latter unit became responsible for all marketing, customer insights, communications and design activities, with the aim of simplifying the structure, clarifying roles and responsibilities and making decisions faster. This was followed by a reduction in the number of product categories that P&G competes in from 16 to 10, and a reduction in the number of brands in its portfolio from 170 to 65. This was in response to the growth in online shopping and faster innovation cycles driven by better customer insights through Big Data and analytics.

Structural changes are not restricted to large multinationals like P&G. Chobani is a US yoghurt manufacturer, which was named one of the 10 most innovative companies in the world by *Fast Company* magazine in 2017. In that year, it decided to abolish its marketing, sales and insights departments and combine them all into one unit called the 'generating demand department'. The goal was to operate a more team-based structure that allowed customer insights to be central to all key decisions. Such collaboration is reflected in the fact that, for example, sales people often accompany researchers to focus group sessions, while marketing, sales and other functions can have input in market research studies. The merging of the marketing and sales functions appears to be on the increase, with Coca-Cola having a *chief growth officer* and Mars describing the marketing role as effectively a *chief demand officer*. Similarly, in the UK, companies like John Lewis have a *customer director*, while British Airways has a *director of customer experience*. As new imperatives, such as customer experience, data-led insights and digital marketing, grow in importance, further innovations in the marketing organization are inevitable.

Based on: Eleftheriou-Smith, 2014;[25] Neff, 2014;[26] Vizard, 2018;[27] Whiteside, 2017[28]

Assessing marketing strategies

Finally, all marketing plans need to be evaluated to determine whether the objectives set out at the beginning of the plan have been achieved or not. One of the criticisms frequently levelled at the marketing profession is that it does not do a good job of demonstrating how its efforts benefit the organization. Control systems need to be put in place to ensure that marketing resources are spent wisely.

Control systems

The aim of control systems is to evaluate the results of the marketing plan so that corrective action can be taken if performance does not match objectives. Short-term control systems can plot results against objectives on a daily, weekly, monthly, quarterly and/or annual basis. Measures include sales, profits, costs and cash flow. Strategic control systems are more long term. Managers need to stand back from week-by-week and month-by-month results to critically reassess whether their plans are in line with their capabilities and the environment.

Where this kind of long-term control perspective is lacking, it may result in the pursuit of plans that have lost strategic credibility. New competition, changes in technology and moving customer requirements may have rendered old plans obsolete. This, of course, returns the planning process to the beginning since this kind of fundamental review is conducted in the marketing audit. It is the activity of assessing internal capabilities and external opportunities and threats that results in a SWOT analysis. This outcome may mean a redefinition of the business mission, and, as we have seen, changes in marketing objectives and strategies to realign the business with its environment.

How, though, do the stages in marketing planning that we have looked at relate to the fundamental planning questions stated earlier in this chapter? Table 12.4 shows this relationship. The question 'Where are we now?' is answered by the business mission definition, the marketing audit and SWOT analysis. 'Where would we like to be?' is determined by the setting of marketing objectives. 'How do we get there?' refers to marketing strategy, marketing mix decisions, organization and implementation.

Marketing metrics

A key area of **control** is that of marketing metrics. The marketing discipline has traditionally been criticized for the quality of its metrics. For example, sales revenues are an important metric, but many of the factors influencing sales levels are outside the control of marketers, such as economic conditions or competitor activity. And, as we saw in Chapter 1, because marketers have not been good at measuring what they do, they are often poorly represented in corporate boardrooms compared with disciplines such as production and finance, although this situation appears to be changing.[29] Much of this is down to the complexity of marketing performance measurement, which comprises attitudinal, behavioural and financial variables that are often weakly interrelated.[30] In addition, marketing budgets are often the first to be cut when companies need to make cost savings.

As a result, more attention than ever is being paid to the metrics used to measure marketing activity. A vast array of potential metrics can be identified.[31] One study of US firms found that the most common marketing metrics in use were awareness (41 per cent), total customers (37 per cent) and market share (32 per cent). The most common financial metrics in use were total volume (units or sales 43 per cent), return-on-investment (36 per cent) and net profits (28 per cent).[32] In the main, there are two key elements of marketing measurement, namely, the effectiveness of operational marketing activity and the impact of marketing on the bottom line. Measuring the former is contingent on the type of marketing activity undertaken. For example, distribution activity can be measured by inventory levels, markdowns, facings and out-of-stock levels. As we saw in the previous chapters, one of the attractions of digital marketing communications techniques is the rich amount of control data they generate. For example, Facebook's advertising campaigns can be measured on a daily basis, and metrics like reach, click-throughs, conversions and cost can be assessed. But, ultimately, marketing decisions must contribute to increasing profits by increasing sales volumes, increasing prices or reducing unit costs.[33] The most common metrics in use in UK firms are shown in Table 12.5.

Table 12.4 Key questions and the process of marketing planning

Key questions	Stages in marketing planning
Where are we now and how did we get there?	Business mission Marketing audit SWOT analysis
Where would we like to be?	Marketing objectives
How do we get there?	Marketing strategy Marketing mix decisions Organization Implementation

Table 12.5 The use of marketing metrics in UK firms

Rank	Metric	% using measure	% rating it as important
1	Profit/profitability	92	80
2	Sales, value and/or volume	91	71
3	Gross margin	81	66
4	Awareness	78	28
5	Market share (value/volume)	78	37
6	Number of new products	73	18
7	Relative price	70	36
8	Customer dissatisfaction	69	45
9	Customer satisfaction	68	48
10	Distribution/availability	66	18

Source: Based on Ambler, Kokkinaki and Puntoni, 2004[34]

Effective marketing planning

Various authors[35,36,37] have attributed the following benefits to marketing planning.

1 *Consistency*: the plan provides a focal point for decisions and actions. By reference to a common plan, decisions by the same manager over time, and by different managers, should be more consistent and actions co-ordinated more effectively.

2 *Encourages the monitoring of change*: the planning process forces managers to step away from day-to-day problems and review the impact of change on the business from a strategic perspective.

3 *Encourages organizational adaptation*: the underlying premise of planning is that the organization should adapt to match its environment. Marketing planning, therefore, promotes the necessity to accept the inevitability of change. This is an important consideration since adaptive capability has been shown to be linked to superior performance.[38]

4 *Stimulates achievement*: the planning process focuses on objectives, strategies and results. It encourages people to ask 'What can we achieve given our capabilities?' As such, it motivates people, who otherwise might be content to accept much lower standards of performance, to set new horizons for objectives.

5 *Resource allocation*: the planning process asks fundamental questions about resource allocation. For example, which products and services should receive high investment (build), which should be maintained (hold), which should have resources withdrawn slowly (harvest), and which should have resources withdrawn immediately (divest).

6 *Competitive advantage*: planning promotes the search for sources of competitive advantage.

However, it should be borne in mind that this logical planning process, sometimes referred to as synoptic, may be at variance with the culture of the business, which may plan effectively using an *incremental* approach.[39] The style of planning must match business culture.[40] Saker and Speed argue that the considerable demands on managers in terms of time and effort implied by the synoptic marketing planning process may mean that alternative planning schemes are more appropriate, particularly for small companies.[41]

An incremental planning approach is more focused on problems, in that the process begins with the realization of a problem (for example, a fall-off in orders) and continues with an attempt to identify a solution. As solutions to problems form, so strategy emerges. However, little attempt is made to integrate consciously the individual decisions that could possibly affect one another. Strategy is viewed as a loosely linked group of decisions that are handled individually. Nevertheless, its effect may be to attune the business to its environment through its problem-solving nature. Its drawback is that the lack of broad situation analysis and strategy option generation renders the incremental approach less comprehensive. For some companies, however, its inherent practicality, rather than its rationality, may support its use.[42]

Problems in making planning work

Research into the marketing planning approaches of commercial firms has discovered that most companies did not practise the kinds of systematic planning procedure described in this chapter and, of those that did, many did not enjoy the rewards described above.[43] However, others have shown that there is a relationship between planning and commercial success (e.g. Armstrong and McDonald).[44,45] The problem is that the 'contextual difficulties' associated with the process of marketing planning are substantial and need to be understood. In as much as forewarned is forearmed, the following paragraphs offer a checklist of potential problems that have to be faced by those charged with making marketing planning work.

Political

Marketing planning is a process of resource allocation. The outcome of the process is an allocation of more funds to some products and departments, and the same or less to others (see Exhibit 12.9). Since power bases, career opportunities and salaries are often tied to whether an area is fast or slow growing, it is not surprising that managers view planning as a highly political activity. An example is a European bank whose planning process resulted in the decision to insist that its retail branch managers divert certain types of loan application to the industrial/merchant banking arm of the group, where the return was greater. This was required because the plan was designed to optimize the return to the group as a whole. However, the consequence of this was considerable friction between the divisions concerned because the decision lowered the performance of the retail branch.

Opportunity cost

Some busy managers take the view that marketing planning is a time-wasting process that interferes with the need to deal with day-to-day problems. They view the opportunity cost of spending two or three days away at a hotel thrashing out long-term plans as too high. This difficulty may be compounded by the fact that people who are attracted to the hectic pace of managerial life may be the type who prefer to live that way. Hence, they may be ill at ease with the thought of a long period of sedate contemplation.

Exhibit 12.9 As part of its plan to meet its financial difficulties, UK retailer Homebase announced in 2018 that it was closing 42 of its 241 stores in the UK and Ireland.

Reward systems

In business, reward systems are increasingly being geared to the short term. More and more incentives and bonuses are linked not just to annual but to quarterly results. Managers may thus overemphasize short-term issues and underemphasize medium- and long-term concerns if there is a conflict of time. Marketing planning, then, may be viewed as of secondary importance. For example, as it sought to respond to competitive challenges in the personal computer business by emphasizing long-term initiatives that drove sales, Dell Computer Corporation incurred the wrath of institutional investors who wanted to see more emphasis on short-term profits.[46]

Information

A systematic marketing planning system needs informational inputs in order to function effectively. Market share, size and growth rates are basic inputs into the marketing audit, but may be unavailable. More perversely, information may wilfully be withheld by those with vested interests who, recognizing that knowledge is power, distort the true situation to protect their position in the planning process.

Culture

Efforts to establish a systematic marketing planning process may be at odds with the culture of an organization. As we have already seen, businesses may 'plan' by making incremental decisions. Hence, the strategic planning system may challenge the status quo and be seen as a threat. In other cases, the values and beliefs of some managers may be altogether hostile to a planning system.

How to handle marketing planning problems

Various authors[47,48] have proposed the following recommendations for minimizing the impact of these problems.

1 *Senior management support*: top management must be committed to planning and be seen by middle management to give it total support. This should be ongoing support, not a short-term fad.
2 *Match the planning system to the culture of the business*: how the marketing planning process is managed should be consistent with the culture of the organization. For example, in some organizations the top-down/ bottom-up balance will move towards top-down; in other less directive cultures the balance will move towards a more bottom-up planning style.

3 *The reward system*: this should reward the achievement of longer-term objectives rather than focus exclusively on short-term results.

4 *Depoliticize outcomes*: less emphasis should be placed on rewarding managers associated with build (growth) strategies. Recognition of the skills involved in defending share and harvesting products should be made. At General Electric, managers were classified as growers, caretakers and undertakers, and matched to products that were being built, defended or harvested, in recognition of the fact that the skills involved differ according to the strategic objective. No stigma was attached to caretaking or undertaking as each was acknowledged as contributing to the success of the organization.

5 *Clear communication*: plans should be communicated to those charged with implementation.

6 *Training*: marketing personnel should be trained in the necessary marketing knowledge and skills to perform the planning job. Ideally, the management team should attend the same training course so that they each share a common understanding of the concepts and tools involved, and can communicate using the same terminology.

Summary

In this chapter, we have examined the important issues of marketing planning and marketing strategy. The following key issues were addressed.

1. The role of marketing planning is to give direction to the organization's marketing effort and to co-ordinate its activities. It helps to answer core questions like 'Where are we now?', 'Where would we like to be?' and 'How do we get there?'

2. The various stages of the marketing planning process include developing or adjusting the business mission, conducting a marketing audit, conducting a SWOT analysis, setting marketing objectives, deciding on the core strategy, making marketing mix decisions, and organizing, implementing and controlling the marketing effort.

3. The marketing audit is divided into an external audit, which examines environmental and competitive conditions, and an internal audit, which reviews marketing decisions and operating results. The information generated by a marketing audit should guide managerial choices regarding future directions for the organization.

4. Marketing objectives need to be decided at two levels, namely, strategic thrusts and strategic objectives. Strategic thrusts deal with the ways in which the organization can grow; there are four core choices, namely, market penetration, product development, market development and diversification. Strategic objectives are decided for each product and again there are four choices, namely, build, hold, harvest and divest.

5. As well as decisions regarding how to grow, organizations also need to make choices regarding how to compete. Four strategies are available, namely, differentiation, cost leadership, differentiation focus and cost focus. Value chain analysis can assist companies to identify the skills and resources necessary to implement effective competitive strategies.

6. There are a number of rewards to be gained for pursuing careful planning, including consistency, encouraging the monitoring of change, encouraging organizational adaptation, stimulating achievement, resource allocation and competitive advantage.

7. Making planning work is difficult because of office politics, perceived opportunity costs, pressures for short-term results, availability of the necessary information, and cultural issues. However, top management leadership, matching planning to organizational culture, reward systems, and communication and training, can all help to overcome these problems.

Study questions

1. Discuss some of the difficulties that can be encountered in making marketing planning work in an organization. How can these difficulties be overcome?

2. Discuss the role and limitations of the external analysis phase of marketing planning.

3. What is meant by a SWOT analysis? What are the characteristics of an effective SWOT analysis?

4. Compare and contrast a cost leadership strategy with a differentiation strategy. Is it possible to pursue both strategies simultaneously?

5. Discuss why it is important for marketers to be able to measure and justify the effectiveness of marketing activities.

6. Visit www.bplans.com, www.knowthis.com/general/marketplan.htm and www.howstuffworks.com/marketing-plan.htm. Review some of the sample marketing plans available on these sites.

Suggested reading

Burk Wood, M. (2011) *The Marketing Plan Handbook.* London: Pearson.

Day, G.S. (1999) *Market Driven Strategy: Processes for Creating Value.* New York: Free Press.

Feng, H., Morgan, N. and **Rego, L.** (2015) Marketing department power and firm performance, *Journal of Marketing*, 79, 1–20.

Hanssens, D. and **Pauwels, K.** (2016) Demonstrating the value of marketing, *Journal of Marketing*, 80, 173–90.

Mintz, O. and **Currim, I.** (2013) What drives managerial use of marketing and financial metrics and does metrics use affect performance of marketing-mix activities, *Journal of Marketing*, 77, 17–40.

Moorman, C. and **Day, G.** (2016) Organising for marketing excellence, *Journal of Marketing*, 80, 6–35.

Shaw, R. and **Merrick, D.** (2005) *Marketing Payback: Is Your Marketing Profitable?* London: Pearson Education.

References

1. **Bacon, J.** (2016) Marketing in the age of Trump, *Marketingweek.com*. Available at www.marketingweek.com/2016/10/04/marketing-in-the-age-of-trump/ (accessed 3 May 2018); **DeMers, J.** (2016) How Trump won using strategic branding and what entrepreneurs can learn from him, *Entrepreneur .com*. Available at www.entrepreneur.com/article/285124 (accessed 3 May 2016); **Quelch, J.** (2016) 6 lessons from Donald Trump's winning marketing manual, *Fortune.com*. Available at www.fortune.com/2016/11/10/donald-trump-campaign-marketing-success/ (accessed 3 May 2016); **Ritson, M.** (2016) Trump's marketing success shows the power of personality, *Marketingweek.com*. Available at www .marketingweek.com/2016/03/22/mark-ritson-donald-trumps-marketing-success-demonstrates-the-power-of-personality/ (accessed 3 May 2016); **Shen, L.** (2016) Here's how much you could've won by betting on Trump's presidency, *Fortune.com*. Available at www.fortune.com/2016/11/09/donald-trump-president-gamble/ (accessed 3 May 2018).

2. **Varadarajan, R.** (2010) Strategic marketing and marketing strategy: domain, definition, fundamental issues and foundational premises, *Journal of the Academy of Marketing Science*, 38, 119–40.

3. **Piercy, N.** (2002) *Market-led Strategic Change: A Guide to Transforming the Process of Going to Market.* Oxford: Heinemann.

4. **Gunther McGrath, R.** (2013) Transient advantage, *Harvard Business Review*, 91, 62–70.

5. **Ackoff, R.I.**(1987) Mission statements, *Planning Review*, 15(4), 30–2.

6. **Hooley, G.J., Cox, A.J.** and **Adams, A.** (1992) Our five year mission: to boldly go where no man has been before ..., *Journal of Marketing Management*, 8(1), 35–48.

7. **Levitt, T.** (1984) Marketing myopia, *Harvard Business Review*, 4(4), 59–80.

8. **Porter, M.E.** (1980) *Competitive Strategy: Techniques for Analyzing Industries and Competitors.* New York: Free Press.

9. See **Barney, J.** (1991) Firm resources and sustained competitive advantage, *Journal of Management*, 17(1), 99–120; **Teece, D.J., Pisano, G.** and **Sheun, A.** (1997) Dynamic capabilities and strategic management, *Strategic Management Journal*, 18, 509–33.

10. **Nakamoto, M.**(2005) Caught in its own trap: Sony battles to make headway in a networked world, *Financial Times*, 27 January, 17.

11. **Rigby, E.** (2008) DSG contracts with a view to improved service, *Financial Times*, 16 May, 17.

12. **Piercy, N.** (2002) *Market-led Strategic Change: A Guide to Transforming the Process of Going to Market.* Oxford: Heinemann.

13. **Claridge, T., Edwards, D.** and **Sellars, R.** (2016) Curry's PC World: we start with you, *Warc.com*. Available at www.warc.com/content/article/ipa/currys_pc_world_we_start_with_you/108058 (accessed 9 August 2018).

14. **Davidson, L.** (2016) A peek inside Dixon's Carphone's plan to keep customers coming back to its stores, *Telegraph.co.uk*. Available at www.telegraph.co.uk/business/2016/03/11/a-peek-inside-dixons-carphones-plan-to-keep-customers-coming-bac/ (accessed 9 August 2018).

15. **Joseph, S.** (2014) Currys PC World unveils £20 million 'statement' campaign to press home customer values, *Marketingweek.com*. Available at www .marketingweek.com/2014/10/21/currys-pc-world-unveils-20m-statement-campaign-to-press-home-customer-values/ (accessed 9 August 2018).

16. **Simonian, H.** (2010) Emerging markets drive sales for Nestlé, *Financial Times*, 12 August, 20.

17. **Plush, H.** (2016) Would you stay in a 'Ryanair Room'? *Telegraph.co.uk.* Available at www.telegraph.co.uk/travel/news/ryanair-launches-package-holidays-rooms/ (accessed 15 August 2018).

18. **Day, G.S.** (1999) *Market Driven Strategy: Processes for Creating Value.* New York: Free Press.

19. **Kim, S.** (2017) The first class cabin war: Emirates unveils 'zero gravity' flatbeds inspired by NASA, *Telegraph.co.uk.* Available at www.telegraph.co.uk/travel/news/emirates-new-cabins-for-boeing-777/ (accessed 13 August 2018).

20. **Voight, J.** (2014) Emirates is the world's most glamorous airline, *Adweek.com.* Available at www.adweek.com/brand-marketing/emirates-worlds-most-glamorous-airline-160714/ (accessed 13 August 2018).

21. **Fifield, A.** (2003) Kiwibank can afford to hold critics to account, *Financial Times*, 24 April, 11.

22. **Day, G.** (2011) Closing the marketing capabilities gap, *Journal of Marketing*, 75, 183–95.

23. **Drucker, P.F.** (1993) *Management Tasks, Responsibilities, Practices.* New York: Harper & Row, 128.

24. **Homburg, C., Vomberg, A., Enke, M.** and **Grimm, P.** (2015) The loss of the marketing department's influence: is it really happening? And why worry? *Journal of the Academy of Marketing Science*, 43, 1–13; **Feng, H., Morgan, N.** and **Rego, L.** (2015) Marketing department power and firm performance, *Journal of Marketing*, 79, 1–20.

25. **Eleftheriou-Smith, L.** (2014) P&G signals the end of 'marketing' with major restructure, *CampaignLive.co.uk.* Available at www.campaignlive.co.uk/article/p-g-signals-end-marketing-major-restructure/1301294 (accessed 10 August 2018).

26. **Neff, J.** (2014) It's the end of 'marketing' as we know it at Proctor & Gamble, *Adage.com.* Available at www.http://adage.com/article/cmo-strategy/end-marketing-procter-gamble/293918/ (accessed 10 August 2018).

27. **Vizard, S.** (2018) Mars on why its top marketers are becoming 'chief demand officers', *Marketingweek.com.* Available at www.marketingweek.com/2018/08/15/mars-chief-demand-officers/ (accessed 15 August 2018).

28. **Whiteside, S.** (2017) Chobani's new structure magnifies power of insights, *Warc.com.* Available at www.warc.com/content/article/event-reports/chobanis_new_structure_magnifies_power_of_insights/117200 (accessed 10 August 2018).

29. **Feng, H., Morgan, N.** and **Rego, L.** (2015) Marketing department power and firm performance, *Journal of Marketing*, 79, 1–20.

30. **Hanssens, D.** and **Pauwels, K.** (2016) Demonstrating the value of marketing, *Journal of Marketing*, 80, 173–90.

31. **Farris, P.W., Bendle, N.T., Pfeifer, P.E.** and **Reibstein, D.J.** (2006) *Marketing Metrics.* Upper Saddle River, NJ: Wharton.

32. **Mintz, O.** and **Currim, I.** (2013) What drives managerial use of marketing and financial metrics and does metrics use affect performance of marketing-mix activities? *Journal of Marketing*, 77, 17–40.

33. **Shaw, R.** and **Merrick, D.** (2005) *Marketing Payback: Is Your Marketing Profitable?* London: Pearson Education.

34. **Ambler, T., Kokkinaki, F.** and **Puntoni, S.** (2004) Assessing marketing performance: reasons for metrics selection, *Journal of Marketing Management*, 20, 475–98.

35. **Leppard, J.W.** and **McDonald, M.H.B.** (1991) Marketing planning and corporate culture: a conceptual framework which examines management attitudes in the context of marketing planning, *Journal of Marketing Management*, 7(3), 213–36.

36. **Greenley, G.E.** (1986) *The Strategic and Operational Planning of Marketing.* Maidenhead: McGraw-Hill, 185–7.

37. **Terpstra, V.** and **Sarathy, R.** (1991) *International Marketing.* Orlando, FL: Dryden, Ch. 17.

38. **Oktemgil, M.** and **Greenley, G.** (1997) Consequences of high and low adaptive capability in UK companies, *European Journal of Marketing*, 31(7), 445–66.

39. **Raimond, P.** and **Eden, C.** (1990) Making strategy work, *Long Range Planning*, 23(5), 97–105.

40. **Driver, J.C.** (1990) Marketing planning in style, *Quarterly Review of Marketing*, 15(4), 16–21.

41. **Saker, J.** and **Speed, R.** (1992) Corporate culture: is it really a barrier to marketing planning? *Journal of Marketing Management*, 8(2), 177–82. For information on marketing and planning in small and medium-sized firms, see **Carson, D.** (1990) Some exploratory models for assessing small firms' marketing performance: a qualitative approach, *European Journal of Marketing*, 24(11), 8–51; and **Fuller, P.B.** (1994) Assessing marketing in small and medium-sized enterprises, *European Journal of Marketing*, 28(12), 34–9.

42. **O'Shaughnessy, J.** (1995) *Competitive Marketing.* Boston, MA: Allen & Unwin.

43. **Greenley, G.** (1987) An exposition of empirical research into marketing planning, *Journal of Marketing Management*, 3(1), 83–102.

44. **Armstrong, J.S.** (1982) The value of formal planning for strategic decisions: review of empirical research, *Strategic Management Journal*, 3(3), 197–213.

45. **McDonald, M.H.B.** (1984) The theory and practice of marketing planning for industrial goods in international markets. Cranfield Institute of Technology, PhD thesis.

46. **Allison, K.** (2008) Dell's long view irks investors, *Financial Times*, 1 September, 23.

47. **McDonald, M.H.B.** (1984) The theory and practice of marketing planning for industrial goods in international markets. Cranfield Institute of Technology, PhD thesis.

48. **Abell, D.F.** and **Hammond, J.S.** (1979) *Strategic Market Planning.* Englewood Cliffs, NJ: Prentice-Hall.

Introduction

Uber is one of the best-known and most high-profile sharing economy companies to have emerged in the past decade. But, as 2018 comes to a close, the controversial US business appears to be facing many opportunities and threats. It has some significant trends in its favour. The growing penetration of internet services, rapid urbanization, the popularity of sharing services among millennials, and the development of semi-autonomous and autonomous vehicles are all trends that bode well for its mobility app transportation business. But there are many clouds on the horizon too. Uber has had to beat a painful and costly retreat from Southeast Asia after failing to disrupt local markets in the same way that it has in the USA and Europe. It has been dogged with controversies, both externally with taxi organizations and regulators, and internally in terms of its corporate culture and business practices. And, despite rapidly growing revenues, it continues to lose money. It would appear that there will be further interesting twists and turns for this car company in the years ahead.

Company background

Uber Technologies, Inc. – initially known as UberCabs – was founded in 2009 in San Francisco by two friends, Garrett Camp and Travis Kalanick. Both had been serial Silicon Valley entrepreneurs – Camp had co-founded StumbleUpon, a web discovery platform, while Kalanick had founded two companies: Scour, a peer-to-peer file exchange platform, and Red Swoosh, a data-transfer business. The idea for a transportation business apparently first came to the friends while they were in Paris and struggling to find a taxi cab during a snowstorm. Initially, the business was conceived as a private luxury car service for executives and the first version of the app appeared in Apple's App Store in 2010. Customers wishing to use the service had to email Kalanick for a code to access the app. After entering their credit card information, they could then summon a black car service from their phones. The cost of the journey was automatically deducted from the customer's pre-loaded credit card, with Uber keeping 20 per cent of the gross fare and the driver keeping the remainder.

The appeal of accessing transportation services this way quickly became apparent. Prior to Uber, customers had to book private car services well in advance or walk out into the street and hail a taxi. The innovation quickly gained the attention of investors. In February 2011, the company received a major boost when Benchmark Capital led a US$11 million funding round valuing Uber at US$60 million. Benchmark was a recognized Silicon Valley venture capital firm that had provided equity for some well-known technology firms such as Snap, Instagram and Dropbox. Additional investments from other high-profile firms, such as Google Ventures, BlackRock and Menlo Ventures, followed over the next few years. By late 2017, the company had raised US$14 billion in funding, helping to facilitate its growth and expansion throughout the United States and internationally.

However, it was also quick to attract the attention of the regulatory authorities. In 2010, it received 'cease and desist' orders from both the California Public Utilities Commission and the San Francisco Municipal Transportation Agency, demanding that it cease all operations as it was operating without a taxi licence. However, Kalanick did not let this stop him. He believed that he was not in the taxi business, but rather had created a platform to bring drivers and customers together, so he simply changed the company name to Uber and ignored the order.

Disrupting the taxi business model

Like many new technology businesses, Uber was providing a solution for in-built inefficiencies in an existing business system. Hiring a cab was certainly one of those. In many instances, it can be frustratingly difficult for a customer to get a taxi, particularly during periods of high demand. High levels of regulation in cities around the world often left customers with an expensive, inconvenient service. Equally, much of the time, drivers are sitting in their cars simply waiting for customers. All this and yet the global taxi industry was estimated to be worth US$100 billion, so it was almost inevitable that a technology start-up would have a look at this sector. The Uber app, using GPS, mobile computing and Google Maps, connected drivers and passengers together, online and in real time. When a customer needed a car, they could simply go on the app and select from one of the drivers close to their location. It allowed the customer to check the driver's name and their quality rating, ranging from 1 to 5 stars. They could also contact the driver by phone or text if they wished and could track the driver's progress on a map. The app worked in a similar way for drivers, who could choose to pick up a passenger or not, and who could also contact the customer by phone or text. The driver app had additional features, such as 'heat maps', which showed where they were most likely to find customers. It also showed how passengers were rating them, as well as providing a breakdown of their income.

At the end of the journey no money changed hands – the fare was automatically deducted from the customer's account. An email receipt was sent to the customer, who was then invited to rate the driver. Prices were determined by time and distance as well as by the quality of the car being used – for example, a limousine service versus a regular car. In 2012, Uber introduced a concept known as *surge pricing*, a form of dynamic pricing whereby prices were raised during periods of increased demand such as bad weather or when events are taking place in an area. When customers opened the app, they were notified of the 'surge' and had to accept it before they could summon a car.

Uber operated a very lean business model. Its drivers were independent contractors using their own cars. Consequently, they did not receive any of the normal employee benefits and were simply paid on the basis of any journeys completed. They could set their own hours, working as much or as little as the chose and, if they didn't own their own cars, Uber provided them with favourable loan terms to help them purchase their vehicles. The company mainly competed with the taxi services on offer in the various cities in which it operated, although its high profile and success also attracted new ride-sharing entrants into the business, such as Lyft and Sidecar.

Challenges and controversies

Uber's rapid growth has catapulted the company's brand to an unprecedented level of global recognition. However, the journey to date has not all been plain sailing and new challenges are emerging all the time. One particular feature of Uber was its well-documented battles with municipal authorities around the world, which had accused it of flouting local laws and regulations with respect to the provision of transportation services. Key regulations in the sector included the rights to provide public transportation, qualifications and background checks for drivers, and quality and safety checks for vehicles. For example, Uber has been keen to push ahead with the testing of driverless vehicles, an initiative that has been dogged with controversy. In 2016, it began using self-driving Volvo cars in San Francisco but, a week later, permission to do so was revoked by the California authorities. Uber simply moved the programme to Arizona, where one of its cars was involved in a fatal collision with a cyclist.

Stories emerging regarding workplace practices at Uber led to accusations of an overly aggressive corporate culture. For example, in 2017, a female former engineer wrote a blog post alleging that the Uber workplace was riddled with sexual harassment and gender discrimination, which ultimately led to 20 employees being fired. Perhaps the aggressive nature of the company started at the top, where Kalanick was on record as saying that opposition had to be met with 'principled confrontation'. Several other scandals had also emerged, such as it being accused of ordering fake rides from competitors such as Lyft and Gett, which were cancelled at the last minute, that it used its proprietary software to avoid giving rides to government officials and law enforcement officers in some cities, and that it engaged in false advertising, which cost the company US$20 million in compensation. Ultimately, these controversies led to Kalanick being forced to step down as CEO of the company in 2017 to be replaced by Dara Khosrowshahi.

Having validated the business model in the USA, Uber had quickly begun expanding internationally, starting appropriately enough with Paris and from there to other major cities around the world. However, the challenges of international expansion were graphically illustrated by the difficulties that the business experienced in some leading Southeast Asian markets. China was seen as a particularly lucrative market, with its huge, densely populated cities and rapid economic growth fuelling demand for transportation services. However, Uber's battles with complex local regulations and laws meant that it was unable to displace a local rival, DiDi, and it eventually sold its operations there for a 20 per cent stake in Didi and a US$1 billion equity investment. Its experience in India was not a happy one either. Again, despite massive market potential and strong brand awareness, the company struggled with complex local regulations, controversies surrounding the qualifications of its drivers, competition from bike services, internet and mapping issues, as well as a local preference for cash transactions. Eventually, in March 2018, Uber sold off its entire Southeast Asian business (including Cambodia, Indonesia, Malaysia, Myanmar, Philippines, Thailand, Singapore and Vietnam) to local rival Grab for a 27.5 per cent stake in that company.

Of perhaps most concern may be some of the fundamental issues surrounding Uber's business model.

While it has focused heavily on innovations designed to improve the customer's experience, it has not always shown the same level of attention to its drivers. A report in the USA in 2017 showed that only 4 per cent of Uber drivers remain with the company for longer than one year due to the low earnings available for their work and competition from the company's rivals. The knock-on effect of this is that the company is forced into expensive driver recruitment each year, with new drivers offered bonuses of US$1,000 on top of normal compensation. One positive human resources development for the company in 2018 was a US court's decision ruling against drivers who claimed that they should be treated as employees rather than independent contractors. Similarly, its surge pricing model, which initially saw prices jumping to seven times the normal rate during periods of peak demand, has proved particularly unpopular with customers. Stories abounded in the media of customers paying extremely high fares, along with those of drivers 'gaming' the app to force surge pricing to kick in. Uber responded by claiming that surge prices had been reduced to be no more 2.5 times the regular price, but this is another controversy that shows no signs of going away.

Finally, like many rapidly growing tech companies, Uber still has to report a profit. In 2017, it raised more than a few eyebrows by reporting huge sales revenues of US$7.5 billion, but in the same year it lost a staggering US$4.5 billion. The results even led the reputable business magazine *Forbes* to describe Uber's journey as extraordinary in that no venture has ever raised more capital, grown as fast, operated more globally and *lost as much money*. Only time will tell how this exciting story ends!

Questions

1. Conduct an environmental analysis of the transportation services business. How does it explain Uber's success, and what opportunities and threats does it present for the company?
2. Evaluate Uber's competitive strategy. Do you think it can continue to be effective or will it need to be changed?
3. Conduct a value chain analysis of Uber's business. What insights does this provide?

This case was prepared by Professor John Fahy, University of Limerick, from various published sources as a basis for class discussion rather than to show effective or ineffective management.

Glossary

A/B testing comparing two versions of an advert or webpage to assess which works most effectively; sometimes known as split testing

ad hoc research a research project that focuses on a specific problem, collecting data at one point in time with one sample of respondents

administered vertical marketing system a channel situation where a manufacturer that dominates a market through its size and strong brands may exercise considerable power over intermediaries even though they are independent

advertising any paid form of non-personal communication of ideas or products in the prime media (i.e., television, the press, posters, cinema and radio, the Internet and direct marketing)

advertising agency an organization that specializes in providing services such as media selection, creative work, production and campaign planning to clients

advertising message the use of words, symbols and illustrations to communicate to a target audience using prime media

advertising platform the aspect of the seller's product that is most persuasive and relevant to the target consumer

ambient advertising any out-of-home display advertising that does not fall into normal outdoor categories

ambush marketing any activity where a company tries to associate itself or its products with an event without paying any fee to the event owner

animal cruelty an overt and intentional act of violence towards animals, and also includes animal neglect or the failure to provide for the welfare of an animal under one's control (such as not only physical, but also psychological harm, for instance in the form of distress)

attitude the degree to which a customer or prospect likes or dislikes a brand

awareness set the set of brands that the consumer is aware may provide a solution to a problem

beliefs descriptive thoughts that a person holds about something

benefit segmentation the grouping of people based on the different benefits they seek from a product

bonus pack pack giving the customer extra quantity at no additional cost

bounce rate the percentage of visitors to a particular website who navigate away after viewing just one page

brainstorming the technique whereby a group of people generate ideas without initial evaluation; only when the list of ideas is complete is each one then evaluated

brand a distinctive product offering created by the use of a name, symbol, design, packaging, or some combination of these, intended to differentiate it from its competitors

brand equity a measure of the strength of the brand in the marketplace

brand extension the use of an established brand name on a new brand within the same broad market

brand stretching the use of an established brand name for brands in unrelated markets

brand values the core values and characteristics of a brand

business analysis a review of the projected sales, costs and profits for a new product, to establish whether these factors satisfy company objectives

business mission the organization's purpose, usually setting out its competitive domain, which distinguishes the business from others of its type

buying centre a group that is involved in the buying decision; also known as a decision-making unit (DMU) in industrial buying situations

catalogue marketing the sale of products through catalogues distributed to agents and customers, usually by mail or at stores

causal research the study of cause-and-effect relationships

cause-related marketing the commercial activity by which businesses and charities or causes form a partnership with one another to market an image, product or service for mutual benefit

chain of marketing productivity the processes through which marketing activities contribute to the performance of the firm

channel integration the way in which the players in the channel are linked

channel intermediaries organizations that facilitate the distribution of products to customers, also known as distribution intermediaries, marketing intermediaries or middlemen (e.g. agents, wholesalers, distributors and retailers)

channel of distribution the means by which products are moved from the producer to the ultimate consumer

channel strategy the selection of the most effective distribution channel, the most appropriate level of distribution intensity and the degree of channel integration

choice criteria the various attributes (and benefits) people use when evaluating products and services

classical conditioning the process of using an established relationship between a stimulus and a response to cause the learning of the same response to a different stimulus

cognitive dissonance post-purchase concerns of a consumer arising from uncertainty as to whether a decision to purchase was the correct one

cognitive learning the learning of knowledge, and development of beliefs and attitudes without direct reinforcement

communications-based co-branding the linking of two or more existing brands from different companies or business units for the purposes of joint communication

competitive bidding drawing up detailed specifications for a product and putting the contract out to tender

competitor analysis an examination of the nature of actual and potential competitors, their objectives and strategies

concept testing testing new product ideas with potential customers

consumer culture theory (CCT) views consumption less as a rational or conscious activity and more as a socio-cultural or experiential activity that is laden with emotion

consumer decision journey the information search, decision making and consumption journey undertaken by a consumer making a purchase

consumer panel consumers who provide information on their purchases over time

consumer pull the targeting of consumers with communications (e.g. promotions) designed to create demand that will *pull* the product into the distribution chain

consumer-generated advertising advertising messages created for brands by consumers

contextual targeting a form of targeted advertising whereby advertisements are served by automated systems based on the identity of the user and the content displayed

continuous research conducting the same research on the same sample repeatedly to monitor the changes that are taking place over time

contractual vertical marketing system a franchise arrangement (e.g. a franchise) tying producers and resellers together

control the stage in the marketing planning process or cycle when the performance against plan is monitored so that corrective action can be taken, if necessary

cookie a piece of computer code that websites use to help them recognize returning visitors; also helps to identify customers as they travel around the web

corporate vertical marketing system a channel situation where an organization gains control of distribution through ownership

culture the traditions, taboos, values and basic attitudes of the whole society in which an individual lives

custom research research conducted for a single organization to provide specific answers to the questions that it has

customer analysis a survey of who the customers are, what choice criteria they use, how they rate competitive offerings and on what variables they can be segmented

customer benefits those things that a customer values in a product; customer benefits derive from **product features** (see separate entry)

customer brand engagement the level of a customer's cognitive, emotional and behavioural investment in specific brand interactions

customer insight 'knowledge about the customer' that is valuable for a firm and that is distinct from customer information; it is important for firms to understand that 'information requires transformation to generate insight'

customer relationship management (CRM) the methodologies, technologies and e-commerce capabilities used by companies to manage customer relationships

customer satisfaction the fulfilment of customers' requirements or needs

customer value perceived benefits minus perceived sacrifice

customer value proposition a clear statement of the differential benefits offered by a product or service

customized marketing a market coverage strategy where a company decides to target individual customers and to develop separate marketing mixes for each

decision-making process the stages that organizations and people pass through when purchasing a physical product or service

depth interviews the interviewing of consumers individually for perhaps one or two hours with the aim of understanding their attitudes, values, behaviour and/or beliefs

descriptive research the systematic examination of a marketing question in order to draw conclusions

differentiated marketing a market coverage strategy where a company decides to target several market segments and to develop separate marketing mixes for each

differentiation strategy the selection of one or more customer choice criteria, and positioning the offering accordingly to achieve superior customer value

diffusion of innovation the process by which new products or services are adopted in the marketplace

direct marketing (1) acquiring and retaining customers without the use of an intermediary; (2) the distribution of products, information and promotional benefits to target consumers through interactive communication in a way that allows response to be measured

disintermediation the elimination (by the online sources) of the traditional marketing channel intermediaries by product or service providers such as, for instance, between the seller and the buyer (such as an agent, broker or reseller), or between the source and the recipient of information (such as an agency, official or gatekeeper)

distribution analysis an examination of movements in power bases, channel attractiveness, physical distribution and distribution behaviour

distribution push the targeting of channel intermediaries with communications (e.g., promotions) to *push* the product into the distribution chain

Dwell Time the length of time a visitor spends on a webpage before moving to a new page

dynamic pricing the frequent adjustment of prices in response to patterns of demand

e-WOM electronic word-of-mouth marketing is any online positive or negative statements about products or services

earned media refers to publicity gained through promotional efforts other than paid media advertising

economic value to the customer (EVC) the amount a customer would have to pay to make the total life cycle costs of a new and a reference product the same

environmental scanning the process of monitoring and analysing the marketing environment of a company

ethics the moral principles and values that govern the actions and decisions of an individual or group

ethnographic research an approach to research that emphasizes the observation/interviewing of consumers in their natural setting

event sponsorship sponsorship of a sporting or other event

evoked set the set of brands that the consumer seriously evaluates before making a purchase

exclusive distribution an extreme form of selective distribution where only one wholesaler, retailer or industrial distributor is used in a geographical area to sell the products of a particular supplier

exhibition an event that brings buyers and sellers together in a commercial setting

experiential marketing the term used to describe marketing activities that involve the creation of experiences for consumers

experimentation the application of stimuli (e.g. two price levels) to different matched groups under controlled conditions for the purpose of measuring their effect on a variable (e.g., sales)

exploratory research the preliminary exploration of a research area prior to the main data collection stage

family brand name a brand name used for all products in a range

focus group a group, normally of six to eight consumers, brought together for a discussion focusing on an aspect of a company's marketing

focused marketing a market coverage strategy where a company decides to target one market segment with a single marketing mix

franchise a legal contract in which a producer and channel intermediaries agree each other's rights and obligations; the intermediary usually receives marketing, managerial, technical and financial services in return for a fee

full cost pricing pricing so as to include all costs, and based on certain sales volume assumptions

geodemographics the process of grouping households into geographic clusters based on such information as type of accommodation, occupation, number and age of children, and ethnic background

global branding adopting a standardized approach to marketing in all the countries in which the brand is available

going-rate prices prices at the rate generally applicable in the market, focusing on competitors' offerings rather than on company costs

green marketing a practice of marketing that markets environmentally friendly products and services; it can involve a number of things, such as creating an eco-friendly product, using eco-friendly packaging, adopting sustainable business practices or focusing marketing efforts on messages that communicate a product's green benefits

group discussion a group, usually of six to eight consumers, brought together for a discussion focusing on an aspect of a company's marketing strategy

guerrilla marketing a technique that captures the attention of consumers by the creation of highly unusual and unexpected forms of promotional activity

hall tests bringing a sample of target consumers to a room that has been hired so that alternative marketing ideas (e.g., promotions) can be tested

horizontal electronic marketplaces online procurement sites that cross several industries and are typically used to source low-cost supplies such as MRO items

individual brand name a brand name that does not identify a brand with a particular company

information framing the way in which information is presented to people

information processing the process by which a stimulus is received, interpreted, stored in memory and later retrieved

information processing approach sees consumption as largely a rational process - the outcome of a consumer recognizing a need and then engaging in a series of activities to attempt to fulfil that need

information search the identification of alternative ways of problem solving

ingredient co-branding the explicit positioning of a supplier's brand as an ingredient of a product

inseparability a characteristic of services, namely that their production cannot be separated from their consumption

intangibility a characteristic of services, namely that they cannot be touched, seen, tasted or smelled

integrated marketing communications the concept that companies co-ordinate their marketing communications tools to deliver a clear, consistent, credible and competitive message about the organization and its products

intensive distribution the aim of intensive distribution is to provide saturation coverage of the market

internal marketing selecting, training and motivating employees to provide customer satisfaction

just-in-time (JIT) the JIT concept aims to minimize stocks by organizing a supply system that provides materials and components as they are required

key account management an approach to selling that focuses resources on major customers and uses a team selling approach

lifestyle the pattern of living as expressed in a person's activities, interests and opinions

lifestyle segmentation the grouping of people according to their pattern of living as expressed in their activities, interests and opinions

lifetime value of a customer recognition by the company of the potential sales, profits and endorsements that come from a repeat customer who stays with the company for several years

macroenvironment a number of forces tha affect the company itself but also its stakeholders, e.g. sconomic developments, demographic, politics, technological and social developments

marginal cost pricing the calculation of only those costs that are likely to rise as output increases

market analysis a statistical analysis of market size, growth and trends

market intelligence the systematic collection and analysis of publicly available information about consumers, competitors and marketplace developments

market segmentation the process of identifying individuals or organizations with similar characteristics that have significant implications for the determination of marketing strategy

market targeting the choice of market segments to which to sell products and services

market testing the limited launch of a new product to test sales potential

market-driven or outside-in firms seek to anticipate as well as identify consumer needs and build the resource profiles necessary to meet current and anticipated future demand

marketing the delivery of value to customers at a profit

marketing audit a systematic examination of a business's marketing environment, objectives, strategies and activities, with a view to identifying key strategic issues, problem areas and opportunities

marketing concept the achievement of corporate goals through meeting and exceeding customer needs better than the competition

marketing environment the actors and forces that affect a company's capability to operate effectively in providing products and services to its customers

marketing information system a system in which marketing information is formally gathered, stored, analysed and distributed to managers in accordance with their informational needs on a regular, planned basis

marketing mix a framework for the tactical management of the customer relationship, including product, place, price, promotion (the 4Ps); in the case of services, three other elements to be taken into account are process, people and physical evidence

marketing objectives there are two types of marketing objective – strategic thrust, which dictates which products should be sold in which markets, and strategic objectives, which are product-level objectives, such as build, hold, harvest and divest

marketing orientation companies with a marketing orientation focus on customer needs as the primary drivers of organizational performance

marketing planning the process by which businesses analyse the environment and their capabilities, decide upon courses of marketing action and implement those decisions

marketing research the systematic design, collection, analysis and reporting of data relevant to a specific marketing situation

marketing structures the marketing frameworks (organization, training and internal communications) on which marketing activities are based

marketing systems sets of connected parts (information, planning and control) that support the marketing function

media class decision the choice of prime media (i.e., the press, cinema, television, posters, radio) or some combination of these

media vehicle decision the choice of the particular newspaper, magazine, television spot, poster site, etc.

microenvironment the number of forces that adress the internal environment of the firm, such as vision, mission, strategy, resources, processes, products and services.

modified re-buy where a regular requirement for the type of product exists and the buying alternatives are known but sufficient (e.g. a delivery problem has occurred) to require some alteration to the normal supply procedure

money-off promotions sales promotions that discount the normal price

multi-channel retailing A combination of channels, which includes physical stores, direct distribution such as mail order and catalogues, as well as online stores

native advertising paid advertising that matches the form, feel and function of the content of the media on which it appears

neuro-marketing the application of brain research techniques to the study of marketing issues

new task refers to the first-time purchase of a product or input by an organization

omni-channel retailing The design, deployment, coordination, and evaluation of channels to enhance customer value through effective customer acquisition, retention, and development

operant conditioning the use of rewards to generate reinforcement of response

packaging all the activities involved in designing and producing the kind of container or wrapper for the product

parallel co-branding the joining of two or more independent brands to produce a combined brand

parallel importing when importers buy products from distributors in one country and sell them in another to distributors who are not part of the manufacturer's normal distribution; caused by significant price differences for the same product between different countries

pay per click (PPC) the advertiser pays the publisher when the ad is clicked

perception the process by which people select, organize and interpret sensory stimulation into a meaningful picture of the world

perishability a characteristic of services, namely that the capacity of a service business, such as a hotel room, cannot be stored – if it is not occupied, there is lost income that cannot be recovered

permission marketing marketers ask permission before sending advertisements or promotional material to potential customers; in this way customers 'opt in' to the promotion rather than having to 'opt out'

personal selling oral communication with prospective purchasers, with the intention of making a sale

personality the inner psychological characteristics of individuals that lead to consistent responses to their environment

place the distribution channels to be used, outlet locations, methods of transportation

portfolio planning managing groups of brands and product lines

positioning the choice of target market (*where* the company wishes to compete) and differential advantage (*how* the company wishes to compete)

premiums any merchandise offered free or at low cost as an incentive to purchase

price (I) the amount of money paid for a product; (2) the agreed value placed on the exchange by a buyer and seller

price escalation the additional costs incurred in taking products to an international market, including transportation costs, distribution costs, taxes and tariffs, exchange rates and inflation rates

price unbundling pricing each element in the offering so that the price of the total product package is raised

product a good or service offered or performed by an organization or individual, which is capable of satisfying customer needs

product features the characteristics of a product that may or may not convey a customer benefit

product life cycle a four-stage cycle in the life of a product, illustrated as a curve representing the demand; the four stages being introduction, growth, maturity and decline

product line a group of brands that are closely related in terms of the functions and benefits they provide

product placement the deliberate placing of products and/or their logos in movies and television programmes, usually in return for money

product-based co-branding the linking of two or more existing brands from different companies or business units to form a product in which the brand names are visible to the consumer

production orientation a business approach that is inwardly focused either on costs or on a definition of a company in terms of its production facilities

profile segmentation the grouping of people in terms of profile variables such as age and socio-economic group so that marketers can communicate to them

Programmatic advertising the automation of the purchase and sale of digital advertising

promotion the ways in which organizations communicate with customers, both to create awareness of their offerings and to try to engage with and persuade consumers to purchase

prospecting searching for and calling upon potential customers

proximity marketing the use of wireless devices to distribute marketing messages to specific locations

psychographic segmentation the grouping of people according to their lifestyle and personality characteristics

psychological pricing taking into consideration the psychological impact of the price level that is being set

public relations the management of communications and relationships to establish goodwill and mutual understanding between an organization and its public

publicity the communication of a product or business by placing information about it in the media without paying for time or space directly

purchasing power the amount of goods or services that a certain amount of money can buy at a given time

qualitative research a semi-structured, in-depth study of small samples in order to gain insights

quantitative research a structured study of small or large samples using a predetermined list of questions or criteria

real-time bidding (RTB) a means by which advertising inventory is bought and sold on a per-impression basis, via programmatic instantaneous auction

real-time marketing creating a marketing strategy focused on current, relevant trends and immediate feedback from customers

reasoning a more complex form of cognitive learning where conclusions are reached by connected thought

reference group a group of people that influences an individual's attitude or behaviour

relationship marketing the process of creating, maintaining and enhancing strong relationships with customers and other stakeholders

repositioning changing the target market or differential advantage, or both

research brief written document stating the client's requirements

research proposal a document defining what the marketing research agency promises to do for its client and how much it will cost

retail audit a type of continuous research tracking the sales of products through retail outlets

retail positioning the choice of target market and differential advantage for a retail outlet

retargeting a form of advertising by which online advertising is targeted to consumers based on their previous internet activity

retargeting a form of online advertising which enables advertisers to keep their products and brands in front of consumers that have left their websites

reverse marketing the process whereby the buyer attempts to persuade the supplier to provide exactly what the organization wants

rote learning the learning of two or more concepts without conditioning

safety (buffer) stocks stocks or inventory held to cover against uncertainty about resupply lead times

sales force evaluation the measurement of salesperson performance so that strengths and weaknesses can be identified

sales force motivation the motivation of salespeople by a process that involves needs, which set encouraging drives in motion to accomplish goals

sales orientation a business approach that focuses on the development of products and services and the aggressive selling of these offerings as the key to its success

sales promotion incentives to customers or the trade that are designed to stimulate purchase

sampling process a term used in research to denote the selection of a subset of the total population in order to interview them

secondary research data that has already been collected by another researcher for another purpose

selective attention the process by which people screen out those stimuli that are neither meaningful to them nor consistent with their experiences and beliefs

selective distortion the distortion of information received by people according to their existing beliefs and attitudes

selective distribution the use of a limited number of outlets in a geographical area to sell the products of a particular supplier

selective retention the process by which people retain only a selection of messages in memory

self-concept the beliefs a person holds about his or her own attributes

semiotics the study of the correspondence between signs and symbols, and their roles in how we assign meanings

service encounter any interaction between a service provider and a customer

servicescape the environment in which the service is delivered and where the firm and customers interact

shareholder value the returns to a company's shareholders, which grow when the company increases its dividends or its share price rises

social advertising refers to adverts placed on social media platforms like Facebook, Instagram, Twitter, YouTube and Snapchat

social marketing the use of commercial marketing concepts and tools in programmes designed to influence the individual's behaviour to improve their well-being and that of society

societal marketing concept the idea that a company's marketing decisions should consider consumers' wants, the company's requirements, consumers' long-term interests and society's long-run interests

sponsorship a business relationship between a provider of funds, resources or services and an individual, event or organization that offers in return some rights and association that may be used for commercial advantage

straight re-buy refers to a purchase by an organization from a previously approved supplier of a previously purchased item

strategic business unit (SBU) a business or company division serving a distinct group of customers and with a distinct set of competitors, usually strategically autonomous

strategic issues analysis an examination of the suitability of marketing objectives and segmentation bases in the light of changes in the marketplace

strategic objectives product-level objectives relating to the decision to build, hold, harvest or divest products

strategic thrust the decision concerning which products to sell in which markets

sustainable competitive advantage a long-term competitive advantage that is not easily duplicable or surpassable by competitors, e.g. unique employee skills or advanced distribution process, that allow the business to dominate its area of operations and exclude competitors

SWOT analysis a structured approach to evaluating the strategic position of a business by identifying its strengths, weaknesses, opportunities and threats

syndicated research also known as omnibus research, research that is collected by firms on a regular basis and then sold to other firms

target audience the group of people at which an advertisement or message is aimed

target marketing selecting a segment as the focus for a company's offering or communications

test marketing the launch of a new product in one or a few geographic areas chosen to be representative of the intended market

trade-off analysis a measure of the trade-off customers make between price and other product features, so that their effects on product preference can be established

trademark the legal term for a brand name, brand mark or trade character

undifferentiated marketing a market coverage strategy where a company decides to ignore market segment differences and to develop a single marketing mix for the whole market

user-generated content any form of content, such as images, videos, text and audio, that has been posted by users of online platforms

value-based marketing a perspective on marketing that emphasizes how a marketing philosophy and marketing activities contribute to the maximization of shareholder value

variability a characteristic of services, namely that, being delivered by people, the standard of their performance is open to variation

vertical electronic marketplaces online procurement sites that are dedicated to sourcing supplies for producers in one particular industry

vicarious learning learning from others without direct experience or reward

yield management the monitoring of demand or potential demand patterns with a view to adjusting prices

Author index

A

Abell, D.F. and Hammond, J.S. 385
Abraham, M. 94
Ackoff, R.I. 365, 384
Ackoff, R.L. 101, 125
Adams, B. 296–7, 319
Adidas profile 59
adslogans.co.uk 152
Aijo, T.S. 219
Al-Shakhsheer, A., Habiballah, M., Ababne, M. and Alhelalat, J. 246
Allen, R. 319
Allison, K. 385
Allwood, E.H. 296–7, 319
Almquist, E., Cleghorn, J. and Sherer, L. 94
Alter, A. 329–30, 355
Alviro, L., Constantinides, E. and Franco, M. 69, 93
Alwi et al 174
Ambler, T., Kokkinaki, F. and Puntoni, S. 380, 385
Amman, J. 191
Andersen, T. 287
Andersson, H. 355
Ansoff growth matrix 371
appannie.com 357
Ariely, D. 245, 320
Armstrong, J.S. 381, 385
Arnett, G. 103, 123
Arnould, E. and Thompson, C. 93
Aroean, L. and Michaelidou, N. 156
Arora, N. 74, 94
Arnett, C. and Tuten, T. 357
Ashley, C. and Tuten, T. 357
Asquith, R. 124
Associated Press 191
Atwal, G. 96–8, 358–60

B

Bacon, J. 40–41, 60, 384
Bakan, J. 49, 60
Baker, R. 283
Balabanis, G., Stables, R.E. and Philips, H.C. 220
Balta, H. 157
Barber, B. 13, 156
Bardon, N. 156
Barnard, J. 319
Barney, J. 384
Baron, S., Harris, K. and Davies, B.J. 219
Barrett, C. 74, 94
Barry, A. 22
Baskin, S.J. 287
Bell, E. 320
Bellweather Report 33
Benady, D. 321
Benita, J. 287
Bennett, B. 320
Bennett, P.D. 220

Benton, R. 22
Berg, M.D. 137–8, 156
Berkowitz, D. 354, 357
Berkowitz, E.N., Kerin, R.A., Hartley, S.W. and Rudelius, W. 60
Berry, L.L. 219, 220
Berry, L.L. and Parasuraman, A. 220
Berry, L.L., Parasuraman, A. and Zeithaml, V.A. 220
Bertilsson, J. 174, 192
Birchall, J. 124, 219
Bishop, L. 105, 124
Blackwell, R.D., Miniard, P.W. and Engel, J.F. 67, 93
Blitz, R. 246
Boff, L. 90
Boland, M. 357
Boone, J. 22
Booz, Allen & Hamilton 192
Borden, J. 220
Borden, N. 20, 23
Bowen, D.E. and Lawler, L.L. 219
Bowman, J. 321
Bowsher, E. 123
Boyd, S. 157
Brady, J. and Davis, I. 192
Branson, R. 80–81, 94
Brech, P. 192
Broadcasters' Audience Research Board (BARB) 300
Brogger, T.H. 287
Brown, D. 61–3, 158–61
Brown, J.M. 192
Brown, R.G. 320
Brownsell, A. 14, 22
Brynjolfsson, E., Hu, Y.J. and Rahman, M.S. 283
Bryson, D. 96–8, 358–60
Büchmann-Slorup, B. 287
Buckingham, D. 124
Bughin, J., Doogan, J. and Vetvik, O.J. 219
Bulik, B.S. 320
Burrows, D. 93
Burrows, P. 277–8, 283
Business Insider Nordic 287
Butler, P. and Collins, N. 220
Butler, S. 237–8, 246, 265, 282
Buzzell, R.D. and Gale, B.T. 222

C

Cadwalladr, C. and Graham-Harrison, E. 124
Calkins, T. 192
Cambra-Fierro, J.J., Centeno, E., Olavarria, A. and Vasquez-Carrasco, R. 220
Campbell, P. 245
Cardenas, L. and Perrin, J. 355
Carlstrom, V. 205, 219

Carlzon, J. 335, 356
Carroll, C. 26–9
Carson, D. 385
Carter, M. 94, 321
Cavaglieri, C. 246
Cerna, N. 321
CGI, Inc. 287
Chaffey, D. 90, 95
Chaffey, D. and Ellis-Chadwick, F. 334, 357
Chaffey, D. and Smith, P.R. 333, 356
Chakravorti, B. 245
Chapman, B. 35–6, 59
Charles, G. 157
Chartier, T. 123
Chicourel, R. and Poskett, W. 154, 157
Choudhury, M.M. and Harrigan, P. 220
Christensen, S. and Lundgren, E. 205, 219
Christopher, M.C., Payne, A. and Ballantyne, D. 211
Claridge, T., Edwards, D. and Sellars, R. 370–1, 384
Clark, N. 178, 192
Cleary, C. 131
Connan, C. 60
Connolly, K. 43–4, 60
Content Marketing Institute 356
Cooper, R.G. and Kleinschmidt, E.J. 192
Corey, R. 156
Coulter, D. 22
Court, D., Elzinga, D., Mulder, S. and Jorgen Vetvik, O. 94
Coyle, D. 282
Crouch, S. 120, 124
Crouch, S. and Housden, M. 124

D

Dahlander, L. and O'Mahony, S. 192
Damour, L. 93
Daneshkhu, S. 245, 350–1, 357
Darbyshire, R. 321
Davcik, N. and Sharma, D. 191
Davenport, T. 123
Davidson, J.H. 320
Davidson, L. 370–1, 384
Davies, G. 270–1, 283
Davis, B. 320
Davis, P. 22
Day, G. 385
Day, G.S. 192, 385
Day, G.S. and Moorman, C. 22
De Mers, Y. 94
Delamaide, D. 321
DeMers, J. 357, 384
Descubes, I. 284–5
Dias, J., Ionitiu, O., Lhuer, X. and van Ouwerkerk, J. 94
Dillard-Wright, D. 355
Dillman, D. 124

Companies index

Brands index

Subjects index